US Intelligence, the Holocaust and the Nuremberg Trials

Volume 2

History of International Relations, Diplomacy, and Intelligence

Series Editor

Katherine A. S. Sibley
Saint Joseph's University

VOLUME 7/2

US Intelligence, the Holocaust and the Nuremberg Trials

Seeking Accountability for Genocide and Cultural Plunder

Volume 2

By

Michael Salter

LEIDEN • BOSTON
2009

This book is printed on acid-free paper.

Library of Congress Cataloging-in-Publication Data

Salter, Michael.
US intelligence, the Holocaust and the Nuremberg trials : seeking accountability for genocide and cultural plunder / by Michael Salter.
p. cm. — (History of international relations, diplomacy, and intelligence ; 7)
Includes bibliographical references and index.
ISBN 978-90-04-17277-7 (v. 1 : hardback : alk. paper)
1. United States. Office of Strategic Services. 2. World War, 1939–1945—Secret service—United States. 3. Holocaust, Jewish (1939–1945) 4. Nuremberg War Crime Trials, Nuremberg, Germany, 1946–1949. I. Title.
D810.S7S235 2009
341.6'90268—dc22

2008048105

ISSN 1874-0294
ISBN 978 90 04 17320 0 (volume 2)
ISBN 978 90 04 17277 7 (set)

PRINTED IN THE NETHERLANDS

CONTENTS

SOURCES AND ABBREVIATIONS

CIC	US Army, Counter Intelligence Corps
Cornell Collection	General Donovan's Nuremberg files contained in the Rare Books Room, Cornell Law School, Ithaca, New York State, USA.
DRU	Document Research Unit (headed by OSS' Walter Rothschild).
ERR	The Einsatzstab Reichsleiter Rosenberg, Nazi Plunder Agency based in France.
ETO	European Theatre of Opcrations
FEA	US Foreign Economic Administration
FRUS	Foreign Relations of the United States (US official record of diplomatic relations).
GIS	German intelligence system
IMT	International Military Tribunal
ISOS	Intelligence Services Oliver Strachey.
Jackson Papers	R. H. Jackson Papers, Library of Congress, Manuscript Division.
MFA&A	Monuments Fine Arts and Archives Branch of the United States Army
NCA	Nazi Conspiracy and Aggression, (compilation of Nuremberg trial evidence and trial briefs, Washington, 1949.
NSA	National Security Agency (US intelligence body).
OCC	Office of Chief of Counsel (Jackson's American prosecution agency).
OSS	Office of Strategic Services headed by General Donovan.
PRO	Public Records Office, Kew, London: recently renamed 'National Archives'
RG	US NA Record Group.
RSHA	Internal security division of the SS, headed by Kaltenbrunner.
SEA	Staff Evidence Analysis report (summary of Nuremberg documentation on a standard form often written by translators).

SHAEF Southern Hemisphere Allied Expeditionary Force.

WRB War Refugee Board, primarily a Jewish relief organisation created by Roosevelt in 1944.

US NA United States National Archives, Modern Military Archives 2, College Park, Washington DC, USA.

CHAPTER FIVE

OSS' INVESTIGATION OF LOOTED JEWISH ART

The Nazi leaders devoted an inordinate amount of time to cultural matters... Their control of the arts was an important element of their totalitarian system. Similarly, their commitment to amassing both private and state art collections stands as a remarkable aspect of their rule. Never before, with the possible exception of Napoleon and his cohorts, had an entire leadership corps been responsible for the acquisition of so much art. Through purchase and plunder, (the Third Reich was a "kleptocracy"), their harvest amounted to hundreds of thousands of pieces.... One finds a situation in the art world that is analogous to the findings of Christopher Browning and Daniel Goldhagen, who showed that 'ordinary people' participated in the murder of Jews and other victims of the Holocaust.... the two projects were interlinked, part of a continuum. With respect to the cultural sphere, one sees a progression from persecution in the professional realm (dismissing Jewish and left-wing employees) to the expropriation of Jewish property (parts of the efforts to dehumanise the victims) to the spoliation of cultural property of neighboring countries and, in certain cases (especially in the East), outright destruction. In short, the Nazi leaders' cultural policies were inextricably bound up with their racial and geopolitical agendas.[1]

The question of restitution of property confiscated and looted by the Nazis is a general problem, but one that has special implications for the Jews of Germany. Considering the great amount of Jewish community property confiscated by the Nazis, and in view of the small number of surviving German Jews, it is evident that the restitution of even part of this community property would provide sufficient funds for the reconstruction and rehabilitation of the remaining Jewish population. Practical difficulties will undoubtedly arise in cases where Jewish owned establishments were lost by "Aryanization," sale under duress, or outright robbery. In many cases, the property seized will not be possible to identify, or else will be consumed or destroyed. Often those responsible for the wrongs will either be dead, impossible to trace, or financially incapable of making amends for the damage caused. All direct beneficiaries (the State, the Party, corporations, and private persons) should be liable for compensation.[2]

---

[1] Petropoulos, *The Faustian Bargain: The Art World in Nazi Germany*, NY: OUP, 2000, 5–6.

[2] 'Military Government and Problems with Respect to the Jews of Germany' (R&A 1655.25, draft, 14 June 1944): US NA, RG 226, Entry 191, Box 2, Folder by the same

Introduction

This chapter contains an in-depth historical analysis based partly upon the contents of recently declassified intelligence files.[3] It supplies detailed information of both the activities of the Nazi organisations of plunder,[4] and the interventions of OSS officials in this area, and the

name as this report, 14. 'Military Government and Problems with Respect to the Jews of Germany' (R&A 1655.25, draft, 14 June 1944): US NA, RG 226, Entry 191, Box 2, Folder by the same name as this report.

[3] These are scattered across many places with the US National Archives sometimes interspersed with Safehaven and more general war crimes files, as will be clear from the references given throughout this chapter. See, for example, US NA, RG 94, Entry 2599A, Boxes 1–491. Within these boxes are folders on 'Jewish Atrocities', ibid., Box 219, Folder 711.6; ibid., Box 286, Folder 711.6 'War Crimes' (2 folders); ibid., Box 294, Folder 840.3 'Preservation of Works of Art'; ibid., Box 381, Folder 840.3 'Looted Art, *et al.*'; 'Safehaven report 57 (looted art), American Embassy, London, 1945: US NA, RG 226, 'CIA withdrawn-withdrawn collection,' Box 1; 'Looted art, 1945' ibid; 'Alois Miedl, two documents, [looted art] 1945' ibid., Box 3; 'ORION Activities, two documents; looted art, German art personnel, memorandum from Paul Rosenberg, 1945, ibid., Box 4.

[4] For relevant archival records, see *OSS Art Looting Investigation Unit Reports, 1945–46* National Archives Microfilm Publication M1782, Records of the Roberts Commission for the Protection and Salvage of Artistic and Historic Monuments in War Areas, and Records of the Office of the Chief of Naval Operations: US NA, RG 239 and RG 38; US NA, RG 99 'Art Works'; ibid., Box 33, Folder 1 'Report containing information on locating art works looted from Florence, Italy'; ibid., Box 105 Folder 1 'A Report on looting and damage of art works in Europe'; ibid., Box 105, Folder 6 'Consolidated Interrogation Report #2, The Göring Collection.' September 1945; ibid., Box 105, Folder 7 'More Art Loot, Lists of'; ibid., Box 106, Folder 1 'Art Looting Investigation-Biographical Index of Individuals Involved in Art Looting in Europe,' n.d.; Records of the COI/OSS Washington, US NA RG 226, Entry 118A, Box 4, Folder 4 'Looted art treasures', ibid., Box 5, Folder 1, 'Looted art'; ibid., Entry 183, Box 13, Folder 70 'Matisse painting in Switzerland; questionable art dealers' and ibid., Box 18, Folder 94 'report on location and recovery of French and Belgium art treasures'; ibid., Box 29, Folder 170 containing file 6603 'dealing with the dealer in looted art Hans Wendland'; ibid., Box 29, Folder 171 contains 'Safehaven reports, intelligence disseminations, articles, and other documents pertaining to Safehaven activities involving art and German assets; ibid., Entry 190, Box 30, Folder 122 contains 'Stolen Art' giving 'information about looted art in Switzerland' and 'a 10-page report on looted art in Switzerland, dated 5 January 1946; ibid., Folder 123 'Safehaven Memos' on transfers of gold, looted art and cloaking of funds: July 1944–November 1947. There is a large collection of other records at US NA, RG 226, Entry 190, Box 532, Folder 1751 Folder 1743 'Safehaven—art objects looted by Germany; locations and individuals who are in possession of objects.' December 1944–April 1946; ibid., Folder 1747 'Orion Organization—art looting September 1944–January 1946'; ibid., Folder 1748 'Orion Project progress reports January-December 1945'; ibid., Folder 1749 'German and Austrian repositories February 1945–October 1946'; ibid., Folder 1750 'Art Looting Investigation Unit Report of unit's final mission to Europe from 10 June, 1946 to September 24, 1946 dated October 14, 1946'; ibid., Folder 1751; 'Orion Budget and Fiscal'; ibid., Folder 1753 'Inter-Orion Correspondence'; ibid., Folder 1754 'War Department G-5 [Orion]'; ibid., Folder 1755 'State Department [Orion]'; ibid., Box 533, Folder

various institutional and historical contexts in which both these activities took place. The following extensive sections will focus on an area of the work of the OSS in the Nazi war crimes field that has not received sufficient attention in the academic literature on intelligence agencies: its monitoring, investigation and evidence-gathering in relation to works of art that the Nazis looted as an integral part of the Holocaust.[5] The chapter opens with a discussion of the creation of the ALIU, its staffing and administrative structure. It then describes this OSS art units mission objectives, including the creation of master and target lists of wanted individuals. The next topic discussed is this Unit's early wartime operations in Germany, Austria, Italy, Spain and France, and postwar interrogations of those individuals on its high priority 'target lists' who had been detained. What follows next is a series of lengthy sections on art looting and the Holocaust in France, and OSS' investigations of the Göring and Linz Collection. The final sections address problems concerning Switzerland, counter-espionage dimensions of ALIU's work and this Unit's contribution to Holocaust-restitution issues. This chapter will not, however, address how elements of the OSS' work contributed, in various ways, to both the Nuremberg trials evidence and on-going restitution work, a task reserved for the next chapter.[6]

Of necessity, we need to begin by briefly summarising some historical background material as this provides one of the contexts in which OSS officials were operating. It is necessary to understand the nature of such contexts as a precondition for critically appreciating the nature and purpose of their investigative work.

1756 'Art Looting Investigation Unit-Liaison'. See also US NA, RG 226, Entry 118A 'Records of the COI/OSS Washington', Box 4, Folder 4 'Looted art treasures'; ibid., Box 5, Folder 1 'Looted art'.

[5] 'See Security-Classified Reports Concerning Recovery of Looted Art Treasures in Germany 1940–1945': US NA, RG 226, Entry 30, Box 1; 'General Records 1936–1945, 1948–1954; 1955': US NA, RG 94, Entry 2599A, Boxes 1–491. Within these are folders on 'Preservation of Works of Art'; ibid., Box 294, Folder 840.3; ibid., Box 381, Folder 840.3 'Looted Art, *et al.*' See also the Otto Wittmann collection at the Getty Museum: http://www.archives.gov/research/holocaust/art/oss-art-looting-investigation-unit-reports.html, and various other NARA citations listed below.

[6] When finalising this section I noticed that, Nancy Yeide had just published a short but important study entitled: 'The Plunder of Art as a War Crime: The Art Looting Investigation Unit Reports and the Hermann Göring Art Collection', *Rutgers Jnl of Law and Religion*, 8:2 (2007), 1–8. online at http://org.law.rutgers.edu/publications/law-religion/articles/Yeide.pdf. See also Anne Rothfeld, 'Project ORION: An Administrative History of the Art Looting Investigation Unit (ALIU): An Overlooked Page in Intelligence Gathering', (2002) (unpublished thesis on file with University of Maryland, Baltimore County).

From the mid-1930s to the end of the war, different and sometimes competing agencies of the Nazi regime, including Rosenberg's ERR (Einsatzstab Reichsleiter Rosenberg),[7] applied a series of increasingly severe anti-Semitic measures and legal decrees.[8] These authorised the regime's systematic plunder of works of art throughout occupied Europe.[9] Alfred Rosenberg's 'ERR' was the official Nazi office charged with confiscating prominent art collections in France.[10] The ERR operated from 1940 to 1944 and was housed in the *Jeu de Paume* Museum in Paris, a location used as a clearinghouse to process all French confiscations. The definition of Einsatzstab is 'special staff'; whilst the word 'Einsatz' means to 'give effect through action.' Hence, the German phrase signified a special task force. This agency of systematic plunder was created on 17 July 1940 with a mission to: 'battle Judaism and Freemasonry' within the Western territories and the Netherlands.[11] It was, however, only one of many other German bodies involved in this form of war criminality and clashed with a separate section of the German Army and members of Ribbentrop's Foreign Office.

ERR officials acquired specific jurisdiction over Jewish artworks in October 1940. They relied upon the services of SD and Gestapo agents, supported by French officials and informers, to hunt down Jewish properties and then seize valuable works of art and other assets.

[7] For an early account, see 'The Einsatzstab Reichsleiter Rosenberg,' 30 March 1945: NGA, MSS33 (Faison Papers), box 4, Central Control Commission for Germany (British Component), MFA & A Branch. Another ALIU report notes: 'The *Einsatzstab Reichsleiter Rosenberg für die Besetzen Gebiete*' was a special unit formed under *Hauptabteilung III: (Sonderaufgaben)* (Division # 3: Special Projects) of the *Aussenpolitischesamt* (Foreign Political Office) of Reichsleiter Alfred ROSENBERG. Originally, its primary and theoretical function was the collection of political material in the occupied countries, for exploitation in the 'struggle against Jewry and Freemasonry.' *Amt Westen* (The Office for the occupied Countries of the West) became operational in July 1940, with headquarters in Paris. CIR 1, op. cit., 3.

[8] Jonathan Petropoulos, 'German laws and directives bearing on the appropriation of cultural property in the Third Reich.' In *The Spoils of War—World War II and its Aftermath: The Loss, Disappearance, and Recovery of Cultural Property*, NY: Harry N. Abrams, 1997, 106–111. He shows that many of the measures were first tried outside Germany, especially in Austria where the Nazi art plundering methods were tested; and that these laws and directives were closely linked to the Holocaust, with the expropriation of property leading to the other stages of a wider genocide.

[9] Feliciano, *The Lost Museum: The Nazi Conspiracy to Steal the World's Greatest Works of Art*, NY: Basic Books, 1997, 3–5.

[10] Hermann Göring helped establish the ERR.

[11] It represented a special operation within the Hauptabteilung III, Sonderaufgaben (Main Department III, Special Assignments) of Rosenberg's Foreign Policy Office: CIR 1 (ERR), op. cit., 3.

Although such looting did not concentrate exclusively upon items owned by Jews, they were prominent amongst the victims of this type of war criminality.[12] For example, the Nuremberg and other evidence in particular makes it clear that Jews, including owners of many of the well-known art houses within Germany and Europe,[13] fell disproportionately amongst the victims of this type of war crime.[14]

Feliciano recognises that the plundering and destruction of art and other cultural / religious artefacts of European Jews was integral to the wider genocidal dimension of Nazi racial policies:

> Between 1939 and 1944, the Nazis systematically confiscated, stole, or bought works from a number of European collections, or from private collections belonging to wealthy Jewish families, Freemasons, and political opponents.... This story deeply concerns art and culture, symbols of the soul and breadth of a country. By looting French art collectors and dealers the Nazis stole more than mere assets. These wily and tenacious confiscators were also stealing the soul, meaning, and cultural standards of these collectors. Not only do conquerors try to physically obliterate their enemies, but they try to take over the precious art objects they own and patiently collected. The plundering gives us a fair insight into the reason the power of all victors—even recent ones, like in the former Yugoslavia—rests in part on the looting and destruction of the cultural possessions of the enemy. Of course, behind this tightly organised confiscation of art stands the Holocaust, as a backdrop and context.[15]

A distinguishing feature of Nazi art looting was its systematic nature as a legally authorised aspect of official state policy. Both Hitler and Göring regarded their regime's confiscation of Jewish artworks and their reallocation to specific collections, particularly their own, as important policy objectives in their own right for establishing and consolidating a new Fascist order across Europe.[16] Kajetan Mühlmann, one of Göring's suppliers of artworks and 'arguably the single most prolific

[12] Jonathan Petropoulos, *Art as Politics in the Third Reich*, NY: The University of North Carolina Press, 1999.

[13] Much of the information in the next paragraphs draws heavily upon Anne Rothfeld, 'Nazi Looted Art: The Holocaust Records Preservation Project,' Part 1, *Prologue*, Fall 2002, Vol. 34, No. 3.

[14] Feliciano, 1997 op. cit., is an impressive study of the Nazis' looting, with considerable help from a variety of French and other collaborators, of five large-scale and artistically significant French Jewish art collections: the Rothschilds, Paul Rosenberg, Bernheim-Jeunes, David Weills and the Schloss.

[15] Feliciano, 1997 op. cit., 16, 7.

[16] Ibid., 4, 16–19.

plunderer in the twentieth century',[17] personally participated in the formulation of anti-Semitic measures within Austria during 1937–38, which represented a dry run of similar measures later introduced across Germany.[18] In April 1938, Göring issued the 'Decree Regarding the Reporting of Jewish Property', which stated that by no later than 30 June 1938 every Jew in the Reich was required to assess all property owned, domestic and foreign, and to report these findings to Nazi authorities.[19] By the end of 1938, Hitler had enacted another two laws enabling the Nazi authorities to seize and then transfer into non-Jewish ownership, all Jewish businesses, including of course art dealerships; and to seize Jews' personal property. These laws, 'The Ordinance for the Attachment of the Property of the People's and State's Enemies', and 'The Ordinance for the Employment of Jewish Property', were applied throughout the occupied countries.

During 1938, Nazi art confiscations of the collections of Vienna's prominent Jewish families had begun in newly-annexed Austria.[20] Petropoulos notes that Mühlmann: 'played a central role in expropriating the Rothschild's art collection.' He even wrote to Hitler arguing that the 60–70 Million Reichsmarks worth of confiscated Jewish artworks should remain in Austria.[21] Such 'Aryanization', the transfer of ownership of Jewish property to non-Jews, peaked at 33,000 episodes prior to 1939. Only 8,000 of these property transfers were 'legal', at least in the minimal sense of being expressly authorised by the German regime.[22] These measures represented an early stage of what Karl Schleunes termed: 'the twisted road to Auschwitz.'[23] Certainly, amongst functionaries such as Mühlmann, the opportunity of seizing Jewish wealth interpreted as booty, was a material motivation for his important support for this aspect of the Holocaust. Mühlmann and his family personally benefited from widespread 'Aryanization' of Jewish residences and other property in Austria, including that of the Rothschilds.[24]

These legally-authorised racist measures of expropriation formed part of the Nazi regime's wider ideological and 'cultural' programme. This

[17] Petropoulos, 2000 op. cit., 8.
[18] Petropoulos, 1996 op. cit., 188–89.
[19] Rothfeld, 2002 op. cit., pt. 1.
[20] Ibid.
[21] Petropoulos, 1996 op. cit., 190.
[22] Ibid., 187–88.
[23] Ibid., 190.
[24] Ibid.

involved purging German public art museums of supposedly 'decadent', or 'degenerate', art created during the Weimar Republic, (1924–1930),[25] which the regime associated with Jewish and cosmopolitan influences.[26] Hitler, himself a failed painter, advocated a racially-exclusive type of *Volkish* or folk art. This included the paintings of the Old Flemish and Dutch masters,[27] and medieval and Renaissance German and Italian artworks. Other approved types were various baroque pieces, Eighteenth Century French works, and Nineteenth Century German realist paintings depicting, in an idealised manner, German folk culture.[28]

The Nazi regime implemented the specifically anti-Semitic aspect of this ideological programme to newly-occupied territories in a remorseless and systematic way. In 1939, art confiscations followed immediately in the wake of the regime's military invasion and occupation in Poland.[29] This set in motion a pattern that Hitler's officials continued during the Nazis' subsequent invasion and occupation of other European nations during the early 1940's. In January 1940, Hitler gave Alfred Rosenberg, previously the 'philosopher' of Nazism, the task of looting Jewish and Masonic art and other cultural assets, including religious icons and artefacts, across occupied Western Europe.[30] By the autumn of 1940, Hitler ordered Rosenberg to expropriate all Jewish art collections as these were now decreed to be 'ownerless' because their former owners had become reclassified as 'stateless persons', lacking all property rights. ALIU's Detailed Interrogation Report (hereafter 'DIR') No. 5 (Lohse) provides additional details of the secrecy associated with this anti-Semitic measure, which amounted to an implied admission of its illegality:

> Von Behr had explained to him [Lohse] that, in accordance with a Hitler order, "ownerless" Jewish collections were to be requisitioned and sent to Germany, such confiscation being in accord with a special provision of the German-French armistice signed at Compiegne in 1940. Lohse

[25] Shearer West, *The Visual Arts in Germany, 1890–1937: Utopia and Despair*, NY: Rutgers University Press. 2001, 159–205; Peter Adam, *Art of the Third Reich*, NY: Harry Adams Ltd, 1992; and Stephanie Barron, *'Degenerate Art': The Fate of the Avant-Garde in Nazi Germany*, Los Angeles County Museum of Art, 1991; CIR 4 (Linz), op. cit., 47.

[26] These purged items, totalling over 1600, included cubist, expressionist, and impressionist art.

[27] Feliciano, 1997 op. cit., ch. 1.

[28] More generally, see John Willett, *Art and Politics in the Weimar Period: The New Sobriety, 1917–1933*, NY: Da Capo Press, 1978.

[29] Lynn H. Nicholas, *The Rape of Europa: The Fate of Europe's Treasures in the Third Reich and the Second World War*, NY: Vintage, 1995, ch. 1.

[30] J. Petropoulos, 2000 op. cit.

> stated that von Behr told him also that the entire operation had been declared secret by Hitler, and that even the basic text of the special article of the Armistice was not to be divulged; it had been his original impression, and that of his colleagues at the ERR in Paris, that the confiscations were entirely legal and carried out by agreement of the French and German governments.... Lohse was given the initial responsibility for the preparation of a catalog and inventory of the newly confiscated Alphonse Kahn Collection.[31]

In addition to financial and other material factors underpinning the orientations and actions of those, such as Utikal, involved in such confiscations, OSS reports recognised the operation of a racist and violent form of anti-Semitism:

> Prior to the preparation of the BUNJES paper, UTIKAL, on 3 November 1941, had prepared an internal memorandum by way of reply to the protest over confiscation of Jewish-owned art properties, lodged with the German authorities on 25 July 1941 by the French General Commission for Jewish Questions. UTIKAL dismisses all legal considerations in his paper which is, in essence, a violent anti-Semitic harangue, couched in terroristic language.[32]

As well as forming a distinctive policy objective of their wider and racist cultural programme, the Nazi regime directly and indirectly exploited the *subjective consequences* of threatened looting for its potential victims. This fear was exploited as a way of raising additional funds. During early phases of anti-Semitic programmes of persecution, Austrian and other Jews who remained within 'Greater Germany' were subjected to an escalating series of racist decrees. In response to such programmes, some Jews transferred assets into works of art believing, often wrongly, that these would provide a safer and more easily disposable device for holding their family wealth. Others immediately sold their artworks at reduced prices in order to purchase, at punitive cost, official exit visas and taxes.

Lacking foreign currency, particularly Swiss Francs,[33] Hitler's regime also deployed confiscated artworks as a substitute for hard currency when purchasing items vital to its growing war economy.[34] This, together

---

[31] DIR No. 6 (Lohse) op. cit., 2.

[32] Consolidated Interrogation Report (CIR)/(ERR), 78.

[33] This element is regularly noted in CIR reports, e.g., CIR 2 (Göring), op. cit., 18 33, 131, 164: 'The chief reason for the exchanges [of confiscated Jewish art] was the lack of foreign currency' ibid., 128.

[34] CIR 4 (Linz), op. cit., 73–74.

with the criminally dishonest and fraudulent ethos of implicated dealers, is made clear by parts of the OSS' DIR Report on Hans Wendland:

> Wendland has admitted to the practice of giving receipts for sums in excess of those actually paid him by Hofer,[35] and to have given Hofer receipts for objects which were not even purchased from him. Paintings which were sold by Wendland to Hofer in Paris occasionally came to Göring bearing receipts purportedly from Frau Schulzess, Swiss dealer. In this manner, Hofer was able to obtain Swiss francs from Göring in payment for bills which he had settled in French francs. While Wendland admits having given Hofer false receipts to enable him to obtain Swiss francs, he denies ever having cognisance of the use of Frau Schulzess' name in this connection. He excuses this as a common practice in the art market, thus implying that he, at least, has done this on other occasions.[36]

It is clear from this DIR that Göring and Andreas Hofer (his chief adviser), became increasingly desperate for Swiss Francs as the war progressed, and were willing to resort to fraud, or at least to breaches of contract, in their dealings with Wendland and Fischer:

> The chief reason for the exchanges on Göring's side was the lack of foreign currency, the Reichsbank having decided that henceforth its dwindling supply of foreign credits would have to be used for the purchase of items more essential to the war economy than works of art. Wendland states that the exchange arrangements were always unsatisfactory to Fischer and himself and that they would have preferred Swiss francs in payment, as had been originally agreed to by Hofer. But, he states, in each case, after the deliveries had been made in good faith on their part, they were informed by Hofer that payment could not be made in Swiss francs but would have to be made in impressionist and modern French pictures. They are represented as having no alternative but to accept.[37]

Alternatively, confiscated Jewish and other plundered works of art were simply sold in Switzerland, Italy, Holland or France as a way of raising foreign currency.[38] For example, in 1939 the Nazi regime auctioned 126 'degenerate' artworks, including works by van Gogh and Matisse, at

---

[35] Hofer, who began his career as a small-scale Berlin art dealer, had, by 1937, become appointed to Göring's chief art adviser. Their arrangement was that, while acting as Göring's agent with the various privileges and protection this afforded, Hofer could still operate as an independent dealer allowed to keep any work of art that Göring rejected. Plaut, 1946a op. cit.

[36] Wendland DIR, op. cit., 15.

[37] Ibid., 16.

[38] CIR 4 (Linz), op. cit., 67.

the 'Fischer Galerie' in Lucerne, Switzerland.[39] Hofer, Göring's curator, was complicit in the hypocritical practice of taking and then either selling, or using for exchange, examples of disapproved art that the ERR had confiscated from French Jews.[40] In other words, Göring was not such a Nazi purist as to destroy artworks that his regime deemed to be 'decadent' because of their associations with Jewish artists or modern art themes. Instead, and as ALIU officials recognised in their analysis of the following letter from September 1941 from Hofer to Göring, he was willing to acquire approximately 100 examples of such confiscated works from Jewish and other collections. He took these in order to exchange them for other paintings that were more to his own personal taste, that is, old masters and German nineteenth century art:

> Collection of the Jew Rosenberg: I have chosen for you and reserved with Mr. von Behr: 2 Ingres drawings, 7 pictures and one drawing by Corot, one watercolor by Daumier, three pictures by Courbet, one by Pissarro, four pastels and one picture by Degas, one picture by Manet, 5 by Sisley, 3 watercolors by Cézanne, 4 pictures by Monet, 3 drawings and 5 pictures by Renoir, one picture by van Gogh, one picture and two drawings by Seurat and one picture by Toulouse-Lautrec. All are of outstanding quality, and measured by the results of [a recent]...auction, exceedingly cheap and suitable for exchange. I shall bring you...very willing purchasers for it![41]

As an official policy following the lead given by both Hitler and Göring, art looting also provided a source of preferential advancement for German officers seeking official recognition from their superiors as 'dedicated Nazis', and hence internal promotion within the party. Gifts of confiscated artworks to these leaders operated as a strategic form of homage, tribute and ingratiation. From the start of their regime in 1933, Hitler and Göring planned two large art collections: Hitler's *Führermuseum* in Linz, Austria, and the Hermann Göring Collection located at Carinhall, Germany. Later sections of this book will show that both 'benefited' substantially from works confiscated from European Jews.

Scholars trying to reconstruct and understand the nature of Nazi art

---

[39] In relation to Voss, Director of the Linz Museum, and Haberstock, see CIR 4 (Linz), op. cit., 47: 'Voss states that Haberstock used unscrupulous methods to force certain museum directors to exchange, for works by 19th Century German masters like Schuch and Trubner which he was promoting, works which, even if not approved by the Nazis, he could exchange abroad at a handsome profit.' Cf. ibid., 67–68, Attachment 71.

[40] CIR 2 (Göring), op. cit., 11.

[41] Ibid., Attachment 1.

plundering have, for good reasons, relied heavily upon the contents of Allied intelligence records, including interrogation and intercept evidence. This is particularly the case for those records which were composed both at the time this activity was taking place, and during the immediate aftermath of investigative work carried out, at least in part, for the immediate postwar national and international war crimes hearings. Even the gaps in, and limits of, such evidence can be instructive. As Feliciano notes, OSS and other Allied agencies engaged in such intelligence work faced considerable obstacles in seeking to ascertain details, particularly in areas where the interviewees felt they were personally liable for prosecution as Nazi war criminals:

> In order to acquire some solid elementary facts, I was forced to consult many still-classified intelligence documents...conserved in the National Archives and Records in Washington DC.... Once I was able to locate the right documents I soon found the Allies had performed many interrogations. What intrigued me most, as I read the interrogation transcripts, was how frequently those being questioned—mostly art connoisseurs—were stricken with timely bouts of amnesia, becoming unable to remember little or nothing about a piece in question...the closer the interrogators' questions were associated with them, the less they could remember about the period. Once the interrogators moved further away, their memories improved suddenly and remarkably.[42]

In short, and as a matter of official state policy, the Nazis engaged in a systematic and comprehensive form of cultural plunder of Jewish artworks as an integral aspect of the Holocaust. They created special agencies to carry this out, the activities of which were investigated by the OSS and other intelligence agencies, and stored many of these looted works in Hitler and Göring's collection. Researchers in this field have, for good reasons, extensively cited and, in many cases, 'mined' OSS records on Nazi art looting.

The creation of the ALIU[43]

This section retraces the process of negotiation between the Roberts Commission, represented by Francis Henry Taylor, and leading figures within the OSS, particularly senior figures within OSS X-2 and SI

[42] Feliciano, 1997 op. cit., 8.

[43] For overviews see 'X-2 ALIU official history': US NA, RG 226, Entry 99 (OSS Branch Histories), Box 19, Folder 68.

Branches. Taylor was a leading light of the Robert's Commission and Director of America's Metropolitan Museum of Art. He was also the member of the Commission most directly concerned with the protection and recovery of cultural materials within fighting zones. Following the intervention of a colleague, Theodore Sizer, Taylor became increasingly aware of: 'the need for an intelligence connection.'[44] He had experienced frequent difficulties in gaining relevant intelligence on looted art from senior Allied military circles. As Winks notes: 'Further, art historians assigned to SHAEF...were having difficulties with their British counterparts under Sir Leonard Wooley and with both the British and American military because of their generally lowly ranks.'[45]

The work of the OSS in the field of Nazi art looting had, until the autumn of 1944 at least, been largely sporadic and *ad hoc*. Certainly references to art looting are contained in OSS war crimes files,[46] including those consolidated into General Donovan's Nuremberg files during his period as Deputy Chief Prosecutor.[47] It is clear from a number of the references already given in our earlier discussion of the OSS' contribution to the Safehaven programme that OSS staff had been investigating looted works of art where this could have involved the transfer of assets abroad.[48] Prior to the creation of the OSS' art unit, such information, and the intelligence-gathering which underpinned it, had lacked a central focus and dedicated unit within this intelligence agency.

---

[44] Winks, *Cloak and Gown*, NY: Collins, 1987, 303.

[45] Ibid.

[46] Interrogation reports: US NA, RG 226, Entry 158, Box 10, Folders 120–121.

[47] For example, the interrogation report from Hans Frank dated 13 Sept. 1945 includes references to art looting together with information on concentration camps, the Polish educational system, and the legal rights, in Poland, of Germans, Jews, and Poles, respectively. See Cornell Collection, Vol. 13, 31.03.

[48] In addition to earlier references, see 'Washington Secret Intelligence/Special Funds Records' US NA, RG 226, Entry 183, Box 3, Folder 19 'preliminary report on 'Looted Art in Occupied Territories, Neutral Countries and Latin'. The next Box 4, Folder 26 contains Safehaven materials on investigations of 'purchases' from the Rothschilds, whilst Box 6, Folder 32 includes Safehaven reports on art holdings and looting, and Box 6, Folder 46 'Safehaven reports, intelligence documents, and other documents concerning German personnel implicated in looted art; looted art; German looting.' Box 6, Folder 49 contains Safehaven reports 'on the forced sale of art, theft of art, and personnel involved including person working in Göring's interest'; whilst Box 12, Folder 60 contains 'Safehaven reports and other documents pertaining to possible traffic in looted paintings in Norway'; US NA, RG 226, Entry 183, Box 15, Folder 81 contains 'Safehaven reports and other documents pertaining to looted art work'. Ibid., Box 17. Folder 89 'looted art in Switzerland'; ibid. Folder 90 'looted art of Baronne Elizabeth Weiss and her brothers in Budapest, Hungary', January 1946.

Specific OSS R&A Branch materials had, on occasions, been sent to official agencies responsible for investigating art looting, particularly the American Commission for the Protection and Salvage of Artistic and Historic Monuments in War Areas ('the Roberts Commission'), which later recognised their value.[49] These materials included a formal 'Report on Looting and Damaging of Art Works in Europe', and a shorter bulletin: 'German Publicity on Measures for the Protection of Art in Italy'—both distributed in 1943. Indeed, it is arguable that the emergence of the OSS' art unit can be traced back to the positive reception with which the first of these reports were received by the Roberts Commission. As Winks has recognised: 'The report proved so useful to the Commission, OSS were asked to do further research.'[50] The Commission's final report noted how such OSS studies helped set up a closer and encouraging form of institutional cooperation between different bodies:

> These publications inaugurated a close collaboration between the American Commission and the Office of Strategic Services. Data on German art and library personnel collected by the Office of Strategic Services was forwarded to the American Council of Learned Societies Committee in New York and to the Vaucher Commission in London for coordination with their files.[51]

During 1943, however, there was no clear indication that investigative activity connected with Nazi art looting would contribute to war crimes evidence by substantiating criminal charges falling under recognised offences within either domestic or international law. Nor was it even certain that any such trials were definitely going to take place during the immediate postwar years. Furthermore, even if war crimes trials embracing racist forms of cultural plunder were to take place, there were no guarantees at this time that it would be the OSS, as distinct from some other or newly-created organisation, that would be given

[49] 'The Research and Analysis Branch of the Office of Strategic Services had, from the inception of this agency, assembled information on many phases of activity of interest to the Commission. Such pertinent data was transmitted from time to time to the Commission and certain affiliated agencies, and these, in turn, brought additional material to the attention of the Branch.' 'Report of the Roberts Commission for the Protection and Salvage of Artistic and Historic Monuments in War Areas,' (Roberts Commission Report), US Government, Washington: 1946, op. cit., 33.

[50] Winks, 1987 op. cit., 303.

[51] Roberts Commission Report, op. cit., 38–39.

responsibility for gathering and preparing trial evidence. However, by the Autumn of 1944, the OSS leadership was, in pursuits of its own postwar survival, already committed to achieving a prominent institutional position in any future postwar Nazi war crimes trials. They made this commitment notwithstanding the absence of official policy decisions in this field, let alone any allocation of specific institutional responsibilities. The emergence of this institutional imperative in 1944 has been recognised by historians of Nazi art looting, with Nicholas, for example, noting: 'not least the agency was beginning to compile evidence for future war crimes prosecutions.'[52]

The creation of a specific Unit dedicated to the investigation of Nazi art looting was prompted, at least in part, by Roosevelt's Special Commission chaired by Justice Owen Roberts.[53] Rothfeld suggests that preliminary contacts between OSS and members of this Commission began as far back as 1942:

> In September 1942, Francis Henry Taylor and David Bruce, National Gallery of Art board president and as early as 1941 U.S. intelligence chief, discussed the creation of an art investigative unit and the issue of under which federal civilian or military agency the unit could possibly operate. Ideally, at this point, Taylor and Bruce wanted the unit to work alongside yet independently of the military because the military was handling all of the incoming war intelligence reports.... David Bruce and Francis Henry Taylor discussed the possibility of placing the [proposed] unit under former governor Herbert Lehman's newly organized United Nations Refugee and Rehabilitation Agency (UNRRA). Officially established in 1943 to aid European refugees, UNRRA developed from the League of Nations High Commission for Refugees (1921) and the Inter-Governmental Committee on Refugees (1938).[54]

However, these contacts did not result in any further progress until the winter of 1943–1944. At this time, X-2 officials and Taylor engaged in renewed discussions regarding the future establishment of an investigative art unit, and the placement of the unit's officers within combat units.[55]

---

[52] Nicholas, 1995 op. cit., 282.

[53] Records of the Roberts Commission are available from: US NA, RG 239. The Roberts Commission records contain index card boxes divided into different subjects, including art looting suspects, looted art objects, repositories and collectors suspected of obtaining or storing looted art objects, and firms involved in art contraband.

[54] Rothfeld, 2002 op. cit., Chapter Two, 9.

[55] Ibid., 20.

In March 1944, and building upon the progress made in the earlier meetings, Justice Roberts contacted the OSS Director concerning the possibility of creating a special OSS unit dedicated to addressing various aspects of Nazi art looting.[56] In this month, Huntington Cairns, secretary to the Roberts Commission, wrote a letter to Donovan. This sought further assistance from the OSS regarding:

> collection of information on the looting and removal of art objects by the enemy, on damage to such objects, on protective measures taken by the Allies and by the Axis, on enemy art personnel, and on the activities of dealers in art objects in every occupied area.[57]

Donovan then held a meeting with Justice Roberts, representing the Roberts Commission. It was at this meeting that the OSS Director finally agreed to the latter's request for the OSS to create and fund a special art unit. This unit was to assist both the Commission and the US Army's Monuments officers, some of whom had, from late 1943, already been operating in Italy. Donovan probably appreciated that the proposed art unit could contribute significantly to X-2's wider mission of tracking the Nazis' movement of concealed assets, as well as other counter-espionage imperatives.[58] Despite his agreement in principle to the creation of this new body, there was a delay of approximately eight months before the OSS leadership and the Roberts Commission finalised their formal agreement relating to a mutual exchange of art intelligence. According to this Commission, the unit's mission was to include not only the identification and protection of looted works but also the discovery and apprehension of individuals and organisations who were complicit in their systematic theft:[59]

> In March 1944, the Secretary of the Commission, in a letter to Maj. Gen. William J. Donovan, Director of the Office of Strategic Services, requested the further assistance of that organization in the collection of information on the looting and removal of art objects by the enemy, on damage to such objects, on protective measures taken by the Allies and by the Axis, on enemy art personnel, and on the activities of dealers in art objects in every occupied area. Material of this nature was supplied

[56] Plaut, 1997 op. cit., 124.
[57] Report of the Roberts Commission (1946), op. cit., 37–39.
[58] Ibid.
[59] Anthony Cave Brown, (ed) *Secret War Report*, NY: Berkeley Publishing Corporation, 1976, 92–93; *OSS War Report, Vol. I*, 196.

> from time to time by the Office of Strategic Services to the Commission, and through it, to the American Council of Learned Societies Committee in New York.[60]

It was not until the late summer of 1944 that these plans started to take a concrete shape linked to a real institutional outcome. In August 1944, Taylor opened up further lines of communication with David Bruce, chief of OSS SI in London and former US National Gallery board president, who he considered more sympathetic to the investigation of Nazi plunder, and with Whitney Shepardson, overall Head of OSS-SI and Norman Pearson chief of X-2 in London.[61] Bruce's diary from this period notes: 'August 31: Norman Pearson and Hugh Will talked about Francis Taylor's (Director of the Metropolitan Museum) Commission to track down objets d'art stolen by the Germans. They were interested in the possible use of this Commission as cover for X-2.'[62] During this August meeting with Pearson, Taylor had agreed to share the Roberts Commission's extensive private files on art looting with X-2. In return, Pearson promised Taylor OSS funding for a: 'field unit of properly qualified individuals whose chief interest should be the attention to problems in [Taylor's] interests.'[63] Apparently Pearson: 'was pleased to have played a small, but key, role in the work of the OSS Art Looting Project.'[64]

During the next month, Pearson wrote to Murphy describing his meeting with Taylor on 30 August 1944.[65] According to Murphy, their discussion had resulted in: 'mutual exchange of information between our respective files.' It was reported that Murphy and Taylor had recognised that such contacts could be developed further through the establishment of an art investigative unit.[66] In October 1944, Taylor met again with

[60] Roberts Commission Report, 1946 op. cit., 39.

[61] Ibid., 303–4.

[62] Nelson Douglas Lankford (ed), *OSS Against the Reich: The World War II Diaries of Colonel David K. E. Bruce*, Kent, OH: Kent State University Press, 1991, 182.

[63] Pearson to Murphy, 10 September 1944, 'Orion organization': US NA, RG 226, Entry 190, Box 532.

[64] Winks, 1987 op. cit., 303–304.

[65] Norman Pearson, the head of the X-2 operation in London, reported to James Murphy, the Chief of X-2 operations worldwide. Murphy, in turn, supplied X-2 intelligence reports to both David Bruce, then head of the OSS SI operations in London, and General Donovan in Washington.

[66] Pearson to Murphy, 10 September 1944, 'Orion Organization' ibid. Taylor originally suggested enlisted army men for an art investigative unit. For proposed names of personnel, see Taylor to Murphy, 2 October 1944: US NA, RG 239, Box 52.

his old friend David Bruce. Taylor wanted to see if the OSS would be able and willing to aid the objectives of this Commission by establishing an investigative art unit. At this time, Taylor also contacted James R. Murphy, chief of OSS X-2 in Washington, concerning personnel to staff a: 'special unit of [the OSS] organization.'[67] Taylor and Murphy thought that this proposed investigation unit could fulfil each other's future needs and concerns. However progress stalled somewhat over the next months.

OSS officials, including Murphy and Pearson, wanted X-2 staff to begin collecting counter-espionage information by infiltrating the German espionage system in Europe.[68] Certainly by this time, Taylor had come to appreciate that the OSS had strategic reasons, connected with its own existing counter-espionage responsibilities, to infiltrate more agents under cover into Europe, for wanting to engage in a more emphatic form of interagency collaboration with the American Commission:

> Taylor...turned to a more sympathetic source: the OSS. Here was an organisation which did not have to work through army channels. Access was no problem—its ranks were full of friendly academics and the London Office was headed by former National Gallery President David Bruce. Bruce had initiated contact with the Roberts Commission [RC] after his recruitment to the secret agency in 1942. He had wanted to have an OSS analyst attend RC meetings and had hoped to send agents into Europe under MFAA cover, ideas that met with negative responses from everyone: Finley, Eisenhower, and the Army staff. Ignoring these objections, Taylor began discussions with the OSS in London in August 1944. The idea of investigating Nazi looting not only appealed to the RC but fitted in well with the OSS' counterintelligence operation which was compiling dossiers on Nazi agents on the continent who might be a threat after the German military authorities had been defeated.[69]

In his 10 September report to Murphy, Pearson argued that this cooperative effort would directly benefit the interests and programmes of X-2:

> In view of the prospect of hidden art treasures becoming one of many sources for financing underground movements for the Nazis directed from outside Germany, and the fact that the longer the emergence of these

[67] Taylor to Murphy, 2 October 1944, 'Orion Organization': US NA, RG 226, Entry 190, Box 532.
[68] Ibid., 21.
[69] Nicholas, 1995 op. cit., 281–82.

> treasures was delayed the more sinister might be the implication, Taylor's proposition holds certain attractions for the long-range planning of X-2.[70]

The final report of the Robert Commission recognised that the proposed OSS art unit integrated its concern with looted works of art, and the OSS' own long-term interests in the movement and fate of Nazi and German assets, both of which would extend into the post-hostilities period. Furthermore, and in contrast to the more narrowly defined restitution focus of the Roberts Commission, the OSS had a keen interest in broader Safehaven objects, that is: 'in tracing and preventing the flow of assets to places of refuge where they might be used to finance the postwar survival of Nazism.'[71] Pearson thus suggested this proposed art unit should be able to dovetail into X-2's long-term goals by coordinating working relationships with the British intelligence agencies, and by sharing and disseminating information between American and British officials in London.

Pearson and Murphy both recognised that the main function of X-2 was to continually supply the civilian and military agencies with current and useful intelligence data.[72] On the other hand, in his report, Pearson also cautioned that X-2 might perhaps be held responsible for how the art-related intelligence would eventually be deployed by the proposed unit.[73] Anne Rothfeld has argued that the creation of the OSS' Art Looting Investigation Unit needs to be understood in terms of the recognition of a perceived need of the OSS leadership and the Roberts Commission to provide a 'bridge' between their two areas of interest in relation to Nazi looted art:

> the ALIU acted as a "bridge" between the art community's (Roberts Commission) interests of recovering and restituting looted artworks and the intelligence community's interests of finding German agents acting as art dealers and tracing the movement of hidden Nazi assets.... The story of the ALIU was one of bringing together two agencies with different needs and their increasingly shared concerns with the movement and fate of Nazi looted assets.[74]

[70] Pearson to Murphy, 10 September 1944, 2, 'Orion Organization': US NA, RG 226; Entry 190, Box 532.

[71] Nicholas, 1995 op. cit., 282.

[72] Rothfeld, 2002 op. cit., Chapter Two, 21.

[73] Pearson to Murphy, 10 September 1944, op. cit., 2.

[74] Rothfeld, 2002 op. cit., Chapter One, 15 (quoted from a private copy of this remarkable MA thesis kindly supplied by the author, which I gratefully acknowledge).

Arguably, one successful result of these discussions during the late summer of 1944 was Bruce's decision to approve a formal liaison between X-2 and the Roberts Commission.[75] In September matters moved up a gear with the formulation of one the early analytical goals for the proposed Unit prior to the liberation of Europe. This was stated as involving the study of: 'the coordinated files of the various [national] commissions on stolen art in order to identify persons involved and to discover patterns of transmission of these articles, especially into neutral counties'.[76] The idea at this stage was to apply whatever could be found in this way to the proposed Unit's ongoing and later field investigations. In the same month, the OSS contacted Taylor and requested that he begin selecting members for this new unit. The Roberts Commission and the OSS officials urged Taylor to hire fine art professionals in whom he had the personal confidence to carry out this important assignment.[77] In early October 1944, Taylor insisted to Pearson and Murphy that the proposed art unit's integration within X-2 would be vital: 'a unit working under OSS would be of the utmost benefit to the [Roberts] Commission, and [Taylor was] sure that Mr. Cairns [Roberts Commission secretary] would be glad to arrange with [Murphy] for proper cover for your operations in the field.'[78]

Another notable landmark in the emergence of the ALIU was the creation of a blue-print for its mission contained in an anonymous OSS memorandum dated 23 October 1944, presumably written by either Bruce or Murphy. This directly addressed its counter-espionage potential for monitoring dubious individuals connected with Nazism, and tracing any assets they may have concealed. This document emphasised the mutual dependence of tracing and recovering not only assets but also the persons concerned with their looting. In this way, it clarified the OSS' possible contribution to possible restitution for the victims of a systematic programme of Nazi war criminality, of which European Jews were one of the main victims:[79]

[75] Ibid.

[76] Anonymous memorandum, 23 October 1944, 'Orion Organization': US NA, RG 226, Entry 190, Box 532.

[77] Ibid.

[78] Taylor to Murphy, 2 October 1944, 'Orion Organization': US NA, RG 226, Entry 190, Box 532.

[79] Anonymous memorandum, 23 October 1944, 'Orion Organization': US NA, RG 226, Entry 190, Box 532.

> [T]he basic assumption behind the sponsoring of such a unit is that art goods have and may increasingly become a medium of exchange for financing espionage rings as well as the means of providing with nest eggs certain individuals who come within our sphere of interest. Whereas the art missions are ultimately concerned with objects, and X-2 with persons, the tracing of persons on our part may benefit the commissions by locating objects, it is also probable that the tracing of objects may ultimately assist in the location of persons.[80]

This memorandum sought to justify the proposed unit's inclusion within X-2 operations. However, it also recognised that the results of its investigative efforts would, in order to yield significant results, need to be combined with the fruits of other wider X-2 and SI Branch materials. Winks notes that it was X-2's Pearson who: 'proposed that the art historians be formally attached to X-2 and that a "Cultural War Room" be set up in London, as X-2 was able to get higher simulated rank for its personnel and promotion came more easily overseas. This war room provided the central collecting office for: 'all Allied information on enemy [art] looting gained through intelligence channels.'[81] Senior OSS figures recognised that their Art Unit could face problems in establishing: 'special chains of agents composed of art dealers and collectors who might be in a position to discover dealers in clandestine art objects.'[82] Sumner Crosby, from Yale's History of Art Department, worked out the administrative details so that some of the work technically fell under Pearson's command.

The final agreement between the Roberts Commission and Donovan was expressed in an OSS inter-branch directive dated 21 November 1944 authorising the creation of an art unit.[83] It was then approved by the Chief of the X-2 Branch several days later. This memorandum told senior OSS staff that an 'Art Looting Investigation Unit' had been created and was to be located within X-2.[84] Because this unit's goal was to hunt down art thieves and to prevent the movement of German

---

80 Ibid.

81 Anonymous, undated report on the ALIU's creation, 'Orion Organization': US NA, RG 226, Entry 190, Box 532.

82 Ibid.

83 ALIU Final Report, 1 May 1946: US NA, Microfilm M1782.

84 For associated files, see Plaut and Rousseau to Murphy, 21 November 1944, Plaut to Dunn, 29 November 1944; Finley to Murphy, 4 December 1944; and Chief, X-2 Branch to Chief, R&A Branch and Chief, SI Branch, 9 December 1944: US NA, RG 226; Entry 190, Box 532.

and Nazi assets, the OSS gave it the code name, Project Orion, named after the hunter god of Greek mythology. The ALIU's initial budget was made only for a six month period on the grounds that: 'the project is still in an experimental phase.'[85] However, during late January 1945, Donovan approved considerable additional funding of $30,000.[86]

In short, the creation of the ALIU / Orion took place in November 1944 through a codification of an earlier agreement between members of the OSS leadership (including Donovan and David Bruce) and Owen Roberts, acting as chair of The Roberts Commission.

It appears that the various sides to this process broadly welcomed the results of their negotiations. Finley, from the Roberts Commission, welcomed the creation of the ALIU. He informed the X-2 Chief James Murphy that the Roberts Commission was pleased to see the unit working within X-2 and that the shared: 'experience which [the two groups] gain will be of great assistance in the formulation of policies and procedures in connection with restitution.'[87] Furthermore, and as one major study of Nazi art looting recognises:

> The creation of the ALIU was a coup for Taylor and the Roberts Commission, which until then had experienced great difficulty in obtaining information concerning MFA&A [Monuments Fine Arts and Archives Branch of the United States Army] activities in Britain where SHAEF was located. Furthermore, there had been increasing resentment within the Commission at the apparent assumption by the British of control of the entire Allied MFA&A organisation.... Thus, it was that the formation of the OSS ALIU in November 1944 came at a very welcome time for the Roberts Commission.[88]

Within the different branches of the OSS, the reception of the creation of the ALIU also appears to have been positive. Different branch chiefs

[85] Sears to Donovan, 13 January 1945, 'Orion': US NA, M1642, Roll 38, Frame 927–8. For other art looting files in the Director's Files, see 'Art looted by Nazis in Europe 7–18–47, ibid., Roll 101 Frames 1206–1207; Art Looting Investigation Unit, report on 3–10–47; ibid., Roll 46, Frame 407; Art looting report 3–17–47, ibid., Roll 46, Frame 410; Art looting, investigation of 8–19–46, ibid., Roll 112, Frames 300–301; Art looted by Nazis in Europe, OSS documents relating to 7–18–45, ibid., Roll 101, Frames 1206–1207; Art treasures in Europe 3–5–44, ibid., Roll 33, Frames 170–175.

[86] Special Funds, Webb from White, 25 January 1945: ibid., Frame 17.

[87] Finley to Murphy, 4 December 1944, 'Orion Organization': US NA, RG 226, Entry 190, Box 532.

[88] Harclerrode and Pittway, *The Lost Masters*, London: Orion, 2000, 87–89.

recognised that they might be able to benefit from the ALIU sharing its intelligence with their own staff.[89] For instance, a memorandum presumably from Murphy dated 9 December 1944 to the Chiefs of the R&A and the SI Branches indicated that the ALIU would: 'obtain information bearing on enemy espionage and on subversive individuals and activities.'[90] The claim here was the ALIU's creation would allow information to be exchanged between the different OSS branches. In addition, the art unit would be able to both clarify and supply: 'references to art dealers, German museum officials and other individuals or organizations involved in formal confiscation procedure... as well as records of personal or public loss of works of art through enemy action.'[91]

This memorandum also advocated a mutual pooling of relevant OSS intelligence information regarding art looting, and prohibited OSS staff from informing external agencies about the existence of the ALIU.[92] It was also ordered that: 'knowledge [of the ALIU] be restricted within OSS to as few persons as possible.'[93] Pearson's efforts to develop cross-Branch cooperation yielded some fruit. He received a memorandum from the OSS' Biographical Division that offered the ALIU access to its files on enemy personnel who, they believed, were possibly involved in art looting operations.[94]

In January 1945, the OSS leadership was beginning to have real hopes for the ALIU's mission; and set about establishing enhanced external liaisons. Pearson discussed sharing information with other OSS branches, including the section on prisoners-of-war (P/W) and the Military Intelligence Service (MIS). He indicated: 'that individuals under [P/W] control may be in a position to furnish information which would greatly assist in [ALIU's] work.'[95] Within a month of its creation,

---

[89] Rothfeld, 2002 op. cit., Chapter Two, 30.

[90] Anonymous memorandum to Chief, Research and Analysis Branch, Chief, SI Branch, 9 December 1944, 'Orion Organization': US NA, RG 226, Entry 190, Box 532. I am grateful to Anne Rothfeld for her references to this document.

[91] Ibid.

[92] Ibid.

[93] Ibid.

[94] T.W. Reese to Pearson, 8 January 1945, 'Orion Organization': US NA, RG 226, Entry 190, Box 532.

[95] Pearson to Holt, 18 January 1945, 'Orion Organization': US NA, RG 226, Entry 190, Box 532. In his letter to the P/W, Pearson gave a list of questions to ask the POWs designed to assist ALIU investigations. The questions included names of German personnel connected with the movement of looted art and related assets,

James Plaut (the Unit's Chief, see below) also made contact with other agencies including the State Department and the Civil Affairs Division (CAD) of the US War Department. The idea was to seek to further extend interagency liaison and cooperation. State Department liaison could, he suggested, provide his staff with the required protection and movement in neutral countries that could improve their investigations in these states.[96] With respect to the CAD, Plaut was exploiting the fact that MFA&A officials operated under the auspices of CAD, and that this organisation could provide ALIU with 'cover'. Hence, Plaut requested that ALIU staff: 'be permitted to function ostensibly as G-5 Fine Arts and Monuments personnel' in the European and Mediterranean Theaters of Operation.[97] The fact that members of this unit were OSS employees was concealed from other government agencies with MFA&A operating as 'cover' for all external purposes.[98]

Following its creation in November 1944, ALIU officials gained full access to OSS' dossiers on Nazi agents working in Europe who, it was suspected, might play an active role in establishing and funding postwar varieties of Neo-Nazism.[99] Such officials could also officially exploit the extensive documentation developed by the Roberts Commission and associated bodies who had created a card file system with over 75,000 entries. According to an internal OSS memorandum, these described plundered works of art objects, the names of those implicated and biographical information on persons possibly linked to the confiscations and possible espionage activities. They also included information on the possibility of such plundering generating: 'future funds for underground activities directed from outside Germany.'[100] From the start, these dossiers and card files formed an invaluable foundation for the investigative art unit's research and analyses. They also functioned as helpful aids to ALIU's future interrogation of suspected Nazi and German art looters.

---

details of looting operations in the West, and the locations of depositories storing confiscated artworks.

[96] Plaut to Towell, 2 December 1944, 'Liaison': US NA, RG 226, Entry 190, Box 533.

[97] Plaut to Kades, 26 December 1944, 'Liaison': ibid.

[98] Rothfeld, 2002 op. cit., Chapter Two, 21.

[99] Nicholas, 1995 op. cit., 282.

[100] Pearson to Murphy, 10 September 1944, 'Orion Organization': US NA, RG 226, Entry 190, Box 533.

The idea of the OSS X-2 Branch establishing and financing an art looting investigative unit was supposed to harmonise with, and contribute to, X-2's wider counterintelligence activities both generally and in relation to Safehaven projects. In particular, it was designed to contribute to the investigation of the Nazis' use of looted artworks as a highly mobile form of concealed wealth linked to future political agendas. By locating the planned art unit within the X-2 Branch, its personnel would be able to assist the shared goals of the Roberts Commission and X-2 relating to locating and tracking Nazi looted assets and enemy personnel involved in the confiscations.

In short, during 1944, the X-2 Branch had developed a prior interest in exploiting art looting investigative activities both as an objective in itself, and as a 'cover' for wider secret counter-espionage operations. However, it is equally true that the internal culture, resources and institutional practices of this branch tended to foster skills and knowledge that were uniquely valuable in tracking down and investigating this type of war criminality and its perpetrators. Rothfeld correctly notes that ALIU activities continued—but also extended—prior X-2 expertise and interests:

> The OSS and specifically its Counter-intelligence Branch, X-2, were interested in the movement and ultimate disposition of Nazi looted assets. In fact, the OSS's counter-intelligence branch was actively collecting economic intelligence, which would be of interest to the art unit. Additionally, OSS officials considered the movement of art assets as another field potentially full of German and Nazi agents.[101]

Bringing certain art looting intelligence and investigation activities under the auspices of the OSS in general and X-2 in particular, had a number of distinct logistical advantages to the missions of both the Roberts Commission and Donovan's organisation. According to internal OSS memorandum, these stemmed partly from the fact that members of the ALIU were automatically given military titles. These, in turn, granted ALIU officials special rights to travel across liberated Europe and even neutral countries, such as Switzerland.[102] Such officials also became independent from control by the US Army. Instead, they

---

[101] Rothfeld, 2002 op. cit., Chapter Two, 19.

[102] 'As members of an OSS unit...have facilities for movement both in military zones and neutral countries, perhaps not fully enjoyed by the members of other services.' Memo Finley to Hilldring, 28 April 1944: US NA, RG 165, Entry 463 quoted in Nicholas, 1995 op. cit., 282.

liased directly with the Roberts Commission.[103] In addition, the fact that the ALIU was assigned to X-2, rather than to the scholarly OSS R&A Branch which might have appeared at first sight to provide a more obvious home for this unit, yielded additional advantages. These included not only enhanced mobility but also immediate access to the Allies' latest relevant 'Ultra' intelligence data via ISOS (Intelligence Services Oliver Strachey). This was hand-enciphered material named after a senior member of the British Bletchley Park code-breakers. As Winks notes:

> While methodologically the tiny investigation unit might have fallen to R&A, this would not do, for the investigators had to have access to ISOS, as R&A did not, to be able to go immediately behind the advancing troops, and the unit, since it was charged with interrogation, had to have mobility and access to immediate information.[104]

Staffing the new OSS Unit and creating its administrative structure

In terms of staffing, Roberts and Donovan asked Taylor to help select members for the in whom he had personal confidence. Through his recruitment efforts, the unit comprised 10 personnel: 4 commissioned officers, 3 enlisted men, and 3 civilian support staff.[105] Apparently, recruitment continued as late as June 1945.[106] In relation to its staff's background, the ALIU's Final Report states: 'the majority of whom had extensive pre-war experience in fine arts, either as museum officials or in an academic capacity, as well as previous investigative training and experience in World War II.'[107]

Given that the unit dependent upon the skills and quality of its small staff, it is worth examining these in more detail. For the vital post of overall founding ALIU director, Taylor appointed James S. Plaut, who had a wartime background in the Office of Naval Intelligence interrogating captured U Boat personnel and had previously worked for Sachs at the Fogg Museum. Plaut was fluent in both German and French.

---

[103] Nicholas, 1995 op. cit., 282.

[104] Winks 1987 op. cit., 324.

[105] See the introductory essay by Michael Hussey, Michael J. Kurtz, and Greg Bradsher: 'M1782: OSS Art Looting Investigation Unit Reports, 1945–46: http://www.archives.gov/research/holocaust/microfilm-publications/m1782.pdf

[106] ALIU Final Report, 1 May 1946, 1: US NA, RG 239, Box 83.

[107] Ibid.

Taylor had considered that Plaut's: 'talents would be particularly useful in Switzerland where much of the looted works of art [were] probably concealed.'[108] Theodore Rousseau was recruited as 'operations officer'. This appointment stemmed, in part, from Rousseau's pre-war work for the National Gallery of Art in Washington, and his fluency in French, German, Italian, Spanish, and Portuguese. Another factor was Rousseau's prior experience as a naval attaché to Portugal and Spain in 1942–44. According to Taylor, he wanted to recruit Rousseau for the ALIU because there was: 'no naval officer... better equipped to deal with [the] various aspects of civil government and art administration.'[109] According to Plaut, Rousseau and himself: 'shared full responsibility for the unit's activities.'[110] The formal position, however, was that Rousseau had to supervise the European field operations and account directly to Plaut.[111] Other well-qualified individuals with expertise in art were also recruited to the ALIU: S. Lane Faison;[112] Otto Wittmann;[113] L. Sumner Crosby;[114] Charles Sawyer (Washington Liaison),[115] and John Philips (London Office).[116]

Taylor considered Faison as an excellent addition to the ALIU staff because he had studied fine arts in Paris and, like Rousseau, was a skilled linguist.[117] Other members had proven investigative skills related to artworks. For example, whilst working on the Göring collection, John Philips had discovered that a Jan Vermeer painting showed a Seventeenth Century pewter tankard with a lid which had a thumb-piece that was only in production some 200 years later. This exposed one of

[108] Taylor to Murphy, 2 October 1944, 3: US NA, RG 239, Box 52.

[109] Ibid.

[110] See James S. Plaut, 'Investigation of the Major Nazi Art-Confiscation Agencies', in Elizabeth Simpson (ed.) *The Spoils of War*, NY: Harry N. Abrams, 1997, 124.

[111] Plaut and Rousseau to Murphy, 21 November 1944, 3–5, 'Orion Organization: US NA, RG 226, Entry 190, Box 532.

[112] Faison later returned to Germany in 1950 to become Director of the Munich Collecting Point for plundered cultural items.

[113] After the war, he became Director of the Toledo Museum of Art in Toledo, Ohio.

[114] Crosby and Philips had been early recruits to OSS X-2.

[115] He had been Director of the Addison Gallery of American Art in Andover and the Worcester Art Museum in Massachusetts, and later became master of Timothy Dwight college after the war.

[116] Philips had been curator of the Mabel Brady Garvan Collections and professor at Yale University. He was internationally well-known for his artistic judgement and an assistant professor of the history of art. Winks, 1987 op. cit., 304.

[117] Taylor to Murphy, 2 October op. cit.

the most notorious art forgers of the period: Hans Van Meegeren.[118] As Wink's study recognises: 'Such a man, with such an eye, was obviously priceless to an art investigation unit.'[119]

The ALIU's administrative arrangements were designed to co-ordinate its activities in both Washington and Europe. The staff and activities of the ALIU were divided between a Washington administrative HQ, and a London Operations Centre. From January 1945, the Washington headquarters, which was maintained for the full duration of the project, was headed by Charles Sawyer.[120] This HQ: 'was responsible for the administration of the Unit, maintenance of its permanent records, procurement and training of personnel, and integration of field activities.'[121] It also coordinated its information with other American agencies having parallel interests,[122] including in relation to all Safehaven aspects of its investigations.[123] Because it had 'primary responsibility for the administration of the Unit',[124] the Washington base was assigned: 'decisions relating to policy.'[125] This HQ was also responsible for distilling a mass of information received from other agencies so that its operations staff received the best available information in a suitable format.

By contrast, the ALIU's London Field Headquarters, which was also established in January 1945, took responsibility: 'for the planning of all field operations, the reception and collation of material submitted by field representatives and the transmission of such material, and the maintenance of the operational files of the project.'[126] Operational control of field operations within the Unit's established policy agenda

---

[118] See Theodore Sizer, 'John Marshall Philips, 1905–53', *Publications of the Walpole Society*, 43rd Annual Meeting 22 May 1953, 26–41: Yale Univ. Library, MG 453.

[119] Winks, 1987 op. cit., 305.

[120] 'News Reports', *College Art Journal*, Vol. 5, No. 3. (March 1946), 245–252, 252. Sawyer had previously worked with the MFA&A organisation and US Military Civil Affairs units.

[121] Hussey *et al.*, op. cit.

[122] These including the US War Department's Civil Affairs Division; Division of Foreign Funds Control and Customs of the US State Department, and the Allied War Crimes Commission: See Roberts Commission Report, 1946 op. cit., 40.

[123] US Treasury Department, Foreign Economic Administration, and the State Department's, Economic Security Controls Division.

[124] 'Final Report', op. cit., 1.

[125] 'Establishment of Project Orion', 14 December 1944 op. cit., 1: US NA, RG 226, Entry 190, Box 516, Folder 'Art Unit'.

[126] 'Final Report', op. cit., 2.

was clearly delegated to the London Office.[127] This operations section also directly liased with a wide variety of other Allied official bodies working in related areas, including the US Nuremberg prosecutors and US and British agencies responsible for Safehaven investigations.[128] In particular, it: 'maintained an active liaison with the Roberts Commission throughout the war and in the immediate postwar period.'[129] The report of Roberts Commission noted:

> The London office of this Unit was established early in 1945, and close liaison was maintained with representatives of the American Commission, who aided the staff of OSS in the preparation of certain lists needed by the latter's field representatives and by the MFA&A officers in the field. Liaison of the OSS Unit with the Vaucher Commission and with the Economic Warfare Division and the Ministry of Economic Warfare was initially facilitated through the Commission's office.[130]

The ALIU's mission objectives

The nature and scope of the ALIU's original aims and mission were complex. They were geared initially to an anticipated military victory in Europe. According to Plaut, the ALIU was established: 'in anticipation of the forthcoming occupation of Germany by the Allied forces.'[131] Its scope extended throughout Western but not Eastern Europe, as the latter remained within the jurisdiction of the Soviet authorities alone. Given the scale, instrumental effectiveness and scope of Nazi art loot-

[127] 'Establishment of Project Orion', 14 December 1944 op. cit., 1: US NA, RG 226, Entry 190, Box 516, Folder 'Art Unit'.

[128] These included: the Roberts Commission; the Monuments, Fine Arts and Archives Branch of the Civil Affairs Division of US Army G-5 and G-2 divisions; the Economic Security Controls Division of the US State Department; the US Foreign Economic Administration; the Captured Materials and Personnel Branch; the Foreign Funds Control, and the Treasury Department; SHAEF, USFET, U.S. Group Control Commission (Germany); Allied Control Commission (Italy); the Economic Warfare Division (U.S. Embassy, London); the Ministry of Economic Warfare; the British Element (Control Commission, Germany); the Commission de Recuperation Artistique (France); the Netherlands Ryjksbureau voor de Monumentenzord; the British Committee on Preservation and Restitution of Works of Art, Archives, and Other Material in Enemy Hands (Macmillan Committee); and the Interallied Commission for Protection and Restitution of Cultural Material (Vaucher-Gros Commission).

[129] Hussey *et al.*, op. cit. See also Charles Sawyer, 'Report on the Activities of the Office of Strategic Services as they have related to the Roberts Commission,' 27 December 1945: US NA, RG 59, Entry: Lot 62D-4, Box 24 [114005].

[130] Ibid., 30.

[131] Plaut, 1997 op. cit., 124.

ing, the ALIU faced a particularly daunting task.[132] This new Unit's purpose and function was defined in relation to the *perceived gap* in the existing Allied coordination of measures concerning artworks. These stemmed in part from the confused scope of various American agencies in this field with overlapping responsibilities for intelligence-gathering and counter-intelligence. In other words, for Donovan, Roberts and Taylor, the rationale for the work of this new art unit was to supplement and coordinate a number of existing Allied intelligence operations, and thereby prevent the specific theme of art looting from either falling between the gaps of different institutional jurisdictions as it were, or becoming subject to a wasteful duplication of institutional efforts.

Once established, the general aim of the ALIU was embodied in an internal OSS directive of 21 November 1944. It declared that this Unit's key mission objectives combined investigative (evidence-gathering), analytical and restitution elements:

> to collect and disseminate such information bearing on the looting, confiscation and transfer by the enemy of art properties in Europe, and on the individuals or organizations involved in such operations or transactions, as well as be of direct aid to the United States agencies empowered to effect restitution of such properties and prosecute war criminals; [and] to establish the pattern of looting and confiscation in its broader aspects, so as to be guided in the promulgation of plans for ultimate restitution.[133]

A related goal was to: 'provide an intelligence component to the Monuments Fine Arts, and Archives (MFA&A) Branch of the United States Army.'[134] In December 1944, a further OSS directive summarised ALIU's role in terms consistent with the mission of X-2 more generally: 'ORION will obtain substantial information bearing on enemy espionage and on subversive individuals and activities.'[135] This directive stated that:

---

[132] OSS document, 13034 including the interrogation report on Driedrich Wilhelm Kritzinger, State Secretary at the Reich Chancery, regarding foreign art purchases, and Hermann Göring's complicity in art looting and cross references to OSS report XL-15259, July 1945; OSS report XL-15687, 'Information on the organization and activities of the Einsatzstab Rosenberg', headed by Bruno Lohse and von Behr, and a complete personnel list of the ERR in all occupied countries.' These reports include a list of the Parisian private collections and the works looted: OSS report XL-18055, November 1943: US NA, RG 226, Entry 16.

[133] OSS memo, Plaut and Rousseau to James Murphy, Chief OSS X-2 Branch, Fine Arts Project: Orion, 21 November 1944, 1–2: US NA, RG 226, Entry 190, Box 532, Folder 1747.

[134] Plaut, 1997 op. cit., 124.

[135] Saint DH/001 to Saint, 'Establishment of Project Orion', 14 December 1944, 2: US NA, RG 226, Entry 190, Box 516.

> Intelligence particularly useful to Orion in the execution of its mission and presently desired from X-2 field stations will roughly fall into the following categories: a) Information concerning the current activities of art dealers, German and collaborationist museum officials, art scholars and other classes of individuals known or believed to be active in art [looting]. (b) Information concerning Germans and other persons or organizations known or believed to be involved in the confiscation or transfer of art properties, and in other private or official art transactions; information concerning such procedures. (c) Information concerning losses of art objects from private or public collections through enemy activity.[136]

It is possible that leading members of this Unit had considerable scope to exploit the difference between narrower, X-2 specific definitions of their role, which had been developed at the start of the project and reflected X-2 existing priorities at the time, and their own wider interpretations developed subsequently. These included providing substantial assistance in the prosecution of Nazi war criminals and restitution to the rightful owners of works of art that had been unlawfully confiscated. Which of these different aims was the main driving force remained an open question at this stage. The art unit was also required by its mission objectives to actively and effectively liase with the Roberts Commission and other interested agencies.[137] A later section will explore the ALIU's counter-espionage mission concerning the combating of covert Nazi intelligence operations, including the threat of a postwar resurgence of Nazism funded by the sale of looted art works.

Given this work is concerned with the OSS' responses to the Holocaust, it is worth stressing that contributing positively to the restitution of works of art back to their original owners, many of whom were Jewish, remained a key function and rationale for this body. Its leading members regarded themselves as responsible for obtaining: 'substantial information bearing on enemy espionage and on subversive individuals and activities; and establishing: the pattern of looting and confiscation in its broader aspects, so as to be guided in the promulgation of plans for ultimate restitution.'[138] In other words, by broadening the scope of its original terms of reference, the ALIU voluntarily accepted an

[136] Ibid.
[137] Ibid.
[138] Ibid.

enlarged role relating to the restitution of art works, which by implication included Holocaust-restitution.

ALIU's early wartime operations

Most of the investigative work by members of the ALIU took place between November 1944 and the late spring / summer of 1946.[139] Hence, this Unit survived intact the institutional transition from the OSS to the short-lived 'Strategic Services Unit' (SSU) of the US War Department in October 1945. At this time, the OSS was officially disbanded, with only a reduced number of its staff and institutional functions preserved in different branches of the American government, such as the War and State Departments.

Although created in November 1944, the start of sustained investigative work required ALIU personnel to undergo a period of training and indoctrination into X-2's distinctive methods of covert investigation and communications. According to an internal memo, by 13 November 1944: '[Plaut was] now organizing files and general program and liaison here on arts project. Should be able depart London about mid-December and we both feel that [Sawyer] be returned to Washington early December to take over this end.'[140]

In December 1944, an internal OSS statement indicated that: 'Plaut and Rousseau will proceed to the field at an early date to establish personal contacts at all European field stations and to confer with and brief X-2 field personnel with specific Orion Problems.'[141] The completion of this 'field survey' was a pre-condition for the assignment of other ALIU personnel.[142] However, neither Plaut nor Rousseau were able to leave the United States for Europe to begin institutional liaison on the European continent and Britain until early in the new year.

---

[139] See 'Security-Classified Reports Concerning Recovery of Looted Art Treasures in Germany 1940–1945': US NA, RG 226, Entry 30; 'biographical index': US NA, RG 226, Entry 99, Box 106, Folder 1; US NA, RG 226, Entry 99, Box 104, Folders 1, 6, 7; 'Looted Art': US NA, RG 226, Entry 118, Box 4, Folder 4 and Box 5 Folder 1. The Unit's final report is at: US NA, RG 226, Entry 146, Box 253, Folder 3523.

[140] Plaut and Rousseau to Murphy, 21 November 1944, 3–5, 'Orion Organization: US NA, RG 226, Entry 190, Box 532.

[141] 'Establishment of Project Orion', 14 December 1944, 1: US NA, RG 226, Entry 190, Box 516, Folder 'Art Unit'.

[142] Ibid.

From this time onwards, the ALIU became better able to liase directly and independently with other U.S. and British agencies. This was a point noted in Sawyer's early 1945 progress reports to X-2 and Roberts Commission officials. By February 1945, it was possible for this ALIU official to report that the: 'plan of operation for ORION Washington [had been] completed by Lt. Plaut.'[143] Initial investigative work during the first 6 months of 1945 was held back to some extent because of the limited number of ALIU qualified personnel available. This meant that Plaut and Rousseau had to make many trips back and forth between the ALIU's Washington and London offices, even though their primary focus was supposed to be conducting detailed field investigations in liberated Europe. This over-stretching of limited staff resources devoted to investigative work was presumably eased a little once Lane Faison, the final ALIU field operative, arrived in Europe in July 1945.

At this point, it may be useful to outline the operations and priorities of the ALIU. An initial priority for the ALIU's activities in the field was to identify both individuals complicit in looting, and the particular art works which had been confiscated. As Winks notes: 'Looted art was traced, records were compiled on several thousand individuals who had sold art, perhaps improperly, to the enemy, and lists were made of the purchases of German galleries and museums.'[144] Members of the ALIU also analysed the Nazis' general pattern and methodology deployed for their artistic plundering operations.[145] Indeed, the Roberts Commission's report recognised the help it had both given to, and received from, ALIU officials in these matters during the new Unit's difficult first weeks and months of wartime operations. It also acknowledged the early beliefs

---

[143] Sawyer to Sharrar, 7 February 1945, 'Progress reports,': US NA, RG 226, Entry 190, Box 532. These independent liaisons included the Roberts Commission (John A. Gilmore), G-5, War Dept. (Lt. Col. Kades and Maj. Minard), State Dept., Division of Public and Cultural Relations (John S. Dickey, Dr. Kefauver, Dr. Hovde), and G-2, MIS, War Dept., Captured Material and Personnel Branch (Lt. Col. Sweet and Lt. Col. Brown). I am grateful to Anne Rothfeld for this information.

[144] Winks, 1987 op. cit., 303.

[145] The ALIU's creation, operation and progress were also documented sporadically in the OSS Director's own files. See Director's Office and Field Station Records: US NA, RG 226, Entry 190, Box 516, Folder 1723; US NA, RG 226, Entry 190, Box 532, Folders 1747–1751; US NA, RG 226, Entry 190, Box 533, Folder 1756. Other archival sources on the ALIU's work in identifying individuals, companies and processes of looting, including those of the ERR, are contained in the 'Records of the Roberts Commission for the Protection and Salvage of Artistic and Historic Monuments in War Areas': US NA, RG 239, ALIU Subject File, 1940–1946, Entry 73, Boxes 74–83.

of the ALIU's leading members concerning the best way they should proceed to accomplish their formidable tasks, which of course spanned the entire European continent from Holland to Portugal:

> During the early stages, the reports which the Commission had received from the MFA&A officers in the field, and the data assembled by the Committee of the American Council of Learned Societies were used in the preparation of the [OSS] Unit's preliminary list of persons known to be, or suspected of being, connected with art dealing and looting. Later, the Unit provided the Commission with access to intelligence information which was of primary interest, and, with the use of specialized personnel, actively engaged in independent investigations of art looting in Europe. Members of the Unit felt that if restitution of art objects was to be effective, it would be of primary importance to investigate first the devious methods used by the enemy in making extensive acquisitions, and to determine where and how the enemy had hidden or preserved these valuable tangible assets. The investigation of these problems was undertaken in France, Spain, Portugal, Italy, Holland, Switzerland, Austria, and Germany.[146]

The ALIU'S wartime investigations required its staff to analyse many thousands of captured documents, as well as interviewing a good proportion of those it had previously identified as being directly and centrally involved in art looting in various ways.[147] In a 29 November 1944 memorandum to X-2, Plaut suggested that the ALIU should coordinate its operations with those of Captured Personnel and Material Branch in the US War Department. This was because it would be: 'of inestimable value to have German prisoners-of-war screened for fine arts information, and...to have [ALIU officials] advised of the availability for interrogation purposes of any captured personnel known to have been museum officials, history of art scholars, art dealers, and officials who have had any responsibility for, or connection with, confiscation and transfer of such properties.'[148] Unfortunately, it is unclear what became of this proposal.

During early 1945, Plaut rapidly gained a reputation amongst Allied officials engaged in related work for his expertise on German art looting. His specialist knowledge was sought not only concerning who was likely

---

[146] Roberts Commission Report, 1946 op. cit., 39.

[147] Much of the following information is extracted from *The Document Project: Project for the Documentation of Wartime Cultural Losses*: http://docproj.loyola.edu/oss1/index.html, which also now contains links to the full text of the ALIU's Final Report.

[148] Plaut to unnamed X-2 officials, 29 November 1944, 'Orion Organization': US NA, RG 226, Entry 190, Box 532.

to be complicit in this aspect of the Holocaust, but also in relation to those German and Austrian individuals who could be considered 'clean'. The Allied occupation forces could, therefore, recruit or otherwise work with such individuals.[149] Indeed, one feature of a number of later ALIU reports is their identification of individuals who did *not* co-operate with the Nazis, or who even sabotaged aspects of this regime's art looting, such as Professor Hermann Michael.[150] Such material was obviously relevant for the Allied authorities plans for rebuilding German cultural institutions following the proposed purging of active Nazis by means of 'de-Nazification' programmes.

It would be useful at this point to review how ALIU officials gathered intelligence on individuals and networks of individuals. From 15 January 1945 to the end of the European phase of WWII on 8 May 1945, the ALIU's London Office built upon the close liaison it had already established with British, Dutch, and French officials working in the art looting area. It rapidly established itself as the centre of a web of information and knowledge becoming: 'the clearinghouse for all information in Allied hands on this subject.'[151] Indeed, the Roberts Commission Report recognised:

> The Art Looting Investigation Unit, through its London office, worked closely with Allied commissions concerned with art looting, and was regarded as the central depository for all Allied information on enemy looting gained through intelligence channels. Several investigations were made in close collaboration with members of the British Element, Control Council for Germany. The French and Dutch also contributed information at their disposal concerning enemy personnel engaged in art looting, and the Unit's London office was regarded by them as a "Cultural War Room."[152]

Late in January 1945, Rousseau began his investigations in Spain and Portugal concentrating initially on 'German-owned' property in this countries, a project that continued: 'intermittently through 8 May

---

[149] Howe's memoir recalls that: 'Jim Plaut a naval lieutenant at the London office of OSS...would probably have valuable information about German museum personnel. It would be helpful to know the whereabouts of certain German scholars, specifically those whose records were, from our point of view, "clean."' Thomas Carr Howe Jr., *Salt Mines and Castles: The Discovery and Restitution of Looted European Art*, Indianapolis: The Bobbs-Merrill Company, 1946, 20.

[150] CIR 4 (Linz), op. cit., 25.

[151] Hussey *et al.*, op. cit.

[152] Roberts Commission Report, op. cit., 40.

1945 (VE Day.'[153] Nicholas provides additional details of ALIU officials' engagement with a series of specific wartime investigative operations. Acting in conjunction with other Allied intelligence agencies, particularly the British, these officials started to identify a range of individuals whose interrogation could, perhaps, supply vital information. In particular, they sought new leads to other members of various networks of official organisations and art dealers suspected of involvement in art looting, the most important of whom was defined as that of Alois Miedl characterised as: 'German banker, speculator and financial agent of Göring.'[154] Nicholas adds that the extensive research and liaison work carried out by Rousseau and his colleagues had prepared the ground for their interrogation of Miedl:

> the three officers...looked into Alois Miedl's activities in Spain and attempted without success to extradite him. They had done preliminary work in France and England, drawing on the documents collected by the Intelligence agencies of various nations. Since the previous autumn Army authorities had had lists of the Nazi art principals, and Douglas Cooper of British intelligence had been questioning any POWs taken to England who seemed to have art backgrounds. Lists of suggested questions and names of Nazi agencies were [then] distributed to all Intelligence units.[155]

Miedl had worked for Hermann Göring via Hofer. He was at least partly responsible for looting the Jewish-owned Goudstikker art collection and Gallery, and subsequently most of Goudstikker's personal property.[156]

It is worth examining the ALIU's investigation into Miedl's complicities in greater detail as this was, perhaps, the first 'dry run' and test drive of their methodology and operating practices. From early January, Rousseau began his search for confiscated artworks that Miedl was suspected of having concealed in Spain and Portugal.[157] An OSS report from mid-February 1945, whose author is designated as 'Orion' but who was probably Rousseau, made a series of references to 'the Miedl case.'[158] This was characterised as:

---

[153] Final Report, op. cit., 3.

[154] Ibid.

[155] Nicholas, 1995 op. cit., 378–79.

[156] Ibid., 105.

[157] Rothfeld, 2002 op. cit., Chapter 2, 15.

[158] 'Recommendations concerning Orion's activities in Madrid': 13 February, 1945: US NA, RG 226, Entry 210, Box 352, Folder 6.

> by far the most important case which we have at the moment. As it stands, it may prove one of the basic elements in which the whole restitution policy can be established as far as neutral countries are concerned... The following are main points to be stressed: A. The identification of the pictures is the main objective. The Dutch Minister is proceeding with his diplomatic demarches and will keep Mr Butterworth advised. If he fails, we will try the Bilbao personal approach through the British. If this also fails, then we must keep in mind the subversive method, unless it is absolutely impossible. I am willing to do almost anything to get photographs, or failing that, a look at those pictures. B. The present whereabouts of Miedl—the British are working on this at the moment... C. Duval, and the possibility of using him as a source... D. Group of pictures allegedly in Madrid—the investigation of this aspect of the case should be gone into quite urgently because of the possibility of their being sold at any time. An investigation in Khamer's activities, or any source that we have in the German embassy who can get into the storeroom there might help a good deal.[159]

In Spain, Rousseau's early interrogation of Miedl's activities from 1940–1945, which was made possible by the latter's detention there by the Spanish authorities, took place: 'over an extended period of time and in great detail.'[160] Rousseau secured the cooperation the US and Dutch diplomatic missions in Madrid to obtain: 'the permission of the Spanish Government to examine personally the 22 works of art placed in Miedl's name in the Free Port of Bilbao.'[161] Under Rousseau's questioning, Miedl admitted that he had generally acted in his own personal capacity in acquiring and selling looted works of art. He specifically claimed that he had obtained the Jewish-owned Goudstikker Collection through 'legitimate business transactions', despite his close connections with both Göring and Hofer,[162] and that his only motivation was to find a way to support his family during the war.[163] The result of his interrogation was a report: 'The Miedl Case: Reports 1–4' dated, 13 February 1945. The ALIU's Final Report emphasises the importance of this initial investigation both in terms of restitution and, more generally, for the later work of this Unit: 'Not only did the Miedl case become the keystone on subsequent investigations by the Unit of German art looting in Holland, but the Miedl-owned paintings were sequestered

[159] Ibid., 3

[160] Final Report, op. cit., 3.

[161] Ibid.

[162] Sawyer to Towell, 20 June 1945, 'Liaison': US NA, RG 226, Entry 190, Box 533.

[163] Ibid.

by the Spanish Government and placed at the disposition of the Dutch Minister as a result of information presented by the Operations Officer to the Spanish Government.'[164]

Rousseau discovered that, although the Spanish authorities had been willing to detain Miedl, they were not inclined to support further investigations and possible prosecution.[165] Ex-ALIU officer Lane Faison has recalled:[166]

> With the intervention of the U.S. and Dutch diplomatic missions in Madrid, the Operations Officer secured the permission of the Spanish Government to examine personally the 22 works of art placed in Miedl's name in the Free Port of Bilbao. The Miedl case became the keystone in subsequent investigations by the Unit of German art looting in Holland. The Miedl-owned paintings were sequestered by the Spanish Government and placed at the disposition of the Dutch Minister as a result of information presented by the Operations Officer to the Spanish Government. The ALIU was, however, unable to achieve the extradition of Miedl.[167]

It was claimed that one lesson from this case was to alert the ALIU that evidence concerning looted art was: 'most likely to turn up in...any of the normal C.E. [counter-espionage] reports; as, for instance, in the case of Miedl, connected with smuggling, or in any way with the financing of subservice activities.'[168] Another lesson was the importance of networking and personal contacts, including identifying individuals

[164] Final Report, op. cit., 3.

[165] See 'Washington X-2 Branch Personalities Files' 'State Department-FBI memos. Alois Miedl Safehaven activities. Subject reports. November 24, 1944–April 22, 1946': US NA, RG 226, Entry 171, Box 39, Folder 654; ibid., Entry 183, Box 13, Folder 69 'paintings brought into Spain from the Netherlands by Alois Midel [sic].' Plaut reacted angrily to this and wrote to both X-2 in London and Washington and the MEW arguing that the situation had become ridiculous and the investigation will end since there's no governmental cooperation among the Allies, the Dutch, and the Spanish. (I thank Anne Rothfeld for this point).

[166] CIR 2 (Göring) op. cit., 18–19. For further more general OSS records on Miedl, see US NA, RG 226, Entry 210, Box 1: Alois Miedl, [looted art] 1945 and [two documents] Box 3. More generally, see Records of the Roberts Commission for the Protection and Salvage of Artistic and Historic Monuments in War Areas (The Roberts Commission), 1943–1946: US NA, RG 239, Entry 6: US NA Microfilm Publication M1944, roll 9: Folder: Miscellaneous Enclosures 1 and 2 to dispatch No. 19,750 of December 8, 1944, from the Embassy at London, England, regarding Alois Miedel [Miedl] noting that Miedl possessed in Spain paintings by Cézanne, Rembrandt, Van Dyck, Rubens, Jan Steen, and Cranach, and detailing Miedl's activities in the Netherlands and dealings with Göring; London Files, 1943–1945; RG 239, Entry 12, Roll 32 Folder: Cables, British Ministry of Economic Warfare Report on Aloys [Alois] Miedl, 29 December, 1944.

[167] Hussey *et al.*, op. cit.

[168] Ibid., 1.

in Spain who had proven helpful in this case, such as: 'The Dutch minister [who] has been exceedingly helpful in the Miedl case.'[169] A similar point was made with respect to a Mr Titus, who had some connection with the French authorities.[170]

Rousseau made a number of more general points in relation to his investigations in Spain. He noted that although particularly famous and expensive looted works of art would be difficult to sell, those in the second tier were fetching: 'extremely good prices.':

> A work known to be looted could be purchased either for the purpose of keeping it in hiding for several years until the war is forgotten, or for the purpose of exporting it clandestinely for sale in South American. The facility which makes paintings, whether on canvas or panel,... disguised makes this a very tempting proposition to anyone who is willing to undertake it. Ship examiners in Gibraltar or Trinidad are certainly not equipped to trace this kind of smuggled goods.[171]

Under the sub-heading 'Activities to be watched,' he also noted that looted items could be found in various sources. These included private collections, such as that of the Japanese Minister, Suma, who had been reported to have had possession of two suspicious Goyas in Madrid in October 1944 meriting further investigation; hidden amongst otherwise legitimate picture exhibitions or auction sales, or in the hands of art dealers. The latter worked either through galleries, or on a more personal and private way through intermediaries and personal contacts. Rousseau emphasised that: 'The latter are those who bear most watching.'[172] This report then lists the various contacts he had made in Madrid with appropriate expertise to receive and evaluate suspicious works, including an art collector working for the British Embassy, and a member of the US Naval attachés office. In addition, he identified a list of: 'other contacts who have expressed their willingness to pass on to this office any related materials which they could obtain.'[173] This list included a member of the Polish legation, the Dutch Minister, and four private individuals with various direct and indirect connections with aspects of the Spanish art business.[174] Based on an earlier December

[169] Ibid., 2.
[170] Ibid., 3.
[171] Ibid., 1.
[172] Ibid.
[173] Ibid., 3.
[174] Ibid., 3.

1944 report from the Dutch authorities, Rousseau also identified three: 'other suspicious pictures for sale in Madrid', whose origins he had asked the Dutch Minister to investigate further. Rousseau's investigative work in the Miedl case dovetailed into wider X-2 Safehaven concerns at this time, particularly with the role being played by wealthy Germans residing in Portugal and Spain; and their dealings in questionable assets capable to funding a postwar resurgence in Nazism.[175]

In June 1945, X-2 ordered Faison to meet Spanish authorities in order to bring Miedl back into Allied-occupied areas for arrest and subsequent investigations. Miedl was to present himself to American officials. After waiting in vain for ten days in France and Spain for this exchange to take place, Faison was ordered back to Paris from where he travelled to Alt Aussee, Austria to meet up with Rousseau and Plaut to begin interrogation and related work.[176] On the other hand, despite the frustration over extradition, Rousseau's interrogation may have helped motivate the Spanish government to sequester Miedl's paintings and placed them in the custody of the Dutch embassy.[177] In the end, Rousseau's mission was comparatively successful, and both the OSS and the Dutch government came to recognise this.[178] By the end of 1945, the Dutch government had received almost all of the Goudstikker paintings and started the drawn-out process of restituting the pieces to their original Jewish owners.

Pearson, X-2 Chief in London, wrote to General Donovan in May 1945 suggesting that Rousseau's investigation and report into Miedl's activities, and its practical results of its intelligence, could even be considered a: 'cornerstone for Allied restitution policy.'[179] Rousseau's own reflections upon the Miedl case in February 1945 were more cautious and self-critical. He outlined the nature of the ALIU's activities in

---

[175] SAINT, ORION to SAINT, London and Washington, 29 January 1945, 'Cables': US NA, RG 226, Entry 190, Box 533. See also Rousseau's Progress Report to Murphy, Pearson, Plaut, 15 February 1945. 'Cables,' ibid.

[176] 'ALIU Final Report (May 1946),' 3. This paragraph is also based on Rothfeld's personal conversation with S. Lane Faison, April 6–7, 2002, Williamstown, MA. See also Sawyer to Rushin, 21 April 1945, 'Orion Organization': US NA, RG 226, Entry 190, Box 533.

[177] This was a case where restitution to the Paul Rosenberg collection was successful albeit not until the early 1950s. See Sawyer to Towell, 20 June 1945, 'Liaison': US NA, RG 226, Entry 190, Box 533; CIR Nos. 1 and 2, op. cit.

[178] Sawyer to Rushin, 21 April 1945, 'Orion organization': US NA, RG 226, Entry 190, Box 532.

[179] Pearson to Donovan, 20 May 1945, 2, 'Orion Organization': US NA, RG 226, Entry 190, Box 532.

Spain and the lessons that needed to be learned for future investigative work.[180] The Miedl case also helped clarify the importance of *the financing* of art looting activities, the multiple possible hiding places for such works of art, the importance of identifying the type of personnel actually or potentially involved.[181]

The creation of master and target lists

From January through May of 1945, the London analysts and staff of ALIU compiled a 'master list' of over 2,000 individuals using a full range of internal OSS and other sources of information it had secured through its various liaison activities. This 'master list' included Nazis and their collaborators suspected of having been involved in art confiscations and other forms of looting.[182] The ALIU's successful liaison efforts with British, Dutch, and French officials resulted in information that further enriched these files. The Unit's London offices rapidly became: 'the central repository and clearing house for all information in Allied hands on this subject.'[183] Immediately after VE Day (8 May 1945), the ALIU: 'issued to all Allied intelligence teams on the Continent a "high priority" personnel target list' based on the large master list.[184] This contained: 'the names of 21 individuals considered to be the most prominent figures involved in the German operations and wanted urgently for interrogation and subsequent prosecution.'[185] These 21 persons had been selected from the large list for two purposes: 'a) Detention as potential war criminals; b) Investigation in connection with

---

[180] Rousseau to BC001, 13 February 1945: US NA, RG 226, Entry 210, Box 533, Folder 6.

[181] Ibid. See also the ALIU's Progress Report for April 15–30 1945, which stated that successful interrogations occurred in the Miedl case: US NA, RG 226, Entry 190, Box 532.

[182] Final Report, op. cit., 4. Ms. Lambie, an analyst member of the administrative staff in Washington, began receiving the ACLU card files 'of personalities and other material of interest to [ALIU]' reviewed these and other files for the use of the ALIU field operations. See Sawyer to Sharrar, 7 February 1945, 'Progress reports': US NA, RG 226, Entry 190, Box 532.

[183] Final Report, op. cit., 4.

[184] See OSS R&A 'Regular' Intelligence Report No. 14362, August 1945. This target list of 21 German personnel included a brief biographical details in each, and notes that some of those cited are identified as potential war criminals: US NA, RG 226, Entry 19.

[185] Ibid., 4.

their participation in such [looting] activity.'[186] Among the 21 names listed were German art dealers, Walter Andreas Hofer and Karl Haberstock, two of the most active individuals in art confiscations in Europe, who had a particular complicity in the acquisition practices concerning the Linz and Göring collections and the ERR. This list then provided the basis of the ALIU's field operations and interrogations. ALIU officials distributed their 'high priority' personnel target list to all Allied intelligence teams on the European continent. As Winks notes:

> A "target list" of enemy personnel known to have engaged in art looting, who were to be captured and held for interrogation in Germany, was also circulated, and from June to October 1945 those on the list who were captured were interrogated at a special interrogation center in Austria. Particular attention was given to the Hitler museum and library at Linz, to the Göring collection, and to the activities of Einsatzstab Reichsleiter Alfred Rosenberg in France. At a nerve center set up in the Neuschwanstein castle, the unit compiled a register of 21,903 objects confiscated in Paris alone.[187]

The high priority 'shortlist' also specified which particular works of art had, by various techniques, been plundered by these individuals and, where possible, identified their current location. These persons were then sought urgently for interrogation and—if they could gather sufficient relevant and credible evidence—their subsequent prosecution as war criminals.[188] With these specific investigations in newly-liberated parts of Europe, and their compilation of 'wanted lists' and 'high priority' lists during the first full months of their operation during WWII, ALIU officials certainly 'hit the ground running.'[189] Members of the ALIU achieved remarkable results in building up a wider picture of the patterns of the overall process, methodology and impact of Nazi looting operations. This, in turn, helped create the foundations for later

---

[186] 'Safehaven Report: Target List of German Personnel implicated in Looting of European Art Treasures,' 14 August 1945, author unknown, Safehaven Reports, 1944–1945, War Crimes Branch, Records of the Office of the Judge Advocate General (Army): US NA, RG 153, Box 8.

[187] Winks, 1987 op. cit., 303.

[188] Hussey *et al.*, op. cit.; 'By spring 1945, the ALIU had collected significant evidence of looted art hidden in Germany and in neutral countries; new information about individuals who had dealt, bought, or transported works of art during the war; and details about confiscation methods used by the Nazis.' Descriptive summary of Microfilm 1782: http://www.archives.gov/research/microfilm/m1944.pdf

[189] Yeide, 2007 op. cit., 2.

interrogations, improved intelligence and, as a result, led to a growing number of arrests. For instance, the Robert's Commission Report summarised the Unit's following achievements for 'the months before 8 May, 1945:

1. Considerable evidence was furnished to the Commission concerning a large number of works of art missing from the German-occupied countries.
2. Locations of secret deposits of art objects in Germany were reported, evidence of art hidden by the enemy in neutral countries was uncovered;
3. Information concerning enemy personnel involved in art acquisitions was collected, and details of the methods used were explored.
4. As a result of independent investigations, interrogations of enemy personnel, and the examination of documents, the general pattern of art looting by the enemy began to emerge.
5. By VE-day, the Unit had amassed records on several thousand individuals concerned directly or indirectly with art acquisition by the enemy, and much detailed information on German art repositories had been passed on to G-5, SHAEF [Southern Hemisphere Allied Expeditionary Force] for action. It had also prepared a 'target list' of key enemy personnel concerned with art looting to be captured and held for interrogation in Germany. Of this list, the majority was captured...[190]

Furthermore, the initial ALIU field reports sent first to the London office and then to Washington, began to uncover the *modus operandi* of the Nazis' patterns of art confiscations in Europe, including that of the ERR in Paris. The Miedl and Mohnen interrogations tested the quality of the ALIU's collected intelligence data, and helped Plaut and Rousseau plan later ALIU investigations.[191] At this stage, the ALIU claimed its reports had obtained an improved insight sufficient to: 'to distinguish with greater clarity between those transactions which represent traffic in looted art from those that are part of a legitimate international art trade.'[192] In other words, by March and April 1945,

[190] Roberts Commission Report, 1946 op. cit., 39–40.
[191] Rothfeld, 2002 op. cit., Chapter 3, 19.
[192] Yeide, 2007 op. cit., 2.

the ALIU was becoming a fully operational investigative and analytical agency. Plaut and Rousseau reviewed preliminary field surveys and several case studies from other agencies conducted in Europe.[193] Mrs. Lambie, based in ALIU's Washington Office, received and analysed dossiers and intelligence on enemy individuals involved in art looting from this Unit's liaisons in both Washington and London.[194]

This degree of empirical and analytical progress towards the realisation of its mission objectives assisted in the creation of the foundations for later interrogations, and hence improved intelligence. In turn, such progress allowed the occupation authorities to make a growing number of arrests of suspects. In a memorandum dated 20 May 1945 to General Donovan, Norman Pearson noted that the continuous liaisons and flow of intelligence between the ALIU and various Allied agencies, including the War Crimes Commission, Allied counter-intelligence services, and the Roberts Commission, had proved to be especially effective. This flow of information was helped considerably by Plaut and Rousseau's investigative activities in Europe, and the effectiveness of the support provided to them by their administrative staff based in their London and Washington bases.[195]

It should not be thought that the work of the ALIU took place in total isolation from the more general investigative work OSS officials carried out at this time. On the contrary, James Donovan's second 'War Crimes Information Memo' from 30 April specifically addressed the importance of receiving additional information from OSS field stations concerning the Nazis' looting of property. That is, repressive measures involving the: 'removal or confiscation of public or private property, whether done directly or through ostensibly legal methods. All information concerning enemy records or the keeping of such records, which would aid in the... the location of property suspected of having been illegally appropriated.'[196] In short, although only created in November 1944, the ALIU made considerable progress towards

[193] Sawyer to Rushin, 21 April 1945, 'Orion organization': US NA, RG 226, Entry 190, Box 532.

[194] Ibid.

[195] Pearson to Donovan, 20 May 1945, 'Orion organization': US NA, RG 226, Entry 190, Box 532. This noted that in London, the unit was in 'intimate collaboration with MI-6, MEW [Ministry of Economic Warfare (Br.)], and the London representatives of the respective French, Dutch, Belgian, Czech, and Polish services.'

[196] Donovan to Special List, 30 April 1945: Jackson Papers, Box 101, Folder 7.

achieving its objectives during the next six months before the end of hostilities in Europe in May 1945.

Missions to Italy and France

In the wake of the retreat of Axis forces following successive Allied military victories during late 1944 and early 1945, the geographical scope for new investigative work of the ALIU became considerably extended. For example, on 10 March 1945, Plaut was able to travel to Southern Italy to survey the: 'art looting problems in the Mediterranean Theatre of Operations.' This involved conducting investigations over the next months in Naples, Rome and, from 29 March, Florence, before returning to London on 4 May 1945.[197] This mission included overseeing the: 'the interrogation, in Rome, of Wilhelm Mohnen, German espionage agent and minor participant in German official art looting activities in France.'[198] Plaut suspected Mohnen of acting as a German espionage agent. His detailed interrogation yielded little new intelligence but was: 'chiefly productive for broad intelligence purposes.'[199] Plaut worked in Italy until May of 1945, moving between the ALIU offices and the site of his own field investigation, where he worked closely alongside and cooperatively with MFA&A officers.[200] This working relationship was enhanced further by Plaut's investigation into Mohnen's knowledge of art looting methods in France.[201] The placement of ALIU under OSS X-2 was, as already mentioned, originally designed to optimise the possibility of exploiting such potential counter-intelligence opportunities, particularly in contexts where such plunder by art dealers was also functioning as a cover for Nazi intelligence operations.

Plaut's Italian investigations and liaison with MFA&A officers resulted in the Director of the ALIU making a series of 'suggestions for future operations' to OSS' James Angleton, who was then commander of

[197] See, Plaut to Chief, X-2 Branch ETO, 'ORION Project', 5 May 1945, 'Cables': US NA, Entry 190, Box 533.

[198] 'ALIU Final Report' (May 1946), op. cit., 3.

[199] Ibid., 4. See also 'Interim report on German looting of works of art in France', 15 April 1945 (Mohnen interrogation report) cited in ibid., 7.

[200] Ibid., 3–4.

[201] Ibid., 4. See also Pearson to Donovan, 20 May 1945, 2, 'Orion organization': US NA, RG 226, Entry 190, Box 532.

a special OSS counter intelligence unit (SCI/Z) in that country.[202] These included encouraging high-level and centralised liaison between Angleton and both US and British MFA&A officers. Plaut also reported on his efforts to exert pressure on the previously 'apathetic' Italian authorities, who had lacked commitment to recover even previously government-owned art treasures looted by the Nazis, and identified relevant senior officials in the Italian government who should be providing assistance.[203] He also emphasised his work with locally-based OSS officials: 'in an effort to have traced in Northern Italy, the major works missing', and the possibly 'spurious' claim of one private citizen who had previously advised Mussolini and sold works to Göring allegedly 'under coercion'.[204] Plaut could identify only one other example of looting from private collections of individuals.[205] These somewhat limited results could, he claimed, be improved upon through the later interrogation of Dr Gottlieb Reber, a task that was accomplished soon afterwards, and whose results will be discussed later in this book. Plaut also recruited Dr Crico, a: 'British national, born in Aden, and long-term resident of Italy.'[206] Crico had previous relevant professional experience with the British art investigation authorities since 1943. He wanted her to work for the OSS complete with credentials supplied by this intelligence organisation. Such authorisation was needed to permit Dr Crico to move freely across different regions by means of her own private car. The plan was that Dr Crico would be 'attached nominally' with MFA&A for three months in order to: 'investigate the flow of art properties from Central to Northern Italy.'[207] Before leaving Italy, Plaut also wrote a memorandum to regional Director of the MFA&A, Ernest de Wald, urging him to better coordinate his officers' art looting and restitution investigations with the Angleton's operation to the mutual benefit of both parties:

> It is to be hoped that you will take every advantage of the services which Lt. Angleton can place at your disposal; he is able to facilitate the movement of your "jointly controlled operatives", to obtain personnel

[202] Plaut to Angleton, 26 April, 1944: US NA, RG 226, Entry 210, Box 352, Folder 6.
[203] Ibid.
[204] Ibid., 2.
[205] Ibid.
[206] Plaut to Angleton, 'Crico, Dr Albertina,' 27 April 1945: US NA, RG 226, Entry 210, Box 352, Folder 6.
[207] Ibid., 1.

> for purposes of questioning, to conduct security investigations, and to render other services which you may require in this connection. As I have stressed...it will be to our mutual advantage that we use Angleton's channel's of communication (both cable and pouch) to resolve any matters of urgency which, in your estimation, concern this unit....it will be greatly appreciated if you will outline to the MFA&A officers...procedures for the coordination of such investigations, and if you will request transmission to this unit, of relevant information. Lt. Angleton can suggest means of collaboration in each area with the SCI/Z...It is requested particularly that any information bearing on the flight *from Italy* of identifiable works of art, or groups of objects, or of identifiable personnel responsible for removals, be transmitted expeditiously to this unit, so that requisite action, where possible, may be taken.[208]

It appears that some of Plaut's efforts to energise the previously 'apathetic' Italian Government officials had, in his view, begun to yield some fruit, as he also noted:

> The increasingly energetic attitude of the Italian Ministry, as manifest recently by the Siviero sponsorship and the Venturi appointment, is encouraging. Any determination by our personnel of a) the whereabouts of missing objects, and b) the responsibility for their removal warrants positive assistance on the part of the Italian Government in continuing investigations, and should stimulate vigorous official representations both as to legitimate recovery and the prosecution of guilty individuals.[209]

After the liberation of France, ALIU officials provided the reconstituted French authorities in Paris with growing quantities of damning evidence of the complicity of French persons, as well as German nationals, in the art looting dimension of the Holocaust. They provided: 'all information gained during the German operation, and from other sources....affecting French interests.'[210] However, these authorities, for whom the question of extensive French collaboration with the Nazi regime was a difficult political issue, were not initially responsive. As Nicholas notes:

> By late 1944 not one dealer's doors had been closed by the authorities. This seeming insouciance on the part of the French upset the OSS

[208] Plaut to de Wald, 28 April 1945, 'Investigation of German Looting and Removal of Italian Art Properties; Coordination of Operations: US NA, RG 226, Entry 210, Box 352, Folder 6.

[209] Ibid.

[210] Final Report, op. cit., 4–5.

> investigators whose mounting stacks of evidence pointed straight to numerous Paris dealers, but could get little cooperation from their French counterparts, the DGER—the result more of chauvinism and political turmoil than inaction.[211]

However, Rousseau continued to work with the different branches of the French government, including the intelligence services, between late 1945 and February 1946, and: 'acted as informal technical advisor to the French Government in art looting problems.'[212] By May 1946, the ALIU could claim to have materially assisted the French with both restitution and war crimes prosecution work. It: 'was directly responsible for the return to France of a number of invaluable works of art and for the delivery into French custody of several of the Germans most conspicuously involved in the French depredations.'[213] On the other hand, Wittmann's report from the Autumn of 1946[214] recalled that, at the start of the ALIU's investigations, the members of the French DGER had only been active 'to some degree' in investigating French collaborationist art dealers, and that: 'these members had proved to be inefficient and unwilling to co-operate even though their government had a primary interest in the recovery of looted art.'[215] The result was that many of these dealers had, by the summer of 1946, restarted their trade, and may well have exported looted works to the United States and other countries.[216]

ALIU's postwar investigations and interrogations in Germany and Austria

This section will examine evidence of the postwar priorities of the ALIU and how these were realised through their questioning of individuals suspected of being complicit in Nazi art looting. The end of hostilities in early May 1945 finally allowed Plaut's OSS Unit to carry out investigations across Germany itself.[217] Members of the Unit entered Germany

[211] Nicholas, 1995 op. cit., 424.
[212] Final Report, op. cit., 5.
[213] Ibid.
[214] The Getty Research Institute have a number of relevant oral histories including one by Otto Wittmann.
[215] Wittmann, 'Final Mission to Europe', op. cit., 6.
[216] Ibid.
[217] Nicholas, 1995 op. cit., 378.

on 20 May 1945, and began conducting interrogations of individuals named on their high priority 'target list', who had been subsequently detained by Allied Army and intelligence officials.[218] They secured authority from US 12th Army HQ to work in Germany and Austria as 'technical advisers' to war crimes investigations of the JAG department. The work they carried out there will be discussed in detail in a later section. At this time, the Allied Forces Headquarters (AFHQ) requested that the ALIU dispatch one of its members to Italy to interrogate leading members of the German Kunstschutz (The German Commission for the Protection of Works of Art in the Occupied Countries under the direction of the German Army High Command) captured in the fighting in the North. Because of the Unit's impending operation in Germany, a member of the parallel British unit undertook this mission at Plaut's suggestion and then reported back to the ALIU.

For obvious reasons, during the ALIU's postwar investigations in Germany and Austria, Plaut had to establish both a series of priorities and a specific division of labour between his staff, which in turn allowed each of them to develop a *specialist area of expertise*. For example, one of Plaut's team, Faison,[219] has recalled that he was given specific responsibility for investigating the Linz Museum:

> In 1945...[I] spent that summer quizzing Nazi art personnel. My particular task was to find out about Adolf Hitler's massive art collection, which he intended to become the crown jewel in a sort of Acropolis-on-the-Danube in the old Austrian city of Linz. As a great new cultural centre, Linz was to replace Vienna, scene of Hitler's failures as student of art and architecture.[220]

Three members, Plaut, Rousseau, and Faison, with the help of Dutch Army Intelligence officer Captain Jan Vlug, travelled to Germany on 20 May 1945.[221] In late May 1945, Plaut left Italy and Rousseau left Spain to join forces in Austria to begin a programme of interrogations.[222] During May and June 1945, Plaut and Rousseau reviewed current

---

[218] Final Report, op. cit., 5.

[219] The Getty Research Institute have a number of relevant oral histories including one by Lane Faison. Faison's papers are at the National Gallery, with his slides, photos and a few other things at Williams College. I am grateful to Jonathan Petropoulus for this point.

[220] Lane Faison, 'Transfer of Custody to the Germans', in Simpson, 1997 op. cit., 140.

[221] For Plaut's own account of his work: see www.theatlantic.com/unbound/flashbks/nazigold/intro.htm.

[222] Pearson to Donovan, 20 May 1945 op. cit., 2.

ALIU investigations, which at this point had benefited from the results of questioning over 700 individuals suspected of being involved in art looting. 20 of the 21 identified on the ALIU's high priority target list were detained as of June 1945 at the U.S. Judge Advocate General's interrogation center at Alt Aussee, Austria.[223] Working in 'direct liaison' with the 'vanguard of the US Chief of Counsel', as well as with MFA&A officers, and other representatives of the Allied military, Plaut and Rousseau were personally involved in the apprehension of the majority of these 'most wanted' individuals.[224] During the first week of June 1945, and acting in conjunction with the Judge Advocate, 3rd U.S. Army, they succeeded in establishing their special interrogation centre in a 'tall, gabled villa' at the Austrian village of Alt Aussee, which they occupied from 10 June through to the start of October 1945.[225] Jurisdiction of the Alt Aussee villa fell under the U.S. Army Judge Advocate's office, which was at this time gathering information regarding Nazi war crimes. Whilst working at their Austrian base, ALIU personnel interrogated art looting suspects in the order that the Third U.S. Army was able to locate them in occupied Germany and Austria and then transport them to Alt Aussee. This meant that Heinrich Hoffmann, Walter Andreas Hofer, and Bruno Lohse were the first three to be detained and interrogated. On the other hand, the number allotted to the interrogation reports matches closely the 'target number' of the individual concerned, which suggests a greater pattern and logic to this sequence. Hoffmann, for example, was interrogated at Alt Aussee: 'during the period 8–28 June 1945.'[226]

Plaut has recalled the reasons behind their choice of this location: 'an interrogation centre was established in Alt Aussee, Austria, in close proximity to the salt mine where the greatest proportion of Nazi plunder from Western Europe was concealed.'[227] Indeed, later interrogations

---

[223] 'Safehaven Report: Target List of German Personnel implicated in Looting of European Art Treasures,' 14 August 1945, Safehaven Reports, 1944–1945, War Crimes Branch, Records of the Office of the Judge Advocate General (Army): NA, RG 153, Box 8. Faison later joined Plaut and Rousseau here in July 1945.

[224] Final Report, op. cit., 6.

[225] Outgoing cable to SAINT (ORION) London, presumably from Plaut, cable received in ORION office 16 June 1945. 'Cables': US NA, RG 226, Entry 190, Box 533. See also Nicholas, 1995 op. cit., 378. Howe recalls that this 'tall, gabled villa' was a 'commonplace suburban structure, standing behind a stout iron fence with padlocked gates, within a stone's throw of the main highway, and built in the gingerbread style of fifty years ago.' Howe, 1946 op. cit., 131.

[226] DIR Hoffman, op. cit., 1.

[227] Plaut, 1997 op. cit., 124. See also Feliciano, 1997 op. cit., 50 noting that elements

at this base provided further details of how much of the ERR's store of looted works confiscated from French Jews was transported there over a thirteen month period starting on February 1944.[228] Apparently their base for 'intensive investigation of German art-looting activity', which included specially adapted holding cells in the basement, was characterised by a: 'well ordered domesticity', including the services of a cook and waitress.[229] Cells held multiple prisoners, and Karl Haberstock, according to ERR cataloguer Bruno Lohse,[230] 'joined him and Göring's agent, Walter Andreas Hofer,[231] for a good part of their confinement.'[232] In short, at Alt Aussee from 10 June to the start of October, Plaut and his colleagues interrogated art looting personnel who had been hunted and detained. Their detention followed the submission of the Unit's 'high priority' wanted list to various field intelligence agencies, including of course the OSS and US Counter Intelligence Corps (CIC). After interrogation, the majority of the detainees were either: 'placed under house arrest or given into the custody of the US Chief of Counsel, Nuremberg as witnesses in the Nuremberg trials and for ultimate prosecution in subsequent war crimes proceedings.'[233]

There were good reasons for the choice of Alt Aussee as ALIU's operations base. At this time, Plaut recalls that the surrounding area contained a 'compact concentration' of senior Nazi officials implicated in the Holocaust and other war crimes who had fled from Allied advances. This proved beneficial: 'such that we were able to find and detain many of the looting operators close at hand.'[234] The Roberts Commission Report extensively quotes from ALIU's DIR on Hofer, and notes that:

---

of the Rothschild's collection was discovered there concealed in salt mines; CIR 4, op. cit., 13.

[228] DIR 5 (Schiedlausky) op. cit., 3.

[229] 'We could perhaps stop off at Bad Aussee for supper. Two naval officers—Lieutenants Plaut and Rousseau, both of them OSS—had set up a special interrogation center there, an establishment known simply as 'House 71,' and were making an intensive investigation of German art-looting activities. They lived very well, Posey said with a grin. We could do a lot worse than to sample their hospitality. I knew Jim Plaut and Ted Rousseau—in fact had seen them at Versailles not so many weeks ago—so I thought we could prevail on them to take us in.' Howe, 1946 op. cit., 128.

[230] Lohse had acted as Göring's 'special representative' in the ERR. See CIR 4 (Linz), op. cit., 57–58; CIR 2 (Göring) op. cit., 18.

[231] For more details of Hofer, see CIR 2 (Göring) op. cit., 10.

[232] Petropoulos, 2000, op. cit., 94. Hofer was detained between 10 June and 1 September 1945: CIR 2 (Göring), 1.

[233] Final Report, op. cit., 6.

[234] Plaut, 1997 op. cit., 125.

> Early in June 1945, officers of this unit began interrogations at Alt-Aussee, Austria, of nearly a dozen persons intimately connected with the administration of Göring's household, and with his acquisition of works of art. One of these men, Walter Andreas Hofer, was an art dealer and director of the Reichsmarschall's collection and his chief confidential adviser on such matters.[235]

Indeed, Petropoulos notes that within 'House 71 of Alt Aussee', these OSS officials had: 'assembled many of the leading figures of the Third Reich's art world, including Dr Ernst Buchner,[236] Karl Haberstock,[237] Walter Andreas Hofer,[238] Heinrich Hoffmann,[239] Bruno Lohse,[240]

[235] Roberts Commission Report, 1946, op. cit., 76.

[236] Buchner, an expert on pre-modern German artworks, had been Director of the Bavarian State Paintings Museum, which meant that he oversaw a network of 15 museums. According to Petropoulos, he 'evolved into a politicized accomplice of the Nazi leaders in the initiative to amass huge collections' including the looting of the Ghent and Bouts altar works.

[237] Haberstock was chief agent for the Linz collection and a Berlin art dealer who bought and sold Hitler's works of art). He was also a Berlin Art dealer who was 'active in all occupied countries' and sold to both Hitler and Göring. CIR 2 (Göring), 2 and Reference K. Haberstock was detained for 36 days and proved generally co-operative. Petropoulos, 2000 op. cit., 94; CIR 4 (Linz), op. cit., 47–48. Haberstock and Dequoy/Wildenstein had developed a close business relationship noted in postwar OSS report: 'Haberstock states that he always understood that the money was being paid to a secret account which would ultimately have been at the disposal of M. Georges Wildenstein.' Anonymous OSS report, 'Special Report on the firm of Wildenstein & Cie,' August 1945: US NA, RG 260, Entry 446; OSS Cooper Report, 20 September 1945 (cited in Nicholas op. cit., 159–60 and 453); Petropoulos, 2000 op. cit., 89.

[238] Director of the Göring Collection and Göring's chief purchasing agent CIR 2 (Göring), op. cit., 165.

[239] Hoffmann was Hitler's art adviser, who was further interrogated at Nuremberg. See CIR 4 (Linz), op. cit., 43–45. Feliciano, 1997 op. cit., 21 noting that: 'Hitler had begun creating his own art collection in the 1920's and 1930's, using his portrait photographer Heinrich Hoffmann as a broker.'

[240] Lohse was a Munich art dealer, had served as executive officer of the Einsatzstab Reichsleiter Rosenberg (ERR) in Paris. CIR 1 describes Dr. Bruno Lohse as: 'member of the Paris art staff from February 1941, subsequently its Deputy Director, and special representative of GÖRING in the E.R.R. Ibid., 49. See DIR No. 6, Subject: Bruno Lohse. Plaut states: 'Other members of the Göring entourage were less venal. Young Bruno Lohse, tall, athletic, and Prussian, was a serious art student, a convinced Nazi, and a dreamer. Struck by his attractive manner and his sincerity, Göring had singled him out from von Behr's staff and made him deputy director and his personal agent. Much of the French wrath over the indignities of the Einsatzstab is visited, justifiably, on Lohse, who, in his National Socialist zeal and his worship of Göring, organized and dominated important looting operations, convinced that in so doing he was serving his state and his chief with real nobility.' Plaut, 1946a op. cit.

Kajetan Mühlmann[241] and Hermann Voss.'[242] Six other individuals who were being interrogated in relation to matters other than the Linz collection were also questioned at Alt Aussee concerning their knowledge of acquisitions for this collection.[243] Plaut recalls that:

> What of the men around Göring, the satellites who carried out the Reichsmarschall's bidding? In the months after V-E Day, their American captors came to know some of them well—questioned them, talked to them, watched them. At the modest summer house in the mountains of the Salzkammergut where they had been rounded up for intensive interrogation, they were observed at close hand for weeks on end as the whole fantastic story of Nazi looting was gradually unfolded. A singularly diverse group, they had—apart from a mutual interest in art and in Göring—virtually nothing in common.[244]

In some cases, Rousseau and Plaut invited their opposite numbers in the British, French and Dutch agencies to attend and even participate these interrogations as part of their own distinct investigations.

At this point it may be useful to address the lines of questioning developing during interrogations, and what these revealed about the roles and motivations of those being interrogated. The interrogators addressed a range of themes, some of which were common to most of their subjects, including their biographical and professional background, the emergence of their involvement with the Nazi movement or prominent figures in it, such as Göring and Hitler, knowledge of the actions and institutional positions of others on the ALIU wanted list,[245] and their complicity in distinctly anti-Semitic aspects of art looting, including the activities of the ERR.[246] The topics for interrogation were thus varied but all were related to the following four strands of

---

[241] Mühlmann was a well-educated member of Austrian intelligentsia attaining a PhD from University of Innsbruck at the age of 28 years in 1926, Petropoulos, 1996b op. cit., 179. He was later made a 'special commissioner for the safeguarding of works of art in the occupied territories'. He kept offices in Berlin, Vienna, Warsaw, Cracow and The Hague from which he acted as 'official purchaser' for both Hitler and Göring, 'with a special staff at his disposal': CIR 2 (Göring), op. cit., 2.

[242] Voss was second director of the Linz Special Commission in charge of acquisitions following the death of the previous founding Director Hans Posse.

[243] Mühlmann, Hofer, Limberger, Lohse, Buchner and Bornheim: CIR 4 (Linz), op. cit., preface.

[244] Plaut 1946a op. cit.

[245] DIR 2 (Buchner) op. cit., 2, which clarified the administrative hierarchy with the Linz Museum.

[246] Ibid., 4.

the ALIU's overall mission: the identification of networks of individuals complicit in looting, ascertaining their degrees of comparative responsibility and centrality; analysing the methodology deployed during such acquisition; and, finally, ascertaining the current location of the fruits of such illegal acts.[247]

For example, one topic was the organisation of the acquisition of artworks for Hitler's Linz Museum, and the curious logic behind the strange appointment on 15 March 1943 of Hermann Voss to the post of provisional Director of this expanding collection. It was well known that Voss was an anti-Nazi and friend of several German Jews.[248] In addition, most of the resulting DIR reports ended with a conclusion that included recommendations as to whether or not their subjects merited prosecution as war criminals, or further interrogation by the MFA&A, or—in some cases—exploitation for the purpose of locating and identifying recovered art works.[249] Of course, ALIU officials also pursued other, more specific lines of questioning where the individual was, for example, involved with or knowledgeable about the acquisition policies of either the Linz Museum,[250] or the ERR, or both.[251] Whilst, evidence concerning the corroboration of detainees' statements was not included in every ALIU interrogation report, discrepancies were generally highlighted and illustrated with examples.

There is an interesting relationship between the resulting Detailed Interrogation Reports (DIRs) and the Consolidated Interrogation Reports (CIRs). The former summarise the interrogation record and its implications with respect to a specific individual; whereas the latter are thematic and relate to specific institutions. The CIR's tend to consolidate and summarise relevant information contained in one or sometimes more DIRs. For example, DIR 7, relating to Göring's personal secretary Gisela Limberger, notes: 'The major portion of her testimony has been included in CIR No. 2, The Göring Collection, as one of its most important sources. This report is intended to give a more detailed account of her duties in the Göring organization and to determine as far as possible the extent of her responsibilities in the

---

[247] DIR No. 9 (Hofer), op. cit., Attachment 3.
[248] CIR 4 (Linz), op. cit., 12, 15; DIR 12 (Voss) op. cit., 1.
[249] DIR 1 (Hoffmann) op. cit., 8.
[250] These points will be substantiated and illustrated below.
[251] DIR 2 (Buchner) op. cit., 4.

formation of the collection.'[252] In some cases, such as DIR 3 on Robert Scholz, the DIR is classified as merely 'supplementary' to CIR 1 (ERR). Some DIRs were completed after the relevant CIRs as was the case with Haberstock's interrogation report which is dated summer 1946, many months after the CIR 4 (Linz) was finished.[253]

The first of ALIU's CIRs, completed by Plaut on 15 August 1945 and addressing the ERR's looting activities in France, identifies the following interrogations and captured records as *particularly relevant* sources for its investigations:

> The following individuals, listed as sources, were detained and interrogated at a special investigation centre in Austria during the period 10 June–15 August 1945:
>
> 1. Dr. Robert SCHOLZ, chief adviser to Reichsleiter ROSENBERG in art matters; Bereichsleiter (Divisional Director) of the Rosenberg *Amt Bildende Kunst* (Office for Pictorial Arts), Berlin.
> 2. Dr. Bruno LOHSE, special art representative of GÖRING in France and Deputy Director of the ROSENBERG art staff in Paris.
> 3. Dr. Günther SCHIEDLAUSKY, member of the E.R.R. and keeper of the E.R.R. deposits in Germany (Interrogated at Neuschwanstein/ Füssen, Bavaria, on 10–11 July 1945).
> 4. Karl KRESS, photographer attached to the E.R.R. staff.
> 5. Gustav ROCHLITZ, German art dealer active in Paris, who conducted important transactions with the E.R.R.
> 6. Walter Andreas HOFER, art dealer; principle buyer for GÖRING, and Director of his gallery at Carinhall.
> 7. Fräulein Gisela LIMBERGER, GÖRING's personal librarian and secretary, and keeper of the records of the GÖRING Collection.
>
> The files of the EINSATZSTAB ROSENBERG, still largely intact, were examined at Neuschwanstein / Füssen, Bavaria and constitute a primary source of information.[254]

Questions of individual responsibility for anti-Semitic war crimes are addressed more directly in the DIRs and the CIR on Göring. By contrast, issues of *organisational* liability under future war crimes hearings are dealt with more clearly in the CIRs on the ERR and the Linz organisation. Buchner, for instance, was pressed on his personal knowledge of, and complicity in, the ERR's plunder of Jewish works of art. He

[252] DIR No. 7 (Limberger), op. cit., 1.

[253] 'The information contained in this report has been obtained from sources and documents which have come to hand since the publication of CIR 4.' DIR No. 13 (Haberstock) May 1946, op. cit., 1.

[254] CIR 1, op. cit., 2.

was even confronted with examples of pictures which Rousseau knew the ERR had plundered and previously shown to Buchner at Munich. Typically he admitted the facts but denied possessing any subjective knowledge that these items had in fact been looted from Jewish collections. The DIR report clearly reflects how Rousseau intensively pursued this theme of Buchner's various contacts with the ERR and those of his staff, notwithstanding the latter's denials. The interrogators' pressure resulted in the disclosure of a series of his official complicities, despite his claimed lack of personal enthusiasm, or support for, the Nazi regime's anti-Semitic art looting:

> Buchner states that as Director General of the Bavarian Collections, it was his official duty to attend sales of confiscated pictures and to make choices for his own museums, taking his turn after the Director of Linz. He claims that he never bought such pictures on his own initiative. He adds that he was never in favor of the anti-Semitic laws, and cites as evidence to confirm this the fact that he is perhaps the only German museum director to have preserved for his museums the collection of paintings by the Jewish painter Liebermann. Payments for the confiscated pictures were made directly to the people concerned by the Ministry which had authority for the museums.[255]

ALIU officials also carried out a number of interrogations specifically relevant to the Linz Museum at other locations, such as Munich.[256] One ALIU report recalls that:

> Individuals were detained for varying periods. Karl Haberstock, for example, was detained for 36 days. Some of those interrogated were more cooperative than others. Karl Haberstock, the most active and successful German art dealer during the war, was relatively cooperative. Walter Andreas Hofer...seemed to remember every transaction, and provided details of certain of them with ease while avoiding those that revealed his own venality.[257] Kajetan Mühlmann, the chief figure in the organized German looting of art of Poland and the Netherlands, twice attempted to escape and initially responded with contempt. However, he eventually talked a great deal. Bruno Lohse's...knowledge was encyclopaedic, and, hoping to please his captors, he held back nothing. Equally responsive was Gisela Limberger, Göring's secretary, who, while professing her own innocence, became a fountainhead of incriminating information.[258]

---

[255] DIR 2 (Buchner) op. cit., 5–6.

[256] Dietrich, Reger, Gurlitt, Weinmueller, Ruprecht and Kluge: CIR 4 (Linz), op. cit., preface.

[257] CIR 2 (Göring) op. cit., 32.

[258] Plaut, 1997 op. cit., 124.

Cells at Alt Aussee held multiple prisoners, and Karl Haberstock, according to ERR cataloguer Bruno Lohse,[259] 'joined him and Göring's agent, Walter Andreas Hofer,[260] for a good part of their confinement.'[261] Over the three month period from June to September 1945, ALIU officials operated full-time from their Alt Aussee base carrying out these interrogations. Rothfeld notes certain limitations and ambiguities in our knowledge of what took place stemming from the nature of the surviving records and the loose and varied format of the resulting DIR reports:

> Unfortunately, only some of the ALIU interrogation reports included evidence that corroborated the information provided by other interviewees. The reports do not clearly indicate whether or not the ALIU believed the accounts being described to them. The ALIU had confirmation from other detained art looting suspects as to what specific information each of them knew in regards to their colleagues' actions. The ALIU had no set questions for each of their interrogations, which made corroborating testimony more difficult. The exact questions asked in the interrogations did not appear in the reports; they were merely summaries of what the ALIU member discovered during the interrogation session. This could have led to several layers of interpretation by the ALIU.[262]

These and other related points are best discussed and illustrated with specific examples.

ALIU officials interrogated Buchner from 30 June through to 31 July 1945.[263] He was questioned in part concerning his knowledge of the role of Linz Museum's acquisition policies in the cultural plunder aspect of the Holocaust, particularly in respect to his claim that: 'Linz always had the first choice of the pictures confiscated from the Jewish collections.'[264] Buchner was also pressed concerning his role in the reassignment of such confiscated collections to Museums he personally controlled.[265]

---

[259] Lohse had acted as Göring's 'special representative' in the ERR. See CIR 4 (Linz), op. cit., 57–58; CIR 2 (Göring) op. cit., 18.

[260] For more details of Hofer, see CIR 2 (Göring) op. cit., 10.

[261] Petropoulos, 2000, op. cit., 94. Hofer was detained between 10 June and 1 September 1945: CIR 2 (Göring), 1.

[262] Rothfeld, 2002 op. cit., Chapter 4, 1.

[263] DIR 2 (Buchner), op. cit., 1.

[264] Ibid., 2.

[265] 'In 1939 at the time of the wholesale confiscation of Jewish property carried out by the Nazis in Munich, Buchner took his turn, after Posse [Linz Director], in choosing for his museums from the pictures which had been taken. He says that the

The OSS interrogators deployed a number of different techniques both to obtain and then test the credibility of the information disclosed during extensive questioning. One of these was to probe detainees on a certain point on which, but not known to the subject of the interrogation, these interrogators already possessed adequate documentary evidence, and then confront them with any discrepancies requiring explanation. This could be termed an ambush strategy designed to test whether the detainee was telling the truth on those points which had already been established in order to establish their credibility in relation to *other* areas where they could possibly provide genuinely new information to fill gaps in the ALIU's current knowledge.

Another of this Unit's interrogation tactics was to test claims against the statements of earlier detainees, or even to bring two detainees into the same room so that one could make a statement about a disputed point in person and in the presence of the person who was, for his or her own strategic reasons, denying it. In addition, for those detainees who had held senior posts associated with Nazi art looting organisations or dealers with close associations with Göring, the OSS interrogators appeared to adopt the stance of 'guilty until proved innocent'. Proof was taken as the agreement between the detainees' claims on the one hand, and the implications of external source material on the other.

Lane Faison's interrogation report on Hermann Voss provides some examples of these techniques, including the sceptical cross referencing of postwar claims to evidence of wartime actions:

> Voss represents himself as a person of strong anti-Nazi sympathies who accepted the Linz position only with the idea of saving the pictures and handing them over, intact and inventorized, to the Allies who he felt certain would win the war. Voss' case therefore rests on his demonstrating, first his anti-Nazi ideals up to March 1943, when he accepted the Linz position; and second, an unchanging attitude thereafter, together with actions suitable to such an attitude.[266]

This placing of the onus on the detainees to prove their case, based on a presumption of prior guilt, meant that the statements of other detainees with relevant experience became a relevant source for cross-checking such claims. Voss' DIR finally accepted that his anti-Nazi views and

confiscations were the result of a Hitler order according to which all Jewish collections were to be put at the disposal of Prof. Posse so that he could choose from them for the Linz Museum.' Ibid., 4.

[266] DIR No. 12 (Voss), op. cit., 3.

stance had been confirmed by other detainees and witnesses interviewed:[267] 'Reactions to the appointment of Voss appear to have been one of wide-spread surprise. Hofer, Lohse Kajetan Mühlmann...and Haberstock all testify to this effect....'[268] Where Voss pressed his claims to total innocence to extremes by expressing resentment and surprise at having been treated as possible war crimes defendants in the first place, the ALIU interrogators appeared to have been left distinctly unimpressed, a point that will become clearer when we review their recommendation for his prosecution as a war criminal:

> Voss complains of the abruptness of his reception and incarceration at Wiesbaden, and appears surprised that the Americans did not know all about him and welcome him as the saviour of valuable works of art. He expected that no one would question his motives in becoming the Sonderbeauftragter of Linz, that he would be able to return to Dresden without incident as soon as he had finished his business in Wiesbaden, and that the Americans would transport his wife, himself and his belongings out of the Russian zone.[269]

At the end of WWII in Europe on 8 May 1945, Voss had travelled to Wiesbaden, Germany, to offer his help in locating looted art previously destined for the Linz Museum.[270] ALIU officials interrogated him in their Alt Aussee base from one month beginning on 15 August 1945.[271] Nicholas notes:

> It never seemed to occur to him that his wartime activities would be viewed as criminal by the Allies; he expected that the Americans would arrange for his wife and his personal papers to be brought from Dresden so that he could donate them to some public institution or university, where no doubt he planned to continue his studies...He was, therefore, quite amazed to be arrested immediately by Walter Farmer and sent off to Alt Aussee to be interrogated.[272]

The summary and conclusion to this detainee's interrogation report shows that his various defensive claims had received a distinctly unsympathetic reaction, something worsened by Voss' inconsistency, inability to adequately explain discrepancies, and his various transparent attempts at evasion and selective amnesia:

---

[267] Ibid.
[268] Ibid., 7.
[269] Ibid., 20.
[270] Nicholas, 1995 op. cit., 379.
[271] DIR 12, (Voss), op. cit., 6–20.
[272] Nicholas, 1995 op. cit., 380; DIR No. 12, 'Hermann Voss' op. cit.

> In the absence of complete documentation, the part played by Hermann Voss in Hitler's scheme of things is not altogether clear... During a month of interrogation, he impressed his several questioners very unfavourably. It was their unanimous opinion that Voss' character is vacillating, and that he is an extraordinarily conceited and ambitious man. His constant reliance on failure of memory to explain discrepancies in his testimony did not improve the atmosphere of interrogations... He constantly evaded the question of moral responsibility involved in accepting the position of Sonderbeauftragter of the Linz Museum... since he was able to hand over to Reimer almost all administrative detail and all the direct dealings with the Party bosses, he claims immunity from the consequences. [A]s a result of his decision, Voss became involved in the most elaborate expedition on the history of art dealing, under artificial economic conditions designed by the Nazis as one of the subtler methods of despoiling occupied territories.[273]

The last point concerning voluntary participation in a flow of artistic works from France and other parts of Nazi-occupied Europe to German collections could perhaps have been applied to all those they interrogated, included those such as Limberger, Göring's personal secretary, who they exonerated fully.

The next paragraphs will summarise a number of points relevant to the overall theme of this book that emerged during individual interrogations. Hofer's interrogation revealed some surprising modest qualities of the background and abilities of someone who had both worked closely with the deputy leader of Nazi Germany, Göring, and fully exploited the reflected power and influence this brought him. Indeed, Rousseau noted how Hofer had even become 'Göring's alter ego as far as the Collection was concerned.'[274] He further recorded that:

> with most of Europe cowering in terror of the Luftwaffe, Hofer proudly flaunted his title... it was engraved on his business cards and his stationery, and it was thus that he insisted on being known wherever he went. He was extremely jealous of his position. He suspected that others were constantly plotting to displace him, and his attitude to all who approached the Reichsmarschall was hostile...[275] [Yet] Before he began his work for Göring he had been comparatively unknown, and as soon as he rose to prominence the fear of being displaced prevented him from forming any close associations in the art world.[276]

[273] Ibid., 20–22.
[274] DIR No. 9 op. cit., 2.
[275] Ibid.
[276] DIR No. 9 (Hofer) op. cit., 4–5.

Another remarkable fact that emerged from his interrogation was Hofer's ability to have continued working as an independent dealer, despite both acting as curator for the Göring collection and having already sold his own collection to the Reichsmarschall.[277] Hofer's interrogation also revealed his complicity in specifically anti-Semitic acts of looting carried out in close cooperation with the ERR, which extended even to making independent trips to Paris to earmark specific items owned by French Jews that might in the future be subject to confiscation:

> There is undeniable proof that he alone went to the Jeu de Paume and chose the confiscated paintings from the Paul Rosenberg Collection for the exchange with Wendland (see reference B, Attachments 1 and 55). The confiscated Impressionist paintings for the exchange with Fischer of Lucerne were officially given out to Hofer by the ERR staff... That he was not only fully informed about the activities of the ERR, but also repeatedly both advised Göring and sometimes acted on his own initiative to obtain confiscated objects for the Collection, is proven by his own letters to his chief.... he strongly advised Göring to take certain specific pictures from the Rothschild Collections, and drew his attention in particular to their "voluminous collection of modern family jewelry."[278]

One aspect of this complicity was his connection with the Foreign Enemy Protection Commandos that involved freezing dealings in actual or potentially Jewish art works stored in safe deposit boxes in French banks, including the Joseph Rottier collection.[279] His interrogation report noted that Hofer took pride in forcing down the price he paid for confiscated works of art and encouraged Göring to follow suit: 'Hofer inspired and encouraged Göring in his natural tendency to be mean and avaricious.'[280] Hofer was 'at least as responsible as his chief for the methods employed and for the choice of the majority of the objects.'[281] Rousseau also reported that: '[Hofer] laughingly told how he had offered the painter [Georges] Braque a speedy release of his mistakenly confiscated collection if he would be willing to sell his Cranach, a picture which Hofer knew he never intended to part with.'[282]

---

[277] Ibid., Attachment 2 (list of Hofer's independent sales).
[278] Ibid., 2–3.
[279] Ibid., 3.
[280] Ibid., 4.
[281] Ibid., 1.
[282] Ibid. 4.

Howe recalls meeting Hofer at the OSS' Alt Aussee base where he was being interrogated. He provides evidence of the effectiveness of the interrogation techniques that Plaut's team were deploying, and discusses some of the beneficial side-effects concerning the rescuing of damaged works of art:

> Hofer had been arrested shortly after the close of hostilities. He had been a "guest" at House 71 for some weeks now, and was being grilled daily by our "cloak and dagger boys." They were probing into his activities of the past few years and had already extracted an amazing lot of information for incorporation into an exhaustive report on the Göring collection and "how it grew." Hofer was just one of a long procession of witnesses who were being questioned by Plaut and Rousseau in the course of their tireless investigation of the artistic depredations of the top Nazis. These OSS officers knew their business. With infinite patience, they were cross-examining their witnesses and gradually extracting information which was to lend an authentic fascination to their reports.[283]

Howe then provides some additional recollections of the quantity, type and value of the information that Plaut's team of officials were able to extract from Hofer's interrogation. He also discusses the 'convenient' and selective memory lapses from which Hofer pretended to suffer whenever ALIU staff raised questions related to his own personal complicity in Nazi war crimes:

> We turned back to the subject of Hofer, who had not yet finished his daily constitutional and could be seen still pacing back and forth below us. He was, they said, a voluble witness and had an extraordinary memory. He could recall minute details of complicated transactions which had taken place several years before. On one occasion Hofer had recommended an exchange of half a dozen paintings of secondary importance for two of the very first quality. As I recall, the deal involved a group of seventeenth century Dutch pictures on the one hand, and two Bouchers on the others. Hofer had been able to reel off the names of all of them and even give the price of each. It was just such feats of memory, they said with a laugh, that made his vague and indefinite answers to certain other questions seem more than merely inconsistent.[284]

Howe further recalls that Plaut and Rousseau deployed the tactic of directly confronting Hofer's selective memory with specific paintings from the Göring collection. They had taken Hofer and his wife to

---

[283] Howe, 1946 op. cit., 132–33.
[284] Ibid., 133–34.

inspect a number of these works. This was a tactic which produced a flood of new information mixed with an irritating stream of less relevant details:

> They had been quizzing him about certain pictures in the collection and he had wanted to refresh his memory by having a look at them. They pointed to a stocky German dressed in grey tweeds who stood a little distance away talking with a tall, angular woman. We recognized him as the man we had seen pacing the garden at House 71 weeks before—the evening Lamont and I first reported to George at the mine. That was his wife, they said.... Hofer was a loquacious passenger. All the way to Bad Aussee he kept up a line of incessant chatter, half in English, half in German, on all sorts of subjects.... I was getting bored with this chatterbox when he suddenly began to talk about Göring and his pictures. We asked him the obvious question: What did Göring really like when it came to paintings? Well, he was fond of Cranach. Yes, we knew that. And Rubens; he had greatly admired Rubens. And many of the Dutch masters of the seventeenth century. But according to Hofer it was he who had directed the Reichsmarschall's taste. Then, to my surprise, he mentioned Vermeer. Did we know about the Vermeer which Göring had bought? After that he went into a lengthy account of the purchase, leading up to it with an involved story of the secrecy surrounding the transaction, which had many confusing details. When we pulled up before House 71, Hofer was still going strong. Lamont and I were worn out.[285]

The interrogations served to confirm the view of ALIU officials that, despite Hofer's protestations of innocence, in his role as Director of Göring's collection and 'chief confidential operator', he was massively complicit in Göring's plunder of works of art. Their reports concluded: 'He appears to have trusted no one, a sentiment which was heartily reciprocated by most of those who came into contact with him...He is chiefly responsible for many of the methods used, and it is due to his influence that the collection assumed its present form (See Reference F).'[286]

---

[285] Ibid., 181.

[286] CIR 2 (Göring), 1 and DIR No. 9 (Hofer), op. cit., 4. Plaut later recalled: 'Curator Walter Andreas Hofer, short, red-haired, and beady-eyed, was a product of the hard, Berlin school of urbanity. In the early twenties he had been a salesman in the art firm of his brother-in-law, a Jew, whom he superseded quickly in Nazi patronage after 1933. Initially, he merely offered pictures for sale to Göring, but the relationship strengthened, and in 1937 he replaced a well-known expert as the Reichsmarschall's adviser in art matters. Hofer played his master shrewdly. He insisted on maintaining his independent dealer status even after being appointed director of the Göring Collection. Refusing a salary, he worked wholly on commission and, as Göring's official

In addition, ALIU interrogations indicated that, between April 1941 and November 1943, Hofer had played a central coordinating role in arranging, for a secret commission, the exchange of looted Jewish works through the Fischer Gallery in Lucerne Switzerland, a process which will be discussed in more detail later.[287] Hofer's frequent trips to Switzerland and Holland, made largely on behalf of Göring, prompted OSS officials to suspect that, given the modest status of his openly declared postwar assets, he must have hidden away some of his wealth in these countries.[288] Rousseau's 'recommendations for action' with respect to Hofer stated: 'As regards art looting, Hofer is in every way as guilty as Göring. It is the recommendation of this Unit that he be held as a material witness in Göring's trial and that he be indicted himself as a war criminal.'[289]

Under close questioning, Haberstock revealed a decidedly ambiguous and extraordinarily ruthless quality combined with a high degree of caution. His displays of anti-Semitism appeared in part to be made for business purposes as he maintained fruitful and friendly contacts with a number of Jewish dealers. Rousseau noted that he: 'never liked risks, and he always saw to it that he had something to fall back on should his plans miscarry. Even after he became a Nazi, he maintained his

buyer, brought to bear the manifold advantages of power and backing which his position implied. The flexibility of this arrangement permitted him to keep for himself anything which Göring did not want for the collection, a factor which gave him an incalculable advantage over his business competitors, in view of the vast scope of his sources. He had facilities for travel, for foreign exchange, and for promising 'official protection' to certain select victims of Nazi persecution, in return for which he received purchase rights to their works of art. Göring insisted that Hofer rule on every painting acquired for the collection, another obvious discriminatory weapon which he did not hesitate to use against his colleagues. Hofer travelled incessantly throughout the war, always preceding Göring on excursions to the occupied countries and preparing the scene for the regal descent into the art markets. Often he went alone, reporting constantly on his 'finds' to his chief by telephone or letter. The documentation reveals that Hofer took the lead at all times in determining the choice of objects, the methods of bargaining, and the nature of 'payment.' Consistently with the Nazi code of ethics, Hofer even cheated Göring. Often he falsified bills and receipts, working against Göring's interests in collusion with other agents. Just after V-E Day, Walter Andreas Hofer put in a jaunty appearance at Berchtesgaden, proudly exhibited the Göring Collection to ranking American officers, and posed for *Life*. Today, much chastened, he is behind bars at Nuremberg.' 1946a op. cit.

[287] DIR 9 (Hofer), 6, and Attachment 2.

[288] Ibid., 8.

[289] DIR No. 9 (Hofer), op. cit., 9.

membership in International Rotary.'[290] Other OSS interrogations with some of the victims of Haberstock's ruthlessness revealed that this dealer had the power to make and break the careers of others.[291] Rousseau's interrogation also noted that: 'Haberstock's career was crowned with his appointment by Hitler as chief adviser to Posse.'[292] This, together with letters of authorisation from Posse, Göring and Bormann, as well as various senior military figures, allowed Haberstock considerable freedom of movement and influence.[293] Other parts of this interrogation addressed the controversial question of the alleged involvement, perhaps through intermediaries, of certain Jewish firms, such as George Wildenstein, in sales of looted and other art works to Göring and Hitler.[294] Through their interrogations and analysis of documentation, ALIU officials identified 82 people with whom Haberstock conducted business in France alone.[295] Their study of Voss revealed that the new director of the Linz project had expressly blocked Haberstock's plans to benefit personally from various large-scale anti-Semitic thefts of art work including those in France, such as the Mannheimer Collection.[296]

It must not be thought that the handful of ALIU officials involved in these field operations were involved in a relatively straightforward task. On the contrary, they faced considerable problems in tracking down important sources, as well as securing credible information from those who they successfully detained. Some suspects, who had a good idea of their status as wanted war criminals, decided to be unhelpful to the fulfilment of the ALIU's mission. For example, DIR No. 3 notes with respect to Scholz:

> Personally, Scholz is shrewd, hypocritical and unreliable. He made a poor impression on his interrogators by attempting throughout to minimise his own responsibility, cloud the dominant issues, and implicate his collaborators... Under interrogation, Scholz attempted frequently to defend the "legality" of the Einsatzstab confiscations; yet he stated on several occa-

[290] DIR No. 13 op. cit., 1.

[291] Philips and Sutton, 'Report on Preliminary Interrogation of P. W. Alfred Hentzen', 22 June 1945: US NA, RG 239, Entry 81.

[292] DIR 13 op. cit., 2; cf. CIR 4 (Linz), Attachment 49.

[293] Ibid.

[294] Ibid., 4. See also an anonymous OSS report in Wildenstein from August 1945 that noted that 'Haberstock states that he always understood that the money was being paid to a secret account which would ultimately have been at the disposal of M. George Wildenstein.': US NA, RG 260, Entry 483.

[295] CIR4 (Linz) op. cit., Attachment 48.

[296] CIR 4 (ERR) Attachment 35a.

> sions that he had always been convinced that the question of title would have to be referred to an international commission upon the termination of hostilities, and that the activity of the Eisensatzstab had been salutary in preventing the "wanton" destruction and loss of a substantial portion of the cultural heritage of Europe.... Scholz stated...that throughout his career he remained a professional art critic, painter and museum director. The magnitude of his responsibilities within the Rosenberg organization gives the lie to those statements.[297]

Nicholas has noted a number of additional difficulties ALIU officials faced in tracking down the full range of persons on its target lists:

> It took longer to track down ERR executive Gerhard Utikal, who knew all too well what was in store for him and had started working on a farm under an assumed name. His wife and small children were found in a small Bavarian town. When: "Confronted with the alternative of either revealing her husband's whereabouts or of being interned herself," she yielded his address.[298]

Worse still, a number of individuals the ALIU sought for interrogation, had recently committed suicide, including Bunjes and von Behr, with Plaut describing the latter someone: 'universally regarded today as the person most responsible for the organized looting of France'.[299] The

---

[297] DIR No. 3 (Scholz), op. cit., 4.

[298] Nicholas, 1995 op. cit., 380 summarising and then quoting Horn report, 27 November 1945, and Howe to Horn, December 28 1945: US NA, RG 260, Entry 32.

[299] On von Behr, Chief of the Paris office of the ERR, CIR 2 (Göring), op. cit., 21. Plaut notes: 'Kurt von Behr, the autocratic chief of the Einsatzstab Paris office, universally regarded today as the person most responsible for the organized looting of France, gave dramatic evidence of awareness of his own guilt by committing suicide at Schloss Bans at the instant of its investiture by the American forces. When the proud Baron was found, he was seated next to his wife, an aristocratic Englishwoman, in the library of a family estate. A few minutes before, the Baron and his lady had toasted each other in poisoned champagne, delicately writing finis to an extraordinary career. Von Behr was the black sheep of an old Mecklenburg family. Between the wars he served as adjutant to the Duke of Saxe-Coburg and held a minor diplomatic post in Italy, which he was obliged to relinquish when his name cropped up in an insurance scandal. In 1940 von Behr rejoined Saxe-Coburg, now a distinguished old gentleman and head of the German Red Cross, and was sent to France. Through Göring, he was appointed director of the Einsatzstab Paris office, a position which he held while discharging certain nebulous duties with the Red Cross. Intensely vain, von Behr always wore elaborate uniforms though he remained a civilian. He treated the professional members of his staff patronizingly and drove them hard. He resorted to any practice calculated to bring in objects of value, traded actively on the side, and used the wherewithal to court the favor of Germans in high places with lavish gifts and entertainment. While the German High Command found him pompous and rather ridiculous, von Behr nevertheless became a central figure in occupation society. He is said to have had a table reserved at Maxim's every evening for two years, and to have

latter was found with his wife in their apartment in Schloss Banz, near Banberg, after both had taken cyanide.[300] For these and other logistical reasons, it did not prove possible to interrogate all relevant individuals substantially implicated in Nazi art looting.[301]

Certainly, ALIU officials confronted real challenges in their efforts to extract relevant and truthful information from individuals, many of whom were facing possible criminal trial and punishment, and therefore had every reason to adopt strategies of evasion and deceit. On Plaut's account, the OSS interrogators faced a series of difficulties stemming from the selective amnesia of specific detainees. Howe has recalled that OSS investigators faced problems with certain complicit individuals of dubious truthfulness who were seeking to improve their position at the expense of others:

> When...Lincoln Kirstein[302] had arrived at Alt Aussee in May, he had identified himself as one of the ringleaders of the Austrian resistance movement and vociferously claimed the credit of saving the mine [the artwork collection stored there]. Since then he had been working in the mine office. Captain Posey had given him permission to make a routine check of the books and archives stored there. He was such a talkative fellow that we kept out of his way as much as possible. And we didn't like his habit of praising himself at the expense of others. He was forever running to Plaut and Rousseau at House 71 with written and oral reports, warning them to beware of this or that man in the mine organization.[303]

Nicholas gives other examples of the initial resistance to interrogation of other suspects:

---

entertained generals and diplomats, artists, and U-boat officers or fliers on triumphal leave. In 1942 he came to Göring's birthday party in Berlin, bringing as a proud offering the original copy of the Versailles peace treaty and a manuscript letter from Richard Wagner to Napoleon III. These were presented to the Reichsmarschall appropriately in the name of the Einsatzstab, which had, of course, simply confiscated them in France for the occasion.' Plaut, 1946a op. cit.

[300] Nicholas, 1995 op. cit., 379.

[301] For example, Posse and Martin Bormann had died, whilst other 'key figures' including Reimer, Göpel, Herest, Wolffhardt and von Hessen, 'are still unaccounted for.' CIR 4 (Linz), op. cit., preface: 'No claims for completeness, therefore, can be made for the present report. It is hoped, however, that any information subsequently acquired will supplement, rather than alter, its contents.' Ibid. See also CIR 2 (Göring), op. cit., 174.

[302] There may be a mistake here as I gather from Jonathan Petropoulos that Lincoln Kirstein was an American who later founded the New York City Ballet.

[303] Howe, 1946 op. cit., 184.

> The work of arrest and interrogation was not so pleasant: Frau Dietrich dropped all the charm she had displayed to the Fuehrer when Lain Faison came for her account books, but soon calmed down when she saw the pistol (never used) which he wore. Once in captivity, the German art purveyors spoke volumes.[304]

Other members of Nazi art looting networks refused to cooperate fully. They either withheld specific details of their transactions, including the current whereabouts of Jewish art works, or adopted a stance of evasion. The ALIU's DIR on Wendland is instructive here:

> Hans Wendland has stated during interrogation that he was at one time in possession of a considerable fortune, but that during the past several years these assets have dwindled to a few objects of art, and considerable debts. While this statement is borne out to some extent by the modest manner in which he had lived in Rome since April 1946, where, he states, he lived on 250 Swiss francs a month, it must not be assumed that the following list of assets as reported by Wendland is complete. Even were the list complete, his art possessions would still represent a sizeable fortune. Wendland has refused to reveal the present whereabouts of certain of his paintings on the ground that they are being held for him by Swiss and French friends, who would be open to serious prosecution by their own countries were it known that they are concealing assets of a German national. Following is a list of Wendland's assets, arranged by country, which must be accepted with the above reservations...[305]

Dir 4 (Rochlitz) contains additional details of the sceptical approach ALIU investigators were obliged to adopt with respect to the selective and self-interested interpretations of many of their subjects. It notes that Rochlitz's claim that he was forced against his will and opposition to Nazi anti-Semitism to sell and exchange confiscated Jewish works of art to German visitors to Paris was: 'refuted by all other cognizant informants.'[306] Plaut also rejected Rochlitz's claim that he always anticipated that such confiscated items would ultimately be restored to their rightful owners, and had, from the start, been willing to cooperate with any such process of restitution.[307] The report goes on to provide extensive details of Rochlitz's transactions involving confiscated Jewish artworks with the ERR. These included 18 exchanges through which

---

304 Nicholas, 1995 op. cit., 379.
305 DIR (Wendland) op. cit., 22.
306 DIR No. 4 (Rochlitz), op. cit., 3.
307 Ibid., 5.

he received 82 confiscated paintings from the Rosenberg, Bernstein and Kahn collections, most of which were negotiated with Dr. Bruno Lohse, Göring's representative with this plundering organisation.[308] Rochlitz admitted to selling 31 of these and retaining 32 others.[309] In return for his voluntary cooperation with the ERR, which resulted in a series of exchanges of such artworks, Rochlitz received not only excess profits but also a highly valuable travel pass authorised by Göring himself. This provided him with unlimited travel between occupied and unoccupied France.

According to DIR 9, the revealing evidence disclosed during Hofer's interrogation was achieved despite his persistent attempts at evasion and self-exoneration. The interrogation of Hofer concerning Göring's tendency to acquire artworks by means of forced exchanges, also presented challenges. According to the ALIU report, these were at least partially resolved by comparing Hofer's verbal statements with the contents of documentation of which he was unaware that his interrogators possessed: 'Under interrogation, he at first denied any knowledge of the exchanges but after being confronted with documents proving him to be a liar he admitted having a part in all the negotiations.'[310] Rousseau's report highlighted the extent to which Hofer had tried to minimise his role and influence on Göring by posing as an independent art dealer despite, during the war, having cultivated the opposite impression as 'Göring's alter ego as far as the Collection was concerned.'[311] This interrogation emphasised another of Hofer's self-serving—but ultimately counterproductive—deceits he made in relation to the confiscation, acquisition and exchange of French Jewish collections:

> Throughout his interrogation Hofer has tried to give the impression that his part in the building up of the Collection was limited to advising Göring with regard to "legal" purchases. However, the evidence, and in many cases his own admissions, have played a leading part in almost every aspect of its formation. He began by stating that he was never consulted in the choice of works of art from confiscated collections [ERR].

---

[308] On the events that led to Lohse being appropriated into Göring's staff in practice, which began with their meeting at ERR HQ during an exhibition of confiscated artworks, see DIR No. 6 (Lohse) op. cit., 2–3.

[309] Of course, if Rochlitz received 82 works from the ERR through trades, and sold 31 and retained 32, this raises the question of what in fact happened to the other 19?

[310] CIR 2 (Göring), op. cit., 128.

[311] DIR No. 9 (Hofer), op. cit., 2.

> However, he later admitted that, as early as 1940, he chose objects from such collections... Though repeatedly questioned on the subject, he at first denied having any but the most superficial knowledge of Göring's transactions with the ERR. In contradiction to this, Lohse, Borchers and Kress all say that he almost always preceded the Reichsmarschall's visits to the Jeu de Paume, and, generally speaking, played an active part in all the proceedings.... In a letter of 2 September 1941, he urgently advised Göring to have the confiscated collections of the "Jew Paul Rosenberg and Braque" transferred from Bordeaux to Paris and the collection of "the Jews Andre and Jean Seligmann" from the Credit Lyonnais bank, to the Jeu de Paume. He added that he had made the necessary arrangements with Herr von Behr. He also claimed almost complete ignorance of the Göring exchanges with the ERR... but the documents show that on 23 November 1942 he himself signed the exchange "contract" which gave a painting by Utrillo confiscated from the Bernheim Collection to the "Jew Loebl" in exchange for the entire art library of the Kleinberger Gallery. When confronted with the evidence, Hofer declared that he could not remember having done it, that he must have put his signature to a blank piece of paper![312]

Another example of Rousseau exposing contradictions in Hofer's various alibis concerned the latter's role in the financial aspects of purchasing artworks for the Göring Collection, including once again those from Jewish collections seized by the ERR:

> Here again the documentary evidence and his own later admissions show his statement to be untrue. He was well aware of the financial aspects of every deal in which he took a part. In bargaining he was second to none, not even to his chief.... Hofer's own letters to Göring are full of references to financial matters and to his success in bring down prices. He insisted on a low appraisal for the confiscated Paul Rosenberg pictures,... although he was well aware of their value on the German market.[313]

Rousseau's summary and recommendation section concerning Hofer clearly expresses the degree of frustration generated by both the latter's deceitful conduct, evasiveness and inability to tell a consistent story during his interrogation, viewed as further evidence of his more general criminal dishonesty. Hofer's less credible statements were checked against the implications not only of available documentation, which he would not have been aware that ALIU possessed, but also against the statements of fellow-detainees such as Dr Bruno Lohse:

[312] Ibid., 2.
[313] Ibid., 3.

> The examination of his activity as an independent dealer has revealed him to be consistently dishonest and underhanded, and to have deceived even his own master. The opinion of Hofer's character gained from the evidence has been thoroughly confirmed by his behavior under interrogation. He repeatedly lied and changed his story. When cornered, he repeatedly tried to get out of difficulties by putting the blame on others. An example of this occurred with Lohse, whom he accused of lying about his (Hofer's) activity in the Jeu de Paume. However, when the two were confronted, he again changed his story and admitted that Lohse was right.... In short, his insincerity and dishonesty have been so consistently shameless that in a man of different character they would have been insulting to the intelligence of his interrogators. However, in his case they simply prove once more that Hofer was a small-time crook and hanger-on of another somewhat but not much bigger gangster, the Reichsmarschall.[314]

Given Hofer's chronic inability to stick to a credible cover story and evade the truth of his actions, and the extensive details of transactions involving looted artworks that he could either provide or at least confirm, his interrogation must be regarded as largely successful, despite the time and effort that Rousseau was forced to expend upon him.

ALIU officials did manage to secure at least the partial cooperation of a significant proportion of the other key players in Nazi art looting. This resulted in considerable new insights into the part played by cultural plunder in singling out Jews and other groups for persecution. Buchner, for instance, helped Rousseau clarify differences in how the Nazis reacted to confiscated private collections and 'Aryanized' art dealerships:

> Buchner says that there was a difference between the manner of handling confiscated dealer property and private collections. The latter were simply collected and shown in an exhibition gallery, where they were looked over by buyers for the German museums. What was not bought was later auctioned off. Dealers' collections [by contrast] were kept as part of the equipment of the dealer's shop, and were taken over with it. In some cases the Nazis would put one of their own men in to carry on the firm's business instead of its former owner. This was the case with the following: (1) Helbing...(2) Bernheiner...(3) The Heinemann galleries...(4) the Fleischmann galleries...[315]

The DIR on Bornheim provides extensive details of its subjects' involvement in the voluntary and relatively benign 'Aryanization' of a Jewish-

---

[314] Ibid., 9.
[315] DIR No. 2 (Buchner), op. cit., 5.

owned art gallery in Munich, Franz Drey. This process was accomplished on terms that gave a comparative measure of protection to the owner and aspects of Drey's stock, which he was prohibited from taking abroad: 'Drey wanted to leave Germany because of the recent death of his father and the increasing difficulties which were being made for German Jews.'[316] This DIR also records details of the cooperation its subject afforded to his OSS interrogators, and their appreciation for this: 'Bornheim has made a good impression on this interrogators. He has consistently told the truth, he has volunteered significant information, and he has willingly supplied from his files what documentation still existed after the destruction of his business premises. His declarations have often been confirmed by the statements of other reliable witnesses and by documents.'[317] On the other hand, the same report points out that although he was personally innocent of any participation in art looting, Bornheim still exploited opportunities the early phase of the Holocaust opened up for his art business:

> He was a small German dealer who rose to considerable prominence and wealth under the Nazi regime, and with the help of one of its foremost exponents, the Reichsmarschall. Although the "Aryanization" of the Drey firm may have been carried out with the consent of its former owners, and may indeed have protected their interests in some respects; as far as Bornheim was concerned, it was a great step forward, and one made possible by the Nazi anti-Semitic laws.[318]

The ALIU's recommendation was that he: 'be held as a material witness in the Göring trial, and that he subsequently be placed at the disposition of the French Government for purposes of restitution.'[319]

The DIR report on Lohse affirms the apparent success of the interrogation process, helped by this ERR official's candour and willingness to provide full details of acts of this agency's anti-Semitic confiscations:

> Lohse had been under interrogation for an extended period. The apparent candor of his statements and the directness of his answers have at all times impressed his interrogators favourably. On no occasion has he attempted to deny his personal responsibility for acts committed under orders as a member of the Eisensatzstab Rosenberg, nor has he shown any inclination to minimise the significance of his activity on behalf of Göring. His

[316] DIR No. 11 (Bornheim), op. cit., 1; ibid. Attachment 1.
[317] Ibid., 7.
[318] Ibid., 7.
[319] Ibid.

> statements concerning colleagues and business associations—often in the face of accusations against him by the individual under discussion—appear to have been made truthfully and without bias.[320]

Hoffmann and Buchner were also largely cooperative, although the latter sought to gain credit for his alleged subversion of anti-Semitic confiscation in the Goldschmidt case.[321] Buchner did, however, admit his complicity in visiting an: 'exhibition of confiscated Jewish pictures at the Baer Gallery in Munich (Kaulbach Strasse) which had been taken over by the Nazis. He says that he also visited a few confiscated private collections but rarely made any purchases.'[322]

Rousseau's interrogation report on Limberger, Göring's personal secretary, almost congratulates itself for the fruits of its efforts, suggesting that this person's actions deserve a sympathetic interpretation. This is despite what could be seen as both her proximity and assistance to a central figure in Nazi art looting:

> She has made an excellent impression on her interrogators. Though reserved at first she answered all questions without hesitation and as she became more familiar with the purpose of the investigation she volunteered important information. Her story has been consistent throughout. She has never changed it and her statements have frequently been confirmed by documentary evidence or the testimony of other witnesses. It is clear that she had no personal responsibility whatever in the formation of the Göring Collection...The evidence shows that on the rare number of occasions when she did exercise her influence it tended to be for the good. It was because of her intervention that Göring did not accept the loot from the Monte Cassino as had been intended by Hofer, and it was she who finally persuaded Göring to make a complete listing of the objects taken from the Einsatzstab Rosenberg.... Fraulein Limberger has made a very real contribution to the solution of many of the problems presented by this investigation...She is without doubt one of the most important sources which can be drawn upon in building a case against him. It is the recommendation of this Unit that she be held as a voluntary witness pending the trial of Göring.[323]

---

[320] DIR No. 6 (Lohse), op. cit., 10.

[321] Ibid., 4: '[H]e claims to have himself broken the law by concealing the August Goldschmidt Collection which he had on loan in the Alte Pinakotek at the time.... Attachment A is a list of all pictures confiscated in Munich.' Ibid.

[322] Ibid.

[323] DIR 7 (Limberger), op. cit., 3.

With respect to the benefits gained from these especially cooperative subjects, Plaut has recalled that: 'Like all such "round up" activities, a relatively small number of detainees provided the most significant information.'[324] Plaut concludes that the ALIU: 'benefited from the revelations of a few individuals who had been centrally involved in the looting process.'[325] The interrogators were even successful in gaining admissions from many individuals that undermined both their own alibis and those of others. For example, Buchner had initially maintained that the order he received from the Reich Chancellery in June 1942 stated that: 'the [Ghent] altarpiece [by the Van Eyck brothers] was not being confiscated by the German Reich, but was being put out of danger from air attacks so that it could eventually be restored to its legal owners.'[326] This had been looted from a chateau in the South of France by Bucher accompanied by an armed detachment. However, when subjected to repeated interrogation he eventually confessed 'in an unguarded moment' that, at the relevant time, he had been aware that this artwork had always been destined for the Kaiser Friedrich Museum in Berlin (now the Bode Museum).[327]

His interrogation also revealed that Buchner possessed strong nationalist sentiments for German expansionism: 'Any conversation with [Buchner] on his own subject, German painting, reveals at once his fixed belief in a greater Germany—whether the Fuehrer be Friedrich the Great, William II, or Hitler.'[328] On the other hand, Rousseau noted that Buchner: 'was one of the very few German Museum directors who succeeded in holding on to their collections of "degenerate" art.'[329] Buchner had also been complicit in gaining benefits from the Nazis' pre-war and anti-Semitic 'Aryanization' measures, which resulted in Jewish art gallery owners loosing their collections with minimal compensation.[330] Buchner had stored works of art looted in this way, and

[324] Plaut, 1997 op. cit., 125.
[325] Ibid.
[326] DIR 2, op. cit., 3; Petropoulos, 2000 op. cit., 34; cf. William Honan, *Treasure Hunt: A New York Times Reporter Tracks the Quedlinburg Hoard*, NY: Delta, 1997, 28. Honan recounts how one of these altar panels was plundered from the Cathedral of St. Bavo in Ghent in 1934; Carr 1946 op. cit., 144–48.
[327] DIR No. 2, op. cit., 3.
[328] Ibid., 10.
[329] Ibid. For a slight revision to this conclusion, see Petropoulos, 2000 op. cit., 25.
[330] Dir 2, op. cit., 5.

even exploited his contacts with the Gestapo to arrange for the purchase of especially choice items for his own collections.

He was able to secure many of the Jewish-owned works that Posse decided not to acquire for the Linz project, including items from the 'Aryanized' Bernheimer firm and the Baer Gallery.[331] In total he acquired, often under conditions of coercion and implied threat: 'at least twenty-eight works that had been taken from Jews, including paintings by Delacroix and Trübner.'[332] In addition, the OSS interrogators also managed to extract from Buchner the concession that he had maintained close contacts with other dealers involved in anti-Semitic looting, including Hofer, Hoffman and Haberstock.[333] With respect to the Linz Museum, Buchner revealed that during 1943 he had assumed a semi-official position within the management of this collection which involved assisting with the process of authentication and ultimate acquisition, including items looted from the Jewish Schloss collection. This role, for which he was paid well, i.e., some RM 500 per consultation, followed his earlier sales to Linz of works from the Bavarian State Gallery that he directed.[334]

The ALIU's interrogators also exploited information gained from one detainee to further pursue lines of inquiry with others. For example, Buchner was confronted with various claims made by Hoffmann, which the former denied and offered an alternative account.[335] In this way, a small number of individuals ended up providing a 'windfall' of information opening up a considerable number of the most important leads. Plaut recalls that interrogators sometimes had to confront members of Göring's staff with documentary evidence of the latter's dishonesty in order to break the spell that Göring had cast over many of his more fanatically loyal subordinates:

> So apt was the master of Carinhall in concealing his true nature from his followers that Fraulein Limberger, Lohse, and several others, on being shown the documentary evidence of Göring's crimes, his deceits, and

[331] Ibid., 4; CIR 4 (Linz) op. cit., Attachment 33 Posse to Bormann, 26 November 1940.
[332] Petropoulos, 2000 op. cit., 27; Dir No. 2, op. cit., 4–5, and Attachment D that lists the works.
[333] DIR No. 2 (Buchner), op. cit., 1, 6–9; CIR 4 (Linz) op. cit., 53.
[334] DIR No. 2 op. cit., 2; CIR 4 (Linz), Attachment 27.
[335] DIR No. 2 (Buchner), op. cit., 7.

> his inherent cheapness, actually became despondent and irreconcilable in their personal disillusion.[336]

As one would expect, the theme of the integral connection between art looting anti-Semitism was more strongly emphasised in some of the DIR reports than in others. For instance, the DIR on Haberstock report noted:

> Haberstock's entire career was based on two principles: anti-Semitism and Germanic chauvinism. He is said to have been a vociferous anti-Semite from the beginning, and to have attracted a certain clientele in this way, particularly in Berlin during the twenties,... This clientele, drawn mostly from reactionary German circles, had a natural taste for 19th century German art, as opposed to the "degenerate" French products of the same period or their progressive German contemporaries. [Yet], throughout the period of Jewish persecution he helped certain of his Jewish colleagues to escape. All of this he pointed to as evidence of his decent and liberal instincts.[337]

The interrogators expressed concern that Haberstock had apparently actively sought information from former Berlin art dealer Alexender Ball on the whereabouts of Guy de Rothschild, a prominent French Jew: 'the implications of such a revelation are exceedingly grave, and Ball should be brought to account.'[338] The suggestion here is that Haberstock was helping Nazi officials locate Jewish owners of artworks. The same report noted Haberstock claim to have helped 'liberate' the Jewish dealer 'Friedlander' from detention in Holland sometime in 1940.[339] On the other hand, this defensive claim cut in two directions. The ALIU authors of this report highlighted Haberstock's alleged failure to provide protection for some of his Jewish colleagues and associates, such as August Mayer (aka Henri Antoine), a well-known authority on Spanish paintings:

> Mayer disappeared in 1944, and Wendland reported that he met his end in the gas chamber. The details of his work for German dealers during this period are not clear; nor is the story of his falling into the hands of the SS—in spite of the possibilities of protection he enjoyed from Haberstock and others.[340]

336 Plaut, 1946a op. cit.
337 DIR No. 13 (Haberstock), op. cit., 1.
338 Ibid., 6.
339 Ibid., 7.
340 Ibid.

As a result, one of the authors' conclusions was that: 'It is recommended urgently that Haberstock be questioned further regarding his knowledge of the activities of Fabiani and Ball, and in particular, the disappearance of Mayer.'[341]

The theme of anti-Semitism, including the confiscation of Jewish Collections and the ERR, was also prominent in the DIR on Voss, and the latter's role as Director of the Linz Museum. This report noted a contradiction between Voss' well-known opposition to Nazi ideology and his later willingness to accept a leading role in a prominent Museum dedicated to Nazi-approved art and containing a substantial selection of items confiscated from European Jews:

> Voss soon [1933–34] had difficulties with the Nazi Party because of "cosmopolitan and democratic tendencies", and friendship with many Jewish colleagues. Late in 1933, he lost his directorship of the Kaiser Friedrich Museum, Berlin, where Koetsceau was appointed to this position over his head, as successor to Dr Friedlander, recently ousted on racial grounds.[342]

The authors clearly pressed Voss on his subjective knowledge of the partial reliance of the Linz project upon confiscated materials when he was first offered the job as director: 'Voss states he was entirely ignorant of how the Linz project had been managed... Voss insists that no mention was made of any confiscated works having come into the Linz collection.'[343] Unsurprisingly, under interrogation Voss disassociated himself from ERR and denied having visited the ERR or acquired works from this source:[344] 'Concerning the Einsatzstab Rosenberg, Voss repeatedly denied ever having heard of it before March 1943. In later interrogations, however, he admitted having a general idea of the work of this organization, but could not be more specific. Lohse believes that the Einsatzstab Rosenberg was known to all museum directors in Germany.... Lohse, Borchers and Schiedlausky all state that Voss never came to the Jeu de Paume.'[345] Voss was anxious to minimise any association between his period as Director and the acquisition of confiscated works, by attributing the latter to the poli-

---

341 Ibid.

342 DIR No. 12 (Voss), op. cit., 2.

343 Ibid., 4. also ibid., 12 re his job interview with Bormann and Hitler: 'nothing was said of confiscated material'.

344 Ibid., 13.

345 Ibid., 5.

cies of his predecessor, Hans Posse. However, when his interrogators subjected his story to close probing, he became unable to sustain this self-exonerating account:

> When he learned after taking office that some of the Linz paintings were confiscated material, he considered that to have been Posse's affair. He determined, however, to do what he could to keep other confiscated works from being added to the Linz collections. In this desire he was opposed by Oertel, who had warm Party sympathies, and he had to bring Reiner around to this view.... Under further interrogation, however, Voss...states that the confiscated paintings were bound to go somewhere, and what difference did it make! For example, he once accepted several confiscated pictures at Wiesbaden. Though in every instance the Museum paid for them, Voss is by no means certain that the owner received the money, except in [one case].[346]

Voss' interrogation report shows that he was to be held accountable for accepting all aspects of his formal job responsibilities, even those which in practice he refused to take advantage of, or which did not in practice materialise. Furthermore, it appears that his personal decision not to accept confiscated Jewish artworks for the Linz collections was not judged to count as a substantial mitigating factor as far as the ALIU were concerned:

> It appears to be true that Voss personally accepted no looted art for Linz, but as Posse's successor he inherited a vast store of confiscated works. He accepted the Schloss Collection under very dubious circumstances, and he was officially named expert in charge of final distribution of all confiscated works of art held by the ERR,...and likewise all works of art confiscated by the SS in Greater Germany and all occupied territories.[347]

In addition to his involvement with the ERR, ALIU interrogators gave a sceptical interpretation to Voss' questionable involvements with the purchase of the Schloss Collection, which had been confiscated by the French authorities under pressure from the Nazi authorities: 'Several months after Voss took office, some 250 pictures from the Schloss Collection (French Jewish) were acquired by purchase for Linz under questionable circumstances. During interrogation, Voss brought up this subject of his own accord, with the idea of demonstrating that if anything was wrong, he had acted in good faith and was not

[346] Ibid., 8–9.
[347] Ibid., 23.

responsible.'[348] The interrogators then confronted him with contrary evidence from another detainee at Alt Aussee:

> Voss learned about the pictures from Goepel, after they had been brought to Paris, but prior to the negotiations which were carried out between the German Embassy in Paris and the Vichy Government. He...instructed Goepel to go ahead with the purchase, cautioning him, however, "to proceed with utmost fairness to France." The fact that the sale had been forced by the Vichy government, potentially under German pressure, was not enough to stay Voss' hand. He states that in any case "things had gone too far for me to stop them." He had an uncomfortable moment when told, during interrogation, that the circumstances were dubious enough to make Göring order Lohse to stop all purchase proceedings on this account. He states that he had not known of Göring's interest in the pictures, but the truth of this assertion is very doubtful.... Voss' position in all this intrigue is the unenviable one of a professed lover of France who kept his hands clean by leaving the dirty work to others and not asking too many questions.[349]

The interrogators pressed Voss particularly hard concerning his personal knowledge and involvement in the confiscation of the Jewish Schloss collection and its acquisition by Linz Museum.[350] This DIR report emphasised noted that Voss had learned about the pictures from his subordinate Göpel, albeit *after* they had been already been brought to Paris, but *prior to* the negotiations which were carried out between the German Embassy in Paris and the Vichy Government. This meant that, as far as his interrogators were concerned, Voss had to assume responsibility not for the initial decision to confiscate the artworks but for their subsequent fate. Furthermore, his various self-interested denials of the possibility of ever having the possibility of acting differently in this situation lacked all credibility.[351]

This is a point that, with some further elaboration and justification, his interrogators made even more strongly in their conclusion of the main points against Voss:

> In the Schloss affair, Voss' activity was particularly questionable.... It is clear from testimony given by Lohse in Voss' presence, which Voss was unable to refute, that he learned fully of the details of the case from Lohse...on or about 25 April 1943. This was well before the sale, and not

[348] Ibid., 16.
[349] Ibid., 17–18.
[350] Ibid., 16.
[351] Ibid., 17–18.

> many days after he had received Goepel's written report on the affair...it is clear, however, that he had the chance to stop proceedings and that he did not, even though he was sufficiently informed as to what he was getting into. He could have taken the position that the pictures were below the Linz standard, if he did not dare to refuse them outright. He states that he used this ruse on some occasions to keep confiscated items out of the Linz collections, but he had been unable to cite any example. In short, his contention that "things had gone too far for me to stop them" falls apart when closely examined.[352]

In short, the theme of the relationship between Voss, the acquisition practices of the Linz Museum and Nazi anti-Semitism was a prominent theme in the DIR dedicated to Voss. It was clearly a major factor in their recommendation that the Allied authorities prosecute him as a war criminal and, in the meantime, he be put to work in restitution projects: 'It is recommended that Voss be detained as a potential war criminal for the forthcoming War Crimes trials. Pending these trials, it is recommended that Voss be utilized at the Central Collecting Point...Munich in inventorizing the Linz collections for whatever redistribution is deemed advisable.'[353]

The sections of the DIRs entitled 'Conclusions and Recommendations' are often particularly relevant for the purposes of the present book. They sought to balance evidence of complicity in the Holocaust with various mitigating factors, including passive resistance to aspects of this genocidal programme. This part of the report on Buchner, for example, stated:

> Ernst Buchner is probably honest when he says that he was out of sympathy with such manifestations of Nazism as the persecution of the Jews and the campaigns against "degenerate" art. It is doubtless also true that he joined the Party largely because it was necessary for his position. To date the evidence has not revealed him as a Nazi zealot. Other more fanatical party members have confirmed that they considered him lukewarm at best. He was one of the few German museum directors who succeeded in holding on to their collections of "degenerate" art. He protested publicly against the Party condemnation of Rembrandt as a Jew, and his known to have personally protected at least one Jewish collection. These considerations, however, are of secondary importance, and tend to obscure the real issue. For the world at large and for the German public in particular, the outstanding fact...is that he, the son of a well-known

[352] Ibid., 23.
[353] Ibid.

> Munich painter, and himself reputedly the most important living authority on German painting, held the position of head of the Bavarian State Collections, as a member of the Nazi Party, under the Nazi regime. No amount of passive resistance could counterbalance the moral effect of his official allegiance.... These men bear a heavy responsibility to the mass of their compatriots, for they provided the fanatics and criminals with the necessary cloak of respectability.[354]

After having balanced these factors, Rousseau concluded: '(a) that Buchner be kept under house arrest at the disposition of the MFA&A authorities, and (b) that he placed on the list of those officials who are to be prohibited permanently from holding any position in a newly constituted German fine arts administration.'[355] Certain of the ALIU's recommendations gave greater weight to mitigating factors, even in the case of convinced Nazis such as Schiedlausky. Indeed, these recommendations made a point of concentrating more upon the actions, impact and implications of those it interrogated, including postwar cooperation with the Allies, than their degree of commitment to the Nazi ideology.[356]

On the other hand, whilst they recognised mitigating factors in the case of individuals drafted into the ERR against their will, ALIU officials were particularly negative about the actions of art dealers, such as Rochlitz, who had voluntarily and extensively collaborated with the ERR's disposition of scores of confiscated Jewish artworks purely for personal gain, and whose interrogation had revealed a high degree of evasion, cowardice and dishonesty:

> It has been established that Rochlitz, perhaps more than any other individual, sought and derived personal and material gain from the depredations of the Einsatzstab Rosenberg. He has taken elaborate measures to convince his interrogators that the exchanges with the Einsatzstab to which he was a party were forced upon him, and that he was threatened with "consequences" if he demurred; however, at no time has he claimed ignorance of the fact that the 82 paintings which he received from the Einsatzstab were works confiscated from French Jewish collections. Politically, Rochlitz had no genuine convictions. He appears to have acted at all times in his own interests as an unscrupulous opportunist.[357]

---

354 DIR No. 2 (Buchner), op. cit., 10.

355 Ibid.

356 DIR No. 5 (Schiedlausky) op. cit., 3.

357 DIR No. 4 (Rochlitz), op. cit., 11.

Because his crimes were committed in France against French interests, it was recommended that he be tried as a war criminal by the newly-reconstituted French authorities. Alternatively: 'it is recommended that he be tried as a war criminal by the US authorities.'[358]

The concluding 'recommendations for action' section of the DIR on Lohse is especially interesting. Despite previously recognising his apparent honesty and helpfulness under interrogation, and his credible denials of various accusations as to his individual conduct, including threatening Jews for personal gain, Plaut stated:

> It is recommended that every effort [be made] to bring under interrogation those individuals in a position to verify his statements... Whereas Lohse appears to have been victimised in large measure by the jealousy of his colleagues, there can be no doubt that he played a leading part in the confiscation of Jewish art properties conducted by the Einsatzstab Rosenberg in Paris. It is recommended, therefore, that he be held as a material witness in such war crimes proceedings as may be directed against Einstatzstab Rosenberg personnel, and that, if tried as a war criminal, the severity of the charges brought against him be determined by the extent to which his complicity in Einstatzstab operations is judged to have been criminal.[359]

There were clear difficulties of extracting credible information from some of those interrogated. For example, the CIR on Linz addressed Hoffmann's claims that he never 'purchased' for Linz any art that had been looted from the Jewish owners of the Jaffe collection, which amounted to some 30 different paintings. However, Plaut's team were able to rebut this claim by means of clear and extensive documentary evidence to the contrary. He continued to deny the implications of such counter-evidence.[360] This example suggests that interrogators refused to accept at face value the statements of implicated detainees. On some occasions at least, they successfully cross referenced these claims with other evidence stemming from both other statements and captured records, including those from specialist art transportation companies.[361] The DIR on Hoffmann notes that:

> The interrogation of Hoffmann is a thankless task. He is an alcoholic and has all the weaknesses that go with that vice. His memory is bad and

[358] Ibid., 12.
[359] DIR No. 6 (Lohse), op. cit., 14.
[360] CIR 4 (Linz), op. cit., 44–45, which discusses three major works from Jaffe.
[361] Ibid., 44, 79.

> he changes his story from day to day, according to what he thinks will please his interrogators most... He curses and praises Hitler alternately. Above all, his chief concern is the future of his material possessions. He appeared more upset about the theft of his linen than by the unfavourable reports about his immediate family.[362]

The ALIU's specific DIR on Wendland also discusses the source of the difficulties ALIU interrogators faced in establishing both this detainee's degree of personal responsibility for art looting, and the location of certain of these art works:

> The exact degree of his culpability in the events in which he figured is difficult to determine. The lack of access to his records concealed in Switzerland and elsewhere and his convenient as well as chronic bad memory, made it well-nigh impossible to pin him down to any exact or definite assertions. During the interrogations he may be said to have proved willing to talk but reluctant to communicate.[363]

Another ALIU report notes, perhaps with a measure of intense frustration, that:

> [A]dmissions do not come easily to Kajetan Mühlmann, but during interrogation he stated that he was ashamed of two actions in his career of "safeguarding" works of art: the exchange he forced... for Göring's benefit,[364] and the sale of the extensive Jewish Mannheimer collection for the benefit of the Fuehrer. In both instances, he considers he was doing the dirty work for superiors.[365]

Based on his free admissions during interrogations, it became clear that Mühlmann had been complicit in the looting, through forced sale at massively underestimated prices, of part of the Jewish Jaffe collection sent to the Netherlands. The German-Jewish owners of this collection had fled to London after having sent part of its contents to the Netherlands for safekeeping.[366] After some weak and initial denials, Mühlmann's interrogation produced similar admissions with respect to the Lugt collection, which also was formerly Jewish-owned. Mühlmann also made a series of claims that sought to exonerate himself, including

---

[362] DIR No. 1 (Hoffmann), op. cit., 1.

[363] Wendland DIR, op. cit., 25.

[364] See also CIR 2 (Göring), op. cit. 139–141.

[365] CIR 4 (Linz), op. cit., 37–38.

[366] CIR 4 (Linz), op. cit., 45; CIR Mühlmann, op. cit., for an account of what Nicholas op. cit. 102, refers to as 'the distinctly unsavoury methods' employed by Plietzsche on behalf of Mühlmann concerning the Jaffe collection.

suggesting that he had actively sought to preserve existing collections, and to protect both Austrian and Polish artworks from confiscation.[367] Yet, even he did not attempt to conceal his doubts regarding the essentially criminal nature of the art confiscation activities of the Nazi regime of which he was a part: 'The Third Reich had to lose the war because this war was based on robbery and on a system of injustice and violence that could only be broken from the outside. Every individual has to now pay personally for the mortgage which the German people has accepted.'[368] He did not impress his OSS interrogators, with Vlug noting: 'Rotterdam was still burning when Kajetan Mühlmann in his SS uniform arrived in Holland to take up the task of his Dienststelle.'[369]

Despite Mühlmann's apparent freedom of action and the profits he was reaping, his interrogation report suggested that Mühlmann's activities as a semi-official agency for Nazi art looting remained highly vulnerable to punitive acts from his German masters. Although complicit in the Holocaust, his actions always risked the accusation of favouring one Nazi leader's requests for sought-after artworks over those of another, something which could lead to grave repercussions from their rivals. He stated to OSS officers that: 'the competition between Hitler and Göring caused a pressure from which one could not escape.... I personally was in a very difficult position.'[370] In the autumn of 1944, Ernst Kaltenbrunner, head of the dreaded Reich Security Main Office which included the Gestapo, informed him that Martin Bormann had threatened to have him detained in a concentration camp. This was because of his failure to secure enough high quality works of art for Hitler's Linz Museum.[371] This threat followed an earlier dispute during October 1943 with Hans Frank, Nazi General Governor of Poland. Later Göring had threatened to imprison Mühlmann after finding out that, following Hans Frank's direct orders, he had taken Leonardo da Vinci's *Lady with an Ermine* and transported it from Berlin back to Cracow.[372] OSS interrogations and other reports suggest Mühlmann withdrew from active art dealings towards the end of the war; whilst still

---

[367] On Polish confiscations, see CIR 2 (Göring) op. cit., 32.
[368] CIR 3 (Mühlmann), op. cit., 57.
[369] 'Report on Objects Removed to Germany from Holland, Belgium and France During the German occupation on [sic] these Countries', Amsterdam: Report of Stichting Nederlands Kunstbesit, 25 December 1945, 5.
[370] Vlug, op. cit., quoted in Petropolous, 2000 op. cit., 195.
[371] Ibid., 52.
[372] Petropolous, 2000 op. cit., 195.

maintaining a residence in Vienna. This was searched by OSS agents for its artworks in the early spring of 1945.[373] Here, they recovered a triptych that came from a Jewish art dealer named Rosenbaum.[374]

Plaut has recently recalled that: 'In his interrogations, Faison received a number of windfalls. Because our "network" grew, we were led to Gustav Rochlitz, one of Göring's chief art procurers, who had taken refuge in a nearby village.[375] Rousseau and I apprehended him and drove him to Paris, where he was detained by the French authorities.'[376] Howe recalls additional details concerning these OSS official's dealings with Rochlitz, which included a successful element of Holocaust-restitution work:

> The last morning of our stay at Füssen, Lamont and I had a special mission to perform. A German art dealer named Gustav Rochlitz was living at Gipsmühle, a five-minute drive from Hohenschwangau, the small village below the castle. For a number of years Rochlitz had had a gallery in Paris. His dealings with the Nazis, in particular his trafficking in confiscated pictures, had been the subject of special investigation by Lieutenants Plaut and Rousseau, our OSS friends. They were the two American naval officers who were preparing an exhaustive report on the activities of the infamous *Einsatzstab Rosenberg*. They had interrogated Rochlitz and placed him under house arrest. In his possession were twenty-two modern French paintings, including works by Dérain, Matisse and Picasso, formerly belonging to well known Jewish collections. He had obtained them from Göring and other leading Nazis in exchange for old master paintings. We were to relieve Herr Rochlitz of these canvases.[377]

In a number of cases, after detainees had been fully interrogated by a combination of Rousseau, Platt and Laison they were handed over to other military intelligence officials, such as US 3rd US Army CIC staff, for subsequent detention at Munich. In Hoffmann's case, this was followed by his movement initially to 7th Army Intelligence Center, Augsburg, followed by a later transfer back into the custody of MFA&A officials in Munich.[378] Later ALIU staff retuned to this location to conduct further detailed interrogations of a large number of major

373 Petropoulos, 1996b op. cit., 200.

374 Vlug, *Report on Objects Removed to Germany*, op. cit., 12, 101.

375 On this point, see also CIR 4 (Linz), op. cit., 55.

376 Plaut, 1997 op. cit., 125.

377 Howe 1946 op. cit., 49.

378 DIR No. 1 (Hoffmann), op. cit., 1.

participants in Nazi art looting operations, suspects, and informants, an activity which continued until the late spring of 1946. After being exhaustively interviewed, Lohse was handed over to the French authorities and was later imprisoned for his war crimes.[379]

After gathering intelligence information from their programme of interrogations, ALIU members wrote thirteen DIRs: 'on the interrogation of leading conspirators';[380] and three major Consolidated Interrogation Reports (CIRs).[381] The contents of these DIRs include descriptions of Nazi looting activities, attempts to transport and sell such contraband, and the current locations of looted art.[382] In addition, these reports

[379] Plaut, 1997 op. cit., 125.

[380] Ibid. These DIRs comprise: Report No. 1, Heinrich Hoffman, July 1945; Report No. 2, Ernst Buchner, July 1945; Report No. 3, Robert Scholz, August 1945; Report No. 4, Gustav Rochlitz, August 1945; Report No. 5, Gunther Schiedlausky, August 1945; Report No. 6, Bruno Lohse, August 1945; Report No. 7, Gisela Limberger, September 1945; Report No. 9, Walter Andreas Hofer, September 1945; Report No. 10, Karl Kress, August 1945; Report No. 11, Walter Bornheim, September 1945; Report No. 12, Herman Voss, September 1945; Report No. 13, Karl Haberstock, May 1946. These are now available on microfilm from the US National Archives, M1782; The entire collection of the OSS interrogation reports (4 consolidated and 15 detailed) is found in the US NA, RG 38, Entry 98A, Strategic Services Unit, ALIU, Box 421; US NA, RG 239, Entry 73, Strategic Services Unit, ALIU, Box 83; and RG 239, Entry 74, Strategic Services Unit, ALIU, Box 84. Other DIRs are found at US NA, RG 226, Entry 190, Box 294, Folder 1366 'Interrogation reports nos. 1 (Heinrich Hoffman), 2 (Ernst Buchner), 7 (Gisela Limberger), 9 (Walter Andreas Hofer), 11 (Walter Bornheim), and 12 (Hermann Voss).

[381] Yeide, 2007 op. cit., 2. 366; US NA, RG 226, Entry 190, Box 294, Folder 400 'Art Looting I—Göring Collection-copy of Consolidated Interrogation Report No. 2 'The Göring Collection,' covering the history and formation of the collection and methods used by Göring to obtain items, September 15, 1945; ibid., Folder 401 'Art Looting II-Göring Collection-Attachments to report in Folder 400'. For additional archival references, see ALIU Detailed Interrogation Reports, 1945–1946: US NA, RG 239, Entry 74, Boxes 84–84A, Records of the Roberts Commission for the Protection and Salvage of Artistic and Historic Monuments in War Areas. Arranged numerically by report numbers 1–13, with report number eight not being used. 'Investigation of Dr. Kajrtan Muehlmann, 1945–1948' was a separate summary completed by the Dutch Officer Jan Vlug and is located in the Ardelia Hall Collection, Records of U.S. Occupation Headquarters, World War II (OMGUS), Restitution Research Records 1933–1950: US NA, RG 260, Box 435.

[382] See 'Art Looting Investigation Unit's Detailed Interrogation Reports' 1945–1946, Records of the Roberts Commission for the Protection and Salvage of Artistic and Historic Monuments in War Areas, US NA, RG 239, Entry 74, Boxes 84–84A. Arranged numerically by report numbers 1–13, with report number 8 not being used. 'Investigation of Dr. Kajetan Mühlmann, 1945–1948,' a distinct report by Jan Vlug, is located in the Restitution Research Records, 1933–1950, Box 435, Ardelia Hall Collection, OMGUS, Records of U.S. Occupation Headquarters, World War II, US NA RG 260.

contain detailed descriptions and dimensions of specific looted artworks and collections, information on the selling and purchasing prices, and the names of purchasing agents, art dealers and auction houses.

As already illustrated, each DIR addressed the activities and degree of individual responsibility of a specific individual complicit in the Nazi bureaucracy. For instance, ALIU's DIR on Karl Haberstock revealed he was one of the major suppliers of looted art to the Nazi leadership. Haberstock and his associates were highly successful in identifying business opportunities dealing with at least eighty-two individuals within France alone,[383] and he used a number of French collaborators to act as his agents.[384] And there were others, in addition to the familiar associates, who sought out Haberstock. The Duveen brothers in Paris, for example, merited explicit credit in an OSS report for being rare exceptions to this general rule. They had refused to meet with Haberstock on 12 December 1940, and thereafter conducted no business with him.[385] Interrogations of others revealed that although this dealer did not deal directly with the ERR, largely because he had been 'outmanoeuvred and never had a chance to profit from the exchanges', works of art which this Nazi plunder organisation had originally acquired nevertheless passed through his hands.[386] Rousseau's interrogation report on Haberstock culminated in a recommendation that he be prosecuted as a war criminal because of his close association with the Nazi looting apparatus, particularly through his close association with Hans Posse, Director of the Linz Museum, who owed his position largely to Haberstock's recommendation:

> It is recommended that he be tried on the same level as the leading members of the Sonderauftrag (Special Project) Linz. He was, beyond any possible doubt, one of the individuals most responsible for the policies and activities of this group, which dominated German official purchasing and confiscation of works of art from 1939 through 1944.[387]

---

[383] Supplement to CIR 4 (Linz), op. cit., Attachment 48.

[384] DIR 13, op. cit., 5.

[385] Duveen to Haberstock 12 December 1940: US NA, 260, Entry 446; Haberstock to Breitenbach 13 August 1947: NGA MSS 3 (Faison Papers), Box 2, Central Control Commission for Germany (British Component), MFA&A Branch cited in Petropoulos, 2000 op. cit., 89.

[386] DIR 4 (Rochlitz) op. cit., 6–7; Philips and Sutton, 'Report on Preliminary Interrogation of P.W. Alfred Hentzen', 22 June 1945: US NA, RG 239, Entry 81.

[387] DIR 13 (Haberstock) op. cit., 7.

As Yeide notes, the DIRs contain a wealth of detail that remains of considerable historical interest in critically exploring the various claims, selective interpretations and alibis associated with this aspect of the Holocaust, which is not found in other available reports:

> The information in the DIRs created by the ALIU was utilized in the CIRs, but the DIRs are useful documents in their own right. The DIRs summarize interviews with available key players involved in the Nazi confiscation of art and cultural property and are usefully checked against one another for confirmation or contradiction of alleged facts.[388]

For example, the DIR on Bornheim contains rich details concerning processes of 'Aryanization' by which formerly-Jewish art dealerships were placed in the name of 'gentiles'. These include the Drew business located in Munich containing artworks valued at RM 300,000, but which had been 'Aryanized' in 1936 for a mere RM 30,000.[389] The Drew family then emigrated to New York with only a limited number of their remaining assets.[390]

Amongst the various DIRs that was important as a source for the later lengthy CIR on the Linz Museum was DIR 1 (Heinrich Hoffmann).[391] Rousseau's report drew upon Hoffmann's intimacy with Hitler's personal motivations for selecting this location, where the latter had spent his youth, as a new cultural and artistic centre to rival and ultimately displace Vienna and even Berlin.[392] It also extracted from Hoffmann considerable details of the internal organisation, funding, 'methods of acquisition' and management of the Linz Museum, and the responsibility of its second Director, Hermann Voss, for the acquisition of the Jewish Schloss collection.[393] Rousseau notes that it was works of art plundered from Jews that provided many of the earliest items for this new centre, and that even here one theft was later compounded by both other fraudulent activities and Hitler's resulting efforts to optimise his museum's benefits from such anti-Semitic looting:

[388] Yeide, 2007 op. cit., 6.

[389] Albeit subject to a possible buy-back after five years and safe-holding of certain important works regarded as 'German national treasures.'

[390] See DIR Bornheim: US NA, RG 239, Entry 84.

[391] Gerard Aalders, *Nazi Looting: The Plunder of Dutch Jewry during the Second World War*, NY: Berg, 2004, 248.

[392] DIR 1 (Hoffmann), op. cit., 3.

[393] Ibid., 4.

> As was customary with the Nazis, among the first sources of pictures for the Museum were the confiscated collections of German and Austrian Jews. Hoffmann says that the first of these to be considered was the Alphonse Rothschild collection, which he visited in the company of Hitler and Gauleiter Burkel in Vienna. However, Burkel, who was associated in some way with art dealer Haberstock, did not send the best of the collection, but kept it for himself. As a result of the scandal which followed, Hitler decided that he would place the responsibility for such selections on one man, the Director of the Linz Museum.[394]

Rousseau's interrogation of Hoffmann revealed details of the generally anti-Semitic atmosphere that surrounded art dealers close to the Nazi inner circle, including the perceived need of dealers such as Maria Dietrich to conceal any family connections with Jews whether through birth or marriage.[395]

This DIR also noted Hoffmann's status as an early and ideologically-committed member of the Nazi Party, having joined the movement in 1922 as member number 59. This status as an 'old fighter' gave him special privileges, influence and access to Hitler's inner circle. This continued after the Nazis' seizure of power in 1933–34 and through the first half of the war period. However, such access ended during 1943 when both Martin Bormann and Eva Braun succeeded in isolating Hoffmann. He exploited this to promote the generally racist and certainly anti-Semitic distinction between 'healthy' and 'degenerate' artworks, rooted in dubious biological analogies that excluded works of art associated with Jewish and/or cosmopolitanism origins and associations:

> After the Nazi accession to power and during World War II he was a prominent political figure. His special and favourite sphere of activity was art. He played a leading role in the campaign against "degenerate art" and it was under his orders that an attempt was made to remove all traces of it from German museums. Later he became the official patron of the modern art which flourished in Germany with Nazi approval... Broadly speaking, Hitler placed him in charge of presenting art to the people of the Third Reich and seeing that they got the right sort.[396]

This ALIU report expresses scepticism of Hoffmann's various alibis, including his claim not to have ever acted in a self-interested, profit seek-

---

[394] Ibid., 3.

[395] Ibid., 5. Dietrich had been married to a Turkish Jew, Almas, but reverted to her maiden name 'for more Aryan appearances' Ibid.

[396] Ibid., 1.

ing way, or as representing himself as an agent for the Linz Museum: 'In spite of these denials, the evidence shows that Hoffmann not only bought works of art, representing himself as an official representative of the Fuehrer, but also sometimes did a little picture dealing on the side for his own profit.'[397] Rousseau reacted with equal scepticism to Hoffmann's claim to have avoided dealing in works originally looted from Jews: 'He protests that he never bought a picture which had formerly been in a confiscated Jewish Collection. However, he admits that he never inquired about the immediate provenance of anything he bought, even if it was from Mühlmann of whose [anti-Semitic looting] activities he was well aware.'[398]

Rousseau also extracted incriminating statements from Hoffmann concerning the actions and orientations of other dealers, such as Karl Haberstock and Andreas Hofer, who were also scheduled for later interrogation.[399] Plaut managed to extract details of the wrangling associated with the fate of a number of confiscated Jewish collections and/or those subjected to forced sales, including the Goudstikker collection[400] and works of art looted from the Rothschilds by the ERR in France, such as works by Vermeer (*The Astronomer*) and Boucher (*Portrait of a Lady*). Despite Hitler's reluctance to include confiscated works from Jewish sources in official publicity material, they were nevertheless included in the Linz Museum.[401]

The ALIU's DIR on Scholz, a senior visual arts adviser to the ERR based in Berlin,[402] is also revealing. Plaut's report noted a tension between Scholz's own defensive claims and the implications of available evidence regarding the confiscation Jewish collections:

> Under interrogation, he has sought to convey the impression that he was personally responsible only for the orderly cataloguing and "safe-keeping"—in well-fitted deposits—of the works of art confiscated by the Branch of the Rosenberg office which he in no way controlled. Detailed

[397] Ibid., 2.
[398] Ibid., 7.
[399] Ibid., 6.
[400] Miedl played a key role in the acquisition of the Goudstikker collection. See the articles in the new catalogue, Bruce Museum (Ct.), *Reclaimed: Paintings from the Collection of Jacques Goudstikker*, Yale University Press, 2008.
[401] DIR 1 (Hoffmann), op. cit., 7, reference 2.
[402] Scholz was appointed coleader with Kurt von Behr of the ERR's Special Staff Visual Arts which was sometimes described as Special Staff Louvre, within this organisation's Amt Westen (Western Office). Scholz also supervised up to ten art historians and professional staff of the Sonderstab Bildende Kunst who catalogued the plunder: CIR 1 (ERR), op. cit., 15–16.

> interrogation, however, has developed the following points: (a) that Scholz was at all times empowered to control the assignment of personnel to, and removal from, the special art staff of the Einsatzstab; (b) that he took an active, possibly the leading part, in the preparation and execution of the 28 exchanges of confiscated paintings which the Einsatzstab conducted; and that he ordered and directed the compilation of a list of confiscated Impressionist paintings, which were to be made available for exchange or sale by the E.R.R. (c) that he represented Rosenberg directly in relations with the Reichschancery, other party organizations, and the German military, where questions of broad policy related to art matters were involved.[403]

This DIR also noted that Scholz: 'was responsible not only for the scientific recording of all art objects confiscated by the ERR and for their shipment to Germany, but for the maintenance of the various deposits within Greater Germany to which the confiscated material was brought.'[404] This report addressed one vital issue relating to Holocaust restitution: the extensive detailed records of the ERR. Prior to the German military collapse in April 1945, Scholz became responsible for the 21,903 artworks the ERR had confiscated from French Jews and removed to Germany, the last transport taking place on 15 July 1944. Part of this responsibility was the protection of the ERR inventories, including a card catalogue and photographic file. These were vital to the Allies' postwar task of identifying the plunder and determining actual ownership prior to possible restitution.

In defiance of explicit orders from the Nazi Party Chancellery, that is, indirectly from Martin Bormann, to destroy documentary evidence of anti-Semitic plunder, the DIR on Scholz noted that he had sent his deputy, Bruno Lohse, from the ERR Paris branch to safeguard these records. Scholz also wrote a letter to Lohse and ERR photographer and art historian Günther Schiedlausky, ordering the two to safeguard these confiscated Jewish artworks and associated records and: 'turn them over to the American authorities at such time as Füssen might be occupied.'[405] This point could, perhaps, be taken as a limited mitigating factor.

This DIR also suggested that, unlike the majority of those implicated in looting who were motivated largely by greed, Scholz's was a committed and ideologically-driven Nazi. He had been concerned to promote

[403] DIR 3, 4.
[404] Ibid.
[405] Ibid.

a racially determined German Volk, which would be 'free' of Jewish and other supposedly alien elements. Plaut's report noted:

> [It] is believed that the motivation for Scholz' activity with the Einsatzstab was essentially ideological rather than material, and that he derived no financial profit from the confiscations effected with his knowledge and under his direction. In addition to his salary as Bereichsleiter, Scholz claimed to have received a monthly expense allowance of RM 300, and to have received no further compensation whatsoever. This statement is believed to be accurate.[406]

It further suggested that: 'It has not been established finally to what degree Scholz personally initiated German policy...all the evidence at hand would indicate that he was a burning protagonist of National Socialist cultural ideology, and that he participated actively in the "struggle against Jews, Freemasons and enemies of the Reich."'[407] This OSS report further stated: 'Scholz is considered, instead, to have sponsored the commercial exploitation for Germany of such material as was "unsuitable" ideologically for importation into the Reich.'[408]

Another DIR on Gustav Rochlitz corroborated this impression of Scholz as an exclusively politically-driven looter: 'Scholz talked frequently in almost hysterical terms about the 'degenerate' nature of all modem French painting, and stated that this material would under no circumstances be taken to Germany.'[409] Another DIR, relating to Bruno Lohse, also reveals further details relating to the actual process of decision-making and delegation within the ERR that would not otherwise have been clear from formal organisational charts, such as Scholz's extensive delegation of responsibilities to his deputies Lohse and Borchers.[410] The DIR on Rochlitz provides extensive biographical details of how he first became complicit in the buying and selling of artworks the ERR had confiscated from French Jews, relying from early 1941 onwards partly on Bruno Lohse to act as his intermediary. He conducted business with Göring's agents as well.[411]

In order to provide a fuller flavour of the focus and structure of these DIRs without trawling through the detailed contents of each one

---

406 Ibid.
407 DIR 3, 3.
408 DIR 3, 4.
409 DIR 4, 5
410 DIR 4, 3. This is confirmed by DIR No. 6 (Lohse) op. cit., 3.
411 DIR 4, 2.

individually, I will now summarise the key elements of ALIU's DIR: 'Hans Wendland', which Otto Wittmann, co-wrote with Taper from MFA&A following ten days of intensive joint interrogation starting 5 September 1946. This report, completed long after the main work of the ALIU had been brought to a close, can be interpreted as a case study of more general features of the attitudes and tactics of interrogators, and certain defensive attempts by their subjects to evade admissions of culpability and optimise any possible mitigating claims.

Wendland had been identified by both the Allied 'Proclaimed List' during the war, and the Allied Repatriation List. Because of the delay in securing his arrest in Switzerland and extradition to Germany,[412] this was issued on 18 September 1946, far later than most of the other DIRs and CIRs. It can, therefore, be taken to have incorporated many of the lessons from the structure, style and content of these earlier ALIU reports. At this late stage, the report fell under the auspices of not only the OSS (by now revamped in a reduced form as the Strategic Services Unit or SSU), but also the Office of Military Government For Germany (U.S.) Economics Division, Restitution Branch Monuments, Fine Arts, And Archives Section. The report had a wide circulation, including US Army Military Intelligence (G-2), various branches of the US State[413] and Treasury Departments,[414] and various branches of the British and American Armies' MFA&A departments.[415] In addition to a brief introduction and final summary, the structure of the report contains four substantive sections: Wendland's 'personal history', 'dealings and dealer relations', 'traffic in confiscated art' and 'personal assets'. It also includes cross references to seven earlier ALIU reports.[416]

---

[412] Wendland was arrested in Rome by the American Forces on 25 July 1946 at the request of the American Legation, Berne. After a preliminary interrogation there, he was transferred to Oberursel near Frankfurt on or around 22 August., he was returned to Germany in accordance with a request from the United States Department of State. He was returned within the next week to the Internment Camp at Oberursel for further disposition.

[413] These included its Division of Foreign Activity Correlation 2 copies; Division of Economic Security Control (for Retention and distribution to London, Paris, Rome, and Berne) 6 copies; Division for Occupied Areas, Arts and Monuments Section 2 copies.

[414] The Foreign Funds Control 1 section.

[415] In addition, copies were sent to the French authorities including Commission de Recuperation Artistique and the Ministry of Justice (Seine Tribunal), and to the Holland's Dutch Nederlands Ryjksbureau voor de Monumentenzord.

[416] CIR No. 1, The Einstatzstab Rosenberg; 2. CIR No. 2, The Göring Collection; 3. DIR No. 4, Gustav Rochlitz; 4. DIR No. 6, Bruno Lohse; 5. DIR No. 9, Walter

This report's introduction notes the centrality of Wendland to an extensive network that both serviced Göring's collection and played a key part in the looting of Jewish artworks in France and their ultimate disposition in Switzerland, the base of his operations:

> Hans Adolf Wendland is, in relation to the history of the complex web of art looting and acquisition spun by the Nazis, the most important German figure whose base of operations was a neutral country—Switzerland. He was one of the most agile and informed contacts of Walter Andres Hofer, "Director of the Art Collection of the Reichsmarshall". He figured, whether wittingly or not, as the receiver of confiscated art in the first exchange of paintings from French private collections effected by the Einsatzstab Rosenberg, and subsequently participated in three other exchanges with Göring's agent, playing an important role in the importation of these works of art into Switzerland.[417]

By cross referencing his answers to other interview material, ALIU officials characterised Wendland's network in terms that were closer to a Mafia operation or criminal syndicate, than a legitimate circle of business people:

> Hofer has stated that during the war Wendland was a kind of unofficial "king" of the Paris art world.... Capitalizing upon his German citizenship in a land occupied by Germans, and upon his wide pre-war acquaintanceship in the Paris art market, Wendland became a kind of advisor and guide to many of the French dealers anxious to do business with Germans. He gradually formed an informal syndicate of the French dealers, Boitel, Perdoux, and Loebel. Hofer states that he was connected with the Dequoy-Fabiani combination, and he is known to have had interests in the Mandle-Birthschanksy group. Just how formalized were these dealing syndicates formed by or participated in by Wendland is difficult to ascertain.[418]

Hofer's interrogation in particular became an important source of information. Hofer and his counterparts Hans Wendland in Switzerland and Achilles Boitel in Paris developed a close relationship that OSS officers characterised as a 'dealing syndicate.'[419]

It is a common feature of interrogation accounts that the interviewee seeks, by way of mitigation, to place great emphasis upon any support

Andreas Hofer; 6. DIR No. 13, Karl Haberstock; 7. Final Report, Art Looting Investigation Unit.

[417] DIR Wendland, op. cit., introduction.

[418] Ibid., 6–7.

[419] DIR No. 9: Walter Andreas Hofer op. cit., 7.

or protection they could possibly claim to have provided for members of Jewish and other persecuted groups, and the risks they ran with the Nazi regime by doing this. Under the heading of: 'A. Aid to Jewish Dealers' this DIR notes:

> In his own defense, Wendland claims to have aided Jewish dealers to avoid German confiscation of their works of art. Wendland states he was able to rescue four paintings belonging to Alfred Weinberger from sequestration by the Devisenschutzkommando in Paris in 1941. These paintings, which included a Goya "Portrait of an Old Man", and a Patinir and two others had formerly been sold by Wendland to Weinberger, and Wendland claims that by means of an old catalogue he was able to convince the German authorities that the paintings still belonged to him. The paintings were taken to Switzerland where they all still remain in Wendland's possession, with the exception of one painting which was returned to Weinberger. An Altdorfer owned by the Jewish dealer, Paul Graupe, now in New York, together possibly with several other paintings belonging to the same dealer, were given to Wendland by Graupe's former partner, Arthur Goldschmit. Wendland states that the Altdorfer was sent to Carl Bueming of Darmstadt, who was to transmit it to Switzerland. Wendland does not know where it now is.[420]

The report refuses, of course, to take Wendland's defensive claims in mitigation at face value. Its authors suggest that factors other than altruism in favour of the victims of Nazism had probably been a more important factor shaping Wendland's actions. It notes, for example, his exploitation of the threat of confiscation to acquire a part share of Jewish works of art. The appropriate test here to distinguish between clear resistance to Nazi art looting and complicity in this aspect of the Holocaust was not whether Wendland and others had 'safeguarded' Jewish-owned works of art. Instead, it was whether such war crimes suspects had, in practice, already secured the safe return of such items to their rightful owners on their own initiative:

> Wendland cites these cases, among others, as examples of assistance to Jewish colleagues at considerable trouble and some danger to himself. It is known, however, that he held a certain financial interest in at least some of those objects, and the possibility must not be overlooked that he may have gained a share in all of the pictures for his trouble. It is significant that of all the objects which Wendland obtained in this manner, he can cite only one picture which he has until now returned to its owner.[421]

---

[420] Ibid.
[421] Ibid., 12.

ALIU's DIR on Lohse expresses a similar concern to highlight any evidence of mitigating aid its subject provided for actually persecuted Jews, or others who would have become victims of the Holocaust without official protection. For example, it emphasised Lohse's role in connection with Allen Loebl, Jewish director of the Galerie Garin (formerly Kleinberger):

> Lohse stated...that he met Loebl shortly after he arrived in Paris; and that he had made an agreement with Loebl, protecting him against anti-Jewish action, in return for which Lohse received first option for Göring on any works of art passing through Loebl's hands. In addition, he secured the release of Loebl's brother, Manon, from the concentration camp at Drancy on two occasions.... Loebl was Lohse's adviser and intermediary in a substantial number of transactions, and "spotted" pictures for him.[422]

It is likely that the OSS interrogators' suspicious attitude towards many self-interested defensive claims further intensified following their experience of debunking the blatant lies told by Hofer and other members of this network. Certainly, the interrogators' tactics were successful in extracting damaging information from Wendland concerning his complicity in anti-Semitic looting, the incriminating details of which he had concealed from his formal records. Such activities had taken place against a wider context of secrecy and criminal deception amongst his network, which included resorting to bribery and related 'compromises':

> He admits to claiming pictures as his own which in fact did not belong to him in connection with his rescue of Jewish owned art in France. He claims reluctance to reveal all of his transactions in France during the war on the grounds that some of the deals represented collusion to evade French taxes, duties, etc., and could therefore be harmful to his French associates. He admits freely transactions in black market exchanges of currency on numerous occasions. He claims to have kept few records or books of his transactions. He claims to have had a special arrangement with the Swiss whereby he paid income tax only on a "standard of living" basis. He speaks frequently of bribery to minor government officials, and has several times suggested to his present interrogators the possibility of certain compromises.[423]

[422] DIR No. 6 (Lohse), op. cit., 6.
[423] DIR (Wendland), op. cit., 12–13.

It is clear from this report that Wendland's interrogators pushed him hard concerning his contacts and dealings with the main official body responsible for the systematic looting of Jewish art, the ERR. In the immediate postwar context of ongoing war crimes trials, Wendland was—for obvious reasons—particularly anxious to distance and disassociate himself, as far as possible, from both this organisation or other dealers who were involved with it. Wendland was particularly sensitive to the accusation that he had drawn upon his past dealings and contacts to help ERR officials track down hidden Jewish works:

> Wendland denies any official relationship with the ERR or with any of its staff; and he apparently knew very few of its members. He states that he visited the Jeu de Paume but once during the war, the occasion being during one of his last trips to Paris, early in 1943. He knew, but claims to have been no friend of, von Behr, whom he describes as "a man that a decent German would not give his hand to." It was not until late November 1942, that he made the acquaintance of Lohse. The occasion which brought them together was an involved transaction in which Wuester, in order to make a Delacroix and Courbet from the ERR available to his sponsor, Ribbentrop, bought from Wendland and made available to Göring through Lohse and the ERR a Gobelin tapestry and an Albert Cuyp. Wendland categorically denies the charge that he had ever through Dinglage, informed the ERR of the whereabouts of hidden Jewish property. Wendland states that it was only after late November 1942, when he made the acquaintance of Lohse, that he began to understand the workings of the ERR. Until that time, he says the secrecy of the affair had kept it well concealed from him.[424]

In order to assess the credibility of Wendland's claims, the ALIU / MFA&A interrogators cross-referenced and then contextualised them with other evidence derived from both other interrogation sessions and documentary sources. Amongst this evidence was information concerning the nature of the criminal, or at least semi-criminal, network with which Wendland chose to associate, and the presumed state of play of his subjective knowledge and orientation concerning the trade in the fruits of anti-Semitic looting:

> However, if he had no personal friends among the ERR staff at first, Wendland was at least intimately acquainted with men like Dinglage, von Behr's cousin, and the collaborator Boitel, who would have been well able to describe to him the German activities in the Jeu de Paume.

[424] Ibid., 13.

> He had extensive business relationships with such dealers as Rochlitz, Birtschansky, Loebel and others, many of whom have since been indicted by the French government as collaborationists and dealers in looted art. Finally he had, while in Switzerland or during his journeys through unoccupied France, the opportunity of knowing Jews whose property had been confiscated or was in danger of it, and, in fact, he points out that he took what he describes as daring steps to rescue this property. It is therefore difficult to believe that a person in Wendland's circumstances could have remained completely and innocently unaware that Jewish owned property was being confiscated and used as loot for exchange purposes. Whether he was aware or not, the basic fact remains that Wendland acted as a party to at least four exchanges in which he, alone or in connection with Theodor Fischer, received works of art which had been looted by the Nazis from private art collections.[425]

In terms of his complicity with the Holocaust, one of the more damning sections of this DIR report concerned Wendland's 'exchange with the ERR through Rochlitz'. The exchange included Wendland receiving the following paintings confiscated from Jewish owners: Corot, *Mother and Child* and Matisse, *Women at a Table* (both Rosenberg-Bernstein Collection); Degas, *Madame Camus at the Piano* and Braque, *Still Life* (both Kann Collection). Here, this report draws attention to the discrepancies between established evidence, including Rochlitz's account of this exchange, and Wendland's defensive claims and attempts at self-justification:

> The exchange occurred 3 March 1941. Wendland gave his shares in an alleged Titian, "Man with a Beard" and a Jan Weenix, and he is said by Rochlitz to have received six modern French paintings. This took place during Wendland's first visit to Paris after the occupation; coincidentally, perhaps, this also represented the first exchange that the ERR had effected. From evidence presented in DIR 4 and CIR 1 of the OSS Art Looting Investigation Unit, the background of this affair may be reconstructed as follows:...The entrance of Wendland into this affair at this moment of impasse was...providential for the Nazis. Without seeing the Titian (which at that time was probably at the Jeu de Paume for Göring's inspection) Wendland agreed to buy Birthschansky's share (for 12,000 dollars) and to receive, upon consummation of the exchange, six of the eleven modern pictures. These pictures, according to Rochlitz's statement in DIR 4, were delivered to Wendland in Paris. Wendland's version of the affair presents substantial differences with that outlined above....[426]

[425] Ibid.
[426] Ibid., 16.

The next section of this DIR addresses the three exchanges that the 'Wendland-Fischer combination' made with Hofer, Göring's curator. It notes critically that: 'Wendland has been evasive on this subject.'[427] Wendland's strategy was to accept that he had participated in the exchange of what he later realised were confiscated Jewish artworks. However, and for obvious reasons, he denied that at the relevant time he had ever known, or had good reason to appreciate, that this was the case. He also rejected the accusation that he had ever possessed any intent to engage in this form of war criminality. Although Wendland went to Berlin and made the selection of pictures, he claimed:

> that neither he nor Fischer suspected the provenance of the pictures. Although they knew that the exchange was being made on Göring's behalf, Hofer assured them in the name of the Reichsmarschall, that the affair was beyond doubt, legal and honourable. And, as a sign of their good faith in this matter, Wendland cites the fact that Fischer immediately invited art experts and museum officials to see the pictures, began preparing a catalogue and arranging an exhibit. The revelation of the fact that the pictures acquired were loot came, states Wendland, late in 1942.[428]

This DIR then proceeds to address an important, if somewhat ironic, restitution issue raised by the question of whether Wendland and Fischer were, as they claim, acting in good faith and lacked subjective knowledge of the provenance of these pictures. This issue: 'is of considerable importance... since, according to the United States-Swiss Agreement of February, 1946, concerning restitution Fischer stands to be recompensed by the Swiss government for these pictures if it can be established that he acquired the pictures in good faith.'[429] The remainder of the main body of this report describes in considerable depth the details and context of each exchange Wendland was involved in during the spring and summer of 1941. For our purposes, it is particularly important to recognise that those works of art were originally confiscated from the Jewish Rosenberg,[430] Levy-Benzion, Kannand and Lindenbaum collections.

Finally, this DIR on Wendland contains a conclusion summing up the significance of his role in Nazi art looting, and attributes levels of responsibility and culpability for this type of war criminality. It also

---

[427] Ibid.
[428] Ibid., 16–17.
[429] Ibid., 17.
[430] These included paintings by Monet, Cort, and Sisley.

contains a recommendation that effectively this individual be imprisoned, at least until he makes a fuller disclosure of his involvement and its fruits:

> Wendland cannot be considered to have been a guiding spirit in the main art looting activities of the times, but he was one of those who were eager to profit from these activities.... It is recommended that he be retained in custody until such time as conclusive investigations may be made in Switzerland and France, the full extent and nature of his assets revealed, and the disposition of these assets determined.[431]

In short, Wendland's DIR is an important illustration of the tactics of ALIU interrogators, their cross-referencing of his claims against information extracted from other sources and interrogations, and the critical testing of his defensive claims.

More generally, the DIRs provided some but not all of the raw information for the ALIU's larger and thematic 'Consolidated Interrogation Reports' (i.e., CIRs).[432] Plaut recalls that: 'The results of our interrogations are incorporated in three major reports, dealing with the most comprehensive looting efforts.'[433] The Roberts Commission report noted that, in addition to summarising the implications of the DIRs, these larger reports brought together: 'earlier investigations in other European areas, as well as from inspection of large numbers of captured enemy documents.'[434] The CIR series completed during the life-time of this Unit comprised the operations of the Einsatzstab Reichsleiter Rosenberg (ERR) in France (CIR 1), written by Plaut,[435] the Göring Collection (CIR 2),[436] and the proposed Führer Museum at Linz, Austria (Hitler's hometown, CIR 4).[437] CIR 3 on Kajetan Mühlmann was only published later as a joint OSS-Dutch enterprise.

Each of these CIRs contains materials relevant to our understanding of the cultural plunder dimensions of the Holocaust. However, it

[431] Ibid., 25.
[432] See US NA, RG 226, Entry 99, Box 105, copy NGA curatorial files; Yeide, 2007 op. cit., 2.
[433] Plaut, 1997 op. cit., 124.
[434] Roberts Commission Report, 1946 op. cit., 40.
[435] J. Plaut, 'Activity of the ERR in France' (CIR 1), 15 August 1945: US NA, RG 239, Entry 85.
[436] T. Rousseau, 'The Göring Collection' (CIR 2), 15 September 1945: US NA, RG 239, Boxes 85–85A. These reports are also available at US NA, RG 260, Records of the United States Occupation Headquarters WWII, Ardelia Hall Collection, Box 450. OSS files.
[437] S. Faison, CIR 4 (Linz) op. cit.

is CIR 1 that is focused uniquely upon anti-Semitic forms of plunder within France. This is clear from the Plaut's own description of the focus of his report:

> This report is intended as a comparatively definite study of the most elaborate and extensive art looting operation undertaken by the Germans in World War II—namely, the confiscation by the Einsatzstab Rosenberg of Jewish-owned collections in France. The information contained herein has been derived from the detailed interrogation of key German personnel and the analysis of official German documents.[438]

Each of these more comprehensive and thematic reports integrates incriminating materials contained in individual DIRs and other sources, and includes lengthy supplements supported by a series of pertinent documents. Fitzgerald's judgement on the high quality of these reports merits quotation:

> These reports are marvels of exhaustive research, in-depth analysis and sophisticated judgment. They simply have not been surpassed. Rousseau devoted himself to plumbing Göring's vast appetite for art and in the process delivered some of the most penetrating analyses of this man who was then awaiting trial at Nuremberg. Rousseau did not write to count beans but to convey the centrality of art to the Nazi program.... Faisan meticulously analysed Hitler's even more grandiose plans for a museum of art in Linz, Austria, where the Fuhrer had spent part of his youth. There were several British adjuncts to the team, notably Douglas Cooper, the foremost collector of Cubism in the 1930s. He applied his vast knowledge of the art market to uncovering the extensive trade funnelled through neutral Switzerland. All of the reports are supplemented with weighty files—copies of essential Nazi documents and face-to-face interrogations of the dealers, agents and principals involved.[439]

The contents and structure of the CIR 4 concerning the Linz Museum illustrates and gives some flavour of the nature and utility of the three larger reports.[440] Indeed, the preface to this document provides a useful

---

[438] CIR 1, op. cit., 1.

[439] Michael Fitzgerald, (chairman of the fine arts department of Trinity College in Hartford, Conn.), review of 'Lost Museum', *Art in America*, February 1998, 2.

[440] CIR 1 is similar, consisting of: i. Introductory Note: Sources; I. Organization And Authority; Ii. Development Of Einsatzstab Activity In France; (a) The GÖRING Relationship; (b) 'Revision' of the Mission; the *M-Action*; (c) Internal and External Conflict; III. Confiscation In Practice And In Theory; (a) Methods Employed by the Einsatzstab; (b) Official French Protests and German Justification; (c) Analysis Of Confiscation; IV. Disposition Of Confiscated Material; (a) Objects Brought to Germany—General; i. *Difficulty of Transportation and Storage*; (b) Objects Acquired by GÖRING; (c) Objects

summary reflecting how this unit's reports retained a focus upon the specific objectives of its original mission:

> This report concerns the collections of paintings, arms and armour, coins, books, sculpture, furniture and objets d'art which Hitler intended to present to the city of Linz. It has three functions: (1) to identify the personalities involved, and the particular role played by each: (2) to classify the methods employed in amassing the collections; (3) to indicate the sources from which the works were obtained. The information contained herein was derived from documents and from interrogations.[441]

CIR 4 opens with a historical analysis of how the idea for this Museum originated, and the structure and activities of its organisation and operation between 1939–1945 in Austria, Poland, France, Holland, Belgium and Italy. It then addresses the personnel and organisation of this institution.[442]

In short, the DIRs and CIRs provide ample examples of the lines of questioning ALIU officials pursued during their interrogation at Alt Aussee of those complicit in the Nazi regime's art looting, the results and measure of success of these investigations. They provide evidence that the specifically anti-Jewish dimension of such looting was not ignored, and that indeed this remained a recurring theme throughout many, if not all, of the DIRs and CIRs these officials produced for war crimes prosecutors and other agencies responsible for restitution.

The final operational chapter of ALIU's work: Spring 1946–September 1946

Following the dissolution of the ALIU, Otto Wittmann was kept on as a one-person investigator to write a concluding chapter for this Unit, partly following the recommendation on 19 April of the section of the US State Department responsible for Safehaven work: The Division of Economic Security Controls.[443] The 'Final mission to Europe'

Acquired for HITLER; (d) Exchanges; i. *Summary*; ii. *Policy and Method*; V. Details Of Exchanges; Vi. E.R.R. Personnel Active In France; (a) Executive (b) Professional Specialists (c) Confidential Assistants (d) Photographic Staff (e) Secretarial (f) General VII. ATTACHMENTS.

[441] CIR 4 (Linz), op. cit., preface (i.).

[442] For additional details relevant to the potential utility of this report within the Nuremberg process, see below.

[443] See Otto Wittmann, Jr., 'Art Looting Investigation Unit, Final Mission to Europe' 10 June 1946–24 September 1946, 14 October 1946, (hereafter 'Final Mission'), 1: US

involved Wittmann carrying out a four month survey of developments and remaining problems in France, England, Germany, Switzerland, Sweden and Denmark. He was charged with ensuring that other US Government agencies, including Allied Military Government over Germany, picked up where the ALIU was leaving off by becoming engaged in: 'continuous investigations and controls initiated by this Unit.' His other somewhat open-ended and widely defined task was to confer with Foreign Government agencies working on Nazi art looting, and: 'survey the extent of continuing traffic in looted art [and] undertake certain concluding investigations of problems connected with art looting.'[444]

Wittmann used Paris as his base camp, and he liased with French intelligence and government officials active in this field, one of which, the French Restitution Commission: 'requested additional aid in the apprehension and interrogation of certain German nationals known to have been connected with art looting in France.'[445] He discovered that the French intelligence services had not kept their side of an agreement to monitor and investigate 'collaborationist art dealers'.[446] Wittmann's investigation of the state of play of domestic prosecutions revealed that only the more complicit dealers, of which he secured the current list,[447] had been prosecuted. Others dealers within this category had been punished merely by administrative means, such as prohibitions of future trading in art.[448] He had to refer the request for additional investigative assistance in the American Zone of Germany to the intelligence officer of MFA&A.[449]

Wittmann's survey of the state of play in Germany included efforts to encourage the further 'development of an expanded art intelligence organization which could incorporate certain phases of the work which this Unit had formerly undertaken in Germany, and to continue the close liaison which this Unit has always had with the MFA&A.'[450] This

NA, RG 239, Entry 73, Box 83, Subject Files, 1940–1946. Wittmann wrote this report on SSU/War Department letterhead as the OSS was officially disbanded at this time. His report was distributed to the Division of Economic Security Controls, State Dept., and the Division of Occupied Areas, Arts and Monuments Section, State Dept.

[444] Ibid., 2.
[445] Ibid., 3.
[446] Ibid., 4.
[447] Ibid., Appendix A.
[448] Ibid., 5.
[449] Ibid., 6.
[450] Ibid., 14.

plan for an enhanced investigative and intelligence group was agreed by the MFA&A, as was Wittmann's suggestion of closer liaison with State Department officials working on related Safehaven projects. He also succeeded in encouraging a formal system for the licensing of German art dealers, using ALIU's reports as a basis for screening out those who had participated in the acquisition or sale of looted artworks, and a system of positive permission for works of art produced before 1850.[451]

The conclusion of this part of the report noted that: 'there are still several Germans active in this field during the war who should be interrogated. The problem of German art looting in the East has never been properly explored.'[452] It expressed the hope that with the expansion of the intelligence and investigation side of the MFA&A: 'these remaining problems will be solved.'[453]

Having explained aspects of the institutional and logistical elements of the ALIU's role, and the nature of its mission and the format of its investigative reports, it is now timely to adopt a more thematic approach. The remainder of this chapter will devote a subsection to the following more specific themes: art looting and the Holocaust within France, the Göring Collection, the Linz Collection, problems concerning Switzerland, counter-espionage aspects and restitution issues. The analysis of the ALIU's contribution to the Nuremberg war crimes trials process will be deferred to the final chapter, where OSS' other inputs in this legal process are discussed.

Art looting and the Holocaust in France

In France, whose capital was then a key European centre and market for art, a number of major international collections of art were owned by French Jews.[454] Integral to the Holocaust in France was a series of German decrees that declared French Jews to be 'non-citizens' and / or 'enemies of the state' under the Vichy emigrant laws. On 30 June 1940, General Keitel, Commander in Chief of the Wehrmacht, referring to an order from Hitler, directed that both private and public French art

[451] Ibid., 15.
[452] Ibid., 16.
[453] Ibid., 17.
[454] CIR 2 (Göring) op. cit., 33.

possessions be safeguarded against possible loss. This in effect authorised the seizure of Jewish property. Within less than one hundred days after the Germans had overrun France, that is on 17 September 1940, Keitel directed, on Hitler's authority, that any disposition of French property subsequent to 1 September 1939 was null and void. Keitel directed the Chief of the German High Command in France to give all assistance to Rosenberg in the confiscation of so-called 'ownerless Jewish possessions.' Keitel stated that Rosenberg: 'has received clear instructions from the Fuehrer personally governing the right of seizure; he is entitled to transport to Germany cultural goods which appear valuable to him and to safeguard them there. The Führer has reserved for himself the right of decision as to their use.'[455] Furthermore, the ERR, which had been created in the meantime, was required to make seizures of Jewish-owned works and to transport these to Germany, where Hitler would decide upon their disposition.[456]

On 5 November 1940, Göring issued a decree in Paris that extended formally the authority of the Einsatzstab to include the confiscation of 'ownerless' Jewish art collections. This fundamentally altered the emphasis of the Einsatzstab mission so as to make such activity its primary function. Prior to this decree, such activity had been the nominal responsibility of the German military commander for France and the German Embassy in Paris. Göring's 'special representative' in the ERR, Bruno Lohse, was responsible for arranging exhibits of confiscated Jewish and other works of art for the Reichsmarschall's personal inspection, and to arrange transportation of any selected works back to Carinhall.[457]

On 18 November 1940, Hitler ordered through Reichsminister Lammers, that all confiscated works of art were to be brought to Germany and placed at his personal disposal, and that all matters relating there were to be the responsibility of the Director of the Dresden Painting Gallery, Dr. Posse.[458]

One of Plaut's ALIU reports notes that on 18 December 1941, three months before the deportations of Jews in France began in March 1942,

---

[455] Quoted in Plaut, 1946a, op. cit.

[456] CIR 4 (Linz), op. cit., 7. On 5 September, Rosenberg made a similar announcement.

[457] CIR 2 (Göring), op. cit., 18.

[458] CIR 1, op. cit., 3.

Alfred Rosenberg sought and—within two weeks—received Hitler's authorization to seize all personal possessions of French Jews who were targeted for deportation or who had fled abroad for understandable reasons. CIR 1 translated and then attached this order as follows:

Memorandum for the Führer

SUBJECT: Jewish Property in France.

As a consequence of the Fuehrer's order concerning safeguarding of Jewish cultural possessions, a great number of Jewish dwellings have remained unguarded. The result has been that in the course of time many articles of furniture have disappeared, since naturally a watch could not be carried out. Throughout the EAST the administration found frightful living conditions, and the possibilities of procurement are so limited that practically nothing more can be purchased. I therefore request the Fuehrer to approve the seizure of all furniture of Jews who have fled or those who are about to flee, in PARIS as throughout the occupied WESTERN territories, to supply furniture, as far as possible, for the administration in the EAST.

BERLIN, 18 December 1941.

(Signed) ROSENBERG.[459]

In other words, confiscated Jewish property was to be distributed between party members and German army staff in the Eastern occupied territories.[460]

These 'legal' decrees were rapidly acted upon setting in motion extensive and escalating acts of anti-Semitic plunder, which included but were not confined to artworks. Following German occupation in June 1940, Jewish collections became an early target of official Nazi looting policies. Keitel's decree initiated what Plaut described as:

> the most extensive and highly organized series of thefts devised by a nation in modern times: the wholesale seizure, by Rosenberg's special task force (*Einsatzstab*), of 203 French private collections containing some 21,000 works of art. This was a carefully conceived operation, aimed at the cultural debilitation of the strongest of the fallen nations, since France's purest heritage lay in the hands of her enlightened collectors.[461]

---

459 CIR 1, op. cit., Attachments 4 and 5.
460 Ibid., 9.
461 Ibid.

In addition to the actions of the ERR, separate Hitler and Göring commissions were also engaged in plunder within France to enrich the holdings of these leading Nazi leaders. Plaut's report on the ERR noted that during the opening months of 1942, the Nazi regime systematically looted property from the accommodation of French Jews who had fled, or were about to leave, their homes. These items included furniture and household effects. Such persecution was particularly intense within Paris. As already noted, this material was plundered initially in order to meet the needs of German occupation administrators in Eastern Europe, but eligibility was later extended to various other police and security officials within Germany.[462]

ALIU officials noted how, ironically, Nazi cultural plunder from rival German organisations and their agents yielded economic benefits to French collaborators and their agents working on commission. Plaut recalled:

> Aided by Göring's largesse, and under Baron von Behr's determined leadership, the Einsatzstab Rosenberg evolved swiftly into a well-oiled machine for the systematic plunder of France. The operations were remarkably simple. Since, under the prevailing code, any non-Aryan property was fair game, and since a striking proportion of the good works of art privately held in France were in the large and well-known Jewish collections, the field was fertile and the pickings easy. To be sure, most of the property owners had taken flight before the Nazis and were hiding out in the country, or in unoccupied France, or abroad. In many instances, their collections had gone underground with them, so that von Behr's hirelings had to ferret them out. Unfortunately, there was no dearth of collaborationist *indicateurs*, ever ready to sell their information, and themselves, to the German intelligence services. Von Behr had free access to the files of the French collaborationist police force, the Gestapo, and the Security Service (*Sicherheitsdienst*), and worked so closely with these organizations that their representatives usually accompanied Einsatzstab personnel on house raids.[463]

Wartime conditions, including the creation of a large number of refugees as well as other events more closely related to the Holocaust, ensured a frantic rush to sell artworks to German dealers and their agents. The latter, who visited Paris in droves, were widely known to be willing to pay inflated prices in the dubious 'occupation currency' that had cost their country nothing, even for so-called 'degenerate art'. This

---

[462] Ibid., Attachment 5, 18 December 1941; Feliciano, 1997 op. cit., 39.
[463] Plaut, 1946a op. cit.

currency gave such dealers a twenty-to-one advantage over the franc, allowing them to make a hundred per cent profit on their return to Germany.[464] This heightened economic activity, in turn, boosted the prices on the Paris art market, which enjoyed an economic boom.[465] A variety of French collaborationist art dealers exploited such economic conditions to make large profits from selling and exchanging many hundred cheaply acquired artworks confiscated from their Jewish owners. Yeide's study of the ALIU reports recognises that the cultural plundering aspect of the Holocaust, which resulted in a mass of Jewish-owned looted art becoming available for sale to Göring and other leading Nazis, had fundamentally altered the Parisian art market to the disadvantage of Jews and to the benefit of those French collaborators willing to materially benefit from anti-Semitic persecution:

> While the major players of the pre-war Parisian art market were Jews who had fled the country, leaving their stock and personal collections to be confiscated, there was also a ready network of dealers willing to sell to the Reichsmarschall [Göring]. A lively art market flourished throughout the war in Paris. The Hôtel Drouot had its most successful years of the century during the German Occupation, resuming sales a few months after the Germans arrived in June 1940.[466]

As already noted, in September 1939, the Nazi regime gave Rosenberg's ERR organisation exclusive power over art looting in France. This regime allocated over 60 specialist German officers to the ERR's art confiscation programme, including art historians, museum workers, librarians, archivists, photographers and secretaries. Plaut notes that although a civilian unit, the Einsatzstab: 'worked in a strict military environment, even wearing a uniform which caused no little confusion among the terror-stricken French hangers-on because of its paradoxical resemblance to that of the SS.'[467]

ERR officials exercised considerable powers regarding transportation and securing cooperation from other state officials.[468] ERR staff looted extensively from wealthy Jews, such as the Rothschild,[469] David-Weill,

---

[464] CIR 2 (Göring) op. cit., 33.
[465] CIR 4 (Linz), op. cit., 38.
[466] Yeide, 2007 op. cit., 5.
[467] Plaut, 1946a op. cit.
[468] Feliciano, 1997 op. cit., 4.
[469] Ibid., Ch. 1 noting that Vermeer's *Astronomer* owned by the Rothschild Family was seized by the ERR in 1940 and declared 'property of the Third Reich.' Ibid., 15: 'on September 6 [1940] Maurice de Rothschild's mansion was searched and number of

and Seligmann families.[470] Plaut has recalled that the Nazis' plunder of valuable Jewish art collections was combined with attempts to vindicate wider anti-Semitic ideologies:

> Early in the occupation of France, the confiscation of valuable properties had become an issue of some magnitude in high Nazi circles. Largely at Göring's instigation, the German Embassy in Paris, the Foreign Currency Control Administration (*Devisenschutzkommando*), and the Alien Property Administration (*Feindvermögenverwaltung*) had made fruitful raids on the fabulous Rothschild holdings, which—as was the case with considerable portions of the country's private cultural treasure—were stored in the family's châteaux and its large Paris town houses, famous throughout France. Simultaneously, and consistently with their formal mandate, a small group of Nazi scholars attached to the Rosenberg office were combing the libraries and archives of the occupied countries in search of material for exploitation as propaganda in the "ideological struggle against Jewry and Freemasonry."[471]

According to Plaut's Consolidation Interrogation Report, (CIR 1), which was based on both interviews with leading participants incriminated in Nazi art looting activities and a study of original German documentation,[472] the ERR represented the: 'most elaborate and extensive art looting operation undertaken by the Germans in World War II.'[473] Here, we need to recall that between April 1941 and July 1944, 4174 cases containing at least 22,000 items, were shipped out from the ERR base in Paris for many different collections within Germany,

---

his works of art seized.' Ibid. 34, Ch. 4. Louis V Rothschild (1882–1955) was arrested in Vienna in 1938 and his house and hunting lodge were fully looted and all art items seized: 3978 of them were stored in the castle of Neuschwanstein. The rest—about 50—were stolen or lost. He was only granted an exit visa for the USA by paying a large sum and giving up title to all of his Austrian assets.' Ibid., 34, Ch. 4.

[470] Ibid., 33–34: 'In July 1940, the contents of a number of galleries belonging to Jews, such as the one owned by...Jaques Seligmann...were seized.' Ibid.

[471] Plaut, 1946a op. cit.

[472] 'Einsatzstab of Reichsleiter Rosenberg's' later renamed to Einsatzstab Reichsleiter Rosenberg *für die besetzten Gebiete*).

[473] CIR No. 1 (ERR), op. cit., 2. Recent scholarship has discussed the ERR's plunder of Western European cultural items. See Patricia Kennedy Grimsted, 'Roads to Ratibor: Library and Archival Plunder by the Einsatzstab Reichsleiter Rosenberg' *Holocaust and Genocide Studies* 2005 19(3): 390–458; Donald E. Collins and Herbert P. Rothfeder, 'The Einsatzstab Reichsleiter Rosenberg and the Looting of Jewish and Masonic Libraries during World War II,' *Journal of Library History* 18 (Winter 1983): 21–36; Joshua Starr, 'Jewish Cultural Property under Nazi Control,' *Jewish Social Studies* 12 (January 1950): 32–45; Leslie I. Poste 'Books Go Home from the Wars,' 73 *Library Journal*, No. 21 (December 1948): 1699–704.

including of course Linz and Carinhall.[474] In one sense, these figures are misleading because they fail to highlight the fact that the majority of the looting from Jewish collections took place during the *first two years* of German occupation, yielding such a quantity of materials that ERR staff responsible for its classification and cataloguing became overwhelmed.[475] Plaut notes:

> One of the art historians admitted under interrogation that, by mid-November, 1940, virtually the entire contents of the several Rothschild Collections, totalling 5009 objects; the Alfonse Kann Collection, comprising 1202 objects; and those of Weil-Picard, with 123, and Wildenstein, with 302, were already in hand. Dr. Robert Scholz, the Berlin director of all Einsatzstab administration, stated categorically that the great majority of works of art seized in the entire course of Einsatzstab operations—which lasted, technically, from September, 1940, until the fall of Paris in August, 1944—were already in the Jeu de Paume when he arrived there early in 1941. This is vivid evidence of the swiftness with which the task force worked. Several great collections, and many others of real consequence, were confiscated later, but the initial seizures came hard on the heels of the German military victory in France, and at the moment when German prestige, largely because of the fear and chaos which it inspired, was at its highest. Moreover, the strategy laid down for the confiscations called for the early seizure of the great—and the obvious—concentrations; these constituted, both numerically and qualitatively, the most important "take" of the Einsatzstab.[476]

Plaut's CIR 1 (ERR) recognised that the Nazis looted a considerable quantity and range of Jewish items and provides the following break-

---

[474] CIR 1 (ERR), op. cit., 53. This is confirmed in DIR 5 (Schiedlausky) op. cit., 2, which notes that: 'in November 1940... the most significant portions of the Rothschild Collection had already been confiscated, as well as the Kahn Collections at St. Germain and the Weil-Picard, David Weill, Wildenstein and Seligmann Collections.' Ibid.

[475] 'SCHOLZ stated categorically that the great majority of the works of art seized during the course of the entire Einsatzstab action were already in hand when he arrived in PARIS early in 1941. The flow of confiscated material, toward the end of 1940 and in the beginning of 1941, was characterized as so swift that the art historians, in any event, could not have kept up with the incoming collections. Later, following the change in administration, greater selectivity was shown and examination of potential seizable material was undertaken by one of the art historians prior to confiscation. LOHSE stated, however, that with the exception of the Max WASSERMANN Collection and portions of the David WEILL Collection, no group of important objects was confiscated after the early months. The monthly reports of E.R.R. acquisitions generally listed no more than five or six objects obtained, and these of low quality. There was a certain resurgence of activity when the *M-Action* was initiated in 1942, but this was described by LOHSE as irregular and circumstantial.' CIR 1 (ERR), op. cit., 17–18.

[476] Plaut, 1946a op. cit.

down: 10,890 artworks, 583 sculptures, 2477 pieces of 17th and 18th Century furniture, 583 tapestries, carpets, embroideries etc, 5825 *objets d'art*, 1286 works of Asiatic art, 259 items of classical antiquity.[477] In addition, this ALIU report provides details of which Jewish Collections were particularly subject to such looting: 2687 items were looted from the David Weill collection, 1202 from that of Alphonse Kahn, 989 from that of Levy de Benzion and 302 from Georges Wildenstein's collection. Other figures are acknowledged to be only fractions of the total numbers of works confiscated from other Jewish collections, these being 558 from Seligmann and 123 from Weil-Picard.[478] The value at that time was estimated to be one billion dollars.

This CIR also noted that, whilst the plundering operations against French Jews were systematic, the internal organisation of this agency was often characterised by intrigue and bitter rivalries, which led to: 'hysterical slander and counter-accusations.'[479] Lohse revealed under Plaut's interrogation that internal relations were disrupted by: 'a series of petty intrigues precipitated by the jealousy of several women members of the staff and by general envy of his favored position in relation to Göring.'[480] Furthermore, it appears that one of the ERR officials, Rose Valland, a former curator of the Jeu de Paume prior to the Nazi occupation, was in fact secretly working against the Nazis. She kept meticulous records on which items the ERR were transporting to which particular destinations in Germany.

These records, which according to DIR 6 (Lohse) had been ordered to be destroyed,[481] were later used for the investigative restitution operations of the ALIU and other Allied agencies, and are sometimes referred to in OSS reports as a 'French source'. Plaut states:

> The Musée du Jeu de Paume in the Tuileries became the focal point of German looting activity in France. Taken over by von Behr complete with its French staff—including the Director, Mlle. Rose Valland, who observed the proceedings closely and who today, as a captain in the French WAC, is a key figure in her government's restitution proceedings—it was turned into a collecting point for the "safeguarded" material. Here, once a collection had been brought in by van from its place of origin, the Einsatzstab "scholars" took over, authenticating, cataloguing, inventorying,

[477] CIR 1 (ERR) op. cit., 20.
[478] Ibid.
[479] Ibid., 53.
[480] DIR No. 6 (Lohse) op. cit., 2.
[481] Lohse credits Scholz for the decision to ignore this order, ibid., 4.

> and photographing every object. All the painstaking thoroughness of the German method was lavished on the job, with the neat result that the Einsatzstab files were discovered intact at its headquarters in Germany after the American break-through, and the vast complications of Allied restitution procedure were immeasurably simplified.[482]

DIR 6 (Lohse) notes that following von Behr's departure, responsibility for supervising such confiscations fell to either Lohse or Borchers, with the logistical side of securing their physical removal to Jeu de Paume being delegated to Fleischre.[483] ERR officials, whose Chief was Alfred Rosenberg, sometimes competed with other Nazi agencies that had also been given responsibility for carrying out art looting in France: the German Army's Kunstschultz,[484] and the Germany Embassy in Paris operating under the French Ministry of Foreign Affairs.[485] From 30 June 1940, the Kunstschultz was authorised to place: 'all art objects... belonging to individuals, and Jews in particular,... into safekeeping... under the supervision of the German embassy.'[486] ALIU reports note that the rivalry between senior Nazi ministers, including between Bormann, Rosenberg, Göring and Ribbentrop, also exerted an impact on the art looting operations in France.[487]

One ALIU report on the ERR noted that there were internal tensions between the French authorities and the ERR, with the former making occasional complaints to the latter regarding its plundering operations. Objections by the French were treated with contempt.[488] The German authorities argued that Jewish property fell outside the category of French property demanding respect under the surrender treaty. One ALIU report notes that the combination of formal 'legal' authorisation with the Nazis' creation of the ERR as an institutional mechanism

[482] Plaut, 1946a op. cit.

[483] DIR No. 6 (Lohse) op. cit., 5.

[484] Feliciano, 1997 op. cit., 34.

[485] CIR 4 (Linz), op. cit., 9; Feliciano, 1997 op. cit., 4–5. CIR 4 notes: 'Prior to the establishment of the ERR in Paris, confiscations were carried out by the German Embassy. The loot was turned over to the ERR (Rothschild items so acquired were given the title "BoR"'). CIR 4 (Linz), op. cit., 60.

[486] Cited in Feliciano, 1997 op. cit., 33.

[487] CIR 4 (Linz), op. cit., 13, 15, 43.

[488] Plaut notes that: 'It is of parenthetical interest that the Vichy government, whatever its more significant political conciliations, demonstrated courage and aptitude in bombarding the German High Command with communications designed to preserve the cultural heritage of France. The ultimate success of this policy is shown in the insignificant number of officially owned works of art which left the country in German hands.' Plaut, 1946a op. cit.

to give practical effect to anti-Semitic plunder within France, meant that the artworks, and other assets of this group, were—as previously discussed—declared in principle to be 'ownerless'. Hence, by default, ownership in them was defined as having reverted back in practice to the Nazi regime:

> During these developments [ERR confiscation of artworks from French Jews and their transfer to Germany for Hitler or Göring's collections], the theory was developed that Article 46 of the Hague Convention did not apply to Jews and Freemasons, because the Compiegne armistice of June 1940 had been concluded with the French people, of which they were not a legitimate part. This idea is found in Bunje's report of October 1941. (See reference A, page 18).[489]

In August 1942, Dr Bunjes,[490] acting on orders from Göring given three months previously, provided an attempted justification along classic Nazi anti-Semitic lines. His document entitled 'French Protests against the Safeguarding of Ownerless Jewish Art Properties in Occupied France', assigned the blame for French objections towards the Musées Director, Jaujard and his staff. The closing part of Bunjes' letter stated: 'Only...when the Fuehrer has made the final decision as to disposition of the safeguarded art treasures, can the French Government receive a final answer.'[491]

CIR 1 provides a critical analysis of the supposedly 'legal' rationale that Göring commissioned Bunjes to write concerning their confiscation of the artworks of French Jews and Freemasons, and for their refusal to respond sympathetically to: 'the numerous official Vichy protests lodged with the German authorities on the subject of the ruthless and illegal plundering by the Einsatzstab Rosenberg.[492] The Bunjes report explained the measures taken, provided a detailed analysis of the French protests, and suggested concrete counterarguments. Bunjes argued that the real motive for the French protests was the French authorities' attempts to deceive Germany and to undermine its occupation, not

---

[489] CIR 4 (Linz), op. cit., 8.

[490] Bunjes was director of the Franco-German Art Historical Institute in Paris and Hermann Göring's first major art purchasing agent in France. On Bunjes work for Göring, see CIR 2 (Göring), op. cit., 21.

[491] CIR 1 (ERR), op. cit., Attachment 9.

[492] Plaut, 1946a op. cit. In a later section, we will show how Göring came to exercise considerable control over the operations of Rosenberg's ERR.

least by systematic anti-German cultural propaganda that ignored the more relevant question of the legitimate German claims for the return of cultural materials destroyed by French soldiers in Germany after 1918. For example Bunjes' report stated:

> These treasures if transferred into money values, could be made effective tomorrow against Germany in the form of tanks or planes...yet their return has not even been demanded by the Reich. The further French request for access by its government officials to those localities in France where German personnel are taking inventory of confiscated material would, if granted, simply invite French espionage. Moreover, the affirmation of the Louvre that the French people would lose valuable national works of art through the aforementioned safeguardings is refuted by the fact that many of the safeguarded works stem from great masters of German origin or are under the influence of the German spirit.... All French arguments...are voided by the Führerbefehl [Hitler decree] of September 17, 1940, according to which all lawsuits regarding bequests, gifts, etc., are not recognized.... Only when these measures are completed and when the Führer has made the final decision as to the disposition of the safeguarded art treasures can the French government receive a final answer.[493]

The main thrust of ALIU's analysis of this would-be legal rationalisation is particularly critical. It argues that 'The Einsatzstab confiscations not only were conducted under the authority of the Hitler order of 18 November 1940, but were cloaked by the fictitious pretext of adherence to international law.'[494] It dismissed Bunjes explanation of: 'the ingratitude of the French state and the French people for the altruistic efforts of the Einsatzstab, without which the destruction and loss of invaluable cultural material would have been inevitable.'[495] The ALIU analysis even describes Bunjes report as: 'a pinnacle in the literature of political treachery.'[496] It describes the self-interested 'legal justification' for the German action as 'blatantly transparent', and as a disingenuous attempt to exploit a loophole in international law:[497]

> The Hague Convention of 1907, signed by Germany and France, and observed in the armistice terms of May 1940 calls in Article 46 for the inviolability, among other things, of private property (ATTACHMENT

[493] Quoted in Plaut, 1946a op. cit.
[494] CIR 1 (ERR), op. cit., 19.
[495] Ibid.
[496] Ibid.
[497] Ibid.

> 9A). BUNJES states, however, that the Compiegne armistice of 1940 was a pact made by Germany with the French state and the French people, but not with Jews and Freemasons, and that the Reich, accordingly, was not bound to respect the rights of Jewish property owners; further, that the Jews, in company with Communists, had made innumerable attempts since the signing of the armistice on the lives and persons of Wehrmacht personnel and German civilians, so that even sterner measures had to be taken to suppress Jewish lawlessness. BUNJES contends that the basis for the French protests, and petitions for the return of ownerless Jewish property, is the desire on the part of the French government to deceive Germany and further the prosecution of subversive activity against the Reich.... (The BUNJES paper is reproduced in its entirety (and in translation) in ATTACHMENT 9.)[498]

CIR 1 provides a useful summary of the creation and operations of the ERR. This merits quotation not only in terms of the information it contains, such as the complicities of the German Army leader General Keitel and Göring, but also for how it illustrates and substantiates its claims with a range of potential trial evidence in the form of documentary 'attachments'. These were designed to operate as a draft prosecution brief and meet the criteria concerning the linkage between general claims and specific documentary proof that the OSS General Counsel, James Donovan, had previously requested for all reports potentially relevant to the Nuremberg process. CIR 1 summarises the actions and culpabilities of von Behr in a manner that is particularly helpful for the purposes of revealing lines of responsibility for the essentially lawless, as well as officially-organised, aspects of anti-Jewish cultural plunder in France. It provides interesting clues as to his relationship with both Göring and Rosenberg:

> *German Red Cross Oberfuehrer Baron Kurt von BEHR*, Deputy Director of Amt Westen, Director of the Paris E.R.R. Kunststab, and subsequently Director of Dienststelle Westen and the *M-Action*. [looting of mobile personal property] Von BEHR, as confirmed by all sources, was the individual in France chiefly responsible for the looting of Jewish art collections, both in the "controlled" active phase of the Einsatzstab and the subsequent wild confiscations of the *M-Action*. The awareness of his own guilt let to his suicide at Schloss Banz/Lichtenfels at the time of the American occupation. Middle-aged member of an aristocratic Mecklenburg family, von BEHR utilised his position in the E.R.R. as a stepping-stone to personal prominence in German war circles in Paris and, possibly, to acquire objects of value for himself. All sources are agreed

---

[498] Ibid.

> that he initiated, directed, and personally conducted the majority of the E.R.R. confiscations without fear of consequence, without legal pretext and without respect for the ownership or quality of the works of art seized. He was impatient with all suggestions for moderation in confiscation, or for orderly cataloguing of objects received. Von BEHR was under orders from ROSENBERG to represent the Reichsleiter on the occasion of GÖRING's frequent visits to Paris. He shared this honour with UTIKAL and they vied for GÖRING's favors. LOHSE cites as an illustration of von BEHR's desire to please GÖRING the fact that he came to Berlin for the Reichsmarschall's birthday in 1942, bringing with him as a birthday gift the original copy of the Versailles peace treaty with all signatures, and an original letter from Richard Wagner to Napoleon III. These were documents confiscated by the E.R.R.[499]

The next paragraphs exposes once again the centrality of Göring's not so hidden hand in this aspect of the Holocaust, and the sheer gangster quality of the ERR's methods and leadership. These even resorted to the deployment of both French collaborationist and SS personnel to terrorise the victims of art looting, with the latter's political intelligence division (SD) assisting ERR's actions:

> Von BEHR was wholly unscrupulous in his depredations, and in the use of criminal and near-criminal types to carry them out. He is stated to have resorted to any practises calculated to bring in objects of value, and have courted the favor of persons in high places by lavish gifts and entertainment, the wherewithal being gained through the activities of the Einsatzstab. He treated the professional members of his staff patronizingly, and was bitterly opposed through out by SCHOLZ, von INGRAM and LOHSE, all of whom protested either to ROSENBERG or to GÖRING over his disgraceful actions. Von BEHR worked closely with the French Commissioner for Jewish Problems, Darquier de PELLEPOIX and, according to LOHSE with industrialist/art dealer, BOITEL. Of the several "V-manner" (confidential informants) whom he employed, PFANNSTIEL appears to have been the most prominent. In addition to the E.R.R. confiscations which von BEHR directed, he was stated to have: (a) proposed the *M-Action*; (b) forced E.R.R. personnel to collaborate with Sicherheitsdienst in 1941 in searching for Jews wanted by the S.D. In this connection, he attended frequent conferences of the Judenreferat of the S.D., both receiving and contributing information leading to the apprehension of Jews and confiscation of their property. Later as Director of the *M-Action*, he placed Jews as forced labor repairing and packing confiscated furnishings, and ran a "little concentration camp" in Paris. (c) initiated action leading to the confiscation/sale of the Schloss Collection

[499] CIR 1 (ERR), op. cit., 47–48.

> in 1943. (d) proposed to UTIKAL in 1944, at the time of the rout of German armies in France, that a new M-Action be organised in the Arnheim (Holland) area, and be undertaken by the E.R.R., rather than by his Dienststelle Westen.[500]

Immediately after the end of the war, the ALIU provided French authorities with considerable detailed information on German looting that was directly, or even indirectly, relevant to France and French interests. This had been gathered largely during their early wartime investigations in newly-liberated France from November 1944. Between September 1945 and February 1946, ALIU officials worked closely with and advised their counterparts in the French Commission de Recuperation Artistique, the Ministry of Justice, and the French intelligence agencies. This cooperation resulted not only in the return of art taken from a number of French Jews but also the detention of several Germans who had been complicit in such looting.[501] For example, whilst based in Austria, Plaut and Rousseau personally apprehended Gustav Rochlitz, one of Göring's chief art procurers, from his hideaway in a nearby village, and transported him to the French authorities in Paris. On 15 August 1945, Plaut filed his major CIR report, 'The Activities of the Einsatzstab Rosenberg in France.'[502]

Taper's recollections of the work of Allied officials also cast new light upon a specifically Holocaust-related theme: the ALIU's investigation of artworks the Nazi regime and its proxies looted from French Jews. It addresses the practical consequences in terms of both art restitution and arrests of a number of those complicit in this aspect of the Holocaust:[503]

> Of these interrogations, the most extensive and significant was one I conducted together with Otto Wittman Jr., an OSS officer, of the art dealer Hans Wendland. A shadowy rather slippery figure, Wendland was the key link in the complex of transactions by which important artworks confiscated from French Jewish collections by the... ERR passed through the hands of Göring and then made their way by diplomatic pouch to

---

[500] Ibid., 48–49. See also DIR 3, 2 which, with respect to Scholz and von Behr's conflict: 'The personal and ideological conflict between the two men was the dominant element in the internal relations of the Einsatzstab.'

[501] Hussey *et al.*, op. cit.

[502] CIR 1 (ERR), op. cit., preface.

[503] See Taper and Wittman, 'Detailed Interrogation Report' subject: Hans Wendland', 18 September, 1946 discussed in Simpson, 1997 op. cit., 137.

> Switzerland for sale by the Fischer Gallery of Lucerne. Wittmann and I questioned Wendland for ten straight days at the Wannsee Interrogation center in Berlin to establish a coherent, authoritative history of this unsavoury episode in the history of art dealings, and of Wendland's role in it. The report we assembled provided possible whereabouts of a number of important paintings that had been questionably acquired. It also led to the extradition of Wendland to France.[504]

CIR 1 recognises the personal complicity in this aspect of the Holocaust in France of not only Alfred Rosenberg, but also his fellow Nuremberg defendant, General Keitel, and a connection with the offence contained in Article 6 of the Nuremberg Charter of 'waging aggressive war' it recognised that: The conquest of France offered unparalleled opportunities for further acquisitions, whether by confiscation or purchase.

CIR 1 notes that the blatantly illegal actions of the ERR in looting Jewish works of art and other cultural items, together with suspicions that it may be trespassing upon the jurisdiction of the SS, meant that this organisation suffered from low prestige and opposition from a number of other branches of the Nazi regime. This opposition, particularly that of German military circles, affected the ERR in various ways, which its leadership tried with little success to counteract:

> The felonious activity of the Einsatzstab was deplored by many German officials, who contested its legitimacy and attempted to obstruct its operations. Count METTERNICH, head of the *Kunstschutz*, the German military organisation for the protection of works of art, condemned von BEHR publicly whenever possible, and the military organisation as a whole was antipathetic to what it considered a disgraceful political action. ROSENBERG, aware of the low repute in which his organisation was held by the German military, encouraged von BEHR to entertain extensively, in the hope that the prestige of the Einsatzstab would gain accordingly. It is of parenthetical interest that HIMMLER, following HITLER's restatement of policy (in March 1942) whereby the E.R.R. was to have the sole right of confiscation of archives, libraries and cultural material, wrote to ROSENBERG to determine the rights of the *Sicherheitsdienst* and the *Sicherheitspolizei* in the confiscation and exploitation of documentary material bearing on enemies of the Reich. ROSENBERG thereupon agreed to the transmittal to HIMMLER's organisations of all police documents, and sought to assure HIMMLER that the Einsatzstab was in no sense attempting to usurp the authority of the *Sicherheitsdienst* and the *Sicherheitspolizei*. For a considerable period, the confiscatory

[504] Taper, 1997 op. cit., 137.

> prerogatives of the Einsatzstab were jeopardized by the firm opposition of HIMMLER and LAMMERS, whose influence in Army circles was sufficiently strong to minimise the cooperation extended the Einsatzstab by military units.[505]

CIR 1 also provides extensive details of the ERR's changing senior staff, including the positions of von Behr and Utikal, and their specific functions within this organisation in relation to confiscated artworks This information was obviously vital to the needs of the Nuremberg and other war crimes prosecutors to identify clear lines of command, and hence criminal responsibility.[506]

Later this report identifies various internal conflicts between Scholz and von Behr for example, charts the changing and complex divisions of responsibilities for anti-Semitic looting, and identifies some of the dishonest motivations and strategies that underpinned these.[507] Once again, Plaut was able to identify a real tension between formal positions of responsibility, and how different parts of the ERR were led somewhat chaotically in practice:

> On 25 March 1942, von BEHR was appointed *Leiter der Dienststelle Westen des Ostministeriums* (Direct of the Western Branch of the Ministry for the Occupied Countries of the East). General dissatisfaction with von BEHR's conduct of the Paris art staff had existed from the beginning, and there was an open breach in his relations with SCHOLZ and the professional art historians. Von BEHR's high-handed methods and utter disregard for the intrinsic value of the confiscated material, coupled with his excessive vanity and selfish ambition, had produced a chaotic condition within the Einsatzstab.... On 14 January 1942, ROSENBERG requested of HITLER's headquarters that the mission be placed under the jurisdic-

[505] CIR 1 (ERR) op. cit., 14.

[506] '*Amt Westen* was directed at the outset of Stabsfuehrer Dr. EBERT, assisted by the German Red Cross Oberfuehrer, Kurt von BEHR. This office was located in Paris, with headquarters in the Hotel Commodore. In addition to a staff of photographers, the Paris *Dienststelle*, commanded a small group of professional art historians who worked as a unit designated as the *Arbeitsgruppe Louvre*. The function of this unit was the methodical preparation for transport to Germany of all works of art received through confiscation, and a comprehensive inventory thereof. At the outset, this group comprised Doctors SCHIEDLAUSKY, WIRTH, ESSER, JERCHEL, KUNTZE, and several research assistants. Early in 1941, EBERT was forced to retire because of an injury suffered in an automobile accident. He was succeeded by Stabsfuehrer Gerhard UTIKAL, who, however, was given complete responsibility for the activities of the Einsatzstab in all countries, with offices in Berlin and the title of *Hauptstellenleiter des Aussenpolitisches Amt und Leiter des E.R.R.* Simultaneously, von BEHR was made responsible for all Einsatzstab operations in France.' Ibid., 3–4.

[507] See also DIR No. 3 (Scholz), op. cit., 2.

tion of the Reichsminister for the Occupied Territories of the East, as he felt unable to cope with the problems attendant to such confiscation and transfer through extant Einsatzstab channels. Accordingly, on 25 March 1942, the Reichsminister ordered the establishment in Paris of *Dienststelle West*, with subsidiary branches throughout France, Belgium and the Netherlands, and with von BEHR in full control. This newly inaugurated confiscation activity was known as the *M-Action*, and von BEHR in his new capacity was ordered to relinquish control of the Paris art staff of the Einsatzstab, inasmuch as the *M-Action* was to be entirely divorced from the Einsatzstab mission as of 1 May 1942. Von BEHR was stated to have considered that the *M-Action* would enable him to discover and manipulate personally a large number of valuable objects, which as "furniture" would not be subjected to the careful scrutiny and inventory which had been prescribed for valuable art collections seized by the Einsatzstab. All sources are agreed that von BEHR proposed the *M-Action* to ROSENBERG as a means of achieving a freer hand and a greater prestige. In theory, von BEHR's activity as Director of the Einsatzstab art staff ceased with his appointment as Director of *Dienststelle West*. SCHOLZ was given full professional responsibility for the art staff, and Lieutenant Hermann von INGRAM was made its administrator and business manager. A Dr. BRETMAUER took over von BEHR's administrative duties with the Einsatzstab. Von BEHR was, in fact, not deposed as head of the art staff until January 1943.[508]

CIR 1 also addresses the often chaotic methods through which Jewish artworks from the Rothschild and other collections were subjected to confiscation supported by members of repressive agencies, such as the SD and collaborationist French police officials. According to Plaut's review of earlier interrogations, the stereotype of ruthless German efficiency directed by a centralised system of command and control, was hardly borne out by evidence of the largely *ad hoc* nature of the ERR's confiscation practices at least prior to Rosenberg's acceptance of the recommendations of Scholz's report:

The manner in which collections of works of art were obtained by the Einsatzstab in its early stages of activity is described by all informants as chaotic. As the initial confiscations were effected by the German military command in France and the German Embassy, the Einsatzstab became operational at a moment when these collective seizures were already widespread. SCHOLZ stated that EBERT, UTIKAL and von BEHR never communicated with Berlin to receive instructions for the disposal of a given collection which had been located.... The early seizures were directed by two-non-professional "technical assistants" to von BEHR,

[508] CIR 1 (Err) op. cit., 8–9.

> named BRAUMUELLER and BUSSE. These men worked without inventories and, following leads which they received from the collaborationist French police, effected wholesale confiscations and turned over the accumulated material to the Einsatzstab. SCHOLZ states that members of the French police force accompanied BRAUMUELLER and BUSSE on their expeditions to facilitate the confiscations. Information was also received from the Sicherheitsdienst [SD].[509]

The ALIU also noted that, despite a high degree of internal conflict amongst its leadership and a number of chaotic operating practices, the ERR had rapidly become a central agency in anti-Semitic art looting. By 8 August 1944, the ERR had raided and plundered 71619 dwellings and shipped over 1079373 cubic metres of such goods in 29436 railway cars. Indeed, Plaut recalls that, notwithstanding Göring's considerable assistance concerning logistical issues, transportation of this amount of looted items raised serious problems:

> Shipments to Germany were obstructed, in spite of Göring's help, by a severe shortage of adequate rolling stock. For the first and most important transfer (in April, 1941) 30 special baggage cars—of the heated type normally attached to de luxe passenger trains—were requisitioned from every corner of the Reich. The train carried the choicest items from the Rothschild, Seligmann, Wildenstein, and David-Weill Collections to the principal Einsatzstab repository, set up at Schloss Neuschwanstein, the castle of the mad King Ludwig which nestles in the foothills of the Bavarian Alps. A special Luftwaffe detachment rode the train as armed guard, and the material was three days in transit. A second major shipment, comprising 28 carloads, took place in October, 1941. Thereafter, partly because of the inordinate difficulties of transport, partly because the most valuable pieces had already been transferred to Germany, the loot was brought in piecemeal, and placed—through to the end of 1943—in the six special Einsatzstab depots—at Neuschwanstein, Nickolsburg, Chiemsee, Buxheim, Kogl, and Seisenegg.[510]

---

[509] Ibid., 15. See also DIR No. 6 (Lohse) op. cit., 2: 'The initial confiscations . . . were conducted by confidential assistants of von Behr, who were unaccompanied and unadvised by the professional art historians attached to the special staff. . . . [Later] it became standard procedure to have one of the art historians accompany responsible ERR personnel to the premises where confiscations were to take place. Lohse as well as Borchers, Kuntze, Bammann, Fraeulein von Tomforde and other members of the art staff, engaged in this activity. It was their function to control the scope of the confiscation in terms of the intrinsic value of the objects of art under consideration, and to eliminate the irresponsible seizure of miscellaneous, comparatively valueless items. . . . Lohse was obliged, furthermore, to determine, through the French Commission for Jewish Problems and the Sicherheitsdienst whether the prospective seizures encompassed properties abandoned by Jewish owners.' DIR No. 6 (Lohse) op. cit., 4.

[510] Plaut, 1946a op. cit.

CIR 2 provides extensive details of Göring's active complicities in those aspects of the Holocaust in France concerned with art looting, and the extent to which around half of his massive art collection at Carinhall stemmed from this type of cultural plunder. It notes that his agents resorted to all manner of ingenious devices to extend the scope of Nazi confiscations, largely at the expense of Jews:

> Works of art confiscated from "enemies of the state" [i.e., Jews and Freemasons] form an important part of the Göring Collection. It can be fairly estimated that they constitute almost fifty per cent of its total, the ERR alone supplying in the neighbourhood of seven hundred objects. Göring considered confiscated property as a source for his collection from the outset. There is abundant evidence that he and his agents were constantly in search of new possibilities in this respect. More than once, private collections were frozen... until it was proved the owner was not a Jew. Letters from Hofer to Göring show that on such occasions he stood by hoping the outcome of the investigation would make it possible for him to step in and choose for the Reichsmarschall (see Attachment 1). In the case of the Kronig collection, three pictures were already in Berlin when the owner was discovered to be "Aryan". They were later returned...[511]

The OSS reported that Scholz entrusted much responsibility to his ERR deputies in Paris, art historians Bruno Lohse and Walter Borchers.[512] Scholz attempted with some success to sell (or barter) so-called 'degenerate' works of art, including those associated with Jewish artists. DIR No. 3 states: 'Scholz is considered, instead, to have sponsored the commercial exploitation for Germany of such material as was "unsuitable" ideologically for importation into the Reich.'[513] In early 1942, he even tried to give effect to Göring's order for Rosenberg's office to take on the project of liquidating the remaining works of 'degenerate' art that had been seized in the Reich. The OSS report noted the importance of Scholz's systematic work for Göring's plunder, in that he: 'was responsible not only for the scientific recording of all art objects confiscated by the ERR and for their shipment to Germany, but for

[511] CIR 2 (Göring), op. cit., 23.

[512] DIR 6 (Bruno Lohse), op. cit., 3. CIR 1 describes Dr. Walter Borchers as follows: 'Obergefreiter in the Luftwaffe, came to the Paris art staff later than the aforementioned art historians. He was highly esteemed by SCHOLZ as a first-rate scholar, and ultimately was placed in charge of the *Arbeitsgruppe Louvre* in all professional matters. At the time of von BEHR's removal, BORCHERS shared this responsibility with LOHSE, but because of the latter's unwillingness to devote the majority of his time to research, cataloguing, etc., SCHOLZ placed BORCHERS in charge and removed LOHSE completely some months thereafter.' Ibid., 52.

[513] DIR 3, op. cit., 4.

the maintenance of the various deposits within Greater Germany to which the confiscated material was brought.'[514]

With respect to Scholz's personal complicity in the Holocaust, DIR 3 states: 'It has not been established finally to what degree Scholz personally initiated German policy with respect to the confiscation of Jewish-owned art properties in occupied countries; all the evidence at hand would indicate that he was a burning protagonist of National Socialist cultural ideology, and that he participated actively in the "struggle against Jews, Freemasons and enemies of the Reich."'[515] The CIR report devoted to Göring notes that his various trips to the ERR's Paris HQ prompted rivalries with other leading Nazis who competed over the spoils from their regime's looting of various Jewish collections, including those of the Rothschilds, Seligman and Rosenberg.[516]

ALIU investigations also revealed that, in 1943, Göring was implicated in aspects of the Schloss affair, partly through his covert use of ERR's M-Aktion officials and Lohse. This had involved the confiscation of a Jewish collection ostensibly by French Vichy Government officials, and then sold in large part to Germans including for the Linz Museum. However, despite being kept 'in the loop' of all developments by Lohse, Göring eventually thought better of including any of the confiscated works in his own collection as he considered them: 'too hot to handle'.[517] Göring's reluctance to accept these looted artworks stemmed from the negative rumours associated with the way in which the confiscation process had been carried out. This had already been exposed as a German looting operation, which had been poorly camouflaged as an internal French affair.[518] Another factor was Göring's temporary shortage of sufficient ready cash.[519]

CIR 2 notes that Göring's actions in France combined a willingness to confiscate Jewish artistic works with a public display of reluctance to be associated with 'crude undisguised looting'.[520] Hence, *de facto* confiscations were disguised by: 'always managing to find a way of giving at least the appearance of honesty, by a token payment or promise thereof

---

[514] Ibid., 3.
[515] Ibid.
[516] CIR 2 (Göring), op. cit., 148; Nicholas, 1995 op. cit., 129.
[517] CIR 4 (Linz), op. cit., 33.
[518] DIR (Lohse), op. cit., 9.
[519] CIR 4 (Linz), op. cit., 30.
[520] CIR 2 (Göring), op. cit., 23.

to the confiscation authorities.'[521] This strategy of cloaking dishonesty with a veneer of legality explains why Göring and his agents refused any 'official' connection with the ERR. However, at the same time, they: 'nevertheless used them to the fullest extent possible. Göring backed their actions through his position as Reichsmarschall, as is shown by his order of 5 November 1945. (See Attachment 3).'[522]

Furthermore, CIR 4 noted that Göring benefited substantially from the confiscation of the Rothschild collections. In 1940, all four of the Rothschild family heirs were stripped of their French citizenship and—over the next year—suffered the loss of over 5000 pieces of their concealed artworks and other property.[523] Many of these items were sent to supplement Göring's already swollen art collection, with a comparatively small number, 53 paintings including Vermeer's *Astronomer* and Boucher's *Portrait of Madame Pompadour*, assigned on 8 February 1941 to Hitler's Linz Museum project.[524] With the exception of one or two objects, these artworks came entirely from the Rothschild and Seligmann collections, confiscated at the start of the German occupation of France.[525]

Göring sought out a Vermeer and was frustrated at loosing out on the Rothschild's *Astronomer* to the Linz Collection. Hence, he managed to secure from his agent, Alois Miedl, another Vermeer *Christ with the Woman taken in Adultery*. He only paid for this work by means of a forced exchange for a collection of vastly inferior works.[526] CIR 1 notes that although the formal position was that Jewish works confiscated by the

[521] Ibid., 24.

[522] Ibid.

[523] Feliciano, 1997 op. cit., 44–45.

[524] CIR 4 (Linz), op. cit., 59 noting, with considerable specific details of individual works of art, that: 'Of the large quantity of Jewish-owned works seized by the ERR in Paris, only 53 came to Linz. See Attachment 56.); cf. Feliciano, 1997 op. cit., 46–47; Nicholas, 1995 op. cit., 131. 'In Paris most of the works of art which were taken over by the ERR from the Rothschild and other Jewish collections were absorbed by Reichsmarschall Göring; but 53 items, specially selected by Posse and identified by Göring at the Jeu de Paume, were shipped to the Fuehrerbau in Munich and became an important addition to the Linz Museum. (See Attachment 56). According to Heinrich Hoffmann, two of these items... were to been reproduced in the special article on the Linz Museum.' CIR 4 (Linz), op. cit., 27, Attachment 56.

[525] The selection was made at the Jeu de Paume on 5 February 1941. Most of the artworks were packed in their original Rothschild cases, and the entire selection was send on Göring's personal train to Munich. Two large Bouchers and four tapestries from the Rothschild Collection could not be fitted on the train, and were later sent to Füssen. CIR 1 (ERR), op. cit., 23–24.

[526] CIR 2 (Göring), op. cit., 62.

ERR remained within the jurisdiction of Hitler's Linz Museum collection, it was Göring who managed to appropriate the lion's share of this loot. In short, largely through his agents, Göring engaged in a number of exchanges in which he received high value items, including a Rembrandt, in return for other artworks originally looted from the Paul Rosenberg collection, and a van Gogh previously owned by Miriam de Rothschild.[527]

CIR 2 provides additional details on Göring's direct and indirect complicity in this forced sale of a major Jewish collection in France,[528] which included Rembrant's *Two Philosophers*. It also recognises the: 'very favourable' nature of the price Göring paid: a point recognised even by Hofer.[529] More generally, Göring exploited the practice of creating a massive discrepancy between the ERR's appraisals of the value of confiscated Jewish works, and their true market value as estimated by Hofer.[530] This OSS report also reminds us that Miedl, who was involved in many of these transactions, had his own interest in currying favour with Göring: the need to protect his Jewish wife from persecution.[531] A deal Miedl brokered on Göring's behalf with the Goudstikker family had various anti-Semitic aspects in that a number of the paintings were co-owned by other Jews, who alone received no compensation for the loss of their shared interest in these works.[532]

ALIU officials also accused Göring of engaging, through his agent Bunjes,[533] in substantial looting of art camouflaged as 'cultural exchanges'

527 Ibid., Attachment 1, Hofer to Göring, 26 September 1941; cf. ibid., 168.

528 Assuming the firms in questions had not already been 'Ayranized'.

529 Ibid., 72.

530 Ibid., 137 noting 'striking' discrepancies here of up to 24 times: 'in other words, this 'degenerate' art had little value when it was being taken from the French but when he [Hofer] and Göring wanted to use the pictures for their own purposes, they multiplied the Paris appraisal by 20 times or more....it was interest rather than ideology which made Göring and Hofer insist on the low appraisals for the impressionists in the Jeu de Paume' Ibid., 138–39.

531 Ibid., 72. Plaut notes: 'Aloys Miedl, long-time friend of Göring and Heinrich Hoffmann, left Germany some time before the war because his wife was a Jewess. This stocky Bavarian was an ardent mountain climber. His other ruling passion was speculation, in everything from Rembrandts to Canadian timber. A shrewd financier, he negotiated the sale of the celebrated Goudstikker Collection of Amsterdam for Göring, and is even said to have tried at one time to purchase the island of Anticosti in the Gulf of St. Lawrence for a German syndicate. Miedl played a game of duplicity for many years, possibly to protect his family, more likely for personal gain. He is believed to be awaiting repatriation from Spain to Germany, whence he will doubtless be taken to Holland to answer serious charges by the Dutch government.' Plaut, 1946a op. cit.

532 CIR 2 (Göring) op. cit., 73.

533 For further details on Bunjes, see ibid., 20.

with French governmental officials. These 'exchanges' allowed Göring to secure a number of high value artworks from the Louvre. Amongst these works was *Renaud et Armide* by Coypel. This had originally been confiscated from the Jewish Seligman collection in Paris.[534] Hence, ALIU officials classified this so-called 'cultural exchange' as essentially a sham device to disguise the illegal seizure of art works from the major French National Gallery. Another forced sale in France concerned the Jewish Mannheimer collection, which Mühlmann secured largely for Göring's benefit.[535] ALIU officials uncovered other evidence of forced sales and exchanges with respect to the Wildenstein Collection in Paris. Its Jewish owners were forced, through the interventions and threats of Haberstock, to exchange other works they controlled in return for looted 'degenerate' modern works that the Nazis' otherwise sought to banish.[536]

The ALIU singled out the plundering of the Schloss collection of 333 paintings in 1943 as: 'Perhaps the best example of acquisition for the Linz Museum by forced sale.'[537] This involved the plunder of a major Jewish collection in the unoccupied zone of France, which was chiefly noted for signed and dated pictures by Dutch Masters. The element of coercion here involved the detention and arrest of different members of the Schloss family, a number of whom were seized whilst travelling to a funeral.[538] The Vichy government, led in this affair by Abel Bonnard and Louis Darquier de Pellepoix, collaborated with Göring and other leading Nazis to confiscate these paintings; and then transfer them to Paris for later liquidation.[539] The two governments created an involuntary sale of these artworks for a fraction of their market price, in which the Linz agents secured 262 works, the Louvre took 49 superior pieces 'at a stipulated price',[540] with a Vichy-appointed agent named Lefranc selling off the remainder.[541] In other words, the results of this plunder were largely divided between the Vichy government and agents for the Linz Museum. The Jewish family who owned the collection did not receive the amount they were promised. Although dressed up as a

[534] Ibid., 13–14.
[535] CIR 4 (Linz) Attachment 35A.
[536] OSS / Cooper Report, 20 September 1945 (cited in Nicholas 1995 op. cit., 159–60 and 453); Nuremberg document 015–PS.
[537] CIR 4 (Linz), op. cit., 29.
[538] DIR Lohse, op. cit.; CIR 4 (Linz) op. cit., 29–34.
[539] Ibid., 29–34; DIR Lohse, op. cit.
[540] CIR 4 (Linz), op. cit., 29, Attachment 26 (statement by Lohse).
[541] Petropolous, 1996 op. cit., 192.

forced sale, rather than an outright act of racist plunder, ALIU officials emphasised that ultimately:

> The Schloss family did not receive any payment for the paintings. The Vichy government never paid the 18,975,000 French francs it owed, and the 50,000,000 French francs paid by the Germans went into the fund of the organisation of Darquier de Pellepoix.... the degree of good faith attending the whole proceedings is well illustrated by the fate of the 21 (or 22) paintings which were not acquired either for the Louve or for Linz. By the original agreement [with the Schloss family] any left-overs were to revert to the owners. None was ever returned.[542]

According to the ALIU, this collaboration by French officials was: 'forced by German pressure on the Vichy government.'[543]

One ALIU report highlighted: 'a sensational discrepancy between estimated price and apparent value with respect to Schloss #39... this picture was listed by Catroux at only 100 francs.'[544] However, the same work was then sold on by Postma to a former Director of the Louvre for 300,000 francs. CIR 4 (Linz) indicates that these 262 paintings from the Schloss collection later constituted approximately half of Voss' total acquisitions for the Linz collection for 1943–1944.[545] With respect to Voss, it commented that: 'His most questionable activity still remains the purchase of the Schloss collection.'[546] The Schloss affair was later characterised by OSS officers as: 'the best example of acquisition for Linz by forced sale.'[547] Under interrogation, Göpel denied playing a central role in this aspect of the Holocaust. He maintained that his function was confined to merely cataloguing in oversized type Hitler's existing collection, and transferring negatives of the artworks to Hitler personally for his inspection.[548] This defensive claim was, however, later contradicted by Linz Museum director Hermann Voss who claimed: 'it was Göpel who came to know of the Schloss collection, which by some error had been brought to Paris, and he conceived the idea of acquiring it partly for Linz.'[549] Furthermore, after a number of these

542 CIR 4 (Linz), op. cit., 31, 33.
543 Ibid., 32.
544 Ibid., 31.
545 Ibid., 18.
546 Ibid.
547 Ibid., 29.
548 Ibid., 33.
549 Ibid., Attachment 27.

262 Schloss pictures were not considered of sufficient quality for the Linz museum, it was Göpel who purchased some of them.[550]

A number of OSS interrogations highlighted other strategic and geopolitical aspects of the Holocaust in France, which supplemented both crudely anti-Semitic motivations, and those founded on basic greed:

> In 1945, Dr Robert Scholtz, section head of Rosenberg's Amt Bildende Kunst stated under interrogation by James S. Plaut... that early in World War II a special commission had inventoried all objets d'art and cultural items removed from Germany by the French during World War I. Accordingly, the confiscations from France most certainly were intended as reparations payments for everything that Germany had lost to the French; seizure of Jewish property provided a good basis for this effort, and the 'antiGerman' sentiment of Jews and freemasons was a convenient excuse.[551]

Göring visited Paris about 20 times during the war. He was represented in this European centre for art by a predatory network headed by Hofer, Bornheim, Lohse and Angerer.[552] ALIU's analysis of captured records suggested that Göring removed 596 items of art from the ERR's Paris HQ in the period up to 20 October 1942.[553]

Not content with obtaining Jewish and other artworks looted by the ERR, he also intervened with other German confiscation authorities, such as the Germany Army's *Kunstschutz*. These officials soon came to recognise that Göring was a driving force behind the confiscation of Jewish works in France.[554] Indeed, even leading officials of this body who disapproved of art confiscations, such as Count Wolff-Metternich, eventually succumbed to Göring's pressure to assist his agents loot Jewish private collections. During the months immediately after the defeat of France, they did so by supplying secret police officials and former employees of Jewish dealers skilled in tracking down these hidden collections:

> Turner used the section for the confiscation of Jewish owned property, and collaborated with Göring in this connection.... When Hofer, Angerer and

[550] Ibid., 34.
[551] Willem de Vries, 'Sonderstab Musik: Music Confiscations by the Einsatzstab Reichsleiter Rosenberg under the Nazi Occupation of Western Europe', Amsterdam: Amsterdam University Press, 1996, 107.
[552] CIR 2 (Göring) op. cit., 34.
[553] Ibid., 24.
[554] Ibid.

> Fritz Schmidt came to Paris, Turner put at their disposal an agent of the French Sureté Generale (Secret Police) and Mlle. Lucie Botton... formerly an employee of Seligmann Brothers who guided them to repositories where Jewish collections were stored. During these visits, Göring's agents chose what they considered desirable, and the objects were later sent to the Jeu de Paume, where they were kept for the Reichsmarschall to see on his next visit to Paris.[555]

CIR 2 then provides an extensive list, derived from Hofer's interrogation, of the Jewish collections located in Paris that Göring subjected to this form of looting, including Bacri Freres, Graupe Jonas, and Wildenstein (located outside Paris).[556]

Göring also fully exploited the German-Belgium division of the Foreign Currency Authority of German Military Government's Finance Ministry, particularly the Franco-Belgium branch, to freeze or seize Jewish artworks stored in banks that came under this agency's authority. This was headed by Minister Michel, a friend of Göring:

> Michel instructed Staffeldt to place his facilities at the Reichsmarschall's disposition, and this was done in the following way: When the Devisenschutzkommando discovered an art collection in the vaults of one of its banks which came under their authority, and then advised Göring's stabsant. If one of Göring's agents happened to be in Paris at the time, he visited the collection in the Bank and indicate what he considered desireable for Göring. A record of this was made... and the objects chosen were later sent to the E.R.R. (Jeu de Paume) to await Göring's next visit.... Sometimes the collections were sent straight to the Jeu de Paume without a previous examination... [but] in the name of the Reichsmarschall.[557]

CIR 2 provides an extensive list of this form of looting, identifying the collections of Dr Wasermann, Soloman Flavian, Dr Erlanger, Issac Hamburger, Seligmann, Paul Rosenberg, Stern, Weiss, Dreyfus, Jacobson, Thierry (nee Rothschild), Sarah Rosenstein, Rothschild and Wilderstein in Paris as amongst the victims of this form of plunder.[558]

The ALIU final report, which has prompted a book on the Linz Collection once it was declassified in 1964,[559] included an extended

---

555 Ibid., 25.

556 Ibid.

557 Ibid., 26–27.

558 Ibid., 27, 148.

559 David Roxan, Ken Wanstall, *The Rape of Art: The Story of Hitler's Plunder of the*

bibliographical listing of French and German individuals, including French, Austrian and German Jews, alleged to have been involved in looting Jewish works of art in France. For instance, it records that M. Armilhon [partly illegible], Legal Head of the Vichy Government's Bureau of Claims of the Commission for Jewish Affairs, was: 'reportedly involved in the Schloss Collection affair.'[560] In addition, Alexander Ball is listed as a 'German-Jewish refugee dealer' who allegedly acted as an: 'intermediary for Haberstock in the sale of pictures from the unoccupied zone'. He was: 'Also believed to have informed on the whereabouts of prominent Jews, notably Guy de Rothschild. (See DIR 13).'[561] The entry for Herbert Engel lists him as: 'Austrian Jewish refugee dealer, son of Hugo Engel. Acted as agent in unoccupied France for Haberstock and his father...probably now in Switzerland.'[562] Hugo Engel's entry describes him as being an: 'Austrian Jewish dealer, active in France and Switzerland in official German interests. Close collaborator of Wendland and Loebel, and Haberstock's chief Paris agent. Associated in Switzerland with Max Glant...See CIR 4, DIRs 2, 6, 13'.[563] German Jews, including Goldschmidt, are also identified as art dealers who dealt with Fischer, Wendland, Haberstock and others central to the Nazi art confiscation processes.[564] The entry for Parisian Ali Loebel states that he is a:

> Dealer of Austro-Hungarian Jewish descent. Director and leading spirit of the firm Kleinberger & Co., "Aryanized" under the name of E. Garin during the war. Center of the informal art dealing syndicate comprising Wendland, Perdoux, Mandl, Boitel, Dequory, Engel. Sold chiefly to Lohse, Hofer and Haberstock, for whom he travelled as agent in unoccupied France...See CIRs 1, 2, 4, DIRs 6, 9, 19. Indicted by the French Government.[565]

It appears from the OSS Final Report that certain potential Jewish victims of the Holocaust decided that partial collaboration with the Nazi authorities responsible for art looting could help them survive the

---

Great Masterpieces of Europe, NY: Coward-McCann, 1965. Their preface strongly attacks the lack of declassification of other ALIU reports.

[560] Final Report, op. cit., 87.

[561] Ibid., 88.

[562] Ibid., 101.

[563] Ibid., 101. See also CIR 4 (Linz), op. cit., 67.

[564] Final Report, op. cit., 104. Fischerin Lucerne and C. W. Buemming in Darmstadt also worked in tandem. See CIR No. 4, op. cit., 48.

[565] Final Report, op. cit., 112.

evolving genocide. For example, Loebel's business partner and brother, Manon, is reported to have been: 'twice freed from concentration camps through the efforts of Lohse. See CIR 2, DIR 6.'[566]

CIR 4 contains other examples of German Jewish collaboration, in many cases following expectations or promises of protection for family members threatened with detention in concentration and death camps.[567] For example, following the interventions of Göpel, Dr Vitale Bloch, an Eastern European Jew who had dealt in art in Berlin and London, received protection from 'anti-Semitic laws' whilst he was resident in The Netherlands: 'in exchange he advised Goepel in his purchases for Linz and gave him first refusal on anything he found in the market. He is said to be Friedlander's most intimate friend. Between them they formed the centre of the collaborationist art world.... He was in contact with Hofer, Lohse and Mühlmann.'[568]

It appears, however, that even active collaboration by Jews in Nazi art looting operations against their co-religionists could not always protect them from extermination during the Holocaust. For example, the entry in the ALIU final report for Antoine Henri Mayer states that he was a:

> well known Jewish art expert and authority on Spanish painting. Consulted by Lohse, Wendland, Herbert Engel and others. Disappeared 1944. Believed murdered by the SS in the gas chambers. Used cover name Antoine for negotiations with the Germans. See CIR 4, DIR 13.[569]

CIR 2 (Göring) contains other similar examples of failed collaboration with Hofer by German Jewish refugees.[570]

Other non-Jews who, for a reward, allegedly betrayed their Jewish compatriots are also identified by the OSS' Final Report.[571] French persons who actively benefited from anti-Semitic confiscations of Jewish artworks, such as Roger Dequoy, are listed. So are their last

---

[566] Ibid.

[567] CIR 4 (Göring) 87 re Wetzlar who willingly cooperated with Mühlmann but 'cooled off after Mühlmann had been unsuccessful in liberating his daughter's fiancé from a concentration camp.' Ibid. See other similar entries for Kurt and Legat noting their desire to protect Jewish or half-Jewish family members as a key motivation for collaboration: ibid., 89.

[568] Ibid., 88.

[569] Final Report, op. cit., 114.

[570] CIR 2 (Göring), op. cit. 87 on 'Abt' who 'ended up in a concentration camp.'

[571] Final Report, op. cit., 126 entry Visconti.

known addresses.[572] This report also supplies details of French nationals, including Lucie Botton, who allegedly assisted the German authorities locate: 'the French repositories where Jewish collections were stored. Also believed to have dealt with Hofer. (See CIR 2).'[573] ALIU officials made similar allegations of active collaboration with the ERR concerning the looting of French Jews with respect to entries for Daber,[574] von Dinlage,[575] and Dubourg.[576]

Other references describe more ambiguous situations where individuals appear to have gained advantages from the outcome of anti-Semitic confiscations, which they did not necessarily engage in personally. For example, an entry on Benier, an assistant in the Jewish art firm located in Paris, states that he had taken over: 'the business in 1943 after Stora was forced to leave because of Jewish persecutions. Said to have been in constant touch with Stora after the latter's departure. Prior to 1943 Stora had worked with Angerer, Hofer and Bornheim. (See CIR 2).'[577]

The ALIU Final Report also identifies some of those individuals who took a more active role in the 'Aryanization' of Jewish collections. These included Charles Montag, a Swiss borne but naturalised French dealer and artist. This report claims he was:

> involved in the 'Aryanization' of the Bernheim Jeune and Wildenstein [partly illegible] firms.... instrumental in the sale of several looted pictures to Swiss clients. Former drawing master of Winston Churchill, and has professed Allied sentiments.[578]

Other entries record the details of Jeune Bernheim, a: 'well-known Jewish art firm whose collections were seized by the Germans. It is reported that two million French Francs, two Renoirs and a Cézanne were sent by Jean Bernheim to Switzerland in 1944 through the Japanese diplomatic pouch.'[579] Other listings describe who allegedly

---

[572] Ibid., Dequoy entry, ibid., 98. See also CIR 4 (Linz), op. cit., 32 which notes that this person had helped Haberstock and Destrem 'Aryanize' the Wildenstein firm' of which Dequoy then became the owner in 1941 to prevent its outright confiscation by the ERR.

[573] Final Report, op. cit., 93.

[574] Ibid., 98.

[575] Ibid., 99.

[576] Ibid., 100.

[577] Ibid., 90.

[578] Ibid., 116.

[579] Ibid., 90.

purchased looted Jewish works, including the Rosenberg Collection,[580] and identify individuals involved in contraband who had already been arrested. The Final Report also provides details of individuals, such as Mile Bosc, who allegedly: 'held pictures from Jewish collections sequestered by the Germans.'[581] For example, a Cypriot-borne but naturalised Frenchman, Petrides, who the ALIU classified as: 'one of the most active collaborationist dealers', was identified as a purchaser of: 'paintings looted by the ERR from the Paul Rosenberg collection, and which he later sold to Zervos.... (See CIR 1, DIR 4.)'[582] The report names others involved in the looting of this collection, including Renou Colle who were a: 'firm of art dealers who handled looted art, notably from the Paul Rosenberg Collection.'[583]

The OSS' Final Report also provides details of specific police and security force officials, such as Cloup, Jacquin, and Lienhardt[584] and others working for the ERR, such as Gobbert and Mann,[585] who allegedly played significant roles in the confiscations themselves, including with respect to the Schloss Collection.[586] As already noted, this Jewish collection, which ironically contained many of the Dutch and Flemish old masters that Hitler particularly valued,[587] was the object of investigation by both German and French collaborationist individuals and agencies.[588] The ALIU report suggests that Jean Lefranc was a 'leading collaborationist dealer' and: 'Vichy-appointed administrator of the Schloss collection, and personally responsible for its liquidation. See CIRs 2, 4, DIR 6.'[589] It also listed Darquier de Pellepoix, then based in Madrid, and formerly Vichy Commissioner for Jewish Affairs (1942–44) as: 'involved in confiscation of the Schloss Collection. See CIRs 1, 4.'[590]

580 Ibid., Bernier entry, 91.
581 Ibid., 92.
582 Ibid., 118.
583 Ibid., 120.
584 Ibid., 107, 111.
585 Ibid., 104, 113.
586 Ibid., 97.
587 Feliciano, 1997 op. cit., 44–45.
588 On Von Hummel's role in the Schloss affair, see CIR 4 (Linz), op. cit., 16.
589 Final Report, op. cit., 110. On the Schloss collection and Lefranc's role, see Feliciano, op. cit., ch. 8; and Final Report, op. cit., Postma entry, 119 for further details of a Dutch art dealer complicit in Lefranc's activities.
590 Ibid., 118.

A series of other more general OSS intelligence reports monitored the traffic in Gauguin's *Christ Jaune*, formerly in the Rosenberg collection at Paris, but then apparently moved to Geneva, Switzerland. These reports identify this Gauguin as a work that German forces, under the Chief of the 'Einsatzstab Reichsleiter Rosenberg' (ERR), Baron Kurt von Behr, looted from a collection in Bordeaux, France, and which Behr then exchanged with a German art dealer, Gustav Rochlitz. The OSS reports also noted that Gauguin's work had been rediscovered in Paris in September 1945.[591]

In short, and in pursuit of both strands of its prosecution and restitution objectives, ALIU officials conducted extensive and detailed investigations into the Nazis' systematic policy of art looting in France as an integral aspect of the Holocaust. On the basis of captured records, recovered art works and interrogation transcripts, they provided considerable details and examples of who the victims were, which works were looted and through which institutional mechanism.[592] The ALIU's Final Report identifies who was complicit in the looting process, and where the plundered works of art may still be located. They exposed massive collaboration by numerous French art dealers, and instances of greed, knowing deception and interpersonal betrayal, even by a small number of French and German Jews.

Investigating the Göring collection

It is worth addressing ALIU's analysis of Hermann Göring's role in some detail. He was the highest ranking Nazi on trial at the IMT; and was widely acknowledged as the leading figure amongst the Nuremberg defendants. Göring also faced considerable prosecution evidence concerning his complicity in art looting across Nazi-occupied Europe.[593] Yeide recognises that:

---

[591] OSS document 12414, July 1945 (Regular Intelligence Reports) cross-referenced to later OSS documents, XL-14045 and XL-16427: US NA, RG 226, Entry 16.

[592] CIR 4 (Linz), op. cit., 8.

[593] For German sources on Göring and art looting, see Gunther Haase, *Die Kunstsammlung des Reichsmarchalls Hermann Göring: Eine Documentation* Ed. Q, Berlin: 2000; Ilse Von Zur Mühlen, *Die Kunstsammlung Hermann Görings: Ein Provenienzbericht der Bayerischen Staatsgemaeldesammlungen*, edition q im Quintessenz Verlag; Auflage: 1 2000.

> Reichsmarschall Hermann Göring, second in command in Nazi Germany, was second only to Hitler in the acquisition of art by whatever means necessary. In fact, his collecting activities were even more passionate than those of Hitler, whose ultimate goal was the creation of the world's largest museum to glorify the German people. In contrast, Göring's motive was significantly more egotistic—his desire was his own glorification. Goring planned for his collection to become a museum, probably housed in his estate at Carinhall, on the occasion of his 60th birthday.[594]

Based on captured ERR records, CIR 2 records numerous artworks that ERR officials had released to Göring.[595] By 1945, Göring had acquired, mainly by confiscation from Jews and other 'enemies of the state', over one thousand new paintings. Indeed, fom the beginning, confiscated Jewish property was one of the main sources for Göring's collection. In 1945, ALIU officers calculated that Göring's art collection consisted of 1,375 paintings, 250 sculptures, and 168 tapestries.[596] Under the sub-heading 'Objects Acquired by Göring', CIR 1 provides details figures for this source:

> Approximately 700 objects from the Einsatzstab were selected for the GÖRING collection. Shipments of this material from Paris to Berlin took place on 8 February 1941, 15 March 1941, 3 May 1941, 15 August 1941, 2 December 1941, 14 March 1942, 15 May 1942, and 24 November 1942. The standard procedure for the selection of this material was that GÖRING would give eleventh hour notice of his intention to visit Paris and would go to the Jeu de Paume personally to make his selection from the material placed on exhibition there by the Einsatzstab staff. According to SCHOLZ, LOHSE and SCHIEDLAUSKY, he was accompanied on all but one or two occasions by HOFER, to whom he deferred invariably in the matter of choice. In most instances, the material selected was packed in the Jeu de Paume and taken out at once to the GÖRING special train, as it was stated that the Reichsmarschall wished whenever possible to have his acquisitions accompany him back to Germany.[597]

---

[594] Yeide, 2007, op. cit. 3.
[595] CIR 2, op. cit., Attachment 5.
[596] Ibid., 174.
[597] CIR 1 (ERR), op. cit., 23. Petropoulos notes that although Göring relied to some extent on his agents and representatives to select works of art from the ERR, he was personally involved in selecting the bulk of material that his collection derived from this source: 'Göring employed a hands-on method of collecting—even when the items involved were tainted by their having been obtained by force. His twenty visits to the Jeu de Paume between November 1940 and November 1942, where he inspected the booty taken in by the ERR and removed at least 594 pieces for his own collection, are a prime example of him not shying away from potentially embarrassing situations.' Petropoulos, *Art as Politics*, 1996, 190 based on CIR 2 (Göring), op. cit., 157.

Plaut notes that approximately 50 percent of the Göring collection consisted of works of art from 'enemies of the Reich', that is mainly Jewish collections, and that sources outside of France also made an extensive contribution.[598]

Aside from Hofer, the ALIU report on Göring's art acquisitions identified eight individuals as "purchasing agents": Sepp Angerer, (an art merchant who traded 'degenerate art' abroad); Walter Bornheim, (an art dealer based in Munich); Kajetan Mühlmann, (who scoured Poland and the Netherlands for works to Göring's taste);[599] Bruno Lohse, (a Berlin art dealer who Göring drafted into the Luftwaffe as a liaison to the ERR in Paris); Alois Miedl, (an art dealer based in the Netherlands who sold artworks to both Hitler and Göring); Gottlieb Reber, (a German living in Lucerne, Switzerland who purchased works in Italy);[600] Hermann Bunjes, (the Paris-based ERR official); and Kurt von Behr, (the Chief of the main ERR commando in France and probably Göring's main connection to this plundering organisation.)[601]

The preparation of the case against Göring was initially entrusted to OSS staff as a 'dry run' to test how well the prosecution's case would work in a particularly high profile case. This meant that OSS staff involved in trial preparation had to give high priority to the task of gathering evidence of this defendant's war crimes, including of course his complicity in art looting. Indeed, the X-2 progress report for June 1945 noted: 'Other activities of the War Room include the study and dissemination of materials from captured documents of varying importance. Of particular value to the Art Unit has been the register of Göring's art transactions.'[602] The Roberts Commission report contains additional details of the range and type of sources, including

[598] 'Einsatzstab Rosenberg was but one of the many channels of illicit acquisition used by Göring. Other loot entered Carinhall from Italy and Poland, through the offices of the SS and the Wehrmacht; from France, through the German Embassy and the Military High Command; and from Belgium and Holland, through the freezing of 'enemy assets' by the Foreign Currency Control Administration. As nearly as can be estimated, approximately 50 per cent of the objects which made up the Göring Collection were acquired through purchase or forced sale. The remainder was outright loot.' Plaut, 1946a op. cit.

[599] He had made early contacts with Göring's family during the mid-1930's, including visits to Göring's family home. Petropoulos, 1996b op. cit., 181.

[600] CIR 2 (Göring), op. cit., 20.

[601] CIR 2 (Göring), op. cit., 174. DIR 4 (Linz), op. cit., and DIR Hans Wendland, op. cit.

[602] X-2 Progress Report, June 1945: US NA, RG 226, Entry 99, Box 120, Folder 1.

both interrogation transcripts and original administrative records, which ALIU sought and obtained in preparing their investigation into Göring's art plundering:

> In preparation for documenting the history of Göring's international art dealings, careful investigations were made of the various trains in and near Berchtesgaden, and a large baggage car was found on a siding strewn with books and papers. Hofer,... stated that there were 200 cases belonging to Göring and him when the car left Veldenstein. Germans, displaced persons, and Allied soldiers had apparently ransacked and looted it, some papers being burned. The remainder was collected, taken to Munich, and a large part of it was loaned temporarily to the Art Looting Investigation Unit of the Office of Strategic Services. This Unit assembled a large collection of documents dating back to 1940, interrogated dozens of persons connected with the wide ramifications of the artistic activity of the Marshal and, as a result of these studies, prepared a detailed report on the expansion of a collection that contained, by the time of his downfall, about 1,375 paintings, 250 sculptures, 108 tapestries, 2,000 pieces of period furniture, 60 Persian and French rugs, 75 stained glass windows, and 175 objets d'art.[603]

As German political and military success expanded the territorial scope of the Nazi regime, Göring sought—often in competition with the German Army and diplomats—to build up a world class art collection ultimately to be devoted to the German nation at 'Carinhall', his large hunting lodge.[604] Plaut has graphically summarised the overblown grandeur of Göring's ambitions and the pseudo-imperial vision of this collection:

> Photographs of Carinhall, his fabled estate laid waste in the Russian advance northeast of Berlin, point up dramatically the aspirations of the Number Two Nazi. A gigantic, rambling structure compounded of ponderous stone and concrete, Carinhall was a strange fusion of the most flamboyant elements of the storied past with the inflated sterility of official Nazi architecture. Set down with a fine sense of isolation in the midst of a rich hunting preserve, it was destined, for a brief moment in history, to project with forceful grandeur the pose its master so studiously cultivated, of Reichsmarschall Göring, feudal seigneur, peerless huntsman, and enlightened patron of the arts. A seemingly endless series of great rooms—salons, dining halls, studies, and libraries—held, until the Allied bombings threatened them, the spectacular booty of a continent, installed always with more theater than taste, yet breathtaking in its innate richness and its scope. Here were the Cranachs and Titians, the massive plate,

[603] Roberts Commission Report, 1946 op. cit., 140.

[604] Feliciano, 1997 op. cit., 32–33.

> and the Gobelin tapestries brought in from France and Italy on a scale worthy of the great despot. Here, too, were the abominations of taste, the nineteenth century's overpowering, fleshy nudes, the "strength through joy" figures of Nazi sculptors, the empty furnishings of the Third Reich. And here were the rich birthday offerings, the coveted sixteenth-century German paintings purchased by Göring's agents with funds contributed by Nazi industrialists in return for favors rendered. Showplace of the Reich, Carinhall *was* Göring, his sanctuary and his shrine, the perfect meeting ground of Rubens and the stuffed bull moose. Wearing the new crown of empire and with the spoils of Europe as its necklace, Carinhall would emerge after the German victory as a national shrine without parallel. Göring had even planned, with the Führer's consent, to build a special railway connecting the estate with Berlin, so that it might become the foremost Mecca for tourists in the Reich.[605]

During his interrogations at Nuremberg, the records of which formed part of General Donovan's collection of documents, Göring defended his acquisition of art objects as involving unproblematic purchases either by private transaction, or through auction via the many art dealers with whom he did business. He maintained that his ultimate aim was to put these artworks stored at Carinhall in a public gallery open to the German people. Until such a gallery could be established, he assumed the role of custodian of this art collection.[606]

OSS reports also note that Göring had exploited a large-scale network of well-connected and, in some cases, aristocratic individuals to procure looted and other artworks, including valuable items of jewellery confiscated from the Rothschild families.[607] This means of obtaining artworks even exploited and abused diplomatic privileges, such as sealed diplomatic pouches,[608] in order to transfer works of art.[609]

Plaut's immediate postwar account of his investigative work as the Chief of the ALIU devotes considerable attention to Göring's questionable strategies for acquiring works of art. It notes his key role located at the centre of a web of agents and dealers engaged in a concerted and systematic process of cultural plundering across Nazi-occupied Europe, and also records the negative impact of their activities:

> Göring himself was a passionate and active collector. The evidence of his preoccupation throughout the war years with the formation of the

---

[605] Plaut, 1946(a) op. cit.
[606] Donovan Collection, Vol. 14, subdivision 35.
[607] CIR 2 (Göring), op. cit. 152.
[608] Ibid., 135.
[609] Ibid., op. cit., 97. Göring employed Ambassador Mackensen to arrange this subterfuge.

> Göring Collection, even at times when the very destiny of Germany was being shaped by his thinking, is astounding.... Göring was the heart of German looting and its inspiration. Without his strength, his zeal, and his formidable backing, not a single one of the German organizations formed to carry out the prodigious task could have accomplished its mission.... Göring 's lawyer at Nuremberg called him a Renaissance man, failing to mention that he wished to be one but never quite measured up. Because the Reichsmarschall was obsessed with the desire to become a latter-day Medici, the artistic domain of Europe became, of necessity, his playground.... The Allied investigations of German looting, proceeding from diverse points of view and in many directions, always happened, sooner or later, upon a common denominator: the intimate relationship of Göring to the problem. It became increasingly apparent that his tentacles stretched across Europe—east to Poland in the person of his agent, Mühlmann; south to Switzerland and Italy, where Hofer, "Curator of Carinhall," and Angerer, dealer in tapestries and member of the German Intelligence, were tirelessly active on his behalf; west to France and Holland, where these men were joined by a host of others working directly or indirectly to swell the amazing body of the Reichsmarschall's loot.... Göring left his ugly mark on European culture by the ruthless pursuit of foreign treasure to adorn a monstrous vanity.[610]

In keeping with his grand ambitions, Göring had allocated considerable financial resources to his art fund. This maintained an average monetary balance of two million Reichsmarks to cover the expenses of both acquiring and maintaining his personal art collection.[611]

Göring was second only to Hitler in the scope and extent of his looting of Jewish works of art. Although Göring's collecting was dramatic and personal, Hitler's acquisitions benefited from being an official government project organised through a high-powered 'Special Linz Commission.' Göring controlled less agents than those employed by the Linz Museum, who also enjoyed unlimited funds. In the event of any obvious conflict, Hitler's interests generally prevailed as Göring tended to withdraw from negotiations if Linz interests were directly engaged. One example was Memling's *Portrait of a Man*, owned by Prince Corsini of Florence. In this case, Hofer deferred to Prince Philipp of Hessen, an agent for Linz, who bought it for between five and six million lire.[612] Göring also made a number of 'gifts' to Linz to

[610] Plaut, 'Loot For The Master Race', *The Atlantic*, Sept. 1946, Vol. 178 No. 9 (hereafter Plaut 1946a).

[611] CIR 2 (Göring) op. cit., 8.

[612] Plaut, 1946b op. cit.

curry favour from Hitler, including: 'a personal selection of 53 masterpieces confiscated from the Rothschild Collections in Paris.'[613] However, Göring reluctantly deferred to Hitler when there seemed little alternative in practice. He recognised that certain high profile pieces, such as a Vermeer's *Astronomer*, which he could have taken for Carinhall, was better left for Hitler's Linz Museum. Indeed, although Göring issued orders that contained specific subcategories recognising Hitler's priority in principle, in practice, a 'finders keepers' practice generally prevailed.[614]

The Linz CIR noted the complicity of Göring in providing all manner of assistance to the ERR's anti-Semitic plunder of Jewish-owned art in France:

> Reichsmarschall Göring, active on behalf of his own collection for Carinhall, classified seized Jewish works destined for Germany in an order dated 5 November 1940. (See Attachment 7). These works over which the Fuehrer reserved the right to decide disposition came first; those desired for enlargement of Göring's own collection came second; and those destined for Party purposes follow in due course.... in fact, acquisitions in Paris for the Fuehrer collection played second fiddle to Göring's activities...[615]

Under the heading, Göring's connection with Linz, one ALIU report stated:

> The Reichsmarschall's connection was chiefly as a competitor, but not entirely so. He made a few birthday gifts of works of art to the Fuehrer. In February 1941, he earmarked 53 confiscated works for Linz at the ERR in Paris. (See Attachment 56).... From later correspondence... it transpires that three of the pictures designated for Linz went to Carinhall instead. (See Reference A, Attachments 12 and 13).[616]

Göring's art looting was connected to Nazi military aggression, not least through his sponsorship of others, including Mühlmann. The latter organised both the process and the institutional outcomes of particularly brutal programmes of confiscation across German-occupied Europe. Indeed, Petropolous notes:

> With the German's success in the Polish campaign in September 1939, Göring found himself in a position to offer Mühlmann a post in the

[613] Ibid.

[614] CIR 2 (Göring), op. cit.; cf. Nicholas, 1995 op. cit., 127–29 for a more extensive summary.

[615] CIR 4 (Linz), op. cit., 7.

[616] Ibid., 8.

> occupation administration. Göring testified at Nuremberg that Mühlmann had approached him with a request to confiscate art, in which case, this represents a startling case of a policy initiative coming from a secondary leader.[617]

On 6 October 1939, Göring appointed Mühlmann as his special agent for securing artistic treasures in Poland, granting him wide ranging powers to confiscate Jewish property. Mühlmann was responsible: 'for forming a cadre of agents to locate, transport and catalogue the artworks in Poland.'[618] Petropoulos recognises how he later extended the techniques of plunder tested out in Poland to other parts of Europe:

> as usual Mühlmann adapted to his surroundings, and just as he had created brutal looting commandos in Poland, he was able with equal ease to establish a type of art dealership for processing plunder from departed Jews and other enemies.... Mühlmann's operation became a relatively sophisticated operation: with Headquarters in the Hague...he eventually opened branches in Amsterdam, Brussels, Paris, Berlin, and Vienna. Because his agency received works from different branches of the Nazi Bureaucracy—the SD and the Reichskommissariat for Enemy Property stand out as the two key sources—it in many ways resembled a clearing house. Records show that the *Dienststelle* Mühlmann sold at least 1,114 artworks during the war. Such apparent niceties could not conceal the essence of Mühlmann's project, which was to expropriate the artistic property of Jews and other enemies of the regime, and to ensure that the booty flowed in an orderly manner to the top Nazi leaders.[619]

Petropoulos also notes that 'Mühlmann and his staff had worked very expeditiously in Poland—he reported to Hitler that: 'within six months almost the entire artistic property of the land was seized.'[620] One part of Mühlmann's written Nuremberg trial evidence was presented to the court on 19 November 1945. It confirmed that Hans Frank's policy was to loot and send back to Germany 'all important artworks' from private and public collections in Poland: 'for the completion of German art holdings' (see Appendix 3 below).

From the autumn of 1940, Göring effectively gained control of the actions of the ERR officials, at least with respect to artworks that

---

[617] Petropoulos, 1996b op. cit., 191. On the trial evidence given on 14 March 1946, see IMT 11, 352 and Nuremberg document PS-2219 discussed in more detail in Appendix 2 below.
[618] Petropoulos, 1996b op. cit., 191.
[619] Ibid., 198.
[620] Ibid., 196.

he was particularly interested in acquiring for this own collection.[621] Göring then relied heavily upon his direct personal authority over Kurt von Behr, the ERR's Director of French operations, the advice of art historian and Deputy Director of the ERR, Dr Bruno Lohse, and the activities of his agent and the curator of Carinhall, Walter Hofer.[622] In France, Walter Bornheim, an art dealer and Director of a Munich Art Gallery, was also highly active on Göring's behalf and 'under his special protection.'[623]

In November 1940, Göring extended, by his own decree, the jurisdiction of the ERR over Jewish works of art into the occupied zone of France, works that were officially declared as 'ownerless'.[624] ALIU reports revealed that even this highly permissive precondition for seizures of such works was flouted in practice: 'Lohse stated that to the best of his belief, no seizure was ever effected by the ERR unless the owner had actually fled; but he admitted that this principle was not applied in the indiscriminate confiscations undertaken by von Behr and the Dienststelle Westen in the course of the M-Action.'[625] Plaut's immediate postwar articles also emphasised the point that, partly but not exclusively by means of this decree, Göring succeeded in usurping the ERR from its original leadership and moulding its role to his own different purposes. He achieved this without ever needing to wrest formal control of the ERR away from Rosenberg, who therefore retained the various organisational problems whilst Göring creamed off a mass of artworks for his personal collection:

> The presence of the Rosenberg group in France appears to have suggested to Göring the means of formalizing the confiscation of art treasures which the other German agencies then engaged in this activity considered both distasteful and somewhat out of their line. In any case, a Göring order of November 5, 1940, issued in Paris, extended the authority of the Einsatzstab Rosenberg to include the "safeguarding of ownerless Jewish collections" and, indeed, altered the emphasis of the entire Rosenberg mission so as to make such undertakings its primary function. It is indicative of Göring's power that he could issue a directive affecting vitally the operations of an organization over which he had no formal administrative control.[626]

---

621 Feliciano, 1997 op. cit., 4–5, 33, 36.
622 Ibid., 36.
623 CIR 2 (Göring), 2.
624 Feliciano, 1997 op. cit., 40.
625 DIR No. 6 (Lohse) op. cit., 5.
626 Plaut, 1946a op. cit.

As Feliciano recognises: 'It was under Göring's control that the ERR undertook its largest confiscations of works of art from the most renowned Jewish collections.'[627] Petropoulos, summarising a CIR report, notes:

> Göring quickly co-opted the plundering agency for his own purposes, as he directed some seven hundred paintings from the Jeu de Paume depot to his collection at Carinhall near Berlin. These manoeuvres were not entirely secret, as he made twenty trips to the Jeu de Paume between 3 November 1940 and 27 November 1942 to select the works he desired. Yet his refusal to make payment, despite promises to the contrary, and other acts of subterfuge (such as removing works before they could be inventoried) were the result of his surreptitious co-optation of ERR staff members—most notably von Behr, Utikal, and art historian Bruno Lohse.[628]

CIR 1 (ERR) indicates that Göring's control over aspects of the ERR's activities in France during late 1941 caused a degree of tension with Rosenberg. The latter sought, on occasions, to both investigate and counteract the Reichsmarschall's efforts through the interventions of his assistant Scholz. Such tensions led Bormann to intervene against both Rosenberg and Scholz, and confirm that it was Hans Posse who had prior claims and priority on behalf of Hitler's Linz Museum.[629] Göring's power over the ERR, and hence access to looted Jewish artworks stored in the Jeu de Paume, was unsuccessfully challenged in the Spring of 1941. Rosenberg sent Scholz to block a proposed transportation of artworks to the Göring Collection. In turn, the failure of Rosenberg's attempted challenge of Göring's dominant role presumably served to consolidate the Reichsmarschall's authority over the ERR even further.[630]

---

627 Ibid., 40.

628 Petropolous, 2000 op. cit., 131–32 citing ALIU's CIR 1, op. cit., 15.

629 CIR 1, op. cit., Attachment 4; CIR 4 (Linz) op. cit., Attachments 56A and 56B; cf. Nicholas, 1995 op. cit., 130. OSS maintained a biographical record on Hans Posse dated 29 May 1945 which Donovan included in his Nuremberg files: Cornell Collection, Vol. 17 Subdivision 53 'Others Investigated or Interrogated'.

630 'Immediately after BUNJES' visit, ROSENBERG dispatched SCHOLZ to Paris, in an attempt to block another large transfer of Einsatzstab material by GÖRING to Germany. SCHOLZ arrived in Paris, and was informed by von BEHR that the works in question were being placed in two freight cars attached to GÖRING's special train. When SCHOLZ remonstrated with UTIKAL and von BEHR over the irregularity of this procedure, he was told bluntly that nothing could be done to stop the GÖRING transfer as it was in fact already taking place. Early in 1941, GÖRING selected Dr. Bruno LOHSE, one of the art historians attached to the Paris *Dienststelle* of the Einsatzstab, as his personal representative. The arrangement was made with von BEHR's

Plaut also confirms that Göring's 'abuse' of the ERR staff, particularly von Behr, for personal gain was internally contested between Schloss[631] and von Behr, and that such conflict proved key to the future development and operations of this plundering body:

> The personal and ideological conflict between the two men was the dominant element in the internal relations of the Einsatzstab.... The two delivered a report to Rosenberg in August 1942 that stressed the chaotic conditions under which the professional art historians, through lack of adequate personnel and constant friction with von Behr, had been obliged to report....von Behr was ousted from his position at the head of the art staff in Paris early in 1943, and Scholz took the dominant role in the professional guidance of the staff, von Ingram assuming the primary responsibility for its administration.[632]

For reasons that we have already amply illustrated, Plaut's CIR 1 on the ERR devotes an entire section to the theme of 'the Göring relationship'. This focus is vital because of the characteristic contradiction between formal administrative responsibilities in principle, and Göring's real control through his 'personal sponsorship' and direction of key ERR staff, which Rosenberg was unable to successfully resist. For the purposes of the present section, Plaut's report on the sources of Rosenberg's *de facto* subordination to Göring, including ERR's lack of the required logistical support, merits extensive citation:

> It is of the utmost significance that, whereas the confiscations of the Einsatzstab in France were conducted under authority vested in the Rosenberg office by the Reichschancellery (HITLER), the important

approval, and LOHSE continued to work with the *Arbeitsgruppe Louvre*, but was accorded independent status for the *Sonderauftrag Göring* (Special GÖRING Mission). LOHSE was given credentials signed by GÖRING which ordered all German military and civil units to facilitate his mission. Within the Einsatzstab, he was given the responsibility, with SCHIEDLAUKSY, of arranging exhibitions of confiscated works of art which he thought GÖRING might wish to acquire for himself.... SCHIEDLAUSKY stated that from November 1940 through December 1941 he had been obliged to arrange ten exhibitions for GÖRING, and that these exhibitions took place on the following dates:

3 November	1940	1 May	1941
5 '	1940	3 May	1941
5 February	1941	13 August	1941
11 March	1941	15 '	1941
14 '	'1941	4 December	1941' Ibid., 7.

[631] For Scholz's nephew, who had the same last name, see DIR No. 10: Karl Kress op. cit., (15 August 1945), 2.

[632] DIR 3 (Scholz), op. cit., 2.

> operations were dominated by GÖRING. The function of the Einsatzstab on GÖRING's behalf was in formal contradiction to the HITLER order of 18 November 1940; but GÖRING, through personal sponsorship of the project, contrived to exploit its activity in his own interest from 1940 through 1942. First, ROSENBERG, while he felt constrained to carry out the HITLER order literally, was not strong enough politically to oppose GÖRING on even terms. Second, GÖRING's command of the Luftwaffe enabled him to supply the Einsatzstab with much-needed motor transport, military escort personnel and such operational perquisites as the organization was unable to obtain from other sources. Early in December 1940,...SCHOLZ was sent to Paris in order to determine the extent of GÖRING's interest in the Einsatzstab and the effect of such interest on the activity of the Paris staff. On arrival, SCHOLZ was told by EBERT and von BEHR that GÖRING had received HITLER's permission to examine the collections already confiscated, and to decide what should be done with them. SCHOLZ received the impression that EBERT and von BEHR were working entirely in GÖRING's interest, and that GÖRING, who had already visited Paris, had begun to select confiscated works of art for his own collection.[633]

CIR 1 provided additional factual details of the extent of Göring's involvement with the ERR, including the frequency of his visits to its Paris HQ to acquire new works. It also notes 'Göring's domination' of this body and its leadership, which emphasised that the latter treated Göring, rather than Rosenberg, as their most powerful chief. This material is important to establish Göring's personal culpability for the ERR's central role in the plundering aspect of the Holocaust, whilst reducing the culpability of his fellow Nuremberg defendant Rosenberg:

> GÖRING's domination of the Einsatzstab is most clearly indicated by the fact that, on numerous occasions, von BEHR received word that GÖRING would be in Paris within forty-eight hours, and wished to have shown to him the most recently confiscated material. At such times, von BEHR would put his entire staff to work to arrange a special exhibition in the Musee du Jeu de Paume of newly acquired collections, always with emphasis on those objects which it was believed GÖRING would wish to take for himself. GÖRING is known to have visited the Jeu de Paume on the following dates:

3 and 5 November	1940	13 and 15 August	1941
5 February	1941	2, 3 and 4 December	1941
3, 11 and 14 March	1941	25 February	1942
7 April	1941	14 March	1942

[633] CIR 1 (ERR), op. cit., 5–6.

1 and 3 May	1941	14 May	1942
9 July	1941	24 and 27 November	1942

The extent of his interest is manifest in these figures.[634]

DIR 5 also provides additional details of which particular Jewish collections ERR officials, such as Schiedlausky, were expected to put on display during these private exhibitions arranged for Göring's benefit.[635]

Indeed, CIR 1's account of Rosenberg portrays him as a weak figure and indecisive figure compared with Göring, lacking access to the centre of power. He lacked any real control over the anti-Semitic organisation that bore his name, and certainly was either unable or unwilling to benefit personally from its looting activities. Under the heading of 'E.R.R. Personnel Active in France', the ALIU downplayed the role of one Nuremberg defendant, Rosenberg, in a manner that was designed to place even greater emphasis upon both the extent and depth of Göring's complicity:

> *Reichsleiter Alfred ROSENBERG.* As HITLER's Deputy for the Supervision of the Total Spiritual and Political Indoctrination and Education of the NSDAP, he was directly responsible for all activity of the Einsatzstab. In addition, his function as Reichsminister for the Occupied Territories of the East was used as authority for the conduct of the nefarious *M-Action*, which was allied to, although administratively separate from, the E.R.R. SCHOLTZ and LOHSE both described ROSENBERG as the kind of man who was always strongly influenced by the last person to see him, and as a man without political strength or political courage. SCHOLZ stated that ROSENBERG deplored personally the necessity for undertaking the Einsatzstab mission, except insofar as the results of such activity could be made felt in the dissemination of National Socialist cultural propaganda. He resented GÖRING's domination of the Einsatzstab, but did nothing to counteract it. ROSENBERG was stated also to have been influenced unduly by forceful personalities within his organisation. Thus, whereas SCHOLZ was closest to him professionally, von BEHR and UTIKAL were able to act with virtual independence because of their personal influence upon him.[636]

In this report, Plaut contrasted Rosenberg's formal responsibilities with his *de facto* role for the Nazis' looting of Jewish art collections. He suggested that, in this respect at least, von Behr and Utikal, who

[634] Ibid., 9.
[635] DIR 5 (Schiedlausky) op. cit., 2, discussing the confiscated Jewish Seligmann Collection.
[636] CIR 1 (ERR), op. cit., 46.

exploited Göring's patronage, were at least as culpable for this aspect of the Holocaust as their administrative chief:

> ROSENBERG's position in the Party hierarchy was well below the level of GÖRING, GOEBBELS, RIBBENTROP, HIMMLER and BORMANN during the war years...This fact contributed to the lack of standing of the Einsatzstab in the Reichschancellery, and made it imperative for the organisation to accept GÖRING's offers of personnel, transport, etc., in order that it might conduct its affairs with some degree of efficiency. Both SCHOLZ and LOHSE have affirmed that ROSENBERG acquired no works of art through the Einsatzstab confiscations, nor did he seek personal financial profit therefrom. LOHSE stated that ROSENBERG visited the E.R.R. in Paris on only two occasions. The Einsatzstab was a constant source of irritation to him, and on more than one occasion he was heard to say, "Don't ever mention the word "Einsatzstab" to me again."[637]

Plaut's postwar account confirms and extends these points. He notes that Rosenberg lacked political stature in the Nazi Party hierarchy sufficient to procure the trained personnel, transportation, and other elements essential to the effective implementation of the confiscation program, particularly in the light of the heavy concurrent demands of the combatant military and the forces of occupation. He was also handicapped seriously by: 'the disdain of the High Command and its unwillingness to cooperate with his agency in the planning and execution of the depredations'. Another source of problems was Rosenberg's bitter personal feud with Martin Bormann that blocked access to Hitler during any crisis.

Plaut also noted that von Behr appealed 'out of channels' to Göring. The latter: 'responded handsomely in his capacity as commander of the

[637] Ibid. Plaut reiterated many of these points in his postwar articles: 'Reichsleiter Alfred Rosenberg was in no position to carry out the Göring directive.... Most important, Rosenberg himself was not keen on the confiscations. He regarded the Einsatzstab as a bastard offspring and its program as incompatible with the aims of the Party bureau for National Socialist political indoctrination (the *Amt Rosenberg*). In his view, the Rosenberg office was not simply a headquarters for raiding parties. Several of his deputies emphasized, under interrogation, that Rosenberg chafed at the problems attendant to the looting operations, that he had no interest in art and sought no personal gain from the seizures. Without support from Berlin, the Einsatzstab was virtually paralysed. Without experts to separate the wheat from the chaff and without the means to ship the loot to Germany, the 'safeguardings' would have become an empty, and politically dangerous, gesture.... It is not remarkable that Göring was unopposed in his selection of the choicest confiscated items, despite the Hitler order prescribing retention of all material pending the Führer's decision as to disposal.' 1946a, op. cit.

Luftwaffe, ordering art historians in the German Air Force transferred to duty in Paris, supplying shippers, photographers, packers, and drivers from the ranks, and putting Luftwaffe motor transport, freight cars, even special cargo planes, at von Behr's disposal.'

Plaut concludes that, 'from top to bottom the Einsatzstab became a Göring show under the Rosenberg flag.'[638] Plaut also highlights that Göring's frequent visits to the ERR's HQ were not distracted by his wartime responsibilities as deputy head of state and chief of the Luftwaffe. He argues that the senior ERR staffs' deference to Göring, particularly that of von Behr, was more than symbolic. It extended to allowing this Nazi leader to have the pick of artworks confiscated from Jewish collections, even though this was, in one sense, a violation of the original mission of this organisation to 'safeguard' such works:

> Whenever he visited Paris during the occupation, the notorious Baron Kurt von Behr, director of the Einsatzstab Rosenberg Paris office, would receive word forty-eight hours in advance that the Reichsmarschall intended to make a visit. By the time Göring arrived, a special exhibition of selected works of art, recently confiscated by the Einsatzstab from French collections, would have been arranged at the Musée du Jeu de Paume by von Behr's minions. Between November, 1940, and January, 1943, Göring visited the Jeu de Paume, for the express purpose of choosing new loot for Carinhall, no fewer than twenty-one times; he was there a week before the bombing of Coventry, three days before Pearl Harbor, and two weeks after the landings in Africa! Following conferences of state at the Quai d'Orsay, he would summon Hofer or Lohse, his younger purchasing agent who doubled as deputy director of the Einsatzstab. Then the procession of "eligible" works for purchase would begin, and would often consume most of the day, for, after looking at the pictures brought in, he would frequently go out to visit the shops of dealers whom he favored.[639]

Plaut's ALIU report also suggests that Göring's power was delegated to his personal representatives, such as Bunjes and then later to Dr. Bruno Lohse:

> GÖRING was seldom opposed in his choice of Einsatzstab material for his own collection. It has been learned from several sources that POSSE was reluctant to implement HITLER's order giving him full authority over the disposal of the confiscated collections. As POSSE had unlimited funds for purchase, he did not wish to be burdened with the responsibility

[638] Plaut, 1946a op. cit.
[639] Ibid.

> for such material. In addition, he was a sick man and came infrequently to Paris. At the outset, GÖRING had no personal representative in the Einsatzstab. All sources are agreed that von BEHR acted wholeheartedly in GÖRING's interest, so as to ingratiate himself with the Reichsmarschall and to secure his own position. Also, it has been established that Dr. BUNJES, never a member of the Einsatzstab, but present in Paris as Director of the German Art Historical Institute, acted initially as an advisor to GÖRING. In March 1941, BUNJES came to Berlin, bringing with him a large portfolio containing photographs of Einsatzstab material which he wished to present for GÖRING's approval. BUNJES met with ROSENBERG and UTIKAL to discuss the availability of such items for GÖRING.[640]

The measure of Göring's *de facto* power was further shown by his ability to both postpone the removal of von Behr from his overall responsibility for artworks until December 1943, and—in the meantime—defy the express orders of Rosenberg, the nominal chief of the ERR:

> It was stated that he had managed to prolong his activity with the art staff by asking GÖRING, on the occasion of the latter's periodic visits to Paris, to legitimatize his activity temporarily; and that this went on for some months. It was also stated that during this interim period of reorganization the art staff of the Einsatzstab continued to function as heretofore, and that GÖRING remained unopposed in his efforts to exploit confiscated material.... On 18 June 1942, ROSENBERG wrote GÖRING to the effect that it would no longer be possible for the Einsatzstab to make available works of art for GÖRING's personal selection. ROSENBERG emphasised that he was grateful both for the personal support which GÖRING had given the undertaking, and for his material assistance in having supplied transport and personnel. He stated that the professional art historians employed by the Einsatzstab would remain at GÖRING's disposal for all questions of consultation and advice, and that it would be entirely in order for GÖRING to retain LOHSE and his assistants for "special duties" (ATTACHMENT 8). In spite of ROSENBERG's letter, von BEHR continued to provide GÖRING with confiscated works of art, and the terms of the letter did not take effect until von BEHR's final removal six months later.[641]

CIR 1 also recognises that Göring's influence and ability to subvert the ERR's original mission, chain of command and weak senior leadership was reflected in internal conflicts, low morale, and hence bouts of inef-

[640] CIR 1 (ERR), op. cit., 6–7.
[641] CIR 1 (ERR), op. cit., 10.

ficiency, affecting many of ERR's administrative staff.[642] Unfortunately, these negative effects upon staff morale did not prevent the ERR from becoming an extremely fruitful source of Jewish looted art for the Göring Collection. Indeed, Göring's access to the ERR's repository of looted art works allowed him to select approximately 500 items.[643] These, together with approximately 1000 other plundered artworks, were then transported back to Germany on one of his 4 private trains.[644] Whilst, as already noted, the ERR was supposed to fall within the jurisdiction of Hitler, CIR 1 records that it was Göring—rather than Posse or Voss—who personally selected for the Linz museum works that this agency had confiscated. This exercise of authority both reflected and reinforced his personal domination over the ERR's operations.[645]

Plaut's postwar articles emphasise the wide geographical range of Göring's looting activities, including so-called 'regular purchases', which required the frequent deployment of his special train to take the fruits of his war criminality back to Carinhall:

642 'The efficiency of the Einsatzstab undertaking was jeopardized consistently through lack of authoritative direction and by internal friction. Most important, the GÖRING monopoly undermined morale, in that the staff was precluded from carrying out its basic (HITLER) directive. ROSENBERG's political weakness in the Party hierarchy, moreover, made itself felt even in the lower echelons of his organisation. SCHOLZ stated, for instance, that ROSENBERG, though Minister for the Occupied Territories of the East, as well as Reichsleiter, was unable to obtain an audience with HITLER for a period of nine months; and that this fact was common gossip among his subordinates. Both LOHSE and SCHOLZ have referred repeatedly to the feuds which existed between ROSENBERG and GOEBBELS, ROSENBERG and BORMANN, and BORMANN and GÖRING, the repercussions of which were felt strongly in the conduct of Einsatzstab activities.... Von BEHR, characterised by SCHOLZ, LOHSE and others as an unscrupulous egomaniac, antagonized the professional art historians serving under him, both through his gangster-like methods and his highly patronizing attitude.... LOHSE provoked the resentment and jealousy of his fellow-workers through the enjoyment of special privileges in the execution of his mission for GÖRING. He is known to have clashed with his colleagues on several occasions.' Ibid., 11–12.

643 CIR 1 (ERR), op. cit., 6; CIR 2 (Linz), op. cit., Attachment 5; Feliciano, 1997 op. cit., 36–37.

644 Ibid., 37–38.

645 'SCHIEDLAUSKY and LOHSE stated that GÖRING undertook the selection for HITLER personally in the Jeu de Paume. This is borne out by a letter dated 19 July 1941 from SCHOLZ to POSSE, in which SCHOLZ replies to questions raised in a letter from POSSE with respect to the material selected for HITLER. POSSE had made a tentative selection of objects from photographs submitted to HITLER during the first stages of confiscation proceedings, but GÖRING subsequently conferred with HITLER and was authorized to make the selection on the occasion of his visit to Paris in February 1941 (see ATTACHMENTS 12 and 13).' CIR 1 (ERR), op. cit., 24.

> His luxurious special train (later discovered by French and American troops at Berchtesgaden and used by Eisenhower) figured prominently in the formation of the Göring Collection. On the return trip to Germany following each of Göring's excursions to the occupied countries, it would carry back his most recent acquisitions—Einsatzstab loot from French collections, presents from collaborationist officials, and the Reichsmarschall's own "legitimate" purchases from the Paris dealers or the collectors of Brussels and Amsterdam, who were paid off handsomely in the unsupported paper occupation currency (*Reichskassenscheine*) printed in Germany.[646]

One of sources for the Göring Collection were purchases of artworks, a proportion of which had previously been looted from Jewish collections and then sold on the open market. Amongst the many items from plundered Jewish collections that Göring acquired were 16 highly valuable paintings from the Rosenberg collection located at Bordeaux, and previously looted by the ERR on 14 September 1941.[647] Outside of France and Belgium, Göring and his agents plundered Jewish artworks in Holland. This took place mainly through the services of Mühlmann's organisation, Dienstatelle Mühlmann, following up on official confiscations by Seyss-Inquart's officials. Seyss-Inquart had issued a decree requiring Jews to give up their property to the Aryanized Bankhaus Lippmann, Rosenthal and Co. in Amsterdam. Through an intermediary organisation, Mühlmann then received such works for valuation and sale or transfer to various Nazi leaders and Nuremberg defendants, including Ernst Kaltenbrunner, von Schirach and Hans Frank:[648]

> When a collection had been confiscated, the Dienstatelle Mühlmann was informed, and Plietzsch or Kieslinger made their choice. Göring acquired few objects from Dutch confiscation collections. The most important were the Openheim [partly illegible] and the Jaffe collections owned by Jews.[649]

Mühlmann also purchased confiscated Jewish works for Göring that had been appropriated by German military government agencies.[650]

---

[646] Plaut, 1946a op. cit.

[647] CIR 2 (Göring), op. cit. 132, 135.

[648] Mühlmann had established a close alliance with Seyss-Inquart, an attorney from Moravia, and the two men 'teamed up in Vienna, Crakow and the Hague.' Petropoulos, 1996b op. cit., 199, 181 respectively.

[649] CIR 2 (Göring) op. cit., 29.

[650] CIR 2 (Göring) op. cit., 84. These were obtained from the Lippmann-Rosenthal premises in Amsterdam which was used as 'The central depot for all Jewish collections confiscated by the Feind Vermoegen Stelle.' Ibid.

An important member of Dienstatelle Mühlmann was Mrytel Frank, a German-Jewish refugee, who enjoyed partial protection from anti-Semitic persecution because of personal contacts with the Nazi SD organisation.[651]

Not all of Göring's art acquisitions stemmed from the direct confiscation and looting activities of the ERR or the Dienstatelle Mühlmann. CIR 1 summarises the general character of Göring's *resort to exchange* as a device for building up his collection, and the role played by ERR officials controlled by the Reichsmarschall in this form of plunder of Jewish collections:

> From February 1941 through November 1943, the Einsatzstab conducted 28 formal exchanges of confiscated paintings with 6 individuals. In most cases, the works exchanged by the Einsatzstab were French paintings of the late 19th and the 20th century, confiscated chiefly from the ROSENBERG-BERNSTEIN Collection. 18 of the 28 exchanges were arranged with the German dealer, Gustav ROCHLITZ.... Eighteen of the exchanges were conducted on behalf of GÖRING: six or seven for HITLER and the Reichschancellery; one, possibly two, for RIBBENTROP, and one for BORMANN. Von BEHR is believed to have arranged a single exchange on his own behalf, and GÖRING received the entire art library of the Jewish dealer, Allen LOEBL, in "token" exchange for one E.R.R.- confiscated painting by Utrillo. This exchange was implemented by LOHSE and HOFER and was not conducted through normal Einsatzstab channels. The contract, dated 23 November 1942, was signed by HOFER. The Utrillo was from the BERNHEIM Collection.[652]

Interrogations by ALIU officials were not able to arrive at a consistent account of who within the ERR first thought up the idea of using exchanges as a method of by-passing internal Nazi regulations prohibiting the importation of so-called 'degenerate' art, including French Impressionist and 20th century paintings. They were, however, able to detect the guiding hand and interests of Göring behind many of these transactions. Nearly all the main perpetrators were either directly or indirectly controlled by the Reichsmarschall, who they knew preferred forced exchanges on favourable terms to outright purchase. Göring's preference stemmed from the fact that this mode of acquisition retained the semblance of legality, including market appraisal, despite operating in practice as a form of outright plunder involving no real costs:

---

651 CIR 2 (Göring) op. cit., 79.
652 CIR 1 (ERR), op. cit., 25–26.

> Rather than allow this abundance of highly saleable material [of "degenerate art"] to lie fallow, however, the Einsatzstab was prepared to sacrifice certain ideological considerations to the interests of commercial exploitation. It has not been possible to ascertain finally who conceived the idea for the exchanges. HOFER attributes it to von BEHR and LOHSE jointly, with the observation that they initiated the exchanges as a means of "enriching" the GÖRING collection.... the exchanges of such material for old masters and German 19th century paintings in the trade were sufficiently flagrant. ROCHLITZ stated that he was forced by LOHSE to propose the series of exchanges in which he was involved, and was threatened with "the consequences" should he fail to comply with GÖRING's wishes (see Detailed Interrogation Report No. 4—Subject: Gustav ROCHLITZ). GÖRING was stated by LOHSE to have preferred acquisition by exchange rather than purchase whenever possible. SCHOLZ and LOHSE denied categorically that ROCHLITZ had been forced in any way to participate in the exchanges, and were agreed that he had seen in these transactions a means of (a) making large profits, (b) gaining a prominent position in German art circles, and (c) winning personal favors from GÖRING. There is abundant evidence to support their contention. In almost every exchange, the *quid pro quo* was balanced heavily in Rochlitz' favor. For example, he acquired celebrated masterpieces by Cezanne, Corot and Degas, together with eight pictures by Renoir, Sisley, Picasso, Matisse, and Braque, in the first exchange (3 March 1941), in return for a highly questionable Titian portrait and a pedestrian work by Jan Weenix. A comparable disproportion persisted throughout most of the exchanges. A letter from UTIKAL to Reichsleiter ROSENBERG of 18 February 1941 (ATTACHMENT 14) stresses GÖRING's desire to have such confiscated material as is "unworthy" to come to Germany used in this manner, and invites ROSENBERG's attention to the initial proposals for exchange. In all exchanges undertaken for GÖRING, BELTRAND was called in to make an appraisal of the objects in question. This procedure was "consistent" with GÖRING's method of acquisition from the E.R.R., as the appraisals were to form the basis of ultimate payment by GÖRING. Characteristic exchange contract and appraisal forms are appended (ATTACHMENTS 16 and 17).[653]

In addition to these and other examples of coercive exchanges, Göring made a number of purchases on the open market through established dealers, such as Bornheim from Munich, who also assisted in purchasing items for the Linz Collection and other collectors.[654] However, the introduction to the CIR Report on Göring made it clear that it would be a mistake to rely upon an assumed *clear-cut* distinction between legally

[653] Ibid., 26–27.
[654] DIR Bornheim, op. cit.

unproblematic purchases (and exchanges) of Jewish owned works, and their outright plunder and confiscations without compensation:

> a preliminary study of... the methods used by the Reichsmarschall of the Third Reich to strip the occupied countries of Europe of a large part of their artistic heritage. This widespread enterprise, which worked in the shadow of the occupying forces, took the form of both looting and of so-called "legal" purchase.[655]

CIR 2 also records details of the sham nature of Göring's exchanges with the French National Gallery, the Louvre, which were conducted against the background of severe threats. This involved the 'payment' to the French government by the Germans of: 'a picture which the latter had previously stolen from a Frenchman'.[656]

Behind Göring's apparently voluntary exchanges and purchases lay the threat of murder, and of course the Holocaust. CIR 2 also noted that Angerer exploited the fear associated with Göring's name both to extract favours and subject less compliant individuals to real threat. Through his influence upon Göring, Angerer: 'was able to have at least one person released from a concentration camp through his request to Göring.'[657] There was, however, a more sinister side of the same coin:

> On two known occasions he used the threat of the Gestapo to extract paintings from an unwilling dealer. This happened both times in the case of Bornheim, who reports that in 1937 Angerer called him up and obliged him by threats of Gestapo intervention to sell first the Cumberland Tapestry (Bervais ca. 1700) and later the Maximilian Court Tapestry (Brussels 16th Century'). The former went to Hitler, and the latter to Göring.[658]

The OSS investigators discovered that Göring could also resort to threats and the exploitation of vulnerabilities amongst Jewish dealers in need of protection from Nazi persecution. As Petropoulos notes:

> Art dealers who did business with Göring sometimes encountered threats, either explicit or veiled. Gustav Rochlitz, a German dealer with a sullied reputation who was based in Paris as of 1933, told OSS interrogators that when negotiating the sale of Titian *Portrait of a Man* and Jan Weenix *Still Life*, Göring communicated to him through his representative, Bruno

[655] CIR 2 (Göring), op. cit., 1.
[656] CIR 2 (Göring), op. cit., 143.
[657] CIR 2 (Göring), op. cit., 14.
[658] CIR 2 (Göring), op. cit., 14.

> Lohse, that his asking price was *trop chère* and that he would "have to take the consequences" of not entering into the transaction according to the stated terms. On a number of occasions Göring did business with Jews in the occupied west. While one might argue that he offered them protection, he also exploited the situation for his own profit.[659]

ALIU reports discuss specific examples of where Göring exploited his power to exert direct personal coercion upon Jewish families, or families which included Jewish members, and who were fearful of their fate under Nazi rule. For example, Pieter de Boer, who had become a major seller of artworks to the Germans in Holland, was sufficiently intimidated by Göring's visit to one of his collections that he parted with various works of art. These included a precious altar piece and fifteen pictures, which he would have preferred to have retained. After succumbing to this threat, the de Boer firm received a measure of support from Göring and his agents, which allowed them to prosper.[660]

Following his master's lead, Hofer exploited the fact that he was widely seen as closely associated with Göring for purposes of extortion. He both threatened Jewish owners and then, in classic gangster fashion, offered them protection in return for their artworks. For instance, CIR 2 accuses Hofer of exploiting his status as Göring's curator to offer protection to persecuted Jews and others in exchange for artworks sought by either himself or Göring. Hofer had identified 19th Century French paintings sought by Göring. He then discovered items within the Paul Rosenberg collection that could be exchanged for them.[661] CIR 2 also refers to Hofer: 'promising protection to those persecuted by the Nazis in exchange for the sale of something which he might desire.'[662] Göring, acting through his agent Hofer, protected the German-Jewish art expert Professor Friedlander and Vitale Bloch from measures of Nazi anti-Semitic persecution. However, Göring's protection was provided in exchange for their consultancy services on artworks of interest to the Reichsmarschall:[663]

---

[659] 1996 op. cit., 194 based upon DIR 4.

[660] On de Boer's dealings with Göring more generally, see CIR 2 (Göring), op. cit., 148.

[661] CIR 2 (Göring), op. cit., 10–13 and Attachments 1, 17.

[662] Ibid., 10.

[663] 'Report on Amsterdam' by Waterhouse, 13 May 1945: US NA, RG 239, Entry 83; and 'Traduction #3448 for J Vlug': US NA, RG 239, Entry 79. 'Göpel's chief advisor in Holland was Vitale Bloch, a Russian Jewish dealer at the Hague. Goepel had protected him from the anti-Semitic laws, and in return received first refusal on whatever Bloch discovered on the market... He was highly regarded as a connoisseur, and was a close friend of Friedlander.' CIR 4 (Linz), op. cit., 47.

> Collaborationist circles, both professional and amateur, seem to have centred around Friedlander, the well-known German art historian and specialist in early Flemish painting, who was formerly with the Kaiser Friedrich Museum, Berlin. In spite of his being a Jew and a refugee, he was treated with care and respect by the Germans. Hofer, Lohse and Mühlmann all claim a part in protecting him from anti-Semitic laws. He wrote expertise for both the Dutch and the Germans, and he sometimes gave the latter tips about the location of interesting pictures. His chief confidant and helper was Vitale Bloch...[664]

Hofer was, however, rather selective in these offers of protection from anti-Semitic persecution. He initially refused, for example, to come to the aid of his Jewish brother-in-law, Kurt Bachstitz. This was despite the professional help he had previously received from Bachstitz. Eventually, when the family situation became acute, Hofer relented gaining travel visas to Switzerland, albeit only after having first secured extensive material benefits for himself. According to the ALIU, these benefits took the form of extra artworks for both himself and Göring as a precondition, and as hostages for Bachstitz's future silence on this matter.[665] Hofer's extortion and exploitation formed one part of a wider pattern of dishonest practices: 'In this he followed the line set down by Göring to use every available advantage over the seller, and to bring him down to rock bottom prices.'[666]

Miedl, another member of Göring's network, introduced Hofer to Hans Tietje, a German businessman with a Jewish wife and three equally vulnerable daughters. Tietje: 'duly sold him a nice Cranach, *Madonna and Child*.'[667] CIR 2 notes: 'He had never been known to sell, but on this occasion he saw the advantages to be gained through the connection to Göring and decided to do so.'[668] Another person who Miedl exploited was Fritz Gutmann, a German-Jew anxious to escape from Holland. Miedl 'purchased' three sixteenth century silver cups from Gutmann.[669] Miedl's efforts to please Göring, and to act almost as a member of his staff, were based at least partially on coercion linked to the unfolding Holocaust: 'Göring's hold on him came from the fact

[664] CIR 2 (Göring), op. cit., 63.
[665] Ibid., 74.
[666] Ibid., 11.
[667] Nicholas, 1995 op. cit., 105.
[668] CIR 2 (Göring), op. cit., 69.
[669] Ibid., 65–74. Petropolous has reminded the author of the fate of the Gutmanns: Fritz was beaten to death by Goering's agents in Berlin dying en route to Thereseinstadt, and his wife was killed in Auschwitz.

that he protected Miedl's Jewish wife.... the reason for this sale was that Miedl... wanted to send his wife and family to Switzerland for protection against the anti-Jewish laws.'[670]

In short, ALIU officials recognised a broad spectrum of potentially criminal actions committed by Göring. These included not only all direct and indirect acts of outright anti-Semitic looting and plunder by his agents or proxies in other organisations such as the ERR, but also *forced* sales and exchanges.[671] In the latter case, there was merely *the appearance* of regular legality serving only to disguise violent acts of plunder:

> The use of the exchange as a method of acquisition is a most significant aspect of the formation of Göring's Collection. The Reichsmarschall of the Greater German Reich showed that he considered property confiscated by his government for "ideological" reasons to be his own to dispose of as he saw fit, and that he would resort to any trick however low, if it got him what he wanted. The exchanges establish once and for all the identity of those people outside of Germany who, for personal profit, were willing to be Göring's accomplices... Hofer in his letters to Göring repeatedly refers to confiscated pictures as desirable for exchange purposes. See Attachment 1. Under interrogation, he... admitted having a part in all the negotiations.[672]

Since such sales and exchanges took place against the background of more overt acts of violence, there always remained an element of force, and even physical threat, underpinning all Göring's negotiations for artworks. The reference to the fact that his collection was acquired in the 'shadow of occupying forces', part of whose 'widespread enterprise' involved deliberate policies of cultural plunder, is significant. This, in turn, meant that all such so-called legal 'agreements' for the sale or exchange of Jewish art works between theoretically 'equal' private individuals, still remained doubtful. They lacked the vital element of freely given and genuine consent. For example, Plaut recalls that Hofer exploited European Jews' well-founded fears of persecution and death to extort their artworks:

> For Göring's account, Curator Hofer "accepted" cherished heirlooms from certain proud Jewish families in the Netherlands. In return, he

---

[670] Ibid., 19, 150 respectively.

[671] Ibid., 141 re the exchange of parts of the Rothschild collections confiscated by the ERR.

[672] Ibid., 128.

> provided funds far below the value of the offering, supplementing payment with an official German *laissez passer* or a Swiss passport, to be used by these benighted people in their flight from the Nazis! Agent Lohse, writing to Göring's secretary, requested that he be "permitted to arrange for placing at my disposal by the Gestapo the two Jews, the Brothers L., for further work in the Reichsmarschall's interests." Göring's secretary replied: "You are to make sure that this matter is handled so as to avoid having the Reichsmarschall's name mentioned in connection with Jews. If possible, handle it all under cover."...He [Hofer] had facilities for travel, for foreign exchange, and for promising "official protection" to certain select victims of Nazi persecution, in return for which he received purchase rights to their works of art.[673]

The ALIU's critique of one of Göring's most frequently deployed devices, the sham contract of sale and exchange, explains why their report on his collection devotes considerable space, amounting to over 50 percent of the overall report, to the methods he directly or indirectly deployed to make purchases, sales and exchanges of artworks: 'here an attempt is made to analyse the first two stages of the process of so-called 'legal purchase': (1) the method of operations used by Göring and his agents, and (2) the relationship between them and the persons from whom they made their acquisitions.'[674] The very fact that these aspects of acquisition were not only included but also given such close scrutiny is significant. It is testament to the OSS officials' considered view that, in many cases, a close study of even apparently 'lawful' purchases, sales and exchanges of artworks by leading Nazis could also be treated as providing substantial evidence of war criminality.

The ALIU argued that Göring's unlawful plans for extortion were often carried out through the actions of members of his immediate staff, including his Chief of Personal Staff, Dr Gritzbach. For instance, CIR 2 highlights examples of how Gritzbach was: 'used by his chief to apply pressure upon people who were unwilling to part with objects desired by Göring. There is evidence of this in the cases of both Renders and Miedl.'[675] Göring's decision to appoint someone as blatantly dishonest as Hofer to the post of curator of his entire collection, was significant. ALIU officials further alleged that Göring had chosen to employ only one comparatively honest agent, Bornheim. The fact that this quality made Bornheim stand out from the rest of Göring's network is clear

[673] Plaut, 1946a op. cit.
[674] Ibid., 1.
[675] CIR 2 (Göring) op. cit., 6.

evidence of the general climate of dishonesty and plunder that permeated Göring's style of acquiring and dealing in art.[676] His appointment of dishonest agents represented Göring's own commitment to the institutionalisation of an essentially coercive and criminal acquisitions policy involving the plunder of Jewish works, at least wherever such theft was deemed 'necessary' to secure a particular work of art:

> The documents recording the telephone conversations and the letter themselves give positive proof that Hofer played a decisive part in the choice of pictures, in the method of bargaining, and the decision as to the nature of payment. In spite of his own denials, it has been established that he encouraged Göring to take over or, as he put it, "purchase", confiscated collections in France. On one occasion he draws attention to the Rothschild collection... In the case of the Brague Collection, he tells his chief, with some pride, of how he offered Brague the chance of a speedy release of his property, which had been illegally taken in the first place, on condition that he be willing to sell a picture which he, Hofer, admits he knew Brague had never intended to part with. (See Attachment 1). Göring supplied the initial impulse, but Hofer is the man principally responsible for the method by which objects were acquired.[677]

Hofer's centrality to Göring's operations meant of course that he could provide OSS officials with important information under interrogation concerning the details of these activities. In turn, these officials noted that Hofer developed a series of contacts with others who shared his lack of scruples in both benefiting from and exploiting the Holocaust. Wendland, for example, was a key Hofer contact: 'The most important of these was Hans Wendland, who operated in France and Switzer land, and who seems to have had a hand in every deal.'[678] Wendland's extensive network relevant to his work for Göring included Boitel, Perdoux and the French Jewish dealer Loebl:[679] 'In the combination, Wendland represented the international interests; Boitel the financial; Loebl the Paris art market; and Perdoux contacts throughout France, particularly in the provinces. All four were unscrupulous, and they must have dealt in millions.'[680] Other key contacts were Sepp Angerer:

---

[676] 'Walter Bornheim: there is no evidence that to date he was associated at any time with... Enemy Property Control or Foreign Currency Authorities or the ERR. Nor does he ever appear to have used his position with Göring to exert pressure on those who were unwilling to sell.' Ibid., 16.

[677] Ibid., 12.

[678] Ibid., 3.

[679] Ibid., 34.

[680] Ibid.

'next to Hofer, Angerer is the most important of Göring's agents',[681] and Kajetan Mühlmann.[682]

Mühlmann proved to be a lucrative source of confiscated Jewish works of art for the Göring collection: 'When Jewish collections were confiscated, Mühlmann's assistants were advised, and they made their choice at the same time as Goepel, the Linz representative at the Hague.'[683] With respect to the complicities that Angerer shared with Göring concerning this aspect of the Holocaust, CIR 2 noted:

> He first came into contact with Göring when he sold him works of art taken from the confiscated Jewish collections in Vienna.... When Göring wanted to make an anonymous sale of some of his objects at auction, it was camouflaged under the name of Angerer's firm.... Hofer says he [Angerer] was responsible for the first shipments of confiscated works of art from France to Carinhall.[684]

Hofer's network (with the exception of Bornheim) treated all property confiscated from Jews and other 'enemies of the state' as a potential source for Göring's collection.[685] Plaut recalls that, on occasions, Göring resorted to direct and personal intimidation of the owners of artworks who had refused to sell him items:

> Occasionally, when hard pressed, Göring showed his true colors, as in the case of a prominent Belgian whose collection he coveted. Göring wrote to him personally in 1941 as follows: Mr. M. reported to me on the discussions he had with you concerning your collection of paintings, and informed me that you had again withdrawn from your earlier position and not yet arrived at a settlement. I have instructed M. to communicate with you again concerning the final terms.... Should you this time again not be able to decide, then I would be compelled to withdraw my offer, *and things would go their normal way, without my being able to do anything to impede their course.* [Emphasis added.]
>
> With German greetings, H. GÖRING.[686]

---

681 Ibid., 13. Angerer could conceal a number of Göring's sales on the open market, ibid., 156.

682 Mühlmann attempted to please both Hitler and Göring, the latter demanded to receive first refusal on any items not chosen by the Linz Museum despite the complaints this generated from Seyss-Inquart. Ibid., 17.

683 Ibid., 18.

684 Ibid., 16, 13, 14 respectively.

685 Ibid., Ch. 5 'Confiscations'.

686 Plaut, 1946a, op. cit.

Certain DIRs include accounts of Göring's subordinates Hofer, Lohse and Wendland that are directly relevant to Göring's complicity in the Holocaust.[687] For example, Rousseau's DIR on Hofer includes a series of attachments identifying the dealers who Göring's curator had worked with, and his storehouses for works he acquired during 1945, which were later used to reclaim these items.[688]

Göring also bought works directly from various dealers such as Mühlmann, who made considerable profit through supplying Göring (and Hitler) with Jewish artworks he had purchased very cheaply across Europe. Mühlmann had established offices in the Hague, Netherlands. Their function was to list any enemy property and open bank accounts for Göring and other high officials, and liase with Hofer concerning possible purchases. Göring personally visited the Netherlands in May 1940 to oversee developments.[689] Through Mühlmann, Göring acquired a series of paintings by German artists 'unjustly removed from the fatherland' at drastically reduced prices.[690] ALIU officials compiled a list of Mühlmann's transactions, which spread over 75 pages of single spaced typed A4 pages.[691]

Göring's acquisitions in the Netherlands, effected through the Mühlmann agency, also contributed to the Holocaust,[692] albeit in a more complex way than in France. Yeide, for example, notes:

> In German-occupied Holland, most of Göring's art acquisitions were also through dealers. In general, fewer large Jewish collections were subject to confiscation in Holland than in France. For those that could be confiscated, the Nazi organization Dienstatelle Kajetan Mühlmann functioned like an art dealer. It obtained works either through the Enemy Property Administration (Feindvermögensverwaltung)—which from 1942 onwards had access to the property that Jews were required to turn over to the Bankhaus Lippmann Rosenthal—or directly from dealers or collectors willing to sell. The Dienststelle then offered the assembled art objects to the Nazi elite, including Göring, Hitler, Himmler, Hoffmann and others, while turning a tidy profit.[693]

[687] Yeide, 2007 op. cit., 6.
[688] Ibid.
[689] CIR 3 (Mühlmann), December 25 1945 by Vlug: US NA, RG 260, Entry 394.
[690] Ibid., 29, 46; CIR No. 2, 'Göring Collection', op. cit., 139.
[691] DIR Mühlmann, op. cit.
[692] CIR 4 (Linz), op. cit., 17.
[693] Yeide, 2007 op. cit., 5.

Gifts to Göring from friends and other important Nazis were another source for this collection. These were often based on the results of this Nazi leader's extensive reviews of artworks within Nazi-occupied Europe.[694] During the first two years of the war, Hofer helped Göring create a 'gift list' of pre-approved works of art.[695] CIR 4 notes that after receiving a number of 'unsuitable' works of art as acts of homage, Göring created a type of reserve, or gift-list, to which those seeking to make such presents could turn:[696] 'Göring...invited the attention of would-be donors to an already selected group of items acceptable for his collection.'[697] In fact from 1937, all donors needed to do was to write a cheque to his 'Art Fund' knowing that this would be used to finance a confiscated work of art that Göring had pre-approved but had not yet purchased for himself. There were many different donors and wealthy individuals, such as Philip Reemtsma who donated over RM 1 million per year.[698] Angerer,[699] Hofer[700] and Haberstock's firm all assisted in this process.[701] Howe recalls the proactive steps that Hofer used with respect to this device for extracting funds for the Göring collection:

> A shrewd and enterprising Berlin dealer before the war, Hofer had succeeded in ingratiating himself with the Reichsmarschall. He, more than any other single individual, had been responsible for shaping Göring's taste and had played the stellar role in building up his priceless collection of Old Masters. Some of his methods had been ingenious. He was credited with having devised the system of "birthday gifts"—a scheme whereby important objects were added to the collection at no cost to the Reichsmarschall. Each year, before Göring's birthday on January twelfth, Hofer wrote letters to wealthy industrialists and businessmen suggesting that the Reichsmarschall would be gratified to receive a token of their continued regard for him. Then he would designate a specific work of art—and the price. More often than not, the piece in question had already been acquired. The prospective donor had only to foot the bill. Now and then the victim of this shakedown protested the price, but he usually came through. In Hofer, the Reichsmarschall had a henchman

[694] CIR 2 (Göring), op. cit., 32, 162.
[695] Ibid.
[696] Ibid., 17, 33, 162 for other examples of such homage.
[697] CIR 4 (Linz), op. cit., 26.
[698] 'Göring interrogation' 22 December 1945: US NA, RG 260, Entry 172; and 'Birthday lists': US NA, RG 260, Entry 82.
[699] Originally a tapestry merchant.
[700] Hofer's wife maintained the condition of the artworks.
[701] CIR 2 (Göring), op. cit.

> as rapacious and greedy as himself. And Hofer had possessed what his master lacked—a wide knowledge of European collections and the international art market. Göring had been a gold mine and Hofer had made the most of it.[702]

Hofer became central to the acquisition of confiscated art, including his knowledge of Göring's self-interested concerns regarding works of art he received as birthday gifts looted from *public* collections, such as Montecassino, a blatant war crime under the 1907 Hague Regulations.[703] As the Roberts Commission Report notes in its extensive quotation of ALIU's DIR on Hofer:

> Hofer...said he first became informed of the appearance of these [confiscated] works of art in December 1943, when:...he was called to Reinickendorf [near Berlin], the headquarters of the Hermann Göring Division, by a group of officers who revealed to him that they had brought the objects to Berlin with the intention of presenting them to Göring as a surprise for his birthday [12th January].... The cases containing works of art were moved to Carinhall and there Gritzbach, Brauchtitsch, and Hofer set to work preparing them with the other presents for their chief.... About a year later, in February 1945, Göring suddenly ordered Hofer to take all works of art from Montecassino to the Reichskanzlei, where they were to be given to Reichsleiter Martin Bormann, who, he said, was to send them to Munich. Hofer carried out these instructions and from then on heard no more about the objects. However, there was also found the log book of the mine at Alt-Aussee, where parts of the collections of the Einsatzstab Rosenberg and of Hider were also stored. Entries in this log book show that the Montecassino works of art arrived there in a shipment on March 28, 1945, and record a telephone conversation in which von Hummel, Bormann's secretary, announced their arrival, referring to them as "the most important works from Reichsmarschall Göring's collection."[704]

In short, various ALIU reports produced weighty evidence of Göring's personal and institutional complicity in the cultural plunder aspect of the Holocaust. In building up his massive personal collection, he resorted through the ERR to outright and extensive confiscation of large Jewish collections of art, as well as the coerced sales and exchanges. He even exploited the climate of anti-Semitic persecution as a form of extortion to 'purchase' at bargain prices works he was unable to confiscate directly, sometimes by offering a dubious form of protection for Jew-

[702] Howe, 1946 op. cit., 132.
[703] See also CIR 2 (Göring), op. cit., 29–31.
[704] Roberts Commission Report, 1946 op. cit., 76.

ish or half-Jewish members of the families of art dealers. In short, the ALIU report on the Göring Collection blames Hofer for establishing the main confiscation methods deployed to create this collection, and for maintaining its detailed records of contract of sale or exchange. Between them, Göring set the tone for a series of dishonest practices which, with one exception, his agents and curator willingly followed and extended at the expense of the victims of Nazi persecution, particularly European Jews.

The looting of Jewish artworks as a source for Hitler's Linz Museum

The second most important driving factor in the Nazi regime's looting of Jewish works of art was the policy of furnishing Hitler's planned Linz Museum. Plaut has noted the combination of grand cultural, personal and political ambitions that underlay Hitler's attempts to build up a world famous art collection within his Linz Museum:

> Hitler's absorption with art, however, centred in his elaborate plans for the Austrian town in Linz, in the region where he was born. He envisaged Linz as the future seat of the new German *Kultur*, and lavished all his limited pictorial talent and architectural training on a vast project which would realize this ambition. Personal resentment toward the cosmopolitan milieu of Vienna, which symbolized the unhappy struggle of his formative years, burned as strongly within the Führer as the sentimental hankering after the places of his boyhood. He was determined that Linz should supplant Vienna as the Austrian capital, and that its new prominence should cement the Austro-German bond so vital to the salutary growth of National Socialism.[705]

Interrogations by ALIU officials confirmed that Hitler had planned to develop the proposed Linz Museum to outshine both Vienna and Berlin as a centre of art and official ceremony.[706] Under interrogation, Voss, denied ever having been: 'consulted concerning the [Linz] building:

---

[705] Plaut, 1946b op. cit.

[706] 'Like many a small town boy who made good, Adolf Hitler wanted the home folks to bask in his success. Linz was the center of the region graced by the accident of Der Fuehrer's birth...It was natural, therefore, that Linz should figure prominently in his post-victory plans. Hitler always disliked the cosmopolitan atmosphere of Vienna. His dreams for Linz thus became part of a general policy to reduce Vienna's importance both politically and culturally. (See Attachment 4). He determined to push the growth of centers more in harmony with nationalist conceptions of Austro-German, and more specifically Austro-Bavarian, culture.' CIR 4 (Linz), op. cit., 1.

that he saw the plans only once, and Flick answered his criticisms by asserting that the prescription was Hitler's and nothing could be done about it.'[707] Plaut notes that Hitler devoted considerable time and resources to the Linz project, whose size and scope was consciously designed to radiate Nazism's imperial 'success'. By implication, this suggested to other leading Nazis that the acquisition and appreciation of artworks, particularly those of Germanic 19th Century realist and Volkish kind, formed an integral part of the leader's vision of the wider National Socialist project:

> Until he was caught up in the maelstrom of a world war, Hitler devoted a disproportionate amount of time and energy, for a Chief of State, to the plans for Linz, personally creating the architectural scheme for an imposing array of public buildings, and setting the formula for an art collection which was to specialize heavily in his beloved, mawkish German school of the nineteenth century. His private library, discovered by the American Army deep in Austria, contained scores of completed architectural renderings for the Linz project, of which the Führer-museum was to be a single edifice related to the whole, comprising a great library (with an initial quota of 250,000 volumes), a theater, and a separate collection of armor. German painting of the nineteenth century was to be assembled in such quantity that, should the need arise for a separate building to house the monumental collection, it could be integrated successfully with the master plan. The Führer-museum, with a colonnaded façade about 500 feet long, the design paralleling that of the great Haus für Deutsche Kunst already erected in Munich, would stand on the site of the present Linz railroad station, which was to be moved four kilometers to the south. Roderich Fick, the official architect, made his drawings entirely from Hitler's personal prescriptions. A bound volume of 75 pages, entitled *The Future Economic Status of the City of Linz*, also found in Hitler's library, spells out his dream for a modern industrial metropolis, with a greatly increased population and all the attributes with which lavish expenditure and city planning could endow the capital of his empire. The study was prepared at his direction by the Economic and Research Section, Oberdonau Department of the Interior.[708]

The Linz project derived its authority from the highest level of the Reich Chancellery. Reichsminister Lammers, President of the Reich Chancellery, and Dr. Helmut von Hummel,[709] Special Assistant to

[707] CIR 4 (Linz), op. cit., 2.

[708] Plaut, 1946b op. cit.

[709] Plaut notes that: 'Von Hummel, a particularly vicious Nazi, may still be at large. His last official act was to order a case of confiscated gold coins brought to him at Berchtesgaden on May 1, 1945, after which he disappeared.' Plaut, 1946b op. cit.

Bormann, were senior state officials accountable only to Bormann and Hitler. These administrators created the directives authorising the confiscation and purchase of Jewish and other art works. The Special Linz Commission, under Hans Posse, employed around twenty specialists in paintings, prints, coins, and armour, a librarian, an architect, photographers, and restorers.

On 26 June 1939, Hitler appointed Posse, a well-known art historian and—as already noted—Director of the Dresden Painting Gallery since 1913: 'to build up the new art museum for Linz Donau' once it became apparent that the growing collection of looted art, much of which stemmed from anti-Semitic persecutions, needed organisation.[710] As the founding Director of the Linz Museum, Posse was empowered to:

> choose what he wanted from art coming in from the confiscated collections of Jews and other "undesirable persons" in Austria and Czechoslovakia.... In June 1940 he had [already] acquired 465 paintings in one year alone....by the end of 1944...the Linz museum contained more than eight thousand items.[711]

Posse must have known of his complicity in the Holocaust. As Petropoulos notes:

> Despite all these purchases [c. 8000 paintings],[712] Posse could have no illusions about his project. At the outset he was charged with cataloguing the plundered art taken from Vienna's Jews, which by January 1939 numbered in the thousands and was valued, according to Himmler, at between RM 60–70 million. (One Nazi bureaucrat estimated in 1939 that "70 percent of the art in private hands was in the hands of non-Aryans)".[713]

CIR 4 revealed that Posse had actively selected artworks looted from German Jews in Munich, and exploited opportunities afforded by the German invasion of Poland.[714] Posse had been described as having: 'worked fanatically to the very end.'[715] His funeral was a state occasion

[710] CIR 4 (Linz), op. cit., 4, and Attachment One.
[711] Feliciano, 1997 op. cit., 22–23.
[712] In fact, the correct figure for works actually forming part of the Linz Museum may well be nearer 1,000 despite the fact that the Linz agents still acquired the number of paintings listed in the ALIU reports, with the difference being accounted for by the fact that not all the works would have gone to Linz. I am grateful to Jonathan Petropoulos for pointing this out to me.
[713] Petropoulos, 2000 op. cit., 52–53.
[714] CIR 4, (Linz), op. cit., Attachment Five, Posse to Bormann 14 December 1939.
[715] Plaut, 1946b op. cit.

with Goebbels reading the eulogy. He became: 'the most powerful individual in the amassing of art treasures for the new Germany.'[716] Posse secured over 2,500 objects for the Linz collection during his three years, a figure that excludes many thousands of confiscated works which were potential acquisitions. Plaut gives an example of how under Posse famous works were acquired at a discounted price through coercion:

> His greatest coup, undeniably, was the "purchase" of the famous Vermeer, *The Artist in His Studio*, from the Czernin family of Vienna in the autumn of 1940, under occult circumstances. One of Europe's greatest masterpieces, the Vermeer had been sought by collectors all over the world for many years, but the owners would not sell. Posse and Bormann appear to have tried to attach the Vermeer originally for non-payment of taxes... Suddenly and inexplicably, the asking price dropped... to 1,650,000 Reich marks, a ridiculously low amount in the inflated art market of the war. Posse was ordered to Vienna instantly, and what was obviously a forced sale of the painting was consummated with the Cozening through the intervention of Reichsleiter Baldur von Schirach.[717]

Posse also acquired Rubens *Ganymede*, as a 'gift' from Vienna in exchange for confiscated porcelains. A letter from Posse to Bormann, dated 10 June 1940, sums up the official attitude toward purchases for the Linz Collection:

> The special delegate for the safeguarding of art and cultural properties has just returned from Holland. He notified me today that there exists at the moment a particularly favourable opportunity to purchase valuable works of art from Dutch dealers and private owners *in German currency*. Even though a large number of important works have doubtless been removed recently from Holland, I believe that the trade still contains many objects which are desirable for the Führer's collection, and which may be acquired without foreign exchange.[718]

In March 1941, an account of 500,000 Reichsmarks was created for Posse's personal use at the Reichskreditbank in Paris, with a similar amount made available to him at the German Embassy in Rome. By mid-March 1941, Posse told Bormann, who oversaw aspects of the Linz project for Hitler, that he had spent 8,522,348 Reichsmarks in the purchase of art works. This figure excluded many of the high-cost major purchases from Hitler's agents.[719] Linz certainly became the main

[716] Ibid.
[717] Ibid.
[718] Quoted in Plaut, 1946b op. cit.
[719] Plaut, 1946b op. cit.

beneficiary of the looting of French Jewish collections. Of the 21,000 objects seized in France, Linz acquired all but the 700 which Göring had already reserved for himself, a situation which matched that of Poland and Austria.[720] CIR 4 (Linz) notes that:

> In his first report, dated 20 October 1939, Posse outlined his suggestions for distributing works of art looted from Viennese Jews. The lists state the provenance of these works in full detail. (See Attachment 72)...Posse's inventory of the Linz collection, dated 31 July 1940, lists many additional items. (See Attachment 73; note that the symbol "W" signifies that the item in question was confiscated in Vienna.)[721]

ALIU officials also accused Posse of complicity in selecting for this museum part of a collection of valuable armour and coins he knew to have been looted in 1941 from the Rothschild collection in Vienna.[722] Plaut argued that Hitler recognised from the outset that illegal cultural plunder from major Jewish collections was to form a major source of the Linz Collection, and that this was manifested in his guilty and secretive behaviour in relation to this collection:

> Either through an early presentiment of guilt or as a tactical measure, Hitler ordered the Linz project, with all its ramifications, to be treated as a government secret. The idea that loot, as in the plans for Göring's Carinhall, was fundamental in the formation of the Linz Collection became clear to the project's personnel as early as October, 1939, when Dr. Hans Posse, Director of the *Sonderauftrag* (Special Commission), presented to Martin Bormann, for Hitler's approval, a list of 182 pictures which he had selected for Linz from the confiscated collections of the Viennese branch of the Rothschild family. In July, 1940, Posse was able to list 324 paintings already acquired for Linz, and every one of the 182 confiscated works previously recommended figured in the list.[723]

OSS officials documented 68 dealers in Germany alone who transferred works of art to the Linz project.[724] With respect to Posse's acquisitions, one ALIU report concluded that, although most items were secured through voluntary purchases on the market, confiscations without compensation from Jews, particularly the Rothschilds, had played an important role:

---

[720] Ibid.
[721] CIR 4 (Linz), op. cit., 68.
[722] Ibid., 20, 72.
[723] Plaut, 1946b op. cit.
[724] CIR 4 (Linz) op. cit., Attachment 54.

> confiscation played a basic role as a method of acquisition. Each major division of the collection...paintings, armour, coins, and the Linz Library—got off to a good start by outright confiscation of important collections...some of the outstanding examples of confiscation are given here to indicate the scale on which this method was practiced. The entire collections of Alphons and Louis Rothschild, containing hundreds of items of painting, objets d'art, armour, coins and rare books, were seized shortly after the occupation of Vienna, and no payment of any kind was ever made.[725]

Members of the ALIU discovered that Buchner, as part of his contribution to the Nazification of German art, had met personally with Hitler, and later agreed to transfer 18 items from the museums he controlled to the Linz collection, a process termed 'deaccessioning.'[726]

The DIRs contain evidence of the involvement of a number of German Jews and individuals with half-Jewish children in Nazi art looting for the Linz collection. For example, two reports contain details of the activities of Maria Almas-Dietrich. She was a prolific and highly aggressive German art dealer who supplied Hitler's proposed collection in Linz with over 270 works, many of which were of poor quality or even forgeries. Almas-Dietrich reportedly had a half-Jewish daughter by a German-American-Jew, and later married another Jew. As a result, she was denied German citizenship until 1940. Even then, she encountered further serious difficulties with the Gestapo, which meant she had to hide her daughter in her shop. Hoffmann apparently rescued her from the Gestapo in 1943.[727]

One ALIU report states that the starting, or default, position for the Linz Museum's acquisition policy was to seek to exploit any possible opportunity for plunder before even considering making a purchase.[728] Plaut challenges the idea that during the context of an unfolding genocide, purchases fell outside the zone of cultural plunder, emphasising that racist distinctions underpinned both types of acquisition.[729] He

---

[725] Ibid., 27.

[726] Ibid., Attachment 76.

[727] DIR (Hoffmann) op. cit., and CIR 4 (Linz), op. cit.

[728] CIR 4 (Linz), op. cit., 38: 'Purchase was the normal method acquisition where circumstances did not offer the possibility of confiscation (whether or not disguised as safeguarding) or forced sale.'

[729] 'It is worth emphasizing, with respect to the acquisitions for Linz, that the difference between loot and purchase was merely a technical one. Where works of art were held by the downtrodden Poles and Czechs, or by 'non-Aryan' Dutch or French nationals, confiscation was the accepted method. This was in accordance with the

further recalls that Linz officials, together with their agents and informants, actively exploited opportunities for plundering Jewish and other collections created by Nazi military occupations of Central and Eastern Europe, and that the threat and undercurrent of violence remained a pervasive factor:

> Two months after the invasion of Holland, Posse established an office at The Hague, appearing there in the role of *Referent für Sonderfragen* (Adviser on "Special Questions"). Belgium and Holland proved to be fertile ground. Posse's informers and middlemen, supported actively by the Seyss-Inquart government, were able to tap rich sources through confiscation and "purchase." The richest acquisitions of Linz in the Netherlands was the major portion of the Mannheimer Collection (purchased in 1944 for 2,000,000 gulden less than the Dutch authorities asked, following a Seyss-Inquart threat to confiscate the whole as enemy property). It contained such treasures as Rembrandt's *Jewish Doctor*. The remainder of the collection was acquired subsequently in France, also by forced sale.[730]

Following the death of Posse in December 1942, Hitler eventually named Hermann Voss to head the Linz museum in April 1943.[731] Posse's successor continued the anti-Semitic looting policies of his predecessor, albeit with less energy and efficiency. Voss also appears to have exploited the fear of persecution of one of De Boer's Jewish employees in order to extort four panels by Jan Breughel representing the elements. These were taken from the De Boers' private collection but only after these owners had received confirmation of their Jewish employee's safe escape into a neutral country.[732] Under interrogation, Voss claimed to have purchased over 3,000 paintings for Linz between 1943 and 1944, at a total cost of 150,000 Reichsmarks. Despite a measure of exaggeration, Plaut concluded that: 'he was fully as active as Posse in swelling the total.'[733]

Nazi doctrine of oppression. Where political expediency, as in the case of the 'Italian ally' and the 'worthy French opponent,' called for good will toward the New Order, the velvet glove approach was used, with an unprecedented outlay of German funds as lure. Purchases of important items—with German occupation currency wherever possible—accompanied the wholesale seizures, and often were conducted by the same officials. Dealers and agents swarmed into Paris, many armed with special Linz certificates, which formalized their status and assured their precedence in the art grab bag.' Plaut, 1946b op. cit.

[730] Ibid.

[731] DIR 12, 'Hermann Voss', 7, 22–23: US NA, RG 239, Entry 74, Boxes 84–85.

[732] CIR 2 (Göring), op. cit., 74–76.

[733] Plaut, 1946b op. cit.

Furthermore, CIR 4 suggested that even apparently regular and 'voluntary' purchases of artworks for occupation currency which were paid in full still cannot be treated as falling outside the realm of unlawful plunder. This is particularly the case if one considers the wider national and economic contexts:

> In the foregoing discussion of financial arrangements, it should be kept in mind that the paper money which was exchanged in occupied territory for works of art had no real backing. In effect, these "purchases" were only a more devious and more palatable form of looting than outright confiscation. It makes no difference, at least to the economy of the occupied territories, how carefully legalised the form of such sales was made to appear. The German buyers well knew what all this added up to; and the collaborators were willing to take a short-range personal gain at the cost of long-range national bankruptcy.[734]

This analysis has interesting, and perhaps even radical, legal implications. It suggests a basis on which transactions that appear on the surface at least to be instances of the unlawful legal principle of 'freedom of contract' can, nevertheless, be interpreted as examples of art looting.

CIR 1 contains a highly incriminating and illuminating attachment providing details of correspondence from 16 July 1941 between Posse and Scholz. This exchange concerned the ERR's collection of artworks from Jewish collections being supplied to the Linz Collection. It merits quotation as evidence of the prevailing attitude of casual disregard for the ownership claims of the original Jewish owners of these artworks:

> Honorable Director:
>
> Permit me to solicit once more your kind assistance with regard to the art objects from the Rothschild collection and other Jewish collections. Last year, in the autumn, the Fuehrer was shown a collection of photos from which I was ordered to make a selection of those pictures which might be suitable for the Fuehrer-Museum in Linz (Group I) or which might be employed for decorative purposes (Group II). I have informed Reichsleiter Bormann of this matter. On February 8, 1941, a part of these pictures were carried from the Jeu de Paume to Munich, two schedules enclosed, photo-copies of which were sent to me. After their arrival in Munich, the pictures were photographed in the Fuehrerbau. From the photos and the two schedules it is indicated that the greater part of the pictures, of which photos had been previously shown to the Fuehrer, had not been brought to Munich. Instead of the "Pompadour in the

[734] CIR 4 (Linz), op. cit., 42.

Garden" by Boucher, the well-known version of "Madame Pompadour in the Salon," from the collection of Marries de Rothschild, which did not figure in the erstwhile group of photographs, was sent. Another version of this picture had already been seized from the Rothschilds in Vienna, and had been transferred by permission of the Fuehrer to the Vienna Kunsthistorisches Museum. I am enclosing a list of the pictures still missing, and I should be very much obliged to you if you would help me to settle the matter or tell me who is competent to do so. Moreover, it would be desirable, in the light of the order given me by the Fuehrer, should I be able to get a survey of the total stock of works of art seized in France."[735]

CIR 4 provides extensive details of the internal administrative procedures and bureaucratic dimensions of this cultural plunder aspect of the Holocaust: that is, how:

> the collections of Aphons and Loius Rothschild in Vienna, first Jewish collections to be confiscated, were presented to Hitler by Gauleiter Bürckel,[736] after a little official prodding. Other Viennese Jewish collections soon followed. On 20 October 1939 Posse submitted a long list to Bormann, for the Führer's approval, of his proposed selection of objects from these confiscated sources (See Attachment 72). Of a total of 269 pictures, 122 were proposed for Linz (plus a "reserve" of 60), 44 for the Kunsthistorisches Institut in Vienna, and 43 to other museums in Vienna, Innsbruck and Graz.[737]

This ALIU report then discusses the content of various incriminating letters from Posse asserting his authority to appropriate artworks not only from confiscated but also 'safeguarded' collections, and Martin Bormann's explicit authorisation of this policy in July 1939. CIR 4 also refers its readers to additional material concerning the anti-Semitic looting in Austria of the Lanckoronsky and Bondy collections.[738] In many ways, ALIU officials concluded that these Nazi practices served as a blue-print and testing ground for later confiscations across Nazi-occupied Europe.[739] CIR 4 then reviews other documentary evidence relevant to the Holocaust:

[735] CIR 1 (ERR), op. cit., Attachment 11.

[736] CIR 4 (Linz), op. cit., 9 notes the Rothschild collection formed the largest part of the artworks looted for the Linz Museum.

[737] Ibid., 5.

[738] Ibid., 5, and Attachment 5.

[739] Ibid., 7, and Attachment 8.

> In an inventory of 31 July 1940, Posse listed 342 paintings acquired for Linz, not including more than 150 paintings held in reserve for decorative and other purposes. (See Attachment 73). While some of these works were purchased, the greater part were acquired through confiscation of Jewish collections in Vienna. All of the 182 paintings recommended for acquisition on 20 October 1939 appear in this inventory.[740]

This CIR also noted that, whilst Jewish collections were singled out for confiscation in Western and Central Europe, looting policy in Poland was indiscriminate in that 'Poles should keep nothing.'[741] As with so many other areas of Nazi rule, there were fundamental inconsistencies between official policies and actual practices in Nazi-occupied Poland. Plaut, for example, notes:

> On November 25, 1939, traveling under orders issued by Bormann, Posse arrived in Poland to examine for their interest to Linz the repositories of looted Polish art established at Warsaw and Cracow by Dr. Hans Frank's General Government. Three weeks later, he recommended formally to the Reich Chancellery that the world-famous Leonardo, Raphael, and Rembrandt paintings from the Czartoryski Collection be reserved for Linz. Though it was official doctrine that all Polish art works, in churches, museums, and private hands, were eligible for confiscation, the policy called also for the retention of the booty in Poland. Hence, few Polish-owned masterpieces found their way into Germany. (The great Veit Stoss alter from Cracow, which was shipped to Nuremberg in a specially constructed van, and the lovely Bellotto paintings from Warsaw were notable exceptions).[742]

By means of both interrogations and a close analysis of captured records, ALIU officials identified sixty eight dealers in Germany alone who had sold works to Führermuseum agents.[743] They discovered that Posse had to make special requests regarding those works of art originally looted from Poland but then stored by Mühlmann for Göring in Berlin,[744] a small number of which, including a Raphael, Leonardo da Vinci and a Rembrandt, he believed would fill gaps in the Linz Collection. Posse had also developed a list of German masters located in areas further east, on the assumption that these could become available with further

[740] Ibid., 5.
[741] Ibid., 6. For confirmation of this attitude in relation to the Göring Collection, see CIR 2 (Göring), op. cit., 32.
[742] Plaut, 1946b op. cit.
[743] Supplement to CIR 4 (Linz), op. cit., Attachment 54, 'List of German Dealers Not Specifically Discussed in Chapter IV 'Who Sold to Linz.'
[744] CIR 2 (Göring), op. cit., 31.

German military success against the Soviet Union.[745] The latter point is important legally as it shows an integral linkage between planned looting and anticipated invasions of other countries as part of a wider strategy of 'waging aggressive war', one of the key Nuremberg charges.

ALIU staff discovered that, in addition to the activities of the Museum's two Directors, art looting depended upon the services of a wider network of individuals, some of whose actions were directly effected by other aspects of the Holocaust, including the need to seek protection from policies of anti-Semitic persecution. As already noted, a key task for ALIU officials was to identify the core members of this and other such networks for the purposes of both restitution and potential prosecution for war crimes. ALIU staff even interrogated, albeit with little success, Posse's elderly widow, who clearly knew little of the details of her deceased husband's work at Linz.[746] However, interrogations of members of the Linz network, such as Voss were far more successful. For example, it became clear from this interrogation that Posse had employed a number of consultants. These included Göpel, who rapidly became a Linz 'expert' and chief procurer in the Netherlands for this collection.[747] Göpel's acquisitions in the occupied West included transactions negotiated with Vitale Bloch, a Russian Jewish dealer. An OSS report notes: 'Göpel had protected him from the anti-Semitic laws, and in return received first refusal on whatever Bloch discovered on the art market.'[748] Göpel frequently travelled to France in search of artworks, and became involved in the Schloss affair.[749]

In addition to outright confiscations, ALIU officials discovered that, between 1940 and 1941, the Linz Museum had acquired artwork from Buchner and others. These had been arbitrarily 'de-accessioned' from other collections, often with the direct authorisation or, at least general support, of Hitler himself.[750] These officials later discovered that Posse had been required to sell confiscated works from Jewish and other looted collections that were not judged suitable for the Linz Museum.[751]

[745] 'Posse inspection report for Martin Bormann', November 1939: CIR 4 (Linz), op. cit., Attachment Five.

[746] Parkhurst Memo, 6 July 1945: US NA, RG 260, Entry 33.

[747] CIR 4 (Linz), op. cit., 46.

[748] Ibid.

[749] Ibid.

[750] CIR 4 (Linz), 56; Supplement to CIR 4, Attachment 76; Petropoulos, 2000 op. cit., 32.

[751] DIR (Buchner), op. cit.

Nevertheless, between 1943 and 1945, Voss had purchased approximately twelve hundred paintings for Linz, mainly works composed by nineteenth-century German artists.[752]

In short, from April 1943, Hermann Voss assumed the role of Director of the Linz collection as well as the Wiesbaden Gallery. He continued the established range of methods for building up Hitler's collection that Posse had devised and was therefore: 'caught squarely in the flow of loot. With the pattern already established and the machinery smoothly in motion, Voss, a weakly scholar, simply went along.'[753] The ALIU's investigations of the Linz museum addressed many of the major themes of its study of the Göring Collection. Many of these, such as the challenge to apparently 'lawful' purchases of artworks, contained potentially important implications for both war crimes trials and Holocaust-restitution programmes.

Problems concerning Switzerland and other national contexts

Holocaust-restitution efforts, as well as wider studies of Nazi art looting, have highlighted the problematic role that formally 'neutral' Swiss authorities and banks played in supporting aspects of Nazi genocide.[754] As Feliciano's study of the looting of French Jews notes:

> The role played by Switzerland in the Nazi art-confiscation in France also started acquiring a clear shape. The French-Swiss art connection was a well-established one...few have specifically looked into the art found in that country. I have, and what I found out is intriguing and disquieting.[755]

The significance of the ALIU's work in Switzerland, particularly those investigations that culminated in its Final Report,[756] is addressed and placed in a wider context by a number of legal studies.[757] Nicholas notes that:

---

752 DIR 12, op. cit.: 22–23; cf. CIR 4 (Linz), op. cit., 16.

753 Plaut, 1946b op. cit.

754 Thomas Buomberger, Raubkunst, Kunstraub: *Die Schweiz und der Handel mit gestohlenen Kulturgütern zur Zeit des Zweiten Weltkriegs*, Orell Füssli: 1998; Esther Tisa Francini, Fluchtgut-Raubgut: *Der Transfer von Kulturgütern in und über Die Schweiz 1933–1945 und die Frage der Restitution* Chronos: 2001.

755 Feliciano, 1997 op. cit., 9.

756 The report is available at: http://docproj.loyola.edu.

757 For example, see Diane Walton Kelly, 'Leave No Stone Unturned: The Search

> After the war...hundreds of thousands of works were returned to their owners, but, of course, not everything was found or claimed. In the neutral countries, after the war, the Office of the Secret Service ('OSS') and British Intelligence sent teams to Switzerland, Portugal, and Spain to trace looted works. These teams were authorized, in certain instances, to represent the recuperation commissions of other Allied nations. Although their initial reception in Switzerland was warm, they soon ran into great resistance.... But, as soon as Allied pressure decreased, the matter died down. The OSS art unit was withdrawn from Switzerland in January 1946. By 1946, the OSS had traced only about seventy-five pictures to Switzerland, which is another reason the Swiss federal government gave for not pushing the investigation.[758]

Rousseau and Plaut conducted investigations in Switzerland from 20 November 1945 through to 10 January 1946: 'under the aegis of the Economic Counsellor to the American legation at Bern. The Chief problem under consideration was the flow to Switzerland, and the concealment there, of works of art looted by the Germans in the occupied countries.'[759] They liased with American diplomatic authorities in an effort to secure greater cooperation and relevant information from the Swiss.[760] In addition to supplying the fruits of their investigations to the Swiss, they also interrogated a number of German and Swiss nationals.[761]

The DIR report on Wendland emphasises the longstanding, if largely informal, nature of his links with Theodor Fischer, owner of the Fischer Gallery in Lucerne. It notes that: 'Fischer, through his large gallery and auction house in Lucerne became the most important outlet for the works of art ferreted out by Wendland.'[762] Wendland's criminality also extended to violations of Swiss law. As a German citizen prohibited from private sales, he had no option but to sell through a Swiss intermediary. And yet:

> He has however admitted selling some art in Switzerland, and explains this by saying that he sold only enough to cover his actual living expenses

for Art Stolen by the Nazis and the Legal Rules Governing Restitution of Stolen Art', 9 *Fordham Media & Entertainment and Law Journal* (1999) 549; Lynn Nicholas, 'Neutrality, Morality, And The Holocaust; The Rape of European Art', *14 Am. U. Int'l L. Rev.* 237, (1998).

[758] Op. cit., 24.

[759] Final Report, op. cit., 5.

[760] Ibid., 5.

[761] Ibid.

[762] Wendland DIR report, 1946 op. cit., 12.

> in Switzerland—an arrangement which he feels was legal under the Swiss laws.... Certainly all evidence indicates that it was Wendland who chose, and persuaded Fischer to accept, the looted art which came to the Galerie Fischer during the war through exchanges with the Germans.[763]

When discussing the activities of Göring and Hofer, we have already addressed and illustrated with a number of specific examples the role played by the Fischer gallery in the sale of art looted from Jewish owners. Although relevant to the current topic, the details of these various transactions will not, however, be repeated here. With respect to art looted in Switzerland, two reports, produced under the auspices of the US State Department made full use of ALIU research. The findings of ALIU investigations gathered elsewhere but relevant to Switzerland were presented to the Swiss federal political department for use by their federal customs and Office of Compensation.[764]

The ALIU's Mühlmann interrogation report summarises additional detailed evidence it had gathered concerning the role played by Switzerland in Göring's looting operations, particularly the Fischer Gallery in Lucerne.[765] Through buying and selling the fruits of smuggling operations from Germany into Switzerland, this gallery facilitated different aspects of Göring's art looting. Amongst artworks the Fischer Gallery was involved with were included 6 items looted from the Rosenberg and Rothschild collections, which had been transported to Lucerne by means of the diplomatic pouch of the German legation.[766]

Wittmann's final 'winding up' report following his survey of developments in the summer and autumn of 1946, which included liaison with State Department officials with Safehaven responsibilities in this area, came to some rather downbeat conclusions:

> Switzerland still remains the most important unsolved problem in the "Safehaven" aspects of enemy looting of art. Despite the [ALIU] investigations which were carried out here by members of this Unit and Mr Douglas Cooper of the British Element C.C.... there still remain many unsolved questions. Members of the Economic Security Controls Division of the American Legation in Berne still maintain an active interest in this subject and were of considerable assistance during my stay.... In general, the Swiss have agreed to continue the investigations of art transactions

[763] Ibid.

[764] The detailed results of the Swiss operation were incorporated in State Department Safehaven Reports No. 148, 9 December 1945, and No. 229, 5 January, 1946.

[765] CIR 2 (Göring), op. cit. 128–129.

[766] DIR (Mühlmann), op. cit., 4.

> in Switzerland during the war, which had been started by this Unit and by the British.... Swiss dealers who collaborated with the Germans are once more carrying on their businesses as usual and that there has been a considerable amount of traffic in art between collaborationist art dealers of France, Holland and Switzerland since the conclusion of the war.[767]

Wittmann's efforts to intensify Swiss investigations included holding meetings with relevant government officials of the Swiss Compensation Office, where they were given 'detailed reports' of ongoing investigations they had conducted into the Fischer Gallery in Lucerne. These officials requested further assistance from the Americans on this case. In addition, they disclosed details of three other Swiss firms, based in Zurich and Lugano, suspected of involvement in looted art, together with two other art firms in Basel that were soon to be investigated. These officials also told Wittmann of the 'extremely disappointing' results of a census of wartime art purchases, which required doubtful acquisitions to be reported. His conclusion was that:

> It would seem that the Swiss are continuing a policy of strict neutrality in the recovery and return of looted works of art, and are taking limited action to recover such assets. The 76 paintings which appeared on the Allied Lists have, with the exception of 2 or 3 pictures, been collected by the Swiss and sequestered in the Berne Museum, until such time as their ultimate disposition is determined. But aside from these pictures...no other looted works of art have been recovered. It is hoped that the report on Hans Wendland will assist in the clearing up of some of the remaining problems regarding this subject, and that it may lead to the recovery of certain other objects of art.[768]

The results of some aspects of the ALIU's investigations in this country were incorporated into State Department Safehaven Reports 148 and 229.[769]

In short, the ALIU's own summary of its efforts in this country is, despite its best efforts, rather negative, with the blame largely residing with the reluctance of the Swiss authorities to prioritise the interests of the mainly Jewish victims of Nazi art looting over those of Swiss nationals who collaborated with the agents of the looters.

The ALIU also wrote reports on looting activities in particular nations. These included: *Report on Objects Removed to Germany from Holland,*

---

[767] Wittmann, 'Final Mission to Europe', op. cit., 11–13.
[768] Ibid., 13.
[769] Final Report, op. cit., 5.

Belgium and France during the German Occupation on the Countries, focusing upon the Netherlands. It was written by Jean Vlug, a Dutch national and intelligence officer who worked closely with the OSS unit.[770] For a short period, OSS officials also worked with their MFA&A colleagues in the Netherlands investigating the activities of art dealers and experts, such as Friedlander and Vitale Bloch, who had assisted in cultural plunder. Waterhouse reported that the latter: 'is now busily reinsuring himself by turning King's evidence'. He stated that art dealer Peter de Boer was seeking: 'to get on any commission of Dutch experts which might eventually go to Germany to examine restitution claims...perhaps to cover some of his own traces.'[771]

Counter-espionage dimensions of ALIU's work

One of the original premises behind the creation of the ALIU was that the network of art dealers complicit in the cultural plunder aspect of the Holocaust would include a number of individuals using this role as a front for espionage activities. There was, therefore, a *distinctly counter-intelligence dimension* to the ALIU's role.[772] At this time, American and British intelligence operations were gathering information on Nazis who might prove capable of posing a threat to Allied interests, even after Hitler's military surrender. During 1944–45, the Allied policy was to counteract postwar espionage and the transfer of stolen assets, including the plunder associated with the Holocaust: 'to places of refuge where they might be used to finance the postwar survival of Nazism.'[773] In other words, one wartime concern of the OSS leadership in 1943–44 was to neutralise the financing of a postwar resurgence in Nazism by means of the sale outside Europe of looted art and other assets, many of which stemmed from the Holocaust. It was even possible that complicit art

---

[770] Nicholas, 1995 op. cit., 380. Its full title is Detailed Interrogation Report No. 1: Kajetan Mühlmann and the Dienststelle Mühlmann, 25 December 1945. The report includes inventories of art objects purchased (with prices), stolen or confiscated in areas under German occupation. The later CIR describes Mühlmann as: 'obstinate, he has no conscience, he does not care about Art, he is a *liar* and a *vile* person.' CIR 3, Dienststelle Mühlmann' op. cit., 12, and also available from the Getty Museum: http://www.getty.edu/research/conducting_research/provenance_index/holocaust.html.

[771] AMG report 159, Annex X, Report on the Western Provinces of Holland', May 1945: US NA, RG 239, Entry 27; cf. Nicholas, 1995 op. cit., 426.

[772] This is examined in more detail in later section devoted to this topic.

[773] Nicholas, 1995 op. cit., 282.

dealers could contribute to such covert postwar actions. These various counter-intelligence factors, taken together with a need to be physically located as close to the European continent as possible, probably explain why Donovan placed the newly-created ALIU under the administrative control of the London Office of the OSS' X-2 Branch.[774]

American archivists have recognised this specifically counter-espionage dimension:[775]

> The ALIU was established at a time when it had become apparent that the Germans intended to proceed with plans for subversive action after the cessation of hostilities, and were making arrangements for a supply of funds during the post-hostilities period. Various sorts of treasure, in the form of items of small bulk but great value (e.g., jewels, paintings, objets d'art), which could be converted into money, had been stolen or otherwise acquired and were being secretly stored in various places in Europe.... The Branch sought these individuals as sources of information on current and future enemy activities and plans, and because it believed that certain Nazi agents would be using art-confiscation activities to conceal their true roles as espionage agents.[776]

Other commentators, including Petropolous, have noted that art-dealing, a notoriously secret and sometimes murky field of activity, was suspected of providing a potential cover for postwar espionage, which OSS officials and US Army Counter-Intelligence Corp officers (CIC) were responsible for hunting down:

> the art-dealing business has always attracted people of dubious ethics. This was why the OSS expected that they would find dealers involved in espionage: although spying is not necessarily unethical, the OSS art experts took it for granted that the dealers would engage in covert activities and were willing to double-cross people.[777]

In this respect, Plaut has noted that his 'special intelligence unit' was 'code-named Project Orion because we truly were the hunters.'[778]

---

[774] ALIU Memorandum, 'Establishment of Project Orion, Standing Order No. 2, function and organization of Orion field headquarters', London, 14 December, 1944–February 27, 1945: US NA, RG 226, Entry 190, Folder 1723.

[775] Nicholas, 1995 op. cit., 282; See Safehaven report 57 (looted art), American Embassy, London, 1945: US NA, RG 226, Entry 210, Box 1 and entries entitled 'Looted art' ibid., Boxes 2 and 3.

[776] See the archivists summary at: http://www.archives.gov/research/microfilm/m1782.pdf

[777] Petropolous, 2000 op. cit., 105.

[778] Plaut, 1997 op. cit., 124.

The premise that Nazi art looting served partly as a cover for secret counterespionage activities was only partially confirmed by the OSS Unit's investigations. The major example of OSS reports uncovering a counterintelligence dimension was Prince Philipp of Hessen (1896–1980), nephew of Kaiser Wilhelm II and relative of Queen Victoria of Britain, and President of Hesse-Nassau.[779] Philipp had married Princess Mafalda, the daughter of King Vittorio Emmanuele III of Italy. Immediately before and during WWII, he exploited his aristocratic background to not only engage in art procurement for Göring and Hitler but also to practice secret diplomacy and espionage.[780] Philipp became Posse's chief agent for art purchases for the Linz museum in Italy.[781] As Petropolous notes:

> Philipp took advantage of Hitler's interest in art as a means of currying favour with the dictator but also found acquiring artworks to be a source of excitement. He worked closely with Hans Posse—they made three trips together to Italy in 1941 alone—and Posse referred to these trips as "acquisition hunts" (*Erwerbungsjagd*). The OSS agents determined that between March 1941 and March 1942 alone, Philipp obtained an estimated eighty-eight paintings for Hitler, of which the most important were the Corsini Memling, *Portrait of a Man*, and a *Leda and the Swan*, then attributed to Leonardo da Vinci, from the Spiridon collection.[782] Most of the works were, naturally, of Italian origin and were in private collections. Posse also recommended that Prince Philipp concentrate on seventeenth—and eighteenth-century works, believing it difficult to obtain scarce top-quality Renaissance pieces. But artists who were represented on this OSS list included Titian, Tintoretto, Tiepolo, and Raphael.[783]

Following the overthrow of Mussolini in 1943, the Nazi regime eventually turned against Philipp and he was detained in Dachau concentration camp, where his wife died after having been reassigned to the camp brothel.[784] He cooperated with the Americans by testifying at the Flos-

[779] CIR 4 (Linz), op. cit., 10–11, 53; Supplement to CIR No. 4, Attachment 71, 'Posse to Bormann, 25 May 1941'.

[780] Ibid., 10, noting that von Hessen effectively scouted for Posse, and placed his art expertise at Posse's service.

[781] Ibid., 53.

[782] The painting *Leda and the Swan* was believed to be a real Leonardo during the Third Reich, but it has subsequently been down-graded to "school of." Hence in fact Hitler lacked any works by Leonardo, with the finest works arguably being the two Vermeers. I am grateful to Jonathan Petropoulos for pointing this out to me.

[783] Petropolous, 2000 op. cit., 107.

[784] CIR 4 (Linz), op. cit., 53.

senbürg and Dachau war crimes trials. However, this did not prevent his later prosecution and punishment from a Hessen De-Nazification court in December 1947, which sentenced him to two years forced labour and confiscated 30 percent of his property.[785]

There was some, albeit rather weak, evidence that Mühlmann and Angerer were both involved in covert intelligence work for the Political Intelligence section of Himmler's SS, the SD.[786] Certainly, the American Counter Intelligence Corps identified Mühlmann as a member of a covert Nazi 'fifth column' in Austria; whilst Wilhelm Hoettl declared that he was one of Heydrich's SD agents from 1934–38. Certainly, the Austrian authorities had arrested him on this ground in 1935.[787]

ALIU officials uncovered another possible counter-espionage dimension in their investigation of the 'Gold Coin Mystery'. This concerned apparently coordinated attempts during the closing months of the war by a number of senior Nazi officials, including Bormann, Utikal and von Hummel, to appropriate the Linz collection of many thousand gold coins and other similar collections at three different locations. The fullest account of this episode is contained in CIR 1:

> SHIEDLAUSKY stated that UTIKAL arrived at Schloss Neuschwanstein/Füssen on the night of 26 April 1945, and ordered him to hand over any gold which was stored in the E.R.R. deposit. SHIEDLAUSKY gave him the only gold available, namely one small oblong wooden case containing a few gold and silver coins of moderate value. According to SHIEDLAUSKY, these were 6 gold and 7 silver Persian coins of 1798; 23 gold coins of European states, each in a small envelope; one gold medal, circa 1720, portraying the Empress Elizabeth of Russia, and commemorating peace with Turkey, in a red leather case. UTIKAL signed a receipt for the gold and left Nueschwanstein on 27 April 1945 with his wife and two children, in an automobile driven by OPFER. He informed SHIEDLAUSKY that he was taking the gold coins to Reichsschatzmeister SCHWARTZ in Munich, acting on ROSENBERG's personal orders. KRESS, one of UTIKAL's closest followers, stated that he was awakened by UTIKAL and ZOELFEL at Schloss Kogl on the night of 3–4 May 1945, and that ZOELFEL asked "Is the chest of gold for us here at Kogl?" KRESS answered that he did not know, whereupon UTIKAL replied "It must be. We have to take it with us for safekeeping and for

[785] Petropolous, 2000 op. cit., 108.
[786] Plaut, 1946a op. cit. notes that Angerer was a 'member of the German Intelligence.'
[787] Petropoulos, 1996b op. cit., 181.

> reconstruction of the Party." KRESS referred them to SCHOLZ, who confirmed that there was no gold at Kogl, and UTIKAL then left with his companions.[788]

Despite the express reference to the postwar reconstruction of the Nazi Party, the counter-espionage dimensions of this episode is not highlighted by Plaut's report. However, CIR 4, which was written later, does raise the possibility that these searches for gold and art works should remain of 'special interest' because of their likely use:

> to finance Nazi underground activities.... when the incidents... all occurring within a week's time—are added up, a pattern of Nazi underground activity seems to emerge. As the chief protagonists, Bormann and von Hummel, are still at large, and Gerhard Utikal has only just been captured, the mystery of the gold coins is not yet solved. Any trail leading to Bormann, obviously, offers the highest incentive.[789]

Counterintelligence themes are also apparent in the ALIU's DIR on Hans Wendland. Wendland, a Swiss-based German citizen who worked closely with Hofer and therefore indirectly Göring, discovered that free passage from occupied to unoccupied France was fairly easy to obtain from minor German officials in Paris through bribery. Wendland's apparent freedom of movement across national borders during wartime provoked considerable suspicion. Indeed, this DIR devotes an entire subsection to this theme under the heading: 'C. Suspicions of Espionage':

> This apparent ease of travel between Switzerland, Germany, occupied and unoccupied France during Germany's most successful years was at once an important factor in Wendland's large and profitable transactions, a privilege enjoyed by few other art agents, and a source of serious suspicion of espionage. Wendland himself has stated that although he would have liked to have had one, he never held a travel authority from Göring or any other high Nazi official, a fact that has been corroborated by Hofer. Wendland explains this freedom of travel by saying that he was always able to secure a visa for Berlin from a friend in the German Embassy at Berne. From Berlin, he states, that he was able to obtain the necessary red pass to go to Paris through a Colonel Tueppen, purchaser of supplies for the Abwehr. This he claims was possible with a small bribe of four kilograms of chocolate.[790]

---

[788] CIR 1 (ERR), op. cit., 47.
[789] CIR 4 (Linz), op. cit., 22.
[790] DIR (Wendland) op. cit., 9.

ALIU officials did not take these claims at face value. Indeed, the ALIU/MFA&A report contains a strong suggestion that, although unproven, Wendland still had a case to answer on the question of espionage. This was largely due to his contacts with Tueppen, who had been an employee of the German Intelligence Service:

> With the exceptions of his first and last trips, Wendland says that he always obtained permission to enter France through Colonel Tueppen. He professes to have been greatly surprised when he learned during the war that Colonel Tueppen was reported to be a paymaster for agents of the German Intelligence Service. Twice in 1942 Wendland was interrogated by the Swiss police regarding suspected espionage—once in the summer of that year, and more intensively on 22 December. Although no formal charges were ever brought against him by the Swiss, it is significant that after the second interrogation the Swiss refused his further exit permits except for the one occasion in 1943 when he went to Paris ostensibly to obtain his own blocked property. It was also after this second interrogation that the Swiss, according to Wendland, requested him to leave the large hotels where he had been accustomed to live and move to a small city. It was for this reason that he rented the villa at Versoix. Certainly, whatever may be the implications of espionage, it is difficult to believe that his numerous permits to Paris were obtained from Colonel Tueppen merely for the price of four kilograms of chocolate.[791]

This suspicion was not further followed up, at least not by members of the ALIU. It is, however, possible that other developments regarding Wendland occurred involving US or British intelligence staff, which have yet to be declassified.

Addressing Holocaust-restitution issues

This section will examine the relation of the ALIU's overall mission to Holocaust and related restitution issues, including the role of such restitution in both this Unit's mission and the range of practical activities Plaut's staff undertook in order to achieve this objective.

Insofar as the European Jewry were foremost amongst the groups subjected to art plunder, it follows that the any practical commitment to restitution would, if at least partially successful and developed in an even-handed manner, disproportionately 'benefit' this particular victim group, although of course in this context restoration of stolen

[791] Ibid., 9–10.

goods only represents a 'benefit' compared with total non-restitution. Whilst legal accountability through prosecution for Nazi war crimes remained one aim of ALIU's overall programme, it did not entirely overshadow the second strand of the ALIU's mission: the practical effort of restitution of looted assets to the families of Jewish and other victims of this organised theft.[792] By means of a 14 December 1944 memorandum, the OSS and the Roberts Commission both formally agreed to the ALIU's role in investigations with restitution implications.[793] This memorandum emphasised that ALIU purposes included presenting 'evidence on which the proper authorities can base general restitution policy', and obtaining: 'information on the personnel and methods of German looting organizations.'[794] The memorandum also clarified what type of information and intelligence the unit would collect for such restitution:

a) Information concerning the wartime activities of art dealers, German and collaborationist museum officials, art scholars, others believed to be active in art trade.
b) Information concerning Germans and other persons or organizations known to have been involved in the confiscations and/or transfers of art properties, and information concerning such procedures.
c) Information concerning loss of art objects from private or public collections through enemy activity.[795]

Plaut maintained that his Unit's analysis of intelligence information was: 'the primary ORION mission and [constituted] the contribution which ORION [made] to the formulation of long-range policy relative to restitution.' Plaut outlined this role for both the Washington and London offices, and requested the Washington office to rapidly supply all necessary materials relevant to restitution.[796] Furthermore,

[792] OSS memo, Plaut and Rousseau to James Murphy, Chief OSS X-2 Branch: Fine Arts Project: Orion, 1–2, US NA, RG 226, Box 532, Folder 1747; cf. NARA Press Release: http://www.archives.gov/press/press-releases/2001/nr01–59.html; Plaut, 1997 op. cit., 94.

[793] SAINT DH/001 to SAINT, 14 December 1944, 1, 'Art Unit,': US NA, RG 226, Entry 190, Box 516.

[794] Ibid.

[795] Ibid., 2.

[796] See Plaut, Standing Order No. 1, 9 January 1945, 1–4, 'Orion Organization': US NA, RG 226, Entry 190, Box 532.

Plaut established positive liaison with British and other Allied agencies which had a specific remit in restitution, or compensation in lieu of restitution issues. These included the British Vaucher Commission, which possessed extensive dossiers on enemy personnel complicit in art looting, and—with more direct relevance—the Macmillan Commission. Both of these commissions shared their intelligence with ALIU officials. The British Ministry of Economic Warfare also supplied Plaut's Unit with information concerning the identity and suspected location of Nazi and German assets. As Rothfeld notes: 'All of these agencies' intelligence data became useful to ALIU's efforts toward putting together the "puzzle" pieces of the confiscated artworks.'[797]

The following are the main ways in which members of the ALIU and their superiors engaged in activities relevant, directly or indirectly, to the restitution of looted artworks:

1. Agreeing to include restitution as an integral part of the ALIU's overall mission objectives and rationale.
2. Identifying and interrogating individuals with knowledge of the whereabouts of Jewish and other looted artworks, and including issues relevant to restitution amongst the questions put to these detainees.
3. Producing DIRs and CIRs in a format and with content that was immediately relevant to restitution, which included all known details of the origins and current location of looted items.
4. Actively tracing the wartime and immediate postwar movement of looted artworks as these passed through many different hands and, on occasions, across national borders.
5. Investigating the origins of works already recovered.
6. Examining the role of plunder agencies, such as the ERR, auctioneers and transport companies complicit in the seizure and movement of artworks, whose surviving records provide clues as to the likely location of stolen paintings.
7. Producing reports that provided a basis for the longer-term work of other Allied officials working on restitution projects long after the dissolution of the ALIU.
8. Requiring, in various ways, detainees at Alt Aussee who possessed knowledge that was considered relevant to postwar restitution to

[797] Rothfeld, 2002 op. cit., Chapter 3, 10.

lend active support for the identification and ultimate restoration of looted works of art, with the threat of prosecution as a sanction for non-compliance.
9. Negotiating with the relevant authorities in neutral countries, particularly Switzerland, to minimise obstacles to restitution, including supplying additional information that assisted with positive changes of their policy on this issue.
10. Initiating a process where the UN would maintain a registry of stolen and recovered works of art to better facilitate postwar restitution of artworks to the origin owners.

In practice, these elements cannot always be neatly separated out and analysed in isolation, any more than the restitution element can be entirely distinguished from the other ALIU objectives, including the securing of evidence relevant to war crimes prosecution.

The seriousness with which ALIU officials took their obligations towards restitution is especially clear from the 'recommendations' of DIR reports, which specifically gave some measure of credit, albeit only in mitigation, to individuals who had, for whatever reasons, facilitated their efforts at Holocaust-restitution:

> Schiedlausky was a confirmed National Socialist, who appears to have no quarrel with the "ideological" basis for the confiscations effected by the Einsatzstab Rosenberg in France. In spite of his political convictions and his acknowledged complicity, it is believed that he acted in good faith within the limits of his assignment. There is no evidence available to indicate that he ever gained personal profit...or that he initiated or participated in looting operations. He belonged to the more moderate, professionally responsible element of the Einsatzstab, which prepared inventories through which it has become possible to trace and make available for restitution the great majority of the works confiscated. Schiedlausky is believed to have made a conscientious effort (irrespective of the motives involved) to bring some method and order out of the chaotic welter of Einsatzstab seizures. Unless it should be determined that all Einsatzstab personnel are to be held responsible personally for the criminal acts perpetrated by the organization, there appears to be no tangible basis for the retention of Schiedlausky as a war criminal[798]

This recommendation did, however, suggest that he be held in custody as a 'material witness' for later war crimes trials of ERR personnel,

[798] DIR No. 5 (Schiedlausky) op. cit., 3.

and that—by way of making amends for his complicities—he be put to work: 'in a controlled technical capacity in the work of checking and sorting objects confiscated by the E.R.R., preparatory to their final disposition.'[799] Other DIRs reported that works of art recovered from the subjects of ALIU interrogations had been returned to MFA&A colleagues for purposes of ultimate restitution.[800] Mühlmann was also given credit by Plaut's staff for his willingness to assist in aspects of postwar restitution.[801]

In furtherance of their restitution aims, many of the DIR reports contain extensive lists of specific works of art confiscated by the ERR and bought, sold and exchanged in France, Switzerland and Germany, for example, by various profit-seeking dealers, such as Rochlitz.[802] These reports also identified, as far as possible, details concerning the current whereabouts of confiscated works, and identified confiscated items which had apparently 'gone missing' and where restitution could prove more difficult.[803] Yeide rightly notes that in addition to retracing the extent and victims of this massive programme of cultural plunder, ALIU officials were able to use captured ERR records to assist in future restitution efforts for the benefit of the victims of this type of war criminality:[804]

> Despite the Nazis' intent to eradicate the Jewish people from whom art objects were confiscated in France and elsewhere under the ERR, the organization kept meticulous records of its activities, including the sources of the plunder.... The ERR materials provided Plaut and the other ALIU members the documentation needed to assess the scope of ERR activities in occupied France. Moreover, the materials were of vital use in the identification of recovered art and the restitution of art to pre-war owners.[805]

---

799 Ibid.

800 See for example DIR No. 4 (Rochlitz) op. cit., 12.

801 Petropoulos, 1996b op. cit., 178.

802 DIR No. 4 (Rochlitz), op. cit., 3–5, 6–8. See also CIR 1 (ERR) op. cit., Chapter 5.

803 DIR No. 4 (Rochlitz), op. cit., 9–11.

804 ERR Card File, US, NA Microfilm publication M1942, 2003.

805 Yeide, 2007 op. cit., 2–3. This writer also states: 'ERR staff prepared inventory cards for each object, arranged by an alpha-numeric code derived from the name of the collector from whom the object had been seized and the number of individual items within that collection. The ERR card file is astonishing in its level of detail. Objects are catalogued not only physically (i.e., media, dimensions, condition) but also given a brief textual description and, in some cases, an art historical bibliography. Moreover the cards are augmented by photographs arranged by the same alpha-numeric code.' Ibid.

Plaut's postwar writings confirm this point noting that:

> All the painstaking thoroughness of the German method was lavished on the job, with the neat result that the Einsatzstab files were discovered intact at its headquarters in Germany after the American break-through, and the vast complications of Allied restitution procedure were immeasurably simplified.[806]

ALIU officials reported on areas where uncertainty of present and future restitution of looted artworks remained a problem, such as artworks stolen from in Poland, whilst also noting important leads.[807] Wherever possible, their DIR and CIR reports highlighted the current location of looted artworks, and all available information they could gather to assist the victims of art looting track down and recover their works.[808] For example, DIR 2 contains an attachment consisting of: 'a list of all paintings from confiscated Jewish collections or dealers' stocks bought by Buchner for his museums. The provenance, the inventory number, and the name of the repository where they are located at present, is given in each case.'[809] The ALIU's Final Report provides information concerning claimed *locations* of artworks confiscated from the Rosenberg and other Jewish collections, and which had been displayed in other galleries in Paris,[810] or which collaborationists have, perhaps to improve their own postwar standing, returned to their Jewish victims.[811] It also supplied information on Paris companies, such as Jonemann, that, on behalf of the ERR, allegedly transported large quantities of works of art looted from the Paul Rosenberg Collection,[812] not least because their

[806] Plaut, 1946a op. cit.

[807] Plaut for example wrote: 'The chaotic internal situations wrought by subsequent military events has left undetermined the fate of much of the Polish treasure. The Czartoryski paintings desired by Posse never came to Linz, but they were recovered, as well as a group of 30 Dürer drawings which were at one time kept at the Führerhauptquartier in Berlin. These were the only notable 'benefice' from Poland.' Plaut, 1946b op. cit.

[808] For example, Plaut recalls that: 'the loot was brought in piecemeal, and placed—through the end of 1943—in the six special Einsatzstab depots—at Neuschwanstein, Nickolsburg, Chiemsee, Buxheim, Kogl, and Seisenegg.' Plaut, 1946a op. cit.

[809] DIR 2 (Buchner) op. cit., 5.

[810] Drouand entry, ibid., 99.

[811] Martin Fabiani is listed as 'with Dequoy, the arch-collaborationist of the Paris dealer Milieu. Received looted objects from the ERR by undetermined means. Has personally returned 24 pictures to Paul Rosenberg.', ibid., 101.

[812] For internal OSS-ALIU memorandum on this collection, see 'ORION Activities, two documents; looted art, German art personnel, memorandum from Paul Rosenberg, 1945': US NA, RG 226, Entry 210, Box 4.

records are important sources of evidence of the locations of current pieces.[813] In addition, Allied military officials clearly saw ALIU staff as the right people to report the discovery of items probably stolen from victims of the Holocaust by members or associates of RSHA staff, who of course controlled the death and concentration camps.[814]

Other aspects of the ALIU's restitution related activities included recovering photographs of looted works to assist their reinstatement.[815] A typical example of the provision of detailed information regarding coerced exchanges vital for restitution is contained in CIR 1:

> V. DETAILS OF EXCHANGES
>
> (Note: Information gained with respect to the sources and disposition of objects involved, appraisal values, circumstances of the various exchanges, etc., varies in relation to the amount of documentation available and to the details obtained from participants.)
>
> # 1. 3 March 1941, with ROCHLITZ, in Paris (for GÖRING).
>
> *E.R.R. gave:*

1. Braque	*Still Life with Grapes and Peaches* Oil, 45 × 94 cm. Signed: Braque 27 (from the KANN Coll.)
2. Cézanne	*Douleur* Oil, 168 × 126 cm. (from the KANN Coll.)
3. Corot	*Mother and Child in Woods* Oil, 133 × 97 cm. Signed: Corot (from the ROSENBERG-BERNSTEIN Coll.)
4. Degas	*Madame Camus at the Piano* Oil, 140 × 95 cm. Signed: Degas (from the KANN Coll.)
5. Matisse	*Woman at a Table* Oil, 80 × 100 cm. Signed: Henri Matisse 40 (from the ROSENBERG-BERNSTEIN Coll.)

813 ALIU Final Report, op. cit., 107.

814 Michaelis to Rousseau, 11 June, 1945, 'Location of Paintings': US NA 260, Box 450, Folder ERR 1940–44.

815 CIR 2 (Göring), op. cit., 24, 33, 165.

6. Matisse — *Still Life: Flowers and Pineapples*
Oil, 80 × 100 cm.
Signed: Henri Matisse 40
(from the ROSENBERG-BERNSTEIN Coll.)

7. Matisse — *Sleeping Woman at a Table*
Oil, 80 × 100 cm.
Signed: 40 Henri Matisse
(from the ROSENBERG-BERNSTEIN Coll.)

8. Picasso — *Women at the Races*
Oil, 47 × 62 cm.
Signed: Picasso
(from the LINDENBAUM Coll.)

9. Picasso — *Mother and Child*
Oil, 133 × 197 cm.
Signed: Picasso Biarritz 1918
(from the ROSENBERG-BERNSTEIN Coll.)

10. Renoir — *Reclining Woman in Summer Dress*
Oil, 29 × 46 cm.
Signed: Renoir

11. Sisley — *Spring Landscape*
Oil, 54 × 74 cm.
Signed: Sisley 89
(from the Georges BERNHEIM Coll.)[816]

CIR 4 (Linz) also contains a summary of the records of specific works of looted art and other cultural items which the ALIU had recovered.

Many ALIU reports attempted not only to identify who looted which artworks, such as those of the Schloss collection, but also where a number of these were likely to be hidden or stored awaiting restitution to their rightful owners.[817] For example, ALIU officials monitored the movement of the Göring Collection between Carinhall and Berchtesgaden in 1945.[818] Furthermore, the DIR on Wendland notes the

---

[816] CIR 1 (ERR), op. cit., 27.

[817] CIR 2 (Göring), op. cit., 171; CIR 4 (Linz), op. cit., 23 noting that only 22 of the 262 paintings looted from the Schloss collection for the Linz Museum had, at this time, been located. Ibid., This report also retraces who later acquired particular works from this Jewish collection, and restitution of items plundered for the Linz collection on the basis of ALIU lists. See ibid., 34, 59.

[818] See 'Orion: Interim Report on Hermann Göring's Collection of Looted Art', 6 June 1945, Appendix C: French Works of Art Obtained by Former Reichsmarschall Hermann Göring, 19 May 1945, Paul Kubala, Maj, MI, Commanding: US NA, RG 239 / Roberts Commission Subject Files, Microfilm Publication M1944, Reel 89. See also CIR 2 (Göring), op. cit., 170–72.

suspected whereabouts in Switzerland of a considerable amount of artworks looted from French Jews during the Nazis' occupation:

> Le Coultre Warehouse, Geneva: About 60 to 80 paintings. Of these approximately 30 or more were acquired in France during, or since, the occupation. Galerie Fischer, Lucerne: About 20 paintings and drawings of which many were acquired in France during the occupation.... Swiss friends: Approximately 20 of his best paintings acquired in France since 1940 are being held for him by about five Swiss friends (probably art dealers). These pictures include the following: Fragonard "*Children*"; Goya "*Portrait of a Child*"; Goya "*Sketch*"; Mabuse "*Madonna*" and "*Titan/Tintoretto*"; Rubens "*Seneca*"; van Geyen "*Landscape van der Neer*"[819]

CIR 1 also took great care to address the immediate and then later destinations of various Jewish collections that the ERR had looted. It provides as detailed answers to these questions as the captured ERR and other records allowed:

> In conformity with the HITLER order of 18 November 1940, the greater part of the material confiscated by the Einsatzstab was sent to Germany for safekeeping and for HITLER's ultimate disposition. The SCHOLZ report of July 1944 records 29 shipments into the Reich during the period April 1941 to July 1944. The shipments comprised 138 freight carloads, containing 4,174 cases of work destined for 6 separate protected deposits. These deposits were:
>
> 1. Schloss Neuschwanstein (Kreis Füssen)
> 2. Schloss Chiemsee (Herreninsel, Kreis Traunstein)
> 3. Cloister Buxheim (Kreis Memmingen)
> 4. Schloss Kogl (St. Georgen/(Kreis Vöcklabruck)
> 5. Schloss Seisenegg (Kreis Amstetten)
> 6. Schloss Nickolsburg (Kreis Nickolsburg)
>
> The first shipment of Einsatzstab material from France to Germany took place in April 1941. Shipments continued to the above-mentioned deposits through February 1944, at which time the Reichschancellery, because of the increasing danger from air raids, ordered the major deposits evacuated and their contents brought to Alt Aussee, Austria, for storage in the Steinberg salt mine.[820]

As already noted, one of the ways in which ALIU officials contributed to the restitution aspect of their mission was by applying pressure to the detainees they interrogated to reveal additional details of the location of

---

[819] DIR Wendland, op. cit., 24.
[820] CIR 1 (ERR), op. cit., 21.

looted works. Indeed, Plaut notes: 'From June 1945 until the spring of 1946, leading participants in Nazi art looting operations were detained for varying periods of time and helped to...identify the whereabouts of countless masterpieces.'[821]

As already noted, ALIU officials attempted to actively intervene with authorities in neutral countries that had not proved especially cooperative in facilitating restitution. ALIU personnel can claim a measure of credit for gaining greater co-operation in Holocaust-restitution efforts from the Swiss authorities. In cooperation with the Economic Counsellor to the American Legation at Bern, members of Plaut's Unit conducted investigations in Switzerland between 20 November 1945 and 10 January 1946. These focused upon the transportation and concealment of looted art works. In December 1945 and again in January 1946, Plaut and Rousseau travelled to Switzerland: 'to seek the cooperation of the Swiss government in the restitution of looted art that had found its way through many complex and devious channels into the hands of private collectors and art dealers: namely Emil Buhrle, the arms manufacturer, and Theodor Fischer, the well-known dealer and auctioneer.'[822] They also conducted research into the role played by Swiss or Swiss-based dealers. The initial reaction of the Swiss Federal Government to Plaut and Rousseau's investigations was to be: 'uncooperative but in time bowing to international pressure, they helped to expedite the restitution process.'[823]

Wittmann's final ALIU report from the Autumn of 1946 reinforces the impression of other evidence that members of this unit were particularly concerned to ensure that the start they had made on the restitution aspect of their overall mission was not to whither on the vine as it were. He reported that:

> Since it was felt by this Unit and by most of the other agencies involved with the same problem during the war, that after the conclusion of all active investigations there should eventually be a central international file of reports concerning art looting during the war, together with lists and photographs of art objects still uncovered. I talked with the following persons [in London] concerning this problem...It was agreed that such a file, including lists of persons who were active in art looting during the war, catalogues of art objects which are still missing, photographic files of

[821] Plaut, 1997 op. cit., 124. For additional details of interrogation and the liaisons needed to secure them from other agencies, see Howe, 1946 op. cit., 183.

[822] Plaut, 1997 op. cit., 125.

[823] Ibid.

> as many of these objects as possible, should go far to prohibit the illegal traffic in stolen works of art in the future. It is recognized that probably most of the looted art still missing will remain under cover for the next 5 or 10 years and will only appear on the market when it is felt that active interest in their recovery has ceased.[824]

The upshot was that a proposal of this kind was agreed to be presented to the first formal UNESCO meeting in November 1946, which was considering an international art programme.

ALIU staff concerned with restitution were assisted by the fruits of their own previous investigations. Taper, an intelligence official of the MFA&A from 1946–48, recalls:

> And it [the Wendland interrogation] also provided, I understand, some of the documentation needed to persuade the Swiss government to change its policy in regard to wartime art transactions that had occurred—a policy of traditional leniency favouring the dealers, whilst putting virtually impossible obstacles in the way of those who had been victimised and who in postwar years were seeking to recover what had been taken from them.[825]

Taper has also recognised that even after the dissolution of the ALIU, its reports were sufficiently rich to provide 'new leads' for later art looting investigators with direct responsibility for restitution:

> Those of us, like me, who came along after the War Department's OSS had done its superb reports on art looting found them an invaluable basis for our own investigations. Throughout my tenure, we sought to enlarge and build on that foundation by continued questioning of the principal players—such art advisers as Hans Posse, Karl Haberstock, Walter Hofer, and Mühlmann—as well as art dealers such as Hans Wendland, and others...and new leads would develop that we could act on or that would shed further light on the murky history in which they had been involved.[826]

As part of their restitution responsibilities, ALIU staff fully exploited the highly detailed captured inventories of looted art from private and public collections in Belgium, France, Italy, and the Netherlands.[827] This allowed these OSS officials to better determine: 'locations of storage and identifying virtually every object in Nazi custody that was confiscated

---

[824] Wittmann, 'Final Mission to Europe', op. cit., 7.
[825] Taper, 1997 op. cit., 137.
[826] Bernard Taper, 'Investigating Art Looting for the MFA&A' in Simpson, 1997 op. cit., 137.
[827] Plaut, 1997 op. cit., 125.

from these countries.'[828] Concerning the Netherlands, one report noted that: 'the ERR also had a Holland branch, with offices in Amsterdam, with Schmidt-Stahler in charge. Through this agency, important Jewish depositories were liquidated at the Lippmann-Rosenthal Bank, and some of the material went to Linz.'[829]

The ALIU's Final Report issued in May 1946 expressed concern that it had not been possible to afford restitution to a significant proportion of looted art, and that a considerable number of pieces had been relocated to Switzerland, Sweden, Spain, Portugal and to the Americas:

> From information obtained, there appear to be three significant problems of containing transfer [of assets to the USA]. Relaxation of wartime controls on former collaborationist dealers, presence of assets being held for the benefit of collaborationist dealers by their American colleagues, importation because of the relaxation of wartime controls on works of art of questionable origin.... It is likely that a considerable volume of loot may have reached the South American continent. Further investigation will be required with particular reference to movement from South America of looted works of art.[830]

Copies of the ALIU's various reports were, according to the Roberts Commission Report: 'of considerable assistance to the Allied restitution authorities in Germany'.[831] Indeed, there is evidence that those officials involved professionally in art restitution, whose work in this field continued after the disbandment of the OSS unit in the late spring of 1946, found that the ALIU's reports continued to provide particularly helpful guides to their ongoing work. They provided the foundation and guiding principles for future restitution work. As Harclerode and Pittaway note: 'The work of the Allies MFA&A staff and of the OSS ALIU proved to prophetic as well as profitable. In addition to seeking out the principle figures in the Nazi looting programme, they were laying down the basic principles of restitution practice for their successors.'[832] Breitenbach, who worked for the MFA&A organization, has also recalled that:

[828] Ibid.
[829] CIR 4 (Linz), op. cit., 9.
[830] ALIU Final Report, 1 May 1946 op. cit., 5: Getty Research Institute, Box 910130, file 8.
[831] Roberts Commission Report, 1946 op. cit., 40.
[832] Harclerode and Pittaway, 2000 op. cit., 331.

> In the summer of 1945 many of the leading figures of the Nazi art world were interned together in the enclosures of Alt-Aussee. As a result of intensive questioning, the basic facts about Nazi art looting were established and laid down in the excellent OSS Consolidated Interrogation Reports, which became the standard reference document for all later art intelligence work. By studying these reports it became evident that much might be gained by a more detailed questioning of the leading Nazi art dealers. They could in the first place be useful in the identification at the Collecting Point of restitutable objects which had passed through their hands; secondly, they could reveal the names of others who were still holding on to such material; and finally they were in some cases found to be themselves still in the possession of art objects from the occupied countries.[833]

At this point, it would be useful to describe the evaluations of those representing Jewish victims of Nazi art looting. Certainly, Jewish organisations concerned with Holocaust-restitution efforts have valued various OSS ALIU reports. For example, the Final Report has recently been excerpted and distributed privately by the Commission for Art Recovery of the World Jewish Congress and excerpted by *The Art Newspaper* (No. 88, January 1999). Whilst the work of this unit largely came to an end in the Spring of 1946, apart from a one-person concluding mission to Europe, those who followed up on its work recognised the importance of its accomplishments, and sought to develop these further.

CIR 1 contains additional information regarding the ERR that was directly relevant to difficult Holocaust restitution issues in France, which stemmed from the chaotic methods through which many acquisitions were obtained:

> Instead, it was stated that the Einsatzstab employed a number of irresponsible men who would simply collect a truckload of objects and carry them off to the Jeu de Paume. SCHIEDLAUSKY and the other art historians would be working in the Jeu de Paume on inventories, when some stranger would come in with a carload of works of art and simply say, "These are from ROTHSCHILD," or "These are from the Avenue du Bois," leave them and disappear. More often than not, SCHIEDLAUSKY would never again see the same man. When, at a later date, a conscientious attempt would be made to reconstruct the process of seizure

[833] Edgar Breitenbach, 'Historical Survey of the Activities of the Intelligence Department, MFA & A Section, OMGB, 1946–1949,' *College Art Journal*, Vol. 9, No. 2. (Winter, 1949–1950), 192–198, 193.

> and to inventory all objects which had been brought in a particular lot, it would already have become impossible to ascertain the source of a large quantity of material, which remained classified "unknown."[834]

A more detailed assessment of the relative successes and failures of the ALIU in the field of Holocaust-restitution is, however, extremely difficult to make. Part of this problem is that the resources of this small group of OSS officials could, at best, barely make a dent in the massive restitution issues which they, and other agencies operating in this field, had to confront. Between 1945 and 1952, American forces made various efforts to restore stolen art to its original owners. Individuals were required to file their claims through their own national governments, documenting their claims with photographs, invoices, inventory listings, or publications.[835] Sol Chaneles, a commentator on art looting, suggests that over 16 million objects were inventoried by the American forces in Germany.[836] Between 1952 and 1962, West Germany returned more than a million works of art to their rightful owners and heirs. Hence, the overwhelming majority of the pieces were not returned to their owners because they had died during the war and in concentration camps or, if alive, were unable to prove their ownership. Chaneles also points out that many recovered artworks were 'permanently borrowed' by American troops, often being mailed home for later sale through galleries. Furthermore, although the reports of the ALIU were distributed to restitution agencies, they remained classified until the 1970's partly to prevent false claims for missing art, but also to conceal the nature and scope of collaboration and profiteering by French, Dutch, and other art dealers.[837] Recent claims for the restitution of artworks are still being considered by the German government, but of course it is difficult to establish proof of ownership.

This may explain why between 1964 and 1979, only three claims were made, and two of them were settled quickly. Many of the four thousand looted pieces still in the possession of the German government awaiting valid restitution claims are displayed in museums.[838] The

[834] Ibid., 15.

[835] John E. Conklin, *Art Crime*, Westport, CT: Praeger, 1994, 221.

[836] Cited in John Dornberg, 'The Mounting Embarrassment of Germany's Nazi Treasures,' *Art News 87* (September 1988), 130–41.

[837] Chamberlin Russell, *Loot! The Heritage of Plunder*. New York: Facts on File, 1983.

[838] Dornberg, 1988 op. cit.

impact of the somewhat lacklustre commitment of postwar European governments from 1945 to the late-1990's, (when far more serious initiatives were finally launched) in actively pursuing Holocaust-Restitution issues, even those highlighted in ALIU reports, can hardly be laid at the door of these OSS officials. Indeed, in numerous places, these reports contained pleas for such subsequent 'follow-up' work to be undertaken in each of the countries victimised by this aspects of the Holocaust.[839]

In short, ALIU officials included restitution as an integral part of their overall mission objectives and rationale, and regularly acted upon this by identifying and interrogating individuals they suspected of knowing the likely whereabouts of looted artworks. This Unit's DIRs and CIRs addressed issues and materials that were immediately relevant to the work of restitution; whilst operations often succeeded in tracing the wartime and immediate postwar movement of looted artworks even across national borders. In addition, ALIU officials exploited captured ERR and other German records to reveal both the origins of works already recovered, the location of undiscovered artworks and additional details of the role of such plunder agencies. The CIRs and DIRs provided the principles basis for the longer-term work of other Allied officials working on restitution projects. On the international front, ALIU staff negotiated with the Swiss and succeeded in lessening some of the obstacles to restitution, and began a process of the creation of a UN registry of stolen and recovered works of art.

In the spring of 1946: 'it was determined that the...Orion Project had fulfilled its chief functions with the issuance of three Consolidated Interrogation Reports, twelve detailed Interrogation Reports, a final report, and several other reports, the Director, SSU, felt that in order to conclude satisfactorily the work of this unit, a member of the project should undertake a concluding mission to Europe.'[840] In other words, despite surviving the transformation of the OSS into the far smaller SSU of the US War Department, the leadership of the latter determined that the completion of these reports and their deployment by, for example the Nuremberg prosecutors and MFA&A officials more directly responsible for restitution issues, meant that the reason for the ALIU's existence had come to an end.

[839] CIR 2 (Göring), op. cit., 1.
[840] ALIU 'Final Mission to Europe', op. cit.

The ALIU's achievements and frustrations

This lengthy chapter has covered a wide range of themes partly contained within the contents of recently declassified intelligence files. It has mined these files to supply detailed information on both the activities of the Nazi organisations of plunder, and the interventions of OSS officials in the art looting field, and the various institutional and historical contexts in which both these activities took place. The sections of this chapter have provided a mass of details of OSS' war crimes work that has not to date received sufficient attention in the academic literature on intelligence agencies: its monitoring, investigation and evidence-gathering in relation to works of art that the Nazis looted as an integral part of the Holocaust. The chapter has retraced the process through which senior memners of the OSS and the Roberts Commission decided to create the ALIU, appoint staff and devise its administrative structure and broad mission objectives, which included gathering evidence for the war crimes prosecutors and assisting with the restitution process. The operational dimensions of work in various European states have also been described, including the ALIU's creation of master and target lists of wanted individuals, which provided the basis for later interrogations in Alt Aussee. This chapter has also analysed in considerable detail the Plaut, Rousseau and Laison's relative success in extracting information stemming from the Holocaust and related plunder from often uncooperative subjects. The final operational phase of ALIU's work, which unfolded between spring 1946 and September 1946, was clearly premature in that it left a considerable amount of unfinished business.

This chapter has also discussed in considerable detail art looting and the Holocaust in France, and OSS' investigations of both the Göring and Linz Collections, which became the destination of a largely proportion of confiscated Jewish art works. The final sections addressed problems concerning achieving restitution of looted artworks from Switzerland, various counter-espionage dimensions of ALIU's work linked to the detection of Nazi espionage networks and their funding, and the ALIU's contribution to Holocaust-restitution issues.

Overall the ALIU officials were comparatively successful in achieving their objectives, with Plaut suggesting: 'The results of our activities far outstripped the scale of the operation.'[841] Recent commentators have

[841] 1946, op. cit., 125.

noted that although this relatively small unit faced an almost impossible task within a short time period, its positive achievements were remarkable. Before setting these out, it is first necessary to emphasise those specific points where it had not fully completed its mission, at least not to its own full satisfaction.

Various reports note 'gaps in the story of their coverage of topics, such as the Linz Museum, because officials had not been able to interrogate specific individuals, such as Voss' assistant Reimer.[842] For example, the ALIU's final report identifies a number of activities that it considered important in principle but, for reasons of limited time and personnel, was unable to finalise. These included a planned CIR 3 on German 'Methods of Acquisition', a proposed DIR 15 and DIR 8 on, respectively, Rose Bauer (Kajetan Mühlmann's secretary) and Mühlmann himself. Although Mühlmann, a major participant in the Nazis' looting of art in both Poland and the Netherlands, had been interrogated in Austria during August 1945 and later by Capt. Jan Vlug, Royal Netherlands Army, the planned collaborative U.S.-Dutch report was not forthcoming during the life-span of the ALIU. Nor was the planned DIR No. 14 on Maria Dietrich, an art dealer. However, ALIU officials included a full account of her activities in their Consolidated Interrogation Report No. 4 addressing the Linz Museum.

The ALIU Final Report identified other outstanding problems that had not been fully resolved by its own efforts, despite falling within the broad terms of its mission, and which given an extension of time and additional resources could perhaps have been better resolved. In relation to the ERR, these included:

> the question of the clandestine disposal of looted works of art by members of that organization, for private gain, has not been answered. Positive evidence of such activity is available in the form of paintings discovered in Switzerland and in the testimony of Martin Fablani, presently under indictment by the French Ministry of Justice. The activities of the ERR in other countries, Belgium, Holland, and the occupied territories of the East, have been insufficiently explored.[843]

The same report also expresses disappointment at the results of its investigations into the ERR's chaotically and separately organised 'M-Action', the: 'wholesale confiscation of household goods and furnishings of French Jewish families in 1943 and 1944, and the disposal thereof

---

[842] CIR 4 (Linz), op. cit., 24.

[843] Final Report, op. cit., 9.

by sale or shipment to Germany.'[844] Since they did not fall within the definition of 'artworks', these aspects of Holocaust-restitution fell outside the scope of the ALIU; and yet they were still identified as part of this Unit's unfinished business.

With respect to the investigation of the Göring Collection, the Final Report noted that its investigations had been restricted by the 'pre-mature release from Allied custody' of Angerer, a: 'prominent purchasing agent for Göring and suspected member of the GIS [German Intelligence Service].[845] This meant that members of the ALIU could not fulfil their counter-espionage role of uncovering: 'the use of art purchasing as a cover for espionage.'[846] This point was amplified in relation to the ALIU's more general failure to investigate a special service within Himmler's SS: 'established for the acquisition of works of art used to finance intelligence operations, and headed by SS Standartfuehrer Spazil.'[847] The inability to detain and interrogate the head of Göring's personal office, Dr Eric Gritzbach, was also identified as a problem that impeded the ALIU from gaining a fuller knowledge of the Göring organisation.[848] We have already noted the failure of Plaut and Rousseau to secure the extradition of Alois Miedl for interrogation prior to his transfer and prosecution by the Dutch authorities, and the Final Report includes a request that, if he was ever extradited from Spain to Holland, the Dutch interrogation records should be sought.[849]

This report also recognises that the termination of its operational activities took place before it was possible to properly exploit: 'eleven volumes of records from the Reichschancery, bearing on the activities of the Special Linz Commission.'[850] The scope and activities of two other agencies involved in the Nazis' looting of art were not fully investigated by the ALIU: The German Embassy in Paris and Enemy Property Control.[851] Other recognised limitations include the lack of coverage of Eastern Europe, unresolved questions regarding the purchasing activities of German museums in occupied countries, and the impact of the purchasing activities of private dealers in occupied and

[844] Ibid.
[845] Ibid., 10.
[846] Ibid.
[847] Ibid., 12.
[848] Ibid., 10.
[849] Ibid.
[850] Ibid., 11.
[851] Ibid.

neutral countries. In terms of unfinished investigations in Western states, the Final Report noted that the activities in Switzerland of Wendland, Fischer, Reber, Skira and von Frey needed further investigation, especially following the serious complications created by the: 'abrupt and surprising withdrawal of the British representative [Douglas Cooper] from the investigations being conducted jointly with this Unit.'[852] It also recognised that much Nazi loot was likely to have been exported to Latin America with some items then smuggled, or even openly transferred, into the United States, a worrying state of affairs which warranted: 'further investigation.'[853]

Wittmann's report also noted that his colleagues: 'were unable to visit this country [Sweden] during the war, although it was felt that as a neutral country, it may have been a logical place for German concealment of looted art. The points Wittmann made with respect to Sweden applied equally to Denmark, where works of art associated with the Fischer Gallery had been transferred.[854] Several reports emanating from confidential sources there during the war had suggested this possibility.'[855] Certain dealers who had exchanged works of dubious origins with Karl Haberstock had escaped the interrogation that they clearly merited.[856]

Commentators on the work of this Unit, particularly the extensive details and listings contained in its final report, have noted some additional problems:

> It must be stressed that this list has several limitations. First, the appearance of a name does not necessarily implicate that person, directly or indirectly, in the looting of art or handling of stolen works. The presence of a name on the list indicates only that the name came up in connection with the investigation. The names can serve to alert those conducting research into the provenance of an artwork—yes, works that passed through the hands of individuals on this list may have been looted—but not all of the individuals on this list were guilty of criminal behavior. Second, although the ALIU personnel conducted invaluable inquiries, the reports cannot necessarily be considered complete, and they do contain inadvertent errors. This was inevitable because many of the subjects intentionally tried to deceive their interrogators, and because available

852 Ibid., 13.
853 Ibid.
854 Ibid., 20.
855 ALIU 'Final Mission to Europe', op. cit., 18.
856 Ibid., 19.

> documentation was at times insufficient. Some mistakes are relatively minor—an umlaut, for example, might be missing from a name. In other cases, the reports do not characterize an event or an individual in an entirely accurate manner. It appears, for example, that the extent of Karl Haberstock's anti-Semitism is exaggerated in DIR No. 13. These reports were draft documents and should be treated that way.[857]

Yet, having alerted readers to these limitations, the authors note: 'Despite these limitations, the ALIU reports are among the most valuable resources available concerning the Nazi art looting programs.'[858]

The positive achievements included making substantial progress on both strands of its original mandate: the location of concealed works of looted art and the identification and detention of individuals suspected of being complicit in this type of war criminality. Fahy credits the OSS unit with effective but nonetheless limited achievements in this extensive field, noting that postwar political developments and omissions of other agencies failed to extend or capitalise upon its work in the field of restitution:

> The ALIU of the US Office of Strategic Studies was one of the agencies to effect recovery of a great deal of art. But other objects escaped war destruction only to be lost or ignobly dispersed, and postwar politics further complicated matters. The US Army dropped one particular investigation in 1949 when the territory in question became part of East Germany. Last year, this case emerged as one of the greatest art thefts-and diplomatic retrievals of the century.[859]

Hussey *et al.* endorse this conclusion: 'The ALIU work at Alt Aussee clarified the nature of the looting process and identified the whereabouts of countless masterpieces. Its work also contributed to the Nuremberg trials.'[860] The Roberts Commission also concluded that, given the challenging historical context and reasonally conditions in which it had to operate, this Unit had performed well, noting:

> It was through the efforts of the Art Looting Investigation Unit of the Office of Strategic Services, in company with other Allied agencies, that the entire German art looting organization, a highly developed and effec-

[857] 'The Documentation Project, Project for the Documentation of Wartime Cultural Losses, The Art Looting Investigation Unit Final Report' http://docproj.loyola.edu/oss1/index.html.

[858] Ibid.

[859] Anne Fahy, *Collections Management*, London: Routledge, 1995, 107.

[860] Hussey *et al.*, op. cit.

tive machine, was exposed, its leading members arrested, and information furnished which has assisted restitution authorities in discovering and effecting the return of a large percentage of the works of art looted by the Nazis throughout Europe in World War II.[861]

Ardelia Hall, a senior US State Department official, publicly commended the positive art restitution work of ALIU official Faison in continuing the work of his Unit in a later but related institutional context:

> It is questionable whether without the painstaking efforts which were exerted by the MFA&A officers and their German assistants, if so large a percentage of the restitutable property would have been identified and returned to their proper owners. An important contribution to the difficult and exacting task of identification was made during the past year by Professor S. Lane Faison, when he was Director of the Munich Collecting Point. He brought to these complex problems his valuable experience as a former... member of the OSS.[862]

Certainly within a few weeks of operations within continental Europe, Plaut and Rousseau had gained a positive reception and reputation even amongst initially sceptical sources, such as the US Army's MFA&A establishment. By March these officials asked the ALIU to supply them with any 'hot news' that: 'would be immediately useful to [the] MFA&A Officers in the field during the operational phase.' In return, Hathaway promised that the MFA&A would: 'gather any and all information that [the MFA&A] might stumble on for [the ALIU's] edification and use.'[863] This exchange of information points to reciprocity and cooperation among intelligence agencies and growing respect for the ALIU's work.

Having reviewed the achievements and frustrations it is difficult to avoid the conclusion that the closure of the ALIU in the late spring of 1946 was pre-mature since their investigations were heading towards some damning conclusions of the role that Switzerland and other neutral countries played in this field. Furthermore, whilst ALIU reports were deployed in the Nuremberg trials, the expertise of this Unit could certainly have been better deployed as part-time consultants for the full

---

[861] Roberts Commission, 1946 op. cit., 40.

[862] Ardelia R. Hall, 'The Transfer of Residual Works of Art from Munich to Austria', *College Art Journal*, Vol. 11, No. 3. (Spring, 1952), 192–194, 193.

[863] LaFarge to Hathaway, 4 March 1945, 'Orion Organization' US NA, RG 226, Entry 190, Box 532.

duration of these trials (an issue discussed more fully in the next chapter). A similar points applies to the premature ending of their largely effectively liaison with the MFA&A. Lacking a central art unit pressing the American, British, Dutch, Swiss and French authorities for concerted action, a number of Nazis and their collaborators against whom the ALIU had begun to amass damning evidence, managed to avoid being arrested, tried, and sentenced. One result of this was that the business in looted art went underground and became prosperous, before emerging virtually exonerated by official neglect.

CHAPTER SIX

PREPARING EVIDENCE OF THE HOLOCAUST: OSS' SUPPORT FOR THE NUREMBERG PROCESS

Introduction

This chapter summarises the many different ways in which OSS staff prepared actual or potential trial evidence stemming from the Holocaust for the Nuremberg prosecutors.

In mid-April 1945, as the European war was coming to an end, James Donovan issued the first of many 'war crimes information memoranda'. This reminded OSS staff that amongst the war aims of the Allies was the arrest and prosecution of Nazi war criminals responsible for atrocities, particularly against civilians. It summarised various Allied declarations; and informed OSS personnel that General Donovan had already committed their organisation to support and realise these war aims since at least 15 December 1944.[1] This memo also reminded OSS staff of Roosevelt's statement concerning: 'the continuing German massacre of Jews' and the determination to track down and bring to justice not only the leaders who issued orders but also the functionaries who implemented them across Nazi-occupied Europe. James Donovan quoted Roosevelt as follows:[2] 'All who knowingly take part in the deportation of Jews to their death in Poland... are equally guilty with the executioner. All who share the guilt shall share the punishment.'[3] He also requested that OSS staff based in the field should provide full evidence of atrocities suitable for capturing policy-makers implicated in Nazi atrocities, as well as those lower-level officials guilty of specific acts of persecution:

> Information should be as precise as possible, and should include all available details concerning the identity of the accused and victims, and the location, time and nature of the acts done. Witnesses should also be identified

---

[1] 'War Crimes Information Memo #1', 12 April 1945, Jackson Papers, Box 101, Folder 7.

[2] Ibid.

[3] Ibid.

> as fully as possible, whether by name or status or other description, and any leads to additional information should be given. All cases should be examined for evidence of a general policy or of systematic terror. The War Crimes office wants especially to have documents such as military or political orders, instructions, or declarations of policy which may serve to connect high personalities with the actual commission of crimes. Original and certified copies of such documents are needed, together with a full account of their acquisition, location, custody and reproduction.[4]

A second 'War Crimes Information Memo' from 30 April included an order for James Donovan to receive more detailed types of evidence, including evidence relevant to the successful prosecution of those complicit in the Holocaust. He specifically sought information from his colleagues relevant to the restitution of looted property:

> The following categories are the most obvious examples... 1. Atrocities: Killing; torture; rape; physical violence; confinement; mistreatment; deliberate or wanton neglect; and similar acts against the person, whether done in isolated cases or as part of an economic or political plan. 2.... All repressive measures... execution of hostages; collective penalties; deportation; forced labor... destruction, removal or confiscation of public or private property, whether done directly or through ostensibly legal methods.... 4. Persecution of minority groups (racial, religious or political) within enemy states.... 6. The connection of a military unit, or the unit of a police or other organisation, with the commission of a war crime, particularly if individual criminals are not known.... 8. All information concerning enemy records or the keeping of such records, which would aid in the identification of persons suspected of war crimes or in the location of property suspected of having been illegally appropriated.[5]

Clearly this request for information embraced nearly all those types of Nazi activities that have since become known as the Holocaust.

The remainder of this chapter will discuss how OSS staff responded to this call for trial evidence of Nazi atrocities, giving particular attention to materials relating to the Holocaust. It will summarise many of the other more general forms of assistance that OSS staff provided for these prosecutors giving particular emphasis to the Holocaust. Given that the previous chapter was devoted to the contributions made by members of the ALIU, for reasons of continuity, the first section of this chapter will discuss their contribution to the Nuremberg process in relation to the Nazis plunder of art. It will assess the various forms

---

[4] Memo to special list, 30 April 1945: Jackson Papers, op. cit. Box 101, Folder 7.

[5] Donovan to Special List, 30 April 1945: Jackson Papers, Box 101, Folder 7.

of support ALIU staff and their written reports provided for the Nuremberg war crimes prosecutors. This will complete the theme of art looting for present purposes.

The next cluster of sections discuss relevant wartime and postwar Research and Analysis (R&A) Reports addressing different aspects of the Holocaust. Most, if not all, of the R&A Branch's reports addressing Nazi war crimes in general, and the Holocaust in particular, were influenced by Franz Neumann's controversial 'spearhead theory' of anti-Semitism. Hence, our second section needs to discuss this theory before sections three and four examine the presence of the Holocaust within both wartime R&A reports, which were written before there was any clear decision to hold war crimes trials at all, and postwar reports respectively. The fourth section will discuss not only R&A reports specially commissioned by Justice Jackson, but also the role at Nuremberg of the Neumann group. Members of this group acted as specialist consultants to the prosecutors trying to ensure that they gained the optimal benefit from these reports and related documentation. The next topic, which draws together certain earlier threads, is the work of the R&A Jewish Desk both in preparing a draft brief on the Holocaust for the prosecutors and as acting as consultants more generally.

Of course, OSS R&A reports were not the only contribution that OSS staff made to Holocaust-related issues at Nuremberg. No less significant was the production and deployment of the 'R Series' of Nuremberg evidence. This stemmed from the analytical and editing work of OSS' Document Research Unit based within this agency's London Field Office. Hence, the sixth section addresses how Nuremberg prosecutors deployed certain of these materials to establish and prove elements of the Holocaust. The final section will examine the contribution of OSS' Jack Taylor in highlighting the nature and methodology of mass slaughter in Mauthausen extermination camp.

At this point it is worth reminding ourselves of the offences contained in Article 6 of the Nuremberg Charter with which the Nuremberg defendants, including the 'criminal organisations', were charged. These were:

- 'Crimes against the peace' (Count Two of the indictment), e.g., 'planning, preparation, initiation and waging aggressive war'.
- Traditional war crimes against the 'laws and customs of war' (Count Three), such as the maltreatment of captured soldiers.

– 'Crimes against humanity' (charged under Count Four), including the 'persecution, enslavement, deportation and murder' of civilian populations 'before or during the war.'
– In addition, Count One of this indictment also created the new offence of formulating or participating in a 'conspiracy' or 'common plan' to commit the crimes defined in the Counts Two, Three and Four.[6]

The ALIU's contributions to the Nuremberg process

Yeide recognises correctly that the two strands of the ALIU's mission, that of restitution and assistance with prosecution of war criminals, were essentially interconnected:

> While the ALIU's primary mission was to gather intelligence on the nature and scope of Nazi looting, in performing this mission it contributed directly to the prosecution of war criminals at the Nuremberg Tribunal. Not only did the ALIU make recommendations as to who should be tried and who should be held as key witnesses, it also provided its reports to the War Crimes Commission.[7]

Art plundering became one of the charges contained in the Nuremberg indictment: an aspect of 'persecution' on 'racial or religious grounds' forming a subset of 'crimes against humanity' under Article Six of the Nuremberg Charter. It also fell under one of a number of more traditional war crimes, that is, offences against the established laws of war embracing the 1907 Hague Regulations, which were restated in Article 6.[8]

As already noted, one of the key objectives in creating the ALIU was to provide evidence for war crimes prosecutors concerning the culpabilities of Nazi officials and others, such as French collaborators, who had participated in different ways in the Holocaust. ALIU's original objectives emphasise this point: 'Its mission was...to provide evidence for the prosecution of Nazi leaders at the Nuremberg trials.'[9] With respect to this second objective, which is particularly relevant for present

---

[6] For additional details, see *The Judgement of Nuremberg: 1946*, London: HMSO, 1999, 1–6.
[7] 2007 op. cit. 7.
[8] For additional discussion of the law relevant to cultural plunder deployed at the Nuremberg trials, see Appendix One below.
[9] Plaut, 1997 op. cit. 94.

purposes, it was also responsible for gathering evidence: 'on individuals or organizations involved in such operations or transactions, as will be of direct aid to the United States agencies empowered to effect prosecution of war criminals.'[10] Indeed, the Unit received both authority and sponsorship to operate as technical advisers to the Judge Advocate, 3rd U.S. Army, who was conducting an investigation of German art looting on behalf of the Judge Advocate (War Crimes), 12th Army Group.[11] The jurisdiction of their Alt Aussee interrogation centre fell under this office, which at this time was collecting information regarding Nazi war crimes. US Army G-5 section sought evidence from these interrogations for the upcoming trials, particularly in connection with cultural plunder. At this time, the UN War Crimes Commission was also interested in punishing persons guilty of looting art works and other crimes against property.[12] It is not surprising, therefore, that the Unit's final report,[13] listed Jackson's organisation as one of the Allied agencies with whom members maintained a particularly close liaison, including distributing numerous copies of its various DIR and CIR reports.[14]

The ALIU's commitment to the vigorous and comprehensive prosecution of those complicit in anti-Semitic and other forms of Nazi art looting is clear. It is evident from how Plaut emphasised this aspect of their mission, which arguably was implicit from the start, in his January 1945 memorandum outlining the Washington office's administrative functions. In this document, Plaut stated that one of the key purposes of ALIU's primary mission was: 'to prosecute war criminals.'[15] There is no evidence that this element was being forced upon a reluctant Plaut. On the contrary, this emphasis upon preparing materials suitable for the successful prosecution of art looters appears to have stemmed initially from Plaut. It may have gained additional momentum from the shift in OSS policy at this time, which had particular relevance to X-2 branch

---

[10] OSS memo, Plaut and Rousseau to James Murphy, Chief OSS X-2 Branch: Fine Arts Project: Orion, 1–2, RG 226, Box 532, Folder 1747 cf. NARA Press Release: http://www.archives.gov/press/press-releases/2001/nr01–59.html.

[11] Nicholas, 1995 op. cit. 378. See OSS Art Looting Investigation Reports: http://www.archives.gov/research/holocaust/microfilm-publications/m1782.pdf.

[12] Rothfeld, 2002 op. cit. Chapter 3, 19.

[13] War Department, Strategic Services Unit, 'Art Looting Investigation Unit Final Report', Washington, DC: OSS, ALIU, 1 May 1946: http://docproj.loyola.edu.

[14] 'Final Report', 1946 op. cit. para. 4.

[15] Plaut, Standing Order No. 1, 9 January 1945, 4, 'Orion Organization': US NA, RG 226, Entry 190, Box 532.

work, to give greater emphasis to the investigation of Nazi war crimes in general. Rothfeld suggests that:

> Once the ALIU investigated and interrogated enemy personnel involved in art looting and realized the extensiveness of the devious methods employed in art confiscations, it may well have recommended to the X-2 Branch and OSS officials that those Germans and Nazis involved in art looting be charged with war crimes.[16]

Between November 1944 and January 1945 when this additional purpose was added, the ALIU had yet to conduct any interrogations; the unit was busy establishing the Washington and London offices, contacting government and civilian agencies for possible liaisons, and hiring its staff. In any event, by the time the Nuremberg Trials began in late 1945, certainly the ALIU's investigations into German and Nazi art looting led to the charge of "The Plunder of Art Treasures" being included.[17] In some ways, this January 1945 mention of war crimes might have been an attempt by the ALIU to obtain more recognition from agencies such as the War Department and the War Crimes Commission, in addition to having the ALIU's mission and accomplishments held in more esteem, and thus aided more by various Allied agencies.

Some of these suggestions merit more extensive research and corroboration. It is conceivable that the inclusion of a prosecution brief on Nazi art looting could have emerged *irrespective* of the existence and contributions of the ALIU. This was because it was one of the less controversial and legally innovative aspects of the charges brought against the Nuremberg defendants because the legal basis stemmed from Article 46 (spoliation of property by an occupying power) of the Hague Regulations of 1907.

On the other hand, the very existence of the ALIU, and its relatively high profile and productivity in terms of reports with an obvious relevance to the Nuremberg process, also helped provide a focus for other branches of the OSS reporting on the activities of Nazis in this area of cultural plunder.[18] For instance, OSS intelligence reports

---

[16] Rothfeld, 2002 op. cit. Chapter 3, 8.

[17] Office of United States Chief of Counsel for Prosecution of Axis Criminality, *Nazi Conspiracy and Aggression*, Vol. 1 ('The Red Series'), Washington: United States Government Printing Office, 1946, 1097–1116.

[18] Examples include a series of recently declassified OSS reports including: 'Letter concerning art stolen by Benito Mussolini and Hermann Göring, 1946(?); Letter/attached report on stolen art from Göring Collection, 1946; Library belonging to Mr.

noted the manner in which the black market in Vienna had, during the mid-summer of 1944, become awash with looted art works stolen from Hungarian Jews.[19] Dulles and his subordinates at Wiesbaden defined these and related operations as a key part of their immediate postwar role, at least until they were given good reason to prioritise competing anti-communist imperatives:

> When Allen Dulles first moved into Germany [May 1945] he saw as his principal mission something which, he believed, might well bring the Western Allies and the Russians together in common cause now that the war was over: the rounding up of the big Nazis who had gone into hiding, the chasing down of hidden Nazi funds, the uncovering of stolen treasures which the Nazis' had plundered from occupied Europe.[20]

William Casey worked under Allen Dulles in OSS Wiesbaden, Germany. Casey recalls that their OSS-Germany office was called upon to provide considerable help on war crimes related issues. These included providing support for the various OSS officials investigating works of art looted by Göring and other Nuremberg defendants, such as Rosenberg.[21] Dulles and Casey were also supportive of the Nuremberg process by responding to the frequent requests made by the head of the OSS, General Donovan, for OSS staff to locate and take statements from possible witnesses based in Austria, Germany or Allied POW camps further afield.[22] The support provided by Dulles' operation in Germany

Nikolajevsky; looted art, 1947; Looted art, 1946; Max Winkler and Dr. Wener Schuber and stolen assets, 1946; ORION Files, 1947; ORION Project, looted art, 1947; Reports prepared by the OSS Art Looting Investigation Unit, 1946; Stolen art from Stersing by Benito Mussolini and Hermann Göring, 1946; Transfer of files of the OSS Art Looting Investigation Unit, 1947: All at US NA, RG 226, Entry 210, Box 5. See also Coordination of information relative to German art looting, two documents, 1945; Correspondence relating to OSS relation with the Roberts Commission, four documents, 1943–1944; Looted art, 2 documents, 1945; Michel Olian, looted assets, 1946; ORION Progress Report for August 1945; British report on recovered stolen art, 1945: Report in trip to Italy regarding ORION and looted art, 1945: all at US NA, RG 226, Entry 210, Box 6; Looted art, 6 documents, 1945; Watch List, looted art, 1945: all at US NA, RG 226, Entry 210, Box 7. German seizure of works of art, Province of Perugia, Italy, 1945; at US NA, RG 226, Entry 210, Box 8.

[19] Intelligence report 76693, June 1944 discussed in report 64123: US NA, RG 226, Entry 16.

[20] Moseley, op. cit. 227.

[21] See 'Security-Classified Correspondence of the OSS Mission to Germany 1944–1945': US NA, RG 226, Entry 81, Boxes 1–3.

[22] Casey recalls: '[S]ome of these [immediate postwar OSS] activities demanded a fair amount of my attention. One of these was the War Crimes Trials.' William Casey, *The Secret War Against Hitler*, Washington: Regnery, 1988, 218.

was based on access to wartime intelligence sources and contacts that, in all likelihood, would not otherwise have found their way into the hands of these prosecutors.[23]

Recently declassified archival records of the OSS include detailed reports on the art stolen, or extorted, from the Weiss family,[24] and other European Jews.[25] There are also considerable details in various OSS files regarding the extensive monitoring of individuals involved in, or the recipients of, the trade in looted works.[26] OSS records of interrogations with Nuremberg defendants included information on art looting,[27] as did files this agency built up with respect to the Interagency Safehaven Programme.[28] OSS files also recorded the suspicion that Felix Kersten, a Finnish masseur resident in Sweden, had obtained looted paintings and other art objects from Himmler as a reward for his regular treatment for the SS Chief's various ailments.[29] It also appears that Walter Rothschild, Chief of the OSS Document Research Unit which prepared a number of important dossiers for the Nuremberg prosecutors that ultimately comprised the R-Series collection of trials evidence,[30] took an interest in materials secured by the OSS' Art Looting Investigation Unit, as original copies have been discovered amongst his papers.[31]

---

[23] A similar point can be made with respect to the OSS' Document Research Unit headed by Walter Rothschild based in London.

[24] OSS reports, XL-27559 (containing a list of looted paintings) October 1945; XL-34364 (December 1945): US NA, RG 226, Entry 19.

[25] OSS report 17003, September 1945, includes a list of paintings the Gestapo allegedly stole from Fritz D. Heinman, a Jewish art gallery owner, formerly of Munich, Germany, who moved to Lucerne, Switzerland: US NA, RG 226, Entry 19.

[26] OSS document XL-2771 also addressing other OSS sources and investigations including the monitoring of Alois Miedl, Göring's agent, reportedly selling looted works of art in Spain. XL-5615; XL-6604; XL-6650; XL-8897; XL-9404; XL-10465; XL-12609; XL-13972; XL-13974; XL-20392; XL-24097; XL-11366 (Looted Art in Occupied Territories, Neutral Countries and Latin America', Foreign Economic Administration publication) May 1945: US NA, RG 226, Entry 19. The latter includes information about Germany policy regarding the official and semi-official seizure of art in occupied territories, including the role of the Task Force Rosenberg, various individual agents and buyers with these territories and beyond, including Latin America.

[27] For examples of OSS-7th Army interrogations of Göring, Ley and Funk re such looting, see: US NA, RG 226, Entry 158, Box 1, Folders 1–4, and US NA, RG 226, Entry 158, Box 10, Folders 120–21.

[28] Safehaven reports, August 1944–June 1946: US NA, RG 226, Entry 127, Box 26, Folder 190.

[29] OSS reports XL-11281 and XL-11568, both June 1945: US NA, RG 226, Entry 19.

[30] Salter 2007, ch. 7.

[31] http://www.rothschildarchive.org/ib/articles/AR2003.pdf.

OSS biographic reports on Hans Frank, including his interrogation records and those of his subordinates, such as Generaloberst Johannes Blaskowitz, included references to both the Nazis' persecution of the Jews generally, and to OSS officials' efforts to recover looted art works in particular.[32] Other OSS reports contained evidence of the senior Germans involved in the looting of French works of art, including biographical data, their activities, and complicity in the looting of Jewish collections. These reports typically record where the looted assets were sent, and identify the German art galleries and senior Nazi officials who were building up private collections of such looted assets.[33] Yet, all these intelligence files, or parts of records, were relatively 'homeless' until the ALIU was able to provide a central focus and rationale for such materials. This in turn presumably strengthened the perception that such intelligence on this aspect of the Holocaust fell within the scope of the OSS.

For reasons already discussed in the last chapter, the defendants against whom the ALIU gathered the majority of evidence were, of course, Hermann Göring, followed some way behind by Alfred Rosenberg, The bulk of the remainder of this chapter will address this evidence. Nicholas argues that, by mid-June 1945, ALIU staff had made considerable progress by identifying and detaining possible war crimes suspects; and thereby laying the foundations for intense interrogations to yield possible trial evidence: 'Mühlmann, Lohse, Hofer, Göring's Secretary Gisela Limberger,[34] and all the Reichsmarschall's records were in custody.'[35] Specific ALIU reports, including CIR 1, present details of the last known addresses, family location and sightings of leading perpetrators of anti-Semitic cultural plunder who had yet to be detained. With respect to Utikal, a leading figure in the ERR, it stated:

> According to LOHSE, he was strongly influenced by von BEHR, although nominally his superior, and shared von BEHR's desire to achieve personal prominence by placing the facilities of the E.R.R. at GÖRING's disposal. In this connection, LOHSE stated that UTIKAL supported all of GÖRING's choices of Einsatzstab material, saying "Hermann can have anything he wants." UTIKAL's whereabouts remain unknown. He

---

[32] OSS document XL-13148, cross-referenced to OSS report XL-16836, July 1945 and XL-17651 'Biographical information on Frank', September 1945: US NA, RG 226, Entry 19.

[33] OSS document 15175, September 1945: US NA, RG 226, Entry 16.

[34] For further details of her role, see CIR 2 (Göring) op. cit. 7–8.

[35] Nicholas, 1995 op. cit. 378–89.

> was last seen at Schloss Kogl (by SCHOLZ and KRESS) on the night of 3–4 May 1945, and left there in an automobile with several other members of the E.R.R. (ZOELFEL, OPFER and TOST) in the direction of Linz, having said that he wanted to get to "the unoccupied portion of Silesia."... UTIKAL's family has been located at Acheleschwaig/Saulgrub, 19 kilometres south of Peiting on the Munich—Germisch-Partenkirchen road, in the state-owned house supervised by Michael BRANDNER, where they arrived on 28 April 1945. His family comprises: Margot UTIKAL, wife; Ekkehardt UTIKAL, son, born 8 March 1938; and Roswithe UTIKAL, daughter, born 13 March 1945. A questionable source gives UTIKAL's possible present whereabouts as Schloss Sandersdorf, north of Ingolstadt, Bavaria.[36]

The present author's research confirms Fitzgerald's generally positive conclusion on the fruits of the ALIU's investigations concerning the identification of potential war crimes defendants culpable, in different ways, in the Holocaust:

> By far the most revealing sources, however, are the reports prepared by Allied forces to support prosecutions at the Nuremberg trials and guide restitution. Soon after the liberation of Paris in August 1944, a small team of investigators swept into action. Their uniforms were rag-tag, a bit of British Army and American Navy that made sentries across Europe wary, but their qualifications were top-notch. All were highly trained art historians (a couple had studied with Paul Sachs at Harvard's Fogg Museum) and seasoned interrogators wise to the intricacies of the art market. James Plaut,... had spent most of the war grilling U-boat crews.... Operating under extremely chaotic conditions and great time pressure during the final months of the war and its immediate aftermath, they did a remarkable job of reconstructing the Nazis' vast enterprise, sorting out slippery cases of collaboration, and naming the chief perpetrators.[37]

The ALIU's work not only contributed to, but also overlapped with, the activities of their colleagues within the OSS' Biographical Records section. During 1945, the latter were building up incriminating biographical files on actual and potential Nuremberg defendants, including those complicit within anti-Semitic forms of cultural plunder. These included Alfred Rosenberg, Hermann Göring,[38] and Hans Frank, the

---

[36] CIR 1 (ERR), op. cit. 47.

[37] Michael Fitzgerald, Review of 'The Lost Museum' *Art in America*, February 1998.

[38] 'Göring', May–June 1945 (including information on art looting): US NA, RG 226, Entry 146, Folder 439.

Nazis' Polish Governor.[39] As already noted, Hitler had placed Rosenberg in charge of confiscating art treasures from Nazi-occupied countries, and of liasing with both Hermann Göring and Field Marshal Wilhelm Keitel, another Nuremberg defendant.

Indeed, it is possible to find considerable overlap in the substantive points, including legal arguments, made by ALIU documentation, and the detailed report the OSS R&A Branch contributed for the Nuremberg prosecutors: 'Nazi Spoliation of Property in Occupied Europe.' This document, submitted in draft on 24 July 1945 and approved by the OCC Prosecution Review Board, formed part of the wider series of reports Justice Jackson commissioned the R&A Branch to write under the general heading of Principal Nazi Organizations Involved in the Commission of War Crimes: R&A 3113.2.[40] In common with the ALIU analysis, this report gave a broad definition to 'spoliation' to include otherwise lawful acts of taxation and purchase of goods from occupied states which ought to be classified as war crimes because of their disproportionate extent and context of coercion. It addressed the illegality of both the means and the extent of the Nazis' economic exploitation of such states:[41]

> In the category of acts constituting spoliation of individual property belong not only acts of outright robbery, confiscation, seizure and destruction of property (owned e.g., by Jews, Poles, Russians), but also acts which had the outright appearance of legality—that is purchases with a price paid by the German buyers. To lay bare the true character of such deals it is necessary to scrutinize the methods by which, and the circumstances under which, private owners were induced to consent to the sale of their property to the Germans.[42]

This echoes a perennial theme in the ALIU's CIR reports relating to the sham character of apparently lawful purchases and exchanges of Jewish artworks. A similar point applies to this report's emphasis upon the impact of gross economic exploitation as a device for weakening the viability and destroying the previous standard of living of occupied

[39] Nuremberg documentation on art plunder include: Trial Documents 1015-PS and 172-PS and, re the ERR, 1015-PS.
[40] US NA, RG 238, Entry 52F, Box 9.
[41] Ibid., 1.
[42] Ibid.

states, which thereby linked art looting to German criminal aggression and conquest.[43]

Part of the ALIU's brief was to highlight the criminal actions and motivations of specific individuals and entire organisations *which merited prosecution at the Nuremberg trials*. More specifically, and as already noted in passing, ALIU officials recommended that certain individuals, whose art looting activities it had investigated, be tried as war criminals, including Ernst Buchner, Karl Haberstock,[44] Göpel and Andreas Hofer.[45] Indeed, the ALIU's interrogation report on Haberstock indicates that he was interviewed at Nuremberg.[46] Others who were interrogated, such as Limberger and Kress, an art photographer with the ERR, were specifically cleared of any involvement with large-scale art looting sufficient to merit prosecution as war crimes defendants: 'Kress is a "little man" with a weak personality. It is conceivable that he engaged in some petty thievery, but it is not likely that he was involved in any large scale, illegal transfers of art objects. No action is recommended.'[47] In addition, DIR 3 stated:

> Aside from Alfred Rosenberg himself [who became a Nuremberg defendant], Scholz is the highest-ranking former official of the Einsatzstab Rosenberg presently in Allied custody. Von Behr, unquestionably the leading sponsor of organised looting in France, is dead by suicide; and Gerhard Utikal...has not been found. Under the circumstances, Scholz must be held personally responsible, with Rosenberg, for the implementation of all art confiscations undertaken by the Einsatzstab Rosenberg. It is the recommendation of this Unit that he be tried as a war criminal and the severity of charges brought against him be determined by the extent of which complicity in this organized looting operation is judged to have been criminal.[48]

---

[43] Ibid., 2.

[44] 'It is recommended that he be tried on the same level as the leading members of the Sonderauftrag Linz. He was, beyond any possible doubt, one of the individuals most responsible for the policies and activities of this group which dominated German official purchasing and confiscation of works of art from 1939 through 1944.' DIR No. 13 (Haberstock), op. cit. 7.

[45] US NA, RG 239, Entry 77, ALIU, 'German Personnel Connected with Art Looting.' J. Petropoulos, 'The Art World in Nazi Germany', in Francis R. Nicosia, Jonathan Huener, *The Arts in Nazi Germany: Continuity, Conformity, Change*, NY: Berghahn Books, 2006, 135–159, 146.

[46] The report notes: 'In custody of US Chief of Counsel, Nuremberg, as a material witness in war crimes proceedings.' DIR No. 13 (Haberstock) May 1946, op. cit. 1.

[47] DIR No. 10 (Karl Kress), op. cit. 2.

[48] DIR No. 3 (Scholz), op. cit. 4.

Rousseau's CIR 2 also concluded that Hofer, who had been evasive as well as dishonest during his interrogations, merited prosecution as: 'a small time crook' as well as a war criminal who should be forced to give testimony against Göring.'[49] Both Hofer and his wife were later taken into 'protective custody' despite rendering assistance to the Allied authorities in identifying, classifying and securing the physical condition of Göring's collection of looted art.[50] A postwar French Military Tribunal brought charges against Hofer for art plundering and he was convicted in his absence and sentenced to ten years imprisonment.[51] The final ALIU report records whether or not named individuals had been, or were at the time of writing, being charged with crimes by the postwar French authorities.[52] This was clearly important information not only to avoid a duplication of investigative and prosecution efforts but also because French trials could themselves also provide additional evidence against other war criminals complicit in this aspect of the Holocaust.

In addition, various ALIU reports contain recommendations as to who the Allied authorities should consider prosecuting at different national and international courts. For example, the role of French collaborators within Nazi art looting in Paris should, they argued, be left to domestic French courts as their crimes were committed against the cultural heritage and economic well-being of that particular nation:

> The collaborationists, of course, were willing to take immediate personal profit at the risk of ultimate national bankruptcy. Their fate is wholly the concern of the appropriate national governments; but it is hoped that this report contains information useful for whatever investigations may ensue.[53]

ALIU reports are peppered with the names and criminal activities of a number of defendants tried as 'major war criminals' before the International Military Tribunal (IMT) at Nuremberg 1945–46. This is particularly true of those most centrally involved: Göring and Rosenberg of course. However, the culpability of other defendants are addressed

[49] DIR 9, op. cit. 9. See also CIR 2 (Göring) op. cit. 10.

[50] James Rorimer, *Survival: The Salvage and Protection of Art In War*, NY: Abelard Press, 1950, 205–08. Hofer's own account is contained in statements from June 1945 and September 1947: US NA, RG 260, Box 481 (cited in Yeide, 2007 op. cit. n. 29).

[51] Petropoulos, 2000 op. cit. 105.

[52] OSS Final Report, op. cit. Klein entry, 108.

[53] CIR 4 (Linz), op. cit. 85.

also. These included Hitler's private secretary, Martin Bormann (whose fate was then unknown but who was nevertheless tried and convicted in his absence),[54] and Seyss-Inquart, who was responsible for overseeing art looting in the Netherlands and whose record regarding the Holocaust was one of the worst of the Military Governors.[55] With respect to Bormann, the Linz CIR noted:

> Hitler's deputy and secretary, whose power in party circles never ceased to grow, was hardly less energetic in Linz affairs than Hitler himself. All correspondence went through his office, and great quantities of it were handled by Bormann personally....Posse was more independent but it is clear that Bormann both warmly supported him and kept a close watch on all his activities. In the Hitler-Göring feud, Bormann represented the Fuehrer against Rosenberg, whose ERR was dominated by the Reichsmarschall. Voss could not have been appointed without Bormann's approval. He was deeply involved in confiscations; even as late as January 1945 he ordered Himmler to have all material confiscated by SS units transferred to the Fuehrer's handling. (See Attachment 17).[56]

The important legal question of the essentially criminal motivations and intent behind Göring's art looting activity, which of course is a vital element of proof in criminal proceedings, was closely examined by CIR 2. This report noted a remarkable combination of this defendant's public 'stubbornness and conceit' on the one hand, and: 'a certain weakness and humility in private.'[57] Göring's actions appeared to be motivated by: 'his all-embracing acquisitiveness. There were no limits to his desires as far the Collection was concerned.'[58] Indeed, he was: 'a passionate collector.'[59] Another feature picked out by this report was Göring's basic greed and dishonesty, his:

> avarice—an unexpected trait in a man who must have had unlimited resources at his disposal. The witnesses are unanimous in declaring that he always bargained, no matter how small the amount involved...The

[54] CIR 4 (Linz), op. cit. 15–16, 40. Bormann issued travel and authorisation certificates to Posse and others that granted enormous privileges during wartime conditions, including receiving high priority cooperation from regional German authorities. Ibid., 40. Bormann also authorised all foreign currency exchanges, ibid., 41.

[55] CIR 4 (Linz), op. cit. 20, 36, 46, 63; Petropoulos notes, with respect to the Holocaust, that Seyss-Inquart: 'played a leading role 117,000 of the 140,000 Jews, one of the highest fatality ratios.' Petropoulos, 1996b op. cit. 197.

[56] CIR 4 (Linz), op. cit. 15.

[57] CIR 2 (Göring), op. cit. 3.

[58] CIR 2 (Göring), op. cit. 3.

[59] CIR 2 (Göring), op. cit. 4.

> correspondence reveals that he was always slow in paying his bill. All in all he hated to part with money.'[60]

CIR 1 maintained that Göring's dealings with the ERR's looted artworks were a typical mixture of deceitful displays of 'good intentions', combined with a hypocritical desire to appear to be complying with accepted legal requirements to pay a market price:

> The procedure whereby GÖRING "legitimatized" his acquisition of Einsatzstab material was as follows: In the summer of 1940, with the reported concurrence of the Louvre authorities and on the BUNJES' recommendation, GÖRING appointed M. Jacques BELTRAND, a French artist, as "official appraiser" for the French Government. Once GÖRING, through von BEHR, LOHSE, and Walter Andreas HOFER his chief buyer who inevitably accompanied him on the trips to Paris—had decided what material he wished to acquire from the current Einsatzstab lot, BELTRAND would appraise the objects in question. The appraisal lists were held by the Einsatzstab, and were ultimately forwarded to GÖRING's headquarters in Berlin for filing against future payment. It has been determined conclusively that: (a) GÖRING did not pay the Einsatzstab—or any other organization or individual—for the works of art acquired in this manner, and (b) no method of payment was ever established.[61]

Another ALIU report noted: 'the absurdly low appraisals made by M, Jacques Beltrand on paintings confiscated by the Einsatzstab which have been selected for the Göring Collection, have been condemned by all sources... Beltrand, a timid and negative individual, made the low appraisals out of fear of the Germans, notably Göring.'[62]

The implication of these various points for the ALIU officials was that the deceitful character of Göring's hypocritical displays of studious concern for the requirements of legality were, in fact, vital evidence of the depth of his criminal orientation. Plaut later supplemented his critique of Göring's pretence to pay for ERR items as little more than a smokescreen to conceal his ingenious tactics to avoid, delay or minimise any measure of payment. His dishonesty and extortion even extended to cheating Hitler and issuing threats:

> His proposals to "pay" the Einsatzstab Rosenberg were arrant subterfuge, as he was informed both by Alfred Rosenberg and by the Party Treasurer,

[60] CIR 2 (Göring), op. cit. 3–4.
[61] CIR 1 (ERR), op. cit. 8.
[62] DIR No. 6 (Lohse), op. cit. 11.

> Schwarz, that there was no machinery, no channel, no payee, in existence for such a transaction. In sum, Göring resorted to every conceivable device to fill the walls and the coffers of Carinhall, bargaining, cheating, even invoking where necessary the prestige of German arms or the terrible threat of intervention by the Gestapo. Whereas the basic directive of November 18, 1940, the potent Führerbefehl, reserved for the Chief of the Nazi State the formal right of disposition over all cultural goods confiscated from the occupied countries, Göring, capitalizing on Hitler's relative apathy in these matters, kept the bulk of the loot for himself.[63]

In other words, despite his regular promises to the contrary, Göring refused to make payment for confiscated Jewish artworks from the ERR. Plaut's immediate postwar articles have confirmed the conclusions of ALIU reports on the criminally dishonest and mean-spirited character of Göring's orientation, which he had every reason to try to camouflage behind a cover of scrupulous concern for the appearance of regularity and financial probity:

> His vicious penny-pinching tactics cast a strange light on Göring's longing to attain the stature of a grand seigneur. Lavish in his tastes to a degree unparalleled in our times, and with unlimited resources at his disposal, he was nonetheless disposed to bargain over every transaction and was slow in paying his bills. The practice distressed Göring's agents, who thought such bickering unworthy of his exalted position. To be sure, the Reichsmarschall was scrupulously careful to maintain front, to be *korrekt* in his dealings. He would not permit a confiscated painting to be hung at Carinhall; he would not put personal pressure on an owner reluctant to part with an object; he would not accept thanks—in the form of valuable gifts—from Jews whom he had helped. By his own admission at Nuremberg, he made determined efforts to "pay" for the more than 700 looted masterpieces which he had received from the Rosenberg organization; and he was confident that his prodigious amassing of European treasures would be applauded by the peoples of the Axis. Had he not declared that Carinhall, with all its contents, was to become a national monument on his sixtieth birthday?[64]

Göring also engaged in other acts of deceit that corroborated the OSS officials' conclusions concerning his basically criminal intent and orientation. These included removing confiscated Jewish works of art before they could be inventoried. This was possible through: 'his surreptitious co-optation of ERR staff members—most notably von Behr, Utikal,

[63] Plaut, 1946a op. cit.
[64] Ibid.

and art historian Bruno Lohse.'[65] His greed even extended to selling confiscated Jewish works from, for example, the Rosenberg collection not because of any shortage of funds but simply because he enjoyed the process of buying low and selling high.[66] He simply enjoyed acquiring looted Jewish works from the ERR through exchange because: 'they cost him nothing. However, when he himself made a sale his prices were among the highest, as for example, in the case of Miedl, who paid RM 750,000 for six pictures, five of which had cost Göring nothing.'[67] Plaut recalls that:

> The dirty work was carried on by his agents. French Impressionist pictures,—splendid Renoirs and Cézannes and Van Goghs,—"ineligible" for hanging because they were "degenerate art," were very useful for other purposes. Having cost Göring nothing, several hundred of them were exchanged in France and Switzerland for second-rate Cranachs and Holbeins which, as works of unblemished origin, could then grace the proud walls of Carinhall.[68]

The DIR on Wendland indicates that, through Hofer, Göring was even willing to defraud members of his own supply and distribution networks, including Fischer and Wendland who played a vital role in the sale and exchange of looted art in Switzerland. Göring carried out such fraud by withholding important items that he had previously agreed to include in an exchange of 'degenerate' impressionist paintings for old masters, including works by Van Gogh:

> When the first shipment of Impressionist pictures arrived in Lucerne late in 1941, Wendland noted that four of the finest pictures he had chosen were missing. These Wendland names as a Van Gogh "Man with a Pipe", a Jan Steen, and possibly a Van Gogh landscape and a Cézanne portrait. Hofer explained their absence by the cock-and-bull story that they were hanging in Göring's bedroom and that Göring's nephew, a lieutenant, had grown too fond of them to bear to part with them. In 1943 Wendland accompanied Buehrle and a Zurich lawyer to a bank vault in Zurich for the purpose of viewing some paintings which, according to the lawyer who was the custodian of the key to the vault, were being offered for sale by a Dutch firm. The paintings were recognized by Wendland as

[65] Petropolous, 2000 op. cit. 131–32 citing ALIU's CIR 1, op. cit. 15.
[66] CIR 2 (Göring), op cit. 149, 157.
[67] CIR 2 (Göring), op. cit. 157.
[68] Plaut, 1946a op. cit.

> the four missing paintings which were supposed to be adorning Göring's bedroom, and he advised Buehrle against buying them.[69]

Furthermore, Göring's apparent reluctance to acquire works of art directly from confiscated Jewish sources (as distinct from so-called 'purchases' from the ERR) could not be considered to constitute an implicit critique of racist forms of Nazi art looting. On the contrary, the explanation is far more self-interested and concerned with this defendant's anxiety over potential blackmail. Göring: 'was afraid that the picture might be stolen property or that a Jew might be planning to sell something to him and use the sale for blackmail later on.'[70] The other negative motivation was a desire to cover up his own basic dishonesty and eagerness to benefit personally from anti-Semitic persecution and confiscation by putting on a deceptive show of legality:

> Finally, Göring always wanted to maintain the appearance of being "correct". He would not consider having anything on his walls which had been confiscated. He always "intended" to pay for the objects which he took from the ERR. He never accepted presents from Jews who received favours from him. The idea of putting pressure to sell on the unwilling owner of an object which he wanted was unthinkable. However, as will be seen in what follows, this was merely the face he presented, or tried to present, to the outside world. The truth is that Göring was a consummate hypocrite.[71]

As CIR 2 states:

> Göring's attitude towards [Nazi] confiscations was characteristic. He fought shy of crude, undisguised looting; but he wanted the works of art, and so he took them, always managing to find a way of giving at least the appearance of honesty, by a token payment or promise thereof to the confiscation authorities. Although he and his agents never had an official connection with the German confiscation organizations, they nevertheless used them to the fullest extent possible. Göring backed their action through his position as Reichsmarschall, as is shown by his order of 4 November 1940.[72]

This report further noted that such was Göring's control over the ERR's confiscation policies and practices, which were directed mainly against Jews, that senior members of the Kunstschutz (German Army

[69] DIR Wendland, op. cit. 22.
[70] CIR 2 (Göring), op. cit. 145.
[71] CIR 2 (Göring), op. cit. 4.
[72] CIR 2 (Göring), op. cit. 23–24.

Monuments and Arts division) argued that Göring's order be supplemented to recognise that the ERR acted 'under my direction'.[73] In other words, one expression of Göring's criminal dishonesty was his aim to give the appearance of engaging only in legitimate art acquisitions. The appearance of sham legality even extended to: 'a policy of ostentatiously refusing gifts from anyone who was indebted to him for protection against anti-Semitic laws or help in obtaining a visa to a neutral country.'[74] Indeed, OSS officials discovered examples where he deliberately avoided transactions tainted in blatant illegality, including the confiscation of the Jewish Schloss Collection in France.[75] A further example of Göring's hypocritical approach was his refusal to accept artworks looted from a Naples Museum as a birthday present.[76] Plaut notes that Göring's actions in this respect were typical of wider hypocritical practices within the Nazi regime, which cloaked war criminality with: 'an elaborate, fictitious pretext of legality.'[77]

Rousseau's CIR report also pointed out that other features of how Göring organised his staff associated with art acquisition also reveals a greater similarity with the guilty and furtive practices of gangsters, than those of a deputy head of state an advanced modern nation:

> There was an unwritten law... that the employees themselves should, under no circumstances, hold conversations about their respective jobs outside of what was necessary for the successful prosecution of business. In fact, Göring appears to have basically distrusted everyone. He never took anyone totally into his confidence. This tendency to distrust increased... at the end of the war he had brought all branches of his activities under his direct control. This is a curious trait in a man whose external manner appeared so expansive and friendly.... his financial dealings in art matters was characterised by secrecy and a manifest desire to maintain appearances—to be correct.... True to the precepts of National Socialism, Göring was scrupulous in his efforts to cloak his shadiest dealings in the appearance of normal business practice... it was always his

[73] Ibid., 24.

[74] CIR 2 (Göring), op. cit. 158.

[75] CIR 4 (Linz), op. cit. 30–33.

[76] CIR 2 (Göring), op. cit. 29–30.

[77] 'It was preordained by the official Nazi conscience that these depredations, in common with many of the more heinous crimes committed by the Party, should be cloaked by an elaborate, fictitious pretext of legality. A notable series of documents took shape through the war years, which afford us a broad vista of Nazi rationalization hard at work.' Plaut, 1946a op. cit.

> declared intention to pay for the pictures chosen in the Jeu de Paume ... However ... the objects remain unpaid to this day.[78]

CIR 2 also quotes other examples of Göring's attempts to conceal his own fundamental dishonesty and willingness to evade even German laws and international agreements when it was to his financial advantage to do so.[79]

The very structure of the CIR reports appear to have been designed to facilitate their use as raw material for Nuremberg prosecution briefs. For instance, the second chapter of CIR 4 (Linz) is particularly relevant in terms of the identification of possible individuals meriting prosecution as war criminals. It outlines the 'personalities of the Linz Commission', including the role played by 'the party bosses' and Nuremberg defendants: Hermann Göring and Martin Bormann. This chapter also describes the role and function of this Commission's internal senior management, including its two Directors, Posse and Voss, as well as briefly identifying its 'lesser functionaries'. What was equally important from the perspective of the Nuremberg prosecutors, Chapter Three provides a detailed analysis of the 'methods of acquisition' of looted artworks. It shows how these ranged from the apparently less problematic types, such as outright gifts to Hitler and voluntary sales, through to confiscations of private Jewish collections without compensation, and 'forced sales', including the 'Schloss affair'. The next chapter identifies the respective roles played by members of a wider network. They were shown to have been a hub of Nazi officials, such as Hoffmann, Mühlmann and Göpel,[80] who were surrounded by an outer ring of main and lesser dealers and agents operating across Europe.

Chapter Five discusses the various sources from which Hitler's Linz Museum acquired its works of art. It outlines where Nazi plunder organisations, including the ERR, looted the private collections of French Jews, such as Paul Rothschild. The remaining chapters a briefly describe the acquisitions for the Linz Library, including the confiscation of Jewish libraries, and the scope of the overall Linz collections. The report finishes with various 'conclusions and recommendations', and is sourced throughout with original documentation to substantiate the

[78] CIR 2 (Göring), op. cit. 5, 157.
[79] CIR 2 (Göring), op. cit. 81.
[80] Goepel was implicated in the Schloss affair. CIR 4 (Linz), op. cit. 46.

various accusations against Göring, Rosenberg and others in a manner that resembles an extended prosecution brief.

Rousseau's CIR 2 (Göring) adopts a broadly similar but not identical set of aims and structure, which—as before—was designed for selective re-writing as raw material for final Nuremberg prosecution briefs. It repeatedly emphasises that Göring proved willing to evade not only Swiss and international legal regulations but also German law governing the import and export of art works.[81] In short, the ALIU's emphasis upon the blatant dishonesty and illegality of many of Göring's activities, is designed to assist with their preparation of material proving this defendant's criminal intent, a key theme of any war crimes prosecution brief.

Following a brief introduction, CIR 2 (Göring) discusses the sources, 'the origin and character of the collection' and 'personnel'. It then outlines the different methods of acquisition this defendant deployed: 'confiscations', 'purchases', 'exchanges' and 'sales'. The final chapters describe the financial aspects of this collection, its 'administration and care' and 'transportation'. The tail piece of some 200 pages of highly detailed information, including attachments and references, is a series of suitably pithy 'conclusions and recommendations'. This, I suspect, is where many of those who received copies, including the Nuremberg prosecution staff, would have started their reading. CIR 2 (Göring) is supported by an extensive list of attachments. These include letters of authorisation, memorandum regarding confiscations, transportation records, postwar statements, and directives incriminating many of those individuals mentioned above. As with CIR 4 (Linz), such references were deployed as supportive evidence substantiating the various accusations contained in the previous 84 pages of this report. Indeed, these attachments were set out in a way that made them suitable for adaptation into the distinctive format of Nuremberg trial briefs and associated 'document books'.

Furthermore, Plaut and his officials contributed substantial evidence to French and other authorities. This, in turn, contributed to the arrest, trial and punishment of over 20 French art dealers, whilst their German colleagues, Lohse and Rochlitz, were also jailed. It is likely that the physical descriptions gathered and contained in various ALIU reports

[81] CIR 2 (Göring), op. cit. 135, 139, 163, 169, 176.

assisted in this process.[82] Indeed, Rochlitz had been: 'gleefully delivered to Paris by James Plaut after a long ride across France in an unheated Jeep.'[83] Haberstock's information was so damaging to the Nazi leaders, particularly to Göring, that the Americans decided to send him to testify at the Nuremberg trials as a prosecution witness on Nazi art theft. Indeed, Petropoulos notes:

> Haberstock, with his knowledge of the Linz Project and ERR operations, as well as his familiarity with the other Nazi leaders, was one of the key witnesses with respect to art plundering. His testimony, in which he described nearly all the figures in the Nazi art world, is further evidence of how tight-knit the circle really was.... Haberstock earned his release in part because of his cooperation, in part because of his fragile health:... But more importantly, Haberstock avoided criminal prosecution and gained his release because he was able to rally defenders who testified that he had saved lives and actively resisted the regime.[84]

Not surprisingly, given that they had been written largely for the purpose, the Nuremberg prosecutors extensively borrowed material from both CIR 2 and CIR 1. They had received six copies of both shortly after their completion on 15 September 1945.[85] The structure, content and potential usefulness of CIR 2 for these prosecutors merits brief analysis. It claims to be:

> a preliminary study of the history and formation of the Herman Göring Collection, and of the methods used by the Reichsmarschall of the Third Reich to strip the occupied countries of Europe of a large part of their artistic heritage. This widespread enterprise, which worked in the shadow of the occupying forces, took the form of both looting and of so-called "legal" purchase.[86]

As such, it appears to have been designed to contribute to a number of categories of offences about which the Nuremberg prosecutors were, during the late summer of 1945, building up detailed evidence for a variety of trial briefs. These included the 'economic case' against the Nazi leadership regarding 'state on state' forms of cultural plunder contrary to the 1907 Hague Conventions. The prosecutors would have

---

[82] For example, see CIR 4 (Linz), op. cit. 16, 19, 53.

[83] Nicholas, 1995 op. cit. 426.

[84] Petropoulos, 2000 op. cit. 95.

[85] CIR 2 (Göring) op. cit. distribution list notes that 6 copies were assigned to the 'U.S. Chief of Counsel, Nuremberg', whilst the British MI 5 and MI 6 received two copies each.

[86] CIR 2 (Göring), op. cit. 1.

found within Rousseau's report some extremely damaging, but also well-substantiated, summaries of Göring's key role within the Nazis' plunder of artworks. It provides sufficient incriminating details of his actions and motivations to:

> dispel any illusion that might remain about Göring as the "best" of the Nazis. In this one pursuit in which he might have shown himself to be in fact a different type of man, he was the prototype of all the worst in National Socialism. He was cruel, grasping, deceitful and hypocritical...well suited to take his place with Hitler, Himmler, Goebbels and the rest.[87]

Plaut also recalls that: 'As the Nuremberg trials drew near, Rousseau interrogated Göring in prison and found him despondent, indifferent, and degradingly unheroic.'[88]

The CIR on the Linz Museum (CIR 4) makes a number of shrewd observations concerning the criminal intentions that infused the entire project. ALIU interrogations of members of this Museum clearly reveal these subjective elements, whose demonstration can be vital to criminal proof. The latter disclosed how even Hitler sought to disguise the fact that many of the works his agents acquired for the Linz Museum stemmed from either confiscations or forced sales from private Jewish sources in France and elsewhere, including the Rothschilds, Lugt and Jaffe collections:[89]

> Even Hoffmann's articles on accession...were subjected to the Fuehrer's personal scrutiny, and no mention was allowed of anything which had been confiscated...In the same way, Hitler forbade [illegible] to exhibit any confiscated objects designated for the Viennese museums....If Hoffmann can be believed, the Fuhrer ordered him to delete any mention of the acquisition of these confiscated pictures...no work from the confiscated collections of Vienna and Paris was mentioned in the article. See DIR 1, Heinrich Hoffmann, 7....By Ruprecht's own statement, the Linz armour collection was built up almost entirely from confiscated sources, Prague and Vienna being the most important. The Coin collection was likewise solidly based on units seized from Austrian foundations. In Holland, the Dienststelle Mühlmann engaged in confiscation as well as

[87] CIR 2 (Göring), op. cit. 176. See also Nicholas, 1995 op. cit. 380–81.

[88] Plaut, 1997 op. cit. 125.

[89] On one occasion concerning a looted Rubens, Hitler had difficulties accepting this for Linz in a direct and transparent way, preferring the 'devious manoeuvre' of having it presented to him as a gift from the people of Vienna: CIR 4 (Linz), op. cit. 28–29, Attachment 25.

> purchase. Among the items for which Linz made no payment are many works from the Fritz Lugt and the Alphons Jaffe collections.[90]

ALIU officials also suggested that the acquisition from the Czernin family of Vermeer's *The Artist in his Studio*, 'perhaps the outstanding painting in the Linz collection', took place in ambiguous circumstances resembling a forced sale.[91]

The clear implication of the emphasis that ALIU officials placed on the display of guilt and secrecy is that many senior officials of the Linz museum could not credibly deny personal knowledge of the criminal nature of many of the methods they deployed to acquire artworks. These could have been readily apparent from the covert and guilty behaviour of the German head of state himself:

> Hitler took extraordinary precautions to clothe all Linz transactions in the appearance of legality....Special Nazi law covered the seizure of Jewish and enemy property....Nevertheless the Sonderauftrag Linz [special commission] had first claim upon all works of art looted by the Germans. Both actually and potentially it was the major recipient of works of art confiscated or acquired by forced sale...Most important of all, the Fuehrer had prior choice from the entire stock of material confiscated by the ERR. (See Attachments 9 and 16).[92]

This analysis of evidence of the subjective knowledge and intentions of leading members of the Linz Commission was, of course, vital to demonstrating individual, or even perhaps criminal organisational, liability in any war crimes or other trial.

CIR 4 (Linz) also contains other specific materials that either anticipated, or were specifically geared to, a range of issues the Nuremberg trials raised directly. These include the attempts by some defendants to hide behind the defence of 'just following orders', that is, the Nazis' 'leadership principle' under which full or part responsibilities is ascribed to whoever is assigned ultimate command:

> At the current Nuremberg trials, the Fuehrerprinzip is under attack as a valid legal escape for decisions made by highly placed government officials. The Nazi laws under which Jewish and enemy property was confiscated are also being challenged. If the prosecution wins its case before the tribunal, a legal basis will exist for bringing the *Sonderauftrag Linz* to trial

[90] CIR 4 (Linz), op. cit. 4, 27.
[91] CIR 4 (Linz), op. cit. 35.
[92] CIR 4 (Linz), op. cit. 85.

> as a criminal organisation, since it was in the highest category of Nazi looting enterprises.[93]

Another strand to the ALIU's argument addressed the possibility that the prosecution's attempt to establish criminal liability for 'criminal organisations' *per se*, including the various bodies affiliated to the Nazi Party. CIR 4 advocated that the management of the Linz Museum be prosecuted as a criminal organisation, which would afford it analogous status to Himmler's SS at the Nuremberg trials.[94] If the Linz Commission could be interpreted as falling within the scope of organisational liability, then voluntary membership of such an organisation would, in itself, constitute a war crime. Such membership could then be recognised as constituting an offence resulting in individual punishment for the leading members. Of course, the extent of the punishment might depend on these members' specific degrees of complicity, and would need to take into account all mitigating factors. The latter could include any measure of postwar cooperation with the Allies' restitution efforts:

> Of course *forced* sale (as exemplified in the Schloss and Mannheimer affairs [both Jewish collections]) does not differ in principle from confiscation....The superficially legal purchases which were made by Linz agents furthered a deliberate Nazi attempt to ruin the national economy of the defeated peoples. The Nazis exchanged unbacked paper money for real property. Such "purchases" amounted to a more palatable form of looting than outright confiscation....It is recommended: (1) that the *Sonderauftrag Linz* (Linz Special Commission) be declared a criminal organisation; (2) that the members of the *Sonderauftrag Linz* stand trial by virtue of their membership, consideration being given to their relative importance and individual actions....to clarify recommendation (2) above, the reader should consult the organisation chart...the leading figures all share the responsibility for the actions of the Commission. Other than Hitler and Posse (deceased) they are: Martin Bormann, who controlled the organisation as Hitler's direct representative; von Hummel, Voss, Dworschak, Ruprecht and Wolffhardt. The four names might be described as departmental heads, but Voss' department was by far the most important....Both Reimer and Reger, who inventorised the collections at Munich and supervised shipments to the repositories, deserve consideration for their efficient handling of an enormous amount of detail. Without their work, the task of making restitution of the contents of the Linz art collection would be far more difficult than it is.[95]

---

93 Ibid., 85.
94 Ibid., 86.
95 Ibid., 85–86.

A further recommendation was that individuals implicated in Nazi art transactions, even apparently 'legal' purchases, should nevertheless face possible legal accountability. Their prosecution should be considered irrespective of their degree of personal knowledge or intentions, as conspirators complicit within what objectively amounted to a wider and systematically organised and executed programme of economic plunder, underpinned by anti-Semitic and other racist ideologies:

> Looting always accompanies war; but Nazi looting, and especially Nazi art looting, was different. It was officially planned and expertly carried out. Looted art gave tone to an otherwise bare New Order. In the progress to enhance the cultural prestige of the Master Race, the *Sonderauftrag Linz* was the master organisation. Its work had a symbolic value far beyond the mere gathering of an art collection for Adolf Hitler. Operating within the intellectual limits of Nazi philosophy, it barred the work of nearly every non-German artist who flourished after 1800 [it] was an argument for the modern primacy of Germany. With its immense resources and its official prestige, the *Sonderauftrag Linz* tried to bring all art under the shadow of the Swastika. For a time it did.[96]

CIR 2 also emphasised the connection between Göring's art acquisitions and a central charge at the Nuremberg trials, that the defendants had conspired to 'wage aggressive war', noting that the former depended upon the latter: 'the enormous majority of his transactions...were made possible only by the war and never could have been carried out under normal conditions.'[97] Göring's direct and indirect threats of violence, together with his resort to an 'invasion currency', made a nonsense out of even those transactions which were disguised as straightforward voluntary 'sales'.[98] CIR 2 specifically linked plunder to the overall 'Nazi conspiracy' to wage aggressive war, the proof of which was key to the Nuremberg prosecutors' case: 'As an outgrowth of the Nazi regime the collection grew simultaneously with the expansion of German power. In 1939, it numbered about 200 objects. When its growth was cut short by defeat the total head count reached over 2000.'[99]

CIR 2 also made it clear that the Allied authorities had identified such cultural plunder, even apparently voluntary types, as a war crime

[96] Ibid., 87.
[97] CIR 2 (Göring), op. cit. 163.
[98] Ibid.
[99] Ibid., 174.

for which there would be legal and other retribution. This was because acts of looting could be said to have occurred:

> Even if the transaction was not made under duress, and payment was properly completed, no German dealer can now claim ownership because he "paid money" for what he took away. Whether he understood how his government was destroying the financial structure of occupied territories does not matter. Allied policy on this question was constantly broadcast from the first years of the war. It is recommended:...(3) that the German art dealers and agents who bought for Linz be investigated on a purely individual basis, since their only official connection with the *Sonderauftrag Linz* was through the occasional and tenuous link of a Linz travel certificate. [However] among the agents, Goepel occupies a special place. As the official Linz representative in Holland, he held a government position, and received a salary through the office of Seyss-Inquart. Recommendation (2) applies to Goepel, therefore as well as recommendation (3).[100]

Plaut even argued that over and above the personal enrichment and self-glorification of Göring and Hitler and, to a lesser extent, their agents and subordinates in the art looting field, lay a policy of weakening the cultural distinctiveness and vitality of occupied territories in a way that contravened international laws of war:

> The looting of Europe was not merely an official and expert operation designed to enrich the Nazi state and increase the prestige of Hitler and Göring. By contributing to the impoverishment of the occupied and satellite countries, and by exalting Germanic art (while banning all liberal work of the last hundred years), the looting machine remained within the framework of National Socialist philosophy. The failure of German arms must not blind us to the lasting implications of Hitler's attempt to corrupt the culture of Europe and to reduce all art to the Nazi formula.[101]

The ever-expanding results of process of the ALIU's investigations apparently strengthened the resolve of ALIU officials. It made them even more determined to ensure that those Germans and collaborators who had centrally participated in what was increasingly being understood as a massive, cynical and systematic programme of art looting, faced exposure, and ideally punishment, for their activities.[102]

Within the CIRs, ALIU officials included punitive recommendations to the Nuremberg prosecutors. For example, Lane Faison's CIR report

[100] CIR 4 (Linz), op. cit. 86.
[101] Plaut, 1946b op. cit.
[102] Nicholas, 1995 op. cit. 380.

on the Linz Museum suggested that the entire organisation be included within the Nuremberg Charter's definition of a 'criminal organisation', and be prosecuted as such, akin to Himmler's SS.[103] This was because Nazi plunder of art was of a new and different racist character and magnitude from that carried out in an *ad hoc* manner by previous military victors. It had been: 'Officially planned and expertly carried out...to enhance the cultural prestige of the Master Race.'[104] Nicholas notes:

> Reports and questioning produced endless examples of betrayal and corruption, and the extraordinary ability of the Germans to compartmentalise and rationalise their actions.... they were only protecting the art; they were only following orders. These statements were backed by reams of stamped and notarised testimonials from wives, doctors, and colleagues who always mentioned that those being questioned helped this or that Jew, and only gave lip service to the Nazi party.[105]

Other evidence suggests that the ERR records that Plaut supplied to General Donovan, then America's Deputy Chief Nuremberg prosecutor, was particularly well-received, with the General stating that these constituted: 'the most damning evidence of Nazi looting that had been acquired.'[106] Donovan's recently released Nuremberg files at Cornell University include extensive handwritten and signed reports documenting the General's interrogation of Göring. Donovan was monitoring the evidence that Göring's defence lawyer was seeking to obtain, presumably to offset the risk of being ambushed in court by material that the trial lawyers were unaware of, and had no effective reply to.[107] Donovan's interest may be based on his desire to undertake the prestigious role of cross-examining Göring personally. These new materials provide evidence that Göring's reputation as the most defiant of the Nuremberg defendants is unjustified. It is now clear that this defendant had been willing to co-operate with Donovan's plan's to have the former Deputy to Hitler 'sell out' his fellow defendants during

---

[103] Supplement to CIR 4 (Linz), 86.

[104] CIR 4 (Linz), op. cit. 86.

[105] Nicholas, 1995 op. cit. 380.

[106] Charles J. Kunzelman, 'Some Trials, Tribulations, and Successes of the Monuments, Fine Arts and Archives Teams in the European Theatre During WWII', Military Affairs 52:2, 56–60, 59.

[107] See Roger Barrett JAGD to Donovan, 13 November, 1945. This reports on a list of documents examined by Göring's lawyer, Dr Stahmar, noting that he examined one British file not on the American list: UK 62 'Note from Secret Files: 23.1.42' indicating Hitler's 'determination to remove all Jews from Europe.' Cornell Collection, op. cit. Vol. 18, 60.12.

trial testimony conducted by the OSS Director himself. According to Dunlop, Donovan:

> [S]pent ten days alone interrogating him... One day he confronted Göring with details of his looting [based on studies by the OSS Art Looting investigators and presumably others]. He had intended to open a new museum to house the art, according to the report: 'Either in Berlin or at Carinhall in which a railroad was to be built from Berlin to bring tourists.[108]

When interrogating Göring, Donovan would have had in front of him the OSS/R&A 'dry run' trial brief on this defendant, prepared over the early summer, which contained various dossiers of his role in looting and other crimes. Indeed, his personal files from this time at Nuremberg contained an entire subsection of evidence sourced largely, but not exclusively, from his own staff. This included summaries of statements of Ritter, and interrogation records relating to Göring's dealings with both Bruno Lohse and Karl Haberstock.[109] Other materials in this collection related to Göring's personal complicities in art looting.[110]

At this point, it may be useful to review archival evidence that suggests that many of the key findings and conclusions of the ALIU's efforts were included in the source documents from which the prosecutors extracted evidence for their various trial briefs against both Rosenberg and Göring. As Rosenfeld notes:

> ALIU turned over the reports and copies of captured evidence used during the interrogations to the War Crimes Commission to provide supporting evidence for prosecutors at both the trials of both Herman Göring and Alfred Rosenberg at the War Crimes Trials.[111] Thus Plaut's January 1945 vision for punishing those involved in art looting was not totally unrealistic; Plaut and the ALIU could be credited for having this charge created and at least being able to detain individuals in preparation they hoped for prosecution for their crimes.[112]

---

[108] Dunlop, op. cit. 481.

[109] See Cornell Collection, sub-section 19. The former addresses Lohse's activities as a member of the ERR, primarily the acquisition, via confiscation, of art objects in his role as Göring's purchasing agent in Paris for paintings. The Haberstock record provides details of Haberstock's collecting work on behalf of both Hitler and Göring and avoids references to outright confiscations.

[110] Ibid., Volume XCIX (no subsection): 'French Works of Art Obtained by Former Reichsmarschall Hermann Göring.' In this document, Göring refers to his willingness to return the art treasures he acquired during the war.

[111] ALIU Final Report (May 1946), op. cit. 6.

[112] Rosenfeld, 1992 op. cit. Chapter 3, 20.

Here, we must bear in mind that the prosecution, whose ambit in terms of the historical period, the location and scope of war crimes was exceptionally wide, was prepared at great speed. Hence, fulsome acknowledgement in footnotes for example of the various agencies that originally supplied different pieces of key evidence is not contained in any of these trial briefs. These contain various claims concerning the actions and intentions of defendants illustrated and supported by various largely documentary sources, especially those created the Nazis themselves created.

This means that ideally researchers would have to examine the administrative documentation contained in both the Nuremberg and OSS war crimes files, and identify dossiers of evidence that the ALIU team supplied to the Nuremberg prosecutors through OSS-OCC liaison channels. Then, in order to identify examples of ALIU evidence exerting some direct and tangible impact, we would have to examine the Nuremberg indictment and trial briefs (the underlying basis for many courtroom statements by the prosecutors), and the actual transcript of the Nuremberg trials. Finally, a complete project would require researchers to examine the Judges' own final judgement to see if any of the prosecutors' allegations that appear to have been based fully, or at least partly, on ALIU reports were accepted as valid incriminating evidence meriting special mention. Such an ideal project would take us beyond the scope of the present book, although certain material relevant to it is included as Appendix One.

A number of items of trial evidence deployed within the Nuremberg trials stemmed directly or indirectly from the investigative work of ALIU officials. For example, when investigating the ERR's complicity in the Holocaust, officials searched for its former Director von Behr. Whilst the latter and his wife had already committed suicide, in their apartment's cellars they discovered: 'all the records of Rosenberg's ill-fated Ministry, which now would be used as evidence at Nuremberg. Haberstock and his records were found nearby at the castle of the Baron von Pollnitz.... Gurlitt was there too.'[113]

Furthermore, CIR 1 forwarded various translated German documents incriminating a number of the Nuremberg defendants, including one

[113] Nicholas, 1995 op. cit. 379. Gurlitt was appointed by Posse to be his agent in Paris: 'Because he was half-Jewish, Gurlitt shied away from Nazi circles. Many of his transactions in Paris were arranged through a Dutch dealer.' CIR 4 (Linz), op. cit. 51.

concerning General Keitel.[114] This was an order the latter had made on 17 September 1940 to his Army subordinate in France. This document became American evidence 138-PS, and was fully used in prosecutor Walther Brudno's trial brief, as the following extract makes clear:

> Keitel issued a further order to the Chief of the OKH, France, on 17 September 1940, providing:
>
> The ownership status before the war in France, prior to the declaration of war on 1 September 1939, shall be the criterion. "Ownership transfers to the French state or similar transfers completed after this date are irrelevant and legally invalid (for example, Polish and Slovak libraries in Paris, possessions of the Palais Rothschild or other ownerless Jewish possessions). Reservations regarding search, seizure and transportation to Germany on the basis of the above reasons will not be recognized.
>
> Reichsleiter Rosenberg and/or his deputy Reichshauptstellenleiter Ebert has received clear instructions from the Fuehrer personally governing the right of seizure; he is entitled to transport to Germany cultural goods which appear valuable to him and to safeguard them there. The fuehrer has reserved for himself the decision as to their use.
>
> It is requested that the services in question be informed correspondingly. (138-PS)
>
> The above order was extended to Belgium on 10 October 1940 (139-PS), and an identical order was issued by the Chief of the OKH to the Armed Forces Commander in The Netherlands on 17 September 1940. (140-PS).[115]

A similar point applies to CIR 1's second attachment, an order from Göring from 5 November 1940, which became Nuremberg evidence item 141-PS. This was quoted from during the Nuremberg trials as Exhibit RF-1309 and—as will be discussed later in an appendix—deployed during the French prosecutor's evidence. This document was also cited in Brudno's brief as follows:

> D. Cooperation of Hermann Göring.
>
> On 5 November 1940, Göring issued an order specifying the distribution to be made of art objects brought to the Louvre. The order lists as second in priority of disposition, "Those art objects which serve to the completion of the Reichsmarschall's collection" and states that the objects will "be packed and shipped to Germany with the assistance of the Luftwaffe." (141-PS)[116]

---

[114] CIR 1, Attachment 1.

[115] Brudno, op. cit. NCA 1, Chapter 14, 'The Plunder of Art Treasures': http://www.yale.edu/lawweb/avalon/imt/document/nca_vol1/chap_14.htm.

[116] Ibid.

However, it was the ALIU's fifth attachment, a secret 'Document Memorandum for the Fuehrer-Concerning: Jewish Possessions in France' dated 18 December 1941, which was perhaps the most cited piece of trial evidence. It was used in the trial brief entitled 'The Persecution of the Jews'.[117]

> Rosenberg's notion of the means to be taken against the Jews is expressed in a secret "Document Memorandum for the Fuehrer-Concerning: Jewish Possessions in France," dated 18 December 1941. Rosenberg urges plundering and death:
>
> In compliance with the order of the Fuehrer for protection of Jewish cultural possessions, a great number of Jewish dwellings remained unguarded. Consequently, many furnishings have disappeared because a guard could, naturally, not be posted. In the whole East the administration has found terrible conditions of living quarters, and the chances of procurement are so limited that it is not practical to procure any more. Therefore, I beg the Fuehrer to permit the seizure of all Jewish home furnishings of Jews in Paris, who have fled or will leave shortly, and that of Jews living in all parts of the occupied West, to relieve the shortage of furnishings in the administration in the East.
>
> 2. A great number of leading Jews were, after a short examination in Paris, again released. The attempts on the lives of members of the armed forces have not stopped; on the contrary they continue. This reveals an unmistakable plan to disrupt the German-French cooperation, to force Germany to retaliate, and, with this, evoke a new defense on the parts of the French against Germany. I suggest to the Fuehrer that, instead of executing 100 Frenchmen, we substitute 100 Jewish bankers, lawyers, etc. It is the Jews in London and New York who incite the French communists to commit acts of violence, and it seems only fair that the members of this race should pay for this. It is not the little Jews, but the leading Jews in France, who should be held responsible. That would tend to awaken the Anti-Jewish sentiment.
>
> (Signed) A. Rosenberg. (001-PS)

This document was quoted in full on 13 December 1945 as part of the prosecution's case regarding the persecution and annihilation of European Jews, which included much of the corresponding trial brief. It was used to prove the personally anti-Semitic orientation of Rosenberg and his active role in encouraging further acts of persecution and murder:

---

[117] NCA 1, Chapter 12: http://www.yale.edu/lawweb/avalon/imt/document/nca_vol1/chap_12.htm.

> MAJOR WALSH: I have from time to time made reference to certain utterances and actions of the Defendant Rosenberg as one of the leaders and policy makers of the Nazi Party and German State. It is perhaps reasonable to assume that the Defendant Rosenberg will claim for many of his actions that he pursued them pursuant to superior orders. I have before me, however, a captured document, Number 001-PS, marked "secret," dated 18 December 1941, entitled "Documentary Memorandum for the Fuehrer-Concerning Jewish Possessions in France," Exhibit Number USA-282. I dare say that no document before this Tribunal will more clearly evidence the Defendant Rosenberg's personal attitude, his temperament, and convictions toward the Jews more strongly than this memorandum, wherein he, in his own initiative, urges plundering and death. I offer in evidence Document Number 001-PS. The body of the memorandum reads as follows:...[118]

On 16 April 1946, the French prosecutor, Dr Thoma, confronted Rosenberg with this document during the latter's cross examination. The following extract shows that it clearly embarrassed him before the Tribunal:

> DR. THOMA: I now turn to the furniture operation in France, and for that purpose I am showing the defendant Document 001-PS, also Volume II of the French Document Book, and I am asking the defendant to state his views with respect to it. *[The document was submitted to the defendant.]*
> ROSENBERG: Document 001-PS contains, at the beginning, information to the effect that in the East accommodations were found to be so dreadful that I was proposing that ownerless Jewish homes in France and their furniture should be made available for that purpose. This suggestion was approved in a decree issued, by order of the Fuehrer, by the Reich Minister and Chief of the Reich Chancellery on 31 December 1941. In the course of the ever increasing bombardment in Germany, I considered that I no longer could take responsibility for this, and thus I made a suggestion that this furniture should be placed at the disposal of bombed out victims in Germany-which amounted to more than 100,000 people on certain nights that emergency aid would be given to them. In the report of the French Document Book it is stated in the seventh paragraph how the confiscation was carried out: that these deserted apartments were sealed, that they remained sealed for some time in the event of possible claims, and that then the shipment to Germany was carried out. I am aware that this, no doubt, was a serious encroachment on private property; but here again, in connection with previous considerations, I thought about the implications and, finally, of the millions of homeless Germans. I want to emphasize in this connection that I kept myself well informed; that the homes, their owners, and the main contents in the way of furniture were

---

[118] IMT 3, 537.

> recorded in detail in a big book, as a basis for possible negotiations at a later date. In Germany the matter was so arranged that those people who suffered damage by bombing paid for these furnishings and household goods, which were placed at their disposal; and these deliveries were deducted from the claims which they had against the state. That money was paid into a special fund administered by the Minister of Finance. The Document 001-PS contains under Number 2 a suggestion which I myself consider a serious charge against me. This is a suggestion that in view of many murders of Germans in France, not only Frenchmen should be shot as hostages, but that Jewish citizens also were to be called to account. I should like to say that I considered these shootings of hostages, since they were announced publicly, a permissible measure under special circumstances in wartime. The fact that this sort of thing was being done by the Armed Forces appeared to me according to the result of the usual investigations, the more so since it was taking place in a territory, a State with which the German Reich had signed an armistice. Secondly, this happened during a period of excitement, due to the war which had just broken out with the United States of America and to our recollection of the report from the Polish Ambassador, Count Potocki, dated 30 January 1939, which the Tribunal has forbidden to be read.[119]

The French prosecutor also exploited this document.[120]

Another attachment to CIR 1, Göring's letter to Rosenberg on 18 June 1942 was designated as 1118-PS / RF-1314. It was then used in both Brudno's trial brief and quoted during the trial itself to emphasise the anti-Semitic elements of Nazi plunder:

> The National Socialist Party financed the operations of the Einsatzstab Rosenberg. (090-PS; 145-PS) In a letter to Göring, 18 June 1942, Rosenberg voiced the opinion that all art objects and other confiscated items should belong to the National Socialist Party because the Party has been bearing the brunt of the battle against the persons and forces from whom this property was taken. (1118-PS).[121]

During the trial, on 6 February 1946, the French prosecutor's case on art looting cited another part of this document to demonstrate the ERR's subordination in practice to Göring's art looting activities:

> I turn to Page 19 in the brief to quote a very short passage of a letter dated 18 June 1942, signed by Rosenberg and addressed to the Defendant Göring. I offer in evidence a copy of this letter as Document Number RF-1314. Here is the passage which I shall read to the Tribunal. Page

[119] IMT 11. 474–75.

[120] IMT 7, 55.

[121] NCA 1, Chapter 14, op. cit.

> 20 of the brief, Page 2 of the document book: "Some time ago I explicitly approved the instructions given by the Chief of my Einsatzstab, Stabsfuehrer Party member Utikal, that Party member Dr. Lobse of the Bildende Kunst Office be put at your disposal for any purpose you may desire."[122]

One of the CIR attachments that proved to be most damning was the records of ERR. The prosecutors extracted and used these in many different ways during both the various Nuremberg trial briefs, for example that of Brudno, and in the trial itself, including the following statement in Jackson's opening presentation:

> Moreover, this looting was glorified by Rosenberg. Here we have 39 leather-bound tabulated volumes of his inventory, which in due time we will offer in evidence. One cannot but admire the artistry of this Rosenberg report. The Nazi taste was cosmopolitan. Of the 9,455 articles inventoried, there were included 5,255 paintings, 297 sculptures, 1,372 pieces of antique furniture, 307 textiles, and 2,224 small objects of art. Rosenberg observed that there were approximately 10,000 more objects still to be inventoried (015-PS).[123]

The Judgement of the IMT endorsed a number of key contentions contained in, and illustrated by, ALIU reports. These had been presented to the Tribunal indirectly through trial briefs that had borrowed extensively from these OSS reports. A key claim related to the central importance of the actions of Rosenberg's ERR. The IMT certainly endorsed this central point by reference to key items of evidence that the ALIU had itself forwarded to the prosecutors:

> Rosenberg is responsible for a system of organised plunder of both public and private property throughout the invaded countries of Europe. Acting under Hitler's orders of January, 1940, to set up the "Hohe Schule," he organised and directed the "Einsatzstab Rosenberg," which plundered museums and libraries, confiscated art treasures and collections and pillaged private houses. His own reports show the extent of the confiscations. In "Action-M" (Moebel), instituted in December, 1941, at Rosenberg's suggestion, 69,619 Jewish homes were plundered in the West, 38,000 of them in Paris alone, and it took 26,984 railroad cars to transport the confiscated furnishings to Germany. As of 14th July, 1944, more than 21,903 art objects, including famous paintings and museum pieces, had been seized by the Einsatzstab in the West.[124]

---

122 IMT 7, 58.
123 NCA 1, Chapter 5.
124 http://www.yale.edu/lawweb/avalon/imt/proc/judrosen.htm.

Three other ALIU contentions were: the integral role art looting played within a step by step process of persecution that culminated in the Holocaust, the linkage between this anti-Semitic programme and the build up to aggressive war, and the central role Göring played in these matters. The IMT's judgement endorsed these contentions:

> With the seizure of power, the persecution of the Jews was intensified. A series of discriminatory laws were passed... By the autumn of 1938, the Nazi policy towards the Jews had reached the stage where it was directed towards the complete exclusion of Jews from German life. Pogroms were organised which included the burning and demolishing of synagogues, the looting of Jewish businesses, and the arrest of prominent Jewish business men. A collective fine of one billion marks was imposed on the Jews, the seizure of Jewish assets was authorised... certain aspects of this anti-Semitic policy were connected with the plans for aggressive war.... The imposition of a fine of one billion marks was made, and the confiscation of the financial holdings of the Jews was decreed, at a time when German armament expenditure had put the German treasury in difficulties, and when the reduction of expenditure on armaments was being considered. These steps were taken, moreover, with the approval of the defendant Göring, who had been given responsibility for economic matters of this kind, and who was the strongest advocate of an extensive rearmament programme notwithstanding the financial difficulties.... the connection of the anti-Semitic policy with aggressive war was not limited to economic matters.[125]

The transfer of the results of ALIU's investigations to the Nuremberg prosecutors has left only a limited paper trail of documentation. This is possibly because many prosecutors took back home with them their own papers as mementos. However, it is clear from the ALIU reports' distribution lists that the Allied War Crimes Commission received copies of these studies, from which the Nuremberg prosecutors also derived a considerable amount of their information. One of the results of the ALIU's investigations was the gathering of a large portfolio of evidence that formed an important source of an early draft prosecution brief: 'R&A #3152 Göring as a war criminal', which OSS' war crimes staff fed into the Nuremberg process during the mid-summer of 1945.[126]

---

[125] http://www.yale.edu/lawweb/avalon/imt/proc/judwarcr.htm.

[126] R&A 3152, 'Hermann Göring as a War Criminal': Cornell Collection, op. cit. Vol. 26/62.04; US NA, RG 226, M1221. The Preface to this document states, 'In this study it is intended to list the major types of crimes for which Hermann Göring can be indicted, subdivided into more specific types. In identifying Göring's culpability for in each offence, this report attempts 'to outline a) specific acts constituting the type

This brief, which included early findings on Göring's art looting activities, underwent three successive drafts before being approved by the 'Prosecution Review Board'. A more direct indicator is the fact that, from April 1945 to the spring of 1946, Justice Jackson's organisation certainly received at least the majority of the ALIU reports. Before these OSS officials issued their DIR and CIR reports, it is clear that, from as early as June 1945, London X-2 Branch were sending preliminary materials for transmission to these prosecutors via James Donovan, OSS' General Counsel (senior in-house lawyer). James Donovan had been made responsible for the administrative supervision, liaison and coordination of all of OSS' contributions to the Nuremberg process. This included overseeing the activities of the dozens of staff seconded to the OCC from the OSS itself.[127]

Surviving and declassified OSS files record a moderate sized paper trail from the OSS side of the OSS-OCC relationship which merit a brief summary. The records relevant to the prosecution of Göring as a war criminal appear to start on 27 April 1945, a few days before the end of WWII. On that date, OSS staff sent a memorandum reporting on two of the members of a Nazi looting network: Gottfried Friedrich Reber and Cesare Avellino Albergo.[128]

During the following two months it appears that the pace of investigative work expanded with the end of hostilities as a number of other relevant documents concerning art looting from OSS field officers were produced and filed. This postwar flurry of documentation includes a memorandum dated 19 May 1945 providing details of 'French Works of Art Obtained by Former Reichsmarschall Hermann Göring'.[129] Later, on 13 June 1945, ALIU's John Russell sent James Donovan, in his role as OSS war crimes co-ordinator, three copies of this Unit's 'Report on the Art Activities of Hermann Göring' dated 12 June 1945.

---

of crime in question, and the evidence available or still needed for proving such acts; b) the basis for Göring's responsibility for the commission of such acts, including positions held relating to crimes involved, decrees, orders, and other documents bearing on his jurisdictional responsibility, and statements by Göring and others showing his responsibility; as well as the applicable laws and the possible weakness of the evidence.

[127] Salter, 2007 op. cit. 373.

[128] 27 April 1945, Memorandum from Captain Gilbert S. Meldrum, Officer in Charge, for the Officer in Charge, 'Reber, Gottfried Friedrich, Albergo Cesare, Avellino,' regarding his work for Göring in collecting art: US NA, RG 226, Entry 146, Box 35, Folder 443: 'Hermann Göring'.

[129] Ibid. It was written by Maj. Paul Kubala, MI, Commanding, Seventh Army Interrogation Center.

This was explicitly sent: 'for use in the overall OSS project', although subject to the proviso that its further distribution outside OSS at that time required prior clearance from X-2 to avoid risking the security of 'current operations.'[130] The objectives of this report were to clarify the type, extent and methods of Göring's looting in a way that would contribute directly to the preparation of a trial brief against this most senior defendant.

The report itself states that its aims were to: 'sketch briefly the facts, as they are currently known here of several transactions in which Göring is known to have been involved as illustrative of certain types of his activities.' The author's of the X-2's 'Interim Report on Hermann Göring's Collection of Looted Art', which was contained within the wider dossier, provides the caveat that investigations in the field remain ongoing, and hence they: 'will undoubtedly provide a fuller, more documented story of even these activities.' The second aim of this document was: 'to state, and show their importance to Göring's case, the primary sources of information recently made available in the field to X-2 Branch and which are currently being developed by them for...material of a War Crimes interest.'[131]

The main body of the report notes that Göring had collected art from the Nazis' seizure of power in 1933, and that whilst many were purchased lawfully through 'regular dealer channels':

> [O]thers undoubtedly came from the collections of dispossessed German Jews, either through forced sale or outright confiscation. In this light, it is significant that following the Austrian Anschluss, the art collections of Göring and Hitler are known to have increased greatly as the celebrated collections of Austrian Jews, notably the Czernin Collection of Vienna, found their way in to their hands.[132]

This report also alerts OSS prosecutors to the importance for their purposes of the mission and activities of Alfred Rosenberg, soon to be named as a defendant, and the ERR. It notes that the latter organisation was:

> established under the direction of Alfred Rosenberg originally for the confiscation and disposal of Jewish property in Poland and Russia. In

---

[130] Russell to Donovan, 13 June, 1945: US NA, RG 226, Entry 146, Box 35, Folder 443.
[131] Ibid., 1.
[132] Ibid., 1.

> June 1940 it transferred its activities to the West...with a [Paris] staff of several hundred experts, dealers, valuers and minor officials.[133]

This report also provides as two appendixes for use as trial evidence: a partial list of ERR's confiscated works of art, and this body's complete and extensive records of looting activities. It also identifies its leading surviving officials, such as Bruno Lohse characterised as: 'Göring's leading representative in the organisation', and provides brief details of the role played by each of these officials. This document also relays information on Göring's many visits to the ERR's Paris HQ, the Jeu de Paume. For example, this highly incriminating evidence was supplied by one of X-2's undercover informants who, we are told, had: 'worked in the Jeu de Paume throughout the German occupation.'[134] This informant provided details of Göring's complicity in the forced sale of a Van Gogh painting from the Weinberger Collection for 20% of its market value:

> It appears...from captured records...that he came to Paris on February 4th and 5th 1941 and submitted to von Behr [the ERR Director] photographs from confiscated Jewish collections which he and the Fuehrer wanted for themselves.... these items were to be loaded immediately and sent to Germany by special train.[135]

Anticipating CIR 2, this ALIU report also warns the prosecutors not to be deceived by: 'the cover of legality' that Goring, through Lohse, often supplied by means of a 'formal appraisal' of an artwork's monetary value by Jacque Beltran. This appraisal was designed to create the appearance of a proper sale. Yet it operated as a smokescreen because these valuations resulted in: 'figures well below their true worth.'[136] This report further identifies other important members of Göring's network, including Josef Angerer, who supplied Göring with photographs of largely Jewish works looted by the ERR so that he could decide which to select for the Carinhall collection. Such photographs included: 'the

[133] Ibid., 1.

[134] Ibid., 2. It appears that this agent was Rose Valland, an official at the Jeu de Paume. In 1961, she published an account entitled *Le Front de l'art* of how French curators risked their lives in communicating with the French resistance and thereby successful prevented the Nazis from taking control of the treasures of the Louvre and other major museums.

[135] Russell to Donovan, 13 June, 1945: US NA, RG 226, Entry 146, Box 35, Folder 443, 2.

[136] Ibid., 2.

collections of books, furniture and art objects from the Rothschild Palace.'[137] The ALIU report identifies Alois Miedl, Göring's 'old school friend', who was then in ALIU custody, as the latter's 'principal agent in Holland'. Miedl, it claims, was responsible for various forced sales in that country, including 22 paintings from the Goudstikker family, which later formed part of Göring's collection.[138] The Goudstikker firm was originally owned by a Jewish family but became vulnerable to 'Aryanization', and Göring's contact, Alois Miedl, was one of those who intervened to exploit their plight:

> The thought that the Nazis might otherwise confiscate the inventory of this Jewish firm without compensation was brought forth with varying degrees of subtlety by some of the prospective buyers. A quick sale therefore seemed prudent. One of those interested was Alois Miedl, ... He had several times been associated with Göring, knew the Reichsmarschall's sister and had visited Carinhall. Göring had recommended him to Seyss-Inquart and Mühlmann as one familiar with the Dutch market. Mühlmann found that Miedl had gone rather beyond mere familiarity, and had "as a good businessman taken advantage of the panic which had taken place at the invasion" by suggesting to certain Jewish dealers that they sell to him before the Nazis confiscated their stock.[139]

In this interim report for the prosecutors, ALIU officials insisted that a range of other sources, which it lists, still needed to be exploited or further investigated: 'before making a final report.'[140] It also notes that they and other Allied staff acting on their requests, had already succeeded in detaining for interrogation 12 of the 21 individuals the Unit and British authorities had jointly identified as 'high priority targets'. Philips identified future interrogation of the following 4 persons as vital for clarifying Göring's various complicities: Hofer, Miedl, Lohse, and Haberstock.[141] Reber, Hofer's agent for Italy, is also proposed as a suitable case for later interrogation by ALIU officials.[142] Another source identified as meriting further intensive study are the captured ERR files

[137] Ibid., 3.
[138] Ibid., 3.
[139] Nicholas, 1995 op. cit. 105, citing Mühlmann's interrogation by ALIU.
[140] Russell to Donovan, 13 June, 1945: US NA, RG 226, Entry 146, Box 35, Folder 443, 5.
[141] Ibid., 5.
[142] CIR 2 (Göring), op. cit. 20 for further details on Reber.

'found near Füssen. They are being microfilmed and processed and should yield documentary evidence of the first importance.'[143]

This OSS X-2 report also provided the prosecutors with a small dossier of information either developed by ALIU officials, or acquired from other Allied agencies, such as the US Army's Counter Intelligence Corp's interrogation of Gottfried Reber in Italy from 27 April 1945. The latter revealed details of Hofer's attempts in 1941–43 to widen his network of agents working to secure artworks on Göring's behalf, and indicated that Hofer himself had, through marriage, a Jewish brother-in-law who was also a painter and art collector. During this initial interrogation, Reber claimed his role was confined to making trips to Italy, including Florence in the spring of 1941, to make only *voluntary* purchases of paintings on Göring's behalf. Reder suggested that he had never met Göring personally, and that his information on this Nuremberg defendant's art looting activities was only based upon Hofer's occasional conversations with him. Nevertheless, he was able to remember enough of these conversations to identify a number of other art dealers who had taken a more active role in supporting Göring's acquisitions. For example, Reber recalled a conversation with Hofer regarding the latter's difficulties in exercising pressure upon a dealer, Contini, who had been reluctant to part with some paintings sought by Göring. Contini told Reber that Goring had said one day: 'Contini, its too bad you're not a Paris Jew, and I'd just take them away from you.'[144] Reber also provided further incriminating details that confirmed earlier evidence concerning the complicities of the Swiss Fischer Gallery:

> When Göring confiscated the collections of Rosenberg, the famous Jewish art dealer of Paris, the collections were sent directly to Switzerland, where they were addressed to a certain Fischer, antique dealer of Lucerne.... Fischer provided a very important channel for Hofer's purchases in France, and also possibly from other countries.[145]

In mitigation, and with documentary support, Reber claimed that his 'outspoken criticism' of Nazi anti-Semitism had resulted in the withdrawal of his German citizenship in March 1943.

---

[143] Ibid., 5.

[144] US Army's Counter Intelligence Corp's interrogation of Gottfried Reber, 27 April 1945, in ibid.

[145] Ibid.

Shortly after sending this report on 18 June, one of James Donovan's staff, John Jackson, received an additional dossier from ALIU's John Russell. This comprised: 'five translated orders and letters of Goring which formed the subject of our conversation on Saturday', and which the ALIU had secured from various sources, including Lohse. It highlights Göring's letter of 21 November 1940 (outlined below) discussing his use of criminal agents in France to track down and secure the hidden artwork of French Jews, and comments: 'I am informed that we have the names and whereabouts of many of these should they be needed to build a case.... A pouch has been sent requesting verification and the location of the original inasmuch as both men from whom they were obtained are now in the custody of this branch.'[146] These letters were particularly incriminating, including one to Rosenberg boasting at how the ERR's looting of French Jewish works: 'became possible through the fact that I was able to assist your staff through members of my staff.' Another, a letter from Utikal on Göring's office paper to Major von Brauchtitsch, informs him that Scholz, rather than ERR's Director von Behr, will in future be in charge of 'the seizure of art treasures,' and that Lohse must now be treated as Göring's personal representative in the ERR. Also included was Göring's own letter of 1 May 1941 supporting the work of the ERR. It stated that this organisation's work formed part of: 'the battle against Jews... a foremost task of National Socialism during the war'. Göring's letter required all state officials to support this agency of plunder and contained the ominous threat for those who may not fully comply that any difficulties ERR staff encountered had to be reported to him directly. Another document within this dossier was an order from Berlin of 12 March 1941 requiring:

> the unloading of art treasures transported from Paris and Füssen be executed by the person put in charge through the service of Reichsleiter Rosenberg, Staff West, Party Comrades Scholz, Busse, Dr Kunze and Dr Schiedlausky, are responsible for the uploading and the transportation to the place of safe keeping. I direct all services and authorities to give all necessary support to the persons in charge of the execution of this order. [Signed Göring][147]

[146] Russell to Jackson, 18 June, 1945: US NA, RG 226, Entry 146, Box 35, Folder 443.
[147] Ibid.

Göring's letter of 21 November 1940, which as already noted was identified by ALIU officials as a particularly incriminating piece of evidence of Göring's complicity in the Holocaust, merits extensive citation:

> I have promised to support energetically the work of your staff and to place at its disposal that which it could not hitherto obtain, namely, means of transportation and guard personnel, and the Luftwaffe is hereby assigned to give the utmost assistance. In addition, I should like to call to your attention that I have been able to obtain especially valuable cultural goods from Jewish owners. I obtained them from hiding places that were very difficult to find; I discovered these a long time ago, by means of bribery and the employment of French detectives and criminal agents. This activity continues, as does the activity of my foreign exchange investigation authorities scrutinising bank vaults... your staff will then be required to seize the articles and transport them.... In order to complete this collection I have considered the purchase also of some few pieces from confiscated Jewish cultural goods. This pertains chiefly to masters whose works I did not hitherto possess or works necessary to supplement the collection. I submit these things from time to time to the Fuehrer.... up to now there have been about 15 paintings.[148]

This letter also maintains the pretence that these Jewish works were properly purchased for a fair price taking into account the costs of tracking them down in the first place.

It appears from a routing slip to ALIU's 'supplementary report on Hermann Göring' of 25 June 1945, (essentially a short follow up statement from Philips concerning suggestions that Göring owned assets in Portugal) that James Donovan rapidly transmitted all or part of this important dossier to 'Mr Jackson' on 26 June 1945,[149] with another copy sent to the JAG's War Crimes Office, presumably after receiving prior clearance from ALIU officials. Donovan wrote on a slip: 'I am routing this to Mr Jackson as I believe he also is working on the Göring brief.'[150] This suggests that the earlier materials were also sent to Jackson who may have requested additional details. OSS-R&A's Franz Neumann, the senior analyst on Nazi Germany and war crimes research, was also sent a copy.

---

[148] Ibid.

[149] Another possibility is that it was sent to OSS' John Jackson who was preparing the Göring brief for Justice Jackson, and therefore destined for the US Chief Prosecutor only indirectly.

[150] Part of 15 June dossier, op. cit.

As already noted, the ALIU's research was, in part, aimed at providing the basis for war crimes prosecution, and the OSS leadership in general was anxious to ensure that all its resources documenting Nazi war crimes were fully used during the preparation of trial briefs. General Donovan's twin positions from June to December 1945 as both OSS Director and Deputy Chief Counsel for the dominant American prosecution agency, the Office of Chief of Counsel (OCC), ensured that his subordinates gave a high priority to this policy. Indeed, Donovan's own personal files contain a specific section on Art Looting, including Walter Brudno's trial brief on cultural plunder.[151] Strictly speaking Brudno cannot perhaps be regarded as the sole author of 'Plunder of Art Treasures'[152] as Justice Jackson also credits many other individuals for assisting in this and two other trial briefs: 'Persecution of the Jews' (NCA XII), and 'Concentration Camps'.[153] Those credited include a number of OSS lawyers and research analysts such as Seymour Krieger, Frederick Felton, Lt. Daniel F. Margolies, Bernard Meltzer, and Nicholas Doman.[154]

It would be possible, time and space permitting, to fully cross reference the materials contained in the main Nuremberg trial evidence, including both the indictment and legal briefs, with the contents of ALIU's earlier DIR and CIR reports, and identify sections of the former which probably stemmed from the latter. An exhaustive analysis would, however, be excessive for the purposes of this chapter, as it is sufficient to show that many of the key themes and documentary evidence supplied and analysed by these OSS staff were replicated directly or indirectly in materials deployed as trial evidence.[155]

A decisive piece of evidence, which bypasses the need for such an exhaustive survey, is James Plaut's report to a colleague in November 1945. In this report Plaut stated that he had discovered that the Nuremberg prosecutors had already made such extensive use of this Unit's

[151] Cornell Collection, Vol. X / 19.

[152] NCA Vol. 1 Chapter 14.

[153] Ibid.

[154] Preface to NCA: http://www.yale.edu/lawweb/avalon/imt/document/nca_vol1/preface.htm. For additional if incomplete details of the extensive and growing numbers of OSS staff attached to the OCC see James Donovan to OSS Director, 23 July 1945: US NA, Director's Files, M1642, Roll 120, Frame 211–212.

[155] Brudno, 1945 op. cit. 13 is based probably on fuller information contained in CIR 1, 20, whilst Brudno's citation of orders from Göring, which became Nuremberg document PS-141 borrows from the earlier CIR 2, Attachment 3.

CIRs on the Göring collection and the ERR that, despite being called upon as an expert consultant, there was little more he could personally add to their preparation of trial briefs on art plunder:

> I learned almost at once that there was little that any member of this unit could do at Nuremberg at this stage of the game, inasmuch as the briefs were all but completed. It was, however, a source of great gratification that our material, notably the E.R.R. [Einsatzstab Reichsleiter Rosenberg] and the H.G. [Hermann Göring] reports, had been exploited fully both from the standpoint of text and accompanying documentation.... I believe that our obligation to the War Crimes interests has now been discharged fully and effectively.[156]

Our first appendix, which reviews the applicable law on cultural plunder deployed with the Nuremberg trials, provides extensive corroboration of Plaut's conclusion. In outlining how art looting featured in a number of different presentations by prosecutors, it identifies themes, pieces of evidence and arguments that coincided remarkably with those contained in earlier CIR reports.

The remainder of this section will complete our discussion of the contribution of the ALIU to the Nuremberg process by reviewing the evidence of Mühlmann, whose testimony stemmed directly from this Unit's interrogations and recommendation that he be deployed as a witness in these trials. On 18 December 1945, the Nuremberg prosecutors deployed Mühlmann's affidavit, identified as 3042-PS, concerning the organisation of art looting in Poland against both Göring and Hans Frank. This confirmed one of Göring's purely verbal orders. Colonel Storey then adopted its contents as a significant part of the American prosecution's case against these two defendants, and provided a range of additional illustrations:

> Col. Storey: Before I deal with the plunder of the cultural treasures by the Einsatzstab Rosenberg, I wish to reveal briefly the independent plundering operations conducted in the Government General of Occupied Poland by authority of the Defendant Göring and under the supervision of the Defendant Frank, the Governor General. In October 1939 Göring issued a verbal order to a Dr. Mühlmann asking him to undertake the immediate securing of all Polish art treasures. Dr. Mühlmann himself gives evidence of this order in Document Number 3042-PS found in the document book last introduced as Exhibit USA-375... These are consecutive.

[156] Plaut to Wittmann. 8 November 1945, 'Cables': US NA, RG 226, Entry 190, Box 533 cf. Yeide n. 30 also acknowledging Rothfeld op. cit.

> I would like to offer this affidavit and to read it in full. In short, it was obtained in Austria. Kajetan Mühlmann states under oath:
>
> "I have been a member of the NSDAP since 1 April 1938. I was Brigadier General—Oberfuehrer—in the SS. I was never an illegal Nazi. I was the special deputy of the Governor General of Poland, Hans Frank, for the safeguarding of art treasures in the Government General, October 1939 to September 1943. Göring, in his function as chairman of the Reich Defense Committee, had commissioned me with this duty. I confirm that it was the official policy of the Governor General, Hans Frank, to take into custody all important art treasures which belonged to Polish public institutions, private collections, and the Church. I confirm that the art treasures mentioned were actually confiscated; and it is clear to me that they would not have remained in Poland in case of a German victory, but they would have been used to complement German artistic property."—Signed and sworn to by Dr. Mühlmann....
>
> Numerous objects of art: paintings, tapestries, plates, dishes, as well as other dinnerware, were also safeguarded by Frank, who had the Special Deputy deliver these objects to an architect for the purpose of furnishing the castle at Krakow and the Schloss Kressendorf, which were the residences of the Governor General Frank. It was apparently Frank's belief that these items would be safer in his possession, used to grace his table and dazzle his guests, than they would be in the possession of the rightful owners. There is no doubt whatever that virtually the entire art possession of Poland was seized for the use of Germany and would never have been returned in the event of German victory. Dr. Mühlmann, a noted German art authority, who directed the seizure program for the period of 4 years and was endowed by Frank with sufficient authority to promulgate decrees generally applicable throughout the territory, has stated the objectives of the program in no uncertain terms in the affidavit to which I have just referred.[157]

Later, on 8 January 1946, the prosecutors referred once again to Mühlmann's affidavit in specific connection with the complicity of Göring in art looting within Poland. They relied upon his testimony, which they rephrased as an important part of the prosecution's case, supplemented by one of his reports to Göring from 6 July 1943:

> Evidence has also been introduced showing the organized, systematic program of the Nazi conspirators for the cultural impoverishment of every country in Europe. The continuous connection, of the Defendant Göring with these activities has been substantiated. In October 1939 the Defendant Göring requested Dr. Mühlmann to undertake immediately the "securing" of all Polish art treasures. In his affidavit, already offered,

[157] IMT 4, 78–80.

> Dr. Mühlmann states that he was the special deputy of the Governor General of Poland, the Defendant Frank, for the safeguarding of art treasures in the Government General from October 1939 to September 1943, and that the Defendant Göring, in his capacity as Chairman of the Reich Defense Council, had commissioned him with this duty. Mühlmann also confirms that it was the official policy of the Defendant Frank to take into custody all important art treasures which belonged to Polish public institutions, private collections, and the Church, and that such art treasures were actually confiscated. It appears also from a report made by Dr. Mühlmann on 16 July 1943 on his operations that at one time 31 valuable sketches by the artist Albrecht Durer were taken from the Polish collection and personally handed to the Defendant Göring who took them to the Fuehrer's headquarters.

Immediately after this part of their presentation, the prosecutors cited one of the many documents that ALIU officials had forwarded onto them, as previously discussed:

> The part played by Göring in the looting of art by the Einsatzstab Rosenberg has been shown. We refer to Exhibit Number USA-368, which is our Document Number 141-PS, which is an order dated 5 November 1940, already read in evidence, in which Göring directs the chief of the Military Administration in Paris and the Einsatzstab Rosenberg to dispose of the art objects brought to the Louvre in the following priority:
> "1) Those art objects as to the use of which the Fuehrer has reserved the decision for himself;
> 2) Those art objects which serve to complete the Reich Marshal's collection;
> 3) Those art objects and library stocks, which seem of use for the establishment of the Hohe Schule and for Rosenberg's sphere of activities;
> 4) Those art objects suitable for German museums...."
> In view of the high priority afforded by the foregoing order to the completion of the defendant's own collection, it is not surprising to find that Göring continued to aid the operations of the Einsatzstab Rosenberg. It has been established that on 1 May 1941 Göring issued an order under his own signature to all Party, State, and Wehrmacht services, requesting them to give all possible support and assistance to the chief of staff of Reichsleiter Rosenberg. By May 1942 the Defendant Göring was able to boast of the assistance which he had rendered to the work of the Einsatzstab Rosenberg. In our Document 1015(i)-PS which has been read in evidence on Page 1678 of the record, he is shown writing to the Defendant Rosenberg that he personally supports the work of the Einsatzstab wherever he can do so and that accounted for the seizure of such a large number of art objects because he was able to render assistance to the Einsatzstab. Thus, the Defendant Göring's responsibility

> for the planning of the looting of art, which was actually accomplished by the Einsatzstab Rosenberg, would seem clear.[158]

On March 1946, Göring's defense lawyer, Dr Stahmer, realised that Mühlmann's affidavit was damaging to his client's case. After reminding the Tribunal of its exact wording, he gave Göring the opportunity to reinterpret the affidavit to make its implications appear less damning. Once again, Göring was forced to resort to two scarcely credible claims. First, that his main interest lay not in cultural plunder but rather in safeguarding important but abandoned cultural works in Poland, from possible wartime damage. Secondly, that it was not himself but Mühlmann who had actively created policy in this area, albeit within the framework of Hitler's earlier decisions:

> Dr. Stahmer: On 19 November 1945 a Dr. Kajetan Mühlmann made an affidavit, which has been presented by the Prosecution under Document Number 3042-PS. In this it says the following in three short sentences...
>
> Göring: Actually I had nothing directly to do with the safeguarding of art treasures in Poland, absolutely nothing, in my capacity as Chairman of the Ministerial Council for the Reich Defense. However, Mühlmann, whom I knew, did come to see me and told me that he was to take steps for the safeguarding of art treasures there. It was my view too that these art treasures should be safeguarded during the war, regardless of what was to be done with them later, so that no destruction would be possible through fire, bombing, *et cetera*. I want to emphasize now—I shall refer to this matter again later in connection with France—that nothing was taken from these art treasures for my so-called collection. I mention that just incidentally. That these art treasures were actually safeguarded is correct, and was also intended, partly for the reason that the owners were not there. Wherever the owners were present, however—I remember Count Potocki of Lincut, for instance—the art collections were left where they were. The Fuehrer had not yet finally decided what was to be done with these art treasures. He had given an order—and I communicated that by letter to Mühlmann and also, as far as I remember, to Frank—that these art treasures were for the time being to be brought to Konigsberg. Four pictures were to be taken to the safety "bunker" or the safety room of the German Museum in Berlin or to the Kaiser Friederich Museum in Berlin. The Durer drawings in Lemberg also figured here. In this connection I want to mention them now, since the Prosecution has already concerned itself with them. The Durer drawings in Lemberg were not confiscated by us at that time, because Lemberg had become Russian.

[158] IMT 4, 546–547.

> Not until the march against Russia were these Lemberg drawings—as far as I can remember from Mühlmann's story—rescued from the burning city in the battle by a Polish professor, who had hidden from the Russians until that time, and he gave them over to him. They were drawings and he came with them to visit me. Although I am usually very interested in such things I unfortunately did not have time to look at them properly, as I was on my way to the Fuehrer at the moment. I took them along with me and, as Mühlmann has confirmed, delivered them there immediately. Where they went after that I do not know. I believe I have now answered the question about the Polish art treasures. Apart from that there is still the Veit Stoss altar, which was originally made here in Nuremberg, a purely German work. The Fuehrer wished that this altar should come to the Germanisches Museum here in Nuremberg—with that I personally had nothing to do. I merely know about it. What was intended to be done with it finally had not yet been stated. But it is certain that it also would have been mentioned in negotiations for peace.[159]

Göring's claims to rebut Mühlmann's evidence failed, however, to impress the court, as is clear from the Tribunal's final judgement.

One problem for the prosecution was that, on the one hand, it had to rely upon the veracity of Mühlmann's affidavit in order to help substantiate its claims against Göring. Yet, on 7 February 1946 during the presentation of their case against Seyss-Inquart, the French prosecutors had to present evidence of Mühlmann basic dishonesty, indeed complicity in the Holocaust.

> M. Mounier: 'In regard to works of art, the pillage was carried on in the same way. The Defendant Seyss-Inquart must be considered responsible for organizing the removal of works of art from Holland, since he expressly called in his friend, Dr. Mühlmann, who was a specialist in this branch. In this connection I refer to the document submitted by the Economic Section of the French Prosecution under Document Numbers RF-1343 and RF-1344. The Defendant Seyss-Inquart issued a whole series of measures contrary to international law which did considerable harm to the Netherlands. In 1941 the Dutch authorities had established a currency control system which allowed them to keep track of purchases made with German money, either of goods or public funds, with the aim of preventing abuses which would lead to the plundering of Holland's wealth in the form of materials or of currency. On 31 March 1941 the Defendant Seyss-Inquart abolished the "currency" frontier existing between the Reich and the occupied Dutch territory. By so doing, he paved the way for all the abuses committed in monetary matters by the occupying power, in addition to the impossible sums demanded by

[159] IMT 9, 314–15.

Germany to defray the expenses of occupation: 500 million Reichsmarks on 24 March 1941.'[160]

On 12 June 1946, also during the part of the case entrusted to the French prosecutors, Mühlmann's anti-Semitic activities in Holland under the authority of his fellow-Austrian and friend, Seyss-Inquart, once again fell under the spotlight. This prosecutor sought to expose the reality of confiscation and sequestration, in short, cultural plunder, merely dressed up in the Nazis' euphemistic language of the 'safeguarding' of artworks:

M. Debenest: Were there not in the Netherlands certain agencies which were charged with the looting of art objects?
Seyss-Inquart: I cannot call it looting, but at any rate the administration and care of them, and so forth.
M. Debenest: That is your opinion. At any rate there were several agencies?
Seyss-Inquart: Yes.
M. Debenest: You are particularly well acquainted with the agency of Dr. Mühlmann?
Seyss-Inquart: Yes.
M. Debenest: Who called him to the Netherlands?
Seyss-Inquart: I sent Mühlmann to the Netherlands ahead of me so that he could arrange for premises for my offices.
M. Debenest: But it was only to set up your offices?
Seyss-Inquart: At that time, only to set up the offices.
M. Debenest: But later?
Seyss-Inquart: Mühlmann then left and some time after he returned as an agent of the Four Year Plan, for the safeguarding of works of art. It was similar to what took place in Poland.
M. Debenest: What do you understand by "safeguarding"?
Seyss-Inquart: In point of fact—I do not want to talk a lot about it—but actually he had to determine whether there were any works of art in the confiscated fortunes and then he had the task of reporting these works of art to the various Reich offices.
M. Debenest: Only to report them?
Seyss-Inquart: Yes, because the purchasing was taken care of by these various offices themselves. I assume—that is, I know—that he also dealt privately in works of art, as an intermediary.
M. Debenest: Did you also obtain some pictures for yourself through his mediation?
Seyss-Inquart: Yes. Not for myself, but for the purposes that I described yesterday.

---

[160] IMT 7, 103.

M. Debenest: Yes. You also stated yesterday that you had placed in safekeeping a large number of works of art, particularly pictures. What was your purpose in doing this?
Seyss-Inquart: Many works of art I secured only in the sense that when the decree about confiscation of enemy and Jewish property came out, they were secured and liquidated. I bought perhaps three or four pictures which, as I mentioned, were to be presented as gifts to the Museum of Art History in Vienna.
M. Debenest: No, no, I asked you for what purpose you placed these works of art in safety.
Seyss-Inquart: The confiscation of Jewish and enemy property had, as its primary purpose, sequestration; but in time it became clear that these art treasures were being bought by the Reich. These three or four pictures I purchased with the immediate purpose of giving them to certain Reich institutions, the Museum of Art History in Vienna, for instance.
M. Debenest: But there was not only Jewish property there.
Seyss-Inquart: I said enemy property as well, but that was not enemy property in general, but only in cases where a specially hostile attitude towards the Reich was proved. Such property was confiscated also.[161]

Commentators have recently recognised that ALIU reports were: 'used in the trials at Nuremberg of both Göring and Alfred Rosenberg.'[162] Indeed, the following three CIRs were used as trial evidence against Hermann Göring and Alfred Rosenberg: CIR No. 1, 'Activity of the Einsatzstab Rosenberg in France'; CIR No. 2, 'The Göring Collection'; and CIR No. 4, 'Linz: Hitler's Museum and Library'.[163] It is clear that these studies informed, to a significant extent, Nuremberg prosecution documents, including 'The Plunder of Art Treasures'.[164] The positive contribution of ALIU reports to official agencies responsible for Nazi war crimes investigations was recognised by Roberts Commission:

> With the Office of Strategic Services, the Commission cooperated in the formation within that organization of a special unit specifically concerned with the investigation of enemy personnel suspected of participating in art looting activities. A large amount of information regarding German personnel and looting in the cultural field was thus made available to the War Crimes Commission and to the Military Government.[165]

---

[161] IMT 16, 71–74.
[162] Roberts Commission Report, 1946 op. cit. 40.
[163] Hussey *et al.*, op. cit.
[164] 'Office of the Chief of Counsel for Prosecution of Axis Criminality', vol. 1 (Red Series) (1946), 1097–1116.
[165] Roberts Commission, 1946 op. cit. 5. For other positive references, see Ibid., 9,

Whatever achievements ALIU officials could claim with respect to the preparation of evidence that helped convict at least two of the major war criminals at Nuremberg, were, to some extent, offset by the disappointing reaction of their recommends with respect to middle and lower-ranking war criminals who they had shown were implicated in anti-Jewish plunder of artworks. Indeed, aspects of the ALIU's mission were frustrated by the actions and omission of others. As already noted, ALIU officials recommended the prosecution of Ernst Buchner, Walter Hofer. Hermann Voss and Karl Haberstock.[166] However, whilst the evidence of Nazi plunder was gratefully received by the middle and lower ranking prosecutors responsible for preparing specific trial briefs, their recommendations as to the selection of defendants were not acted upon. As Rothfeld notes: 'However, at no fault of the ALIU's, the War Crimes Commission would not charge the art looting suspects with war crimes. The importance of the ALIU's work can be judged by the fact that the War Crimes Commission used the ALIU's findings in the preparation for the trials of Hermann Göring and Alfred Rosenberg. Ultimately, those individuals, art dealers, etc. detained as witnesses were soon released by the Allied occupation forces and the art dealers resumed their businesses in postwar Europe.'[167] Rothfeld also provides a downbeat conclusion with respect to ALIU's role in supporting the Nuremberg process:

> The evidence that the ALIU gathered during the spring and summer of 1945 showed the extent of collaboration that was involved in the process of Nazi art plundering. Once combined and analyzed, the ALIU interrogations would tell a tale of methodical approaches to looting the most famous artworks in Europe for their intended display in either a public German museum or in Göring's and Hitler's private collections. Yet, in the end, although the ALIU was able to investigate the background and activities of hundreds of art looting suspects and actually interrogated 21 prominent individuals, only the two chief Nazis involved in art looting, Göring and Rosenberg, were actually prosecuted. And in their cases, art looting constituted one of the more minor charges.[168]

Indeed, even lower-order trials and de-Nazification hearings failed to secure effective legal accountability, or even impede major art dealers

---

[166] J. Petropoulos, 'The Art World in Nazi Germany', in Francis R. Nicosia, Jonathan Huener, *The Arts in Nazi Germany: Continuity, Conformity, Change*, NY: Berghahn Books, 2006, 135–159, 146.

[167] Rothfeld, 2002 op. cit. Chapter One, 15, and Chapter Two, 1.

[168] Ibid., Chapter 3, 21.

who were complicit in the cultural plunder aspect of the Holocaust from successfully resuming their careers during the postwar era. Buchner had been interrogated at length by the ALIU officials following his arrest on 18 June 1945, and had cooperated with these interrogators, particularly Rousseau, as well as members of Germany's postwar art establishment involved in art restitution and recovery work. Although recognising some ambivalent behaviour, including passive resistance to the Nazis in some respects, Rousseau's recommendation of July 1945 nevertheless remained that Buchner be punished for his complicities:

> No amount of passive resistance could counterbalance the moral effect of his official allegiance. Buchner, one of the countless "white" Germans, prominent men in their communities who, in spite of an inner dislike for Nazism and a realization of its evils, nevertheless agreed to act as its representatives, through a mixture of personal ambition and fear of consequences of standing aside. These men bear a heavy responsibility to the mass of their compatriots, for they provided the fanatics and the criminals with the necessary cloak of respectability...it is recommended (a) that Buchner be kept under house arrest at the disposition of the MFA&A authorities, Third U.S. Army for consultation, and (b) that he be placed on the list of those officials who are to be prohibited permanently from holding any position in a newly constituted German fine arts administration.[169]

In this case, as elsewhere, ALIU recommendations were not fully implemented. Although removed from his official position as head of Bavarian State Galleries and Museum, he passed through compulsory Denazification programme for officials who had served Hitler's regime. Hearings of this kind were carried out by local boards according to the Law for the Liberation from National Socialism and Militarism of 5 March 1946. At these hearings, prosecutors presented available evidence of degrees of complicity; whilst defense lawyers argued whatever points could be made in mitigation or exoneration. Witnesses were called on both sides. If a suspect was convicted, the local Denazification boards had four sentencing categories: major offender; offender; lesser offender; and 'fellow traveller', the least serious option. From 1949, only those placed in the two highest categories faced further prosecution or impediments to public sector employment.[170] Although convicted before the Munich board, which noted his payment of a considerable honorarium

[169] DIR 2, op. cit. 10.
[170] Petropoulos, 2000 op. cit. 43.

from Hitler of RM 30,000, Buchner received the lowest classification of 'fellow traveller'. This was partly because some of his more serious complicities uncovered by the ALIU, including the looting of the Bouts and Van Eycks altar works, was not presented to the Board. This in turn permitted him to return to his former position as General Director of Bavarian State Paintings Collections, albeit subject to a new appointee who had been appointed in the meantime.[171] Hence, Buchner resumed his former rank but not the same position. He received an income from the state for the purposes of art research until another leading and suitable position became available for him. Controversially, on 1 April 1953, he was re-appointed to *de facto* Directorship of his former position, which completed his full rehabilitation, sometime recognised by his award of a Bavarian Service Medal in 1959.[172]

This was not an isolated case of lenient treatment. Haberstock, for example, who was arguably the most successful art dealer associated with the Nazi regime, was tried not by a war crimes court but only by a Denazification tribunal in 1949. He had previously been released from Civilian Internment Camp No. 4 at Hersbruck as a result partly of his cooperation with the Americans in relation to his supply of incriminating evidence for the Nuremberg and other war crimes trials. Another factor was his ability to have a number of Jewish individuals, such as former German Finance Minister Heinrich Albert and Otto von Mendlessohn-Bartholdy, speak up on his behalf through sworn affidavits as someone who had intervened with senior figures in the Nazi leadership to rescue them from persecution and, in some cases, deportation and probably death.[173] He also successfully deployed the contents of a number of documents that ALIU officials had confiscated as part of their earlier investigations.[174] Five months after his initial Denazification hearing of July 1949 at the Ansbach branch of the Main Chamber at Nuremberg, Haberstock succeeded in having his initial fine of DM 200,000 reduced on appeal to 127,000, and his classification as an incriminated Nazi scaled down from Category 3 to Category 4, that is reclassified as a mere 'fellow traveller'. This meant that he could resume his art business in Munich after the war, which he did, leaving his collection to his home city of Augsburg. Haberstock even

[171] Petropoulos, 2006 op. cit. 146.
[172] Petropoulos, 2000 op. cit. 44–46.
[173] Ibid., 95–6.
[174] Ibid., 96.

created a charitable art foundation in his home town, which returned the complement by naming a street after him.[175]

Furthermore, Mühlmann, an Austrian artist-intellectual who had been complicit in the expropriation of the Rothschild art collection in Austria, and had assisted with Göring's plunder operations in Poland and Holland, also received lenient treatment. This was despite having advised both Hans Frank and Göring regarding the confiscation of Jewish and other artwork in both Poland and the Netherlands, and playing a key personal role in both these countries. At the end of the war, Mühlmann cooperated with ALIU by testifying against his superiors and helping locate missing art. He was able to escape from a prison hospital and then virtually avoid legal accountability for his role. As Petropoulos notes:[176]

> Mühlmann's story sheds light on the denouement and aftermath of the war and the ethically problematic environment caused by a devastated continent and a burgeoning Cold War. After cooperating with the United States' Counter Intelligence Corps and Office of Strategic Services / Art Looting Investigation Unit by testifying against his superiors and helping to locate missing art works, Mühlmann procured documents attesting to his supposed activities as a resistance fighter. This deception, as well as a number of useful contacts, enabled him to escape from a prison hospital and quietly live out his life in a lakeside resort near Munich. Mühlmann, like many of the second rank figures, avoided postwar justice.[177]

Mühlmann claimed to have handed Göring over to the Americans at the end of the war and to have resisted the 'scorched earth' resistance policies of Otto Skorzeny, which would have required considerable destruction of all assets.[178] Petropoulos further argues that:

> It is similarly extraordinary to contemplate the reasons why Mühlmann escaped prosecution after the war. His name was placed on the Crowcass (Central Registry of War Crimes and Security Suspects) list, [created at General Donovan's initiative], and the Americans captured him on 15 June 1945 and took him to Camp Markus in western Austria. On 20 July he was transferred to the camp at Payerbach in Upper Austria, where

---

[175] Petropoulos, 2006 op. cit. 145.

[176] J. Petropoulos, 'The Importance of the Second Rank: The Case of the Art Plunderer Kajetan Mühlmann,' in Günter Bischof and Anton Pelinka, '*Austro-Corporatism: Past, Present, Future*', Contemporary Austrian Studies 4, New Brunswick, NJ: Transaction Publishers, 1996, 177–221 (hereafter 1996b).

[177] Petropoulos, 1996b op. cit. 178.

[178] Ibid., 200.

> he was interrogated by CIC unit that worked on culture (also known as Culture Intelligence). They induced him to discuss the deeds of Göring, Seyss-Inquart, Frank, and Kaltenbrunner—blunt and damning testimony that was submitted to the International Military Tribunal at Nuremberg and helped in the convictions and subsequent death sentences of these leaders [PS-3042].[179]

Once again Mühlmann proved evasive under interrogation:

> Regarding his own actions he admitted responsibility in a way similar to Albert Speer: he confessed to a specific and non-capital offence (viz, the expropriation of Jewish Property) but claimed to know nothing about the Holocaust (a bald face lie considering his career), and denied his deed led to personal enrichment.[180]

The CIC returned Mühlmann back to the Austrian authorities in October 1946. However, they demanded a written pledge that he would not be set free without prior American approval. However, Petropoulos notes that this did not mean he was destined to face legal accountability, even that on a par with comparable perpetrators of this aspect of the Holocaust:

> Art plunders rarely faced prosecution after the war. Nonetheless, the only other sub-leader to rival Mühlmann in terms of scale and net worth of the artworks, Robert Scholtz (another Austrian who worked for ERR in France and on the Eastern Front), was turned over to the French and sentenced to five years imprisonment. With similar intentions, the Poles sought Mühlmann's extradition and pressured the Austrians to relinquish him [who]...proved very accomplished at foot dragging. In 1951 for example they falsely claimed that Mühlmann was either in Switzerland or Lichtenstein and that delivering him to Poland was not feasible....Mühlmann evidently placed his hopes in the exculpatory story that he had turned resistance fighter at the end of the war...Mühlmann had papers signed by an American General attesting to his anti-Nazi activities...Gruber [wartime Austrian resistance leader] therefore had signed a certificate...attesting to Mühlmann's role in the resistance....It appears then that both sides collaborated in providing Mühlmann with the certificate of resistance activities....Whether the Americans also assisted Mühlmann as a result of his postwar cooperation with the CIC and protected him...remains difficult to determine. If Mühlmann actually delivered Göring to the Americans in 1945, this deed, along with damning U.S. testimony that proved so useful to prosecutors at Nuremberg, may

---

179 Petropoulos, 1996b op. cit. 201.

180 Ibid., 202.

> have earned him the generous treatment....they allowed him to escape and were indolent in undertaking his capture.[181]

On the other hand, and in conjunction with Dutch intelligence official Klug, ALIU eventually succeeded in gaining Mühlmann's cooperation during interrogation sufficient to produce damning evidence against Göring and Seyss-Inquart during the Nuremberg trials.

After the war, Rousseau and Faison complained bitterly about the rapid rehabilitation of Haberstock, Bruno Lohse and even Rochlitz.[182] It was apparent that many of those art dealers complicit in this aspect of the Holocaust who ALIU officers had recommended be tried as war criminals had escaped this fate. Yeide contrasts the Allies' treatment of Göring with that of his agent Hofer:

> Göring was the highest ranking Nazi official to be tried at the military tribunals at Nuremberg. He was sentenced to death but took his own life just hours before his scheduled execution in October 1946. His curator Hofer fared much better. After his stint as gentleman in residence in Berchtesgaden, and his interrogation by Rousseau at Alt Aussee, he laid low long enough to reemerge as a dealer in the 1960s, living a comfortable life in Munich.[183]

Whilst providing additional information on legal aspects of Hofer's postwar life, Petropoulos reaches a similarly negative conclusion concerning the frustration of one aspect of the ALIU's mission. This writer argues that the ultimately lenient treatment of nearly all of those that ALIU officials had recommended for prosecution as war criminals was far from uncommon:

> Like most other dealers, Walter Hofer escaped justice after the war. The OSS recommended that he be tried as a war criminal, and after being interrogated at Alt Aussee and Nuremberg, Hofer was sent to the internment camp at Hersbruck that also held Haberstock. He was kept in custody longer than his pre-eminent rival and noted this in an appeal for release sent to the Americans in January 1947....Hofer's last public appearance came in May 1950 in a trial instigated by Theodor Fischer: the Swiss dealer sued the Swiss state for compensation after being forced to return artworks in his possession that had been confiscated from the collections of French Jews. The Swiss authorities called Hofer as witness and he insisted that Fischer and the other dealers knew they were

[181] Ibid., 202–203.
[182] Petropoulos, *The Art World in Nazi Germany*', 1996 op. cit. 145–46.
[183] 2007 op. cit. 7.

> acquiring art plundered from French Jews. (The court's findings were inconclusive on this point, and they awarded the dealer partial compensation for the works he was forced to return.) After testifying, Hofer quickly disappeared, and for good reason.... He reportedly passed away in the early 1970s.[184]

This unfortunate story of individuals who ALIU officials had identified as potential war crimes suspects managing to evade full legal accountability for their complicities in the Holocaust, could be multiplied many times over. Petropolous recounts the disappointment felt by ALIU officials when hearing of the revival of the art dealing careers of many of those they investigated as possible war criminals complicit in the Holocaust:

> [T]he dealers were able to revive their careers after the war. In some cases, such as the German born Alexander Ball, who worked in Paris during the war and had dealings with Nazi art looters, they moved to the United States and began anew. It is not clear how many dealers from the Third Reich continued to sell art, but circumstantial evidences suggest that the number is sizeable. The members of the ALIU who, after the war, returned to civilian jobs usually related to the art world would sometimes comment on their former subjects' success at reviving their careers. Theodore Rousseau, who returned to the Metropolitan Museum of Art as a curator of paintings, dropped a note to former colleague S. Lane Faison in November 1948, where he talked about Haberstock's efforts to get off the hook. Rousseau added, "This may amuse you. [It] makes me all the more angry when I think of the wretched Lohse [who was one of the few in prison]. According to the latest news, even [Gustav] Rochlitz [a German dealer involved with the ERR] is out and doing business!" (he had a gallery on the Boulevard Montparnasse in Paris).[185]

This sense sentiment of disappointment that, outside the context of the Nuremberg trials, the prosecution dimension of ALIU's investigative work and overall mission had not been fully realised, is also clearly expressed in Wittmann's concluding report from the autumn of 1946, which noted the particular issues facing the American authorities:

> However, it is alarming to observe that in this first year of peace in Europe, a majority of the collaborationist dealers, collectors, and agents who willingly aided in the cultural despoliation of their own countries have avoided serious prosecution. Many of them, not only nationals of neutral countries, but also of formerly occupied countries are continu-

---

[184] Petropoulos, 2000 op. cit. 105.
[185] Ibid., 109.

> ing their trade. Since the United States will continue to be the most important market for the sale of significant works of art, the problems presented by the continued trade of these persons is of serious concern to us [we] will have to screen carefully objects of art offered...during the next decade....It is strongly urged that continued use be made of the [ALIU] Final Report...in screening visas of art dealers and agents applying for entrance to this country.[186]

Petropolous concludes that the recommendations for punishment of those complicit in Nazi art looting which ALIU officials thoroughly and impressively investigated did not unfortunately result in the prosecutions which they sought. There is also little reason to dispute this writer's appreciation of how the remarkable efforts of the small team of ALIU officials was partly defeated by the actions of other Allied officials, particularly as cold war imperatives took centre stage in the period from 1946:

> Even though Rousseau, Faison, Plaut, and the others in the ALIU performed a remarkable service in documenting the activities of the art dealers who collaborated with the Nazis and even though they recommended in forceful terms that these dealers face criminal charges and be barred from the profession, they were ultimately unsuccessful in preventing the dealers' rehabilitation. Because the experts in the ALIU were shipped back to the United States and demobilized after completing their reports, there was insufficient expertise and motivation among those who remained to keep down these shrewd and self-interested individuals....due to the prevailing atmosphere, in which reconstruction took precedence over justice, the Nazi art dealers were able to resuscitate their careers.[187]

Conclusion

In short, from November 1944, OSS officials made a significant contribution to the investigation of Nazi war crimes concerning the plunder of art and other cultural treasures. This contribution included identifying looted art works and those involved in looting and then selling them. The ALIU performed essential work of lasting value under extraordinarily difficult circumstances. The material presented here goes some way to rehabilitate the reputation of US intelligence officials with respect to this aspect of the Holocaust and to directly connect

[186] Wittmann, 1946 op. cit. 21.
[187] Petropoulos, 2000 op. cit. 110.

the intelligence work to both postwar legal accountability and efforts at restitution. These officials worked in close liaison with the Nuremberg prosecutors both formally and indirectly through the distribution of its reports, which contained a wealth of highly incriminating detail over the role of specific individuals in this dubious trade. Certain individuals involved in his type of war criminality were directly apprehended as a result of this Unit's work; whilst other leading Nazi defendants, such as Göring and Rosenberg, faced additional evidence at the Nuremberg trials stemming from its investigative activities.[188] Individuals involved in later Holocaust-restitution and related activities have, for good reason, also played tribute to the pioneering work and achievements of this small unit, which achieved remarkable results despite facing a daunting task. There has also been national recognition with Faison receiving the French Legion of Honour in 1947 in recognition of his work with the ALIU.[189]

The ALIU supplied a considerable quantity of documentation to the Nuremberg prosecutors which was itself 'plundered' in summary form during the preparation of an important trial brief. The latter was itself extensively deployed during the trial itself. Mühlmann's evidence, contained in a short affidavit, provided damning insider evidence against Göring in particular, which this defendant's lawyer was not able to rebut with sufficient credibility. The apparent incongruity of trusting the evidence of someone who was complicit in the Holocaust was successfully smoothed over, partly by deferring most references to this complicity to later in the trials.

The nature and influence of Neumann's spearhead theory of Nazi anti-Semitism

This section will briefly make a series of points concerning the OSS R&A reports on Nazi war crimes, before setting out in more detail one of the key theories of the Holocaust that underpinned many, if not all, of these: Neumann's spearhead theory. It will also examine certain of the criticisms that have been directed against this theory and consider various counterarguments.

During the opening weeks of preparations for the Nuremberg trials, one of the most important sources of evidence regarding counts one,

---

[188] Rothfeld, 2002 op. cit. pt. 1.
[189] Simpson, 1997 op. cit. 321.

two and four were the extensive series of R&A Reports. OSS research analysts, particularly Neumann's Central European Section, composed these both during the war and immediately afterwards. By the end of September 1944, James Donovan, OSS' General Counsel, was already able to identify six R&A reports that contained significant details of Nazi war criminality.[190] In his capacity as Chief OSS lawyer with a particular interest in future war crimes trials, he noted: 'The contents of the above [6 R&A Reports] have been carefully considered and all information, on the subject of war crimes and war criminals, noted for future use.... It would be appreciated if you should continue to send such information whenever it is available.'[191] This gathering of information, together with its extraction by the General Counsel's office, took place despite the fact that this Branch had, at this time, rarely if ever been asked by Allied leadership to analyse war crimes prosecution as a topic in its own right.

Franz Neumann's theory of the Nazi state exerted considerable influence upon his R&A colleagues, R&A reports on war crimes and later upon the Nuremberg prosecutors. His influence was enhanced through the positive reception given to his major book *Behemoth* (1942/1944).[192] Following its publication, Neumann's classic analysis of National Socialism was critically acclaimed.[193] Its author soon became widely recognised as the leading authority on National Socialism both within and beyond the group of émigré scholars of the Central European sub-section of the OSS' R&A Branch. Despite its neo-Marxist and sociological underpinnings, this work functioned as a major source and reference book for both the OSS and the Nuremberg prosecutors. Indeed, Katz's exemplary summary of the overall thrust of CES' analysis of Nazi war crimes appears especially significant:

> The structure of their case against the Nazi *Behemoth* grew out of Neumann's claim that it was a tightly integrated system, a corporate state managed by an interlocking directorate of political, military and economic leaders. The tactics of the 1920's were only the first act of a

[190] R&A 1482, R&A 1735.29, R&A 1113.39; R&A 1113.59, R&A 1113.75, R&A 1113.76, R&A 1113.76.

[191] General Counsel to Langer, 27 October 1944, Director's Files: US NA, RG 226, M1642, Roll 120.

[192] Oxford: OUP, 1942/1944.

[193] See *Times Literary Supplement's* list of the hundred most influential books published since the Second World War as cited in the Editorial to *The Antioch Review*), 1 January, 1996; Marquardt-Bigman 1997 op. cit.

> tragic drama that closed with total war. Party ideology and party practice were mutually adjusting elements of a single mechanism; domestic terror and foreign aggression issued from the same mandate.[194]

In other words, in their analysis of the institutional criminality of Hitler's regime Reich for Jackson's prosecution office, the CES applied the general framework of *Behemoth* to suggest that the Nuremberg prosecutors should treat the military aspect of Nazism as one element of a wider 'mandate'. Since 1933, this had included committing acts of internal state terrorism and genocide as preparatory steps orientated, from the outset, towards the Nazis' policy of systematic genocide against the Jews. Such internal terrorism, in turn, was connected to, and formed an integral part of, their wider conspiracy to engage in unlawful wars of aggression.

The step-by-step expansion and deepening of the persecution and ultimate extermination of European Jews tended to implicate an 'ever-larger strata' of groups and individuals in German society 'in a collective guilt'. Reiterating a key theme from *Behemoth*,[195] Neumann argues that: 'the compulsion to commit so vast a crime as the physical extermination of the Eastern Jews makes the German Army, the civil service and large masses of perpetrators and accessories in the crime and makes it impossible for them to leave the Nazi boat.' One functional 'benefit' the Nazis gained from this widening out of the scope of complicity in war guilt was to eliminate the possibility of independent peace initiatives by 'non-Nazi members of the ruling class' because 'each and every one of them' will ultimately become: 'stained by the crime that is now being committed.'[196]

Many of the relevant R&A studies that addressed Nazi anti-Semitism were influenced by Neumann's 'spearhead theory' of anti-Semitism set in *Behemoth*. This theory consists of a number of distinct but interrelated propositions. Each of these will now be summarised.

---

[194] Katz 1989 op. cit. 54.

[195] Indeed, the second and revised edition of *Behemoth* states:
'The persecution of the Jews practised by ever increasing broader sectors of the German nation on orders from the Nazis, implicated these sectors in a collective guilt. The participation in such an atrocious crime as the extermination of the East European Jews made the German Wehrmacht, the German civil service and the masses into accomplices and assistants of this crime and thus makes it impossible for them to leave the Nazi boat.' Neumann 1944 op. cit. 552.

[196] Neumann, R&A 1139.9, op. cit. 20.

Contrary to both Nazi and Allied propaganda, Nazi anti-Semitism does not express the innate character, or basic orientation, of the German people. On the contrary, this is a counter-productive myth that led to Allied proposals for future mass sterilisation, which in turn were then re-deployed as internal propaganda by the Nazis.[197] Instead, anti-Semitism is a historically constructed, and hence contingent, social phenomenon, which is integrally connected with the ideological legitimation of the interests of Germany's ruling power-elites.[198]

According to Neumann's analysis, the Nazi regime did not pursue anti-Semitic persecution as an entirely separate 'end in itself'. Instead, such racism formed one vital part of its wider programme of seeking to build up, refine and extend the mechanisms of a totalitarian machinery of social control, and impose a state of fear upon potential dissenters. Both the institutional machinery of repression, and the state of fear it created, were vital to the reproduction of the Nazis' grip upon power.[199] For example, in one R&A report, Neumann argued that:

> the persecution of the Jews, as practiced by National Socialists, is only the prologue of more horrible things to come. The expropriation of the Jews, for instance, is followed by that of the Poles, Czechs, Dutchmen, Frenchman, anti-Nazi Germans, and middle-classes. Not only Jews fall under the executioner's axe but countless others of many races, nationalities, beliefs, and religions. Anti-Semitism is thus the spearhead of terror. The Jews are used as guinea pigs in testing a method of repression.[200]

He also claimed that: 'Domestically, anti-Semitism is still the testing ground for universal terrorist methods directed against all those groups and institutions that are not fully subservient to the Nazi system.'[201] Neumann noted, for example, that the decrees of 1939 directly excluding Jews from handicraft and retail sectors, represented: 'a prologue of the blow directed against the independent middle class.'[202] He further maintained that: 'the physical extermination of the Jews in the spring of 1943 takes place in similar circumstances', that is in the context of the 1943 Labor Mobilization Act which: 'has again deprived hundreds

[197] See also Neumann's 'German Morale after Tunisia' 1943 op. cit. 2.
[198] Neumann, 1944 op. cit. xiii.
[199] Ibid., 550–51.
[200] R&A 1139.9, 'Psychological Warfare: Weekly Roundup' (May 18–24, 1943): Franz Neumann [signed article], 'Anti-Semitism', 17–20 at 17: US NA, RG 59.
[201] Ibid., 19.
[202] Ibid.

of thousands of middle class men of their independence.'[203] These points illustrate the way in which anti-Semitism represented a 'spear-head' preparing the way for the extension of systematic terror to other sectors of German society.

According to the spearhead theory, insofar as a nation largely 'surrenders' to the spearhead of anti-Semitism, then this form of institutional racism plays a functional role in displacing the various democratic bulwarks in Germany against 'totalitarianism' associated with the liberal tradition. Hence, the Nazis' emphasis upon anti-Semitic persecution and ultimately genocide was simultaneously a distinct goal, as well as a key device for the establishment of a 'totalitarian society.'[204]

Neumann maintained that the Nazi leadership implemented measures against Jewry from late 1933 to November 1938 in a strategic and calculating fashion, that is: 'a cold calculated, legal persecution of the Jews in Germany, a step by step enactment of anti-Jewish legislation.'[205] Thus, they made exceptions, e.g., for German-Jewish war veterans, wherever any *consistent* application of their racist principles could have proved counterproductive for other competing interests of the regime, including the population's psychological preparation for war.[206] For example, Neumann claimed that early anti-Semitic campaigns, such as the 1 April 1933 boycott of Jewish businesses, was: 'prematurely broken off at the insistence of Schacht [later to become a Nuremberg defendant] and of the Anglo-American powers, and that the economic disadvantages resulting from this anti-Semitism far outweighed the advantages.'[207] However, Neumann also noted that during the period from the spring 1938 to the end of that year, the Nazis intensified their anti-Semitic persecution through oppressive legislation. This intensification stemmed from the failure of the Western powers to respond forcefully to Hitler's territorial expansionism into Austria and Czechoslovia. Such escalation was associated with the: 'resistance of the democracies against Nazi Germany'. This resistance was: 'put to the most severe test', becoming a challenge which ultimately defeated these democracies. Neumann is clearly suggesting, albeit in a necessarily coded manner, that Western policies of appeasement gave a 'green light' for the pre-planned inten-

[203] Ibid.
[204] Ibid.
[205] Ibid., 18.
[206] Neumann, 1944 op. cit. 550.
[207] Neumann, R&A 1139.9 op. cit. 18.

sification of anti-Semitic persecution, and that: 'it is in this connection that the radical anti-Semitic legislation must be understood.'[208]

For Neumann, within Germany's social hierarchy, the Nazis' racist propaganda against the Jews was directed downwards from its indigenous historical source amongst Germany's ruling elites. This top-down imposition took place by means of the regime's unprecedented mobilisation of the mass media and youth organisations. However, even after a decade of remorseless exposure to anti-Semitic propaganda, such sentiments had not established deep roots amongst most ordinary working-class German people. For Neumann, this explains why the Nazis' gruesome mass killing centres had to be hidden away largely in remote rural areas of Eastern Europe.[209]

The clear implication of Neumann's theory properly understood is that it was precisely because large sectors of the German population, who on the basis of family background, shared religious belief and culture, defined themselves as Jewish, were fully integrated and assimilated into the life of German society, that the Nazi regime needed to devote considerable efforts to misrepresent this group as 'alien'. Such ideological misrepresentation was directed at a nation, the majority of whose citizens never fully accepted the Nazis' virulent and genocidal brand of anti-Semitism, even after a full decade of being subjected to a remorseless stream of official racist propaganda.[210]

Neumann further claimed that apparently 'spontaneous' anti-Semitic demonstrations were, in the views of all independent reporters: 'manipulated from above' as part of a: 'skilfully organised and manipulated manoeuvre.'[211] Even legislation apparently passed as an immediate reaction to 'Jewish terrorism', such as the punitive measures of November and December 1938, was in fact already: 'carefully prepared in advance.'[212] In other words, Neumann rejected the idea that Nazism only provided an institutional outlet for the expression of indigenous forms of German anti-Semitism. Although Neumann did not reveal his sources, these stemmed from intercepted Ultra messages

[208] Ibid., 19.
[209] 1944 op. cit. 551.
[210] Ibid.
[211] Neumann, R&A 1139.9, op. cit. 18.
[212] Ibid.

made available to him from X-2 and then—without revealing their status—R&A Paris.[213]

Through the Nazis' creation of a widespread climate of fear of violence, their distinctive form of anti-Semitism operated to solidify Hitler's regime institutional terror. It did so by forcing individuals to either commit themselves repeatedly and publicly to this regime, or face the threat of detention or worse in concentration camps. Neumann suggested: 'For years, anti-Semitism has served the purpose of forcing all Germans either to identify themselves with Nazism, or pay the price of dissent.' In turn, this led to 'moral and psychological commitments of ever-greater strength', and created a situation: 'where the German people are kept in a perpetual state of tension.' Neumann noted that such tension created a spurious and ideologically generated type of 'solidarity'. Neumann argued that: 'Germans must again decide between accepting the guilt of the regime, or openly resisting it; and the act of acceptance increases the widespread conviction that all Germans must stand or fall with Adolf Hitler.'[214]

The Nazi regime also designed anti-Semitic measures to combat and outflank alternative socialist ideologies which, through gaining majority support within Parliament, threatened the interests of established power elites, including those of leading industrialists. The ideological requirement here was to deflect pre-existing anti-capitalist sentiment away from its material source within the class divisions of an essentially antagonistic social structure. The latter generated a structural need to redirect these sentiments towards the dehumanisation of a social group widely identified in a stereotypical manner with commercial activities: 'The antagonisms within German society are only concealed by an all comprehensive terrorist machine.'[215]

The antagonistic nature of Germany's social structure meant that at the level of ideology, the Nazis had to replace class-based forms of *social integration*, whose resolution required the application of a redistributive agenda, with racial and nationalistic alternatives. Although dressed up for strategic reasons in a 'revolutionary' form of rhetoric, the nationalistic and racist sentiments of Nazi ideology no longer challenged the

---

[213] See the translated transcript of these messages from Heydrich, OSS CID document 125265, regarding Kristallnacht in the Dwork Papers (OSS R&A Jewish Desk files): US NA, RG 200, Box 3, Folder 88.

[214] Neumann, 'German Morale After Tunisia', 1943 op. cit. 2.

[215] Neumann, R&A 1139.9, op. cit. 19.

basic material interests of Germany's prevailing power-elites.[216] For example, it positively supported the interests of the leading industrialists and 'petty bourgeois', many of who directly benefited materially from anti-Semitic measures of 'Aryanization' of property and businesses.[217]

According to Neumann, the Nazis designed their form of anti-Semitic persecution partly to misrepresent acts of domestic repression as an urgent form of national self-defence against an ideologically-constructed 'supreme foe'. This aimed to help legitimate the rationale of the regime in the eyes of the remainder of the population, who could then be characterised in 'volkish' terms as a racially-based and homogeneous 'national community'.

The false and irrational character of the Nazis' racist principles clearly could not gain acceptance through any process of critical and independent scrutiny. Hence, they required a distinctly ideological form of social integration based upon the mobilisation of fear, prejudice and the threat of violence for acts of dissent.[218] The Nazi regime's ideological projection of a racial 'enemy within', who was claimed to possess diametrically opposed qualities to those endorsed and promoted by their own standpoint, helped meet this social requirement.[219] In other words, the Nazi regime could not reproduce the conditions of its future existence on a rational basis. Instead, it had to resort to mythology by projecting itself as a stalwart 'defender' of a supposedly homogeneous national community from the mythical threat posed by an 'enemy of the people'. Establishing the idea that a certain type of enemy had, therefore, become a functional requirement for the perpetuation of Hitler's regime.

Neumann argued that the Nazis singled out the Jewish minority from amongst other groups of potential victims largely for strategic reasons. Other possible victims, such as the Catholic Church or organised labour, were either too strongly supported, or clearly 'too weak', to be credibly

[216] On the strategic deployment of anti-Semitism as a rhetoric designed to have 'revolutionary anti-capitalist appeal', see 'German Morale after Tunisia' 1943 op. cit. 3–4.

[217] See 'The Significance of Prussian Militarism for Nazi Imperialism', R&A 1281, 20 October 1943: US NA, RG 153, Entry 135, Box 6; 'introduction' to 'Sixty-Five leading German Businessmen', R&A 3020, 28 June 1945: US NA, RG 153, Entry 135, Box 14.

[218] See also 'German Morale after Tunisia', 1943 op. cit. 2–3, which analyses anti-Semitism in line with the spearhead theory as a strategy of generalised repressive control through the mobilisation of fear.

[219] Neumann, 1944 op. cit. 550; Marquardt-Bigman, 1994 op. cit. 333.

(mis)represented as a 'supreme foe', who challenged the future of the 'national community'. Unlike religious persecution, only a *specifically racist* form of victimisation was consistent with the Nazis' master race ideology.[220] With considerable bitterness and irony, Neumann noted:

> It is, however, only the Jews that can possibly play this role. National socialism, which has allegedly abolished the class struggle, needs an enemy who, by his very existence, can integrate the antagonistic groups within this society.... It is the Jews who admirably fill the role being neither too strong nor too weak.[221]

The Nazi regime also had to interpret the much-needed myth of a 'supreme foe' as existing both within and outside Germany's national borders. This was needed in order for Nazi ideology to (mis)represent this group as constituting a world-wide 'threat' to the global 'destiny' of the German nation. Hence, at the ideological level, Nazi anti-Semitism contributed to the project of mobilising the population for military expansionism supposedly against a global foe.[222] The Nazis then appealed to the allegedly 'shared' interests of the entire 'national community' as a pretext for embarking upon a period of military expansionism and wars of aggression.[223] Hitler's regime could seek to justify this aggression as both a strategy of vital self-defence, and as a necessary response to the imperative of securing adequate 'living space' for future generations of Germans.[224] The latter was defined in terms of Nazi racial theory to require the elimination of Jews and Slavs from Eastern Europe.

In short, Neumann's spearhead theory rejected the widespread idea that Nazi anti-Semitism represented a sincere expression of the indigenous German (or 'Prussian') 'national character', which was pursed largely for its own sake.[225] Instead, such racism functioned as a strategically formulated and selectively applied ideology, which served the ulterior motives and specific political imperatives of Hitler's regime. One implication of Neumann's theory is to call into question any notion of collective guilt (and hence indiscriminate postwar punishment) for the

[220] Neumann 1944, op. cit. 551.
[221] Neumann, R&A 1139.9, op. cit. 17.
[222] Justice Jackson reiterated this point in his trial evidence on the Holocaust.
[223] See 'The Significance of Prussian Militarism for Nazi Imperialism', R&A 1281, 20 October 1943: US NA, RG 153, Entry 135, Box 6.
[224] Neumann, 1944 op. cit. 550–51.
[225] Ibid.

anti-Semitic practices of the German people as a whole, as distinct from its elites.

By June 1943, Neumann specifically recognised that the 'extermination of the Jews' had become a reality. The intensification of real acts of racist persecution itself played a central role in both Nazi anti-Semitic ideology and institutional policies. It functioned as: 'the means to the attainment of the ultimate objective, namely the destruction of free institutions, beliefs, and groups.'[226] Contrary to his critics, Neumann's approach did not underplay the centrality of such racist genocide. Instead, he argued that it was not possible to understand the essential character of any aspect of Nazism without first appreciating the vital role played by anti-Semitism as a 'constant and consistent policy', albeit one whose: 'manifestations have changed considerably from 1933 to 1943. Indeed, he even claimed: 'It is these changes...which allow us to gain an insight [into] the structure of the Nazi system.'[227] Hence, Neumann was able to suggest that no viable analysis of this system was possible, not even a strictly military approach, which ignored the social and ideological factors that explain the persecution and ultimate extermination of the Jews.

During the period in which he was writing as an OSS R&A analyst, the practical implications of the spearhead theory for Allied psychological warfare was considerable. It was designed to resist the temptation to produce 'anti-anti-Semitic' forms of Allied counter-propaganda that both emphasised and praised the positive contributions of European Jewry. Such a tactic would backfire because it assumed that, amongst the mass of the German population, the racist beliefs fostered by Nazi anti-Semitism were seriously believed or even credible.[228] The next subsection addresses the presence of Neumann's theory within the statements the prosecutors made during the Nuremberg trials.

The spearhead theory at Nuremberg

Katz recognises that, in some respects, the fulsome recognition of a connection between different episodes of the Holocaust came better

---

[226] Neumann, R&A 1139.9, op. cit. 18. Jackson reiterated this point in his Nuremberg trial evidence, see Appendix One.
[227] Ibid.
[228] Ibid., 20.

into focus during the Neumann group's immediate postwar research for the Nuremberg prosecutors. For example, he analyses an R&A report on the Holocaust submitted for Justice Jackson prosecutors' office during the summer of 1945, in which Neumann's war crimes team of analysts had stated:

> It is the purpose of the Prosecution to demonstrate the existence of a common plan or enterprise of the German Government, the Nazi Party, and the German military, industrial, and financial leaders to achieve world domination by war. The destruction of the Jewish people as a whole, although an end in itself, was at the same time linked to and closely tied up with this aim of world conquest.[229]

Katz argues that, although the above précis was initially drafted by Irving Dwork, who was the CES's specialist on Nazi policy towards the Jews, the draft's general analytical approach: 'bears the indelible stamp of Neumann's influence'. It represented: 'an elaboration of the so-called spearhead theory of anti-Semitism that Neumann had worked out some two years before [i.e., in *Behemoth*].[230]

In an important study based on an impressively wide research base, including personal papers and correspondence, Shlomo Aronson has argued that Neumann's spearhead theory and its author's personal orientation had a direct impact upon the interpretation of the Holocaust developed during OSS' provision of evidence for the Nuremberg trials.[231] He focuses upon Irving Dwork's role within OSS' Jewish Desk, a position: 'created in 1943 for the purpose of gathering information on Jewish affairs, including evidence against Nazi war criminals'. Dwork's Washington-based unit was seeking to involve prominent representatives of the Jewish community in the pre-trial preparations. Allegedly, this aim was not realised partly because Dwork's office, and—Shlomo Aronson implies—its particular concerns, occupied only a relatively *low status* within the overall institutional hierarchy of the OSS-R&A Branch. Dwork's endeavours ultimately fell under Neumann's direct supervision, at least once the latter was placed in charge of OSS' war crimes research staff. Aronson provides strong empirical evidence that Dwork's

---

[229] Irving Dwork, R&A 311422, 'Nazi Plans for Dominating Germany and Europe: The Criminal Conspiracy against the Jews', (Draft for War Crimes Staff), 13 August, 1945, [Neumann to Demos], 13 June 1945, Cornell Collection, Vol. 19, 17.

[230] Katz, 1989 op. cit. 56.

[231] S. Aronson, 'Preparations for the Nuremberg Trial: The O.S.S., Charles Dwork, and the Holocaust,' *Holocaust and Genocide Studies*, vol. 12, no. 2 (Fall 1998), 257–281.

Washington desk had built up considerable documentary resources on the Holocaust, but that there had been a persistent failure to employ this information adequately, even in the high-powered preparatory international conference at London during the summer of 1945, which negotiated the Nuremberg Charter on whose legal basis the trials themselves depended for their authority and jurisdiction. Neumann attempted to encourage Dwork, together with his OSS / R&A colleague Duker, to join him in Europe, but they refused.[232] Aronson maintains that: 'Dwork's bureau ultimately had only a minor role in preparing for the Nuremberg trials because the Jewish case was played down during the preparatory phase of the International Military Tribunal'. The reasons for this was because: 'the prosecution did not make full use of the OSS records'.[233] This, in turn, led directly to the failure by the Nuremberg trials to take the unique character of anti-Semitic genocide seriously, a refusal to recognise adequately 'the tragic uniqueness of the Holocaust'. The US prosecution's initial planning for the Tribunal refused to treat the Holocaust as a separate crime, singling out a distinct 'Jewish case' from amongst the 23 million individuals killed during this war as a whole, and for Dwork this—according to Aronson—'limited his role considerably'.[234] Dwork, who had prepared an extensive collection of potential prosecution material on the Holocaust from 1943 onwards, was left: 'bitter and disappointed.'[235]

Aronson introduces the pervasive impact of Neumann's spearhead theory upon the OSS' analysis as one of the major contributing reasons for this alleged institutional failure:

> OSS had very valuable documentation, but which did not reach its 'Jewish expert' Charles Dwork, on time, or rather was simply never used. But for the time being it was OSS' Franz Neumann who, having developed his own opinions about the Holocaust years before, seems to have played the major role in London, at least in preparation for the International Military Tribunal.[236]

An adequate critical analysis of this claim would require close examination of the many hundred pages of draft evidence Neumann's R&A subdivision prepared at the specific request of Justice Jackson and his

[232] Aronson, 1998 op. cit. 270, 267, 271, 272.
[233] Ibid., 269.
[234] Aronson, 2004 op. cit. 322.
[235] Ibid., 326.
[236] Aronson, 1998 op. cit. 269.

senior staff.[237] It would also require a systematic cross-referencing of elements of Neumann's theory with the Nuremberg prosecutors' selective presentation of trial evidence. Although the fulfilment of such a project could generate a book in its own right, the following paragraphs will highlight affinities between the Nuremberg trial evidence relating to the Holocaust, and the spearhead theory of Nazi anti-Semitism.

Even a cursory reading of the completed Nuremberg trial brief on 'The Persecution of the Jews' would highlight elements of the direct application of Neumann's theory. As already noted, the spearhead theory suggests that Nazi anti-Semitism formed part of a project of ideological unification in preparation for territorial expansion through aggressive war. We can find echoes of this in the following extract taken from this trial brief:

> Unification of the German people was essential to successful planning and waging of war....The anti-Jewish policy was part of this plan for unification because it was the conviction of the Nazis that the Jews would not contribute to Germany's military program, but on the contrary would hamper it. The Jew must therefore be eliminated....The treatment of the Jews within Germany was as much a part of the Nazi plan for aggressive war as was the building of armaments and the conscription of manpower.[238]

Neumann's theory emphasised the cynical escalation of radically anti-Semitic propaganda, including the 'top down' indoctrination of the German people, as a calculated and necessary preliminary stage of the Holocaust. This sowed the seeds for later more radical measures of both persecution and military aggression. These included the ultimate physical extermination of European Jewry once a requirement to disguise this genocidal goal no longer appeared to exist. A version of this claim is also found in the trial brief:

---

[237] 'Sachsenhausen Concentration Camp', document 102832 [1944]: US NA, RG 226, Entry 16; 'German Execution of Jews in Occupied Russia', 23 August 1944, ibid. The draft briefs included the following reports US NA, RG 238, Entry 52f, Box 28; R&A 3113.3, 'Legislative Agencies Involved in War Crimes' (Draft for the War Crimes Staff), 28 August 1945: US NA, RG 238, Entry 52f, Box 28; R&A 3113.6, 'The Gestapo', (draft for use of War Crimes Staff), 6 August 1945: US NA, RG 59; R&A 3113.7, 'The Nazi Party, Parts I and II', (Draft for the Use of the War Crimes Staff), 24 July 1945, ibid.

[238] NCA 1, Ch. 12: http://www.yale.edu/lawweb/avalon/imt/document/nca_vol1/chap_12.htm.

> The objective of the elimination and extermination of the Jews, could not be accomplished without certain preliminary measures. One of these was the indoctrination of the German people with hatred against the Jews.[239]
>
> At this point the gradual and mounting campaign against the Jews was prepared for the achievement of its ultimate violent ends. The German people had been indoctrinated, and the seeds of hatred had been sown. The German state was armed and prepared for conquest. The force of world opinion could now safely be ignored. Already the Nazi conspirators had forced out of Germany 200,000 of its former 500,000 Jews. The Nazi-controlled German state was therefore emboldened, and Hitler in anticipation of the aggressive wars already planned cast about for a provocation.[240]

The spearhead theory also suggests that step by step and escalating forms of Nazi anti-Semitism, which were heading towards the physical annihilation of European Jewry, was also designed for exportation into newly-conquered territories. Once again, the following extract gives voice to this idea:

> The first step in accomplishing the purpose of the Nazi Party and the Nazi-dominated state, to eliminate the Jew, was to require a complete registration of all Jews. Inasmuch as the anti-Jewish policy was linked with the program of German aggression, such registration was required not only within the Reich, but successively within the conquered territories.[241]

Furthermore, the idea of a steadily advancing and pre-planned systematic series of anti-Jewish measures was reflected in the trial brief's description of Nazi measures of registration, segregation into ghettos, forced labor, and ultimately extermination through starvation and mass killings by various means. The trial brief even devotes a sub-heading to each of these practices.

If we now turn to Justice Jackson's famous opening speech to the IMT,[242] it is possible to identify additional influences of Neumann's theory. The first of these is that the size and politically weak position of German Jews made them an ideal group for the Nazis' to scapegoat as a 'supreme foe'. Jackson stated:

---

[239] Ibid.

[240] Ibid.

[241] Ibid.

[242] Justice Jackson's opening address, 21 November 1945: http://www.yale.edu/lawweb/avalon/imt/document/nca_vol1/chap_05.htm.

> The most savage and numerous crimes planned and committed by the Nazis were those against the Jews. These in Germany, in 1933, numbered about 500,000....They were few enough to be helpless and numerous enough to be held up as a menace.[243]

A second affinity between Jackson's opening address is with Neumann's idea that Hitler's regime engaged in a continuous, pre-planned and calculated deployment of anti-Semitic ideology and associated policies for ulterior motives, including the subversion of neighbouring democracies prior to their invasion and annexation. Such application of anti-Semitic ideologies and measures took place in a series of escalating and ever-more intense steps, the initially concealed goal of which was the ultimate physical extermination of European Jewry. Jackson expressed a similar idea:

> Let there be no misunderstanding about the charge of persecuting Jews. It is my purpose to show a plan and design, to which all Nazis were fanatically committed, to annihilate all Jewish people. These crimes were organized and promoted by the Party Leadership, executed and protected by the Nazi officials, as we shall convince you by written orders of the Secret State Police itself. The persecution of the Jews was a continuous and deliberate policy. It was a policy directed against other nations as well as against the Jews themselves. Anti-Semitism was promoted to divide and embitter the democratic peoples and to soften their resistance to the Nazi aggression. As Robert Ley declared in Der Angriff on 14 May 1944, "The second German secret weapon is Anti-Semitism because if it is constantly pursued by Germany, it will become a universal problem which all nations will be forced to consider."[244]

A third area of the spearhead theory's influence, which Jackson acknowledges in his very choice of terminology, is that Nazi anti-Jewish measures represented both the thin edge of a wedge, and a testing ground for methodologies of repression. In turn, these paved the way for the extension of repressive, totalitarian measures to other potentially or actually non-compliant groups:

> Anti-Semitism also has been aptly credited with being a "spearhead of terror." The ghetto was the laboratory for testing repressive measures. Jewish property was the first to be expropriated, but the custom grew and included similar measures against Anti-Nazi Germans, Poles, Czechs, Frenchmen, and Belgians. Extermination of the Jews enabled the Nazis

[243] Ibid.
[244] Ibid.

> to bring a practiced hand to similar measures against Poles, Serbs, and Greeks. The plight of the Jew was a constant threat to opposition or discontent among other elements of Europe's population—pacifists, conservatives, communists, Catholics, Protestants, socialist. It was, in fact, a threat to every dissenting opinion and to every non-Nazis' life.[245]

We have already noted Neumann's view of the cynical and calculated nature of the Nazis' deployment of anti-Semitic ideology and direct measures of persecution, which concealed state planned and coordinated attacks on Jews as apparently 'spontaneous' popular uprisings. Such measures began with political disenfranchisement, before later escalating towards more intense, extreme and violent forms of persecution. Furthermore, such anti-Semitism was an integral and official defining ideology of the entire Nazi movement. Jackson's version of this stated:

> The persecution policy against the Jews commenced with nonviolent measures, such as disfranchisement and discriminations against their religion, and the placing of impediments in the way of success in economic life. It moved rapidly to organized mass violence against them, physical isolation in ghettos, deportation, forced labor, mass starvation, and extermination. The Government, the Party formation indicated before you as criminal organizations, the Secret State Police, the Army, private and semipublic associations, and "spontaneous" mobs that were carefully inspired from official sources, were all agencies concerned in this persecution.... The avowed purpose was the destruction of the Jewish people as a whole... as a measure of preparation for war, and as a discipline of conquered peoples.... I advert to them [state crimes against Jews] only to show their magnitude as evidence of a purpose and a knowledge common to all defendants, of an official plan rather than of a capricious policy of some individual commander, and to show such a continuity of Jewish persecution from the rise of the Nazi conspiracy to its collapse as forbids us to believe that any person could be identified with any part of Nazi action without approving this most conspicuous item of its program.[246]

Finally, the spearhead theory interprets Nazi anti-Jewish measures not only as tactics to secure a measure of internal cohesion against a mythical 'internal threat', but also as directed against European democratic states in general, as a subversive prelude to their military invasion and annexation. Jackson borrowed this idea when he claimed:

---

245 Ibid.
246 Ibid.

> As the German frontiers were expanded by war, so the campaign against the Jews expanded. The Nazi plan never was limited to extermination in Germany; always it contemplated extinguishing the Jew in Europe and often in the world. In the west, the Jews were killed and their property taken over. But the campaign achieved its zenith of savagery in the East.... We charge that all atrocities against Jews were the manifestation and culmination of the Nazi plan to which every defendant here was a party.... Determination to destroy the Jews was a binding force which at all times cemented the elements of this conspiracy. On many internal policies there were differences among the defendants. But there is not one of them who has not echoed the rallying cry of Nazism "DEUTSCHLAND ERWACHE JUDA VERRECKE! (Germany AWAKE, JEWRY PERISH!)."[247]

I would be tedious to contrast other prosecutors' claims with each element of Neumann's theory. One representative quotation, selected from many other possible candidates, will suffice. A similar version of the spearhead theory with respect to coercive solidarity is found in Dodd's presentation of the purpose of Nazi concentration and extermination camps. During trial evidence he stated:

> May it please the Tribunal, we propose to offer additional evidence at this time concerning the use of Nazi concentration camps against the people of Germany and allied Nationals. We propose to examine the purposes and the role of the concentration camp in the larger Nazi scheme of things. We propose to show that the concentration camp was one of the fundamental institutions of the Nazi regime, that it was a pillar of the system of terror by which the Nazis consolidated their power over Germany and imposed their ideology upon the German people, that it was really a primary weapon in the battle against the Jews, against the Christian church, against labor, against those who wanted peace, against opposition or non-conformity of any kind. We say it involved the systematic use of terror to achieve the cohesion within Germany which was necessary for the execution of the conspirators' plans for aggression. We propose to show that a concentration camp was one of the principal instruments used by the conspirators for the commission, on an enormous scale, of Crimes against Humanity and War Crimes.[248]

In short, it is possible to detect significant traces of Neumann's spearhead theory of anti-Semitism in both the terminology and substance of two key parts of the Nuremberg evidence: namely, the final prosecution draft on the persecution of the Jews and Jackson's famous

---

[247] Ibid.

[248] IMT 3, 13 December 1945, 494.

opening address. This theory's themes of anti-Semitism as a calculatedly deployed, ideological device to achieve a variety of ulterior goals, including the silencing of domestic opposition, coercive 'social cohesion' and the preparation for, and justification of, aggressive war, are also found in these two core items of Nuremberg trial evidence.

A defence of the impact of the spearhead theory

Having supported and extended Aronson's contention concerning the influential nature of Neumann's theory, the remainder of this section will respond to the criticisms that Aronson and others have made with respect to its alleged negative implications in relation to the vital task of highlighting the Holocaust within the Nuremberg trials. Far from downplaying its importance, as many of his critics maintain, Neumann's work for the OSS specifically emphasised the centrality of Nazi anti-Semitism as:

> [T]he most constant single ideology of the Nazi Party. No other element has so constantly figured in the forefront of Nazi ideologies and Nazi activities... anti-Semitism is the sole ideology that can possibly cement the Nazi Party, and it is this unique function of anti-Semitism that gives it its peculiar character.[249]

In assessing the adequacy of the Neumann group's responses to the Holocaust, it is important for critics to recognise the unprecedented nature of the Nazi extermination, and the understandable suspicion directed against wartime atrocity stories, which—during WWI—were manufactured for propaganda purposes. It is too easy for contemporary critics who have grown accustomed to the various genocidal slaughters from Rwanda to the Balkans, which marred the last 60 years of the 20th century, to ignore the fact that the very expression 'genocide' was only first coined by the OSS consultant Raphael Lemkin during the 1940's. Katz draws attention to the dangers of reconstructing the reports and analysis of Neumann and his German-Jewish émigré colleagues in the light of contemporary insights and sensibilities, including the Zionist model of Jewish identity as that of a distinct nation or people, which—as

---

[249] R&A 1139.9, 'Psychological Warfare: Weekly Roundup' (May 18–24, 1943): Franz Neumann [signed article], 'Anti-Semitism', 17.

Aronson notes—did not widely prevail during the mid-1940's.[250] In this period, German, Italian and Spanish Fascism governed most of Europe, and threatened to achieve even wider global domination.

Katz now rightly insists upon the need for Neumann's critics to acknowledge the implications of the prevailing culture, in which the warped project of deploying the resources of modern technology systematically to eliminate an entire social group represented an unprecedented, and almost inconceivable, idea. Indeed, a former Chief of OSS X-2 Branch, Judge Will, has recalled the sheer shock that firsthand evidence of Nazi genocide within a concentration camp inflicted upon his senses: 'I could go on describing the almost unbelievable horror of what we saw but many of you were there and I don't have to describe it to you. I am sure that whatever camp you were in, it was the same. If I had not seen it, I would not have believed that human beings could do to other human beings what I saw at Buchenwald.'[251] This almost unbelievable quality, even to those witnessing the results at firsthand, was especially the case within a climate of opinion that viewed the history of modernity as an onward march of progress away from feudal barbarism towards ever-greater degrees of civilisation. As Katz notes:

> It must also be considered that the magnitude of the crime itself, a conspiracy to annihilate an entire population, was to many reasonable people literally unbelievable. Today we have absorbed the grim realities of Armenia, Auschwitz, Cambodia, Rwanda, and Bosnia; we have learned to live in a world in which civilians are not 'collateral damage' but are prime targets. We have, in short, lost whatever innocence we might once have claimed. In the early 1940s, however, the concept of genocide did not yet reside so securely in the conscience of the world and this may partially explain why so many people failed to grasp the larger meaning of the reports emanating from Hitler's Europe. That, in any case, is the climate in which United States Office of Strategic Services was operating.[252]

Stuart Hughes's memoirs from his time as an OSS/R&A official also confirm that it was only on visiting the concentration camps immediately after the war that the full enormity and *systematic quality* of the

[250] Aronson, 2004 op. cit. 265–266, noting that even Jacob Robinson was willing to allow other *religious groups* to play the role of *amicus curiae*, thereby weakening the assertion that the Jewish victims belonged to a common 'nation' or 'people.'

[251] See G. J. Yonover, 'Anti-Semitism and Holocaust Denial in the Academy: A Tort Remedy', *Dickinson Law Review*. 101 (1996): 71, citing 'Hubert L. Will, Address at Strasbourg, June 23, 1995', (on file at Judge Will's chambers, Chicago, Ill.).

[252] Katz, 1991 op. cit. 308.

Holocaust started to become apparent. This was notwithstanding that 'reports of systematic extermination had been confirmed ten months before my original departure overseas [i.e. since mid-1944]'.[253]

It is important to recognise the *specific institutional constraints* under which scholars working for the R&A Branch of the OSS operated if their research was ever to exert any impact upon those who commissioned it. Criticisms of the R&A approach to the Holocaust need to take account of the fact that all R&A intelligence reports had to comply with certain external institutional requirements that distinguished them from more impassioned and morally-charged academic or journalistic critiques. In order for their reports (and the viability of the entire R&A Branch which facilitated them) to continue to be taken seriously, they were not allowed to write in the style of academics. Instead, they had to phrase their reports in the impoverished 'objective' style of apparently value-free studies. The latter had to renounce any political or moral commitments, especially those which might appear to be specific to any particular 'interest group'.[254] These reports had to avoid appearing to trespass upon, pre-empt or otherwise usurp the specific policy-making jurisdiction of their ultimate superiors, not least the State Department, Department of War, War Refugee Board and Joint Chiefs of Staff. As Katz notes:

> OSS had entered a crowded field, and it was a condition of its very survival that it gain a reputation for disinterested professionalism. "There is no future in R&A as a pressure group," the researchers were instructed, and on the first suspicion of pleading a special cause, "we will very soon lose our entree to all policy-makers other than those already committed to the same special cause." The fate of the Jews, tragically, was widely regarded within wartime Washington as one more "special cause."[255]

Another pre-condition for Neumann's team to exert practical influence in the Nazi war crimes field, where it possessed undoubted analytical expertise, was the need to achieve close co-operation with colleagues from *other agencies*. Katz emphasises that the direct interpersonal contact between Neumann's CES and Jackson's organisation represented

[253] Hughes, 1990 op. cit. 170.

[254] See 'Functions of the Research and Analysis Branch' 30 October 1942: US NA, RG 226, Entry 45, Box 2, Folder 45; and 'Draft of Proposed Guide to Preparation of Political Reports,': RG 226, Entry 37, Box 5, Folder: Projects Committee Correspondence.

[255] 1998 op. cit.

a considerable improvement over the usually highly diffuse impact of their research reports:

> [I]t may have been in this period that the German legal scholars—Neumann, Kirchheimer, and Henry Kellerman—finally learned that as confident as they were about their own practical expertise, if they wanted to have any serious advisory influence, they must direct their ideas in direct deliberate collaboration with their potential clients and not simply fire them off in the form of reports to be edited, distilled, excerpted, and ignored.[256]

This is an important point indicating that it was precisely in the field of war crimes research that Neumann's R&A group exerted their most direct influence upon the legal reaction to the Holocaust, and where their analysis could directly feed into the definition of the Nazi regime's nature, operation and chain of responsibility. Indeed, Carl Schorske, Neumann's immediate superior within OSS / R&A, suggested to the present writer that: 'war crimes research was as close to operations against the Nazis as R&A ever got'.[257]

Despite the imperative not to be seen as operating on behalf of any interest or pressure group, Neumann's group built up strong institutional connections with official Jewish bodies. Before joining the OSS, Neumann had worked closely with Jewish organisations in New York to secure funding for a research project on anti-Semitism.[258] Later, when supervising draft prosecution briefs, including those related to the Holocaust, Neumann also relied, as a primary source, upon materials and statistical analysis of this genocide supplied by the Institute of Jewish Affairs, the details of which he personally sent to Jackson's advance party in a long memorandum.[259] Indeed, in the evidence submitted to the Nuremberg prosecutors in the R&A report on: 'the conspiracy against the Jews', Neumann's team insisted on including a further document from this Institute. Jackson later reported that he had now accepted the joint R&A and Institute report as the basis for

[256] Katz 1989 op. cit. 51.

[257] Author's Telephone interview with Carl Schorske, 1 July 1998.

[258] 'It was mainly through [Neumann's] efforts that the American Jewish Committee decided in the autumn of 1942 to support the anti-Semitism project.' R. Wiggershaus, *The Frankfurt School*, NY: 1994, 353–354.

[259] See the joint R&A / Institute of Jewish Affairs document: 'Statistics on Jewish Casualties During Axis Domination' August 1945, a revised document updating an earlier study of the same name issued in June 1945: US NA, RG 200, Dwork Papers, Box 3.

the estimation of the numbers of Jews the Nazi regime killed. This extremely detailed study provides a breakdown of estimated killings on a country by country basis. It estimates that the Nazi regime had killed 5,700,000 Jews, defined as those who identify themselves as such on census returns etc.[260] The joint statistical report represented an active institutional collaboration with one group of victims of the Nazi genocide that was not extended to any other persecuted group.

More generally, it is worth recalling OSS-R&A's collaborative work with the Research Institute of the American Jewish Committee, including that of Walter Rothschild based in OSS London Field Office.[261] Aronson quotes a private letter from Nuremberg to Irving Dwork, a colleague who headed OSS' Jewish Affairs Desk in Washington. This referred to how:

> Lt. Rothschild of OSS told me that he has sent to Nuremberg the indictment drawn up by Anglo-Jewish association.... I saw a copy today at Crime Commission. It consists of quotes from the defendants now on trial, which is no contribution. It has, however, many affidavits by refugees here who submitted long lists of names of individuals who were in any manner connected with persecution....[262]

Neumann's team also co-operated fully with, and received the full confidence of, the assorted Jewish émigrés who ran the Wiener Library in London, where prosecution material was also gathered.[263]

Neumann's willingness to work with an outside 'group' lobbying on behalf of Jewish concerns and interests is remarkable. This is particularly the case given that many Anglo-American intelligence officials suspected that certain Jewish groups who had entered into negotiations with the Nazis for purposes of humanitarian relief, possessed Zionist ambitions. In other words, they were seeking to create a Jewish state in what was then British-controlled Palestine.[264] Indeed, in one sense, it reflected an unstated commitment to give considerable recognition to the Holocaust. Neumann had lost members of his own family, including his mother, to Nazi death camps.

---

260 Ibid., 8.

261 More generally on Rothschild, see materials at: US NA, RG 226, Entry 92, Box 246, Frame 378; Entry 190.

262 Aronson, op. cit. 265–266.

263 Kellerman, 1997 op. cit. 346–7.

264 Aronson, 2004 op. cit. 72.

In short, Neumann's spearhead theory of anti-Semitism develops a distinctly functionalist view of that type of Nazi anti-Semitic ideology which underpinned the Holocaust. This influential theory has attracted criticisms from Aronson and others which ignore various key factors, whose inclusion would result in a more sympathetic view of Neumann's approach. This is not just an analytical issue. With reference to the Neumann group within R&A, CES, one of Neumann's R&A colleagues has recently recalled that: 'German-Jewish refugees [such as Neumann, Kirchheimer, Marcuse, Herz] would have been the last people inclined to ignore or discount reports of a Final Solution.'[265]

Our next task is to further develop the approach the Neumann R&A group took to different aspects of the Holocaust in their wartime and immediate postwar reports. It will be important to note where appropriate the influence of the spearhead theory of anti-Semitism within, for example, draft prosecution briefs directly addressing organisational and individual liabilities for this genocide.

Wartime R&A reports on Nazi war crimes

During 1943–44, members of the R&A Branch composed a series of reports on various legal, political and institutional difficulties facing any future prosecution of Nazi war criminals.[266] It also wrote studies addressing the implications for Allied psychological warfare of the attribution of different types of war criminality.[267] Broadly speaking, these wartime reports fall under two distinct types: those concerned with strategic issues in the prosecution of Nazi war criminals responsible for the Holocaust and other crimes; and analysis of specific instances of this genocide. The strategic reports will be examined first.

One of these 'prosecution strategy' reports was entitled 'Problems Concerning the Treatment of War Criminals' (R&A No. 2577) issued

[265] A. Schlesinger, *A Life in the Twentieth Century: Innocent Beginnings, 1917–1950*, Boston: Houghton-Mifflin, 2000, 307.

[266] See R&A 1482, 'The 'Statement of Atrocities' of the Moscow Tripartite Conference,' 10 December 1943; R&A 1113.33, Political Intelligence Report No. 33, s. 1.3: US NA, RG 153, Entry 135, Box 6; R&A 3110, 'Leadership Principle and Criminal Responsibility', 18 July 1945: US NA, RG 238, Entry 52f., Box 28.

[267] See 'The Significance of Prussian Militarism for Nazi Imperialism', R&A 1281, 20 October 1943: US NA, RG 153, Entry 135, Box 6.

in September 1944.[268] In this report, Neumann's sub-group emphasised the difficulties within international law of employing war crimes charges against those involved in the systematic planning, organisation and execution of purely domestic atrocities on a state's own nationals, not least the genocide of Jews:

> A large number of persons have been directly or indirectly involved in such crimes. Declarations hitherto issued do not sufficiently indicate the principles according to which responsibility of such individuals shall be established. a) In cases of massacre of Jews in a concentration camp, may all hierarchical superiors of the executing Gestapo squad, from the district Gestapo chief up to Himmler as Reich Leader SS and chief of the German police, be held responsible, even when no specific order for the commitment of the act can be found?[269]

Implied here is a plea for this outstanding question to be addressed and properly resolved. This R&A report already indicated a possible solution to the problem of the individualistic biases of traditional criminal law. It was a solution that, by drawing upon a creative interpretation of the earlier 'Moscow Statement on Atrocities' of November 1943, effectively turned the Nazis' own conception of the responsibilities of the leadership for atrocities against Jewish and other civilians back upon its practitioners. As a result, those who planned and organised the Holocaust could, despite legal difficulties that could otherwise occur, be caught in the net of legal accountability:

> Under traditional legal procedure the establishment of individual responsibility is required. The Moscow Statement, by referring to persons who have been responsible for or have taken a consenting part in "war crimes", suggests a broader interpretation of the concept of "responsibility" than it has traditionally received. According to the peculiar structure of Nazi organisation and to the "leadership principle" which under the Nazi regime everywhere rules the relationship between members of official organisations, the hierarchical superior is responsible for whatever happens within the functional and territorial sphere of his jurisdiction. Fundamental policies are laid down centrally by Hitler or his associates, with full latitude for the execution of policies being delegated to the sub-leaders

[268] R&A 2577, 'Problems Concerning the Treatment of War Criminals', 28 September 1944, and R&A 2577.2, 'Problems Concerning the Treatment of War Criminals; List of Potential War Criminals Under Proposed US Policy Directives', 30 September 1944: US NA, RG 238, Entry 52f., Box 28. The archival record of R&A 2577.1 states that a near complete draft was completed on 25 September, 1944, so presumably the revised final draft would have been issued within the next few weeks.

[269] R&A 2577.1, op. cit. 4.

> in the various fields and regions. To this broad power corresponds broad responsibility. Since there exists an unbroken chain of command and corresponding obedience from the highest policy-making level down to the lowest level, every act executed at the lower level must be attributed to each of the hierarchical superiors.[270]

Under the heading 'Need for a Policy Directive', the OSS authors maintained that it was necessary for the Allies to include *domestic* atrocities against Jewish and other civilians as a new category of legally recognised war crimes:

> Such a directive should, it is submitted, be constructed with a view to the principles inherent in modern penal law and in international law, because the main criteria for such a selection already exists in national codes and/or in the established principles of international law. It is therefore suggested that this basis would make possible a policy directive clearly established the following acts as war crimes:... F. Atrocities against whole groups in pursuance of a general program of annihilation, such as the massacre of Jews... Such a directive, if issued by the United Nations, would make plain... the scope which the United Nations intend to assign to war crimes and would afford an efficient basis for uniform tripartite action.[271]

The crucial and legally innovative suggestion here was to combine a specifically *sociological interpretation* of the operation of the chain of command within the hierarchical organisational structure of Nazi power-elites, particularly the SS, to a specific prosecution strategy. The latter aimed to pre-empt possible legal defences of those SS official complicit in the Holocaust:

> Since each of them has a share in the elaboration and execution of a policy in a given field, the plea cannot be accepted that he had no knowledge of a specific act or the details of its execution or that he did not order it himself. In other countries such an excuse is usually valid, because acts of officials would be lawful only if authorised by the law of the land; consequently, any excess is attributable to the individual official and not to his hierarchical superiors. Under the Nazis, however, various agencies and organisations, such as the 'SS', have been exempted from legal limitations, so that whatever is done within the broad framework of the Nazi program must be presumed to have official authorisation. Under these circumstances, the only admissible excuse would consist in the proof that the incriminated person did all in his power to prevent the

---

[270] Ibid.
[271] R&A 2577, 3.

> act or that, having been unable to prevent it, he resigned immediately after the commission of the act.[272]

This analysis leads to the suggestion that one of the main possible trial defences for SS officials, ranging from Eichmann through to concentration camp guards, that of obeying 'superior orders', should be heavily qualified. This defence should be defined as contextually inappropriate in the specific case of Nazi war criminals:

> b) It may be desirable to bring to justice not only the instigators of a crime but also those who took part in its immediate execution. The latter, however, may be expected to raise the exception of having acted under binding orders. Such a plea cannot be considered in the case of those who in executing a policy have a certain amount of discretion. It might, however, be pressed by persons who acted under specific orders which left no individual choice.... While many army manuals, among them the American, admit the plea without exception, others favor its admission only under narrowly defined conditions, if at all. It would therefore be desirable to have a policy statement clearly defining the attitude to be taken in this report. Since the authoritarian structure of the Nazi regime makes individual resistance against orders more dangerous and consequently less to be expected than elsewhere, a general prohibition of the plea does not seem warranted. The individual member of an army firing-squad detailed to shoot hostages may very well risk his life if he refuses to obey. While the same justification would apply to members of Party formations such as the SS, the policy statement should take into consideration whether or not such a person had joined the organisation voluntarily. If he did so, he must be assumed to have had full knowledge of the practices and functions of the organisation and can therefore not avoid his share of responsibility.[273]

This OSS report also noted that *jurisdictional issues* are raised by the widespread genocide committed against Jews and other minority groups throughout Nazi occupied Europe, including of course within Germany itself. The Neumann group clearly anticipated problems with any international trial under pre-existing international criminal law because such law did not embrace domestic crimes by, for example, the German state against German or stateless Jews. Hence, for political as well as jurisdictional reasons, it argues that crimes of domestic genocide may be best resolved by deciding to hold trials before *reconstituted German*

[272] Ibid.
[273] Ibid.

courts, where the ordinary law of murder could be deployed against perpetrators of the Holocaust:

> It may well be argued that crimes, such as the persecution of Jews or political opponents, committed in the execution of the general Nazi program, should be considered as war crimes, even when committed against Axis nationals or stateless persons in Axis territory.... It is possible that such cases would most advantageously be brought before the reconstituted German courts. Punishment of Nazi crimes by German courts would, it is submitted, go far to prove to the German people and the whole world that German repudiates the crimes of its former leaders.[274]

It is arguable that this R&A report helped supply elements of the strategic thinking that informed a number of the more innovative charges contained within the Nuremberg Charter. The remit of the 'criminal conspiracy' or 'common plan' charges set out by this Charter was sufficiently wide to encompass the domestic murder of Jews and other groups, including the Nazis' *prewar* acts of anti-Semitic persecution. Despite this, it was senior prosecutor Murray Bernays who has been hailed as the creator of this approach. However, when formulating his influential model from September 1944 onwards Bernays had been working closely with war crimes strategy materials supplied by Neumann's group, including the material we have just been discussing, which clearly influenced his approach. Arguably, the result was an unduly simplified version of a trial strategy based on a single 'common plan' and 'conspiracy'.

Having reviewed the main strategic studies, it is now appropriate to discuss other wartime R&A reports that focus on factual evidence relating to the Holocaust in specific regions of Nazi-occupied Europe. It would be laborious to list each reference to the Holocaust contained in every wartime R&A Report. However, the most important of these, entitled R&A No. 2027, 'The Jews in Hungary' (19 October 1944), merits extensive discussion, not least because it was one of the main R&A wartime reports on aspects of the Holocaust that Neumann ensured was directly fed into the Nuremberg process.

This study addresses the social, political, and economic position of the Jews in Hungary prior to the Nazi occupation. It starts by outlining the economic discrimination and the expropriation of those defined as belonging to this group under the pro-Nazi government. Such

[274] R&A 2577, 12.

discrimination is identified as including the subsequent adoption of a Jewish badge, limitations on employment opportunities and restrictions on movement. This report then discusses later, more extreme measures, such as economic expropriation, reductions in food rations, the establishment of ghettos and concentration camps, followed by mass deportations. It also addresses the question of the responsibility of Hungarian officials, and various public and international reactions. Another topic is the 'Brandt affair'. This involved the proposed trading of Jewish lives for Allied trucks, Allied and neutral attempts at intervention and rescue through to the period ending in September 1944. Finally, the appendixes identify anti-Semitic movements and members of government.[275]

This report notes that, for over 1000 years, Jews had been an integral and assimilated part of the Hungarian population. They had: 'formed a considerable part of the commercial and professional middle classes.' It was the growth of the power and influence of the Nazi regime that motivated Horthy's government to adopt: 'an active anti-Semitic policy both as a means of bartering with Hitler and stealing the thunder from...Nazis'.[276] However, Horthy's government remained the least subservient of the German satellites: 'In order to avoid the complete alienation of the Allies', it refused to follow: 'the Nazi policy to its ultimate goals of expropriation, starvation and extermination.'[277] However, this situation of 'partial toleration' changed on 19 March 1944 when the Nazis' occupied this country:

> Following the German occupation in 1944, new discriminatory legislation was drafted after the Nazi model. Within the space of weeks, the yellow badge was introduced, property confiscated, professional and civil service positions barred to Jews, enterprises closed down, bank accounts blocked, ghettos and concentration camps established, and finally, the bulk of Hungarian Jewry deported. The results of these measures has been expropriation of an estimated 44,000,000,000 [sic] of Jewish property and the deportation of 800,000 Jews, 640,000 apparently to extermination centers.[278]

---

275 This was one of the many R&A reports that General Donovan secured for his prosecution work at Nuremberg. See Cornell Collection, Vol. 106.

276 R&A No. 2027, 'The Jews in Hungary': US NA, RG 226, Entry 191, Box 1.

277 Ibid.

278 Ibid.

Later sections of the report amplify the speed of anti-Semitic persecution in the immediate wake of this occupation:

> While in Germany the political, economic and physical liquidation of the Jews was spread over a period of ten years, in Hungary the same measures were crammed into a few weeks. During the first days of the occupation the stage was set for future anti-Jewish activities...Ten days were allotted for these necessary [state propaganda] preliminaries, and on 30 March the first new anti-Jewish measures were proclaimed.[279]

These measures were based on the definition of Jews contained in Nazi Germany's own law, and were further refined and intensified in May of this year.[280] On 16 April 1944, Jews were required to surrender their ration cards, for which they received alternatives that excluded them from being able to obtain sugar, butter, poppy seeds, paprika, fats and all meats except beef.[281] This month also witnessed the compulsory registration of the accommodation of Jews, which operated as a 'preliminary measure' to their selective expulsion from 'Hungarian towns with large Jewish populations' into ghettos: 'surrounded by barbed wire.'[282] The report provides extensive details of the dates and times of these deportations.[283] It notes:

> the stage was now set for the logical culmination of the program: the deportation and subsequent extermination of Hungarian Jewry....Reports of deportations of Jews began to leak out of Hungary. (Footnote: OSS-CID reports 9, 26, 27 June 1944 and Source S, 25 May 1944). Barred freight cars were said to be discharging their human cargo at various extermination centers.[284]

The deportation of 400,000 Jews from these temporary camps and ghettos continued throughout May and June 1944. Citing a range of secret OSS sources, this report states:[285]

> Prior to their deportation, these Jews were held in primitive quarters for periods of two to four weeks. Living conditions...defy all description. The Jews were herded together without regard to age, sex or health; food, clothing, and water were inadequate; outbreaks of typhus were not

[279] Ibid., 13.
[280] Ibid., 14.
[281] Ibid., 17.
[282] Ibid., 18.
[283] Ibid., 18–19.
[284] Ibid., 19–20.
[285] Ibid., 20–21.

> uncommon. From these camps the deportees were loaded into freight cars sixty to eighty to a car; the doors were nailed shut, and then hauled off to Poland. En route, the lack of food, water and sanitary facilities is reported to have caused numerous deaths, but the bodies were never taken from the cars.... There is little doubt that the majority of these Hungarian Jews were being shipped to the extermination centers... in Eastern Poland.[286]

This report attributes responsibility for: 'over-all Jewish policy to Gestapo agents in Hungary headed by... [Adolf] Eichmann (OSS Source S July 1944)'. However, it extends this guilt to various collaborationist Hungarian state officials, including Ander Jarcas, former Minister of the Interior, and two of his immediate subordinates: Baky and Endre [partly illegible].[287] The report also argues that, whilst the 'anti-Jewish atrocities' were modelled on the prior Nazi model: 'the collaborationist regime has carried them out with such enthusiasm and thoroughness as to merit an equal share in the guilt.'[288]

In terms of public reactions to the Holocaust, the evidence is stated to be mixed. Many Hungarians, including police officers, viciously exploited the overall climate of persecution for their own private enrichment. However, others engaged in passive resistance by shielding their fellow citizens, arranging false baptism certificates and identity papers, and safeguarding Jewish property from seizure.[289] Unusually for an R&A report, whose authors were required to be strictly objective and value-free, the section on 'Intervention and Rescue Measures' expresses a degree of bitterness at the failure of the Allies and others to save more European Jews:

> By the time of the first deportations of Hungarian Jews, some two million Polish Jews had been brutally exterminated, the Jews of Germany, Austria, Czechoslovakia, Greece, and Yugoslavia had been liquidated; and most of the Jewish population of Holland, Belgium, and France had been sent to the 'death camps' of Eastern Europe. The fate of all these millions of European Jews had elicited relatively slight notice from a world more interested in the larger issues of the war.[290]

---

286 Ibid., 21.
287 Ibid., 23
288 Ibid., 23.
289 Ibid., 24.
290 Ibid., 25.

The report then discusses the infamous 'Brandt affair', when a Gestapo official sought to trade the lives of threatened Jews in return for military supplies, such as trucks, on the understanding that these would not be deployed on the Western Front. It highlights the 'combination of blackmail and political warfare' expressed by this proposal, which was ultimately rejected by the Allies. This section recognises that this offer may have formed one part of a wider policy seeking a 'soft peace', including promises of 'immunity from criminal prosecution' for Himmler and others complicit in the Holocaust.[291] It concludes that Allied attempts at rescue had 'come to naught' mainly because of the refusal of SS officials to cooperate with exit visa and transportation arrangements, British policy on Palestine,[292] and logistical problems related to the changing position of the military front line in Eastern Europe.[293]

A second wartime OSS report that discusses the Holocaust in Eastern Europe is R&A 2500.13, German Military Government over Europe: Slovakia, January 1945. This study devoted a section to 'the treatment of Jews' (26–27), noting the rise of ever-harsher anti-Semitic legislation from 1941 under German pressure, based more on racial than religious lines. It outlined which agencies were responsible for the 'systematic application' of these measures, a 'Central Jewish Office...excluding Jews from economic life, Aryanization of property, and the control of the social and economic life of those Jews remaining in Slovakia.'[294] This office, which only notionally represented Jewish interests, actually monitored and registered all Slovakian Jews in order to subject them all the more effectively to anti-Semitic measures ordered by the Central Economic Office. As a result, Jews were eliminated from economic life by 1942. During October of that year, several 'collecting stations' were established for displaced Jews, many of whom were sent to one of five labour camps in this country, or to concentration / death camps in Poland.[295] By 1943, most of the Jewish population had been removed in this way, with the remainder sometimes benefiting from the support of Slovakian friends and neighbours who shielded them from transportation to such camps: 'The fate of the Slovakian Jews in the fall of

[291] Ibid., 26.
[292] On the Palestine dimension, see Aronson, 2004 op. cit.
[293] 'The Jews in Hungary', op. cit. 27–29.
[294] Ibid., 26–27.
[295] Ibid.

1944 resembled that suffered by the Hungarians a few months earlier' [deportation to death camps].[296]

The generic report in this German Military Government series also addresses the systematic use of terroristic violence and murder against Jews and others. Indeed, under the sub-heading 'The Police and SS as Terror Organisations', the OSS report stated quite clearly:

> The sober and methodical steps taken by the Nazis to build up their system of police controls were supplemented by methods of terrorism. The men who created the administrative machinery described above were the same individuals who were responsible for the machine-gunning of civilians packed tightly into cellars or even churches, for the use of gas chambers and crematories for the innocent victims of Nazi racial theories, and for the execution of hostages. The Police and the SS are both responsible for the greatest part of Nazi terrorism.[297]

This report even contrasted the less extreme but still 'brutal' terrorism SS officials practiced in Western Europe in pursuit of: 'the application of Nazi racial theories', with the extensive and unrestrained brutality: 'employed against the unfortunate populations of Eastern Europe.' It noted that: 'In the east, countless thousands went to their death simply because they were Jews or Slavs.'[298]

A number of other OSS-R&A reports that were later fed into the Nuremberg process had not been originally written for the prosecution but still contained extremely valuable materials for Jackson's staff. These included accounts of, for example, the changing institutional and administrative framework of the SS, Gestapo and SD (the SS political intelligence branch),[299] and potential problems caused whenever perpetrators of the Holocaust could gain a safe haven in neutral countries that refuse extradition, such as certain Latin American regimes sympathetic to Fascism. For example, R&A 2465, completed in January 1945, discusses: 'the theory of asylum in International Law'. It describes: 'both the practice of states both before and during the present war and the extent to which policies now existing in non-belligerent states may prove a barrier to the announced purpose of the United Nations to

---

[296] Ibid., 27.
[297] Ibid., 23.
[298] Ibid.
[299] 'German Military Government over Europe: The SS and Police in Occupied Europe', R&A No. 2500.22, January 1945: US NA, RG 153, Entry 136, Box 6.

punish war criminals.'[300] It also identifies possible lessons to be learned from the experience of the Netherlands' grant of political asylum to the German Kaiser after the previous world war, and the practice of other governments that could follow suit at the end of WWII, including Argentina, Eire, Portugal, Spain, Sweden, Switzerland, Turkey and the Vatican.[301] This report also alerts its readers to the continuing problem, or 'barrier', created by the lack of a clear and serviceable legal definition of what precisely constituted 'war crimes' in this context.[302]

Such OSS documents provided the prosecutors with clear overviews of, for example, the complex array of divisions and sub-divisions within the SS. This was particularly vital with respect to Nazi-occupied Eastern Europe. Here, paramilitary killing squads of the Waffen-SS (including the SS Deathhead Formations responsible for concentration camp security), and the Order Police were both implicated in the extermination of Jews, partisans and communists.[303] R&A reports on Nazi war crimes rarely contain extensive and detailed accounts of particular atrocities that firmly linked particular individuals to specific crimes against Jews. However, they do provide important background information clarifying changing patterns of wartime organisation, lines of command and responsibility.[304] These were obviously important studies to orientate the prosecutors responsible for preparing briefs relevant to the destruction of European Jews.

In short, the selection of wartime R&A reports we have examined set out important strategic issues relating to the prosecution of Nazis complicit in the Holocaust, as well providing extensive details relating to 'crimes against humanity' committed by the SS against Hungarian and Slovak Jews. Neumann ensured that both of these documents were fed into the Nuremberg process via the 'document room', from which all the prosecutors gathered materials during their preparation of final trial briefs.

300 Summary 'description' of R&A 2465 by its authors. A copy of this report is contained in Justice Jackson's own office files, Jackson Papers, op. cit. Box 104, Reel 10.
301 Ibid., 15–32.
302 Ibid.
303 R&A No. 2500.22, op. cit.
304 Ibid., 15–18.

The process of composing postwar R&A reports for the OCC

Before discussing the contents and approach of R&A *postwar* reports relevant to the Holocaust, this section will emphasise the context in which these had to be produced. From the outset of the prosecution's trial planning process, Jackson had entrusted Neumann's OSS team with the task of taking charge of the most difficult and innovative aspects of the prosecution strategy. Jackson's trial planning memorandum of May 1945, co-drafted with James Donovan the OSS' General Counsel, made Neumann's team responsible for addressing the problem of how the prosecutors could employ previously untested charges of 'organisational liability' and 'criminal conspiracy' charges.[305] These innovative charges had to be refined to establish a clear and legally recognisable connection between domestic genocide of various minorities, the conspiracy to achieve 'world domination' and violations of previously established legal categories of international law. It is true that the *systematic* quality of the Holocaust as a device of planned state policy was not fully recognised by the early work of Neumann's section. However, their work for the Nuremberg trials rapidly corrected this deficiency through their critical analysis of the institutional nexus involved in planning and executing this genocide.[306]

From mid-May 1945, the R&A Branch had been given responsibility for preparing draft documentation for a number of particularly complex aspects of the overall case, much of which ultimately dominated the opening weeks of the trials. On 9 July 1945, Neumann's immediate superior within CES, Carl Schorske, noted in a recently declassified memo to Sanford Hollis, entitled 'R&A's contribution to the war crimes program', that:

> The R&A Branch is to be responsible for assembling all possible information on the Nazi effort to conquer power in Germany, to prepare Germany for war, and to extend Germany's hegemony of Europe. This task requires not only a description of the unfolding of the Nazi plan but also a thorough analysis of organisations responsible for executing

---

[305] See 'Memorandum on Trial Preparation' 17th May 1945 in James Donovan's files, Hoover Institute Archives, Box 34, Folder 6.

[306] According to Schlesinger and Breitman, the OSS had received reliable eyewitness evidence of death camps from early on, but saw only a quantitative increase in sporadic repression, not an organised plan of systematic genocide, in Chalou 1992 op. cit. 66–8, 106–8.

> it. The information is being written up in such form that it may serve as the basis for the trial briefs to be submitted by the prosecution.[307]

The crucial aspects of this statement are the expectation that the empirical dimension of demonstrating the existence of a 'conspiracy to wage aggressive war' aspect of Jackson's trial plan, a conspiracy which included pre-war atrocities against German and other Jews, was entrusted to Neumann's team. The latter were, by virtue of both their prior background as German émigrés and specialists within German affairs, deemed uniquely qualified to 'flesh out' the institutional details of the proposed 'criminal conspiracy' charge.

By 30 May 1945, James Donovan was able to present an up-beat, if perhaps overstated, 'Progress Report', which stated:

> The Research and Analysis Branch (lawyers of all nations, political scientists, economists, historians, etc.) has undertaken the preparation of (a) detailed outlines of what are conceived to be the two major projects required for proof of the preparation, (b) preparation of a series of approximately 25 trial briefs on the component parts of the case, (c) preparation of proposed findings of fact based upon the foregoing, (d) a tentative list of major German war criminals, compiled on the basis of the planning memorandum and the implementing work done, and (e) a "trial run" on the case against Göring.[308]

Kellerman, Neumann's deputy, also records the OSS' role in the second most important innovation—the charge directed against the SS and other Nazi institutions complicit in the Holocaust and other war crimes of being criminal organisations, akin to organised crime racketeers:

> My specific job was to collate and summarise evidence against the officials, the so called Amtswalter, of the NSDAP, the SS, the SA and the Hitler-jugend, in the form of pre-trial briefs.... We had dossiers on Nazi leaders at all levels and the records of crimes committed against political adversaries, minorities (especially Jews), foreign workers, the mentally ill and others.... Our sources had served [just] as well, or so it seemed at the time. I was overwhelmed with the sheer volume of information available. Yet, as we were to find out later, when the ovens and gas chambers of Auschwitz were opened, we had hardly scratched the surface.[309]

---

[307] This is located in the National Archive's OSS 'war crimes file' op. cit.

[308] 'Progress Report on Preparation of Prosecution' 30 May, 1945: Jackson Papers, op. cit. Box 101, Reel 7.

[309] Kellerman, 1997 op. cit. 339.

The fact that certain institutions, such as the SS and SA, were themselves being considered as criminal organisations in their own right, made the specialist analyses of Neumann's CES team particularly pertinent. Kellerman suggests that from at least May 1945, the CES were under great pressure to produce concrete results serviceable for prosecution purposes:

> We worked under great pressure. Hostilities in Europe had come to an end in May 1945. The trial date was set for later that year. Our preparations in Washington, my briefs included, had to be completed by midsummer. They did not list a full catalogue of Nazi crimes, but enough to illustrate the record and, of course, the involvement of the principle organisations that formed the body politic in the Third Reich.[310]

An internal memo from Neumann and Phoebe Morrison (head of OSS' International Law Unit) maintained that the definition of war crimes should, on the basis of earlier official statements by senior US officials, be extended to cover pre-war aspects of the Holocaust: 'crimes committed by Germans against Germans.' Their proposed draft classifies potential 'war crimes' of domestic repression as falling under four headings: the 'persecution of the Jews'; 'elimination of political opposition'; the 'fight against the churches'; and, finally, 'abuses in police and prison administration'.[311]

In short, the Neumann's sub-section of the R&A Branch was centrally involved within the preparation of research that was designed to make a direct input into prosecution briefs. This was especially the case with respect to the criminal nature of the entire regime and those organisations such as the SS, SD and Gestapo, which had been central to the Holocaust (as distinct from a series of individual acts considered isolation).

For present purposes, it is R&A's contribution to the US prosecution's case against the SS, the Nazi organisation most closely associated with executing the Holocaust, which is of particular relevance. James Donovan's progress report from May 1945 enclosed: 'a careful study of the German organisations guilty of criminal acts and their leaders'; and reported that other studies, including 'devices used to undermine and crush resistance...with instructions to overseas posts' will be made

---

310 Ibid., 340.

311 'The Trial of War Criminals', Neumann and Morrison, 21 May 1945, NA RG 226, Entry 1, Box 2, Folder 6, 3.

available shortly.'[312] Amongst the trial briefs that were then underway were a number relevant to the Holocaust: 'domestic crimes', 'spoliation of property', 'maltreatment of civilians, especially civilian labor' and 'extermination of the Jews.'[313] Each of these briefs included:

> (i) statement of the crimes involved, with citation of [legal] authority; (ii) a statement of the persons and organisations responsible for the crimes and the legal basis of such responsibility; and (iii) a factual analysis and reference or physical attachment of the evidence available (including a list of witnesses and their probable testimony), a statement of the further evidence required, the steps already taken to obtain such evidence and the steps to be taken.[314]

Donovan reminded Jackson that R&A officials then still based in Washington were able only to prepare 'original basic drafts'. This was because: 'a substantial proportion of the best evidence of specific crimes will be found only overseas in time for the international trial.'[315] He also noted that other branches of the OSS were assisting with the supply of relevant factual information. These included OSS' Biographical and Pictorial Records Divisions, The International Committee, which indexed foreign newspaper and periodical reports of atrocities, and the OSS' Foreign Nationalities Branch. The latter: 'is already engaged in a survey to determine the best witnesses to Axis crimes now within the United States. Several persons are already being interrogated.'[316]

The OSS General Counsel also reported that the espionage and counterespionage (SI and X-2) Branches, with numerous field offices overseas in London, Paris, Italy and Germany, had already been mobilised: 'in the procurement of evidence.' Where prosecutors knew the time and place of an atrocity, X-2 officers could use their own resources, based partly on their access to top secret intercepts of Nazi communications, to identify: 'the name of an area commander and his staff at a given time in a certain area.'[317] Monthly progress reports from X-2 Branch reveal that OSS officials had prepared a digest of interrogations of Dr Hermann Schmitz of I. G. Farben and supplied to R&A Branch:

---

312 'Progress Report on Preparation of Prosecution' 30 May 1945: Jackson Papers, op. cit. Box 101, Folder 7.
313 Ibid.
314 Ibid.
315 Ibid.
316 Ibid.
317 Ibid.

'excepts from preliminary Kaltenbrunner interrogation.'[318] Documentary evidence from overseas would be summarised, with the originals microfilmed and then sent back through air pouches.

The majority of OSS war crimes staff based in Washington would soon be sent to Paris and London to gather and analyse further evidence.[319] Donovan informed Jackson that OSS had sent Bill Whitney, a qualified British barrister, to liase with the London War Crimes Commission, various Allied intelligence agencies (CIOS), OSS field office staff in both London and Paris, and the British authorities more generally.[320] The resources of Allen Dulles' officers and intelligence files were being surveyed for potential trial evidence. These included former Gestapo official Han Gisevius: 'with intimate knowledge of its policies who has been secretly serving the United States for several years', and who was then being interrogated in Paris by Col. Amen.[321]

Justice Jackson's surviving office files contain his own copies of a series of R&A reports.[322] He had explicitly recognised both the prior expertise of OSS-R&A staff, and their commitment to this aspect of the case. This is clear from his decision to allocate officials from this organisation, including Lt Samuel Sharp, initial responsibility for preparing the trial brief on anti-Semitic persecution.[323] Interestingly, the R&A officials

---

[318] X-2 Branch Monthly Report of activities for June 1945, 3: US NA, RG 226, Entry 99, Box 120. Folders 1–2.

[319] 'Progress Report on Preparation of Prosecution' 30 May, 1945: Jackson Papers, op. cit. Box 101, Reel 7.

[320] Ibid.

[321] Ibid.

[322] Jackson Papers, op. cit. Box 101, Folder 7 containing for example, R&A 2577: 'problems concerning the treatment of war criminals, 28 September, 1944; R&A 3113 'Legal responsibility in connection with the Purge of 1934.'

[323] See Kaplan and Farr to Bernays, 'Preparation of the OSS case', 9 June 1945: LOC, Jackson Papers, Box 108: 'The trial briefs now being worked on fall under three general headings: (a) Domestic Crimes, (b) Crimes in Occupied Areas, and (c) The Plan for World Domination. The first two cover specific crimes and atrocities, the last will tie these in with the plan. (a) Under the heading Domestic Crimes, the following trial briefs are being prepared: (1) Persecution of the churches; (2) Persecution of the Jews; (3) Elimination of opposition in Germany.... (c) Under the heading The Plan for World Domination, a single trial brief will be prepared... 6. Lt. Schorske pointed out that some of the topics could be taken up in various ways. For example, persecution of the Jews could be taken up as an entity in a single brief, covering both the domestic treatment and the treatment in occupied areas, or the material could be spread over several trial briefs, the domestic material taken up in connection with briefs on occupation policies. The tentative plan is to deal with the whole subject as a single brief. 7. At the present, 18 people in R&A are working on the trial briefs and in addition some of the work has been circulated to outside experts. The following individuals are in charge of each

noted that, as already noted, they had made formal contact with the World Jewish Congress during the period in which they were preparing prosecution documentation, which was to be developed later in joint reports on the Nazis' persecution of Jews.[324]

Having discussed some elements of the process that underpinned the creation of postwar reports addressing aspects of the Holocaust, it is now appropriate to discuss relevant segments of these reports themselves. A series of R&A Reports on Nazi war crimes were specifically commissioned by Justice Jackson over the summer of 1945.[325] These were completed at Washington by the end of September 1945.[326] Earlier wartime R&A reports, including those mentioned above, were also extensively 'mined' in the production of postwar reports specially commissioned by Jackson, particularly the extensive series: 'Principle Nazi organisations involved in war crimes'.[327] It appears that, in preparing and supervising the production of these reports, Neumann and Irving Dwork, from the R&A's Jewish Desk, gathered materials not only from within the OSS but also State Department files, in Dwork's case these involved files 'treating with the Jewish Question.'[328]

There is a further example of a prosecution strategy report in which the commitment of OSS R&A personnel to ensure that the Holocaust was not entirely passed over in favour of atrocities committed on captured prisoners of war for example, is equally clear. This consists of their report on the 'Leadership Principle and Criminal Responsibility', completed in July 1945. Here, as in many other OSS-R&A reports on war crimes, general points are often illustrated by specific reference to the Nazis' extermination of Jews. For instance, Neumann's team specifically cited the mass killing of European Jews as a field where the practical

of the following trial briefs: a. Persecution of the churches—Thorman; b. Persecution of the Jews—Dwork; c. Elimination of political parties—Neumann...'

[324] See R&A Branch 'Monthly Progress Report', April 1945, 'contact with other agencies', NA RG 226, Entry 42, Box 1.

[325] See minutes of the prosecutor's meeting 11 August 1945, noting that full-time OSS staff were to work under either Storey or Amen, and 'work on projects to make studies and furnish us with the end results.' Jackson Papers, Box 107.

[326] R&A Progress Report, September 1945: US NA, RG 226, Entry 99, Box 12, Folder 1.

[327] R&A No. 3113, August 1945: a preliminary draft of which is available in the Cornell Collection, Vol. 106.

[328] They did always return these on time, leaving a documentary record: Burkhart to Pepin, OSS General Counsel, 25 September 1945: Dwork Papers: US NA, RG 200, Box 3, Folder 28.

relevance of the leadership principle could be turned back upon the Nuremberg defendants to bypass various legalistic defences. The latter included pleas of merely following 'superior orders', or claims of lack of proof that a particular defendant possessed the legally required level of subjective intent, or personal knowledge of specific atrocities:

> For example: If a general policy adopted on the highest level of leadership has been to the effect to 'eliminate all Jews from European life once and for all', and if in pursuance of such policy a large part of the Jewish population under Nazi rule has actually been exterminated, the acts of physical extermination may be attributed to all leaders and sub-leaders who, under the highest leadership, had functional and regional jurisdiction in connection with the implementation of the Jewish policies of the Nazi regime. All of them can be presumed to have known the Nazi program and the Nazi policies in this respect, all of them have used their positions to implement them, and all of them have known that in the execution of policy directives no legal restrictions would be observed. Whether or not under such conditions, they have been aware of the particular details of execution in specific cases, appears immaterial.[329]

The most wide ranging of the postwar R&A reports in the former category is entitled: 'Nazi Plans for Dominating Germany and Europe: 'The Master Plan Vol. I.'[330] With respect to the Holocaust, this specifically commissioned series for Jackson's organisation, provides, according to Katz:

> some of the most complete documentation then available on the magnitude of the catastrophe. The researchers at the R&A Branch now faced the task of explicating such an incomprehensible event... the criminal conspiracy to exterminate the European Jews... Having reported regularly on incidents of official violence and terrorism, on mass deportations... on the liquidation of the Polish ghettos, and on the network of concentration camps in Germany, the R&A scholars now attempted to establish for the Nuremberg prosecutors that these numerous acts had been elements of a single, indivisible crime.[331]

This extensive report attempts: 'to demonstrate the existence of a comprehensive Nazi plan for aggression, conquest, and domination in

---

[329] R&A 3110, 'Leadership Principle and Criminal Responsibility', 18 July 1945, 14–15: US NA, RG 238, Entry 52, Box 28.

[330] Dwork Papers, US NA, RG 200, Box 25. It was initially produced as a 12 June 1945 'Outline' report, followed up on 7 August 1945 with a more extensive 'draft' version.

[331] Katz, 1991 op. cit. 302.

Europe and even beyond Europe.' ('Draft' p. 1). As such, it includes the role played in this conspiracy by the Nazis' elimination of political, religious, and ideological opposition generally; and their extermination of the Jews in particular. The report is organised under a series of substantive headings that anticipated a number of offences soon to be formulated as the Nuremberg Charter of August 1945, including crimes against peace/waging aggressive war and the idea of a 'common plan'. These headings cover the Nazis' overthrow of democratic structures as: 'the first part of the plan for aggression.', and include sub-headings on the regime's: 'use of terror and violence' and: 'development of a plan for expansion'. This is followed by an account of the 'elimination of the opposition, and preparation for the war of aggression', under which the 'extermination of the Jews' is the second sub-heading. The final substantive heading is the 'criminal methods in the Nazi occupation policy.'

A component of this series, R&A 3114.2, 'Nazi Plans for Dominating Germany and Europe: Domestic Crimes,' (Draft for The War Crimes Staff, 13 August 1945), also merits discussion. This report into the Nazis' domestic crimes contains a large section on 'The Organization of Terrorism' (32–68), which includes a discussion of the manner and methods by which the Nazis instituted and executed systemic political terror within Germany before the outbreak of WWII. It addresses the distinct, yet related, actions of persecution the Nazi regime undertook against those it defined as its enemies, including the Jews, trade unions, political parties, religious organisations, and the free press. It also discusses various methods of institutional and legal persecution of these groups, including property confiscations and extermination in concentration camps, designed to enforce totalitarian control of the populace. The following quotation, which addresses those measures of Nazi legislation that needed to be immediately repealed upon Allied occupation, is material:

> In other cases there may not even be a question that a law—no matter how proper in form and enactment—cannot stand. In this latter category belongs the so-called racial legislation proper, especially the law for the Protection of German Blood and Honor (15 September 1935) and various decrees reducing the status of Jews to mere slaves.[332]

---

[332] R&A 3114.2, 26–27.

This R&A study also advocated that the Allies should invalidate such anti-Semitic measures from the start of their military occupation of Germany. This was necessary to remove immunity for those who acted according to its terms, including state attorneys and judicial officials. It even argued for the prosecution of: 'the small nucleus of persons principally responsible for its being put on the statute book and enforced.'[333]

A second subsidiary report within the more extensive series 'Nazi Plans for Dominating Germany and Europe' was entitled: 'R&A 3114.1, The Attitude of the NSDAP toward Political Terror, (Draft for Use of the War Crimes Staff, 9 July 1945).' This study records a catalogue of incidents of political terror and organised murder perpetrated by Nazi Party members and assorted minor operatives, both before the Nazi seizure of power in 1933 and shortly afterwards. It contains a listing of Nazi criminals and their German victims, including Jews killed merely because they were Jewish.

The second equally important series of R&A reports that Justice Jackson had commissioned are those relating to the criminal organisations. Before discussing the contents of these particular reports, it would be useful to review some preliminary work, debates and exchanges that underpinned them. Both in the preparation of OSS-R&A Reports and in specific research work for Jackson's organisation, Neumann advocated the view that the Allied authorities should take a particularly severe line against those organisations most closely associated with the persecution of European Jews, including the Waffen-SS. For example, on 21 May 1945, Neumann wrote a detailed analysis for James Donovan for submission to Jackson concerning the legal status of the Waffen SS. This organisation had, despite OSS/R&A previous objections, been exempted from Law No. 5 of the Military Government immediately dissolving the Nazi Party. This had represented a victory for the stance taken by officials within G3 section of the US Army, over the objections of both OSS-R&A staff and the Allied Psychological Warfare Board. The effect, which had already created controversy within the US press, was that Waffen SS officers had been treated as regular officers of the German army, and hence been allowed to retain their personal weapons and even orderlies. Neumann's analysis, informed as it was by his appreciation of the role of Waffen SS

[333] Ibid., 27.

Units in the Holocaust, was clearly aimed at including the Waffen SS as a 'criminal organisation' even before this category had been formally recognised by the Nuremberg Charter of August 1945:

> A legal case can be made for either position, but we doubt that the legal case had much significance. The Combat SS is part of the Army as much as it is part of the SS. This is documented in the following two German laws: Decree[s] of 17 October 1939 [and]...17 April 1940. [citing *Behemoth* 547]. These two decrees exempt the leadership of the SS and the Combat SS from the military jurisdiction of the German Army and establish SS Courts composed of SS men, with SS prosecutors...It follows, therefore, that although Combat SS formation were incorporated into larger army formations...they were nevertheless autonomous units within the armed forces. The SD (...Security Police) is exclusively an SS agency [citing *Behemoth* 545] in spite of the fact that may have swallowed the larger part of the OKW (...Armed Forces Counter-Intelligence) under Admiral Canaris.[334]

Neumann concluded that: 'one could consider indicting at once the whole SS and SD including the Combat SS', with the result that all members would lose privileges and be 'concentrated in camps'.[335]

Neumann's section identified as potential organisational defendants, the SS, SA, Party Press, Ministry of Interior: 'including the various branches of the Police', the Propaganda Ministry and the various High Commands of the Armed Services. They maintained that: 'proof must be established that in the course of conducting their campaigns these organizations and agencies authorized or executed the acts which violated international law'.[336] The inclusion of acts of 'authorization' were clearly designed to encompass acts of planning wartime policy that had taken place within the highest ranks of the military, political and Government organisations. The required type of proof was evidence that these organisations, or sub-divisions, had authorised or executed: 'atrocities and other crimes'; and: 'in doing so exercised a responsibility fully within the limits of their jurisdiction and as a result of an overall policy which directed or envisaged their commission.'[337]

---

[334] See Neumann to James Donovan, 'The Combat SS and War Crimes Trial', 21 May 1945, 2: US NA, RG 226, Entry 1, Box 2, Folder 6.

[335] Ibid.

[336] 'Outline of a Project—Principal Nazi Organizations Involved in War Crimes', R&A 3113, 31 May 1945, 12: US NA, RG 226, Entry 1, Box 2, Folder 7.

[337] Ibid., 15.

Presumably the authors' strategy here was to show that various atrocities were not the result of authorised acts committed randomly by a number of isolated mavericks exceeding their orders (for which no *organisational* liability could be legally attached). Instead, these acts had to be considered as forming an integral and necessary part of the methods designed to realise the Nazis' 'common plan'. The Neumann group argued that although the regime claimed to be abiding by international law, a number of statements of leading figures and various decrees including, for example, the 'total war of extermination' waged on the Eastern front, reveal that the opposite was the case. During a future trial, these should be quoted as: 'proving that the Germans themselves were conscious of the illegality of their actions.'[338] This report referred to the Neumann groups' earlier analysis of German occupation policies. This had emphasised not only the responsibilities of those organisations charged with the specific execution of such policies in the field, but also those of the administrative 'planners'.[339]

Furthermore, in a memo written during a period in which he was responsible for contributing draft indictments,[340] Neumann specifically pressed Justice Jackson and other senior prosecutors to widen the net of organisational defendants. He argued that: 'It appears politically and legally inadequate to indict only the SS, the SD and the Gestapo.'[341] He complained that the SS, which of course was the organisation primarily responsible for organising the genocide of European Jews, was grossly underrepresented, with Kaltenbrunner left as the sole defendant drawn from this organisation. The implication of Neumann's view was that Karl Wolff and other high-ranking SS officials merited inclusion as defendants in the upcoming Nuremberg trials.[342] He argued that the Nazi Party, 'the incarnation of Nazism', should also be included as a specific defendant, albeit defined in a narrow way to exclude merely

---

338 Ibid., 15.

339 R&A No. 2500 series: US NA, RG 153, Entry 135, Box 14.

340 Neumann's draft indictments against the Nuremberg defendants, which are marked 'rough draft unedited', are available at Cornell Collection, Vol. 19.

341 Neumann to Jackson, 'Indictment of Organisations' 14 September 1945, Cornell Law School, Vol. 19.

342 There is a reference to Karl Wolff in James Donovan's progress report to Justice Jackson as someone the OSS wanted prosecuted for his overall command responsibility for killing 15 OSS special operations forces (the so-called Ginny Mission): 'It is expected that sufficient material for trial of those involved (including Gauleiter [sic] Wolff should be available soon' 'Progress Report on Preparation of Prosecution' 30 May, 1945: Jackson Papers, op. cit. Box 101, Reel 7.

affiliated bodies and concentrate upon the leadership groupings: 'as defined by the Party itself.'[343]

Neumann appeared to be pressing Jackson on this point, possibly because Jackson had himself previously indicated that the list of defendants released to the public on 29 August 1945: 'could be added to at any time'. Jackson had noted: 'Since, for example, Kaltenbrunner is the only defendant on the present list to represent the Gestapo, it is likely that another name or names be added to provide adequate representation of that organisation.'[344] Wolff, however, who was Himmler's co-deputy, managed to escape prosecution, not least because of the interventions of Allen Dulles and his staff.[345]

Neumann's group made a specifically legal contribution involving the supervision of the preparation of final trial briefs generally and those relating to the six criminal organisations in particular. They even drew up draft indictments concerning the culpabilities of a number of the individual defendants.[346] As already noted, Neumann even supervised the OSS-R&A's draft prosecution brief against Göring, intended as a 'dry run' to test prosecution trial strategy.[347] Neumann's deputy within the OSS war crimes research unit, Henry Kellerman, personally obtained documentary evidence establishing the first clear linkage between the Nazi party and the notorious Kristallnacht ('crystal night') anti-Semitic attacks. He also attended interrogations establishing the involvement of the German Army in the Holocaust in Eastern Europe.[348]

Having reviewed elements of the institutional processes, actions and debates that underpinned the production of the R&A's postwar reports, it is now appropriate to discuss their contents in some detail, focusing once more upon how they characterised the Holocaust.

---

343 Ibid.

344 'Notes of a Staff Meeting', 31 August 1945: LOC, Jackson Papers, Box 110.

345 Salter, 2007 op. cit.

346 Hulme and Salter, 2002 op. cit. paras. 17–20, 28.

347 Ibid., para. 28. See also 'Progress Report on Preparation of Prosecution' 30 May, 1945: Jackson Papers, op. cit. Box 101, Reel 7: The test case will attempt to give immediate focus to the basic projects and will be continually revised as such projects develop. The first draft should be available within several weeks.' Ibid., p. 6.

348 H. Kellerman, 'Settling Accounts—the Nuremberg Trials', *Leo Baeck Yearbook*, Vol. XLII (1997) 337–55, 346.

The contents of postwar R&A reports relevant to the Holocaust

At this point, it makes sense to review the contents of the series R&A No. 3113. 'Principal Nazi Organizations involved in the Commission of War Crimes', June and August 1945. This extensive report merits close analysis to clarify the materials OSS R&A analysts contributed to the Nuremberg trials process. It contains a section on the 'extermination of the Jews', including references to relevant legislation, the 'question of what happened to the Jewish population' and the 'agencies responsible'. This report identifies the SS , the Rosenberg Ministry and the Reich Ministry of the Interior as the main agencies responsible; whilst also referring to the role this regime's 'Four Year Plan' played in the Holocaust to indicate the systematic and planned nature of such extermination.[349] This report highlights the domestic crimes of the Nazis, including the: 'division of the German citizenry on a racial basis and discrimination against those who were adjudged not to be of German blood.'[350] More directly, it recognises the: 'Destruction of racial minorities and political opponents through underfeeding; sterilization and castration; deprivation of livelihood, clothing, shelter, fuel, sanitation and medical care; deportation for forced labor; work under inhumane conditions.'[351]

This R&A study also addresses 'anti-Jewish policies', including: '(1) legal enactments: special attention will be given to the problem of whether and to what extent a predetermined plan was executed; and to the stages of its execution. (2) The fate of the Jews.'[352] It also grapples with various interpretive issues arising from the then state of international law (prior to the Nuremberg Charter of August 1945) which appeared to obstruct any prosecution for purely 'domestic' crimes against German Jews for example. Neumann's group recognised that a prosecution for the Nazis' pre-war domestic 'terrorism' against such civilians would be difficult unless it could be 'tied in' directly to the proposed 'common plan for world domination' charge. Establishing this connection within a future war crimes trial required a broadly functionalist interpretation of domestic atrocities and other terroristic actions against Jews. In other words, to interpret them as deliberate phases along

[349] At 19: US NA, RG 238, Entry 52 F, Folder 3113.
[350] Ibid., 22.
[351] Ibid., 23.
[352] Ibid., 24.

the path of 'the establishment of total control over Germany', with the latter defined as: 'merely a step in their aim to seize control of Europe and possibly of wider areas.'[353] With respect to proving this functional interpretation within a criminal trial, the authors argued that:

> It requires, however, an analysis of Nazi terrorism and a study of the attitude of the Nazi leaders towards acts of terror committed by subordinates. We shall have to prove—and we can—that already in the period prior to 1933 crimes were considered a necessary and desirable weapon in terrorising the opposition.... This conception of a basic plan for conquest determines also our selection of domestic crimes for analysis. They are: a. Establishment of rigid internal control over the government and all its agencies, religion, administration of justice, education, news dissemination, finance, commerce, industry, labor, and the professions. b. Destruction of all political opposition. c. Division of the German citizenry on a racial basis and discriminating against those who were adjudged not to be of German blood. d. Unlawful expropriation... e. Establishment and perpetuation of Nazi control through the total execution of the Fuhrer principle. f. Destruction of racial minorities and political opponents through underfeeding, sterilization and castration; deprivation of livelihood, clothing, shelter, fuel, sanitation, and medical care; deportation for forced labor; work under inhumane conditions.[354]

One part of this series, R&A report 3113.5, addresses: 'Agencies involved in the Commission of Crimes against Foreign Labor'.[355] The sub-agencies of the Nazi movement that were identified as responsible for domestic crimes were identified as: 'practically the whole Party and Government apparatus', including press and propaganda departments and professional associations. In varying degrees, these could be defined as potential war crimes defendants. However, the SS, SA and SD were particularly culpable, with Himmler's Office Group/Abt. D of the SS who were directly responsible for concentration and death camp atrocities, possessing a quite specific responsibility for domestic persecutions and extermination of Jews.[356] Eichmann worked this section of the SS. This report quotes Hitler's anti-Semitic rationalisation of the Holocaust:

---

[353] R&A 3113 'Outline of a Project—Principal Nazi Organizations Involved in War Crimes', 31 May 1945: US NA, RG 226, Entry 1, Box 2, Folder 7, 20.

[354] Ibid., 20–21.

[355] This was approved by OCC Prosecution Review Board on 3 August 1945.

[356] Ibid., 24.

> We are obliged to depopulate as part of our mission of preserving the German population. We shall have to develop a technique of depopulation. I mean the removal of entire racial units... Nature is cruel; therefore we too may be cruel. If I can send the flower of the German nation into the hell of war without the smallest pity for the spilling of precious German blood, then surely I have the right to remove millions of an inferior race that breeds like vermin.[357]

Another part of the same series, dated as approved by the Prosecution Review Board on 6 August 1945, is entitled simply 'The Gestapo', and contains considerably more material of direct relevance to the theme of this book.[358] Perhaps excessively, this extensive report devotes a full 26 pages to describing the Gestapo's legal basis, formal functions and personnel. It also addresses this criminal organisations' various responsibilities for the Holocaust. Hence, the author devoted a section addressing the 'Administration of Concentration Camps' (27–35), another to an analysis of this organisation's 'criminal responsibilities (36–43), whilst a third section (Appendix No. 3) supplies an: 'official document concerning the liquidation of prisoners.' However references to the complicity of the Gestapo in the Holocaust also pepper other sections of this paper produced by R&A's Dr Henry Kellerman, himself a German-Jewish émigré working in Neumann's Central European Section. For instance it states:

> The execution of Nazi racial policies comprised above all the implementation of the Nazi program to exterminate the Jews inside Germany and, later, in all German-occupied or German dominated Europe. Also included in this program were other such racially 'inferior' groups as gypsies, etc.... The Gestapo in the case of an occupied enemy country immediately followed the military forces and created special teams of Gestapo and SD agents, which could then... begin the round up of political opponents, Jews etc.... Whenever the Nazis invaded another country, the Gestapo was put in charge of "solving" the Jewish question, first with the idea of forcing the Jews to emigrate, later with the purpose of achieving their outright extermination. For this purpose special branches of the Gestapo were established, which on their face appeared as separate agencies not connected with the Gestapo organization, and which besides Gestapo agents, also comprised officials of other agencies connected with the handling of Jewish affairs... Illustrative of the activities of Gestapo offices in occupied territory, the following documents may be cited... an order [from 21 July 1944] by a Commander of Security Police and SD

[357] The source quoted is Hermann Rausschning, *Hitler Speaks*, 140.
[358] R&A Jewish Desk files: US NA, RG 226, RG 226, Entry 191, Box 2.

> to "liquidate"...Jews rather than permit them to be liberated by the advancing enemy.[359]

This report recounts the details of how Adolf Eichmann's sub-group, the Central Office for Jewish Emigration, which initially supervised the emigration of Austrian Jews, extended its remit into Prague and then into other occupied regions, where it took charge of: 'the organization of the mass deportations of the Jews of Europe to Polish ghettos and concentration camps.'[360] It also maps the complicated relationship of the Gestapo to other branches of the SS, including the Higher SS and Police Leaders, such as General Karl Wolff and their inspectors of Security Police and SD, which: 'laid down the regional policies for it and sometimes gave it immediate directives.[361] This report identified Eichmann's Office, the latter's offshoots and 'subordinate agencies' as the specific part of the Gestapo set up: 'to deal with the liquidation of the Jews.'[362] Branches of the SS responsible for the administration of concentration camps, including guard formations, although not formally an integral part of the Gestapo: 'were closely connected with its activities'. Equally, the SD (Political Intelligence section of the SS): 'cooperated intimately with the Gestapo in all phases of its activities.'[363] For example, the section addressing the role of the Gestapo with respect to concentration camps notes: 'For a victim to be detained in a concentration camp meant disappearance from ordinary life and deliverance to the absolute and arbitrary discretion of the Gestapo...Indeed the camps were used for whatever purposes and activity the Gestapo indulged in, from mere detention of political opponents to the mass extermination of Jews.'[364]

This R&A report also made an important distinction between 'ordinary' concentration camps, which existed primarily as slave labour camps for both SS and private enterprises, and those which were more appropriately termed death or extermination camps. In the former case, the maltreatment of inmates certainly: 'led to a high death rate and which in frequent cases was intended to lead to the death of particular inmates.' However, the decisive difference was that this type

[359] Ibid., 11–12, 23.
[360] Ibid., 23.
[361] Ibid., 25.
[362] Ibid.
[363] Ibid.
[364] Ibid., 28.

of concentration camp were: 'not conceived as extermination camps [built] for the purpose of killing all inmates.' By contrast, the Nazis' extermination camps had been created to allow either immediate, or temporarily delayed, exterminations to be carried out systematically on an industrial scale, and as the institutional culmination of a bureaucratic system geared to ensuring a constant supply of new victims:

> later camps came to be established which had the single purpose of being "annihilation" camps for ever-renewed waves of victims.... Extermination camps...most of them in Poland...were established in pursuit of a program starting in 1941 for the physical extermination of all European Jews. According to one source, the program was laid out by Adolf Eichmann, head of the Jewish desk in the central Gestapo Office, and adopted by his superiors leading up to Himmler and Hitler. While exterminations were at first done through mass shooting, it was found that it could be done more efficiently and economically and in a manner less noticeable to outsiders by [killing] in gas chambers large numbers of Jews assembled for this purpose in special camps. Deportation of Jews from the various parts of Europe was systematically organized under the central control of Aichmann [sic] and his staff, members of which followed the military forces into each newly-occupied country in order to start the segregation and eventual deportation of Jews. Special shipments by trains of sealed freight cars, which in themselves frequently constituted the means of exterminating large numbers of the transportees en route, were organized likewise by SS officers from the central Gestapo staff. In each case, a declaration or way-bill addressed to the commander of the extermination camps, had to be made out and handed to the train leader. Without such a letter or a specific order from Aichmann [sic], the commander was not authorized to kill the deportees on arrival. From the end of 1941 on, deported Jews were not killed indiscriminately. Those found capable of working were allowed to live as long as they could work under the inhuman conditions of the camp but were scheduled for eventual slaughter. Those too old, young, or feeble to work were gassed immediately.[365]

This study then considers the different types of criminal offences with which this organisation, and thereby its leading members, could be charged; and which possible legal defence arguments such individuals could then seek to rely upon. It recognises that, although the Gestapo had total immunity from judicial oversight, not even the Nazi regime was as brazen as to afford this organisation the right to engage in mass extermination guaranteed by a specific legal authority. Indeed, the secretive nature of the Nazis' actions implicitly recognised the extra-legality

[365] Ibid., 34–35.

of the Holocaust, and hence their own organisational and individual criminality:

> Wholesale extermination in the annihilation camps was perpetuated without even such flimsy attempts at excuse [by reference to established laws/decrees]. Such acts were kept secret as far as possible and their perpetration denied whenever an allegation was made... a person could be detained in a concentration camp for having made such statements. Such acts can therefore be prosecuted as murder, battery, assaults, libel, enforced prostitution and rape, theft (in the case of confiscations), or any other applicable provision of the German Penal Code.... Crimes committed outside Germany or within Germany against foreigners deported there are even more easily proved as punishable acts. Not only was German Gestapo law—with the exception of annexed territory...—never formally extended... but such acts were clearly violations of the international rules concerning the law of belligerent occupation. Indictments can therefore be based upon the penal laws of the countries concerned. As far as immediate executors of crimes are concerned, the location of their crimes will in most cases be easily found [often via Ultra decrypts held by X-2]. That location could establish which law was applicable.[366]

This report further argued that no members of the Gestapo should be allowed to escape punishment by pleading the defence of following 'superior orders', even with respect to questions of sentencing: 'officials and members of the Gestapo joined that organization voluntarily and therefore have to bear the consequences of their decision.'[367] It also addressed the issue of assigning responsibility for the Holocaust where it could not be proved when or whether Himmler or Hitler issued a direct and written order for this extermination to be carried out. Hence, this report relied, once again, upon the Nazis' own 'leadership principle', which—as already discussed—holds Nazi officials liable for all actions that take place within their own particular sphere of responsibility and jurisdiction, even where it cannot be proven who in practice was directly responsible for initiating them.[368] Clearly this approach was designed to counteract one of the possible defences that Eichmann or Kaltenbrunner, Chief of the SS RSHA, might try to deploy in any future trial. This report also counteracted the anticipated defence that senior Gestapo officials may, in some cases, have exercised some mercy in particular cases towards a 'prospective victim', especially towards the

[366] Ibid., 38–39.
[367] Ibid., 40.
[368] Ibid., 41.

latter stages of the war when military defeat became increasingly clear and the official in question was probably looking for some 'insurance' in the event of later prosecution.[369]

With respect to organisational liability under the Nuremberg Charter allowing members to be convicted of war crimes on the basis of their voluntary membership alone, the author of this study claimed that, despite its origins as a special unit of the conventional police force of Prussia: 'The Gestapo can certainly be included among such organizations.' The report argues that most members came into this agency from pre-existing Nazi Party affiliated organisations, including the SS, and that: 'their membership in itself can therefore be considered as participation in a vast conspiracy.' This was because members of this organization can be taken to have prior knowledge of its criminal purposes, including anti-Semitic persecution.[370] Prosecution of the perpetrators of the Holocaust under this form of criminal liability could, it was argued, also be combined with: 'prosecution for pertinent crimes of those persons who can be shown to have participated in the commission of such crimes.'[371]

Within weeks of this report, one of Neumann's subordinates, Herbert Marcuse (later to become famous as inspiration for the revolutionary students' movement and new left in the late 1960's) supplied the prosecutors with important follow up material. This consisted of detailed and closely footnoted analyses of the Gestapo's origins, unlimited 'legal' powers and repressive functions. These included the inability of its victims to mount a legal challenge to its powers of detention in concentration camps, and the various repressive and murderous activities that its officials carried out in such camps.[372]

The next part of the series that needs to be discussed is R&A No. 3113.7, 'Principal Nazi Organizations Involved in the Commission of War Crimes: The Nazi Party (Parts I-5)' (Draft for the Use of the War Crimes Staff') 10 September 1945. This represented a lengthy series of studies addressing the formation, organization, principles, and aims of the Nazi Party, and how these elements coalesced in a programme that included totalitarian control and war crimes. It provides descriptions,

[369] Ibid., 41.
[370] Ibid., 42–43.
[371] Ibid., 43.
[372] 'Gestapo', Marcuse to Burkhardt, 31 August 1945: OSS Director's Files, US NA, RG 226, M1642, Roll 120.

supported by specific examples, identifying those Nazi organizations and agencies responsible for implementing different aspects of war criminality. These include key elements of the Holocaust, such as anti-Semitic citizenship requirements and discriminatory racial laws, and the expulsion and ultimate extermination of Jews and others. It notes that the party programme from 1920 expressly envisaged: 'Establishment of citizenship on racial grounds [and hence] the expulsion of Jews... Fight against Jewish-materialist spirit'.[373] This report also notes that: 'most of these postulates have been realized.'[374] The programme had been achieved partly through: 'the division of the German citizenry on a racial basis'; 'unlawful expropriation, spoliation and forced sale [of Jewish assets]' and: 'extermination of racial, ethnic and religious minorities'.[375] It attributed early anti-Semitic policies and 'laws', such as the Nuremberg Laws of 1935 and related provisions authorising anti-Semitic plunder by a decree of 1 March 1942, to the highest levels of the Nazi Party leadership, Hitler's own office.[376]

This report also noted the complicity of specific levels of the Party in anti-Semitic programmes. For example, it highlighted the role of Gauleiters in cooperating with the Gestapo and SS: 'in the preparation and execution of the action against the Jews in November 1938, when synagogues were burned, properties invaded and looted, and persons beaten up and arrested in pursuance of a concerted Party action.'[377]

Part 4 of this series on the Nazi Party, dated 24 July 1945, consists of a highly detailed study of the institutional structures and histories of prominent Nazi 'formations', including those directly involved in the Holocaust such as the SS, SD and Gestapo. It sets out and analyses the institutional responsibilities for Nazi racial theory, concentration camps, and the Germanisation, exploitation and extermination of native populations. In order to indicate the probable extent of war crimes complicity, it identifies the respective heads of each formation's numerous subdivisions, describes their respective spheres of duty (and hence legal accountability), and discusses their main activities. Although highly detailed and comprehensive in terms of the totalitarian institutional relations of Nazi organization and their wide scope and reach

---

[373] At 5.
[374] Ibid.
[375] Ibid., 6.
[376] Ibid., 13, cf. 20.
[377] Ibid., 110 citing teletypes issued by Heydrich, 9–10 November 1938.

into all areas of civil society, it was mainly designed as a background guide for the Nuremberg prosecutors, rather than as a prosecution brief in its own right.

As already noted, this R&A report analyses different formations of the Nazi party including the German Labour Front. The latter was shown to have actively contributed to aspects of the Holocaust by excluding Jews from its welfare schemes, as well as engaging in the: 'indoctrination of labor in racial questions.' Education bodies affiliated to the Nazi party also stand accused of practising anti-Semitic racist 'indoctrination' of school students under the guise of 'racial science', not least through: 'the selection of teaching materials conducive to racial hatred and discrimination.' This report also highlighted the anti-Semitic practices of Nazi agencies responsible for agricultural affairs, including anti-Semitic Entailed Farm Legislation, which excluded 'non-Aryans' from the benefits of entailed status. The resulting redistribution operated as a: 'political weapon to achieve a redistribution of farms to persons of ascertainable political reliability':

> Food was also used as a weapon to enforce conformity to German occupation rule. In the incorporated eastern territories, for example, the "loyal Poles" were given the same rations as the Germans while other non-Germans and Jews got about one half of the amounts allotted to the former groups....the withholding of food...was a deliberate policy for the slow starvation of thousands of conquered people.[378]

Another series of R&A reports, which were originally started during 1944 but in some cases revised in the summer of 1945, are entitled: R&A No. 2500 'German Military Government Over Europe'. One part of this series, 'Economic Controls in Occupied Europe' (R&A 2500.15, 28 August 1945), merits particular discussion. As a potential input to the prosecution's 'economic case', to which a series of other R&A reports made a modest contribution,[379] it addresses aspects of

[378] Ibid., 37.

[379] Three in particular are relevant here: R&A No. 3093 'Nazi Changes in the Law of Real Property', (17 June 1945), which discusses the Nazis' confiscation of Jewish assets and the discrimination against Jews holding real and commercial property. R&A No. 3081: 'Nazi Changes in Criminal Procedure', a study outlining aspects of the Nazis' legal disenfranchisement and institutionalised discriminatory treatment of cases involving Jews and Poles. Finally, R&A 3092, 'Nazi inheritance law' 16 July 1945, examines the impact of Nazi policies of anti-Semitism, racial theory and other elements of its ideological programme upon pre-Nazi laws regarding marriage, divorce, adoption and inheritance.

anti-Semitic 'Aryanization', forced labour, and other economic facets of the Nazis' persecution of Jews as an integral part of a wider programme. The authors' 'abstract' summarises this clearly:

> This study treats the direct and indirect methods used by the Germans in controlling, managing, and exploiting the economies of the countries occupied by them before and during the war. In examining the German economic techniques, an effort is made to determine the political objectives behind the various types of economic exploitation.[380]

The main body of the report recognised how Czech Jews running enterprises suffered disproportionately from German business firms penetrating the Protectorate. Such economic penetration was assisted by German agencies deploying both legal and illegal means, including employing: 'the aryanization of Jewish property.' Within Poland, this study noted that whilst: 'the property of the Polish state was transferred to the General Government; Jewish property was sold outright.' A similar pattern was detected with respect to Serbia:

> The "aryanization" of Jewish enterprises was another instrument for the penetration of German business into Serbia. A census of Jewish property was taken and formed the basis of its liquidation with the help of the State Mortgage Bank. The proceeds were taken over by the German military...The disposal of Jewish property was considered important because of its effects on the future economic structure of the country; it was reported that Göring cooperated directly in this matter.[381]

This report also recognised the Nazi regime's 'aryanization' of enterprises in France, including confiscation of Jewish-owned shares.

In short, during the immediate postwar months and working under severe time and logistical restraints and pressures, the Central European Section of the R&A Branch contributed reports on different facets of the Holocaust. Certain of these fleshed out key elements of the prosecutor's wider strategy, linked to the novel 'criminal conspiracy' model, as well as more specific reports setting out the case against organisational defendants, including the Gestapo and the Nazi party. In total, the R&A Branch supplied Justice Jackson with many thousands of pages of extremely detailed analysis of Nazi war crimes, in which different aspects of the Holocaust featured in a significant way. These

---

[380] Ibid.
[381] Ibid., 69.

included the economic exclusion, expropriation and discrimination against Jews, as well as acts of anti-Semitic plunder, detention, forced labour and ultimately physical extermination. The responsibilities of different branches of the SS, including the Gestapo, were discussed extensively, including those of Eichmann's section.

The significance and deployment of R&A reports: the work of the Neumann research group

The importance of the R&A's work in preparing the organisational cases is clear from the following internal memorandum to Bernays, which argues for a structural link to be made between specific and more general institutional analysis of the Nazi state in order to better explain anti-Semitic crimes:

> As indicated in the outline submitted with the OSS Progress Report of 31 May, R&A is doing extensive work on establishing the individuals and organisations responsible for the various crimes charged. One section of each trial brief will be devoted to the individuals and organisations guilty of the offences dealt with in that brief. It seems to us that at some point in the trial it may be necessary to prove the entire structure of the German state and the place where each of the organisation defendants fits into that structure. Thus, we think that it is not enough to show, for example, that the SS is guilty of such crimes as the persecution of the Jews, political murders, and spoliation in occupied areas without at some time proving just what the SS is and its place in the state structure. We recognize the difficulty of such a task in view of the constant charges made in the state structure and its rather fluid character. The set-up in 1934 doubtless differed greatly from the set-up in 1941. But it would seem necessary to prove the general organizational structure at some point of time. Apparently R&A does not contemplate preparing a separate brief on this point but expects the picture to emerge from the various trial briefs. Perhaps we can tell better what would be done along this line after we have examined the first trial briefs.[382]

Senior Nuremberg prosecutors who had reviewed the OSS R&A reports on Nazi Germany and its occupation policies that Neumann supplied, commented that they were most useful background studies. Although not

---

[382] Memorandum To Colonel Bernays, from Benjamin Kaplan, Lt. Col., G.S.C. and Warren F. Farr, Major, J.A.G.D., 9 June 1945: 'Preparation of OSS Case', Jackson Papers, op. cit. Box 108. This quotation is taken from the sub-heading of 'Structure of defendant organisations and German state.'

always directly 'evidentiary' in the manner of a prosecution brief against an individual defendant, they nevertheless contained: 'a considerable amount of evidence buried in them, as [Murray] Bernays suggested and [Telford] Taylor agreed.'[383] Indeed, senior prosecutors regarded them as such a rich source that the services of one of the senior R&A analysts was needed to assist with their interpretation, explanation and selective extraction for prosecution briefs. Hence, it remained the case, that most R&A Reports needed to be extensively supplemented with more detailed and specific evidence linking individuals to particular war crimes, which was available only within continental Europe. Whilst some of this material was supplied from internal OSS sources, many of which have already been discussed, a considerable quantity stemmed from the Allied Armies and Navies.

These various R&A reports also proved useful as guides for members of the Interrogation Division of Jackson's organisation, headed by Colonel Amen. Indeed, internal OCC correspondence indicates that 'Colonel Amen' had appointed: 'a group of men scrutinising the [R&A] studies to get out of them what will be useful to interrogators.'[384] However, by mid-August 1945, and with the future of the OSS itself in doubt, Jackson decided against commissioning any fresh R&A Reports. Instead, he directed OSS and other staff to concentrate on their supplementation with additional documentary and other eyewitness evidence that was only available from continental Europe.[385]

Having discussed a number of the postwar reports, it is now time to examine the subsequent role played by a number of the analysts who wrote them in Neumann's group of research analysts, who sought to ensure their optimal exploitation at Nuremberg during the frantic preparation of the final draft of prosecution briefs. Prior to his leadership of the OSS war crimes research unit, Neumann had been a senior OSS analyst and intellectual leader of a small Central European Section of this agency's interdisciplinary R&A Branch, a number of whose wartime reports have already been discussed. Neumann's role within the Nuremberg process as 'First Chief of Research' for the US prosecution office, had developed from his earlier responsibilities as head of a specially created OSS 'war crimes unit' attached to Jackson's

[383] Minutes of prosecutors meeting 11 August 1945, op. cit.
[384] Ibid.
[385] Ibid.

organisation.[386] Between May and November 1945, during the build up to the Nuremberg trials, the OSS leadership selected Neumann to lead this organisation's 'top-flight' constituency of researchers within the wider interagency partnership that comprised Jackson's prosecution office.[387] At its core, this OSS grouping included a remarkable German-Jewish group of émigré research analysts, including Otto Kirchheimer, and Herbert Marcuse associated with the Frankfurt School of critical social theory. As already noted, and working with Ben Kaplan from Jackson's organisation, members of this OSS unit helped prepare the *most legally innovative* parts of the war crimes prosecution strategy, such as the case against Nazi organisations,[388] and the application of the all-encompassing 'conspiracy' charges to pre-war domestic persecutions, including the Nazis' early anti-Semitic programmes.[389]

Franz Neumann made considerable efforts to have the considerable expertise of his own sub-section of R&A employed as senior consultants within the war crimes process. In this, he was successful. The expertise of Neumann's R&A specialists remained in great demand from Colonels Amen, Bernays, and Story, each of whom insisted that Neumann's group should be attached exclusively to their section of Jackson's organisation.[390] '[E]ach maintains that his work is vital and each maintains that he controls documents which have to be evaluated.'[391] Neumann realised that he was, therefore, in a strong bargaining position as to both the *type* of work his section would be willing to perform, and for which particular section of Jackson's organisation. He exploited this relative

[386] See minutes of prosecutors meeting 11 August 1945, noting that the Neumann group should: 'stay here in the capacity of a consultant to the lawyers who are analysing the R&A studies and trying to put them into evidentiary form.': Jackson Papers, Box 107.

[387] 'War Crimes Program': US NA, RG 226, Entry 37, Box. 6; 'War Crimes' Correspondence May–July 1945; US NA, RG 226, Entry 1, Box 2; 'R&A/Europe-Africa Division progress report', May 1945: US NA, RG 226, Entry 42, Box 1.

[388] See R&A 3113, 'Outline of Project: Principal Nazi Organisations Involved in War Crimes', 6 June 1945: US NA, RG 238, Entry 52f, Box 28; Kellerman, 1997 op. cit. 339–40.

[389] Alderman *et al.*, 'Memorandum for Mr Justice Jackson', 15 August, 1945: LOC, Jackson Papers, Box 107 (recording the attempt by Jackson's senior staff to appropriate the Neumann group: 'It is felt that Neumann and the following selected persons [Kellerman, Marcuse, Eisenberg] who have assisted him heretofore should be put full-time on the staff…and that they should be assigned to Colonel Kaplan on the aspect of the case which he is preparing'.

[390] The next few paragraphs draw heavily upon material I contributed to Hulme and Salter, 2002 op. cit.

[391] Neumann to Kent, 3 August 1945, 1: US NA, RG 226, Entry 1, Box 2, Folder 7.

strength by flatly rejecting Bernays' demand that the R&A specialists on Nazi Germany be simply assimilated in Colonel Bernays' London team. This team was engaged in: 'merely documentary work...abstracting and evaluating whatever documents come in.'[392] Neumann insisted that his specialists would be better deployed in more senior positions 'writing papers', presumably on the strategic and planning aspect of the case. This counterproposal was initially rejected by Bernays, who may, with good reason, have regarded Neumann as a powerful rival in such strategic matters:

> I explained that under no circumstances would I do this work nor would I request the transfer of the [R&A] personnel for this purpose nor would I ever get them over from Washington for this purpose. His answer was that under these circumstances he did not see that I could do anything at all, a reply that made me quite happy. However, in the course of the discussion he retracted, and accepted my view.[393]

Thus, it was clear to both sides of this internal debate that Bernays needed the contribution of Neumann's team more than this team needed Bernays' support. The result of this fraught negotiation was that Bernays had to accept Neumann's request. Having overplayed his hand, Bernays was even forced to agree to Neumann's strong criticism of the organisational failings of his office, including their inadequate use to date of the various R&A reports already commissioned by Justice Jackson. Bernays agreed to assign Lt. Atherton to redress this perceived failing point, to 'start real work' as Neumann expressed it with characteristic self-assurance.[394]

A memorandum from an informal staff meeting involving Telford Taylor, Alderman, Benjamin Kaplan, and Deinard, presented Jackson with the following request: 'It is felt that Neumann...Kellerman, Marcuse, and Eisenberg...who have assisted him hitherto should be put full-time on the staff of the Chief of Counsel and that they should be assigned to Colonel Kaplan on the aspect of the case which he is preparing.'[395] This meant that Neumann's team were assigned to Colonel Kaplan's small team preparing the criminal organisation charges, which consisted of Farr, Johnston, and Murray.[396]

---

[392] Ibid.
[393] Ibid.
[394] Ibid.
[395] 'Memorandum for Mr. Justice Jackson', 15 August 1945: Ibid.
[396] Ibid.

Neumann was also included amongst the personnel who formed part of Jackson's 'advance party' to London and Paris to help prepare for the planned trials.[397] In late July 1945, Jackson appointed Neumann to the specially created post of 'First Chief of Research' for the US prosecution team within Europe. This post had wide-ranging and largely self-defined responsibilities for gathering and assessing evidence of Nazi war criminality within Europe, including persecution based on religion and race.[398] In August 1945, routing himself via Paris, Neumann travelled to Biebrich in Wiesbaden, where the OSS had established their central office for Germany.[399] Here, and later at Nuremberg itself, he helped prepare and supervise a series of indictments against the Nuremberg defendants, with other OSS colleagues responsible for both interrogation and document analysis. Stuart Hughes, who worked as both an interpreter and historical adviser within the OSS sub-section, recalls: 'the staff of experts the omniscient Franz Neumann was assembling for the great trial', and his own supporting role for the US prosecution office in: 'extract[ing] affidavits about the late regime's atrocities from leading anti-Nazi Germans.'[400]

During a pre-trial planning meeting held on 11 August 1945, the senior prosecutors noted that Neumann should: 'stay here [London] in the capacity of a consultant to the lawyers who are analysing the R&A studies and trying to put them into evidentiary form.'[401] Jackson specifically requested that Neumann's expertise was vital to his senior Nuremberg prosecutors. Hence, he was to: 'act in an advisory

[397] Aronson, 1998 op. cit. 267. He was supported by Walter Doer. OSS Washington based R&A contested the depletion of their senior staff for war crimes projects, particularly when Henry Kellerman, John Herz and Eisenberg was added to the group to travel to Europe in late July 1945: Langer to Kent, 'personnel for war crimes work overseas', 16 July 1945: US NA, RG 226, Entry 37, Box 4, Folder: Langer.

[398] Katz, 1989 op. cit. 55–59. This caused resentment amongst other senior prosecutors allocated less discretion to choose their own job specifications.

[399] See Director's Office and Field Station Records, War Crimes Commission May–August 1945; US NA, RG 226, Entry 190, Box 283, Folder 1244; OSS Mission to Germany August 1945: US NA, RG 226, Entry 190, Box 284 Folder 1247; OSS Mission to Germany, August 1944–May 1945; US NA, RG 226, Entry 190, Folders 1251–1253; OSS Mission to Germany October 1944–April 1945; US NA, RG 226, Entry 190, Box. 286, Folder 1266. For more recently declassified sources, see 'Security-Classified Correspondence of the OSS Mission to Germany 1944–1945: US NA, RG 226, Entry 81, Boxes 1–3.

[400] S. Hughes, 1990 op. cit. 176, 175. This evidence included a deposition from Theodor Heuss, who four years later was to be elected the first President of the Bonn Republic.

[401] Ibid.

capacity explaining [R&A] studies etc.'[402] Partly with reference to these R&A reports, Jackson noted that: 'OSS did excellent work of laying foundation [for the case] and there is still room for valuable OSS contribution.'[403]

Neumann complained to his superiors in R&A Washington that OSS' London Field Office had not yet received a full quota of R&A war crimes reports. Although these reports were in use within Jackson's own office, work was being seriously hampered by a shortage of sufficient copies. He requested that this shortfall of R&A Reports be corrected through the assistance of James Donovan, with Alan Evans playing a co-coordinating role between OSS London and Jackson's office.[404]

There is a vital piece of evidence illustrating the importance Neumann attached to ensuring that the Nuremberg prosecutors received the best available evidence that the OSS had gathered on the Holocaust and related Nazi war crimes. It is a long memorandum from Neumann in London to OSS/R&A Washington.[405] It identifies the wide range of reports relevant to the prosecution of Nazi war criminals which the OSS-R&A Central European subsection had produced. It also reveals Neumann's personal commitment to making sure that these studies were fully distributed amongst the relevant US prosecutors directing them towards those aspects of the case where they could would be of greatest benefit. Neumann thus actively campaigned for the greater use of all OSS/R&A war crimes materials by Jackson's office, and personally arranged for their transportation to the prosecution team.

Given the aims of the present book, it is worth reproducing the sections of this memo to both identify and give an adequate impression of the wide range of topics that had previously been analysed by OSS/R&A that were considered relevant to the preparation of prosecution briefs. Far from underplaying the systematic mass murder of European Jews, as some of his critics have alleged,[406] Neumann specifically requested that additional R&A and other OSS reports relevant to the Holocaust be supplied to Jackson's advance party in London. These related to the war crimes committed by SS and associated security and paramilitary forces within Nazi-occupied Europe, including of course

[402] Whitney to Neumann, 14 August 1945: Jackson Papers, op. cit. Box 111.
[403] Ibid.
[404] Ibid.
[405] NND750178: US NA, RG 226, Entry 146, Box 37, Folder 493.
[406] See Michael Salter, 2000 op. cit.

the extermination of civilians. As the following list of required reports shows, Neumann asked for multiple copies of OSS material directly relevant to the Holocaust to be transmitted to selected members of Jackson's staff:

MATERIAL TRANSMITTED TO WAR CRIMES—LONDON[407]

Doc. no.	Title			
Addendum to R&A 3113.1		6/28/45	Reg. Pouch	2
–	15 copies of R&A 2500 "German Military Government over Europe: Western Territories incorporated into the Reich".	8/14/45	Lt Col Seay	
–	5 copies of R&A 2500.10 German Military Government over Europe: the General Government.	8/20/45	Lt Heller	
–	Fifteen copies R&A No. 5114.3 (part one) Nazi Plans for Dominating Germany and Europe, the Criminal Conspiracy against the Jews, Draft for the War Crimes Staff copy numbers 16–30, copy no. 16 is a master copy.	8/20/45	Lt. Heller	
R&A 3113.6	"Gestapo" 15 copies; copy nos 12 to 26 inc. German Military Government Over Europe: Slovakia	18/10/45	Lt. George Demas	
R&A no. 2577.2	Problems concerning the Treatment of War Criminals under proposed US Policy Directives.			
2500.4	The right of political refugees to Asylum in non-belligerent countries.			
1844	Concentration camps in Germany			
1298	The scope and activities of the National Socialist Party in the German Reich.			
F.M.257	Testimony of two escapees from Auschwitz-Birkenhau extermination camp at Oswiecim, Poland			

[407] NND750178: US NA, RG 226, Entry 146, Box 37, Folder 493.

–	Senate Document no. 47—Atrocities and other conditions in concentration camps in Germany.			
–	War Crimes Prosecutions Planning Memorandum dated 17 May 1945.			
–	Memorandum on Trial preparation dated	16 May 1945.		
3113	Principal Nazi organisations involved in war crimes.			
2057	The major German cartel 1930–1944.			2
3114	Nazi plans to dominate Europe			13
–	Organisations responsible for Nazi crimes—Analyses of the changes in certain principles of the family and inheritance law of Germany since 1933 (A draft)			
–	R&A 3113.5 Agencies involved in the Commission of crimes against foreign labor.	8/7/45	Lt. Maley	
–	Memo "Nazi changes in Real Property Law and in family and inheritance law" (Supplementation of OSS Memoranda R&A 3095)	8/7/45	Lt. Maley	
–	R&A 3113.7 "the Nazi Party I and II" Copies #33,34 thru 48 less 44 copy 33 went via Lt. Flisser.	8/7/45	Lt. Maley	
–	Leadership Principle, R&A 3110 copies 16–35.	8/1/45	Lt. Flisser	
–	R&A 3114.5 copies 34–48	8/1/45	Lt. Flisser	
–	Germany, Discriminatory laws, copy no. 37	7/17/45	Lt. Sprecher	
–	R&A 2465	7/17/45	Lt. Sprecher	
–	Supplement to R&A 3152 and 3113.1	7/17/45	Lt. Sprecher	
–	R&A 3114.5	7/17/45	Lt. Sprecher	
–	15 copies of R&A 2500.10 German military Government over Europe. The Gen'l Gov't.	8/20/45	Lt. Heller	
–	NDSPA dated March 1945	8/7/45	Lt. Maley	
–	Three copies (ea.) same as above to the attn of Dr. Neumann.	8/8/45	Cpt. Brincherhoff	

	Cover page Fifteen copies cover page for R&A 3114.8	8/25/45	McDonnell	15
R&A 3114.8	"Nazi plans for dominating Germany and Europe Agencies involved in the commission of crimes against foreign labor.			
3114.2	Five copies of R&A 3114.2, Nazi Plans for Dominating Germany and Europe—Domestic Crimes. Draft for the war crimes staff. (copies 27 through 31).	8/27/45	McDonnell	5
3114.2	Fourteen copies of R&A 3114.2 Nazi plans for dominating Germany and Europe—Domestic crimes. Draft for the war crimes staff. (copies 14 through 25 and 32 and 33).	8/27/4	Sackett	14
–	American Jewish Conference pp. 98–107	6/18/45	J. B. Donovan	1
–	Information memo. #3 dated 10 July 1945 R&A 3172.3 and # 3172.4 Miscellaneous memo. on war criminals, (with attached memorandum from J. L. McDonnell (copies no. 1 each) This document is addressed to Cmdr. Donovan and is to be opened by him only.	7/17/45	Lt. Sprecher	

Neumann's list of relevant OSS R&A reports emphasised the liabilities of Himmler's SS. It included the joint research his own R&A Branch colleagues had completed with Jewish organisations. He also included his own Behemoth (2nd ed., 1944), as well as Arthur Koestler's *Darkness at Noon*, a grim account of Nazi atrocities against Jews and other groups, both for the attention of James Donovan.

It appears that the involvement of the Neumann group of R&A specialists ended on a bitter note. In late October 1945, shortly before the major trial began, Neumann resigned from the OSS-R&A team supervising Nuremberg prosecution briefs. He was replaced as First Chief of Research by his OSS deputy Henry Kellerman, another German-Jewish émigré. Together with other CES staff, Neumann resigned largely because of the hostility shown by various American lawyers, who bitterly resented having their work overseen and corrected by OSS' Jewish-German émigrés. This resentment was unmitigated by the American lawyers' general lack of skills in the German language, and ignorance of the internal organisational structures of the Nazi regime.[408] John Herz's memoir of his time as part of the Neumann group at Nuremberg recalls that the American lawyers were supposed to be working on legal cases involving completely different legal systems, about which they had no idea. Neumann's group of OSS research analysts were there to assist and offset the resulting difficulties:

> [B]ut anyone who possessed the minimum of psychological insight knew that this would not look good. Allowing young, and in addition to that, Jewish, little upstarts to look over their papers injured the gentlemen officers' egos.[409]

The evidence presented in this section suggests that the criticism of Neumann's personal activities and the implications of his spearhead model of Nazi anti-Semitism is largely misplaced. There are considerable reasons for endorsing Katz's judgement relating to the role of the R&A group over the criticisms of Aronson and Bigman:

> Despite allegations regarding their inaction, the Central European scholars of R&A did attempt to monitor the fate of the European Jews.... OSS'... R&A sheltered a community of American and European refugee scholars who helped to keep the fate of Europe's Jews from disappearing entirely from the American military and diplomatic agenda. The record of the OSS in regard to the Nazi program of genocide is not, in the final analysis, particularly impressive, but it is a far cry from the ignorance and indifference that prevailed elsewhere in the US Government.[410]

The Dwork Papers and the R&A Jewish Desk's contribution to the Nuremberg prosecutors

We have already had reason to refer in passing to the fruits of the research activities of the two person R&A Jewish Desk, headed by Dr Irving Dwork and assisted—on a part-time basis—by Abraham Duker.

---

408 Kellerman, 1997 op. cit. 346–7.

409 Herz, 1984 op. cit. 140: Private translation.

410 B. Katz, 'The Holocaust and American Intelligence' in *The Jewish Legacy and the German Conscience*, Rischin and Asher (eds), Berkeley, CA: Judah L. Magnes Museum, 1991, 300, 297.

The following section will focus on the role this Unit played in converting the results of research into the Holocaust largely as it was taking place, into the types of documentation of direct relevance to the Nuremberg prosecutors. These included the creation of a draft trial brief and a series of summaries of the complicities in the Holocaust of each of the 24 defendants belatedly selected by Justice Jackson in time for their inclusion in the formal indictment scheduled for October 1945.

It was General Donovan who created this specialist part-time unit within the OSS R&A Branch, and appointed two staff members who were politically committed to monitoring and exposing crimes against European Jewry, which they interpreted as a specifically genocidal campaign.[411] This unit lacked high-level intelligence clearance, and was not, therefore, familiar with certain 'top secret' evidence gathered by OSS Secret Intelligence and X-2 Branches based upon original copies of electronic intercepts and decrypts.[412] One cluster of the war crimes evidence Duker and Dwork gathered, which is largely preserved together in the US National Archives, consists of 146 folders of records, with fifty-two folders stemming from the German Embassy, Bucharest. This collection includes documents this OSS unit received from other agencies, including the records of the Assistant Secretary of War, the State Department, and the U.S. Office of Censorship.

Duker and Dwork also obtained a range of private papers and publications in French, German, and English that focus upon the Nazis' treatment of Jews during World War II.[413] A second grouping of materials that illustrates the extent to which Duker and Dwork monitored Nazi atrocities against European Jews is contained in the official R&A files. This second cluster contains a wider range of OSS reports: including 'Concentration Camps, Germany'; 'Axis Concentration Camps and Detention Centers in Europe-Basic Handbook', 'Jews in Hungary' (R&A Report 2027, 29 October 1944) and 'Buchenwald Concentration Camp' (24 April 1945, 12 Army Group). This collection also contains additional accounts of atrocities against Hungarian and Polish Jews;

[411] A. G. Duker's position is clear from his piece. 'The War to Annihilate the Jews—The Second Phase.' 12 *Reconstructionist* (November 1, 1946): 10–16. [Arguing absurdly that British policy in Palestine treats the Jews little differently than had Nazi Germany.]

[412] Aronson, 1998 op. cit.

[413] The collection is US NA, RG 200 entitled the Irving Dwork Papers, and is summarised at: http://www.ushmm.org.

and a file of war crimes evidence dated October 1944 from Dulles' OSS-Bern field station. It further includes reports on the 'Conspiracy Against the Jewish People, Germany, 1933–1944' and an 'OSS Report on Rescue Work [for Jewish refugees]' 25 October 1944.[414]

Taken together, the 'Dwork Papers' (originally removed at the end of the war) and the remainder that had always comprised part of the OSS files within the US National Archives in Washington, this collection: 'represents probably the largest single cluster of OSS information about the Holocaust.'[415] It contains an eloquent plea for assistance, made by a member of the Jewish-Polish resistance, stating that extermination was taking place in the Warsaw Ghetto, conveyed to the OSS by Jan Karski.[416]

The Dwork Papers are an underused aspect of the OSS records. For accidental reasons related to their classification, they fall outside the scope of NARA record group 226, the normal hunting ground for OSS researchers. They consist of drafts and working notes and supportive materials that, in essence, amount to a massively extended prosecution brief related to the liability for the Holocaust of most of the Nuremberg defendants, and others that perhaps could and should have been prosecuted for their complicity in this genocide in other postwar trials.

The authors of this collection clearly took very seriously the idea of mapping a mass of evidence, including media accounts, reports from Jewish agencies and otherwise unremarkable OSS documentation related to Nazi-occupied Europe, with a series of anticipated criminal charges. Hence, material relating to the step by step escalation in the intensity of the Nazis' persecution of European Jews is classified under the headings that formed part of the OSS-OCC memorandum of trial preparation as later amended. The guiding idea it seems was to supply material that the prosecutors could easily 'slot into' their wider prosecution briefs. These related, for example, to slave labour, the creation of a dictatorship through the elimination of internal opposition, the division of the German and captured populations according to Nazi anti-Semitic race theories, the plunder of Jewish property and assets and ultimately, the mass killings of the Jews in deaths camps and by

---

[414] See US NA, RG 226, Entry 191, Boxes 1–4; For a full listing, see http://www.archives.gov/research/holocaust/finding-aid/military/rg-226–3h.html.

[415] Breitman and Goda, 2004 op. cit. 12.

[416] US NA, RG 200, Dwork Papers, Box 11, Folder 107.

other means. This material was, it appears, also designed to supplement other prosecution briefs against both individual defendants and 'criminal organisations'. There are, for example, a series of individual entries that are composed in the style of the more general indictments deployed against individual defendants, and which were presumably designed to be incorporated into these so that the complicities in the Holocaust of, for example, Defendants Göring, Rosenberg, Frank and Frick would form part of a wider indictment. The net effect should have been that the complicities of these defendants in different aspects and phases of the Holocaust would have been highlighted and supplemented by the prosecutions' accusations against them for other types of war crime, such as waging aggressive war and violations of the traditional laws and customs of war.

As with many other examples of extensive trial evidence that OSS staff, particularly the R&A Branch officials, fed into the Nuremberg process, only a fraction of the Dwork materials were incorporated into final drafts of prosecution briefs. As a result, it is possible to trace the impact upon these final drafts of some but not all of the examples and arguments contained in the Dwork materials. Of course, there is the possibility that some areas of overlap of examples and arguments between these final drafts and the Dwork materials are coincidental. This is because the prosecutor in question derived some of these from other sources independent of the OSS. It is not possible to pursue this point further because of the absence of clear evidence. What cannot be doubted, however, is that the Nuremberg prosecutors called upon Dwork to supply them with additional material during the summer of 1945, and this is shown by the presence of cables and pouches of materials exchanged between them.[417] The transfer of materials on the Holocaust was predominantly one-way, from OSS-R&A to the Nuremberg prosecutors. However, there were occasional examples of traffic going in the other direction in situation where these prosecutors came across new material on the Holocaust and forwarded this on to Dwork for him to include it in his own draft prosecution brief, or to offer an expert opinion on its authenticity and significance. The refusal of Dwork to accept an assignment at Nuremberg that Neumann had sought for him was probably one factor in diluting the potential impact

[417] See for example the correspondence records of the OCC contained in US NA, RG 238, Entry 52f and g from June and July 1945.

of the extensive materials on the Holocaust that the R&A Jewish Desk had gathered. Another factor was that with only one defendant representing the SS, Kaltenbrunner, the significance of the Holocaust became scaled down to some extent. Even with respect to this defendant, there was, for example, more than sufficient evidence to convict this defendant for traditional war crimes against captured Allied prisoners of war, including members of the OSS' Dawes and Ginny Missions even though this group of victims was comparatively small in comparison with the approximately 6 millions Jews murdered during the Holocaust. Indeed, the fact that German diplomats, even retired ones such as von Papen and Neurath, were more fully represented amongst the Nuremberg defendants than leading SS, SD and Gestapo figures responsible for the administration of the Holocaust, only added to the problem of ensuring that OSS material on this genocide were taken as seriously as they deserved to be.

The most important outcome of the Jewish Desk's preparation for the trials was: R&A No. 3114.3, 'Nazi Plans for Dominating Germany and Europe: The Criminal Conspiracy Against the Jews', Draft for the War Crimes Staff' 13 August 1945. This report merits extensive description and analysis. It summarises the premeditated and incremental character of the Nazi conspiracy to annihilate European Jewry. A series of discriminatory practices including disenfranchisement, economic and religious persecution, starvation, deportation and extermination in concentrations camps and other sites, are linked to the wider Nazi criminal conspiracy. This study quotes the words of the chief Nazi leaders to highlight both the intensity and scope of Nazi anti-Semitism. It argues that the Nazis' intention to exterminate all European Jews was at the heart of their ideology from its inception:

> It is the purpose of the Prosecution to demonstrate the existence of a common plan or enterprise of the German Government, the Nazi Party, and the German military, industrial, and financial leaders to achieve world domination by war. The destruction of the Jewish people as a whole, although an end in itself, was at the same time linked to and closely tied up with this aim of world conquest.[418]

Katz argues that although the above précis was drafted by Dwork the CES's specialist on Nazi policy towards the Jews, the draft: 'bears the

---

[418] Dwork Papers (OSS R&A Jewish Desk files): US NA, RG 200, Box 3, Folder 32, 1.

indelible stamp of Neumann's influence', and represented: 'an elaboration of the so-called spearhead theory of anti-Semitism that Neumann had worked out some two years before.'[419] There is evidence that Dwork and perhaps Duker had to produce this draft brief at great speed and subject to considerable logistical difficulties, especially in connection with its reproduction and distribution:

> Note: Only 12 "master copies" of this report were reproduced with the Appendixes, Exhibit A Statistics on Jewish Casualties' During Axis Domination 'prepared in conjunction with the Institute of Jewish Affairs, New York' (Revised August 1945) and Indemnification and Reparation: Jewish Aspects' from the same source, Exhibit B. Other copies 13—[onwards] lacked these because of pressure on OSS R&A copying services in Washington and 'the urgency of issuing the report.[420]

The empirical or factual elements of this report are relatively straightforward. They are supported by the extensive statistical analysis of Exhibit A, cross-referencing physical extermination to a programme of mass theft, thereby implying that the Nazi genocide included extensive material enrichment:

> The figures in Exhibit A show that, by even the most conservative estimate of the 96,000,000 Jews who lived in Europe (including the USSR) at the time when they came within the reach of Nazi power, 5,700,000 have disappeared—not killed on the battlefields but deliberately put to death. Exhibit B shows that the total estimated Jewish possessions in the countries dominated and/or controlled by Germany amounted to from 6,230 to 8,629 million dollars. Most of the property is now lost—as a consequence not of war damage, but outright robbery.[421]

This report make a series of claims that pursue the difficult task of assimilating the Holocaust into the categories of international criminal law as these had just been expanded considerably by the Nuremberg Charter to include criminal conspiracy, crimes against humanity and waging aggressive war. The idea was show the German Government, the Nazi Party, and the German military, industrial and financial leaders had engaged in a criminal conspiracy to achieve world domination by war and that the persecution of the Jews was one phase in this wider plan.[422] Its authors made considerable efforts to link the Holocaust

---

[419] Katz, *Foreign Intelligence*, Cambridge: Harvard University Press, 1989, 56.
[420] R&A No. 3114.3, op. cit.
[421] Ibid., 5.
[422] Ibid., 2.

with these legal ideas and the requirements for their demonstration by means of trial evidence, even though of course there were little precedents to guide them.

In order to connect the Holocaust to the criminal conspiracy charge, this report argues that the former was not a series of 'isolated instances of individual brutalities' but rather: 'one continuous and indivisible crime—a criminal conspiracy against the Jewish people. All the various anti-Jewish measures...were links in the same chain....were all part and parcel of the same master plan against the Jewish people.'[423] 'It is...equally criminal to *conspire against* a racial, ethnic, religious or political group, and by depriving it of an opportunity to earn a living, indirectly to exterminate it, as it is to indulge in outright murder.'[424]

Equally ambitious but also legally required was the claim that the plan to exterminate European Jewry was formulated and developed long before the first programme of mass killings. Indeed the report argued that it was implicit in 'earlier preparatory phases', including looting of personal property.[425] Hence, 'physical extermination through killings of individuals and groups of mass murders were merely the last step in the plan to exterminate the Jewish people.'[426] The implication of this stance was that: 'the agencies, associations and persons, which engaged in carrying out earlier phases of the plan are equally culpable with those who executed its final phase, that of mass annihilation.'[427]

The idea that the Holocaust, 'although an end in itself', was also part of a wider plan for the Nazis to achieve domestic and ultimately global domination through aggressive war and the threat of such war, represented a practical application of Neumann's 'Spearhead Theory of anti-Semitism', discussed previously. Indeed, it echoes Neumann's point that the Jews were 'unhappily qualified' to be scapegoated: 'for all the ills of Germany—and of the world' because they were sufficiently 'conspicuous enough to make a good target', to be ideologically misrepresented as a threat to Germany but sufficiently weak in reality to: 'prohibit the possibility of a real struggle.'[428]

---

423 Ibid., 1.
424 Ibid.
425 Ibid., 1.
426 Ibid., 1.
427 Ibid., 1.
428 Ibid., 2.

In a further reiteration of the spearhead theory, Dwork's draft brief argued that such racist ideology played a series of functional roles and 'served other Nazi purposes' relevant to the proof of the various Nuremberg charges. By implication, this 'rallying cry' helped create a fictional sense of belonging to a 'people's community' properly united against Jews reinterpreted as a common internal and external enemy. As the Nazi slogan 'Germany unite, Jewry perish' indicates, this ideological process helped prepare the ground for later mobilisations during aggressive wars fought against real military enemies.[429]

In another attempt to link the Holocaust to 'crimes against the peace', Dwork's report argued that the Nazi leadership initially 'veiled' their intent to ultimately achieve a 'complete physical annihilation' of European Jews. During the 'early period' of their advance to political power, 'when Germany had not achieved sufficient strength to challenge the world', this genocidal intent was hidden behind their less extreme expressions of anti-Semitism. However after 1938, and following four years of massive and illegal re-armament of the German army, Air Force, Navy, the German occupation of Austria and the Munich capitulation: 'all restraint was discarded'. Hence, it became possible to allow the exterminationist elements of their ideology to rise to the surface as: 'the aim of destruction of the whole of European Jewry... was proclaimed openly.'[430] In line with the claims of Neumann's spearhead theory, this suggests that the full implications of this irrational ideology was expressed and developed with some measure of strategic calculation, restraint and cynical opportunism by the Nazi leadership.

Another purpose served by Nazi anti-Semitism was, according to this brief, and later repeated almost word for word by Justice Jackson in his opening speech to the IMT, to provide this regime with:

> an effective guinea pig for testing repressive measures. Actions against the Jews became a regular preliminary to similar measures against other elements of Europe's population... not fully subservient to the Nazi system: 'First Jewish property was appropriated, but before long similar measures were taken against anti-Germans, Poles, Czechs, Frenchmen and Belgians. Extermination of Jews was merely the prelude to the annihilation of Greeks, Poles and [others]. This use of anti-Semitism has been aptly described as "a spearhead of terror.[431]

[429] Ibid., 2.
[430] Ibid., 7–8.
[431] Ibid., 3.

This idea that initial measures of cultural and civil persecution of German Jews, such as disenfranchisement, already contained within themselves the seeds for the later anti-Semitic physical extermination programmes across Europe, was vital. It was necessary to make the prosecution's application of the criminal conspiracy idea more credible than perhaps it might otherwise have appeared. Certainly, Dwork repeatedly made this point:

> What is characteristic of the conspiracy against the Jewish people is the pattern, created in Germany, tested in Austria and Czechoslovakia during the period of preparation for the war, and then methodically applied to all countries conquered by Germany. This pattern consisted of a chain of successive and accelerating measures of repression, all aimed at a final result: Disenfranchisement, elimination from economic life, spoliation, enslavement, starvation, deportation, physical torture, and finally, annihilation.[432]

It was claimed that *the subjective* requirements of the conspiracy charge, the Nazi leaders' criminal intent and knowledge, were clearly present from the start, and could certainly be identified both from their choice of policies, and the tactical decision to conceal their agreed plans for mass Jewish extermination from the public. This decision was kept hidden through a resort to abstract and general statements that were short on specifics, even though the specific tactics of mass killing were privately admitted amongst themselves:

> While the policy of uprooting and spiritual and economic destruction was bound of itself to lead to physical destruction, it is certain in any event that from the beginning the intent of physical annihilation existed in the minds of the Nazi top leaders. Obviously, Nazi tactics insisted in holding up the revelation of such major aims until the time was ripe. Hitler admitted this policy in his speech...of 29 November 1935. He then stated: "National Socialism explained to the people only the general principles. As a rule it was silent about tactics."[433]

This report claimed that 'the all-out fight against the Jew is at the bottom of Nazi racial ideology'.[434] Nazi anti-Semitic ideology gave the Nazi leaders: 'the assurance that killing Jews is not murder. This fundamental

[432] Ibid., 5.
[433] Ibid., 9.
[434] Ibid., 7.

conviction unquestionably underlay and motivated the unique policy of the total annihilation of the Jewish people.'[435]

The Nazis' scapegoating of Jews, and their singling out from non-Jews: 'was both a form of bribe and an implied threat. It served to remind the non-Jewish population of occupied Europe that there was one group which had even less rights than they, however bad the situation might be... things could be considerably worse, and that, consequently, cooperation with the Reich would be to their advantage.'[436]

Reiterating a further theme of the spearhead theory, Dwork's paper argued that nother element of the role that the Holocaust played for the wider Nazi conspiracy to achieve world domination through the waging of illegal and extended wars of aggression, lay in casting the web of complicity and 'collective guilt' in war crimes ever-deeper amongst different sectors of the German state and nation:

> In the slaughter of millions of Jews the Nazis implicated the German Army, the civil service, the occupation authorities and quislings, and all their henchmen and accessories. Conscious as most of them were of their complicity, those groups could the more easily be persuaded that the Nazi fate was their fate. Their dread of being called to account could be relied upon as a brake on any desire to sue for a separate peace.[437]

This draft prosecution brief claimed to have identified an even more direct connection with the new Nuremberg offence of 'waging aggressive war': the development of fifth column subversion of neighbouring states prior to their military invasion or territorial absorption through threat of military force: 'Anti-Semitism also proved to be one of Germany's major weapons for political and economic infiltration abroad... leaders of the Third Reich openly declared their intention to disunite and disintegrate the democratic world by invoking anti-Semitism.'[438] This contention, which once again harmonised with Neumann's spearhead model, was supported by quotations from Werner Best, former legal advisor to the Gestapo. The Nazis' idea was that they could stir up anti-Semitism in neighbouring countries as a way of undermining liberal democratic traditions; and thereby paving the way for their replacement by Nazi or related dictatorships.[439] Once an area of Eastern Europe

[435] Ibid., 2.
[436] Ibid., 3.
[437] Ibid., 3.
[438] Ibid., 4.
[439] Ibid., 15–16.

was conquered in pursuit of the Nazis' goal of enhanced 'living space' for the 'master race', then the physical destruction of indigenous Jews and Slavs became a means to achieve this end. Genocide thus took its place in the Nazis' wider pursuit of world domination by waging illegal warfare, the territorial expansion of the German Nation and repressive occupation policies:

> The Nazi conspiracy of total mastery of the world entailed a total war. Its consequence was the new ruthless concept of "biological warfare"... to bring about permanent biological changes. The perfect example of this new Nazi method of biological warfare was the annihilation of the Jewish people.[440]

Once again, Dr Best was quoted in support of this connection, as is Nuremberg defendant Alfred Rosenberg, who, in 1943: 'insisted on the biological necessity of complete physical elimination of the Jews.'[441]

This report also argued that the Nazis' realisation of their conspiracy against the Jewish people amounted to an unprecedented crime against this specific group, which broke a European population trend by dislocating families and resulted in an 'aggregation of physical and mental wrecks.'[442] In addition, their conspiracy further constituted a crime against civilisation and humanity at large. This contention anticipated the prosecution's specific charges of 'crimes against humanity' against a number of the Nuremberg defendants:

> Another consequence of the slaughter of the Jews of Europe cannot be expressed in figures. But the impact of it is even more important to the future of the Jewish people and mankind... there is no need to stress the contribution [Jewish] communities made to the civilisation of their respective countries in all walks of life—medicine, the arts, education, politics, trade, industry, and commerce. Their destruction, carried out systematically and methodically by the Nazis, represents a loss which cannot possibly be recouped. To grasp its significance, one need only imagine what gaps in all branches of our common culture would be evident today if such an annihilation of the Jewish people had been conceived and carried out a century ago.[443]

The attempted proof of these various contentions was demonstrated through a series of 'typical' quotations from 'top Nazi leaders', including

[440] Ibid., 4–5.
[441] Ibid., 16.
[442] Ibid., 6.
[443] Ibid., 6.

Hitler's *Mein Kampf*, the statements of propaganda minister Goebbels, and Nazi Party publications including its own programme and membership pledge. Other types of evidence were references to the logistical means for annihilation, including—from the outbreak of war in September 1939—the reduction of food rations for German Jews to 20% of those allotted to other citizens.[444] This study maintained that, as a matter of fact, the 'lifting of the mask' concerning Nazi anti-Semitism coincided for essential reasons with the 'climax' of: Germany's military preparations for the launch of an aggressive war. The threat to get rid not only of German Jewry but also of the Jews in all European countries to be dominated and controlled was then openly confessed.'[445] Proof of these accusations consisted, in part, of various quotations from official Nazi publications from the period 1938–39, statements from Nuremberg defendants such as Rosenberg, Ley and Göring, and eventually by Hitler himself immediately prior to the launching of the invasion of Poland.[446] Here, Hitler: 'was already looking for the scapegoat to be charged with the guilt for the coming catastrophe.'[447] The claim that Germany needed to create a 'bloc of anti-Semitic states' linked into the so-called justification for the invasion and occupation of its easterly and western neighbours between 1939 and 1940.[448]

Furthermore, this report sought to correlate the intensification of anti-Semitic statements from Nazi leaders with specific events in both the intensification of physical killings and the military expansion of their regime, including the invasion of the Soviet Union.[449] This correlation was made presumably to better tie in the 'conspiracy against the Jews' to the Nuremberg offence of 'waging aggressive war'. For example, it quotes an ominous statement from Ley made in June 1942 regarding the enhanced position of the Nazi regime to 'solve' the 'Jewish problem' following the invasion of Russia, and then notes: 'A few days after this article was published, the deportation to Poland of Jews from all occupied Europe, and their mass slaughter, began.'[450] The final pages of this document quote Nazi leaders admitting the extent to which extermination had already decimated European Jewry in Poland and

[444] Ibid., 8.
[445] Ibid., 12.
[446] Ibid., 12.
[447] Ibid., 12.
[448] Ibid.
[449] Ibid., 15.
[450] Ibid., 15.

Hungary, and statements from official media, noting that: 'By this action five million Jews have been eliminated in these countries alone.'[451]

In addition to the production of this report, there is also evidence that Dwork acted as consultant to the Nuremberg prosecutors on other matters related specifically to the Holocaust, which entailed an exchange of documentation back and forth between OSS Washington and Jackson's organisation. The prosecutors forwarded certain materials addressing, for example, first person accounts of concentration camp atrocities, to Dwork for analysis and possible inclusion in his planned draft prosecution brief.[452] The eventual draft trial he produced was essentially a summary of a far more extensive project developed over the summer and autumn of 1945. The initial plan, which appears to have been written before the formulation of the new offences contained in the Nuremberg Charter of August 1945, relied instead on the earlier Memorandum for Trial Planning. This had been agreed with the OSS in mid-May 1945 and included five numbered major headings with a series of alphabetical sub-headings. The mass of papers contained in the Dwork papers were largely organised through this scheme, with, for example, 2 D written on the respective folders relating to that specific part of the overall plan. The major headings and sub-headings of 'The Criminal Conspiracy against the Jews' consisted of the following, plus a series of supportive alphabetical 'exhibits' intended as potential trial evidence and legal proof:

1. The preconceived plan for a Conspiracy Against the Jews—statistics, property confiscated.
2. The successive stages of crimes committed Against the Jews.
   A. Introduction.
   B. Charge One: Persecution of Religion and Spiritual life.
   C. Charge Two: Disenfranchisement and Stigmatisation.
   D. Charge Three: Economic Destruction.
   E. Charge Four: Ghettoization.
   F. Charge Five: Starvation.

[451] Ibid., 17.

[452] See materials entitled 'Punishment Without Crime: The Time I was Dead', which describe the author's own experiences as a detainee in Buchenwald in 1938. These were forwarded on 1 June 1945 by Ralph Sanford to Jackson, and—after an initial positive assessment by Prosecutor Sidney Alderman were, in turn, sent to Dwork for comment and analysis: Dwork Papers (OSS R&A Jewish Desk files): US NA, RG 200, Box 24.

G. Charge Six: Deportation.
H. Charge Seven: Forced Labor.
I. Charge Eight: Mass Annihilation.
J. Charge Nine Organized Violence.

3. A. Master List of Individuals and Agencies Guilty of Crimes against Jews.
   B. Individual Dossiers—Göring, Streicher etc.
   C. Regional Responsibilities for promulgation and execution of anti-Jewish legislation.
4. Chronology of Anti-Jewish measures, 1933–1945.
5. Suggestions.

Draft versions of many sections intended to add up to a complete case were contained in the Dwork papers. It is clear from a comparison of the draft sections (such as 'economic destruction', 'deportation, 'annihilation' etc), and those knitted together into the final R&A Paper submitted to the Nuremberg prosecutors, that the latter is a considerably edited down and concise version of the former in a different format. This may be explained by the fact that the original drafts were prepared on the basis of the 'Nine Charges' taken from the May 1945 planning memorandum, not the later offences of Article 6 of the Nuremberg Charter that were in fact the basis of the eventual prosecution and trial.

It would be a massive undertaking to further summarise this extensive series of documents that Dwork's Jewish Desk collected during and immediately after the war largely in preparation for later war crimes trials. Notably examples include excerpts from secret intelligence reports acquired by the OSS from surviving detainees of various death camps, some of which became Allied POWs. One of these, whose subject was Erich Meinke [partly illegible], had been detained by the Gestapo in 1942. Under detention in Gestapo camp 21, he witnessed Jews being subjected to specific and sometimes fatal acts of brutality. He was later sent to a branch or transit camp of the more extensive death camp at Lublin, run by SS-Stubef Dominek, where Jews were sent prior to their final destination at the main extermination camp. The latter was run by the head of the SD in Lublin, Muller who, with respect to the Jewish detainees: 'was responsible for their eventual murder.'[453] The subject

[453] Undated report, 'Erich Meinke', Dwork Papers (OSS R&A Jewish Desk files): US NA, RG 200, Box 3, Folder 32, with the annotation that a copy was to be sent to Kellerman as well who was preparing the OSS side of the case against the Gestapo.

had looked up the internal files to discover: 'how many murders of Jews Dominiek alone had been responsible for from 1940–43. He judged it to be 5–6,000 men, women and children'. Within this sub-camp, the death total for Jews was 'around 30,000, whilst in another small camp for Jewesses, the total was 1600. He estimated that, with respect to the main extermination camp as a whole, between 1–15,000,000 German and Austrian Jews had been killed during this period:

> all these Jews were shipped right into the camp from the main railway line in cattle cars.... The Jews were in part shot to death but for the most part gassed to death. A truck brought them to the Asphyxiation chamber. After the chamber was sealed, a panel was opened at one corner and a gas bomb fired in. After half an hour, the corpses were then burned. In the case of Jews, no identification tags were given, in order to make proof of this crime extremely difficult.[454]

Meinke also stated that, in mid-December 1944, he had met one of the SS officials from the main camp at Lublin who: 'told me that all Jews and part of the German prisoners had been shot. From old documents I knew that this action was possible since some...bore the designation "action for clearing out of the prisons."'[455] He also recorded his experiences of seeing a death march of Jews, whose survivors were destined to be shot on the orders of district commissioner Kure [partly illegible], and of hearing from another SS man of how 64,000 Jews were subjected to killing by machine gun, and, when ammunition for this ran out: 'flame throwers were used.'[456] This report concludes by giving a list of possible witnesses who could confirm these details from their own firsthand experiences.[457] (This evidence was repeated and illustrated in the OSS' film evidence entitled *Nazi Concentration Camps*, and shown to the IMT on 29 November 1945).

Dwork's files contain other similar, and even more extensive, first-hand eyewitness reports of ill-treatment and mass killings by gas and other methods that the Nazis had carried out in Lublin and Auschwitz-Birkenau death camps, some of which were supplied by Jewish organisations in

---

A related OSS report dated 2 May 1945 from its R&A staff attached to OSS 2677th (Provisional) regiment, CID document L-127249 later forwarded to the R&A Central European Section, is filed in the Dwork Papers in Box 13, Folder Buchenwald and Lublin.

[454] Ibid.

[455] Ibid., 2.

[456] Ibid.

[457] Ibid.

London and America. A number of passages of these were highlighted presumably for inclusion in Dwork's draft trial brief.[458] The Dwork Papers also include extensive references to source materials concerning the role and structure of Nazi concentration camps, including media reports, studies by Jewish organisations such as the Institute of Jewish Affairs, US Army Military Intelligence Reports on the 'shooting of Jews', reports from the Office of War Information entitled Report on the Condition of Jews in Poland (20 February 1944) and official investigations by the Soviet-Polish Extraordinary Commission from September 1944.[459] Hence, not all of the materials in the Dwork papers stem from Dwork and Duker's own original research because there is documentary evidence of materials being sent in to the OSS by other agencies, including the British army and the Jewish Agency, which the Chief of the R&A Branch, William Langer, made available to Dwork's unit. In other cases, relevant documentation originated from members of the OSS assigned to various field posts, actively tracking down materials from their contacts with other Allied agencies.[460]

It appears that, from at least August 1945, Dwork's correspondence address was given as the OCC's Washington office, based in the Pentagon. During the second half of August 1945, Dwork corresponded with Ben Kaplan on the Jewish aspects of the prosecution case, providing this Nuremberg prosecutor with additional information and supplementations to the draft indictment.[461] On 17 August, he informed Kaplan that he had received the Richter documentation from Budapest, which was the only captured complete records of a Gestapo operation outside of Germany. On the basis of this and other OSS documentation, including the Kasztner and Katzki documents, he argued that he would be able to demonstrate the direct and personal responsibility of Hitler, Himmler, Mueller and Eichmann. Dwork also promised to send copies of all these documentary sources to Kaplan as soon as possible.[462]

Aronson notes: 'Obviously Dwork wanted the "Jewish Cause" to be represented in the prosecution team next to Franz Neumann,

[458] See the selection gathered in a folder 32 of Dwork Papers (OSS R&A Jewish Desk files): US NA, RG 200, Box 3.

[459] 'References on Concentration Camps', 'Mass Annihilation: References' [partly illegible], ibid.

[460] Gideon Hadary to Langer, 'Condition of Jews in Europe', 15 June 1945; Ibid., folder 32.

[461] Aronson, 2004 op. cit. 329 citing a private letter of 17 August 1945.

[462] Ibid.

without success.'[463] Dwork suggested that Jewish representative Dr. Jacob Robinson be called upon to provide specific assistance in addition to his role as a translator.[464] On 23 August 1945, Dwork had sent the OCC copies of a newspaper story entitled 'Proof of Guilt for Murders in Poland is Found' that mentioned a file of documents belonging to SS Gruppenführer Philip Hoffmann, who had not previously featured on the OCC's radar. In response, Kaplan informed Dwork that: 'we have immediately sent word to our man on the continent in charge of collecting documents to [which] those files referred...'[465] This letter indicates that Dwork had been sending 12 copies of each of the extensive collection of files, sections and supporting exhibits concerning the Holocaust, which he had been preparing over the summer of 1945, but that there were less copies supplied of 'exhibits A and B to Part 1' with a lesser shortfall for Exhibit X-5 'Streicher advises foreigners on Jews.' Kaplan also listed other parts of Dwork's work that had been received in OCC's base in London, including vital materials on Poland where of course many of the death camps were located.[466] This is important evidence suggesting that, contrary to previous suggestions in the literature on Dwork's work, significant sections at least of his research had in fact been supplied to the prosecutors.

It would be excessive to describe the contents of the Dwork Papers in exhaustive detail. A flavour is provided by Dwork's carefully prepared summary of 'anti-Jewish Legislation' in each of the Nazi-occupied states of Europe, which distinguishes different forms of persecution, such as disenfranchisement, 'ghettoization', forced labour, and deportation.[467] The title, date, gist and author of each discriminatory measure is summarised on a separate sheet, with a helpful thematic index also provided.[468] Hence, prosecutors seeking to discover which particular anti-Semitic measures defendant Hans Frank had personally authorised, could—by means of this collection—rapidly identify the details.

[463] Ibid.

[464] Robinson later served as deputy counsellor and advisor before and during Adolf Eichmann's trial in Jerusalem in 1960–61.

[465] Kaplan to Dwork, 4 September 1945: US NA, RG 226, Entry 191, Box 1 (OSS R&A Jewish Desk files).

[466] Namely, Part 3 J Organised Violence, Part 3-E Hans Frank; Part 3-C Czechoslovakia, Belgium, France, Holland, Luxembourg, Ostland, Poland, Serbia. Also exhibits L-1 destruction of Synagogues, Paris France, fall of 1941 and L-4 Representative Nazi Publications on Jews, F-12 and Y-13', ibid.

[467] 'Poland': US NA, RG 226, Entry 191, Box 1 (OSS R&A Jewish Desk files).

[468] Ibid.

At the same time, prosecutors seeking to summarise the step by step escalation in anti-Jewish decrees of a particular type could have usefully drawn upon this material. Certainly, Kaplan emphasised its usefulness for their overall case:

> The project is proving very useful in the preparation of the Indictment, which we are now drafting. It will be even more valuable at the trial, with its complete documentation. We have not yet decided precisely in what form to use the project at the trial; but we will feel free to call upon you for assistance in whipping it into shape for the trial if it is decided to make any changes in the form of the project.[469]

On 9th September 1945, Dwork sent 12 copies of his draft prosecution brief on the 'Conspiracy against the Jewish People' to the Nuremberg prosecutors. Replying for the latter, Benjamin Kaplan welcomed these copies and the impressive level of detail and work that had gone into them, and noted their valuable contribution to the prosecution case:

> Your study was really a colossal undertaking, and I was very agreeably surprised to see it come out so well. You have succeeded in a very difficult job of putting together into manageable and useful form a mass of material that was staggering. I want to take this opportunity of congratulating you and your colleagues who worked on the project. I believe that the project will provide the basic background upon which will be built the case so far as the conspiracy against the Jews is concerned and I believe you have made a really significant contribution to our work.[470]

Kaplan further explained the particular types of additional evidence Dwork may be able to help the prosecution with:

> We are moving on ways and means of putting the project into evidentiary shape for the trial and for that purpose 12 working copies are sufficient. As far as the dossiers are concerned, we would like to have them for all the 24 named defendants. The materials we are particularly interested in are those which tie up the conduct at the working level with the individual defendants, or with other higher-ups in the party or government. We are also particularly anxious to use all material that is available on the criminal responsibility of the SD, SS, Gestapo and similar organisations. Another point that is worth all the emphasis we can give it is proof that all the incredible happenings described in your report were the results

469 Ibid., 2.

470 Kaplan to Dwork, 9 September 1945: US NA, RG 226, Entry 191, Box 1 (OSS R&A Jewish Desk files).

> of carefully worked out and deliberately prepared plans by the leaders of the party and state.[471]

As another part of this consultancy role, in late August 1945 Dwork sought additional materials from OCC sources on defendants Fritzsche, Funk, Kaltenbrunner, Neurath, Saukel and Schirach so that he could integrate these with his own extensive files on their complicities in the Holocaust. He also requested any information on the whereabouts of two officials closely associated with the Holocaust: Adolf Eichmann and Gestapo Chief Mueller.[472] Kaplan gave Dwork suggestions as to how further information on the whereabouts of these 'potential defendants' could be obtained, and noted that: 'one of their witnesses had reported seeing Eichmann in Berlin on 17 April of this year but did not know whether or not he was in custody.'[473] With respect to these six defendants, he asked Dwork to supply the prosecutors with: 'some additional material that will be useful.'[474] Kaplan in particular emphasised the importance of gaining additional material from Dwork concerning Kaltenbrunner's complicities in this area, noting his case 'is of extreme importance.' He asked Dwork for any information he had concerning: 'a report that he attended a conference concerning the disposition of the Jews and that the idea of mass-annihilation by gas originated with him. Do you have any documentary evidence concerning such a conference?'[475] In addition, this prosecutor sought: 'quotations from Schirach advocating the mass-annihilation of the Jews?' Finally Kaplan stated: 'We should appreciate whatever material you have concerning the anti-Jewish activities of the six men listed above...as soon as possible since it is expected to use it in the drafting of the Indictment which is a job that has an extremely short deadline.'[476]

In short, there is documentary evidence that the materials that OSS agents and informants gathered, and which the R&A Jewish desk pulled together into a distinct collection, proved of considerable value to the Nuremberg prosecutors both generally, and in preparing the trial indictments.

---

[471] Ibid., 2.
[472] Kaplan to Dwork, 13 September 1945: US NA, RG 226, Entry 191, Box 1 (OSS R&A Jewish Desk files).
[473] Kaplan to Dwork, 9 September 1945, op. cit.
[474] Kaplan to Dwork, 13 September 1945, op. cit.
[475] Ibid.
[476] Ibid.

Some of the material on Nazi art looting that Dwork included in his draft chapters on specific themes was not included in the final R&A report. For example, the draft 'chapter' on 'Economic Destruction' noted:

> Another phase of looting popular with the Nazi hierarchy was that of Jewish art treasures, from both community and private collections. According to captured German documents (contained in exhibit B2) the Reich Foreign Minister (von Neurath) was empowered to seize art treasures in occupied territory, the Reich Propaganda Minister (Goebbels) was empowered to seize materials relating to Germany in countries in occupied Europe, and Göring admits to having "obtained" Jewish art treasures (letter from Göring to Rosenberg dated 21 November 1940). Another document proves the complicity of the Chief of the Reich Chancellery (Dr Lammers), the Reich Minister for the Occupied Territories (Rosenberg), and the Chief of the Army High Command (Keitel) in the seizure of Jewish "cultural goods" (and even furniture) in Western Europe (Exhibit H2). These documents mention no less than 72 Jewish art collections seized in Western Europe, as well as an inventory of 21,903 works of art looted from 200 localities prior to 1 July 1944.[477]

The Exhibit B-2 consists of a report entitled: 'Collection of German letters and memorandum pertaining to confiscation of European Art Treasures' 19 May 1945 taken from Bruno Lohse and Dr Schiedlausky, and then compiled into a dossier by MFA&A officers.[478] Perhaps the most important element is a list of seized Jewish Art Collections.[479]

We have already mentioned the importance Kaplan attached to receiving additional assistance from Dwork concerning evidence of the various Nuremberg defendants' complicities in Holocaust. Therefore, at this point, it is worthwhile to examine Dwork's suggestions for those parts of the formal indictments that related to the Holocaust. Given the importance the present book attaches to the cultural plunder aspect of the Holocaust and OSS' role in monitoring it, the central theme of this book's largest chapter, these aspects in the Jewish Desk's dossiers on Göring and Rosenberg will now be addressed. Those elements of the Göring Dossier, which were designated as III b under the plan already described—that replicate points already made and evidenced in our discussion of the earlier R&A report entitled 'Göring as a War Criminal',

---

[477] 'Economic Destruction', Dwork Papers: US NA, RG 200, Box 19.
[478] Ibid.
[479] Ibid.

which Dwork presumably borrowed in his subsequent contributions to the indictments, will not be repeated in full here.

Göring is accused of belonging: 'to the first rank of those guilty of the criminal conspiracy against the Jews. This is evident from his writings and speeches as Party leader and from his decrees and deeds as a high [partly illegible] government official.... He has a long and continuous record of anti-Jewish activity.'[480] This claim is substantiated by quotations from a series of Göring's public statements from 1933 onwards. Dwork's account of Göring's complicities highlights the fact that this defendant had, in August 1938 when both political repression and military preparations had advanced enough to remove earlier restraints, advocated the complete expulsion of German and Austrian Jews from their countries' economic and political life. Such persecution including reducing food rations for Polish Jews, which led to actual or near-starvation for many.[481] During Göring's powerful role as Commissioner General in charge of the Nazi regime's four year economic plan, he had taken a series of discriminatory measures relating to Jewish property and enterprises, including the registration, freezing and later confiscation of gold, art and other assets, to realise the policy of 'solving' the 'Jewish problem' within the 'next five years.'[482]

For these and other acts of lending high-level institutional and ideological support to each step of the Nazis' early anti-Jewish programme, each of which was substantiated by various 'exhibits' constituting legal evidence and proof, Dwork's draft indictment made a serious charge against Göring. He stood accused of being: 'the chief culprit in the economic destruction of the Jewish population of Europe, which inevitably doomed it to starvation, forced labor and death.'[483] This draft indictment highlighted his role in art looting, accusing Göring of being: 'responsible for the systematic plundering of Jewish art treasures for his own enrichment', and—as an attached 'exhibit'—cites his letter to Rosenberg of 21 November 1940 boasting of his ruthless methods of acquisition, as further proof of this.

The draft indictment on Rosenberg, who of course had administrative responsibility for the ERR, the Nazis' state body responsible for

[480] 'Göring', Dwork Papers: US NA, RG 200, Box 11.
[481] Ibid., 3–4.
[482] Ibid., 3.
[483] Ibid.

plundering Jewish property,[484] claims that this defendant's complicity in the conspiracy against European Jews was two-fold: 'that of instigator and that of perpetrator of crimes against them.'[485] From 1919 onwards, Rosenberg stands accused of engaging in an increasingly severe and intense programme of ideological attack and incitement to violence against the Jews. This was badly disguised as 'education' and 'scientific research' concerning racial principles. He proclaimed that Germany had been the victim of a world-wide Jewish conspiracy and that a: 'Germany purged of the Jews represents the finest flowering of the Aryan race. Jews being the complete antithesis of Aryans must therefore be expelled from Germany.'[486] This genocidal incitement to 'disenfranchisement, spoliation, eviction and finally liquidation of the Jews', took place within books and both populist and 'widespread and influential Party publications.' It was officially sanctioned by this defendant's acceptance of the massively influential position of Party 'Commissioner for the Total Spiritual and Philosophical Indoctrination and Education'.[487] This position as official ideologist of Nazism in general was directly relevant to Rosenberg's endorsement and practice of anti-Semitism in that it: 'gave his judgements on the Jews extraordinary weight' and allowed him: 'free scope to carry on his policies of defamation and incitement to every recess of German life.'[488] There are pages of Dwork's draft indictment containing direct quotes from Rosenberg's anti-Jewish defamations dating back to 1919 and the formation and refinement of the Nazi party programme.

Dwork's charges went further than the creation and distribution of racist and anti-Semitic propaganda both at home and abroad regarding the threat posed to Germany and Europe by the 'Jewish world conspiracy'. Rosenberg's holding of executive positions with the Nazi regimes afforded him with: 'unrestricted opportunities to put his theories into effect.'[489] Hence, this document accused Rosenberg of creating several institutions and agencies that served as all-too practical and material means initially to persecute Jews, and then ultimately: 'facilitate the process of their ultimate elimination.'[490] His propaganda actively

[484] ERR stands for 'Einsatzstab Reichsleiter Rosenberg'.
[485] 'Rosenberg', ibid.
[486] Ibid., 8.
[487] Ibid., 1–2.
[488] Ibid., 3.
[489] Ibid., 2.
[490] Ibid., 4.

endorsed and defended the Nazis' anti-Semitic laws as 'justice', and included a pamphlet distributed in 1944 to all German servicemen and women entitled 'What are we fighting for?', which listed Jews as the foremost enemy despite the fact that, at this stage of the Holocaust: 'two-thirds of European Jewry had already perished.'[491] In particular, the creation of some of these bodies, presumably he meant the ERR (Task Force Rosenberg), devoted to 'safeguarding' Jewish works of art, operated as agencies for plundering 'Jewish cultural wealth...looted from all parts of Europe.'[492]

Rosenberg's appointment as Government minister for Eastern Occupied Territories' had a fateful impact upon East European Jewry: 'As the Party's foremost authority on the Jews, it fell largely upon Rosenberg to decide their fate.'[493] Following the German invasion and occupation of Poland in September 1939, and an earlier policy announcement advocating the creation of special reservations for European Jews: 'Rosenberg at once attempted to realise his reservation idea by the establishment of the Lublin Reservation, 30–50 miles in area....It was planned to place there two million Jews.'[494] From October of this year, Jews from all regions of Poland, Germany and Austria were transported to this reservation, despite the absence of housing, health and other facilities. The result was a concentrated mass of overcrowded and starving human misery that has been vividly described in a number of eyewitness reports whom this brief quotes extensively.[495] The document then recounts how, despite his personal awareness of the inhuman conditions prevailing in the Lublin Reservation and associated ghettos, and following the start of mass annihilation in 1942, Rosenberg continued to call, allegedly as a defensive measure of 'biological necessity', for the expulsion of Jews not only from Greater-Germany but from the whole of the European continent. Dwork claimed that 'nearly all' of the five million Jews who fell under Rosenberg's administrative control 'perished in the "biological purification" advocated by him.'[496] This claim is substantiated by reference to the 'testimony of highly placed prisoners of war' who told their Soviet interrogators that a Nazi regional Governor of Lithuania

[491] Ibid., 12.
[492] Ibid., 5.
[493] Ibid., 14.
[494] Ibid., 15.
[495] Ibid., 16–18.
[496] Ibid., 20.

had: 'exterminated hundreds of thousands of Jews in Lithuania on orders from Rosenberg.'[497]

Of particular interest for present purposes is the evidence Dwork gathered concerning the ERR, the Nazi plunder organisation that, although partly controlled by Göring, bore Rosenberg's name: 'Working in conjunction with the Army High Command. The "Rosenberg commandos" confiscated all Jewish cultural treasures of all types and varieties both private and communal and transferred these to Germany...even furniture....(Exhibit B is a partial list of the private art treasures confiscated by Rosenberg's directions)'[498] Dwork summed up the implications of this analysis and supportive evidence in almost judicial terms:

> Alfred Rosenberg is thus proven guilty as a defamer, inciter, murderer and robber. Defamation of the Jews and incitement to violence against them was the main features of his career. By virtue of his key positions in the Party hierarchy he enjoyed unlimited scope for shaping and directing German policies towards the Jews...He is responsible for the Lublin reservation and its horrible consequences...As minister for the eastern occupied area he is, in fact, responsible for the murder of millions of Jews in Eastern Europe as well as those transported from Western Europe. He is also responsible for the destruction and confiscation of Jewish cultural wealth.[499]

It would be tedious to run through the contents of all the other individual draft indictments, most of which emphasise the combination of ideological incitement to anti-Semitic forms of racism with direct complicity in a series of discriminatory and—in some cases—genocidal measures. A number of short quotations and summaries will suffice.

The first of these to be discussed is the partial draft indictment that Dwork prepared on Defendant Frick, Hitler's Minister of the Interior, and, later Reich Protectorate of Bohemia and Moravia. It states: 'Frick was one of the most ardent protagonists of the racial measures and anti-Jewish persecutions. He not only propagated through writings and speeches the racial theories and carried out their application within Germany, but was the champion of the exportation of these theories abroad.'[500] The dossier then provides a number of examples, supported

497 Ibid.
498 Ibid., 21.
499 Ibid., 22–23.
500 'Frick', 1–2, ibid., Box 14.

by 'exhibits', of Frick's speeches advocating acceptance of 'principles' of pure race and blood. These were made to coincide with, prepare the ground for, or subsequently justify, a series of intensifying measures of state persecution of Jews. Each one of these measures moved a step further towards their ultimate physical extermination. As Minister of the Interior, Frick personally established a large number of these measures of disenfranchisement and expulsion of Jews, and later their non-Jewish partners, from both public and private sector and economic life within Germany, including the professions and even social insurance. Later measures sought to 'stigmatise and humiliate Jews' by attacking expressions of their culture, even the choice of personal names, their practices of ritual slaughter of meat and so forth.[501]

Dwork's dossier on Seyss-Inquart accuses this defendant of complicity in extending German measures of anti-Semitic persecution into Austria following this country's annexation. He is accused of publicly committing himself to the expulsion of the sizeable population of Jews from Vienna, a policy he later facilitated as a government minister responsible for this region. The gravest charge, however, relates to his conduct whilst Reichskommissar for Holland, with 'absolute authority', responsible only to Hitler. In this military governor role, he:

> dedicated himself to the realisation of his preconceived plan to bring about the complete destruction of Dutch Jewry. Of the approximately 150,000 Jews of Holland at the time of the invasion, only a few thousand survived when liberation came. To bring about this result, Seyss-Inquart ruthlessly executed all the crimes encompassed in the Nine Charges. It required more than the ordinary measure of Nazi brutality and barbarism to carry out these crimes in Holland where the population, unlike that of Austria, was for the most part uncooperative.[502]

Between 1940–42, Seyss-Inquart's measures had also included the familiar anti-Jewish programme of economic, civic and political exclusions. From 1942 onwards, this was followed by his government's confiscation of their personal, commercial and cultural property, including works of art, gold and silver jewellery, even silver tableware.[503] In March 1944, he ordered 568 freight ships to transport looted Jewish property back to Germany.[504] Between 1940–41, this defendant required Jews

---

[501] Ibid., 4.
[502] Ibid.
[503] Ibid., 5.
[504] Ibid., 6.

to register at their businesses and then later in March 1944 to: 'surrender their insurance policies—the usual preliminary to deportation and murder.'[505] In addition to these economic crimes, Seyss-Inquart was also responsible for the 'Ghettoization' of the Jews of Holland in specific reserved areas in Amsterdam for instance, which they suffered: 'the agencies of ghetto inmates in other lands until their turn arrived for deportation.'[506] Upon deportation, all Jews aged under 40 including children were, from July 1942, sent to both slave labour and extermination camps in Eastern Europe; whilst those Jews over 40 were transported to concentration camps in Holland and Germany. The monthly quota for the former category was 12,000, designed to round up all Jews by May or June 1943.[507] Dwork insisted that, because of endless toil combined with starvation rations, being sent to such camps was equivalent 'to a death sentence', albeit one whose execution was slightly delayed.[508] Many Jews deported from Holland died en route, whilst others who were considered: 'useless were shot on reaching the German border.'[509] Those who survived the transportation: 'were exterminated in Poland.' Dwork concludes that: 'by the aforementioned methods, Seyss-Inquart brought about the annihilation of the ancient 100,000 Jewish community of Holland. Seyss-Inquart thus bears full guilt for the extinction of the Jews of Holland.'[510]

Other draft indictments, supported by references to numerous exhibits of evidence, follow the similar style and format as those already discussed. Attempts to indict those responsible for Nazi economic policy for participation in the 'conspiracy against the Jewish people' deployed the argument that they contributed to the opening stages of a: 'preconceived plan of the Nazi leaders for the annihilation of the Jewish people'. Since, from the start, the plan envisaged the destruction of this group, then it followed that individuals such as Walther Funk, Hitler's Minister of Economics from 1938, could still be accused of being: 'guilty as an instigator of and accomplice in the formulation and execution of the conspiracy for the annihilation of the Jewish people.'[511] This was because the 'economic destruction', through a series

[505] Ibid.
[506] Ibid., 7–8.
[507] Ibid., 8.
[508] Ibid., 8.
[509] Ibid., 9.
[510] Ibid., 10.
[511] 'Walter Funk' ibid., Box 15.

of increasingly punitive anti-Jewish laws and decrees issued by Funk, was always designed to function as one step along the path towards their ultimate physical annihilation.

It may have been thought that defendant Ribbentrop, Hitler's Foreign Minister, would have fallen outside the scope of Dwork's attentions. This was not the case as his draft indictment argued that, as a member of Hitler's inner circle of advisors and a 'close friend' of Himmler, Ribbentrop was very much part of the 'innermost circle of the Nazi hierarchy' that had devised the overall conspiracy to annihilate European Jews. This meant that: 'he is automatically co-responsible for the entire anti-Jewish policy . . . and the preconceived plan for Jewish annihilation.'[512] Evidence in the form of an interview is then quoted suggesting that this defendant 'clearly revealed advance knowledge of anti-Jewish measures of "ghettoization" that were neither announced nor executed until much later.'[513] Furthermore, and in his capacity as Foreign Minister, Dwork accuses this defendant of possessing:

> a more direct and immediate guilt stemming from the continuous and determined attempts of German agents (official and unofficial) to create and spread anti-Semitism throughout the world, organize anti-Jewish actions, Aryanize German firms abroad, force anti-Jewish policy upon neutral and satellite governments, as well as other more secret and criminal activities normally associated with the SS, SD, and Gestapo. . . . To further these criminal activities, Ribbentrop created . . . a special section . . . to coordinate all anti-Jewish activities of the Foreign Office with those of the . . . SS [RSHA], Gestapo, Staff Rosenberg etc. in order to execute German anti-Jewish policy abroad . . . The organization functioned through [an official with ministerial rank] who had offices in the embassies and legations attached to neutral and satellite countries and were usually members of the SS or Gestapo. . . . They were directly under the Foreign Office and Ribbentrop must be held responsible for their activities. . . . These officials . . . took a leading role in the deportation and extermination of Jews in the countries to which they were attached, the "Aryanization" of German firms abroad, and dissemination of anti-Jewish propaganda.[514]

Dwork's draft indictment also claims that this defendant should be held directly accountable: 'for the confiscation of Jewish property outside Germany. 'This', it is claimed: 'is apparent from a letter from Göring

[512] 'Ribbentrop', 1, ibid.
[513] Ibid.
[514] Ibid., 2–3.

to Rosenberg dated 21 November 1941, which refers to a circular from Foreign Minister proclaiming his responsibility for acquisitions of art treasures in occupied territory.'[515]

Dwork's efforts to establish organizational responsibility as a supplement to, and not a substitute for, purely individual legal accountability, resulted in his claim that guilt should be attributed on a basis that this was:

> not divisible but joint. Those who belonged to the top leadership of the party, of Nazi German government, and of the Wehrmacht machine are jointly and severally responsible for the whole set of crimes committed in the execution, step by step, of the criminal preconceived plan. Even where no direct connection is shown between a definite person to a specific charge, each person is, nevertheless, to be held responsible as a conspirator.[516]

Gathering trial evidence of Nazi genocide from OSS staff

In one sense, it is not possible to draw a clear-cut line between OSS intelligence-gathering and analysis on the one hand, and the preparation of materials of use to the Nuremberg prosecutors on the other. The previous sections of this work have already noted how Fritz Kolbe had provided Dulles and his SI Branch colleagues with important evidence relating to the Holocaust members of the Nazi regime carried out in both Northern Italy and Hungary. During the summer of 1945, the entire collection of Kolbe's materials from Ribbentrop's Foreign Ministry was analysed and then supplied to officials in both R&A Branch and James Donovan's subordinates in the OSS General Counsel's Office. One objective of this was to exploit this collection's potential as trial evidence against a number of potential defendants responsible for atrocities committed against Jewish and other civilians.[517] The OSS even asked Kolbe to give evidence of Nazi war crimes to Justice Jackson in person. The latter personally debriefed Kolbe on 7 July 1945 at the OSS' German base in Wiesbaden, with his diary noting that Kolbe had supplied extensive information of Nazi war crimes based

---

[515] Ibid., 3.

[516] 'Responsibilities', 1–2, ibid., Box 15.

[517] James O'Malley to OSS Director, 14 August 1945: US NA, OSS Director's Files, M1642, Roll 120, Frame 1248.

on the documents he had copied, many of which we know related to the Holocaust:

> We interrogated the other witness who was employed in the German Foreign Office, and who for some years furnished documents out of that office to Dulles in Switzerland. He gave us in great detail the part of different foreign office characters in the activities which he considered criminal. All of these witnesses were anti-Nazi but not anti-German.[518]

Another account of this meeting provides greater details: 'On entering Judge Jackson's office, Fritz Kolbe was introduced for the first time to General Donovan. Donovan was eager to meet the celebrated "George Wood," who had just been called the "prize intelligence source of the war" by the British secret services. "I was introduced by Allen Dulles with very warm words," Fritz wrote to his friend Kocherhaler. The discussion concerned war criminals.'[519] At this meeting, Jackson also debriefed Dulles' other agents and contacts in the anti-Nazi German opposition, including Hans Gisevius and Fabian von Schlabrendorff. Both men had been secreting away incriminating materials supplied to them through Admiral Canaris. Amongst these were: 'all documents referring to the assassination of the Jews.'[520] Jackson's debriefing of Dulles' group of anti-Nazi Germans was recognised as providing useful additional evidence for the Nuremberg prosecutors both on aspects of the Holocaust and Nazi war crimes more generally.[521]

Donovan's own Nuremberg files, which the critics of the OSS' role with respect to the Holocaust rarely if ever refer to, also contain an entire sub-section devoted to the persecution of the Jews. This collection contains over one hundred pages of OSS-R&A and other documentation of such persecution. Amongst this material, much of it stemming from the efforts of his subordinates, including those re-assigned to Jackson's organisation, was a captured German film depicting atrocities against Jews, reports of mobile paramilitary killing squads (*Einsatzgruppe*) and interrogation transcripts of SS officials closely implicated in genocide.[522] A number of these will be discussed

---

[518] Jackson Diary, op. cit. 7 July 1945.

[519] Delattre, 2005 op. cit. 213.

[520] 'Interrogation of Schlabrendorff and Gisevius', 7 July 1945, 2, Jackson Papers, op. cit. Box 102, Reel 8.

[521] Jackson to William Jackson, 12 July 1945: Jackson Papers, op. cit. Box 95.

[522] See Cornell Collection, 17.01 'Von der Einsatzgruppe A durchgefuhrte Judenexekutionen,'; 17.02 'War Crimes and Crimes Against Humanity: Part V: Persecution

more fully below. Of the various victims of Nazi mass murder, including Poles, Slavs more generally, gypsies, communists and homosexuals, this was the *only* sub-division within Donovan's files that singled out the persecution of a specific civilian group.

Donovan and his personal staff at Nuremberg had gathered many other documents relating to the Holocaust from OSS and other sources. These include a graphic account of 'Murder Hospitals' contained in the interrogation of Dr. Wilhelm Gustave Schueppe. This is introduced by a statement to Donovan from, perhaps, an X-2 branch official summarising its evidential value: 'shows that the SD conduct the Nazi program to exterminate political undesirables.' The interrogation report itself describes the Nazis' practice of killing persons of 'inferior races' and others by means of high doses of morphine injected at the Pathological Institute in Kiev. During Schueppe's nine-month tenure, the SD transported a total of between 110,000 to 140,000 Jews and other victims to this location expressly for the purpose of killing them. His statement includes a shocking defence: 'I believe in this system. It is comparable to pruning a tree, thereby removing the old undesirable branches in order to produce the highest yield. In a nation this system must be carried out to prevent decadence.'[523] Yet, Schueppe also confesses that he left Kiev: 'Because my nerves were shot. It is obvious that this type of activity is not pleasant, especially in my case, since I saw it was my highest duty to practice surgery.'[524]

Donovan also commissioned his R&A staff to write a timeline relevant to the prosecution on, for example, key events in the rise of Nazism: 'containing the most important dates in the German history and the history of the Nazi Party from 1918 through 1944.' Dr Henry Kellerman, himself a German Jew, performed this task. His document highlighted the specifically anti-Semitic aspects of this movement.[525] These

of the Jews,' Brady O. Bryson; Frederick L. Felton; Issac Stone; Hans A. Nathan; 17.03 'OCC Brief, Section 1: The Nazi conspirators adopted and publicized a program of relentless persecution of Jews,' S. L. Sharp; S. M. Peyser; 17.04 'R&A No. 3114.3 / Nazi Plans for Dominating Germany and Europe: The Criminal Conspiracy Against the Jews,' 17.05 'Original German 8MM Film of Atrocities Against Jews / Captured in SS Barracks by U.S.; James Box Donovan; 17.06 'Interrogation of Wisliceny, Dieter,' Lt. Col. S. W. Brookhart.

[523] 'Murder Hospitals' Ibid., Vol. 1, final page.

[524] Ibid.

[525] 'Calendar of German History 1918–1944: With Special Reference to the National Socialist Party and the Principal Defendants Indicted by the International Military Tribunal,' 14 November 1945, ibid., Vol. 2, Subdivision, 6.01.

focused on the pre-war anti-Semitism rather than the extermination programme. Kellerman included the SA-organised large-scale pogroms in Berlin on 12 September 1931; the April 1933 Nazi boycott of Jewish shops 'directed by Streicher'; the Nuremberg anti-Semitic race laws of September 1935; the prohibition of Jews from the medical profession in February 1936; the restriction of German state education for Jews in July 1937; and the Jewish pogrom and Göring's decree introducing severe exclusions of Jews from German economic life in November 1938. Donovan also gathered a high quality sectional map illustrating the approximate locations at which Einsatzgruppe A carried out mass killings of Jews in Nazi-occupied Eastern Europe, particularly at Riga, Schaulen, Kauen, Minsk, Krasnogwardeisk, Dunaburg and Reval.[526]

The same section of Donovan's files that address the role of the SS contain an interesting document summarising a Gestapo register of arrests made and dispositions rendered.[527] It shows that many persons are recorded as being arrested only because they were classified as Jews, and notes that: 'Such persons were shot or sent to the annihilation camp at Ausschwitz [sic].' Another document summarises Wilhelm Hoettl's information on Adolf Eichmann, who admitted to having played the primary role in the extermination of European Jewry.[528] It notes that in a report to Himmler, Eichmann estimated that four million Jews were exterminated in the camps and two million killed by the Einsatzgruppen in Russia. However, Himmler suggested that these figures were too low.[529]

In short, General Donovan, his personal staff at Nuremberg and a number of informants such as Kolbe, certainly gathered and generated a number of items of potential trial evidence relevant to the prosecution of individuals and organisations complicit in the Holocaust.

Jack Taylor's evidence on Mauthausen death camp

In addition to R&A Reports, there are other less well-known examples of OSS documentation relevant to the Holocaust feeding into the Nuremberg process. Certain OSS personnel had firsthand experience

---

[526] 'Von der Einsatzgruppe A durchgeführte Judenexekutionen" ibid., Vol. 9, subdivision 17.01.

[527] 'Haftbuch Jahr—1943', n.d., ibid.

[528] 'Concentration Camps; Jews, Persecution of', ibid., Vol. 105.

[529] Ibid.

of Nazi concentration camp atrocities and wrote reports that were transferred into both the Nuremberg process and other allied war crimes trials. For example, OSS' Jack Taylor provided an affidavit regarding his firsthand and eyewitness experiences of Nazi war crimes within the Mauthausen extermination camp.[530] During his detention, Taylor had forced himself to memorize and recall a vast volume of names and details. After liberation but before the Russians took control of this region, he returned to this camp to assist war crimes investigators by collecting every available item of documentation, diaries, photographs and journals.

Taylor used this evidence and his own memory to compile his detailed report concerning Nazi atrocities. His report testified to what he had seen and heard about the crimes at Mauthausen. These included killings by various methods such as the gassing of prisoners twice a day, 120 at a time. The following extracts relating to evidence of Nazi war crimes against Jews and others are taken from this report. They outline Taylor's first impressions of the camp, including his own immediate ill-treatment:

> At dawn on Easter Sunday, 1 April 1945, our 10 SS guards and we 36 prisoners crossed the Danube ferry at Mauthausen, and climbed the hill past the rock-quarry. Several prisoner work parties (Arbeit Kommandos) under heavy SS guard passed by on their way to the quarries. They were the most terrible looking half-dead creatures in filthy ragged stripes and heavy wooden shoes and as they clanked and shuffled along the cobblestones, they reminded me of a group of Frankenstein's. We kidded ourselves saying we would look the same in a few days, but we were all struck with cold dread terror. Above us we could see the high stone wall with electric fence on top and to our left below the regular camp were a group of low windowless buildings, which were originally barns for horses, later for Russian POWs and at this time serving as a 'hospital' (Krankenlager, Sanitateskager or Russian lager). We arrived at a group of buildings just outside the main entrance and were turned over to the Mauthausen SS who didn't waste any time intimidating us. SS Unterscharfuhrer Hans Prellberg was particularly brutal as he slapped, punched, kicked and beat most of us over the head with a cane belonging to a crippled Slovak in our group. Two young Russians and a Hungarian were unmercifully beaten because they did not understand German. All commands were given in German and I had to keep extremely alert to save myself similar

[530] See transcript at http://www.scrapbookpages.com/DachauScrapbook/DachauTrials/Mauthausen03.html; and J. M. Greene *Justice at Dachau*, (London: Broadway Books, 2003), 146–47.

> beatings. We were told certain rules and regulations, the penalty being instant death on all except one, which was merely hanging the victim by his wrists chained behind his back. This slight penalty was for failure to stand at attention and remove one's cap whenever an SS man, regardless of rank, passed or when speaking to an SS man.[531]

Taylor also records the use of summary murder as part of a grim initiation of the next group of inmates, which included the particularly brutal treatment of Jewish inmates:

> When the next group of new prisoners, following us, were having the same rules and regulations announced to them, the speaker said: "and if you attempt to escape and are recaptured, and you will be shot immediately, like this," and simultaneously pulled his pistol and shot an old prisoner standing near, who had just been recaptured after an attempted escape. We were marched through the main gate and lined up outside the shower room where we were individually questioned, slapped, slugged, and beaten with a stick by three SS men in relays for approximately three hours; in addition, some were spat upon. The worst to me was SS Unterscharfuhrer Hans Bruckner who screamed 'you American swine' every time he struck me. He also beat unmercifully a Lt. Glauber, an ISLD agent (Viennese-born, British citizen) mainly because he was a Jew.[532]

Prisoners, Taylor noted, had to work brutal hours under grim conditions. The camp authorities assigned him to work building a new crematorium. This had proved necessary to speed up the killing operations. Taylor stated he had to carry and mix sand, cement and water for the Spanish tile layers:

> We dawdled at our work to delay completion of the crematorium because we knew that the number of executions would double when cremation facilities were available (No gassed or shot bodies could be buried because of evidence) but one Saturday morning, Prellberg and S.S. Hauptscharfuhrer Martin Roth (head of the crematorium) belaboured Kapo Jacinto for his failure to finish the work quickly and informed him that it must be finished and ready for operation on the following day or we (workers) would be the first occupants of the new ovens. Needless to say, we finished the job in the allotted time. The next day, Sunday April 10th, 367 new Czech prisoners, including 40 women, arrived from Czechoslovakia and were marched through the gate straight to the gas chamber and christened the new ovens. Black oily smoke and flames shot out the top of the stacks as healthy flesh and fat was burned as compared to the normal

[531] Report of OSS captain Jack Taylor transcribed in an online American Military Journal: http://www.udtseal.org/oss.html.

[532] Ibid.

> pale yellow smoke from old emaciated prisoners. This yellow smoke and heavy sickening smell of flesh and hair was blown over our barrack 24 hours a day and as hungry as we were, we could not always eat.[533]

Taylor also records that many hundreds of prisoners soon became sick owing to the near starvation diet and unsanitary work and general living conditions. However, it could prove fatal for prisoners to reveal their illnesses to the camp authorities. This was because such reports of illness functioned as a way of selecting weakened individuals for killing:

> I had terrible dysentery and innumerable small sores on my legs and back but I continued to work as best I could to prevent being put on the sick-list and transferred to the 'hospital' (Sanitatslager) where, believe it or not, five sick people were assigned to each single bunk, rations were half 'normal' and infinitesimal amounts of medicine were supplied. Very few ever returned alive from this 'hospital' and the daily death toll at this time from pure starvation was 400 to 500. These were dumped in a huge mass grave on the hill already containing 15,000.[534]

It soon became clear to Taylor that, as an American citizen, he was in a unique position to gather incriminating materials and eyewitness evidence regarding atrocities committed by both Mauthausen camp personnel and their superiors within the SS who had issued orders for the murder of detainees:

> Many of these men said to me, "We're sorry you're here, but, IF you live, it will be a very fortunate thing; for you can tell Americans and they will believe you, but if we try to tell them, they will say it is propaganda." Every nationality trusted me because I was an American where they couldn't trust their own people entirely due to stool-pigeons. Consequently, I was the recipient of hundreds of eyewitness atrocity accounts with first hand evidence in many cases. It was too dangerous to take notes, but I tried to keep mental account of the teller and enough of the story to remind him later when and if the opportunity came to set down the details and get them sworn to. I had seen only a small percentage of the torture, brutality and murder that these men had seen and suffered, but on this basis I was prepared to believe their stories 100%, in most cases. After all, the acts were themselves so terrible that anything worse could hardly be imagined.[535]

---

533 Ibid.
534 Ibid.
535 Ibid.

In addition to the 'normal' methods of execution, 'i.e., gassing, shooting, hanging, etc.', Taylor's report then drew upon the: 'the enclosed sworn statements' regarding the particularly gruesome methods by which SS personnel and their subordinates killed Mauthausen inmates:

> The following examples: clubbing to death with wooden or/iron sticks, shovels, pick-axes, hammer, etc; tearing to pieces by dogs trained especially for this purpose; injection into the heart or veins of magnesium-chlorate, bezine, etc.; exposure naked in sub-zero weather after a hot shower; scalding-water shower followed by cow-tail whipping to break blisters and tear flesh away; mashing in a concrete mixer; drowning; beating men over a 150 foot cliff to the rocks below; beating and driving men into the electric fence or guarded limits where they are shot; forcing to drink a great quantity of water then jumping on the stomach while the prisoner is lying on his back; freezing half-naked in sub-zero, buried alive; eyes gouged out with a stick, teeth knocked out and kicked in the genitals, red hot poker down the throat, etc., etc., etc.[536]

Taylor noted that although Mauthausen was established in 1939 as a subsidiary extermination camp for Dachau, within 12 months: 'it outshone its parent in its grisly business to the extent that it became a full-fledged Class III Concentration Camp, i.e., extermination camp.' He recognised that in the concentration and death camp system, questions of nationality and 'race' operated as a key determinant of killing, with those deemed to be of Slavic races subjected to more intensive extermination: 'The figures on Spanish prisoners are typical of those of the western nations: out of 7,184 arriving in 1940, 2,000 remain alive today in Mauthausen and its subsidiary Gusen. For Russians, Poles and Czechs, the percentage is even worse.'[537]

Taylor's report also highlighted the degrees of individual complicity of different camp officials and others in the preparation and execution of so-called 'medical experiments' regarding typhus and starvation performed on different categories of Mauthausen inmates:

> According to Dr. Podlaha, the head prisoner doctor, prisoners were also executed for some unusual pathological lesion or specimen such as deformities, tattoo, etc. A hunchback and a dwarf, who had come to the notice of one of the SS doctors, were executed and their skeletons cleaned and mounted for specimens. Pathological lesions were collected as specimens, which involved the death of the patient in most cases. Tattoo marks were

---

[536] Ibid.
[537] Ibid.

> practically a death certificate as one of the SS doctors had a hobby of collecting, tanning, and binding them in book form while his wife made lampshades and book-covers from them. Research was carried on in which healthy prisoners were used as guinea pigs. These experiences mainly concerned typhus and the minimum food requirements to sustain life. The former used infected lice with a celluloid cover taped over them to the patient's leg. The latter consisted of a strictly controlled diet in which the results were measured in the number of deaths.[538]

This report identifies those persons who were individually responsible for ordering executions within the camps, an aspect which has obvious relevance to the war crimes prosecution process. It also provides graphic details of how gassing was used as one of the techniques of genocide:

> Executions were carried out on orders from one of three sources: 1. Berlin Tribunal, which was the only official source. 2. Local Gestapo agency where the prisoner was interrogated. 3. Lager Commandant. Ziereis in this case was also the Chief of the Oberdonau (Upper Danube) Tribunal. The normal methods of executions were gassing, shooting and hanging which were all carried out in the Death House. This block long structure had approximately 50 jail cells on the first floor known as Bunker or Arrest in charge of Hauptscharfuhrer Josef Niedermayer. Underneath was the gas chamber, hanging beam, shooting 'gallery' and crematorium in charge of Hauptscharfuhrer Martin Roth. The gas chamber was approximately 15 feet square and fitted as a shower room with tile wainscoting and overhead shower nozzles. The victims were told that they were going to take a shower; all were undressed in the back courtyard and led into the chamber; the heavy air-tight door was slammed and locked and the gas introduced through the shower nozzles. Normal operation was twice daily at 9 AM and 5 PM, 120 victims at each time. Once 220 were packed in and the SS fought each other to look through the small plate glass window in the door and watch them struggle in their agony. They were thrilled with this mass spectacle. Frau Ziereis, the Commandant's wife, came once to see the sight. The gas used was Cyclone B cyanide a granular powder, contained in pint-sized cans and the same used for disinfection of clothing. In a small room, adjacent to the gas chamber, was a steel box connected immediately to a blower, which was in turn connected to the shower system. While wearing a gas mask, the operator bashed in the ends of two cans of powder (one can kill 100 people) with a hammer and after placing them in the box, clamped the lid on hermetically tight and started the blower. (In winter, when the gas would not evaporate fast enough from the powder, steam was introduced into the box from

[538] Ibid.

> the other end.) After two hours, the intake blower was stopped and the larger exhaust blower was turned on for about two hours.[539]

Taylor's document then indicates that towards the end of the war, the Nazi authorities sought to cover their tracks with respect to the use of mass killings through fixed gas chambers. Instead, they resorted to alternative techniques that could be rapidly reconverted back to less murderous purposes.

> Wearing gas masks, the prisoner operators removed the bodies to the cold room (capacity 500) where they were stacked like cordwood awaiting cremation. See enclosure 'Instructions for the service of Pourric Acid Delousing Chambers in K.L.M', by the Chief doctor. It is worded for delousing but the instructions were especially for gas chamber operators. The blowers and gas receptacle were removed by the SS and attempts made to destroy them. In March 1945, Ziereis and Bachmayer (see protocol) ordered all ventilation sealed in the police wagon and a small trap door installed. A group of 30 to 40 prisoners were told that they were being transported to Gusen, a subsidiary camp about 8 km away, were crammed into the wagon, the door locked and a bottle of poison gas dropped through the trap door on an angle iron specially placed to break the bottle. The 'police wagon' was immediately driven to Gusen and after parking for an hour the prisoners were delivered to the crematorium. The same numbers of Gusen prisoners were then loaded into the 'police wagon' for transport to Mauthausen with identical results. From March to October 1944 the car circulated 47 times with an average of 35 victims each way on the round trip, making a total of approximately 3,300. In October, ventilation was installed again, and the police-wagon resumed its original function.[540]

Taylor provided some explanation of the perverse rationale for introducing gassing as a method of killing. Apparently, this was viewed as a positive alternative to other means of execution that, presumably, were even more dehumanising for the executioners:

> Until 1943, daily executions by rifle or tommy-gun were done openly at the back of Block 15 where those waiting to be executed were forced to watch their comrades, three at a time, being mowed down. When gas and injection deaths practically replaced shooting, all shooting was done individually in another small room adjacent to the gas chamber. The victim was told that he was to have his picture taken and was led into their room where a camera was set up on a tripod. He was told to face

539 Ibid.
540 Ibid.

> the corner with his back to the camera and immediately he assumed this position, [when] he was shot in the back of the neck with a small carbine by a SS man standing to his left and slightly behind. Prisoner operators stood behind a door looking through a peephole as to know when to drag the body out. SS Standartenfuhrer Ziereis, Commandant of Mauthausen, personally executed 300 to 400 men here in the above-mentioned manner during 10 shooting 'expeditions' over a period of four months. In the same room as above, where a stairway led down from the street, an 'I' beam was stretched across about 10 feet high with ends embedded in the concrete on either side. From this beam, nooses were suspended which accommodated six strangling victims at a time. Before departing, the SS cut out the beam but the embedded ends are clearly seen.[541]

This report also supplied considerable details of how the increasing quantity of corpses that emerged from this death camp were physically disposed of within industrial grade crematoriums, facilities which Taylor himself had helped construct:

> The crematoriums were large brick structures containing a firebox for burning wood and coal and over this were the ovens fitted with rounded supports at intervals for the bodies. The bodies were carried into the ovens on steel stretchers and with a quarter turn were rolled out. The new crematorium with two ovens could handle twelve bodies at a time, 160 a day and with the old ovens a total of 250 a day. Insufficient cremating facilities held down the number of executions as all bodies showing signs of violent death could not be buried. Gassed bodies were often disfigured from clawing, biting, etc. and chemical analysis of the tissues would show cyanide. All 'violent-death' bodies had this stamp on their paper: 'Die leiche muss aus hygienischen grunden gefert verbreannt werden' (Sic) which says, "The corpse must for hygienic reasons be cremated."[542]

The most incriminating detail that Taylor's report discussed however, was one of the more remarkable pieces of evidence that the Nuremberg prosecutors both cited and directly quoted from in their brief addressing Nazi concentration camps: the Mauthausen camp 'death books'. Taylor had confiscated these books immediately after his liberation to protect them from an order for their destruction issued on 20 April 1945:[543]

> "Official" deaths were listed in Death Books giving cause of death, etc., from which death certificates were issued to: (1) The SS Police Court where the prisoner had been tried. (2) The political department at Mauthausen.

---

541 Ibid.
542 Ibid.
543 J. M. Greene, *Justice at Dachau*, London: Broadway Books, 2003, 146–47.

> (3) The head SS doctor at Mauthausen. (4) A Berlin agency from which reports were sent to next of kin and insurance agencies. From 1939 to April 1942, the causes of death as entered in the Death Book, from which the certificates were prepared, were all absolutely false as they were assigned to a body from a prepared list of 50 causes by a SS soldier, who was not even a medic. Not until 1942, when a few prisoners were allowed to work, were autopsies begun on a few. Enclosed are examples of original death certificates bearing false causes of death and signed by the SS doctors. Tortures and brutalities as stated in the enclosed protocols usually terminated in death but a few remained alive to tell their stories. Enclosed are prison autobiographies of Dr. Ludwig Soswinski, Vienna Communist; Dr. Hans Von Becker, publicity minister for the Schussmig regime; Karl Dieth, lone survivor of the Wels-Linz Communists; Bernard Cechonski, Polish patriot, Ernst Martin, gas works director, Innsbruck; Josef Ulbrecht, bank director Prague; Georg Havelka, electrical and television engineer Prague. The last three named did a spectacular job of withholding valuable documents and obtaining evidence, which will surely hang some of our murderers.[544]

In addition, Taylor was able to record his own efforts, immediately after the liberation, to assist in the preparation of cases for the prosecution of those camp officials he identified as particularly responsible for ordering, organising and carrying out human extermination. Despite his health problems and considerable loss of weight meriting hospitalisation, this OSS Captain discusses the process through which he gathered additional incriminating material:

> I explained [to the American authorities] that much valuable testimony, documents, etc, were available at Mauthausen, and I should return and collect it. I hated to go back, and it was one of the hardest decisions of my life to stick to, but it was an opportunity, which would not long be available. I worked for three weeks collecting testimony, documents, liaison to Colonel Seibel and running down SS men hiding in the area. In the first two weeks I gained over 30 pounds. One of the most important documents was a collection of 15 Death books (Totenbuch) giving names of 'official' deaths for 6 years. These books are labelled 'Mauthausen', 'Gusen' and 'Executions,' and were withheld at the risk of their lives by Ulbrecht and Martin, the prisoner secretaries assigned to this registration. These approximately 3,600 pages have been microfilmed and the books are in the custody of OSS, SALZBURG. Ulbrecht and Martin by means of tiny secret hieroglyphics were able to put down in many cases the true cause of death (gas, injection, etc.) at the same time as the official (false) death cause, i.e., in the '40 '42 book, all those from number 229 on with

[544] Ibid.

'spr' means 'injection death' (injection of foreign material into the heart) and those with 'COIC' means violent exercise to death. In the '42–43 book, all numbers after 3725 with a dot after the place of birth were by injection. Other small notes in relation to the 'official' death cause can be deciphered by Martin and Ulbrecht. After 18 April 1945, all prisoners who have in the 4th column the remark 'Zellenbau' (prison bldg.) were gassed. On April 26 1945, 1157 prisoners died at Mauthausen through starvation, gas, shooting, and clubbing.[545]

After having recorded and documented the details of crimes against humanity committed in the Mauthausen camp, Taylor's report provides details of those who should, in principle, be held legally accountable for such atrocities. He noted:

A list containing the names, ranks and positions held of 354 Mauthausen SS personnel is enclosed including approximately 100 Rogues Gallery pictures, 41 of which are identified. See list of equivalent ranks of SS, Wehrmacht and U.S. Army. Also included are the names and signatures of 13 Mauthausen women 'overseers' who were directly in charge of the women inmates. One of the most remunerative of the rackets was the extraction of all gold from the mouths of the dead. All bodies were stamped 'Examined by dental surgeon' before cremation or burial. Large amounts of gold were thus accumulated supposedly for the SS in Berlin but actually large quantities were stolen and resold in the black-market by hospital and crematorium SS personnel. See reports 'The Removal of Dental Gold from Deceased Prisoners', and 'SS Dentists and dealings with gold teeth'. A list of degenerate SS dentists and doctors from Mauthausen and some of their infamous acts are enclosed. See also a protocol stating that a prisoner had his gold teeth knocked out with a brick by a guard, only to get the gold.[546]

Not surprisingly, the Nuremberg prosecutors deployed aspects of Taylor's report and associated documentation, including the Mauthausen death books, to considerable effect within the trials.[547] This is clear from following extract from the prosecution's case published in the official Nuremberg trial transcript:

But the records which they kept about concentration camps appear to have been quite incomplete. Perhaps the character of the records resulted from the indifference which the Nazis felt for the lives of their victims. But occasionally we find a death book or a set of index cards. For the

545 Ibid.
546 Ibid.
547 Hence, they form part of the Nuremberg prosecutors' public record: 'Records compiled for the IMT trial': US NA RG 238, Entry 3, Box 3.

> most part, nevertheless, the victims apparently faded into an unrecorded death. Reference to a set of death books suggests at once the scale of the concentration camp operations, and we refer now and offer Document Number 493-PS as Exhibit Number USA-251. This exhibit is a set of seven books, the death ledger of the Mauthausen Concentration Camp. Each book has on its cover the word "Totenbuch" (or Death Book)—Mauthausen. In these books were recorded the names of some of the inmates who died or were murdered in this camp, and the books cover the period from January of 1939 to April of 1945. They give the name, the place of birth, the assigned cause of death, and time of death of each individual recorded. In addition each corpse is assigned a serial number, and adding up the total serial numbers for the 5-year period one arrives at the figure of 35,318.[548]

In presenting this evidence, the prosecutors deployed the rhetorical technique of irony to good effect in order to highlight the perversity of how the camp authorities constructed false records of the causes of prisoners' deaths:

> An examination of the books is very revealing insofar as the camp's routine of death is concerned; and I invite the attention of the Tribunal to Volume 5 from Pages 568 to 582, a photostatic copy of which has been passed to the Tribunal. These pages cover death entries made for the 19th day of March 1945 between 15 minutes past 1 in the morning until 2 o'clock in the afternoon. In this space of 12 and three-quarter hours, on these records, 203 persons are reported as having died. They were assigned serial numbers running from 8390 to 8593. The names of the dead are listed. And interestingly enough the victims are all recorded as having died of the same ailment—heart trouble. They died at brief intervals. They died in alphabetical order. The first who died was a man named Ackermann, who died at 1:15 a.m., and the last was a man named Zynger, who died at 2 o'clock in the afternoon. At 20 minutes past 2 o'clock of that same afternoon, according to these records, on the 19th of March 1945, the fatal roll call began again and continued until 4:30 p.m. In a space of 2 hours 75 more persons died, and once again they died all from heart failure and in alphabetical order. We find the entries recorded in the same volume, from Pages 582 through 586. There was another death book found at Camp Mauthausen. It is our Document Number 495-PS and bears Exhibit Number USA-250. This is a single volume, and again has on its cover the words "Death Book—Prisoners of War." And I invite the attention of the Tribunal in particular to Pages 234 through 246. Here the entries record the names of 208 prisoners of war, apparently Russians, who at 15 minutes past midnight on the 10th day of May 1942 were executed at the same time. The book notes that

[548] IMT 3, 516–17, cf. 514.

> the execution was directed by the chief of the SD and the Sipo, at that time Heydrich.[549]

The death books that Taylor secured were not only actually physically presented to the Nuremberg Court, but also referred to within the main prosecution brief on 'Nazi Concentration Camps'.[550] Taylor's report was, it appears, a major source for an official report into conditions at Mauthausen, which was also entered into the Nuremberg evidence.[551] In addition, Taylor provided one of the most gripping pieces of film evidence contained with the OSS atrocity film, *Nazi Concentration Camps*, which was shown in the first two weeks of the Nuremberg proceedings in order to dramatise the meaning and human implications of the Nazi concentration and extermination camp system.

The Holocaust and the OSS' R-Series of Nuremberg evidence

Nuremberg scholars are familiar with the major series of trial evidence known as the PS-Series, named after the contribution of Robert Storey's staff in the Paris Office ('PS' signifying 'Paris Storey'). The scholarship of the OSS and the Nuremberg trials contains little, if any, acknowledgement of the largely successful efforts of OSS' Documentary Research Unit (DRU) headed by First Lieutenant Walter Rothschild.[552] This comprised a small group of research analysts based in this agency's London Field Office, whose work began at the end of June 1945.[553]

---

549 Ibid.

550 *Nazi Conspiracy and Aggression*, Vol. II. (Washington: USGPO, 1946), 949–968, heading 7.

551 Report of the Office of the Judge Advocate General of the Third United States Army, dated 17 June 1945: Nuremberg document 2716-PS.

552 To be fair, Jackson himself provided the following brief acknowledgement in his preface to a selection of Nuremberg documents, the 'Red Series': 'No work in a specialized field would be complete without its own occult paraphernalia, and the curious reader may desire an explanation of the strange wizardry behind the document classification symbols.... The letter 'R' stands for 'Rothschild,' and indicates the documents obtained through the screening activities of Lt. Walter Rothschild of the London branch of OSS.' Nazi Conspiracy & Aggression Volume I, Preface, 14–15 available online at: http://www.nizkor.org/hweb/imt/nca/nca-01/nca-01-00-preface-03.html.

553 See 'to whom it may concern' James Donovan, 29 June 1945 [basically a letter of authorisation on OCC stationary requesting British authorities to cooperate with his search and analysis of incriminating documentation: Jackson Papers, op. cit. Box 101, Reel 7.

One useful way to assess the significance of the R-Series is to ask the following question: how would our understanding of the nature and extent of Nazi atrocities against the Jews have been diminished if the material gathered and analysed by the DRU had not been cited and quoted during the Nuremberg trials? Nuremberg prosecutors, including former OSS personnel, deployed documents from this series in a number of draft and final prosecution briefs.[554] In many cases, these prosecutors used material from the R-series to establish the liability of a number of different individual and collective defendants (i.e. the 'criminal organisations') culpable for different aspects of the Holocaust.

Original and captured German documents included within the R-Series give precise details of the racist measures of genocide and ethnic purging that Nazi officials used to confiscate the farms, factories and other real estate of different racially-defined categories of Poles. This formed part of the Nazis' wider attempts to 'Germanise' parts of the Polish population: 'as rapidly as possible.' For example, this series contains detailed decrees that Himmler's office had issued regarding a policy of seeking to 'reclaim' individuals resident in Poland who originally had a German ethnic background but who had since become 'Polandised'. One of the potentially fatal sanctions such individuals faced for any non-compliance was detention in a concentration camp. On this point, R-112 proved of assistance. It consisted of a bundle of Himmler's decrees from February–July 1942 authorising the persecution and compulsory 'Germanisation' of Poles, including of course Polish Jews.[555] This dossier contributed to Warren Farr's trial brief on the SS.[556] Today such 'Germanisation' would be recognised as a form of genocide in that it undermined the basis for the survival of the Polish people as a distinct group and nation.[557]

---

[554] Drafts briefs produced by Thomas Lambert and Lt Col. George Seay (OSS) used R-Series documents on pages 38, 54, 40 41: Cornell Collection, op. cit. Vol. 2, pt.1 / 7.09.

[555] R-112: Brand, 'Racial Germans who do not apply for entry into the list for repatriation of German ethnic groups', NCA 7, 108–114.

[556] See the undated and untitled document mapping prosecution documentation to specific trial briefs contained in Jackson Papers, op. cit. Box 101, Reel 7.

[557] SS Brigadier Führer General, 'Instructions for Internal Use on the Application of the Law Concerning the Property of Poles', 15 April, 1941, NCA 7, 61–3, supported by specific standard forms to authorise such confiscations of farms and factories, and statistical reports on the 'success' of such measures to date yielding a grant total of 955, 536 estates and just under 9 million hectares of land (63–65, 65–67, and R-91: SS Brigade Leader Greifelt to Himmler, 23 February, 1941, NCA 7, 68–70).

Amongst the groups who the Nazi regime subjected to gross violations of basic rights were Hungarian Jews. Nuremberg prosecutors deployed R-124. This dossier contained the minutes of Defendant Speer's discussion with Hitler on April 6 and 7 1944, and which were found to support its claim that the Nazi authorities subjected this group to deportation, followed by often fatal forms of forced labour within concentration camps:

> [T]he plan to start the war was coupled with the plan to wage the war through the use of illegal sources of labor to maintain production. Hitler, in announcing his plan to attack Poland, had already foreshadowed the slave-labor program as one of its corollaries when he cryptically pointed out to the Defendants Göring, Raeder, Keitel, and others that the Polish population 'will be available as a source of labor'... This was part of the plan made good by Frank, who as Governor General notified Göring that he would supply 'at least one million male and female agricultural and industrial workers to the Reich' (1374-PS), and by Sauckel, whose impressments throughout occupied territory aggregated numbers equal to the total population of some of the smaller nations of Europe. Here also comes to the surface the link between war labor and concentration camps, a manpower source that was increasingly used and with increasing cruelty.... One hundred thousand Jews were brought from Hungary to augment the camps' manpower (R-124).[558]

Major Farr's trial presentation focused on evidence from R-124 concerning the role the concentration camp system played in the abuse of Jewish labour:

> In April 1944 the SS was called on to produce even more laborers—this time 100,000 Jews from Hungary. The Tribunal will recall the minutes of the Defendant Speer's discussion with Hitler on April 6 and 7, 1944, which were found in our Document R-124 at Page 36 and were read to the Court in evidence as Exhibit Number USA-179—minutes in which Speer referred to Hitler's statement that he would call on the Reichsfuehrer SS to produce 100,000 Jews from Hungary.... It was through the SS that the conspirators squeezed the last drop of labor from such prisoners. I refer to a statement by the Defendant Speer which appears in our Document R-124 at Page 13 of the translation... I quote: Speer: "We have to come to an arrangement with the Reichsfuehrer SS as soon as possible so that PW's he picks up are made available for our purposes. The Reichsfuehrer SS gets from 30,000 to 40,000 men per month."[559]

558 IMT 19, 412.
559 IMT 4, 196–97.

British prosecutor Shawcross also relied upon and quoted R-114 to demonstrate the essentially racist character of German occupation policies within Western Europe. These verged upon the genocidal in the sense of attacking the long term survival of particular ethnic groups deemed to be racially 'inferior':

> The method applied in Alsace was deportation. A captured report reads: "The first expulsion action was carried out in Alsace in the period from July to December 1940 in the course of which 105,000 persons were either expelled or prevented from returning. They were in the main Jews, gypsies and other foreign racial elements, criminals, antisocial, and incurably insane persons, and in addition Frenchmen, and Francophiles. The patois-speaking population was combed out by these series of deportations in the same way as the other Alsatians." (Document Number R-114). The report goes on to state that new deportations are being prepared and after reciting the categories affected, sums up the measures being taken: "...the problem of race has been given first consideration and this in such a manner that persons of racial value are to be deported to Germany proper and racially inferior persons to France."[560]

Since R-114 featured not only in Major Warren Farr's trial brief on the SS[561] but also in Judge Parker's judgement summarising the most incriminating dossier of evidence presented during the trial, it is worthwhile to examine its contents more closely.[562] This bundle of evidence indicates that Gauleiter Wagner, who controlled German-occupied areas of Alsace, prepared plans and took measures leading to the expulsion and deportation of Jews, Gypsies, and 'other foreign racial elements' within the Alsatian civilian population as a means of punishment and compulsory Germanization. Between July and December 1940 in the Alsace region, 105,000 persons were either expelled or prevented from returning.

R-114 also includes a memorandum, dated 4 August 1942, recording the details of a meeting of high SS and police officials that had been convened to receive the reports of the Gauleiter relating to the racist Alsatian deportations. The Gauleiter stated that the Führer had given him permission: 'to cleanse Alsace of all foreign, sick, or unreliable elements'; and that he highlighted the political necessity of further

---

[560] IMT 19, 498.

[561] See the undated and untitled document mapping prosecution documentation to specific trial briefs contained in Jackson Papers, op. cit. Box 101, Reel 7.

[562] IMT, Judgement, Judge Parker (no page numbers) but available online at http://www.yale.edu/lawweb/avalon/imt/proc/judwarcr.htm.

deportations. The memorandum further records that the SS and police officials present at the conference approved the Gauleiter's proposals for further expulsions determined on Nazi racial criteria.

Having cited and quoted from R-114,[563] Judge Shawcross then explicitly linked such policies of deportation and Germanisation to the Nazis' more obviously genocidal policies of sterilisation and extermination of Slavs, including of course Slavic Jews, within Eastern Europe. This programme was directed against individuals and groups not regarded as immediately useful to the Nazi war economy:

> Listen to Bormann's directives for the Eastern territory summarized by one of Rosenberg's subordinates. I quote: "The Slavs are to work for us. Insofar as we do not need them, they may die. Therefore, compulsory vaccination and German health services are superfluous. The fertility of the Slavs is undesirable. They may use contraceptives or practice abortion; the more the better. Education is dangerous. It is enough if they can count up to a hundred. At best an education which produces useful stooges for us is admissible" (Document Number R-36).[564]

This document was cited as a particularly telling piece of evidence by Judge Parker in his contribution to the Tribunal's judgement.[565]

In setting out the prosecution's economic case, which deeply implicated defendant Rosenberg, prosecutor Walter Brudno argued that:

> I come now to the final phase of the case against the Defendant Rosenberg. We have seen how he aided the Nazi rise to power and directed the psychological preparation of the German people for waging of aggressive war. I will now offer proof of his responsibility for the planning and execution of War Crimes and Crimes against Humanity committed in the vast areas of the occupied East, which he administered for over 3 years. These areas included the Baltic States, White Ruthenia, the Ukraine, and the eastern portion of Poland....

Brudno cited R-135: 'to illustrate the manner in which Rosenberg participated in the criminal activities conducted within his jurisdiction'. He then highlighted the casual brutality of 'harvesting' the body parts of victims of Nazi mass murder:

---

563 The prosecution used part of this dossier in other contexts including to demonstrate the complicity of the Nazi Party's Leadership Corps in war crimes. See IMT 4, 57.

564 IMT 19, 498–9.

565 IMT, Judgement, Judge Parker, op. cit.

> I call your attention to the document numbered R-135, which was previously introduced as Exhibit Number USA-289. In this document the prison warden of Minsk reports that 516 German and Russian Jews had been killed, and called attention to the fact that valuable gold had been lost due to the failure to knock out the fillings of the victims' teeth before they were done away with. These activities took place in the prison at Minsk, a prison which...was directly under the supervision of the Ministry for the occupied east.[566]

Parts of this evidence from R-135 impressed Judge Parker sufficiently for him to cite them in his final judgement.[567]

Contrary to allegations that OSS staff at Nuremberg took little interest in the persecution and extermination of European Jews, R-108 provides a report from the Anglo-Jewish association on the: 'systematic terrorisation of the Jews of Germany by the Gestapo since 1933'. This gave the names of the thirteen government officials most closely involved with the Holocaust. It also contains a list of witnesses and their addresses. Furthermore, R-108 supplies evidence that Defendant Hjalmar Schacht was indirectly implicated in the persecution of Jews through his formulation of economic policies that led to the removal of many Jews from economic life: 'exposing them to starvation.' The prosecution trial brief on 'Nazi Concentration Camps' also included three significant items from the R-Series.[568] Major Walsh's presentation to the Tribunal, which was entitled 'The Persecution of the Jews,' was explicitly supported by a 'document book of translated evidence' including a selection from the R-Series.[569] One of these, R-129 also contributed to Warren Farr's Trial Brief on the SS.[570]

Another document the Rothschild group supplied to the Nuremberg prosecutions contained additional evidence that the OSS and its Direc-

---

[566] IMT 5, 62.

[567] IMT, Judgement: Judge Parker, 'War Crimes and Crimes Against Humanity', (no pages) http://www.yale.edu/lawweb/avalon/imt/proc/judwarcr.htm.

[568] R-91 Telegram from Mueller, SS Gruppenführer to Reichsführer SS, 16 December 1942. (USA 241): NCA, VIII, 60; R-124 Speer's conference minutes of Central Planning Board, 1942–44, concerning labor supply. (USA 179): NCA.VIII, 146; R-129 Letter and enclosure from Pohl to Himmler, 30 April 1942, concerning concentration camps. (USA 217): NCA 8, 198. The report is contained in NCA 1, ch. 11.

[569] IMT 2, 378. For example, R-135: 'Letter to Rosenberg enclosing secret reports from Kube on German atrocities in the East', 18 June 1943, found in Himmler's personal files. (USA 289): NCA 8, 205 also deployed in 'The persecution of the Jews' brief: NCA 1, Ch. 12.

[570] See the undated and untitled document mapping prosecution documentation to specific trial briefs contained in Jackson Papers, op. cit. Box 101, Reel 7.

tor were taking the Nazis' genocidal actions most seriously. This document is a copy of a letter from Koch to Defendant Rosenberg enclosing two secret reports from Himmler's personal files on various: 'German atrocities committed in the East' i.e., the killings of civilian Jews and Russians by both the German army and the SS. The complaints related not to the extermination policies themselves, but rather to the *chosen methods* of killing and disposing of corpses. These are noted as including mass burnings to death in barns of men, women and children, and the non-burial of corpses. These complaints highlighted the potentially negative impact these practices could exert upon public order, i.e., the risk of 'alienating the population'. Thus, it provided crucial rebuttal trial evidence that: 'Rosenberg was well aware of atrocities committed in the area under his jurisdiction.'[571]

The Nazis' persecution of the Jews was further highlighted by R-143. This dossier contains an analysis of Himmler's decree from 19 December 1939, which was based on an earlier decree by Göring confiscating: 'all valuables owned by Poles and Jews in the Eastern territories'.[572] The R-Series, also includes details of the Nazis' use of 'special courts' as an instrument of racist persecution of both Jews and Poles. One document within this dossier provides evidence of how the Nazi regime subjected these groups, which of course overlapped in some measure, to extraordinary penalties for undefined offences; whilst also denying members the traditional protections of the criminal law. For example, offences by Poles or Jews against other Poles and Jews could attract a sentence set below the minimum sentence that would otherwise apply to all other classes of defendant.[573]

Other R-Series evidence related to the Holocaust includes documents providing details of secret communications between Himmler and Gestapo Chief Mueller regarding the selection of different categories of Jews for transportation to Auschwitz-Birkenau concentration/death camps. This letter includes the chilling statement that the proposed 45,000 Jews selected for transportation during late December and January 1943: 'should yield... 10–15,000 people fit for work.'[574] Obviously, this acknowledges, albeit in an implicit manner, that the remaining

[571] R-135, SEA 28 September, 1945: Cornell Collection, Vol. 20, pt. 2.

[572] R-143, SEA 3 October 1945: Ibid.

[573] R-96: 'Penal Law against Poles and Jews in the Annexed Eastern Territories', Dr Schlegelberger to Reich Minister of Justice, 17 April 1941.

[574] Mueller to Himmler, 16 December 1942: NCA 8, 60 USA Trial Exhibit 241.

30–35,000 individuals, who were children, sick or infirm, would be exterminated immediately upon their arrival. Another part of the R-Series includes a memorandum from Heydrich, Head of the SS Security Police, who was later assassinated by partisans trained by British Intelligence, that includes the following remarkable claim: 'It may be safely assumed that there will be no more Jews in the annexed Eastern Territories.' Heydrich's statement was made long after the option of deportation of Jews to Madagascar had been closed by the military situation; and thus provides further self-incrimination regarding the Nazis' Holocaust.[575]

Furthermore, R-102 summarises a captured 'situation report' containing grim details of the numbers of Jews and captured partisans (including children) killed by German Einsatzgruppen (Task Forces) and Sonder Commandos. In a coldly matter of fact manner, this 'top secret' document outlines the systematic arrest, persecution and slaughter of Jews in the Baltic area:

> The male Jews over 16 were arrested with the exception of doctors and the elders. At the present time this action is still in progress. After completion of this action, there will remain only 500 Jewesses and children in the Eastern territory.[576]

Concerning Nazi genocide within the White Ruthenia region, this report also describes how the local populations refused to participate in pogroms against local Jews, and how, as a result, the paramilitary squads adopted an: 'all the more vigorous' policy of extermination. Some of these killings were categorised as responses to specific acts of resistance, anti-Nazi propaganda, refusal to work or sabotage. However, in many other locations Nazi officials made little pretence that these deaths were anything other part of a systematic programme of racist genocide. For example, it is noted that in Shitomir: '3,145 Jews had to be shot, because from experience they have to be regarded as bearers of Bolshevist propaganda and saboteurs.'[577] In Cherson, this report records that: 'the solution of the Jewish question has been taken up energetically by the task forces of the Security Police and the SD.

---

[575] Attached to R-96: 'Penal Law against Poles and Jews in the Annexed Eastern Territories', Dr Schlegelberger to Reich Minister of Justice, 17 April 1941, NCA 8, 81–83, with the statement itself found at 82.

[576] R-102: 'Activity and Situation Report No. 6 of the Task Forces of the Security Police and the SD in the U.S.S.R.' [for October 1943], NCA 8, 96–103, at 14.

[577] Ibid., 103.

The areas newly occupied by the commandos were purged of Jews.'[578] In other cases, weak 'explanations' of the slaughter were still being made. For example, in Witebsk: 'On account of the extreme danger of an epidemic, a beginning was made to liquidate the Jews of the ghetto...This involved approximately 3000 Jews'.[579] In Ukraine, this situation report records the mass slaughter by local anti-Semitic groups of 33,771 Jews on the 29 and 30 September 1943.[580]

The prosecutors deployed parts of the R-Series reports extensively during their detailed accounts of the extermination of European Jewry. In this context, the content of R-135 (also cited confusingly as 1475-PS),[581] is especially pertinent. This document, consisting of letters from June 1943 from Lohse and Kube to Rosenberg concerning SS atrocities in eastern Europe, contributed to prosecution briefs addressing 'Atrocities against Civilian Populations of Occupied Territories' and 'Forced Labor'.[582] This is because it includes the protest of the Reichskommissar for Ostland to Defendant Rosenberg against the immediate extermination during the 'Cottbus' project of so many Jews without first exploiting them fully as slave labour. His complaint insisted that the locking of men, women, and children into barns and then setting fire to them represented an inappropriate method for combating partisans. This OSS dossier also includes a report of 5 June 1943 by SS Obergruppenführer Von dem Bach, (the General Commissar of White Ruthenia), to the Defendant Rosenberg, noting that: 'The result of the operation, 4,500 enemy dead and 5,000 wounded, suspected of belonging to bands' (partisan groups), who apparently were the individuals burnt to death in the barns. Most incriminating is the admission that only 492 rifles were taken from 4,500 supposedly fully armed 'partisans'.

The Nuremberg prosecutors also linked the content of R-102 to that of R-135 to paint a gruesome picture of the nature and extent of the Nazis' anti-Semitic genocide:

> There are reports which merely tabulate the numbers slaughtered. An example is an account of the work of Einsatzgruppen of SIPO and SD in the East, which relates that: "In Estonia, all Jews were arrested

---

578 Ibid.

579 Ibid., 102.

580 Ibid.

581 Contained in document Book 16-B, Page 81, USA Exhibit 289.

582 See the undated and untitled document mapping prosecution documentation to specific trial briefs contained in Jackson Papers, Box 101, Reel 7.

> immediately upon the arrival of the Wehrmacht. Jewish men and women above the age of 16 and capable of work were drafted for forced labor. Jews were subjected to all sorts of restrictions and all Jewish property was confiscated. All Jewish males above the age of 16 were executed, with the exception of doctors and elders. Only 500 of an original 4,500 Jews remained. Thirty-seven thousand, one hundred eighty persons have been liquidated by the SIPO and SD in White Ruthenia during October. In one town, 337 Jewish women were executed for demonstrating a 'provocative attitude.' In another, 380 Jews were shot for spreading vicious propaganda." And so the report continues, listing town after town, where hundreds of Jews were murdered: In Vitebsk 3,000 Jews were liquidated because of the danger of epidemics. In Kiev 33,771 Jews were executed on September 29 and 30 in retaliation for some fires which were set off there. In Shitomir 3,145 Jews "had to be shot" because, judging from experience they had to be considered as the carriers of Bolshevik propaganda. In Cherson 410 Jews were executed in reprisal against acts of sabotage. In the territory east of the Dnieper, the Jewish problem was 'solved' by the liquidation of 4,891 Jews and by putting the remainder into labor battalions of up to 1,000 persons. (R-102). Other accounts tell not of the slaughter so much as of the depths of degradation to which the tormentors stooped. For example, we will show the report made to Defendant Rosenberg about the army and the SS in the area under Rosenberg's jurisdiction, which recited the following: "Details: In presence of SS man, a Jewish dentist has to break all gold teeth and fillings out of mouths of German and Russian Jews *before* they are executed." Men, women and children are locked into barns and burned alive. Peasants, women and children are shot on the pretext that they are suspected of belonging to bands. (R-135)[583]

In addition to recording programmes of straightforward executions, the Nuremberg prosecutors fully exploited aspects of OSS evidence regarding the extermination of Jews by means of slave labour programmes, essentially a form of delayed killing. Here R-91 was particularly helpful. This was a copy of a telegram from Mueller to Himmler requesting transportation of 45,000 Jews to Auschwitz concentration camp. The prosecutors had previously used this document in their preparation of trial briefs addressing the 'Establishment and Operation of

[583] IMT 4, 293–4. The R-135 document, the report of Gunther the prison warden at Minsk made on 31 May 1943, to the General Commissioner for White Ruthenia, in which he pointed out that after 13 April 1943 the SD had pursued a policy of removing all gold teeth, bridgework, and fillings of Jews, an hour or two before they were murdered. This report was used by the OSS prosecutor Whitney Harris as evidence that: 'conditions of horror and cruelty continued to characterize the operations of Einsatzkommandos in the East while Kaltenbrunner was Chief of the Security Police and SD.'

Concentration Camps' and 'Atrocities against Civilian Populations of Occupied Territories', for which Edward Boedeker and Edward Kenyon were responsible respectively. Defendant Saukel was cross-examined by his own lawyer with respect to R-91. This attempt at rebuttal of the clear implications of R-91 indicated that, contrary to his feeble denials, Saukel had played a key role in the rounding up and deportation of Jews, who the Nazi regime were treating as little more than an industrial resource to be worked to death:

> Dr. Servatius: What about the employment of Jewish workers?
> Sauckel: I had nothing to do with the employment of Jews. That was exclusively the task of the Reichsfuehrer of the SS.
> Dr. Servatius: I submit the Document R-91. That is Exhibit USA-241, and Exhibit RF-347.... It is a letter from the Chief of Security Police and SD Muller to the Reichsfuehrer SS, field headquarters, dated 16 December 1942. It says there, and I quote: "In connection with the increased assignment of manpower to the... KZ which is ordered to take place before 30 January 1943, the following procedure may be applied in the Jewish sector: total number, 45,000 Jews." Then there is a more detailed specification, and among other things, it says at the end, "3,000 Jews from the occupied territories of the Netherlands," and further, "The number 45,000 includes those unfit for work...." What had you to do with that letter?
> Sauckel: I have just learned of that letter for the first time. I did not know of it before, and I can only emphasize that these transports and this procedure had nothing to do with my work, and that I had nothing to do with them at any time.[584]

Shawcross, President of the IMT, also cited documents from this OSS collection to highlight the complicity of other defendants, such as Frick, and to dismiss the idea that any of the 22 defendants could really deny knowledge of the Holocaust. Here R-96 proved especially helpful. It consisted of four documents showing the history and immediate origin of the law of 4 December 1941 establishing and institutionalising discrimination against Jews and Poles in criminal procedures. This dossier informed the preparation of James Walsh's trial brief 'Persecution of Jews.' During the trial, Shawcross argued:

> Can Frick, as Minister of Interior, have been unaware of the policy to exterminate the Jews? In 1941 one of his subordinates, Heydrich, was writing to another—the Minister of Justice: "...it may safely be assumed that in the future there will be no more Jews in the annexed Eastern

[584] IMT 15, 42.

> Territories." (Document Number R-96). Can he, as Reich Protector for Bohemia and Moravia, deny responsibility for the deportations of thousands of Jews from his territory to the gas chambers of Auschwitz, only a few miles across the frontier?[585]

In short, the R-Series evidence contained a mass of details concerning different aspects of the Holocaust as the Nazis unfolded their programme across both Western and Eastern Europe. The Nuremberg prosecutors deployed many R-Series dossiers effectively during their presentation of trial evidence. A close review of the contents of this series rebuts the suggestion that the OSS either ignored or downplayed the systematic extermination of civilians founded upon the perverse theories of the supremacy of an Aryan 'master race', and the rights of the German nation under Nazi leadership to dominate the whole of Europe. On the contrary, Rothschild's OSS Unit provided highly incriminating documentation of the Nazis' genocidal policies in Eastern Europe.

The value of DCU's work was finally recognised by Justice Jackson in his glowing official tribute to Walter Rothschild. Jackson noted that the work of the latter's OSS unit had been 'invaluable to this mission'. Even before the main party of the US prosecution team had arrived in continental Europe, members of the DRU had established fruitful liaison with a number of other Allied intelligence agencies from whom they secured many important documents. Rothschild's personal contribution had been helped by his skills both as a barrister and a linguist who was fluent in both German and French. It was further enhanced by Rochshild's broad knowledge and: 'intelligent and thorough understanding' of the structures and genocidal policies of Nazi Germany. In addition, Rothschild had, according to Jackson: 'on many occasions materially assisted us with his observations and suggestions' acting partly as a specialist consultant.[586]

Other OSS-sourced evidence of the Holocaust used at Nuremberg

When surveying the evidence used to support Nuremberg trial briefs relevant to the Holocaust, it is possible to recognise many items of trial evidence that OSS staff identified, discussed and analysed in a number

585 IMT 19, 518.

586 Jackson, 'Commendation of Officers' 17 August 1945: Jackson Papers, Box 101, Reel 7.

of the documents we have already examined. With respect to Göring, for example, the prosecution brief on 'The Persecution of the Jews' included materials on anti-Jewish decrees from 1938–39 that Neumann had cited in his draft brief 'Göring as a war criminal' from June 1945. Intercept materials in wartime OSS files, including confidential orders signed by Heydrich relating to the pre-planned pogrom on 10–11 November 1938 (3051-PS), also featured extensively not only in the 'Persecution of the Jews' and 'Concentration Camp' final trials brief, but also in Jackson's opening address to the IMT.[587]

The same is true for documents the OSS originally obtained from the British Foreign Office relating to the Holocaust in Galacia, Poland. These included a report from Lt. Katzmann, General of Police, to Krueger, General of the Police East, dated 20 June 1943, and entitled 'Solution of Jewish Question in Galicia (Nuremberg document L-18). This was originally found within the OSS' internal records,[588] and subsequently taken to Nuremberg where it became part of General Donovan's Nuremberg files.[589] The prosecutors fully exploited the shockingly frank and detailed report concerning the numbers of Jews SS officers killed by various means, and on different pretexts. It also contains an inventory of the loot plundered from the victims of such killings, including dental gold. The use of the key points of this two-page report is worth quoting in full:

> Jews were forced into ghettos in the Polish Province of Galicia. The conditions in these ghettos are described in the report from Katzmann (L-18): "Nothing but catastrophical conditions were found in the ghettos of Rawa-Ruska and Rohatyn... The Jews of Rawa-Ruska, fearing the evacuation, had concealed those suffering from spotted fever in underground holes. When evacuation was to start the police found that 3,000 Jews suffering from spotted fever lay about in this ghetto. In order to destroy this center of pestilence at once every police officer inoculated against spotted fever was called into action. Thus we succeeded to destroy this plagueboil, losing thereby only one officer. Almost the same conditions were found in Rohatyn... Since we received more and more alarming reports on the Jews becoming armed in an ever increasing manner, we started during the last fortnight in June 1943 an action throughout the whole of the district of Galicia with the intent to use strongest measures to destroy the Jewish gangsterdom. Special measures were found necessary during

587 Op. cit.

588 CIA withdrawn/withdrawn collection: US NA, RG 226, Entry 210, Box 6.

589 Cornell Collection, Vol. 1.

> the action to dissolve the ghetto in Lwow where the dug-out mentioned above had been established. Here we had to act brutally from the beginning, in order to avoid losses on our side; we had to blow up, or to burn down several houses. On this occasion the surprising fact arose that we were able to catch about 20,000 Jews instead of 12,000 Jews who had registered. We had to pull at least 3,000 Jewish corpses out of every kind of hiding places; they had committed suicide by taking poison.... Despite the extraordinary burden heaped upon every single SS-police officer, during these actions, mood and spirit of the men were extraordinarily good and praiseworthy from the first to the last day..." (L-18)
>
> These acts of removal and slaughter were not entirely without profit. The report continues: "Together with the evacuation action, we executed the confiscation of Jewish property. Very high amounts were confiscated and paid over to the Special Staff "Reinhard". Apart from furniture and many textile goods, the following amounts were confiscated and turned over to special Staff 'Reinhard'.
>
> "20.952 kilograms of gold wedding rings; 7 Stamp collections, complete; 1 Suit case with pocket knives; 1 basket of fountain pens and propelled pencils; 3 Bags filled with rings-not genuine; 35 wagons of furs." (L-18) The thoroughness of the looting is illustrated by an item listing 11.73 kilograms of gold teeth and inlays. (L-18)[590]

The trial brief exploiting OSS film materials depicting the Nazis' brutal treatment of members of a Jewish ghetto, is also included in Donovan's Nuremberg files,[591] noting that these consisted of:

> a strip of motion picture footage taken, presumably, by a member of the SS, and captured by the United States military forces in an SS barracks near Augsburg, Germany. The film depicts what is believed to be the extermination of a ghetto by Gestapo agents, assisted by military units. The following scenes are representative:
> Scene 2: A naked girl running across the courtyard.
> Scene 3: An older woman being pushed past the camera, and a man in SS uniform standing at the right of the scene.
> Scene 5: A man with a skull cap and a woman are manhandled.
> Scene 14: A half-naked woman runs through the crowd.
> Scene 15: Another half-naked woman runs out of the house.
> Scene 16: Two men drag an old man out.

---

590 'The Persecution of the Jews', op. cit.

591 Cornell Collection, Vol. IX / Subdivision 17.05. The OSS documentation notes that this was secured by James Donovan who was responsible for OSS film evidence on 'Nazi concentration camps' and the regime's rise to power shown at the Nuremberg trials. See Salter 2007 op. cit. 260–76. The full OSS files include two affidavits attesting to the authenticity of this 8mm film captured in SS barracks and to its genuine nature as trial evidence.

> Scene 18: A man in German military uniform, with his back to the camera, watches.
> Scene 24: A general shot of the street; showing fallen bodies and naked women running.
> Scene 32: A shot of the street, showing five fallen bodies.
> Scene 37: A man with a bleeding head is hit again.
> Scene 39: A soldier in German military uniform, with a rifle, stands by as a crowd centers on a man coming out of the house.
> Scene 44: A soldier with a rifle, in German military uniform, walks past a woman clinging to a torn blouse.
> Scene 45: A woman is dragged by her hair across the street.

In addition, the prosecutors made full use of other evidence secured by the ALIU regarding Defendant Rosenberg's role in anti-Semitic plunder in France.[592] This is clear from the following extract from the trial brief: 'The Persecution of the Jews', which will be quoted again here for convenience:

> Rosenberg's notion of the means to be taken against the Jews is expressed in a secret "Document Memorandum for the Fuehrer-Concerning: Jewish Possessions in France," dated 18 December 1941. Rosenberg urges plundering and death:
>
> 1. In compliance with the order of the Fuehrer for protection of Jewish cultural possessions, a great number of Jewish dwellings remained unguarded. Consequently, many furnishings have disappeared because a guard could, naturally, not be posted. In the whole East the administration has found terrible conditions of living quarters, and the chances of procurement are so limited that it is not practical to procure any more. Therefore, I beg the Fuehrer to permit the seizure of all Jewish home furnishings of Jews in Paris, who have fled or will leave shortly, and that of Jews living in all part of the occupied West, to relieve the shortage of furnishings in the administration in the East.
>
> 2. A great number of leading Jews were, after a short examination in Paris, again released. The attempts on the lives of members of the armed forces have not stopped; on the contrary they continue. This reveals an unmistakable plan to disrupt the German-French cooperation, to force Germany to retaliate, and, with this, evoke a new defense on the parts of the French against Germany. I suggest to the Fuehrer that, instead of executing 100 Frenchmen, we substitute 100 Jewish bankers, lawyers, etc. It is the Jews in London and New York who incite the French communists to commit acts of violence, and it seems only fair that the members of this race should pay for this. It is not the little Jews, but the leading Jews

[592] CIR 1, op. cit. Attachments 4 and 5.

> in France, who should be held responsible. That would tend to awaken the Anti-Jewish sentiment.
>
> (Signed) A. Rosenberg. (001-PS)

On the topic of concentration camp evidence, Nuremberg prosecutors made extensive use of the report to which the OSS section assigned to the US Seventh Army contributed on Dachau camp. As Nuremberg document L-159, it was exploited in the trial brief whose substance is well-described by its admittedly inelegant title: 'The Slave Labor Program, the Illegal Use of Prisoners of War, and the Special Responsibility of Sauckel and Speer Therefor.' Under a specific heading most clearly related to the Holocaust, namely, 'The Concentration Camp Program of Extermination Through Work', this brief stated:

> The character of the treatment inflicted on Allied nationals and other victims of concentration camps while they were being worked to death is described in an official report...(L-159). The report states in part:
>
> "...They were forced to sleep on wooden frames covered with wooden boards in tiers of two, three and even four, sometimes with no covering, sometimes with a bundle of dirty rags serving both as pallet and coverlet. Their food consisted generally of about one-half of a pound of black bread per day and a bowl of watery soup for noon and night, and not always that. Owing to the great numbers crowded into a small space and to the lack of adequate sustenance, lice and vermin multiplied, disease became rampant, and those who did not soon die of disease or torture began the long, slow process of starvation....Upon entrance into these camps, newcomers were forced to work either at an adjoining war factory or were placed 'in commando' on various jobs in the vicinity, being returned each night to their stall in the barracks. Generally a German criminal was placed in charge of each 'block' or shed in which the prisoners slept. Periodically he would choose the one prisoner of his block who seemed the most alert or intelligent or showed the most leadership qualities. These would report to the guards' room and would never be heard from again. The generally-accepted belief of the prisoners was that these were shot or gassed or hanged and then cremated. A refusal to work or an infraction of the rules usually meant flogging and other types of torture, such as having the fingernails pulled out, and in each case usually ended in death after extensive suffering. The policies herein described constituted a calculated and diabolical program of planned torture and extermination on the part of those who were in control of the German Government...On the whole, we found this camp to have been operated and administered much in the same manner as Buchenwald had been operated and managed. When the efficiency of the workers decreased as a result of the conditions under which they were required to live, their rations were decreased as punishment. This brought about

> a vicious circle in which the weak became weaker and were ultimately exterminated. (L-159).[593]

This extensive citation was deployed to support the prosecutors' accusation that both Saukel and Speer were knowingly responsible for that aspect of the Holocaust in which initially healthy Jews were deported to slave labour camps where they were, in effect, worked to death:

> Such was the cycle of work, torture, starvation and death for concentration camp labor—labor which Göring, when requesting that more of it be placed at his disposal, said had proved very useful; labor which Speer was "anxious" to use in the factories under his control.[594]

During the trial itself, the prosecution quoted extensively this document early in the proceedings to help corroborate: 'the unspeakably brutal, inhumane, and degrading treatment inflicted [on]... victims of concentration camps, while they were indeed being literally worked to death'.[595] The prosecutor stated that this claim is: 'described in Document L-159', and he then quoted extensively from the parts of the report already quoted above, which will not be repeated.

> I would like to quote from the document briefly, first from Page 14, the last paragraph, and from Page 15, the first two paragraphs, of the English text:... [extract already quoted above]
>
> ...The policy underlying this program, the manner in which it was executed, and the responsibility of the conspirators in connection with it has been dwell upon at length. Therefore, we should like, at this point, to discuss the special responsibility of the Defendant Sauckel....[596]

Later, on 30 January 1946, the French prosecutor, M. Dubost, exploited the same report to help substantiate his claim that the purpose of concentration camps was: '1) to make good the shortage of labor; 2) to eliminate useless forces.' Dubost claimed that the physical destruction of detainees, assumed two different forms. One was 'progressive; the other was brutal':

> Likewise, in the report of a committee set up by General Eisenhower, Document L-159, which we submit under Exhibit Number RF-352, Pages 31, 32, and 33 of the same document book, we read:

---

593 NCA 1, Chapter 10: http://www.yale.edu/lawweb/avalon/imt/document/nca_vol1/chap_10.htm.
594 Ibid.
595 IMT 3, 467, 12 December 1945.
596 Ibid.

> "The purpose of this camp was extermination...... aerolites and other conditions in the concentration camps in Germany.... The mission of this camp was extermination, by starvation, beatings, torture, incredibly crowded sleeping conditions, and sickness. The result of these measures was heightened by the fact that prisoners were obliged to work in an armament factory adjoining the camp which manufactured small fire arms, rifles... The means which were used to carry out this progressive extermination are numerous....[597]

In short, even a brief review of a limited number of examples of Nuremberg evidence relating to the Holocaust involving both death camps and mass killings through the deployment of paramilitary action squads, is sufficient to highlight trial evidence stemming from the OSS' files. The prosecutors prominently deployed a number of these documents in the trial proceedings, including those relating delayed extermination through slave labour within Nazi concentration camps. A thorough and exhaustive study that cross-referenced every item on the Holocaust within OSS records, with each piece of Nuremberg evidence that directly or indirectly touched upon the Holocaust, methodologies of killing and the perpetrators would, in all likelihood, reveal dozens of other examples.

As already noted, General Donovan continued his role as OSS Director whilst also acting as Justice Jackson's deputy. He gathered his own personal staff of experts at Nuremberg, including the jurist and former member of the anti-Nazi German resistance, Fabian Schlabrendorff. Donovan asked Schlabrendorff to review the indictment and make a series of suggestions for its improvement, or at least to alert prosecutors as to any previously unseen difficulties or omissions. Donovan summarised these suggestions in a memorandum he sent directly to Jackson. One of these related to the section addressing: 'crimes against humanity'. He complained that specific atrocities against Jews in Eastern Europe had been underplayed:

> It further occurs to me that the murder by 44 men of 7,000 Russian nationals of Hebrew faith committed in 1941 in Bovvisow has not been mentioned despite that, especially in this case, protests were lodged by German Military Quarters leading to an important inter-German discussions.[598]

---

[597] IMT 6, 333–34, 30 January, 1946: http://www.yale.edu/lawweb/avalon/imt/proc/01-30-46.htm.

[598] Donovan to Jackson, 20 October 1945, Jackson Papers, op. cit. Box 101, Reel 7.

The memoirs of former OSS prosecutors have been quoted already but one in particular merits citation as it concerns anti-Semitic propaganda. In one sense, Drexel Sprecher's had mixed success as a prosecutor. Although he was quickly promoted through the ranks to actually present two cases before the tribunal, only one of these resulted in a conviction. As Sprecher recalls:

> Did the experience live up to my expectations? Well, in many respects, of course, my expectations were overreached, because I was called upon to make two presentations before the International Tribunal. One against Baldur von Schirach, the Hitler Youth leader—he received a sentence of twenty years.[599] The second case was against Hans Fritzsche, the head of the radio division of the propaganda ministry—and he was found not guilty.[600] So I didn't feel that I had done as good a job as I would have liked, with respect to that man who helped encourage Germans to hate Jews, and to hate people he classified as Bolshevists, and of course, he also meant liberals. And I found myself quite unhappy when that decision came down in court, so my expectations were not one hundred percent lived up to.[601]

We can add Sprecher's comments to those we have already quoted from Whitney Harris, who clearly expressed his pride at helping to ascertain new details of the Holocaust for the IMT; whilst also taking notice of Franz Neumann's role in ensuring that OSS materials on the Holocaust reached the prosecutors in sufficient quantities. Considered in the round, it is fair to say that a number of OSS staff took a personal interest in making sure that perpetrators of the Holocaust were brought to justice.

In sum, this chapter opened with a discussion of the ALIU's contributions to the Nuremberg process, which described the important role its reports played in the preparation of trial briefs on cultural plunder. It then addressed the nature and influence of Franz Neumann's controversial 'spearhead theory' of Nazi anti-Semitism. Other sections have discussed wartime and postwar R&A reports on Nazi war crimes that are relevant to the Holocaust, and which, to some extent, reveal

---

599 Hitler Youth or Hitler Jugend encompassed and consumed all youth organizations within Germany. Shortly after Baldur von Schirach became its head in 1933.

600 Hans Fritzsche was a section chief in the Propaganda Ministry underneath Joseph Goebbels and Otto Dietrich, see Taylor 1992: 268. Although he had limited influence over policy decisions, his radio news programme, 'Hans Fritzsche Speaks,' denounced Jews and applauded Germany's aggressions.

601 Sprecher, 1995 op. cit. 213–4.

the influence of Neumann's theory, particularly in relation to Dwork's draft trial brief on the persecution of the Jews. In addition to discussing the contents of written reports, this chapter also assessed the work of the Neumann research group sent to Nuremberg to assist in the practical application of OSS R&A's findings to the final prosecution trial briefs.

OSS officials successfully gathered a vast array of incriminating materials relevant to the Holocaust during the immediate postwar months. Members of this organisation actively sought to publicise atrocities that had taken place, as well as the grim logistical means through which genocide had been accomplished. Mediated through the extensive involvement of General Donovan, Franz Neumann, and other senior and middle ranking OSS staff in the Nuremberg process, much of this evidence proved useful for postwar prosecutions of complicit Nazis. Other sections of this chapter have highlighted the R&A Jewish Desk's significant contributions to the Nuremberg process, the role of OSS staff in gathering trial evidence of Nazi genocide from its own personnel, such as Jack Taylor. The final section has discussed the contents and relative success of OSS' 'R-Series' of Nuremberg evidence stemming from the intelligence-gathering and analytical work of Walter Rothschild's Unit within OSS London, and other OSS-sourced evidence of the Holocaust that was fed into the Nuremberg process.

OVERALL CONCLUSION

This book has provided a close description and analysis of the contents of a wide range of declassified OSS files, which indicate that, contrary to a considerable number of critiques, the OSS played a far more extensive role in the monitoring of the Nazis' genocide against European Jews than was previously recognised. Furthermore, it has been shown that certain OSS officials took considerable risks to engage in a series of practical interventions and interagency collaborations with the US War Refugee Board, the most successful of which took place in the Baltics and, through the sponsorship of the Wallenberg mission, in Hungary.[1] According to specialist scholars, these humanitarian interventions helped save many thousand Jewish lives. OSS staff also made a significant contribution to the exposure of Nazi genocide within liberated concentration camps. This took place both directly, and through their gathering and presentation of damning documentary evidence to the IMT. In addition, largely through the efforts of Franz Neumann, a considerable number of OSS-R&A reports relevant to Nazi atrocities against Jews and others were entered into the raw materials from which Nuremberg prosecutors selected evidence for their trial briefs. The contents of the R-series of trial evidence provided powerful and detailed evidence of the nature and extent of the Holocaust. This is clear from the extent to which such material was selected by the prosecutors and then later singled out as particularly damning by the Nuremberg judges in their final judgements. The OSS succeeded in introducing into court evidence a number of themes relevant to the Holocaust, including Taylor's graphic firsthand testimony of genocide within Mauthausen death camp.

The main argument throughout this book has been that, despite clear examples of misapprehension, omission and inadequate response, many OSS officials and their informants contributed to the building up of an increasingly detailed picture of the Holocaust as this was taking place. This argument has, for the most part, been substantiated by a close reading of declassified OSS war crimes files, including

[1] For OSS documentation, see US NA, RG 226, Entry 37, Folder 6 'War Refugee Board'.

the records and reports of the ALIU and a number of R&A reports commissioned specifically by Jackson's organisation. Through such reports and the R-Series of trial evidence that Rothschild's OSS unit analysed in London, a significant body of OSS information on the Holocaust was ultimately fed into the Nuremberg process. Of course, and despite Neumann's valiant efforts, not all of this was deployed or exploited as well it could have been, but this cannot be laid at the door of the OSS. For example, the work of the ALIU experts was so thorough that Nuremberg prosecutors preparing trials briefs related to the Nazis' cultural plunder needed little additional assistance. Most of the key points from the ALIU's reports had already been included in draft prosecution briefs.

A number of the criticisms directed against Neumann's influential spearhead theory of anti-Semitism, including the idea that it lead to the underplaying of the Holocaust at the Nuremberg trials, have been rebutted. It has been shown that a broadly functionalist theory of this kind, whatever its sociological defects, was precisely what the existing state of international criminal law needed in order to make an integral connection between war crimes and domestic atrocities against Jewish and other civilians. Whilst the work of the OSS' ALIU was not completed, with many of its recommendations for prosecution ignored, those who followed up on this unit's work in the field of Holocaust restitution have paid extensive tribute to the work of OSS officials in this area as laying the foundation of their own later efforts. Virtually all contemporary scholars in this field extensively cite ALIU reports as still providing a mostly reliable basis for historical research and even contemporary litigation. Whilst it is arguable that OSS' contribution to the Safehaven programme cannot be considered especially successful, particularly in respect to Holocaust restitution issues, this stems largely from the fact that looted gold had, in most cases, already been melted down, or mixed in such a way that restitution to the original individual owners was physically impossible. It is worth noting that scholars addressing many of the inefficiencies and problems with this interagency programme have exempted OSS officials from the turf war rivalries that restricted its efficiency, and instead attributed these to rivalries between Treasury, FEA and State Department officials.

Perhaps the most significant failing of the OSS' work lay at the level of analysis: in too many cases, different phases of the Holocaust as a single and unfolding genocidal programme, were reinterpreted as singular and one-off episodes. On the other hand, the failure of intelligence officials to come to terms with an unprecedented phenomena which, at the time it was taking place did not even have a name, was hardly surprising. The event itself, rooted in a particularly vicious form of racism, defied and may still defy rational explanation. With the passing of time much concerning the Nazi's anti-Jewish genocide that was not perceived because it fell within the realm of the unbelievable and inconceivable can be better appreciated, together with the reasons why it has taken so long to gain a better perspective: something which goes some way to exonerating many of the analytical failures of OSS staff.

APPENDIX ONE

THE NUREMBERG LAWS ON CULTURAL PLUNDER

In what follows, I will identify how the prosecutors responsible for drawing up the indictment, effectively a first draft of much of the prosecution's overall case, interpreted the significance of the Nazi art looting as clearly involving acts that were criminal under three of the four counts recognised by the Nuremberg Charter ('criminal conspiracy', 'war crimes' and 'crimes against humanity').

The indictment contains a summary of the offences for which the Nuremberg defendants were charged, a series of claims regarding the policies of the Nazi regime that violated these laws, and statements of the individual and collective responsibility of specific defendants (including 'organisational defendants', such as the Gestapo). It was entered formally into evidence during the second day of the IMT hearings as part of the official trial record. This occurred by means of the tedious process of Alderman and other prosecutors simply reading out its detailed contents to the Tribunal verbatim on 20 November 1945.

Count One of the prosecutors' indictment specifically referred to 'the plunder of public and private property' as an integral aspect of the wider criminal conspiracy to which all the defendants were charged under Article 6(a). This aspect of the indictment also referred to various alleged techniques[1] through which the Nazi leadership put into effect their overall conspiracy, two of which are particularly relevant to our present interest in cultural plunder. This is because firstly they underpinned the racist definition of 'degenerate art' allegedly associated with Jewish, and other supposedly 'alien', influences, and, secondly, they informed aspects of the ALIU's concern, discussed previously, that certain of the individuals they recommended for prosecution as war criminals could seek to evade responsibility by reference to the 'leadership principle':

[1] Characterised as: 'Doctrinal Techniques of the Common Plan or Conspiracy.' http://www.yale.edu/lawweb/avalon/imt/proc/count1.htm.

> To incite others to join in the common plan or conspiracy, and as a means of securing for the Nazi conspirators the highest degree of control over the German community, they put forth, disseminated, and exploited certain doctrines, among others, as follows:
>
> 1. That persons of so-called "German blood" (as specified by the Nazi conspirators) were a "master race" and were accordingly entitled to subjugate, dominate, or exterminate other "races" and peoples;
>
> 2. That the German people should be ruled under the Fuehrerprinzip (Leadership Principle) according to which power was to reside in a Fuehrer from whom sub-leaders were to derive authority in a hierarchical order, each sub-leader to owe unconditional obedience to his immediate superior but to be absolute in his own sphere of jurisdiction; and the power of the leadership was to be unlimited, extending to all phases of public and private life.[2]

The indictment followed a modified version of Neumann's 'spearhead theory' of anti-Semitism.[3] It treated cultural plunder of Jewish art and other property, which is often termed 'despoilment', as a functional aspect of a wider system for consolidating totalitarian control by terrorising with increasingly severe measures all sources of actual and potential opposition to their racist plans:

> (b) In order to make their rule secure from attack and to instil fear in the hearts of the German people, the Nazi conspirators established and extended a system of terror against opponents and supposed or suspected opponents of the regime. They imprisoned such persons without judicial process, holding them in "protective custody" and concentration camps, and subjected them to persecution, degradation, despoilment, enslavement, torture, and murder.
>
> (c) The Nazi conspirators conceived that, in addition to the suppression of distinctively political opposition, it was necessary to suppress or exterminate certain other movements or groups which they regarded as obstacles to their retention of total control in Germany and to the aggressive aims of the conspiracy abroad.[4]

The indictment suggests that the attack on Jewish art and other property needed to be interpreted as one relatively early phase of an escalating process of racist persecution and genocide, based on 'master race' ideas. During this process, policies of anti-Semitic cultural attacks and

---

[2] Ibid.

[3] This controversial approach is discussed in M. Salter, 'The Visibility of the Holocaust: Franz Neumann and the Nuremberg trials': in Fine, R. and Turner, C. (eds.), *Social theory after the Holocaust*, Liverpool: Liverpool University Press, 2000: 197–218.

[4] Indictment op. cit.

plunder of art works represented stepping stones towards a programme of mass and systematic physical extermination, which amounted to their culmination. In order to emphasise the criminal intent, purposes and subjective knowledge of key participants in this conspiracy, the indictment cites as evidence various racist statements of individual members of the Nazi regime who, in their official capacities, were directly implicated in the looting of Jewish art, such as defendant Rosenberg:

> (d) Implementing their "master race" policy, the conspirators joined in a program of relentless persecution of the Jews, designed to exterminate them. Annihilation of the Jews became an official State policy, carried out both by official action and by incitements to mob and individual violence. The conspirators openly avowed their purpose. For example, the Defendant Rosenberg stated: "Anti-Semitism is the unifying element of the reconstruction of Germany." On another occasion he also stated: "Germany will regard the Jewish question as solved only after the very last Jew has left the greater German living space... Europe will have its Jewish question solved only after the very last Jew has left the Continent."... The program of action against the Jews included disfranchisement, stigmatization, denial of civil rights, subjecting their persons and property to violence, deportation, enslavement, enforced labor, starvation, murder, and mass extermination. The extent to which the conspirators succeeded in their purpose can only be estimated, but the annihilation was substantially complete in many localities of Europe. Of the 9,600,000 Jews who lived in the parts of Europe under Nazi domination, it is conservatively estimated that 5,700,000 have disappeared, most of them deliberately put to death by the Nazi conspirators. Only remnants of the Jewish population of Europe remain.[5]

The indictment's analysis of Count Three (Article 6 of the Nuremberg Charter relating to 'traditional' war crimes, including Articles 46 to 56 of the Hague Regulations, 1907), is also relevant to our purposes. It alleged that the defendants had been engaged in racist genocide directed at the civilian population, particularly against Jews:

> They conducted deliberate and systematic genocide, viz., the extermination of racial and national groups, against the civilian populations of certain occupied territories in order to destroy particular races and classes of people and national, racial, or religious groups, particularly Jews, Poles, and Gypsies and others.... Such murders and ill-treatment were contrary to international conventions, in particular to *Article 46 of the Hague*

[5] Ibid., '3. Consolidation of control.'

> *Regulations*, 1907, the laws and customs of war, the general principles of criminal law as derived from the criminal laws of all civilized nations, the internal penal laws of the countries in which such crimes were committed, and to *Article 6 (b)* of the Charter.[6]

Indeed, the indictment's subsection on Count Three included a specific sub-section devoted to cultural plunder. This was interpreted as the Nazis' systematic and deliberate attack on the national economies of occupied states, including undermining their currencies. As forms of extortion, these were designed to unlawfully enrich and 'aggrandise' the wealth and power of the Nazi regime generally, as well as the personal wealth of certain defendants, such as Göring. The looting of art was recognised as a key aspect and element of this wider economic dimension of Nazi war criminality, and the indictment provides a number of examples of Nazi art looting by way of illustration. It also expresses the prosecutors' claims that the 'cover of legality', including allegedly voluntary sales and exchanges that ALIU reports had previously criticised, amounted to little more than a sham. Through their resort to such deceptions, Göring, other defendants and their subordinates attempted to disguise what, in substance, always remained illegal acts of plunder of private and public property. The relevant extracts for our purposes are as follows:

> (E) PLUNDER OF PUBLIC AND PRIVATE PROPERTY
> The defendants ruthlessly exploited the people and the material resources of the countries they occupied, in order to strengthen the Nazi war machine, to depopulate and impoverish the rest of Europe, to enrich themselves and their adherents, and to promote German economic supremacy over Europe. The defendants engaged in the following acts and practices, among others:...
>
> 3. In all the occupied countries, in varying degrees, they confiscated businesses, plants, and other property.
>
> 4. In an attempt to give color of legality to illegal acquisitions of property, they forced owners of property to go through the forms of "voluntary" and "legal" transfers....
>
> 6. By a variety of financial mechanisms, they despoiled all of the occupied countries of essential commodities and accumulated wealth, debased the local currency systems and disrupted the local economies. They financed extensive purchases in occupied countries through clearing

[6] Ibid., (A) Murder and Ill-Treatment of Civilian Populations of or in Occupied Territory and on the High Seas: http://www.yale.edu/lawweb/avalon/imt/proc/count3.htm.

> arrangements by which they exacted loans from the occupied countries. They imposed occupation levies, exacted financial contributions, and issued occupation currency, far in excess of occupation costs. They used these excess funds to finance the purchase of business properties and supplies in the occupied countries....
>
> 9. From their program of terror, slavery, spoliation, and organized outrage, the Nazi conspirators created an instrument for the personal profit and aggrandizement of themselves and their adherents.
>
> These acts were contrary to international conventions, particularly Articles 46 to 56 inclusive of the Hague Regulations, 1907, the laws and customs of war, the general principles of criminal law as derived from the criminal laws of all civilized nations, the internal penal laws of the countries in which such crimes were committed and to Article 6 (b) of the Charter. Particulars (by way of example and without prejudice to the production of evidence of other cases) are as follows:
>
> 1. Western Countries: There was plundered from the Western Countries, from 1940 to 1944, works of art, artistic objects, pictures, plastics, furniture, textiles, antique pieces, and similar articles of enormous value to the number of 21,903....
>
> *Looting and Destruction of Works of Art.* The museums of Nantes, Nancy, Old-Marseilles were looted. Private collections of great value were stolen. In this way Raphaels, Vermeers, Van Dycks, and works of Rubens, Holbein, Rembrandt, Watteau, Boucher disappeared. Germany compelled France to deliver up "The Mystic Lamb" by Van Eyck, which Belgium had entrusted to her....An immense amount of property of every kind was plundered from France, Belgium, Norway, Holland, and Luxembourg....These acts violated Article 50, Hague Regulations, 1907, the laws and customs of war, the general principles of criminal law as derived from the criminal laws of all civilized nations, the internal penal laws of the countries in which such crimes were committed, and Article 6 (b) of the Charter.[7]

Count 4, dealing with the criminalisation by the Nuremberg Charter of 'crimes against humanity', also contained allegations relevant to the Nazis' art looting, or 'despoiling', activities directed against European Jewry and others classified as politically threatening and 'alien' elements within a racist definition of who belonged to the German nation. These activities were addressed under the heading of: '(A) Murder, Extermination, Enslavement, Deportation, and Other Inhumane Acts Committed Against Civilian Populations Before and During the War':

[7] Ibid.

> For the purposes set out above, the defendants adopted a policy of persecution, repression, and extermination of all civilians in Germany who were, or who were believed to be, or who were believed likely to become, hostile to the Nazi Government and the common plan or conspiracy described in Count One. They...subjected them to persecution, degradation, despoilment, enslavement, torture, and murder.[8]

Under the next heading, '(B) Persecution on Political, Racial, and Religious Grounds in Execution of and in Connection with the Common Plan Mentioned in Count One', the indictment made a series of other specific allegations against each of the Nuremberg defendants. These included participating in long-standing acts of cultural plunder and confiscation of personal property. Such acts formed part of the Nazis' wider programme of anti-Semitic persecution designed to give effect to and support other aspects of the overall conspiracy. Furthermore, the escalating deployment of systematic deportation of Jews to concentration and death camps also involved the systematically organised confiscation and plunder of their property, even where this was not the main purpose of this genocidal activity:

> As above stated, in execution of and in connection with the common plan mentioned in Count One, opponents of the German Government were exterminated and persecuted. These persecutions were directed against Jews. They were also directed against persons whose political belief or spiritual aspirations were deemed to be in conflict with the aims of the Nazis. Jews were systematically persecuted since 1933; they were deprived of their liberty, thrown into concentration camps where they were murdered and ill-treated. Their property was confiscated. Hundreds of thousands of Jews were so treated before 1 September 1939. Since 1 September 1939, the persecution of the Jews was redoubled: millions of Jews from Germany and from the occupied Western Countries were sent to the Eastern Countries for extermination.... In November 1938, by orders of the Chief of the Gestapo, anti-Jewish demonstrations all over Germany took place. Jewish property was destroyed, 30,000 Jews were arrested and sent to concentration camps and their property confiscated.[9]

In short, acts of systematic Nazi art looting were embraced, in various ways, by three of the four offences contained in the Nuremberg Charter: namely, Criminal Conspiracy (Count One), War Crimes (Count Three) and Crimes Against Humanity (Count Four). It did not feature

[8] Ibid., http://www.yale.edu/lawweb/avalon/imt/proc/count4.htm.
[9] Ibid.

significantly in the definition of Crimes Against the Peace (waging aggressive war, Count Two).

The next part of the indictment that, for present purposes, merits close examination is the general allegations of the plunder of property the prosecutors made against individual defendants. Göring and Rosenberg are the most important figures here. The material on Göring makes only the following rather general claims, presumably in order to avoid giving the defence lawyers time to attempt a full and detailed rebuttal:

> between 1932 and 1945... [long listing of official positions in the Nazi regime]...The Defendant Göring used the foregoing positions, his personal influence, and his intimate connection with the Fuehrer in such a manner that: He promoted the accession to power of the Nazi conspirators and the consolidation of their control over Germany set forth in *Count One* of the Indictment; and he authorized, directed, and participated in the War Crimes set forth in *Count Three* of the Indictment; and the Crimes against Humanity set forth in *Count Four* of the Indictment, including a wide variety of crimes against persons and *property*. [emphasis added].[10]

The section on Rosenberg follows the same general formulae, stating a list of official positions and then claiming he exploited these to pursue a number of types of illegal activity recognised as such by the Nuremberg Charter:

> he authorized, directed, and participated in the War Crimes set forth in Count Three of the Indictment and the Crimes against Humanity set forth in Count Four of the Indictment, including a wide variety of crimes against persons and property.[11]

This very generalised formulae, with its significant reference to 'crimes against property' as a key part of Count Four, was also used in the indictment of Seyss-Inquart, who the ALIU reports often mentioned as complicit in art looting within the Netherlands.[12]

Following the prosecutors' laborious reading out of the indictment, Justice Jackson delivered his now-famous opening address for the dominant American prosecutors, which anticipated key elements of the overall prosecution case. It is certainly possible to identify aspects of

---

[10] Indictment appendix A: http://www.yale.edu/lawweb/avalon/imt/proc/counta.htm.

[11] Ibid.

[12] Ibid.

the prosecution case contained in the Nuremberg trial transcript which appear to be based largely on, or at the very least entirely consistent with, the content and analysis of various ALIU reports. A number of extracts also rely heavily in documentation recovered by this unit's officials, that originally appeared in the attachments to the point where readers who have previously studied such reports can experience a sense of familiarity.[13]

A number of Jackson's points bear directly or indirectly upon art looting, and therefore merit extensive quotation. Jackson emphasised that amongst the fundamental constitutional protections of the Weimar Republic that the Nazis pressurised the coalition government to suspend indefinitely by means of the Hitler-Hindenburg decree of 28 February 1933 were those of Article 153. This provided protection from confiscation of property without compensation, and of course applied to Jewish works of art within Germany:

> Property is guaranteed by the Constitution. Its content and limits are defined by the laws. Expropriation can only take place for the public benefit and on a legal basis. Adequate compensation shall be granted, unless a Reich law orders otherwise. In the case of dispute concerning the amount of compensation, it shall be possible to submit the matter to the ordinary civil courts, unless Reich laws determine otherwise. Compensation must be paid if the Reich expropriates property belonging to the Lands, Communes, or public utility associations.[14]

Jackson provided an exposition of a difficult and novel legal concept. That is, the idea of holding Nuremberg defendants, of both individual

[13] See IMT, 18 Dec. 45 page 82 Document 136-PS as Exhibit USA-367; Document Number 141-PS (Exhibit USA-368), (a certified copy of an order signed by Göring, dated 5 November 1940). On May 1, 1941 Göring issued an order to all Party, State, and Wehrmacht services, which I am now offering into evidence as 1117-PS, Exhibit USA-384. That is an original bearing Göring's signature. This order requested all Party, State, and Wehrmacht services-and I now quote: '... to give all possible support and assistance to the Chief of Staff of Reichsleiter Rosenberg's Einsatzstab.... The abovementioned persons are requested to report to me on their work, particularly on any difficulties which might arise.' On 30th of May 1942 Göring claimed credit for a large degree of the success of the Einsatzstab. I offer in evidence a captured photostatic copy of a letter from Göring to Rosenberg, showing Göring's signature, which bears our Number 1015(i)-PS, which I offer in evidence as Exhibit USA-385. The last paragraph of this letter states as follows: '... On the other hand I also support personally the work of your Einsatzstab wherever I can do so, and a great part of the seized cultural objects can be accounted for by the fact that I was able to assist the Einsatzstab with my organizations.' Ibid. 86.

[14] Ibid., 111–112.

and organisational types (including potentially the ERR and the Linz Commission), who were complicit in art looting culpable for their knowing participation in a 'criminal conspiracy', or 'common plan', directed towards war:

> In general, our case will disclose these defendants all uniting at some time with the Nazi Party in a plan which they well knew could be accomplished only by an outbreak of war in Europe. Their seizure of the German State, their subjugation of the German people, their terrorism and extermination of dissident elements,... their deliberate and planned criminality toward conquered peoples,—all these are ends for which they acted in concert; and all these are phases of the conspiracy, a conspiracy which reached one goal only to set out for another and more ambitious one. We shall also trace for you the intricate web of organizations which these men formed and utilized to accomplish these ends. We will show how the entire structure of offices and officials was dedicated to the criminal purposes and committed to the use of the criminal methods planned by these defendants and their co-conspirators, many of whom war and suicide have put beyond reach.[15]

Jackson then noted that none of the Nuremberg defendants should be able to argue that he was unaware of the fundamental anti-Semitism of the Nazi party programme. From 1920 onwards, this had included proposals for a series of direct measures of persecution rendering Jews as non-persons, a policy that the leadership had regularly reiterated over later decades:

> The Nazi Party declaration also committed its members to an anti-Semitic program. It declared that no Jew or any person of non-German blood could be a member of the nation. Such persons to be disfranchised, disqualified for office, subject to the alien laws, and entitled to nourishment only after the German population had first been provided for. All who had entered Germany after August 2, 1914 were to be required forthwith to depart, and all non-German immigration was to be prohibited.[16]

Jackson noted that anti-Semitism operated as a key dimension of Nazi policy and was central to its plans for the creation and defense of a 1,000 year Reich:

> The Nazi conspiracy, as we shall show, always contemplated not merely overcoming current opposition but exterminating elements which could not be reconciled with its philosophy of the state. It not only sought to

[15] IMT 2, 104: http://www.yale.edu/lawweb/avalon/imt/proc/11–21–45.htm.
[16] Ibid., 106.

> establish the Nazi "new order" but to secure its sway, as Hitler predicted, "for a thousand years." Nazis were never in doubt or disagreement as to what these dissident elements were.[17]

According to Jackson, the Nazi regime defined these dissident elements and political enemies as the organised German working class, Roman Catholicism and, most relevant for present purposes: 'the Jews.' [Nuremberg document] 1947-PS). Jackson further claimed that the escalating persecution of Jews, which starting with selective confiscations of works of art and other property, culminated in mass killings. This programme has remained a common thread of Nazi domestic and occupation policies both prior to, and then during, the war:

> The warfare against these elements was continuous. The battle in Germany was but a practice skirmish for the worldwide drive against them. We have in point of geography and of time two groups of Crimes against Humanity—one within Germany before and during the war, the other in occupied territory during the war. But the two are not separated in Nazi planning. They are a continuous unfolding of the Nazi plan to exterminate peoples and institutions which might serve as a focus or instrument for overturning their "new world order" at any time.[18]

The American Chief Prosecutor then devoted a lengthy sub-section of his opening address to 'the persecution of Jews.' Only those elements that bear upon the confiscation of art and related property as a form of cultural plunder will be set out below. This, of course, means that Jackson's interpretation of the legal significance of direct physical killings, defined as the most extreme instances of genocide, cannot be discussed at this point. Jackson developed a model of Nazi anti-Semitism that closely follows and expressly acknowledges Franz Neumann's spearhead theory. He defined such systematic racism as *both* an ideological and functional 'testing ground' against a group that was uniquely vulnerable to a process of scapegoating. Having gained experience in deploying terroristic practices against Jews, similar programmes were later extended against *all forms* of opposition to the Nazis' overall programme:

> 3. *Crimes against the Jews*: The most savage and numerous crimes planned and committed by the Nazis were those against the Jews. Those in Germany in 1933 numbered about 500,000. In the aggregate, they had

---

[17] Ibid.

[18] Ibid., 112–113.

made for themselves positions which excited envy, and had accumulated properties which excited the avarice of the Nazis. They were few enough to be helpless and numerous enough to be held up as a menace. Let there be no misunderstanding about the charge of persecuting Jews.... It is my purpose to show a plan and design, to which all Nazis were fanatically committed, to annihilate all Jewish people. These crimes were organized and promoted by the Party leadership, executed and protected by the Nazi officials, as we shall convince you by written orders of the Secret State Police itself. The persecution of the Jews was a continuous and deliberate policy. It was a policy directed against other nations as well as against the Jews themselves. Anti-Semitism was promoted to divide and embitter the democratic peoples and to soften their resistance to the Nazi aggression. As Robert Ley declared in Der Angriff on 14 May 1944: "The second German secret weapon is Anti-Semitism because if it is constantly pursued by Germany, it will become a universal problem which all nations will be forced to consider." Anti-Semitism also has been aptly credited with being a "spearhead of terror." The ghetto was the laboratory for testing repressive measures. Jewish property was the first to be expropriated, but the custom grew and included similar measures against anti-Nazi Germans, Poles, Czechs, Frenchmen, and Belgians. Extermination of the Jews enabled the Nazis to bring a practiced hand to similar measures against Poles, Serbs, and Greeks. The plight of the Jew was a constant threat to opposition or discontent among other elements of Europe's population—pacifists, conservatives, Communists, Catholics, Protestants, Socialists. It was in fact, a threat to every dissenting opinion and to every non-Nazis' life.[19]

Jackson then further developed this aspect of Neumann's spearhead model of anti-Semitism. He emphasised the incremental nature of the 'ratcheting up' of measures of persecution, such as the initially 'measured' confiscations of art and other property from very wealthy Austrian and French Jews, including the Rothschild and Rosenberg art collections. As violations of the property of wealthy and elite groups, as distinct from direct acts of physical violence, such measures of racist persecution were unlikely to generate widespread opposition. However, once these measures of targeted persecution had been completed without arousing mass demonstrations, they were followed by more widespread, far reaching and graver attacks on *all Jews*, which aimed at their ultimate extermination as a distinct group or people:

The persecution policy against the Jews commenced with nonviolent measures, such as disfranchisement and discriminations against their religion,

[19] Ibid., 118.

> and the placing of impediments in the way of success in economic life. It moved rapidly to organized mass violence against them, physical isolation in ghettos, deportation, forced labor, mass starvation, and extermination. The Government, the Party formations indicted before you as criminal organizations, the Secret State Police, the Army, private and semi-public associations, and "spontaneous mobs" that were carefully inspired from official sources, were all agencies that were concerned in this persecution. Nor was it directed against individual Jews for personal bad citizenship or unpopularity. The avowed purpose was the destruction of the Jewish people as a whole, as an end in itself, as a measure of preparation for war, and as a discipline of conquered peoples. History does not record a crime ever perpetrated against so many victims or one ever carried out with such calculated cruelty.... I advert to them only to show their magnitude as evidence of a purpose and a knowledge common to an defendants, of an official plan rather than of a capricious policy of some individual commander, and to show such a continuity of Jewish persecution from the rise of the Nazi conspiracy to its collapse as forbids us to believe that any person could be identified with any part of Nazi action without approving this most conspicuous item in their program.[20]

Jackson was probably attempting to pre-empt the argument from a number of the defendants that they had no knowledge of, or involvement in, such acts of persecution, not even with respect to cultural plunder, and that knowledge of persecution was confined largely to members of the SS or anti-Semitic propagandists, such as defendant Julius Streicher. Instead, and by means of the conspiracy charge, he was attempting to show that each of the defendants, even those in charge of areas not directly concerned with the persecution of the Jews such as Seyss-Inquart or perhaps even Göring, objectively formed part of, and contributed to, a wider criminal plan. Of course, this argument concerning the objective test to be applied when ascertaining membership of the Nazi conspiracy echoed that of earlier CIR reports already discussed. Jackson's opening speech then addressed the escalation of measures of plunder and other forms of persecution contained in a series of anti-Semitic laws and decrees, some of which even anticipated mass murder:

> The most serious of the actions against Jews were outside of any law, but the law itself was employed to some extent. There were the infamous Nuremberg decrees of September 15, 1935 (Reichsgesetzblatt 1935, Part. I, P. 1146). The Jews were segregated into ghettos and put into

[20] Ibid., 119.

> forced labor; they were expelled from their professions; their property was expropriated; all cultural life, the press, the theater, and schools were prohibited them; and the SD was made responsible for them (212-PS, 069-PS).... "The first main goal of the German measures must be strict segregation of Jewry from the rest of the population. In the execution of this, first of all is the seizing of the Jewish populace by the introduction of a registration order and similar appropriate measures.... The entire Jewish property is to be seized and confiscated with exception of that which is necessary for a bare existence. As far as the economical situation permits, the power of disposal of their property is to be taken from the Jews as soon as possible through orders and other measures given by the commissariat, so that the moving of property will quickly cease." "Any cultural activity will be completely forbidden, to the Jew." (212-PS)...Jews as a whole were fined a billion Reichmarks. They were excluded from all businesses and claims against insurance companies for their burned properties were confiscated, all by decree of the Defendant Göring. (Reichsgesetzblatt, 1938, Part I, Pp. 1579–82)...In the West, the Jews were killed and their property taken over. But the campaign achieved its zenith of savagery in the East. ...In Estonia, all Jews were arrested immediately upon the arrival of the Wehrmacht.... Jews were subjected to all sorts of restrictions and all Jewish property was confiscated....For example, we will show the report made to Defendant Rosenberg about the army and the SS in the area under Rosenberg jurisdiction, which recited the following: "Details: In presence of SS man, a Jewish dentist has to break all gold teeth and fillings out of mouth of German and Russian Jews *before* they are executed."[21]

Jackson summed up this part of his presentation with a summary of the implications of his overall argument concerning the place of anti-Semitic persecution, of which confiscations of property formed an integral, if less extreme, early phase. As already noted, ALIU reports emphasised how Göring and his curator and agent Hofer had granted 'protection' from anti-Semitic measures as a reward to those Jews, or half-Jews, who surrendered up their artworks, often at rock bottom prices. Jackson's claim was that, irrespective of any claims by defence lawyers that their client carried out an individual act of 'mercy' towards particular Jewish friends or associates, no defendant can escape liability under Count One. That is, they must accept liability for participating in a wider conspiracy: one which included, as an integral part, an escalating programme of anti-Semitic persecutions of which property confiscations remained an important phase and stepping stone. Such

[21] Ibid., 122, 124.

attempts at mitigation should be disregarded unless, of course, they were underpinned by a complete and public rejection of this very public aspect of the Nazi regime's political programme:

> We charge that all atrocities against Jews were the manifestation and culmination of the Nazi plan to which every defendant here was a party. I know very well that some of these men did take steps to spare some particular Jew for some personal reason from the horrors that awaited the unrescued Jew. Some protested that particular atrocities were excessive, and discredited the general policy. While a few defendants may show efforts to make specific exceptions to the policy of Jewish extermination, I have found no instance in which any defendant opposed the policy itself or sought to revoke or even modify it. Determination to destroy the Jews was a binding force which at all times cemented the elements of this conspiracy. On many internal policies there were differences among the defendants. But there is not one of them who has not echoed the rallying cry of nazism: "Deutschland erwache, Juda verrecke!" (Germany awake, Jewry perish!).[22]

We have already seen how a number of ALIU reports, particularly CIR 2 and CIR 4, linked Nazi programmes of art looting to that of aggressive military expansionism and invasion. Jackson had a pronounced and personal interest in vindicating the idea that the offence of 'crimes against the peace' defined in the Nuremberg Charter, had to be legally vindicated as a properly established part of international criminal law. Hence, this offence took centre stage to the point where the prosecution's presentation of evidence for the conspiracy charge and for crimes against humanity tended to be connected to it. This meant, in practice, the prosecutors reinterpreting even domestic and pre-war policies of anti-Semitism, including art confiscations, as preparations for 'waging aggressive war', and thereby encompassed by this new offence:

> The purpose, as we have seen, of getting rid of the influence of free labor, the churches, and the Jews was to clear their obstruction to the precipitation of aggressive war. If aggressive warfare in violation of treaty obligation is a matter of international cognizance the preparations for it must also be of concern to the international community. Terrorism was the chief instrument for securing the cohesion of the German people in war purposes. Moreover, these cruelties in Germany served as atrocity

[22] Ibid., 127.

> practice to discipline the membership of the criminal organization to follow the pattern later in occupied countries.[23]

Later in his opening speech, Jackson directly addressed the question of the Nazis' art looting, and made a number of points reiterating those found earlier in ALIU reports. These included the economic aspect of such looting, such as substantially weakening the national economies of France and other neighbouring states, and the uniquely systematic and state-organised nature of such plunder. He even referred to the records of the ERR that the ALIU had secured and analysed, before feeding these into the Nuremberg process:

> Not only was there a purpose to debilitate and demoralize the economy of Germany's neighbors for the purpose of destroying their competitive position, but there was looting and pilfering on an unprecedented scale.... But we will show you that looting was not due to the lack of discipline or to the ordinary weaknesses of human nature. The German organized plundering, planned it, disciplined it, and made it official just as he organized everything else, and then he compiled the most meticulous records to show that he had done the best job of looting that was possible under the circumstances. And we have those records. The Defendant Rosenberg was put in charge of a systematic plundering of the art objects of Europe by direct order of Hitler dated 29 January 1940 (136-PS). On the 16th of April 1943 Rosenberg reported that up to the 7th of April, 92 railway cars with 2,775 cases containing art objects had been sent to Germany; and that 53 pieces of art had been shipped to Hitler direct, and 594 to the Defendant Göring. The report mentioned something like 20,000 pieces of seized art and the main locations where they were stored. (015-PS). Moreover this looting was glorified by Rosenberg. Here we have 39 leather-bound tabulated volumes of his inventory, which in due time we will offer in evidence. One cannot but admire the artistry of this Rosenberg report. The Nazi taste was cosmopolitan. Of the 9,455 articles inventoried, there were included 5,255 paintings, 297 sculptures, 1,372 pieces of antique furniture, 307 textiles, and 2,224 small objects of art. Rosenberg observed that there were approximately 10,000 more objects still to be inventoried. (015-PS) Rosenberg himself estimated that the values involved would come close to a billion dollars (090-PS).[24]

In order to further substantiate our claim that there was a considerable overlap between trial evidence and OSS' art looting reports, it is necessary to cite other examples of the former where this overlap is particularly clear. One example stems from the French prosecutors'

[23] Ibid., 127–28.
[24] Ibid., 142.

claim made on 6 February 1946, echoing earlier ALIU CIR conclusions, that the Nazis' art looting needed to be seen as distinctive in the sense of a systematic and state-organised activity of plunder. This remained the case even where these were thinly disguised as 'protection'. In each case, Nazi plunder was linked to the realisation of wider genocidal and racist objectives:

> M. Charles Gerthoffer (Assistant Prosecutor for the French Republic): The Economic Section of the French Delegation had prepared a report on the pillage of works of art in the occupied countries of western Europe.... the American Prosecutor was good enough to inform us that the Defendant Rosenberg intended to maintain that the artistic treasures were collected only in order to be "protected." We consider, from the documents which we are holding at the disposal of the Court, that this cannot be a question of protection only but that this was genuine spoliation; and I am at the Tribunal's disposal to prove this... while offering in evidence the documents which we had already collected. Mr. President, Gentlemen, the pillage of works of art has a cultural significance... the subject of a statement presented by Colonel Storey on 18 December 1945.... As the Tribunal will realize, the leaders of the Reich primarily and systematically seized works of art belonging to private individuals, mostly under the pretext that these individuals were Jews, thus procuring for themselves very valuable means of exchange. In Belgium, Holland, Luxembourg, and France picture galleries, public as well as private collections, ancient furniture, china, and jewellery were stolen. It was not a question of individual looting, of pillaging by soldiers, such as is encountered in all wars and of which we still find examples; this campaign of plunder was carried out in a systematic and disciplined manner. The methods introduced varied in character. Personal judgment and personal initiative could be exercised only insofar as they contributed to the execution of plans already elaborated by the National Socialist leaders before the month of June 1940.[25]

ALIU officials made a related and legally ambitious claim that art looting took many forms other than outright confiscations and forced sale. Furthermore, even apparently regular purchases and exchanges, which gave the appearance of genuine legal contractual transactions, still need to be interpreted as unlawful acts infused with a wider criminal intent, including a calculation of the economic consequences and power-politics at the state to state level. This theme was developed and

[25] IMT 6 February 1946, 51–52: http:// www.yale.edu/lawweb/avalon/imt/proc/02-06-46.htm.

then emphasised once again in the conclusion to the relevant section of the French prosecutor's case:

> There can be no comparison between the pillaging typical of the history of this or that conqueror and practiced throughout the centuries, and the pillaging as understood by the defendants. What prevents any comparison between the past pillaging and the looting practiced by Staff Rosenberg or the National Socialist chiefs, is the difference in purpose, however difficult and delicate a matter it may be to analyse it.... we find the fundamental difference—the National Socialist leaders, when estimating the value of this and that painting or of this or that work of art, wittingly took into account both the standard of aesthetic wealth, that is the value of the object to the individual, and the standard of material wealth, that is its exchange value, an exchange value in which it is a matter of retaining a pledge, if not to facilitate, at least to bring pressure to bear when negotiating future peace treaties, as is evident from the documents submitted to the Tribunal. Whatsoever the pretexts or excuses submitted by the National Socialist leaders when seizing the artistic heritage of western Europe, whether by theft, by so-called preservative confiscations, or by direct purchase from the owners or the markets for the sale of objects of art, the criminal intention is always the same. The German motive was undeniably the establishment of a reserve of securities, if not for the satisfaction of the individual desire, then for the satisfaction of a collective need in conformity with the myth of the "Greater Germany." This reserve of securities would have a triple advantage: A cultural advantage, that is, the advantage of the Hohe Schule. Secondly, an economic advantage, a basis for financial speculation and a reserve of securities easily negotiable in the markets of the world; above all, a reserve of fixed value entirely unaffected by the fluctuations in the cost of raw materials and unaffected either by the lowering or the manipulation of the currency. And, lastly, reserves of securities of political importance in the hands of those negotiating the peace treaties.[26]

The prosecutor's critique of the 'cover of legality, including the use of 'unbacked paper monies', which ALIU reports had repeatedly attacked as a sham behind which the Nazi leaders such as Göring carried out acts of national plunder, was reiterated:

> The Defense will perhaps object that exchanges and purchases on free markets cannot be held against the defendants, because they are in the nature of contracts, and there were agreements, and because equivalents existed. But the facts presented to the Tribunal render it possible to declare that these operations have merely an appearance of regularity, if we remember the conditions under which the contracts were drawn

[26] Ibid., 64.

> up, that the operations were made under duress, or if we consider the rights over the equivalents supplied, equivalents of exchange represented by stolen objects or works of art, by sales paid for in national currencies coming from contributions of a more or less regular nature, and especially by occupational indemnities or clearing operations. Most of these particulars, from the point of view of the general principles of criminal law, are doubly tainted: On the one hand they were paid in stolen currency, since the work of art forming the object of the sale could never legitimately have become the heritage of the purchaser. On the other hand, fraud and deceit tainted a considerable share of the negotiations, as proved by numerous statements, such as the extract from the minutes of M. Rochlitz's statement.[27]

His conclusion further reiterated the key theme of the distinctiveness of Nazi art looting activities as an essentially illegal form of aggression linked to both military expansionism and racist cultural domination. These expressed underlying criminal purposes and were put into effect through deliberate acts of state policy by various state and party backed institutions of plunder:

> I thus come to the conclusion of my presentation... Whatever the markets, whoever the purchasers where the traffic in works of art is concerned, the motive is the same and the methods are the same. It is difficult to conceive that identical acts of pillaging, committed simultaneously in all the occupied countries of western Europe, were not the result of one single will, a ruthless will to dominate in every sphere, which expressed itself in a desire to invest the most irregular acquisitions with an appearance of legality. This is proved by the numerous declarations of the defendants, such as have been submitted to the Tribunal. A will to dominate the cultural sphere was expressed by the intention to extend the "action" of confiscation to ever fresh fields. A will to despoil the occupied countries manifested itself right up to the very last hours of the occupation.... Whatever the reasons of a juridical nature submitted by the Germans to justify the seizures of Jewish property, this property has never lost the character of private property; and it has, for this reason, always remained guaranteed by the clauses of the Hague Convention and especially by Article 46.... As for the fate reserved for the seizures by the National Socialist leaders, the documents produced have sufficiently shown their intentions and their plans.[28]

Gerthoffer's presentation summarises another of ALIU's key findings: the centrality of Rosenberg's ERR to programmes of anti-Semitic

[27] Ibid., 65.
[28] Ibid., 69–70.

plunder, and how these formed an aspect of both racist genocide and military conquest. It also confirmed that certain documentation microfilmed and analysed by the ALIU staff, including the ERR's records, comprised key prosecution evidence:

> The official organization for pillaging was primarily Minister Rosenberg's Einsatzstab for the occupied territories of western Europe and the Netherlands. If this organization was not the sole agent, it was the most important one.... The urge to seize works of art, as well as material wealth, underlies the policy of National Socialist expansion. The behavior in Poland of the Defendant Frank has already given sufficient proof of this. The idea of protecting this valuable booty arose at the time of the invasion of western Europe. From the very beginning, in their haste and their desire to seize as much as they could, several parallel authorities would carry out the confiscations, firstly by the military authorities, either indirectly, as in Holland through the special services of the Devisenschutzkommando or directly as in France through the Department for the Protection of Works of Art. Further, the same mission was entrusted simultaneously to the civil authorities, whether represented by the German Embassy in Paris or, in Holland, the Office for Enemy Property under the auspices of the Reich Commissioner. This plurality of control, moreover, did not end with the establishment of the Rosenberg Staff. This is the first phase in the pillage of works of art.... The second phase opened with the arrival of Einsatzstab Rosenberg which appeared on the scene under the aegis of the Defendant Göring. From now on this Einsatzstab must be considered primarily responsible for the organized pillage. Towards July 1942 a third phase opens in the history of the Staff Rosenberg. The person primarily responsible is the Defendant Alfred Rosenberg. The activities of this staff did not cease in Europe until the liberation. One part of the archives of the Rosenberg services fell into the hands of the French armies; another part, which had been sent to Füssen, was seized by the American Army which also picked up the archives of the Defendant Rosenberg: This is the origin of the PS documents submitted to the Tribunal.

In particular, this prosecutor referred to the importance of documentary evidence, in the form of defendant General Keitel's various orders made in September 1939 that had previously been highlighted in CIR 4, and discussed above:[29]

> The seizure of works of art began with the entrance of the German troops into Holland, Belgium, and France. In Paris, as from the month of June, there was an Embassy service directed by Dr. Von Kunsberg and Dr. Dirksen similar to a specialized service of the Military Governor directed

[29] CIR 4 (Linz), op. cit. 7.

> by Count Wolff Metternich. This order of seizure, in defiance of the Hague Convention, applied to public as well as to private property. The Defendant Keitel, on 30 June 1940, issued an order to the Governor of Paris, General Von Bockelberg. I submit a copy of this order as Document Number RF-1301. Here it is: "The Fuehrer, on receiving the report of the Reich Minister for Foreign Affairs, has issued an order to safeguard for the time being, in addition to objects of art belonging to the French State, also such works of art and antiquities which constitute private property. Especially Jewish private property is to be taken in custody by the occupational power against removal or concealment, after having been labelled with the names of their present French owners. There is no intention of expropriation but certainly of a transfer into our custody to serve as a pawn in the peace negotiations:" Identical measures were soon taken in Holland, Belgium, and Luxembourg.... Beginning with that period, seizures of the most famous French-Jewish art collections were carried out.[30]

Another section of the prosecutor's evidence concerning Keitel's orders, previously highlighted in an attachment to CIR reports, is worth citing in this respect:

> I now come to an order, issued by the Defendant Keitel, on 7 September 1940, [Exhibit Number RF-1310, / 138-PS]. Here is the principal passage: "...Reichsleiter Rosenberg, or his representative Reichshauptstellenleiter Ebert, has received from the Fuehrer, personally, unequivocal instructions concerning the right of confiscation. He is authorized to transport to Germany such objects which appear to him of value and to place them here in security. You are requested to inform the competent military commanders or offices."[31]

It will be recalled that part of the ALIU's dossier of evidence included materials demonstrating the plunder of Jewish artworks, such as that of the Rothschilds, hidden in safe deposit boxes, but which Göring boasted to Rosenberg of having tracked down through criminal agents and others. Again there are clear overlaps:

> Entrusted with the finding and seizing of Jewish collections which had been left "ownerless" in the occupied territories, Staff Rosenberg did not content itself with looting private houses; its activities also applied to the seizure of many trusts, especially of those deposited in strong boxes in banks. This is evident from the passage of the document: "On 26 September 1941 M. Braumuller, acting on Rosenberg's behalf, removed two cases filled with objects of art, which are listed and deposited with

---

[30] IMT 6 February 1946, op. cit. 53.
[31] Ibid., 55.

the agency of the Societe Generate at Arcachon under the name of the depositor, M. Philippe de Rothschild, who has not yet regained his French nationality.[32]

We have already discussed how various ALIU reports highlighted the controlling role that Göring exercised behind the scenes on the actions of ERR officials in France, and how different CIRs contained Göring's order of 5 November 1941 Again this theme was reiterated at Nuremberg:

> This action of Staff Rosenberg was inspired by the orders of the Defendant Göring himself. It is thus that I submit as Exhibit Number RF-1309, a document, discovered by the Army of the United States and filed under Document Number 141-PS, which consists of an order of the Defendant Göring, Paris, dated 5 November 1941 and which extends the activities of Staff Rosenberg. Here is the order: "To carry out the present measures for safeguarding Jewish property taken over by the Chief of the Military Administration in Paris and by Einsatzstab Rosenberg, the following procedure will be observed in connection with the art treasures deposited at the Louvre: "1. Those art objects regarding which the Fuehrer has reserved to himself the right of further disposal, 2. those art objects which could serve to complete the collection of the Reich Marshal, 3. those art objects and libraries which appear suitable for equipping the Hohe Schule within Reichsleiter Rosenberg's sphere of duty."[33]

This chapter has previously discussed the ALIU's analysis of the hypocrisy of Göring and others in profiting from the sale or exchange of artworks that their own racist ideologies condemned as 'degenerate'.[34] Once again, this theme informed the French prosecutor's evidence:

> I come to Page 26 of my brief. Certain of these works of art were considered by the Germans as degenerate, and their admittance into National Socialist territory was forbidden. Theoretically speaking they should have been destroyed; but within the scope of total war economy these pictures, although condemned, were none the less of commercial value and as a means of barter their value was both definite and high. So these pictures, carefully selected from among the great public collections and from private collections, were confiscated; and as already provided for in Section 5 of the decree of 5 November 1940, placed on the French and German art markets. In addition to these condemned pictures, others

[32] Ibid.

[33] IMT 6 February 1946, op. cit. 54.

[34] Göring was hardly alone in this hypocrisy as others, including Mühlmann, stood accused of liking or at least tolerating 'degenerate art.' Petropoulos, 1996b op. cit. 187.

> were set aside as being of lesser interest in the official collections. They formed the object of numerous fraudulent transactions.[35]

A further theme, developed in numerous ALIU reports, was the importance of exploiting the statements, mainly initially secured under interrogation at Alt Aussee and Munich but further developed by later investigations, from a variety of Göring's senior agents and representatives, such as Lohse and Rochlitz:

> We now come to the traffic in works of art. We are not, in this case, dealing with secret and unlawful operations, the personal acts of such-and-such a member of the Rosenberg Service; we are dealing with official operations. Two kinds of operations were currently carried out by the Einsatzstab, that is, exchanges and sales. Exchanges. On this subject we have, by way of an example, the evidence of M. Gustav Rochlitz. I... shall read a passage to the Tribunal. "During the years 1941 and 1942 I exchanged various old pictures for 80 modern ones, delivered by Lohse, who always told me that these exchanges were carried out on Göring's order, and that the pictures received had been intended for Göring. I have since learned that all the pictures given in exchange are contained in the Göring collection. I delivered in exchange about 35 pictures, possibly more." These facts are confirmed by the Defendant Rosenberg himself...[36]

This prosecutor also relied upon quantitative data from the ERR's own records secured and analysed by ALIU officials to provide details of the scale of this agency's looting activities:

> The documents of the Einsatzstab are sufficiently numerous and precise to allow us to establish certain quantitative data. First, the seizures by the General Staff for Art Treasures. The fundamental document is a report of Dr. Scholz, dated 14 July 1944, which we have just mentioned. This is Document Number 1015-PS [RF-1323]. From this report I shall extract only some very brief indications concerning the quantities of art objects carried off. According to this report, 21,903 objects taken from 203 private collections, were removed, notably from the Rothschild, Alphons Kahn, David Well, Levy de Benzion, and the Seligmann brothers collections. According to the same report there were "all told, 29 transports, 137 trucks, and 4,174 cases.[37]

One of the clearest examples of evidence that the ALIU directly supplied into the Nuremberg process was Göring's letter to Rosenberg,

[35] Ibid., 56.
[36] Ibid., 59.
[37] Ibid.

which—as previously discussed—Philips singled out in June 1945 as particularly incriminating:

> The Defendant Göring was the official protector of Staff Rosenberg. He himself wrote to Rosenberg on 21 November 1940, Document Number 1651-PS, a copy of which I submit as Exhibit Number RF-1335, as follows: "I have promised to support energetically the work of your staff and to make available to them what they could not obtain so far, namely, means of transport and guard personnel. The air force has received the order to render utmost assistance."[38]

The identities and role of Göring's network of agents and affiliated dealers that CIR 4 highlighted was also largely replicated in summarised form by Gerthoffer:

> I would point out to the Tribunal that in all the occupied countries the Defendant Göring employed a whole group of buyers, the best known of whom were Dr. Lohse, who was a member of the Einsatzstab, and Hofer. Hofer and Lohse... acted for the defendant most often, however, under their own names. The personal collection of the Defendant Göring flourished considerably.[39]

In short, on a number of points the prosecutors made claims that replicated the central findings of ALIU reports.

A key Nuremberg legal brief was Walter Brudno's, *Plunder of Art Treasures*.[40] This presents the case against the Nazi defendants for the plundering of various works, including books, furniture, sculpture, household furnishings, tapestries, and dozens of other varieties of art objects from European countries under Nazi occupation, and for doing so in a premeditated and systematic fashion. To demonstrate individual liability, it cites decrees, statements and reports of, for instance, Göring, and Rosenberg, which 'validated' these looting operations: 'for the benefit of the German Reich.' These sources are used to provide evidence of the criminal intentions and actions of these major Nuremberg defendants.

Brudno's document follows the conclusions of ALIU reports by giving particular attention to the plundering operations of the ERR, with the assistance of the German Army and various branches of the German police and security services. It argues that art plunder by the

[38] Ibid., 65.
[39] Ibid., 68.
[40] Available online at: http://org.law.rutgers.edu/publications/law-religion/.

ERR and other agencies must be legally considered to represent a war crime under both the Hague Convention and the Nuremberg Charter for which Rosenberg and Göring in particular should be held individually responsible. Such plunder formed part of an officially devised and organised state and Nazi party programme giving effect to Nazi racism, especially anti-Semitism. Virtually all those who the ALIU identified as key players in Nazi art looting, including Alfred Rosenberg; Hermann Göring; Dr. Lammers; Keitel; Bormann; von Behr; Robert Scholz; Utikal; Dr. Mühlmann and Dr. Hans Posse, were also classified as such in this trial brief, and for largely similar reasons. Unlike ALIU reports, it does focus briefly on Nazi cultural plunder in Eastern Europe, particularly Poland. However, Yeide makes the valid point that, although Brudno's trial brief: 'served the impetus to prosecute as war criminals those engaged in the plunder of cultural property', its contents are comparatively superficial, at least compared with the far richer detail contained in the earlier ALIU reports:

> However, by its very nature, the brief only grazes the surface of the scale of these activities and the persons involved. In contrast, a series of reports, created in the late summer and fall of 1945 by the Art Looting Investigation Unit (ALIU) of the Office of Strategic Services, document not just the extent of Nazi looting in occupied Europe, but also the art collections of Nazi leaders, and the key dealers and collaborators in the trade in confiscated art.[41]

This writer also recognises, at least implicitly, that vital material on Göring's decrees contained in CIR 2, Attachment 3, was replicated and exploited in Brudno's trial brief.[42] It is possible to identify a series of factual statements that this brief appears to have taken from various CIR and DIR reports. We can also explain gaps in this Nuremberg document because these stem from the late availability of a ALIU report issued jointly between OSS staff and a member of the Dutch Intelligence Service, Captain Jan Vlug. Indeed, Yeide notes:

---

[41] 1997 op. cit. 1.

[42] 'Brudno describes what he calls the 'cooperation of Hermann Göring' with the ERR and cites an order of the Reichsmarschall's, dated November 5, 1940, in which Göring claims for himself the loot not selected by Hitler personally. In the context of the Brudno brief, this order serves to demonstrate the complicity of the highest ranking Nazis in the plunder of private property in occupied France. Within the context of Göring's art collecting activities, the order has an even broader significance.' Ibid.

In general, the situation in Holland was not addressed in the Brudno document—perhaps because an ALIU-planned DIR on Kajetan Mühlmann was not produced until after the ALIU had issued its final report in May 1946, and therefore was unavailable to Brudno.[43]

[43] 2007 op. cit. 7; cf. 'Report on Activities of ERR in the Netherlands', Nuremberg Document 175-PS CIR 1 (ERR) Attachment 9.

APPENDIX TWO

JACK TAYLOR'S TRIAL EVIDENCE AT THE MAUTHAUSEN TRIAL

In addition to his report and recovery of the Mauthausen 'death books', Taylor was also the first prosecution witness to give evidence for the trial of 61 former personnel employed at this camp. The Allied authorities held this six week trial before an American Military Tribunal at Dachau beginning on 29 March 1946.[1] As the following summary makes clear, Taylor's oral trial testimony both reiterates and elaborates upon his more formal report, which was of course supplied by the OSS to the prosecuting lawyers. All of the defendants were charged with violation of the laws and usages of war, as well as with subjecting foreign nationals to killing, beating, torture, and starvation. Taylor was the only American prosecution witness, and it is possible that the prosecutors regarded his testimony as more credible in the eyes of the Military Tribunal than those of other former prisoners. Greene suggests that the powerful impact of Taylor's earlier appearance in OSS film evidence screened at Nuremberg, *The Nazi Concentration Camps*, prompted the prosecutors' decisions to rely so heavily upon Taylor as their opening witness.[2] Indeed, Taylor's testimony was introduced by the Dachau Trial prosecutors to corroborate the following key element of the charges:

> Mauthausen and its by-camps were nothing more than a many-headed hydra of extermination—and these sixty one men on trial before this court encouraged, aided, abetted, or participated in a common design to subject its prisoners to killings, beatings, and tortures. Prosecution calls Lt. Jack Taylor.[3]

---

[1] For a close analysis of Taylor's testimony based directly upon the massive transcript, see J. M. Greene, *Justice at Dachau*, London: Broadway Books, 2003, extracts from the trial transcript are also cited at http://www.scrapbookpages.com/DachauScrapbook/DachauTrials/Mauthausen03.html; 'Der Bericht des US-Agenten Jack H.Taylor über das Konzentrationslager Mauthausen' in: *Zeitgeschichte* 22 (1995): 318–341, September/October 1995, 318–341. For a summary of the trial, see *Law Reports of the Trials of War Criminals* Vol. 11, London: UN War Crimes Commission, 1949, 6.

[2] Greene, 2003 op. cit. 139.

[3] Cited in ibid., 137–38.

Taylor began his testimony by reiterating the account in his report we have already quoted concerning his initial impressions of Mauthausen and his group's ill-treatment, that is, his initial interrogation reinforced by beatings by SS officials. He testified that, after arriving at Mauthausen camp on 1 April 1945, he was forced to work: 'setting tiles in the new crematorium,' and, with the war clearly lost, that the camp officials: 'were very anxious to have it completed because all the bodies from hanging and beating had to be cremated to destroy the evidence:[4]

> We knew that the only thing that kept the number of violent deaths down was the fact that the crematorium couldn't take care of any more. And we knew that as soon as we finished, the rate would accelerate tremendously because it was a more efficient oven...the regular procedure for the gas chamber was twice a day, one hundred and twenty at a time. I would say that the new crematorium increased the facilities to two hundred and fifty a day.[5]

Taylor testified that the new crematorium was first used on 10 April, 1945.[6]

The prosecutor's questions to this former OSS man were also clearly based on his earlier report, and consisted of requests that he repeat its main points. Taylor's answers placed particular emphasis on those parts of his report that referred to the actions of the defendants, such as Prellberg and Roth, heads of the crematorium, and how the massive death rate amongst camp inmates through gassing and starvation had necessitated more efficient crematoria.[7] Taylor repeated his grim story of the different type of smoke produced by the burning of less starved bodies.[8] In his own direct testimony, prosecutor Lt. Col. William Denson asked Taylor to describe the gas chamber. Taylor replied:

> It was rigged up like a shower room with shower nozzles in the ceiling. New prisoners thought they were going in to have their bath. They were stripped and put in this room naked. Then gas came out of the shower nozzles. The gas was discharged from a thick metal box in the adjoining room[9]

4 Ibid., 138.
5 Ibid. 138–39.
6 Ibid.
7 Ibid.
8 Ibid., 138.
9 Ibid.

In response to the prosecutor's question of how many different forms of killing that he had come in contact with in Mauthausen, Taylor repeated in almost the same words already quoted, the grim list of the different methods that camp officials used to kill prisoners but this time with greater emphasis upon anti-Semitic aspects. He emphasised the particularly brutal mode in which a group of Dutch Jews were killed.[10] Taylor also stated that he had been scheduled to die in the Mauthausen gas chamber on 6 May 1945, but that he had been saved when American troops arrived the day before his planned execution.[11]

Taylor's graphic and personal account of his experiences at this extermination camp clearly disturbed the defence lawyer, Oeding. This lawyer objected to the 'emotionally arousing' and 'inflammatory' level of graphic detail not directly related to the specific actions and guilt of the defendants.[12] Oeding's cross-examination attempted to 'move the tribunal past the emotion of Taylor's testimony.'[13] Taylor stated that, whist detained at the camp, he had seen 'maybe five or six' of the defendants on trial: 'It's been about a year. In their uniforms they look different'.[14]

The OSS Captain stood up well under Oeding's hostile cross-examination. Indeed, Taylor even managed to trap this defence lawyer into pressing him on his knowledge of how camp officials harvested gold fillings. Oeding sought to claim that Taylor's evidence was merely second hand, hearsay evidence. Taylor, however, showed he could substantiate his testimony by reference to his own experience of interviewing

[10] Ibid., 140 That is: 'Gassing, hanging, shooting, beating. There was one particular group of Dutch Jews who were beaten until they jumped over the cliff into the stone quarry. Some that were not killed on the first fall were taken back up and thrown over to be sure. Then there was exposure. Any new transport coming in was forced to stand out in the open, regardless of the time of the year, practically naked. Other forms of killing included clubbing to death with axes or hammers and so forth, tearing to pieces by dogs specially trained for the purpose, injections into the heart and veins with magnesium chloride or benzine, whippings with a cow-tail to tear the flesh away, mashing in a concrete mixer, forcing them to drink a great quantity of water and jumping on the stomach while the prisoner was lying on his back, freezing half-naked in subzero temperatures, buried alive, red-hot poker down the throat. I remember a very prominent Czech general who was held down in the shower room and had a hose forced down his throat. He drowned that way.' Ibid.

[11] Ibid., 142.

[12] Ibid., 141.

[13] Ibid., 143.

[14] Ibid.

a prison dentist immediately after liberation, during which time: 'the prison dentist gave me the last day's collection of extracted teeth with the gold in them.'[15]

Taylor's evidence appeared to impress the court. The Dachau trial ended on 11 May 1946. The Tribunal convicted all sixty one of the accused of: 'participating in a common plan to violate the Laws and Usages of war under the Geneva Convention' and of subjecting: 'foreign nationals to killing, beating, torture, gassing and starvation.' In a 'Special Finding', the tribunal also declared that there was sufficient evidence of death by shootings, gassings, hangings and starvation to find every member of the Mauthausen camp personnel guilty of war crimes. This finding was later used to establish guilt in subsequent war crimes proceedings brought against some of the Kapos at Mauthausen. Of the 61 men who were convicted, 58 were sentenced to death by hanging on 13 May, 1946, and the other three were sentenced to life in prison. Nine of the death sentences were later reduced to life in prison. On May 27 and 28, 1947, the men, whose death sentences had been upheld, were hanged in the yard of the Landsberg prison near Munich.

[15] Ibid., 144.

APPENDIX THREE

RESTITUTION THROUGH PUBLICITY? CONTEMPORARY INTEREST IN OSS' ROLE RELATING TO 'NAZI GOLD'

The appendix will demonstrate that the declassification of OSS files and the subsequent attention paid to them by the media has been a factor in both renewing public interest in looted Nazi gold and prompting restitution efforts, including those involving litigation, taking place many decades after the abolition of the OSS. Part of the recent controversy has included the fact that that OSS-SSU officials had secretly monitored the position of the Swiss authorities during immediate postwar negotiations for the restitution of gold and other assets. As Levin and Dornberg note:

> In response to the Eizenstat report, the Swiss government noted on May 22, 1997 its importance in revealing new details, but in the same breath also noted that most of the issues had been researched in the past. Bern stated that at the conclusion of the Washington Accord in 1946 the parties to the signing realized all essential facts. Thanks to their intelligence sources, the Allies even had precise knowledge of the Swiss negotiating position. Regarding the agreement's implementation, the report confirms in writing that Switzerland had paid the settlement sum at the prevailing value of Sfr. 250 million agreed to in the gold negotiations.[1]

In one sense, this and a host of related issues raise an important question: did the actions of OSS officials in monitoring looted gold from Holocaust victims still manage to exert a positive influence in aiding recent efforts at restitution? More specifically, has the media reaction to the contents of declassified OSS Safehaven materials encouraged and supported a climate of political opinion and debate that has become increasingly oriented towards successful test case litigation and the creation of substantial compensation funds? This is a key question pursued in the remainder of the present appendix.

In early 1996, World Jewish Congress (WJC) leaders, headed by its president Edgar Bronfman, asked US Senator Alfonse D'Amato, the head of the Senate Banking Committee, to look into the supposedly

[1] *The Last Deposit: Swiss Banks and Holocaust Victims' Accounts*, NY: Praeger, 1999, 152.

large quantities of dormant Jewish bank accounts in Swiss banks. These banks had proved obstructive to earlier restitution efforts by victims and their heirs.[2] The WJC claimed that there were billions of dollars in dormant Jewish accounts created during the Nazi era as a way of safekeeping their assets. In late 1995, the WJC had been offered $32 million to settle the matter, which they rejected as an insult. Bradsher recognised that when, in spring 1996, Senator D'Amato began his investigations, which included requests for relevant OSS Safehaven and related records it triggered a renewed public, political and media interest in Holocaust-era assets: 'And what had actually begun as a quest for information on Jewish assets in Swiss banks quickly broadened to include Nazi-looted monetary, or central bank, gold held in the neutral countries of Switzerland, Sweden, Spain, Portugal, Argentina, and Turkey, as well as the gold recovered after the war in Germany.'[3] At this time there was a flood of researchers interested in non-monetary gold, including victims' gold from the death camps, such as dental gold.

British authorities also began to take an active interest in Nazi-looted gold. Several members of Parliament, including Lord Janner and Foreign Secretary Malcolm Rifkind,[4] undertook initiatives in September 1996 which led the Foreign and Commonwealth Office to publish a report written by Gill Bennett, the FCO's chief historian.[5] This report raised serious questions internationally about looted gold, and the wartime actions of Switzerland, which resonated particularly in US Government circles. The resulting debate and publicity created a movement for compensation for Holocaust victims.[6] In early September 1996, President Clinton asked Stuart E. Eizenstat, then Undersecretary of Commerce for International Trade, as well as special envoy of the Department of State on Property Restitution in Central and Eastern Europe, to create an interagency group responsible for preparing a report to: 'describe, to the fullest extent possible, U.S. and

[2] Bradsher, 2002 op. cit. 181.

[3] Ibid.

[4] Bower, 1997 op. cit. 338–339.

[5] Foreign and Commonwealth Office, General Services Command, History Notes, *Nazi Gold: Information from the British Archives*, No. 11, London: Foreign and Commonwealth Office, Sept. 1996. See also Foreign and Commonwealth Office, General Services Command, History Notes, *Nazi Gold: Information from the British Archives*, 2d ed., No. 11 London: Foreign and Commonwealth Office, Jan. 1997; Foreign and Commonwealth Office, General Services Command, History Notes, Nazi Gold: Information.

[6] Bradsher, 2002 op. cit. 183.

Allied efforts to recover and restore...gold and other assets stolen by Nazi Germany.'

At this time, October 1996, class-action lawsuits were filed in the U.S. District Court in Brooklyn against Swiss banks, including Union Bank of Switzerland (UBS). Later, three class-action lawsuits were launched in April 2007 against a number of insurance companies.[7] The plaintiffs sought $20 billion in compensation on the grounds that these banks had obstructed the survivors' efforts to reclaim money that was either deposited in these banks by individuals, or which the Nazis had looted and then transferred to them. In December 1997, and in response to a tide of international criticism, the Swiss passed a law against the destruction of relevant records and created an independent commission of experts to study the Swiss role in World War II under Swiss professor Jean-François Bergier. President Clinton sent Eizenstat to mediate talks and an out of court settlement between the plaintiffs, Jewish leaders and the banks, which continued until August 1998. Also early in 1997, the Swiss established a $200 million fund for Holocaust survivors, which would expand to more than $400 million by 1999.[8]

On 7 May 1997, the Interagency Group on Nazi Assets, headed by Senator Eizenstat, published its report and extensive 'finding aid'.[9] It was based primarily on US NARA's holdings, including OSS and other Safehaven records. This report established that some of looted gold previously regarded as 'monetary gold', and therefore repayable to national governments, was probably looted from individuals, and therefore restitutable to them or their heirs. The report retraces what U.S. officials knew about Nazi looting, when they found out about these actions or those of neutral states, and what efforts the United States

[7] In was not until August 1998 that UBS and Crédit Suisse settled these lawsuits by agreeing to pay $1.25 billion to claimants. By this time, the action had been extended to include four other groups of potential claimants, including those whose looted assets had found their way into Switzerland, slave laborers, and refugees who were turned away by Switzerland. The details of the settlement would take another two years to resolve through the mediation of a U.S. federal court.

[8] Ibid.

[9] U.S. Department of State, *U.S. and Allied Efforts to Recover and Restore Gold and Other Assets Stolen or Hidden by Germany During World War II: Preliminary Study*, coordinated by Stuart E. Eizenstat and prepared by William Z. Slany, Department of State Publication 10468, May 1997, (Eizenstat Preliminary Report). The U.S. House of Representatives reproduced the finding aid as part of the printed Banking Committee hearings of 15 May 1997, on Swiss banks and attempts to recover assets belonging to Holocaust victims.

made to trace and recover such assets into neutral and non-belligerent nations. A second more detailed and wider-ranging Eizenstat report was issued on 8 June, 1998.[10] It addressed the role of the Vatican and neutral countries in looted gold and the fate of the Croatian Ustasha treasury. The report noted that Nazi Germany had purchase a substantial portion of its war effort by using gold to purchase its wartime imports from neutral states, much of this was looted from occupied Europe and victims of the Holocaust.[11] Most of this looted gold was sent to the Swiss National Bank, which converted it into Swiss francs or deposited it in the accounts of other central banks.

The revival of Anglo-American political interest in Holocaust assets summarised above has coincided with and helped inspire a string of media reports, many of which address the contents and implications of declassified OSS reports. From the mid-1990s, the media have begun to take an interest and provide coverage of the issue of 'Nazi Gold' in general, with newly-declassified OSS reports on the Nazis' looting of assets often being treated as authoritative evidence by US politicians and journalists. In one sense, it is remarkable that a report from one of Dulles' agents can still feature as a 'newsworthy' event in comparatively recent controversies. One of the these relates to legal actions by families who had been victimised by Nazi genocide, and who are seeking compensation for the loss of their shared assets. An example of media reports linking OSS war crimes investigations, Swiss Banks and the Nuremberg trials is the following American '*Newsday*' report:

> The Swiss government secretly shipped 280 truckloads of looted Nazi gold to Spain and Portugal during World War II, according to documents from the U.S. Archives unveiled yesterday by Sen. Alfonse D'Amato (R-N.Y). "This is the first evidence that shows it." D'Amato, in a telephone interview from New York, also said the gold was worth 1 billion to 2 billion Swiss francs at the time, the equivalent of $250–500 million in 1940s U.S. dollars. The document, a 1946 top-secret report to the director of the Office of Strategic Services (OSS),...came from an agent in Berne, Switzerland, and was sent to...Donovan. It detailed the numbers of

[10] U.S. Department of State, U.S. and Allied Wartime and Postwar Relations and Negotiations with Argentina, Portugal, Spain, Sweden, and Turkey on Looted Gold and German External Assets and U.S. Concerns About the Fate of the Wartime Ustasha Treasury: *Supplement to* Eizenstat Preliminary Report *Preliminary Study of U.S. and Allied Efforts to Recover and Restore Gold and Other Assets Stolen or Hidden by Germany During World War II*, coordinated by Stuart E. Eizenstat and prepared by William Slany, Department of State Publication 10557 (June 1998).

[11] Bradsher, 2002 op. cit. 190.

> truckloads of gold, and indicated this was "still in Swiss banks. It shows the enormity of the transactions, and that this was not something that the Swiss government was unaware of",... American officials have maintained that the Swiss know more than they are telling about the Nazi gold and assets stored in Swiss banks by Jews during World War II in an attempt to keep that money out of the hands of the Nazis. Several American Holocaust survivors, and families of those who died, claim they still have money in the Swiss accounts that they have been unable to obtain.[12]

Controversies arose during the late 1990's concerning the fate of looted gold, works of art and other financial assets stolen by the Nazis, particularly Hermann Göring, and the considerable support given to the Nazi regime by supposedly 'neutral' Swiss Banks.[13] There has been an understandable political and media inquest into which executive agencies and long-established institutions, including even the Vatican, still have secrets to hide regarding their complicities in assisting Nazis, or their collaborators and supporters, to 'successfully' plunder and retain gold from victims of the Holocaust. This investigation has highlighted segments of OSS intelligence reports, even where these were originally produced for other purposes.

During the mid-1990's, the question of which institutions were allegedly complicit in securing and hiding 'Nazi Gold' and related assets emerged within media coverage. This, in turn, has directly addressed the contents and implications of a number of recently declassified OSS wartime and immediate postwar intelligence reports. Swiss banks in particular have been identified as having a serious case to answer for providing a Safehaven for Nazi funds generally, including remarkably, the accumulated Royalties accruing from Hitler's ridiculous book-length manifesto, *Mein Kampf* [*My Struggle*]. Within this type of journalistic coverage, Allied institutions stand accused of failing to actively pursue such funds as a potential source for Holocaust restitution. For instance, in the second half of 1996, it was reported that OSS documentation suggested—in the words of its headline—that: 'Hitler funds traced to Swiss bank; WWII Allies stayed quiet about account.' The relevant segment of this news story states:

---

[12] E. S. Povich, 'Evidence Swiss Shipped Nazi Gold,' *Washington Bureau*, 13 January, 1997.

[13] See the flurry of books and other publications already cited stemming mainly from the 1990's.

> Adolf Hitler's royalties from Mein Kampf may have been deposited in a Swiss bank account, according to U.S. intelligence reports cited Friday by a Jewish newspaper. The report—the latest linking Swiss banks to funds deposited by Nazis and their Jewish victims—is potentially embarrassing to the United States and other World War II Allies that knew where the money was but never disclosed the information. World Jewish Congress officials tracing Jewish funds found the information among declassified U.S. intelligence documents. It said Max Ammann, Hitler's close associate and the publisher of his racist manifesto, deposited funds for Hitler in the Bern branch of the Union Bank of Switzerland. The Office of Strategic Services, the predecessor to the CIA, titled the 1944 document "Objectionable Activities by Switzerland on Behalf of the Nazis." "It is quite possible that Hitler's foreign exchange revenues from his book and foreign exchange revenues from the Nazi party abroad are held at the Swiss bank," it said. The royalties would have been substantial, as the book—in which a youthful, jailed Hitler outlines his plans for restoring German might and crushing the Jews—had sold 6 million copies by 1940.[14]

This news report continues with a short but helpful précis of earlier developments related to the patchy and controversial response of Swiss banks to wider Holocaust-restitution issues that Jewish organisations have raised directly with the Swiss authorities. The overall impression created is that, to date, these banks had made something less than a full and frank disclosure of all possible sources of funds available for restitution, including gold looted by the Nazi regime from Jews it persecuted and killed. However, agencies within both Britain and the United States have already committed themselves to continuing to press strongly on the issues of accountability, transparency and restitution—partly by following up on the implications of declassified OSS files—until further progress is ultimately achieved:

> This year, Switzerland agreed to bend its famously stiff banking rules to track down money deposited by Jews during the war. The banks say at least $ 32 million is in the dormant accounts; Jewish groups' estimates reach into the billions. Funds tracked down by investigators reporting to an international panel will be given to Holocaust survivors and their families. The Swiss have refused to do the same with Nazi money that found its way to Switzerland. A Union Bank of Switzerland spokesman said the bank had no accounts.... In any case, Robert Vogler said, all German accounts were frozen after the war and searched for "enemy treasure." Any such funds were turned over to the Allies, Vogler said, adding that

[14] *The Chicago Sun-Times*, 8 September 1996.

> the relevant documents were no longer available. Another sore point is the nearly $300 million worth of gold the Nazis smuggled into Switzerland during the war. Jewish groups say the amount substantially exceeds the amount of gold Germany held at the time and likely included gold stolen from Jews and others. The Allies knew about the gold for years. U.S. documents declassified last month show the Allies took about $60 million of the gold at the end of the war. Britain is investigating what it took from the Nazi gold reserves in Switzerland, and Stuart Eizenstat, the U.S. undersecretary of commerce, has promised to do the same.[15]

Rhetorically such news coverage relies, at least in part, for their appeal upon an archaeological metaphor. That is, the idea that OSS' intelligence reports contain factual truths concerning misappropriated Holocaust-related assets, which—largely for strategic reasons—have until now been 'hidden' from the 'public gaze'. The act of declassification and close scrutiny of such records by investigative journalists can, it is presumed, cause a beam of light to illuminate murky corners of the historical record that, for interesting reasons, had been concealed for over 50 years.

For example, in the spring of 1998, *The Guardian* included a news item under the headline: 'The Pope has a problem; The Vatican is still trying to hide what may be ugly secrets about Nazi loot. John Hooper and Richard Norton-Taylor start to look under some stones.' Having set up the parameters and terminological framework within which the significance of relevant OSS records could be converted into a 'news story', this journalistic narrative introduces the records themselves and interprets their significance. Such reconstruction takes place largely according to the requirements of a formulaic script that is underpinned by a wider framework of established historical 'knowledge', including the apparently well-known complicities of British intelligence officials in this controversial field:

> Recently declassified US documents suggest the Ustashe, the Nazi puppet regime in Croatia, smuggled out to the Vatican 80 million pounds worth of gold coins plundered from Jews, Serbs, and Gypsies.... Earlier that year [1945], the Office of Strategic Services, reported that the Vatican was exchanging old British 5 pound and 10 pound notes for new ones through "agents in England". Declassified documents also show the Vatican bank—the Institute for Religious Works—was dealing with the Reichsbank and Swiss banks blacklisted by the Allies. Donald Kenrick,

[15] Ibid.

> of the International Romani Union, told the London conference that 1 million pounds worth of gold jewellery and teeth taken from Gypsies in Croatia ended up in the Vatican. It has long been known that Catholic clerics in Rome used looted gold to smuggle Nazis to South America—a route known as the "ratline"—sometimes with the help of stolen or false Red Cross passports. The Ustashe was extremely close to the Catholic church. Its leader, Ante Pavelic, escaped capture—possibly with the help of British intelligence—and fled to Argentina via Rome.[16]

Having recast this story in terms of 'buried truths coming to light', this raises the question of the challenge posed by both the democratic project of opening up the historical record, and the specific cause of the victims of the Holocaust. The challenge is supposed to stem from the resistance offered by allegedly countervailing 'forces of darkness', strategic silence and closure:

> The Pope's spokesman, Joaquin Navarro-Valls, said after the documents first came to light that the accusations they contained had "no basis in reality". Contacted by the Guardian, Father D'Aniello said "I'm sorry. I can't help you." Father Chappin said: "It is impossible. We who work in the Vatican cannot talk about our work." Vatican insiders say the Pope has a problem. The Holy See's archives are opened up a Papacy at a time—currently they are available to the end of Pius XI's tenure in 1939. If the papers dealing with his successor, Pius XII, were to be released, they would shed light not only on the wartime years but also reveal personal confidences (Pius XII died in 1958) relating to individual Roman Catholics who are still alive. The argument cuts little ice, as the Vatican itself appeared to recognise this week. Archbishop Tauran, under secretary of state, told Janner this week it would release 12 volumes of wartime archives which, in Janner's words, had been "researched some 26 years ago". This suggests the documents have been carefully selected, enabling the Vatican to back up its claim that the archives contain nothing that would embarrass it. As the millennium approaches, Vatican officials say they have agreed to undertake an "examination of conscience". There is no better way to demonstrate this, and—if the Vatican is telling the truth—to back up its denials, than to open up all its wartime archives now.[17]

The passing reference to the claimed role of British Intelligence in assisting the Ustashe escape from the threat posed by postwar legal accountability for the Holocaust is not allowed to redirect questioning

[16] Ibid.
[17] Ibid.

of the presumed truthfulness of OSS files, not least because these have already been mobilised as an untainted source of illumination.[18]

More generally OSS files, including those that contributed to the wider interagency Safehaven project,[19] have been interpreted by journalists as a valuable source of information to substantiate claims by Holocaust survivors and others seeking restitution for their 'Aryanized' assets. Indeed, one *Jerusalem Post* story reports a major financial sponsor of Rabbi Israel Singer's powerful and largely successful campaign for restitution—a movement driven by litigation as well as negotiations with the German and Swiss authorities since at least the 1990s. This sponsor has reportedly paid a considerable sum in wages to independent historical researchers to review the contemporary—as well as purely historical—implications for Holocaust restitution claims related to a vast quantity of OSS Safehaven records:

> "He [Singer] is brilliant, tough and passionate, and he has tremendous energy," declares Edgar Bronfman, the president of the WJC. "It's as though there were 16 of him." (Bronfman says that Singer "sometimes uses me in the background," but he, too, is a vital player: The Report has learned that Bronfman paid more than $1 million for research into documents gathered by the U.S. Office of Strategic Services after World War II in Operation Safehaven, chronicling Swiss collaboration with the Nazis. When the documents were released by former senator Alfonse D'Amato's Senate Banking subcommittee, they deflated the myth of Swiss neutrality, uncovered Swiss financial complicity with the Nazis, and were instrumental in pushing the Swiss into the $1.25 billion settlement.)[20]

The 'revelation by declassified OSS records of Nazi gold scandal' story has often been reported as one campaign within a wider 'battle for justice' between representatives of Holocaust victims on the one hand, who are seeking individual or collective restitution of Jewish assets, and different aspects of the Anglo-American establishment. The latter's complicities can no longer be condoned by reference to lack of relevant knowledge at the time. This is because preliminary indications of the 'true state of affairs' were evident from the revelations contained in declassified OSS files relating, for instance, to this agency's investigations of war crimes within Mauthausen death camp. This was

---

[18] This asks us to believe that, if the relevant files of British intelligence were ever to be fully declassified, one would find a full and frank admission of such complicity in aiding perpetrators of the Holocaust, an assumption that strains credibility.

[19] See chapter 6 above.

[20] 'The Man in the Eye of the Storm', *The Jerusalem Report*, 22 November, 1999.

the camp where OSS' Captain Jack Taylor was detained before later assisting OSS and CIC war crimes investigators at this camp. Aspects of this formulae are evident in the following news item discussing the significance of OSS reports on the extraction of gold dental items from victims of the Holocaust.[21] They not only graphically individualise and personalise the issues but also resort to dramatic labels such as 'Nazi gold in New York':

> GOLD VAULT MAY GUARD NAZI SECRET—THE DAYS BETWEEN. The vault lies under the Federal Reserve Bank.... and holds $112 billion in gold, the biggest stash on Earth. The organization of which Steinberg is executive director believes that more than 2 tons of these lustrous ingots are Nazi booty. "Nazi gold in New York," Steinberg says.... Steinberg further believes that this loot under downtown Manhattan may, by however slight chance, have soul-chilling origins. This fearful suspicion arose from his study of 15,000 secret documents recently declassified after half a century. Document A-57452 from the OSS... is dated June 11, 1945, and titled "Dental Gold from Deceased Prisoners." It notes: "In theory, the director of a concentration camp dental station was required to inspect all deceased prisoners in the camp crematorium, personally to remove any dental gold, and to stamp the body 'Examined by dental surgeon.' He was likewise required to keep a daily log showing in each case the serial number of the deceased and the net amount of gold recovered." In practice, the document says, the extraction was done

---

[21] See 11 June 1945 Report of the Office of Strategic Services, 'Dental Gold from Deceased Prisoners', declassified in 1996: US NA, RG 226 A-57452. This describes the extraction and processing of gold teeth: 'The monthly report submitted to the SS Wirtschaftsbund Verwaltungshauptamt, Amt D III (SS Economic Office, Section D III), Oranienberg/Berlin, by the SS HQ dental stations of all concentration camps, included a secret account of the dental gold recovered from deceased prisoners. The SS Economic Office had ruled that this gold was the property of the SS and that it was to be delivered at specified dates to Section D III... [to be] reissued to members of the Waffen-SS and their families for new dental work. At the Mauthausen concentration camp, where informant was assigned to the dental station, the actual practice was as follows: a. Those prisoners who had a conspicuous amount of dental gold were either assigned to special labor camps where they soon died of hunger and fatigue, or were kept at Mauthausen and taken care of by the SS guards and the prisoners (mostly professional criminals) whom they had appointed overseers and blockleaders. b. A large amount of the gold thus made available for plunder was disposed of directly by the guards and their prisoner accomplices. The rest was collected either in the hospital or crematorium... by low-ranking SS officials. They delivered it, more or less intact, to the director of the dental station... who turned it over... for computation and recording. This was cited in American Holocaust restitution litigation: see In Re HOLOCAUST VICTIM ASSETS LITIGATION (Swiss Banks) SPECIAL MASTER'S PROPOSAL, September 11, 2000, Fn.48: http://www.nyed.uscourts.gov/pub/rulings/cv/1996/667236.pdf. (identified in this proceeding as document number SB 20318).

> by lackeys who had "bitter jurisdictional disputes." The gold then was delivered "more or less intact" to the dental surgeon, who forwarded it to Section D III of the SS Economic Office. The total for one month in Mauthausen concentration camp was 3,085.3 grams, "being from 528 bodies," the document says.[22]

During the second half of 1996, media coverage of Nazi gold issues was only just beginning to emerge sporadically, and then only in rather specialist—if well regarded—newspapers, such as the *Christian Science Monitor*, which in October published the following item:

> Nazi leaders hoped their massive transfer of funds and documents into Switzerland toward the end of WWII would help preserve the Nazi movement, a newly released document indicated. The two-page memo from the Office of Strategic Services, precursor to the CIA, is dated May 9, 1945. It was released by the World Jewish Congress.[23]

It appears from the absence of coverage in the *New York Times*, *Washington Post* and their various British equivalents that, throughout 1996, the World Jewish Congress were struggling to attract mainstream media attention for the 'Nazi gold' issue. However, from the start of 1997 coinciding with the discovery of a growing number of quotable OSS documents on this topic, this particular news story appears to have 'taken off' at least for the next 12–18 months:

> The question of Nazi gold is being investigated by the Senate Banking Committee as part of a larger inquiry into Nazi loot. Its chairman... says he does not have conclusive evidence that Nazi gold of whatever origin is indeed in New York. "Right now, we cannot verify it," D'Amato says. Steinberg and Edgar Bronfman, the president of the World Jewish Congress, remain convinced. They propose that the remaining gold be distributed to Holocaust survivors. "It really has nothing to do with finance... It has a lot to do with justice.... One small measure of justice," Steinberg said.[24]

At the start of 1997, journalists provided additional media coverage concerning *the contemporary*, as well as purely historical, implications of

---

[22] *Daily News* (New York), 22 September 1996. A summary of evidence relating to dental gold at this camp entitled 'protocol of the commander of the Mauthausen Concentration Camp, SS Col. Franz Ziereis' is also contained in Donovan's files: SEA PS-1515, 6 October 1945, Cornell Collection, Vol. 3, Subdivision 20, which reports that '40 kg of gold from the teeth of corpses were confiscated at Auschwitz.'.

[23] 'The News in Brief', *Christian Science Monitor*, (Boston, USA) 23 October, 1996.

[24] Ibid.

recently declassified OSS documentation. Such reporting was often framed, from the start, as a credible accusation to which allegedly guilty parties, including the Swiss authorities, are honour bound to respond. This coverage reported on details of how large and valuable quantities of gold, much of which had been looted from victims of the Holocaust, had been transported across Europe, and the involvement of Swiss banks in this controversial activity. For example, a news agency report from January of that year quoted D'Amato's ambitious claim that the contents of OSS files have now removed any doubts regarding the complicities of Swiss bankers:

> New York Sen. Al D'Amato and American Jewish leaders say they have documents that prove Swiss bankers worked actively on behalf of the Nazis during World War II. D'Amato and the World Jewish Congress released U.S. intelligence reports from 1946 that say the Swiss National Bank sent 280 truck-loads of Nazi gold to Spain and Portugal in the early '40s.... D'Amato released a 1946 top secret report to the director of the Office of Strategic Services (the predecessor of the CIA) that says up to $500 million worth of gold was shipped to Spain and Portugal in trucks bearing the national emblem of Switzerland. He says those shipments were all made between May 1943 and February 1944.... D'Amato has written to the Swiss president, asking who insured the gold, how much it was insured for, and where it all came from, among other questions. Swiss officials could not be reached for comment.[25]

Such coverage often includes not only selected extracts from OSS Safehaven records but also direct—if highly edited—quotations from parties who are currently pursuing this Holocaust restitution issue. In turn, this suggests a level of confidence afforded to the contents of OSS documentation. One source of perceived 'human interest' here is the conjuring up of dramatic images of *sheer brutality* concerning the methods through which gold dental items were extracted from Jews prior to their slaughter, akin to harvesting:

> The banks even had the gold insured by Swiss companies, the documents state. "For the first time since our inquiry began, we have documents confirming that the Swiss were actively involved in shipping gold for the Nazis," U.S. Sen. Alfonse D'Amato (R-N.Y.) said yesterday at a news conference. Elan Steinberg, executive director of the World Jewish Congress, said that gold was stolen from Holocaust victims. "It's like a

[25] 'D'Amato says Swiss laundered Nazi gold', *United Press International*, 12 January, 1997.

> monstrous Indiana Jones movie," said Steinberg. But "it's not the Nazis driving truckloads of stolen gold, it's the Swiss," he said. "This gold was wedding rings, watches, literally gold teeth ripped out of Holocaust victims' mouths." D'Amato, who has been spearheading the drive to trace the whereabouts of the millions of dollars in gold stolen from Holocaust victims, said, "We're following the money." The secret shipments began in May 1943, while the Nazis were putting down the uprising in the Warsaw Ghetto. They ended in February 1944, the same month the Nazis began deporting Hungarian Jews to Auschwitz and U.S. planes began bombing Berlin.[26]

This story opens largely with contemporary reactions to the 'revelations' contained in OSS reports, to the point where there would be no story without them. However, the reports themselves—and the bribery tactics OSS field agents had to deploy to obtain the 'raw' intelligence that informs them—are discussed only in later paragraphs, and then placed in the context of other declassified documentation:

> One 1946 document from the Office of Strategic Services... estimates the value of the gold bars at $250 million to $500 million. And it said the OSS had Swiss truck drivers willing to talk about the shipments in exchange for "10,000 Swiss francs each" and a "new job." Also released yesterday was the 1945 statement of Karl Graupner,[27] a high-ranking Reichsbank executive who told American interrogators that the "Swiss National Bank took care of insuring these transports in the Swiss insurance agencies." Graupner said Nazi gold also was laundered in neutral Sweden and Turkey and in then-Nazi ally Romania. What happened to the gold afterward remains a mystery. According to U.S. intelligence, Swiss businessmen used diplomatic pouches to smuggle a fortune in Nazi loot to South America, some of which is rumored to have wound up in the hands of Eva Peron the Argentine icon and former first lady.[28]

What is particularly interesting is that this story raises, if only in passing, a central analytical issue. That is, the cognitive, ethical and emotional difficulties facing those seeking to come to terms both with the enormity of the Holocaust, and with the implications of the thousands of different types of acts complicit in this programme of genocide, which even extend to secret Swiss diplomatic activity:

---

[26] 'Swiss Shipped Nazi Loot Portugal, Spain Got Gold, Says Document', *Daily News* (New York) 13 January 1997.

[27] Ibid., (Graupner was responsible for gold in the Foreign Exchange Department of the Nazi Reichsbank).

[28] Ibid.

> Swiss banks have admitted profiting from dealings with gold plundered by the Nazis. But while Jewish organizations have accused Switzerland of sitting on up to $7 billion of assets of Jews slaughtered by the Nazis, the Swiss say they have identified just $ 27 million in 775 unclaimed accounts and not all of that belongs to Holocaust victims, they say. Switzerland's only Jewish government minister said yesterday her country fears facing its World War II role. "Just as an individual person needs a psychiatrist to find his way, we need to be confronted with the truth that is being dug up now," she said.[29]

This report continued:

> Excerpts from 1946 dispatch marked "Top Secret" from U.S. intelligence officers in Bern to the director of the Office of Strategic Services...: "Have contacted high-level Swiss who uncovered trail 280 truckloads German gold bars sent from Suisse to Spain and Portugal between May '43 and February '44. Total value estimated between 1,000,000,000 and 2,000,000,000 Swiss Francs. Source willing give full details: Names transport company, customs officials, German officials and officers occupied France, frontier officials Spain, Portugal, Swiss nationals who handled shipments in Spain, consignee banks in Madrid and Lisbon. Gold was shipped for account of Reichsbank. Was taken from vaults of Swiss National Bank Bern and checked by bank officials. Drivers state another like amount gold bearing German marks still remains vaults. Swiss national emblem appeared on every truck. Drivers willing make statements, even testify. However expect lose job or worse, are asking 10,000 Swiss francs each and promise new job. Swiss at frontier and in Spain must also be paid generously. Working closely with U.S. Treasury representative here. He deeply interested due great pressure now being put on Swiss re: German assets. Operation therefore very important and timely. He suggests you contact Orvis Schmid and Joe Friedman of Treasury Department, Washington. Both discreet and know background story. If given green light will ask Amzon (American Zone) arrest and interrogate Germans. Involved them action at Iberian end.[30]

A minority of newspaper coverage of this topic have adopted a more ambitious forms of reporting that takes a more expressly evaluative approach to the perceived implications of the 'Nazi gold' controversy. For instance, an editorial piece in *The Seattle Post-Intelligencer* by columnist

---

[29] Ibid.

[30] Ibid. This report was later summarised in a weekly digest of important news items: see 'That was the week that was' *Daily News* (New York), 18 January 1997: but also included the comment of Elan Steinberg, executive director of the World Jewish Congress, that: 'this gold was wedding rings, watches, literally gold teeth ripped out of Holocaust victims' mouths.'

William Safire described a series of developments that initially appeared to be entirely negative in nature:

> Professionally neutral Switzerland, and especially its secretive banking system, has come under fire for committing the greatest sin a banker can be charged with: not protecting the assets of its depositors, in this case the money of European Jews entrusted to Swiss safekeeping during the Holocaust. When the World Jewish Congress and Sen. Alfonse D'Amato's banking committee asked searching questions about the missing assets, Swiss bankers reacted guiltily, arrogantly and stupidly. They stonewalled for a year; one of their diplomats planned to launch a PR "war" against those demanding an accounting; one big bank was caught shredding records that might prove embarrassing. Such wrongdoing by today's generation of Swiss bankers prompted condemnation of misdeeds of their World War II grandfathers, who helped Hitler by laundering Nazi gold. Unable to deny this, some Swiss bankers pointed their fingers at Sweden, also neutral back then, for doing the same. German bankers, enjoying a little "Schadenfreude" (glee at another's misfortune) at the discomfiture of their banking rivals, hinted that unreturned assets belonging to beneficiaries of victims, with interest compounded, might run as high as a billion dollars. Things got a little ugly last week with politicians threatening a New York boycott against Swiss banking...while the Swiss media (which had courageously ferreted out the bellicose diplomat's internal memo) reported threats of a wave of anti-Semitism if this publicity gave Switzerland a black eye.[31]

He then argued, however, that the controversy regarding the defensive and evasive actions of Swiss banks, which had been prompted by the contents of OSS records highlighted by campaigners: 'could have healthy repercussions' for a number of the parties concerned, even for the reputation of the Swiss authorities who had assisted Dulles' OSS core field office in Berne. Indeed, he argued that the ramifications of this controversy—together with the associated institutional confrontation of uncomfortable aspects of the Nazi legacy more generally (including less extreme forms of contemporary anti-Semitism)—could encourage a more assertive and positive attitude regarding Holocaust-reparations:

> Isn't this terrible? No. This is good for all concerned. It's good for this generation of Swiss, who can at last look their nation's past in the eye. Neutrality was better than Nazi occupation; it meant helping both Axis and Allies (with Allen Dulles of our OSS operating a valuable listening post in Switzerland). And if belated restitution of misappropriated

[31] Ibid.

> deposits assuages this generation's conscience, let it be payback time. It's good for Swiss banking. Rainer Gut, head of Credit Suisse, stepped in to stop the stalling by calling for creation of an initial fund to start restoring the nation's reputation for integrity. That broke the logjam; he understands his industry's need for global trust. Now Paul Volcker, former U.S. central banker who has everyone's trust, can assess the depth of the debt without the harassment of the secrecy-prone. It's good for the Jews. And not just in the partial justice to a massacred generation, with attacks of conscience now extending to French museums. It's the end of the don't-make-trouble syndrome. I ran into the Nobel Prize-winning apostle of remembrance, Elie Wiesel, in a Forum hallway and asked him about the presumed reaction by some angered Swiss against local Jews. "Anti-Semites don't need an excuse to be anti-Semitic," he replied with equanimity. And the Jewish leaders here are not intimidated by the veiled threats of backlash. Times—and Jewish attitudes—have changed.... In his meeting with Koller, Netanyahu said that Switzerland could not leave this as a mystery—that it was best to calm the passions but get to justice. Koller pledged full cooperation in uncovering the truth and has spoken out against anti-Semitism. Committees of the Knesset and Swiss parliament will work together: "You can't bring back the 6 million," Netanyahu told me Sunday night, "but you can do the morally decent thing for victims fast disappearing.... The time has come to do justice to the truth. That's what we expect of Switzerland, and I was assured that's what Switzerland will do."[32]

On the other hand, this upbeat and optimistic editorial interpretation of the Swiss banks controversy was soon counter-balanced by news reports containing rather contrary viewpoints. *The Washington Post*, for example, included a story whose headline stated: 'Swiss Envoy: 'One-Sided' Portrayal May Imperil Fund for Holocaust Victims'. This reported the claim by Swiss Foreign Minister Flavio Cotti concerning the potentially negative implications for Holocaust restitution campaigns of continuing hostile media coverage of this controversy. In what many could interpret as a rather cynical attempt to 'purchase' less critical media coverage by resorting to promises to make large restitution payments in the future providing the tone of such coverage sharply alters, this account stated:

> Cotti warned Friday that his government's plan to provide several hundred million dollars a year to victims of the Holocaust and other tragedies could be jeopardized if Swiss voters are upset by "one-sided" portrayals

[32] 'Switzerland's Banking Snafu Could Have Healthy Repercussions', *The Seattle Post-Intelligencer*, 6 February, 1997.

> of their nation's actions in World War II. Cotti charged that the steady drumbeat of disclosures about Swiss dealings with the Nazis have ignored the contributions of a neutral nation that he noted was praised by former British Prime Minister Winston Churchill as "the sole international force" that linked Britain with European nations occupied by the German Army during the war. The Swiss government has proposed using several hundred million dollars of the annual interest on $7 billion in gold reserves to ease the final years of Holocaust survivors, but stressed that the proposal faces a tough political referendum before Swiss voters. Swiss leaders will work hard to win approval of the plan, he said, but said the recent "indiscriminate" international condemnation of Switzerland's actions during the war had "led to a strong, yet understandable defensive reaction on the part of the Swiss population" that could undermine the plan to make restitution. "The depiction of Switzerland as a willing collaborator and friend of Nazi Germany is historically untenable and perceived by the Swiss people as profoundly unjust," Cotti said.[33]

After firing this warning shot against the implications of 'one-sided' coverage, Cotti was reported as conceding the need for the Swiss commercial and state authorities to face up to the implications of past acts of complicity in aspects of the Holocaust, and no longer ignore historical evidence, including those presumably stemming from recently declassified US intelligence files, which have fuelled this controversy. He argued that, by now doing the right and courageous thing in response to its own earlier acts of complicity, (which comparatively speaking were on a par with those of many others), the Swiss authorities could, perhaps, go some way to restoring aspects of its tarnished international image.

Cotti even managed to secure, perhaps for strategic reasons only, a confirmation of this 'convenient' re-interpretation of events from US Commerce Undersecretary Stuart E. Eizenstat, (former U.S. envoy to the European Union) who was then chairing an investigative committee on this topic:

> But Cotti also was apologetic about those historical acts in which the Swiss did cooperate with Nazi oppression. He stressed during his speech that Switzerland will come to grips publicly with this hitherto little-examined side of its past and promised full disclosure of the documentary record. "The history of Switzerland in the '30s and '40s really contains some very dark moments," Cotti said, "as does the history of other European nations. This is a fact we must accept without ifs and buts. The invention of the so-called Jewish 'J' stamp [for Jewish refugees] and the rejection of...30,000 Jews at the Swiss border was inexcusably wrong. Some of the

[33] *The Washington Post*, 15 March, 1997.

> deals of the Swiss National Bank and other Swiss banks were immoral and outrageous." During his visit yesterday Cotti met with Secretary of State Madeleine K. Albright and Commerce Undersecretary Stuart E. Eizenstat to discuss a massive interagency study by the U.S. government that has reviewed thousands of declassified intelligence documents from the World War II era. "Switzerland will not be judged by what happened 50 years ago in a tumultuous time," Eizenstat said during a meeting with reporters, "but rather be judged by how they react to the report of what happened 50 years ago and how they act upon it."[34]

This news report concluded by alerting its readership to the question of how the shelf-life of the present story—including disclosures of additional complicities of the Swiss and other neutral countries in economic aspects of the Holocaust—would, in all likelihood, be extended. This extension would arise in the wake of the forthcoming publication of the Eizenstat report, which would summarise the contents of numerous OSS and other official documents. In October, 1996, President Clinton had appointed Stuart E. Eizenstat, the Under Secretary of Commerce for International Trade, to head an 11-agency review of the material in the archives:

> U.S. officials say the report...will be based on tens of thousands of declassified documents from the Departments of Defense, State, Treasury, Justice and the Office of Strategic Services. It will describe the findings of a massive effort by U.S. intelligence and military officials during and after the war to identify and track the movement of Nazi assets around the world. It will be "quite precise" about the amounts of gold and other loot that were identified, Eizenstat said in an interview. Officials say parts of the report will be hard reading for several neutral nations, including Switzerland, Sweden and Portugal, which allegedly served as storage depots for the Nazi goods. The Swiss are keenly interested in the findings of the report, because it will disclose a U.S. estimate of the amount of looted gold that was deposited with Swiss bankers, and because they are producing their own study based on Swiss and German archives. After meeting with Cotti, Eizenstat took pains to praise publicly the measures taken by a government that is considered a valued ally in Europe. "I expressed my admiration at the courageous position of the government of Switzerland and the people of Switzerland...to be willing to shine the spotlight of history on their past," Eizenstat said.[35]

Some two weeks later, in mid-March 1997, the very activity of over 100 historical researchers investigating OSS and other files from different

---

[34] Ibid.
[35] Ibid.

branches of the executive involved in Nazi gold issues, itself became a significant part of a news story in the build up to the final publication of the Eizenstat Report. These researchers were sponsored by a variety of bodies ranging from the United States Holocaust Memorial Museum, the Swiss Historical Commission, the Swiss Government, the World Jewish Congress, the Bank for International Settlements in Bern, a law firm representing Swiss banks and another from the Swiss Bankers Association, and several American agencies, including the State Department, the Treasury Department, the Central Intelligence Agency and the Department of the Army. Once again, although the amount of material under review extends to approximately 5,000 cubic feet of papers comprising about 10 million pages, OSS wartime reports on dental gold extracted from death camp victims attracted particular media attention:

> For the last year singly, in pairs and in larger groups—people have been searching in an unlikely place for traces of gold and other treasures looted by the Nazis: the National Archives of the United States. In that period, perhaps 100 private and Government researchers have picked up a paper trail that has offered many clues involving the Swiss role in World War II. They have skimmed or studied uncounted millions of documents that have lain untouched in the half-century since the war ended. Some of the documents had not been seen because, until recently, they were classified as secret.... Some of the newly released material provides stark evidence of what has long been known, like a report obtained from an informer at the Mauthausen concentration camp on May 9, 1945, a day after the formal German surrender was announced. The report, filed by the Office of Strategic Services, then the principal American intelligence agency, cites a meticulous secret record that about 6.8 pounds of gold had been removed from the teeth of 528 bodies. Most of the victims were Jews who had been killed by the Nazis the previous March, just weeks before the war's end.[36]

When the Eizenstat report, entitled 'U.S. and Allied Efforts to Recover and Restore Gold and Other Assets Stolen or Hidden by Germany During World War II,' was finally published in the first week of May 1997, it attracted considerable media attention, including the role of OSS documentation substantiating the Mauthausen dental gold aspect. The final report confirmed the OSS account that Nazi Germany's central bank had smelted gold from Holocaust victims, including tooth fillings

[36] 'Over Here, Paper Chase for Nazi Gold', *The New York Times*, 30 March 1997.

and personal jewellery, and included it in ingots still deposited in Swiss banks. For example, *The Washington Times* reported that:

> Switzerland knowingly accepted tons of Nazi gold looted from conquered European nations and Jewish Holocaust victims during World War II and has held onto most of it, the Clinton administration said in a scathing report yesterday. "There is no question that Switzerland knew, despite their initial protestations to the contrary after the war...that there was looted gold," said Undersecretary of Commerce Stuart Eizenstat, who directed the inquiry. The 200-page report, prepared by State Department chief historian William Slany with the help of 11 U.S. government agencies, confirmed that even gold from the teeth of Holocaust victims was melted down and combined with the bullion that the Nazis stashed in Swiss banks. "Between January 1939 and June 30, 1945, Germany transferred gold worth around $400 million," and worth $3.9 billion today, Mr. Eizenstat said in his report. Of this, the Swiss National Bank retained about $276 million, worth $2.7 billion today, he said. In addition, a large, still unspecified amount of money deposited in Swiss banks by tens of thousands of the Jews who perished in the Holocaust remains in Swiss bank vaults to this day. The heirs and descendants of the victims are still seeking access to it. "For the victims, justice remains elusive....The cumulative facts and conclusions contained in this report should evoke a sense of injustice and a determination to act," said Mr. Eizenstat,...Thomas Borer, the Swiss diplomat who now heads a government task force charged with investigating the issue...said the one major revelation of the report was its confirmation that gold fillings from the teeth of Jews slaughtered in Nazi death camps, along with their other valuables, were melted down to become part of the gold ingots deposited by the Nazis in Swiss banks. "If this is really true, it is grave news of the most shocking nature," he said.[37]

In one sense, the spur given to such investigations by the contents of declassified OSS files forms a loop within an ongoing spiral. This is because one of the results of such subject-specific investigations is that further OSS files are declassified. This, in turn, can act as a catalyst to prompt other campaigns related to Holocaust-restitution that aim to remedy historical injustices. This goal, it is claimed, involves continuing to exert political, diplomatic and moral pressure on contemporary Swiss and other institutions to fully open up a historical record that has been strategically covered up for over 60 years, and to make fulsome financial compensation:

[37] 'Swiss Knew Nazi Gold Was Loot; Still Have Most of It, U.S. Report Says', *The Washington Times*, 8 May 1997.

> Mr. D'Amato, chairman of the Senate banking committee, who has spearheaded U.S. efforts to pressure Switzerland into revealing the extent of its holdings deposited by Holocaust victims, said the Swiss had so far shown only words, not actions, about doing justice to surviving Holocaust victims and their families. "The Swiss have by their own estimates $398 million of gold [in wartime values] worth 10 times that today, close to $4 billion," Mr. D'Amato said. Of that, he said, they returned only $58 million, worth about $500 million today, to individuals and countries after the war. "Instead of returning the largest part they returned 15 percent. That's all they returned," he said. Switzerland has established three commissions to investigate, one of which is headed by former U.S. Federal Reserve Chairman Paul Volcker. But, Mr. D'Amato said, "I haven't seen them do anything." Mr. D'Amato also accused Swiss banks of continuing to cover up their wartime role today. He cited the case of Christophe Meili, a former night watchman at a Swiss bank who revealed that key wartime records this year were being shredded by the bank at which he worked. Mr. Meili subsequently left Switzerland after death threats and threats to kidnap his children.[38]

The media stories discussed so far have contributed to the spiralling effect of political investigations leading to additional controversies concerning Swiss complicities in economic aspects of the Holocaust, which themselves provide an impetus for further rounds of declassification. This process of interaction has been recognised at least implicitly in some of the media coverage itself:

> Earlier this year, the U.S., British and French governments froze a central bank restitution account, administered by the Tripartite Gold Commission, which still has 5.5 tons of Nazi gold worth $63 million. The remaining money could be used for a Holocaust restitution fund. New British Foreign Secretary Robin Cook expressed interest in the idea on Tuesday. Mr. Eizenstat said the United States supported the proposal "to complete the unfinished business of the Second World War, to do justice while its survivors are still alive." Edgar Bronfman, president of the World Jewish Congress, issued an immediate call for the remaining tripartite funds to go to Jewish victims. Mr. Slany said the U.S. government also has declassified and released to the National Archives between 800,000 and 1 million pages on the issue—the most material at any one time in history—including previously unavailable records from the Office of Strategic Services, the Army, and the State, Treasury and Justice departments.[39]

---

[38] Ibid.
[39] Ibid.

The OSS 'dental gold' report has also featured in regional and specialist media coverage of litigation brought by Holocaust survivors in an effort to recover looted assets. Such accounts, which discuss in a dramatic manner the life-stories of specific and named individuals, may have a particular rhetorical appeal as 'human interest' stories. In November 1997, *The Indiana Lawyer* reported that the OSS Mauthausen report was one of the vital keystones of a test case, or 'class action', linking dental gold reports with the Swiss Banks, and the latter's refusal—over at least half a century—to fully honour Holocaust-restitution claims:

> Gisella Weisshaus was a young Jewish girl living in Sighet, Romania, when the Nazi war machine began sweeping over Eastern Europe in the late 1930's. Little did she know that Adolph Hitler's evil plan would involve the extermination of her people.... Following the war, Weisshaus was left without her family or her father's money. Now, after all these years, Weisshaus is suing those who she believes have her money. Weisshaus v. Union Bank of Switzerland, Credit Suisse and Swiss Bank Corporation was filed as a class action in U.S. District Court in Brooklyn, N.Y., in October of 1996. The class represents hundreds of thousands of people worldwide.... Meanwhile, Weisshaus and about 70 relatives also were taken to concentration camps. Weisshaus managed to evade death when she was herded into a line of people who were allowed to live. Her relatives were not as fortunate. After the concentration camps were liberated... She then travelled to Switzerland to find her father's money but was turned away by the banks because she didn't have an account number. Similar stories abound.... Together, damages are estimated at $7 billion. When the Nazis would capture a community, they would take the assets, gold in particular, and transfer them to Swiss banks. The Nazis also collected dental gold from deceased prisoners. According to a document from the Office of Strategic Services in Washington, D.C., the director of a concentration camp dental station was required to inspect all deceased prisoners in the camp crematorium to remove any dental gold. The director was required to keep a daily log showing in each case the serial number of the deceased and the net amount of gold recovered.[40]

As previously noted, this class action was eventually 'settled' on terms that created a large compensation fund for Holocaust restitution purposes.[41] The resulting Settlement Agreement of August 1998 followed discussions facilitated, initially, by Stuart Eizenstat but also involving

---

[40] 'Lost treasures Indy lawyers helping Holocaust survivors get their money back' *The Indiana Lawyer*, 26 November 1997.

[41] More generally, see *Litigating the Holocaust*.

the trial judge included a Settlement Fund of $1.25 billion, in four instalments, over the course of three years.[42]

In short, starting with the mid-1990's, OSS files have contributed to considerable media and public discussion of the complicities of Swiss and other banks in handling gold, a proportion of which was looted from victims of the Holocaust. The newspaper reports on OSS files have been linked with coverage of Nazi gold controversies involving pressure from a variety of sources to force Swiss Banks to stop their historic policy of blocking investigations, and—in this way—to allow individuals to make Holocaust restitution claims. OSS reports on how the Nazis obtained dental gold from the bodies of victims of the Holocaust, and how this and other looted gold bullion was transported across Europe, often with the active co-operation of the 'neutral' Swiss authorities, have been seized upon as factual evidence and ammunition in this wider contestation. Many of the stories are informed by value-judgements concerning the perceived justice of such claims, and the historical injustice of their denial. The resurgence of media interest has both followed and been fuelled by political interests, which in turn has motivated increased archival research in OSS and other related Safehaven records.

Writing in mid-1997 senior archivist Greg Bradsher notes how for the previous 14 months, the US National Archives had experienced a major explosion of public and media interest in 'Nazi Gold':

> Our so-called "Nazi Gold" phenomenon results, in part, because of the interest of many people, as well as foreign governments, to know what happened to the assets Holocaust victims had placed on deposit in Swiss banks and what happened all the gold that the Nazis had looted from the central banks of Europe.[43]

Recent newspaper accounts support this account, and have singled out OSS documentation on dental gold as particularly symbolic. For example, the *New York Times* has noted:

> Some of the newly released material provides stark evidence of what has long been known, like a report obtained from an informer at the Mauthausen concentration camp on May 9, 1945, a day after the formal

[42] In re HOLOCAUST VICTIM ASSETS: 96 Civ. 4849 (ERK) (MDG) LITIGATION: (Consolidated with 99 Civ. 5161 and X 97 Civ. 461) http://www.fonjallaz.net/Suisse+2e-Guerre-Mondiale/Actualites/Le-jugement-de-Korman.html

[43] Bradsher, op. cit.

> German surrender was announced. The report, filed by the Office of Strategic Services, then the principal American intelligence agency, cites a meticulous secret record that about 6.8 pounds of gold had been removed from the teeth of 528 bodies. Most of the victims were Jews who had been killed by the Nazis the previous March, just weeks before the war's end. Some of that gold, the report indicated, had been intended for re-use as tooth fillings for "members of the Waffen SS and their families." But much of it is known to have been melted down and deposited in Swiss banks. That dental gold is a symbolic pebble in a mountain of life savings, artworks and other assets that a dwindling number of concentration camp survivors and their descendants are trying to obtain an accounting of from Switzerland's Government and secretive banks. Some of it was stolen by Nazis and deposited in Switzerland for their personal use or for the Nazi war machine. Some was deposited by Jews and others before they were sent off to concentration camps, in the vain hope that it would be safe in a country whose wartime role is now being questioned.[44]

The declassification or accessing of OSS Safehaven files has also reignited controversy regarding the immediate postwar settlements with 'neutral' states such as Switzerland and Portugal relating to their acquisition of Nazi gold. For example:

> The final result achieved by the Allied negotiating team over seven years of haggling appears even more catastrophic in light of the fact that the American negotiators had in their possession a memo from the American Office of Strategic Services (OSS) dated 7 February 1946, stating that the Portuguese had actually obtained 124 tons of Nazi Gold, and not 44 [the accepted figure].[45]

---

[44] 'Over Here, Paper Chase for Nazi Gold' Irvin Molotsky, *New York Times*, 30 March 1997.

[45] Antonio Louça and Ansgar Schäfer, 'Portugal and the Nazi Gold: The 'Lisbon Connection' in the Sales of Looted Gold by the Third Reich': www1.yadvashem.org/, citing 'Memorandum of Gold Acquisitions by Portugal during the War,' 7 February 1946: US NA, RG 59, Box 4210.

BIBLIOGRAPHY

Adam, Peter, *Art of the Third Reich*, NY: Harry Abrams, 1992.

Aronson, S., 'Preparations for the Nuremberg Trial: The O.S.S., Charles Dwork, and the Holocaust', *Holocaust and Genocide Studies*, vol. 12, no. 2 (Fall 1998).

Barron, Stephanie, *'Degenerate Art': The Fate of the Avant Garde in Nazi Germany*, NY: Harry Abrams, 1991.

Bass, Gary, *Stay the Hand of Vengeance: The Politics of War Crimes Tribunals*, Princeton: Princeton University Press, 2000.

Bauer, Yehuda, *Bartering for Jewish Lives*, New Haven: 1994.

Beer, 'Die Entwicklung der Gaswagen beim Mord an den Juden', *Vierteljahrshefte für Zeitgeschichte* 35(3), 1987.

Bower, Tom, *Blood Money: The Swiss, the Nazis and the Looted Billions*, London: Macmillan, 1997.

Bradsher, Greg, 'Nazi Gold: The Merkers Mine Treasure,' *Prologue* 31 (Spring 1999): 7–21.

——. 'Turning History into Justice: The National Archives and Records Administration and Holocaust-Era Assets, 1996–2001', *Archives and the Public Good: Accountability and Records in Modern Society*, Richard J. Cox and David A. Wallace: Quorum Books, Westport, CT: 2002.

Breitman, Richard, 'American Rescue Activities in Sweden', *Holocaust and Genocide Studies*, 7.2. 02–15.

——. *Official Secrets*, NY: Hilland Wang, 1998.

——. 20 June 2001: 'What Chilean Diplomats Leaned about the Holocaust': http://www.archives.gov/iwg/research-papers/breitman-chilean-diplomats.html.

Breitman, Richard and Aronson, Shlomo, 'The End of the Final Solution? Nazi Plans to Ransom Jews in 1944', *Central European History*, 25.2, 177–203; Quoted in Achim Besgen, *Der Stille Befehl: Medizinalrat Kersten, Himmler und das Dritte Reich*, Munich: Nymphenburger Verlagshandlung, 1960.

Breitman, Richard and Goda, Norman, 'OSS Knowledge of the Holocaust' in Breitman, Richard *et al., US Intelligence and the Nazis*, Washington: IWG-US National Archives, 2004.

Breitman and Naftali, 'Report to the IWG on Previously Classified OSS Records June, 2000'. http://www.archives.gov/iwg/reports/june-2000.html.

Bryan, Ian, and Salter, Michael, 'War Crimes Prosecutors and Intelligence Agencies: The Case for Assessing Their Collaboration', *Intelligence and National Security*, (2001), Vol. 16(3) Autumn 2001, 93–120.

Buomberger, Thomas, Raubkunst, Kunstraub: *Die Schweiz und der Handel mit gestohlenen Kulturgütern zur Zeit des zweiten Weltkriegs*, Orell Füssli: 1998.

Carr-Howe, Thomas, Jr., *Salt Mines and Castles: The Discovery and Restitution of Looted European Art*, Indianapolis: The Bobbs-Merrill Company, 1946, 20.

Casey, William, *The Secret War Against Hitler*, Washington: Regnery, 1988.

Cave-Brown, Anthony, *The Last Hero: Wild Bill Donovan*, NY: Times Books.

——, (ed.) *Secret War Report*, NY: Berkeley Publishing Corporation, 1976, *OSS War Report, Vol. I.*

Cherry, Robert. 'Raoul Wallenberg: Savior of Hungarian Jewry', *Midstream*, April 1995.

Chesnoff, Richard, Z., *Pack of Thieves: How Hitler and Europe Plundered the Jews and Committed the Greatest Theft in History*, New York: Doubleday, 1999.

Conklin, John, E., *Art Crime*, Westport, CT: Praeger, 1994.

Cox, Richard J., and Wallace, David A., (eds.) *Archives and the Public Good: Accountability and Records in Modern Society*, Quorum Books, Westport, CT: 2002.

Dobbs, Michael and Smith, R., Jeffrey, 'New Proof Offered of Serb Atrocities', *Washington Post*, 29 October 1995.

Downs, Jim, *World War II: Tragedy in Slovakia*, Oceanside, California: Liefrink Publishers, 2002.

——. 'Lessons from the Failure of the OSS/SOE Dawes Mission', 2 *The Journal of Intelligence History*, (2002): 29–36.

Dulles, A. W., *Germany's Underground*, New York: Macmillan, 1947.

Dulles, Allen, *The Secret Surrender*, New York: Harper & Row, 1966.

Eastwood, Maggi and Salter, Michael, 'Negotiating *Nolle Prosequi* at Nuremberg: The Case of Captain Zimmer', *Journal of International Criminal Justice*, Vol. 3 (2005) 649–665.

Feingold, Henry L., *The Politics of Rescue: The Roosevelt Administration and the Holocaust, 1938–1945*, New Brunswick, NJ: Rutgers University, 1970.

Fitzgerald, Michael, review of 'Lost Museum', *Art in America*, February 1998, 2.

Francini, Esther, Fluchtgut-Raubgut, Tisa, *Der Transfer von Kulturgütern in und über die Schweiz 1933–1945 und die Frage der Restitution*, Chronos: 2001.

Ganz, Jodi Berlin, 'Heirs without Assets and Assets without Heirs: Recovering and Reclaiming Dormant Swiss Bank Accounts,' *Fordham International Law Journal* 20 (1997) 1306.

Goda, N., 'Manhunts: The Official Search for Notorious Nazis', in *Breitman et al.*, 2004, Ch. 15.

Gordon, David L., and Dangerfield, Royden, J., *The Hidden Weapon; The Story of Economic Warfare*, New York, 1947.

Gould, J., 'Strange Bedfellows: The OSS and the London "Free Germans"', *CSI* Vol. 46: https://www.cia.gov/library/center-for-the-study-of-intelligence/kent-csi/docs/v46i1a03p.htm.

Greene, J., M., *Justice at Dachau*, London: Broadway Books, 2003.

Grimsted, Patricia Kennedy, 'Roads to Ratibor: Library and Archival Plunder by the Einsatzstab Reichsleiter Rosenberg', *Holocaust and Genocide Studies* 2005 19(3): 390–458.

Grose, Peter, *Gentleman Spy: The Life of Allen Dulles*, Boston: Houghton Mifflin & Co., 1994.

Gunther Haase, *Die Kunstsammlung des Reichsmarchalls Hermann Göring: Eine Documentation* Ed. Q, Germany.

Hanyok, R., 'Western Communications Intelligence Systems and the Holocaust,' in *Breitman et al.*, 2004, 443–453.

Harris, Whitney, 'Judgments on Nuremberg: The Past Half Century and Beyond', *Boston College Third World Law Journal*, Spring 1996.

Haynor, P., *Unspeakable Truths: Facing the Challenge of Truth Commissions*, London: Taylor and Francis, 2002.

Hindley, Meredith, 'Negotiating the Boundary of Unconditional Surrender: The War Refugee Board in Sweden and Nazi Proposals to Ransom Jews, 1944–1945', *Holocaust and Genocide Studies*, Vol. 10, (1996) 52–77.

Hinsey F. H. *et al., British Intelligence in the Second World War*, Vol. 2, London: HMSO, 1981.

——. 'The Strategy of Rescue and Relief: The Use of OSS Intelligence by the War Refugee Board in Sweden 1944–5', *Intelligence and National Security* 12 (1997): 145–65.

Honan, William, *Treasure Hunt: A New York Times Reporter Tracks the Quedlinburg Hoard*, NY: Delta, 1997.

Hulme, Claire and Salter, Michael, 'The Nazis' Persecution of Religion as a War Crime: The OSS's Response' *Rutgers Journal of Law and Religion*, Vol. 3, no 1. www.lawandreligion.com.

——. *The Judgement of Nuremberg: 1946*, London: HMSO, 1999.

Jacobson, Philip, 'War crimes court wants SAS to trap Karadzic', Daily Telegraph, 12 March 2000.

Katz, Barry, *Foreign Intelligence*, Cambridge: Harvard University Press, 1989.

Kellerman, H., 'Settling Accounts—the Nuremberg Trials', *Leo Baeck Yearbook*, Vol. XLII (1997) 337–55.

King, Henry T., 'Robert Jackson's Transcendent Influence over Today's World', 68 *ALBLR* 23 (2004), 26–27.

Koch, H. W., 'The Specter of a Separate Peace in the East Russo-German Peace Feelers,' 1942–44,' *Journal of Contemporary History* 10 (1975), 531–49.

Kwiet, Konrad and Matthäus, Jürgen, 'The Nuremberg War Crimes Process', *Contemporary Responses to the Holocaust*, Westport, CT, Praeger, 2004.

——. *Contemporary Responses to the Holocaust*, Westport, CT, Praeger, 2004.

Lankford, Nelson Douglas, (ed.), *OSS Against the Reich: The World War II Diaries of Colonel David K. E. Bruce*, Kent, OH: Kent State University Press, 1991.

Laqueur, W., *The Terrible Secret*, NY: Owl Books, 1998.

Laqueur, Walter, *The Terrible Secret*, London: Weidenfeld and Nicolson, 1980, 13.

Lester, E., *Wallenberg: The Man in the Iron Web*, New Jersey: Prentice Hall, 1982.

Lockwood, C., 'UK passes evidence to war crimes tribunal' *Daily Telegraph*, 21 April 1999.

Lorenz-Meyer, Martin, *Safehaven: The Allied Pursuit of Nazi Assets Abroad*, University of Missouri Press, 2007.

Louça, António, 'The Holocaust Nazi Gold and the Swiss-Portuguese Connection', *Cardozo Law Review*, December, 1998, 498.

Marcuse, Harold, *Legacies of Dachau: The Uses and Abuses of a Concentration Camp, 1933–2001*, Cambridge: CUP, 2001.

Marton, Kati, 'The Liquidation of Raoul Wallenberg; At Last, the True Story Is Out', *The Washington Post*, 22 January 1995.

McPhereson, Nelsen, *American Intelligence in Britain During the Second World War: The OSS in London*, Cass, London, 2003.

Meltzer, Bernard, in the Nuremberg symposium: 'The Fifth Annual Ernst C. Steifel Symposium: 1945–1995: Critical Perspectives on the Nuremberg Trials and State Accountability: Panel I: Telford Taylor Panel: Critical Perspectives on the Nuremberg Trials', published in 12 *N.Y.L. Sch. J. Hum. Rts.* 453, 513 (1995).

Mendelsohn, John, *The Holocaust: Selected Documents in Eighteen Volumes*, Vol. 11: 'The Wannsee Protocol and a 1944 Report on Auschwitz by the OSS', NY: Garland, 1982, Introduction.

——. 'The Holocaust: Records in the National Archives on the Nazi Persecution of Jews', 23 *Prologue* (1984), 23–39.

Mickletz, Jeffrey Craig, 'An Analysis of the $1.25 Billion Settlement Between the Swiss Banks and Holocaust Survivors and Holocaust Victims' Heirs', *Dickinson Journal of International Law. 18 (1999).*

Mühlen, Ilse, *Die Kunstsammlung Hermann Görings: Ein Provenienzbericht der Bayerischen Staatsgemaeldesammlungen*, edition q im Quintessenz Verlag; Auflage: 1 2000.

Naftali, Timothy, 'The CIA and Eichmann's Associates', 2004 op. cit. 337–374.

——. 'CIA and Eichmann's Associates', in R. Breitman et al., *US Intelligence and the Nazis*, 2004 *op. cit.* 339.

NSA, 'Eavesdropping on Hell: Historical Guide to Western Communications Intelligence and the Holocaust, 1939–1945', 2006: http://www.nsa.gov/publications/publi00044.cfm XXX.

Nicholas, Lynn H., *The Rape of Europa: The Fate of Europe's Treasures in the Third Reich and the Second World War*, NY: Vintage, 1995, ch. 1.

Niethammer, Lutz, *Das Mitläuferfabrik: Die Entnazifizierung am Beispiel Bayern*, Berlin: Verlag, 1982, 52.

Ost, Susan and Salter, Michael, 'War Crimes and Legal Immunities: The Complicities of Waffen-SS General Karl Wolff in Nazi Medical Experiments', *Rutgers Journal of Law and Religion*, Vol. 4, 2003, www.lawandreligion.com.

Palmer, Richard, 'Felix Kersten and Count Bernadotte: A Question of Rescue', *Journal of Contemporary History*, Vol. 29, No. 1 (1994) 39–51.

Penkower, Monty N., *The Jews Were Expendable: Free World Diplomacy and the Holocaust*, Chicago: University of Illinois, 1983.

Persico, J., *Casey*, *Piercing The Reich*, NY: Viking, 1979.

——. *The lives and secrets of William J. Casey, from the OSS to the CIA*, NY: Viking, 1990.

——. *Roosevelt's Secret War*, NY: Random House, 2001, 315–20.

Petersen, Neil, H., *From Hitler's Doorstep. The Wartime Intelligence Reports of Allen Dulles, 1942–1945*, University Park, PA: Pennsylvania State University Press, 1996.

Petropoulos, Jonathan, *The Faustian Bargain: The Art World in Nazi Germany*, NY: OUP, 2000.

Plaut, James, 'Loot For The Master Race', *The Atlantic*, Sept. 1946, Vol. 178 No. 9 (Plaut 1946a).

Rickman, Gregg J., *Swiss Banks and Jewish Souls*, New Brunswick, NJ: Transaction, 1999.

Roxan David, Wanstall, Ken, *The Rape of Art: The Story of Hitler's Plunder of the Great Masterpieces of Europe*, NY: Coward-McCann, 1965.

Russell, Chamberlin, *Loot! The Heritage of Plunder*, New York: Facts on File, 1983.

Salter Michael, 'The Visibility of the Holocaust: Franz Neumann and the Nuremberg trials' in Fine, R. and Turner, C. (eds.), *Social Theory after the Holocaust*, Liverpool: Liverpool University Press, 2000.

——. 'The Prosecution of Nazi war criminals and the OSS: the need for a new research agenda', *Jnl of Intelligence History*, 2:1, 2002.

——. 'Unsettling Accounts: Methodological Issues within the Reconstruction of the Role of a US Intelligence Agency within the Nuremberg War Crimes Trials', *Current Legal Issues*, 2003, Vol. 6, *Law and History*, Andrew Lewis and Michael Lobban, (eds.).

——. 'Intelligence Agencies And War Crimes Prosecution: Allen Dulles' Involvement In Witness Testimony At Nuremberg', 2 *Journal of International Criminal Justice*, (2004).

——. *Nazi War Crimes, US Intelligence and Selective Prosecution at Nuremberg: Controversies regarding the role of the Office of Strategic Services*, London: Routledge, 2007.

Schlesinger, Arthur, *A Life in the Twentieth Century: Innocent Beginnings, 1917–1950*, Boston: Houghton-Mifflin, 2000.

Simpson, Christopher, *The Splendid Blond Beast: Money, Law and Genocide in the Twentieth Century*, Maine Monroe: Common Courage Press, 1995.

Spier, Ernst Holze, 19 September, 2001: http://www.archives.gov/iwg/research-papers/barbie-irr-file.html.

Steury, Donald P., 'Tracking Nazi 'Gold': The OSS and Project Safehaven', 9 *Studies in Intelligence* (2000), 35–50: http://www.cia.gov/csi/studies/summer00/art04.html.

Smith, Bradley, *The Shadow Warriors*, NY: Basic Books, 1983.

Smith Jr., Arthur L. *Hitler's Gold: The Story of the Nazi War Loot*, Oxford: Berg Publishers, 1989, 1996.

Smith, Richard, *OSS: The Secret History of America's First Central Intelligence Agency*, Berkeley: Univ. of California Press, 1972.

Vincent, Isabel, *Hitler's Silent Partners: Swiss Banks, Nazi Gold, And The Pursuit Of Justice*, NY: W. Morrow.

Vries, Willem de, 'Sonderstab Musik: Music Confiscations by the Einsatzstab Reichsleiter Rosenberg under the Nazi Occupation of Western Europe', Amsterdam: Amsterdam University Press, 1996.

Wallenberg, Raoul, *Report of the Swedish-Russian Working Group*, Stockholm, 2000, 33: www.sweden.gov.se/content/1/c6/04/11/37/37b7322e.pdf.

'Wallenberg, Was Double Agent', *The Times* (London), 20 March 1990, at 10.

Waller, John H., 'Reichsführer Himmler Pitches Washington', *Studies in Intelligence*, CSI, CSI Publications, Unclassified Studies Volume 46, Number 1, 2002.

Waters, Arthur Donald, *Hitler's Secret Ally*. London: Pertinent Publications, 1992.

West, Shearer, *The Visual Arts in Germany, 1890–1937: Utopia and Despair*, NY: Rutgers University Press. 2001.

Willett, John, *Art and Politics in the Weimar Period: The New Sobriety, 1917–1933*, NY: Da Capo Press, 1978.

Winks, Robin, *Cloak and Gown*, NY: Collins, 1987.

Wistrich, Robert S., *Who's Who in Nazi Germany*, London: Routledge, 1995.

Witte and Tyas, 'A New document on the deportation and murder of Jews during "Eisatz Reinhardt 1942"' *Holocaust and Genocide Studies*, 15, (2001), 468–86.

Wolfe, Robert: http://www.archives.gov/iwg/research-papers/wolfe-statement-september-1999.html.

Yahil, Leni, 'Raoul Wallenberg—His Mission and His Activities in Hungary.' *Yad Vashem Studies* XV: 7–53.

Ziegler, Jean, *The Swiss, The Gold, And The Dead*, tr. John Brownjohn, NY: Harcourt Brace, 1998.

INDEX

History of International Relations, Diplomacy, and Intelligence

Series Editor
Katherine A.S. Sibley

History of International Relations, Diplomacy, and Intelligence is a peer-reviewed book series which seeks to publish high-quality, pioneering works in the history of international relations, broadly conceived. In addition to disseminating original research in traditional areas addressed by this field, including diplomacy, national security, economic conflict, and the role of individuals, this series also embraces the ongoing expansion of the study of international relations into such areas as culture, race, gender, sexuality, and the environment. Its books will encompass as well the often-overlooked role of intelligence and intelligence agencies in shaping foreign relations.
History of International Relations, Diplomacy, and Intelligence actively intends to further engagement between the scholarly community and the policy-making one, by demonstrating the continued importance of past patterns, practices, and policies for today's pressing debates.

1. Berridge, G.R. *Gerald Fitzmaurice (1865-1939), Chief Dragoman of the British Embassy in Turkey*. 2007. ISBN 978 90 04 16035 4
2. Davies, T.R. *The Possibilities of Transnational Activism: the Campaign for Disarmament between the Two World Wars*. 2007. ISBN 978 90 04 16258 7
3. Baxter, C. and A. Stewart (eds.). *Diplomats at War*. British and Commonwealth Diplomacy in Wartime. 2008. ISBN 978 90 04 16897 8
4. Sicking, L. *Colonial Borderlands*. France and the Netherlands in the Atlantic in the 19th Century. 2008. ISBN 978 90 04 16960 9
5. Greenwood, S. *Titan at the Foreign Office*. Gladwyn Jebb and the Shaping of the Modern World. 2008. ISBN 978 90 04 16970 8
6. Davis, S. *Contested Space*. Anglo-American Relations in the Persian Gulf, 1939-1947. 2009. ISBN 978 90 04 17130 5
7. Salter, M. *US Intelligence, the Holocaust and the Nuremberg Trials*. Seeking Accountability for Genocide and Cultural Plunder. (2 Vols.). 2009. ISBN 978 90 04 17277 7